The Paris Opéra

The Paris Opéra

An Encyclopedia of Operas, Ballets, Composers, and Performers

Growth and Grandeur, 1815–1914

A–L

SPIRE PITOU

GREENWOOD PRESS
New York • Westport, Connecticut • London

Library of Congress Cataloging-in-Publication Data

(Revised for volume 3)

Pitou, Spire, 1912-
The Paris Opéra.

Includes bibliographies and indexes.
Contents: [1] Genesis and glory, 1671-1715 — [2] Rococo and romantic, 1715-1815 — [3] Growth and grandeur, 1815-1914.
1. Opéra de Paris—History. 2. Opera—France—Paris—Dictionaries. I. Title.
ML1727.8.P2P5 1983 782.1'0944'361 82-21140
ISBN 0-313-21420-4 (lib. bdg. : v. 1)
ISBN 0-313-24394-8 (lib. bdg. : v. 2)
ISBN 0-313-26218-7 (lib. bdg. : v. 3)

British Library Cataloguing in Publication Data is available.

Library of Congress Catalog Card Number: 82-21140
ISBN 0-313-26218-7 (set)
ISBN 0-313-27782-6 (A-L)
ISBN 0-313-27783-4 (M-Z)

First published in 1990

Greenwood Press, 88 Post Road West, Westport, CT 06881
An imprint of Greenwood Publishing Group, Inc.

Printed in the United States of America

The paper used in this book complies with the Permanent Paper Standard issued by the National Information Standards Organization (Z39.48-1984).

10 9 8 7 6 5 4 3 2 1

TO
MY GRANDCHILDREN,
MICHAEL, DAVID,
CHRISTOPHER, AND
ALLISON PETERS

CONTENTS

Preface ix

Abbreviations xiii

The Encyclopedia 3

Appendix: The Repertory, 1815–1914 1422

Index 1467

PREFACE

The present volume in this current series of publications describing the growth of French opera and ballet is devoted to the multiple aspects of these two types of theatrical activity at the Opéra in Paris following the collapse of the Napoleonic empire in 1815. This portion of the study starts with the return of the Bourbons to the throne of France, and it ends at the moment of total mobilization of all male citizens eligible to serve in the army and navy at the outbreak of World War I in the summer of 1914. The hundred years between Napoleon's departure for St. Helena and Kaiser Wilhelm II's invasion of the northern provinces saw the installation of Louis Philippe's bourgeois monarchy in 1830, the establishment of Napoleon III's empire in 1851, and the inauguration of the Third Republic in 1871. The details of the survival of the operatic and balletic companies at the Opéra during this century of social, political, and military crises have already been related in the first volume of this study, but it may be repeated here that neither the hostile invasions nor the bloody revolutions marking the decades between 1815 and 1914 managed to suppress activity at the Opéra for long.

This nineteenth-century volume has been organized so that information about opera and ballet at the Paris opera house is arranged again in encyclopedia format with entries listed in alphabetical order. Individual entries deal with operas, ballets, singers, dancers, composers, choreographers, librettists, and scenarists. The narrative development or thematic allegations of the operas and ballets are again traced scene by scene or act by act. Basic bibliographies are provided again to offer ready access to supplementary information about the individuals and compositions under scrutiny. Page references are provided for important periodicals and books for the convenience of researchers and more casual readers. The usual cross references to other volumes are provided once again. An asterisk after a proper name indicates that an entry for the starred name is to be found in this volume. Thus, Les Huguenots* signals that this famous Mayerbeer work is discussed herein.

The appendix to this volume presents a bibliographical listing of all lyric and choreographic works first performed at the Opéra between 1 January 1816 and 1 August 1915. This first of six lists includes the entire repertory and gives the composer, librettist, and choreographer contributing to the creation of each composition as well as its title, genre, and the date of its initial performance at the Opéra. The five subsequent bibliographies offer separate chronologically arranged listings for the lyric repertory, the balletic repertory, nonoperatic lyric offerings, dramatic works, and light stage offering.

It must be stated here next that the author of the present encyclopedia has relied heavily upon a number of standard reference books. The especially useful titles have been La Grande Encyclopédie (1886-1902) in 31 vols., Pierre Larousse's Grand dictionnaire universel du XIXe siècle (1866-1890) in 15 vols. with two supplementary vols., Die Musik in Geschicte und Gegenwart: allgemeine Enzyklopädie der Musik (1949-1979) in 17 vols., the Biographie universelle ancienne et moderne in 40 vols., the incomplete Dictionnaire de biographie française (1933-) in 14 vols., and the especially valuable Enciclopedia dello spettacolo (1954-62) in 9 volumes. More specialized in certain respects and quite as useful have been the surveys, dictionaries, and handbooks of ballet, music, or opera compiled by Baril, Beaumont, Cande, Chouguet, Chujoy, Compardon, Gourret, Guest, Hofmann, Koegler, Migel, Mondadori, Nanquette,

Alain Paris, Pougin, Riemann, Sénéchaud, Slonimsky, Oscar Thompson, Tranchefort, and the teams of Clément and Larousse, Kutsch and Riemens, and Brunel and Wolff. The pbulications of Gross, Ewen, Fétis, Grove, and Kobbé have been constantly helpful.

Once again thanks for support and encouragement in the writing of this third volume must be extended to President Arthur Trabant of the University of Delaware. Gratitude is given here for the professional help extended to the author by the library staffs of Yale University and Wesleyan University in Connecticut, of Ocean Country Library and the library of Ocean County College in New Jersey. The cooperation of the library personnel at the University of Pennsylvania, the University of Delaware, and the Library of Congress likewise knew no bounds. Abroad, a great debt of gratitude is owed once more to Mme Martine Kahane and Mlle Marie-José Kerhoas of the Opéra library. Also, I am pleased once again to thank my wife for her patience and vigilance in France and in the United States.

ABBREVIATIONS

AB: Adolphe Boschot, Portraits de musiciens, 2 vols. (Paris: Plon, 1947).

ACD: Anatole Chujoy, The Dance Encyclopedia (New York: A. S. Barnes & Co., 1949).

ACPM: Anatole Chujoy and P. W. Manchester, The Dance Encyclopedia, (New York: Simon and Schuster, 1967).

ADI: Claude Naquette, Anthologie des interprètes (Paris: Stock, 1979).

AEM: Die Musik in Geschichte und Gegenwart: allgemeine Enzyklopädie der Musik, ed. Friedrich Blume, 17 vols. (Kassel u. Basel: Bärenreiter, 1949-79).

AM: L'Art musical, Paris, 1860-70, 1872-94, 1935-36, 1938-39.

APD: Alain Pâris, Dictionnaire des interprètes et de l'interprétation musicale (Paris: Robert Laffont, 1982).

ASSL: André Schaikeovitch, Serge Lifor et le destin du Ballet de l'Opéra (Paris: Editions Richard Masse, 1971).

*The publisher has attempted to compile a thorough list of abbreviations. We regret any omissions in the list that may have occurred, and would appreciate any information from readers regarding abbreviations used in the text not identified in this list.

AWL: Arthur Ware Locke, Music and the Romantic Movement in France (London: Kegan Paul, Trench, Trubner & Co., 1920).

BB: Gerald Goode, The Book of Ballets (New York: Crown Publishers, 1939).

BBD: Baker's Biographical Dictionary of Musicians, ed. Nicolas Slonimsky, 6th ed. (New York: Schirmer Books, 1978).

BCS: Barbara Naomi Cohen-Stratyner, Biographical Dictionary of Dance (New York: Schirmer Books, 1982).

Bio. univ.: Biographie universelle ancienne et moderne, 40 vols. (Paris: Delagrave, n.d.).

BK: Boris Kochno, Diaghilev and the Ballets Russes, trans. Adrienne Foulke (New York and Evanston: Harper and Row, 1970).

BNC: A. V. Arnault, A. Jay, E. Jouy, Biographie nouvelle des contemporains, 20 vols. (Paris: La Librairie historique, 1820).

BOP: Ivor Guest Le Ballet de l'Opéra de Paris, trans. Paul Alexandre (Paris: Théâtre national de l"Opéra, 1976).

CAR: M. D. Calvocoressi and Gerald Abraham, Masters of Russian Music (New York: Alfred A. Knopf, 1936).

CB: Cyril W. Beaumont, Complete Book of Ballets (Garden City, N.Y.: Garden City Publishing Co., 1941).

CBCM: David Ewen, The Complete Book of Classical Music (Englewood Cliffs, N.J.: Prentice-Hall, 1965).

Chouquet: Gustave Chouquet, Histoire de la musique dramatique en France (Paris: F. Didot, 1873).

CODB: Horst Koegler, The Concise Oxford Dictionary of Ballet (London: Oxford University Press, 1977).

COOM: Charles Osborne, The Complete Operas of Mozart: A Critical Guide (New York: Atheneum, 1978).

DBCG: Donald Brook, Composers' Gallery: Biographical Sketches of Contemporary Composers (London: Rockliff, 1946).

DBF: Dictionnaire de biographie française, 14 vols. (Paris: Letouzey et Ané, 1933).

DDD: Jacques Baril, Dictionnaire de danse (Paris: Editions du Seuil, 1964).

DDO: Félix Clément and Pierre Larousse, Dictionnaire des opéras, 2 vols. (reprint ed. New York: Da Capo Press, 1969).

DEC: David Ewen, Composers since 1900: A Biographical and Critical Guide (New York: H. W. Wilson Co. 1969).

DEO: David Ewen, Encyclopedia of the Opera (New York: Hill and Wang, 1963).

DGM: Daniel Gregory Mason, The Romantic Composers (London: Macmillan & Co.; Ltd., 1924).

Diss: Dissertation.

DIx: Dance Index.

D Mgg: Dance Magazine, New York, June 1927, 58 vols.

DNB: Dictionary of National Biography, 29 vols., (London: Oxford University Press, 1963-81).

ECB: Effie B. Carlson, A Bio-Bibliographical Dictionary of Twelve-Tone and Serial Composers (Metuchen, N.J.: The Scarecrow Press, 1970).

EDB: The Encyclopedia of Dance and Ballet, ed. Mary Clarke and David Vaughan (New York: G. P. Putnam's Sons, 1977).

EDS: Enciclopedia dello spettacolo, 9 vols. (Roma: Casa Editrice Le Maschere, 1954-62).

EFC: Jean Gourret, Encyclopédie des, fabuleuses cantatrices de l'Opéra de Paris (Paris: Editions Mengès, 1981).

EGC: David Ewen, Great Composers, 1300-1900: A Biographical and Critical Guide (New York: H. W. Wilson Co. 1966).

ELM: Encyclopédie de la musique, ed. François Michel, 3 vols. (Paris: Fasquelle, 1958-61).

Fel: Clément & Pierre Larousse Dictionnaire des opéras, 2 vols. (reprint ed., New York: Da Capo Press, 1969).

Fétis: F.-J. Fétis, Biographie universelle des musiciens et bibliographie générale de la musique, 8 vols. and 2 suppls. (reprint ed., Brussels: Culture et Civilisation, 1963).

FM: La France musicale, Paris, 1849.

GBAL: George Balanchine, Complete Stories of the Great Ballets, ed. Francis Mason (New York: Doubleday, 1977).

GBGB: George Balanchine and Francis Mason, *101 Stories of the Great Ballets* (Garden City, N.Y.: Doubleday and Co., 1975).

GC: Donald Brook, *International Gallery of Conductors* (Westport, Conn.: Greenwood Press, 1973).

GE: *La Grande Encyclopédie*, 31 vols. (Paris: H. Lamirault et Cie., 1886-1902).

GIR: Claude Nanquette, *Les Grands Interprètes romantiques* (Paris: Arthème Fayard, 1982).

GLMB: Gustave Lanson, *Manuel bibliographique de la littérature française moderne* (Paris: Hachette, 1925).

GMSM: Gérard Mannoni, *Grands Ballets de l'Opéra de Paris* (Paris: Sylvie Messinger et Théâtre national de l'Opéra de Paris, 1982).

Grove: *Grove's Dictionary of Music and Musicians*, ed. Eric Blom, 5th ed., vols. 1-9 and suppl. (New York: St. Martin's Press, 1955).

Grove: (80) or Grove (Macmillan, 80): *The New Grove Dictionary of Music and Musicians*, ed. Stanley Sadie, 20 vols. (London: Macmillan Publishers Limited, 1980).

HAZ: *Dictionnaire du ballet*, a collaboration (Paris: Fernand Hazan, 1957).

HBM: Henri Blaze de Bury, *Musiciens contemporains* (Paris: Michel Lèvy Frères, 1856).

HUT: Alphonse Royer, *Histoire universelle du thèâtre*, 6 vols. (Paris: Paul Ollendorff, 1878).

IBB: Peter Brinson and Clement Crisp, The International Book of Ballet (New York: Stein & Day, 1971).

ICM: The International Encylopedia of Music and Musicians, ed. Oscar Thompson, 6th ed., ed. Nicolas Slonimsky (New York: Dodd, Mead, & Co., 1949).

JB: Jacques Bourgeois, L'Opéra des origines à demain (Paris: Julliard, 1983).

JLJS: Jean Laurent and Julie Sazonova, Serge Lifar, rénovateur du ballet français (Paris, Corrêa, 1960).

KCOB: The New Kobbé's Complete Opera Book, ed. The Earl of Harewood (New York: G. P. Putnam's Sons, 1976).

KOH: Kathleen O'Donnell Hoover, Makers of Opera (New York: H. Bittner and Co., 1948).

KRJ: K. J. Kutsch and Leo Riemans, A Concise Biographical Dictionary of Singers, trans. Harry Earl Jones (New York and London: Chilton Book Co., 1969).

KT: Kenneth Thompson, A Dictionary of Twentieth-Century Composers, 1911-71 (New York: St. Martin's Press, 1973).

Lajarte: Théodore de Lajarte, Bibliothèque musicale du théâtre de l'Opéra (Paris: Librairie des bibliophiles, 1878 reprint ed. in 2 vols., Hildesheim: Georg Olms Verlag, 1969).

Lanson: Gustave Lanson, Manuel bibliographique de la litterature française moderne, 1500-1900 (Paris: Hachette, 1921).

LD: Laurence Davies, The Gallic Muse (New York: A. S. Barnes and Co., 1969).

Lermina: Jules Lermina, Dictionnaire universel illustré biographique et bibliographique de la France contemporaine (Paris: L. Boulanger, c. 1885).

LLD: Serge Lifar, Lelinre de la danse (Paris Journal musical français, 1954).

LOA: Jacques Lonchampt, L'Opéra aujourd'hui (Paris: Du Seuil, 1970).

LOB: Louis Oster, Les Ballets du répertoire courant (Paris: Conquistador, 1955).

LTX: Serge Lifar, Les trois grâces du XXe siècle: Légendes et vérité (Buchet-Chastel: Corrêa, 1957).

LVD: Léandre Vaillat, La Danse à l'Opéra de Paris (Paris Amiot-Dumont, 1951).

LXIX: Pierre Larousse, Grand Dictionnaire universel du XIXe siècle, 15 vols. and 2 suppl. (Paris: Larousse et Boyer, 1866-1890).

MAJO: Gérard Mannoni and Pierre Jouhaud, Les Étoiles de l'Opéra de Paris (Paris: Editions Sylvie Messinger et Théâtre National de l'Opéra de Paris, 1981).

M&L: Music & Letters, 1920.

Martin: Jules Martin, Nos artistes: portraits et biographies (Paris: Librairie de l'annuaire universel, 1905).

MCDE: Milton Cross and David Ewen, The Milton Cross New Encyclopedia of the Great Composers and their Music, 2 vols. (Garden City, N.Y.: Doubleday & Co., 1969).

MCE: The Book of Modern Composers, ed. David Ewen (New York: Alfred A. Knopf, 1950).

MIT: William W. Austin, Music in the 20th Century (New York: W. W. Norton & Co., 1966).

MM: Wallace Brockway & Herbert Weinstock, Men of Music (New York: Simom and Schuster, 1950).

MMFM: Rollo Myers, Modern French Music (New York: Praeger, 1971).

MMR: Monthly Musical Record.

MOC: George Martin, The Opera Companion to Twentieth-Century Opera (New York: Dodd, Mead & Co., 1979).

MOTO: Louis Biancolli and Herbert F. Pesyer, Masters of the Orchestra from Bach to Prokofieff (New York: G. P. Putnam's Sons, 1954).

MPPA: H. Blaze de Bury, Musiciens du passé, du présent et de l'avenir (Paris: Calmann Levy, 1881).

MQ: Musical Quarterly, 68 vols. 1915.

MR: Music Review, 1940.

MSRL: Marcel Sénéchaud, Le Répertoire lyrique d'hier et d'aujourd'hui (Paris: Gérard Billaudot, 1971).

NEO: David Ewen, The New Encyclopedia of the Opera (New York: Hill and Wang, 1971).

NMO: Ernest Newman, More Stories of Famous Operas (New York: Alfred A. Knopf, 1943).

OCM: George Martin, The Opera Companion (New York: Dodd, Mead and Co., 1961).

OEN: Ernest Newman, Great Operas, 2 vols. (New York: Vintage Books, 1958).

OG: Gerhart von Westerman, Opera Guide, ed. Harold Rosenthal, trans. Anne Ross (New York: E. P. Dutton & Co., 1965).

OMEL: Oliver Merlin and Erich Lessing, L'Opéra de Paris (Paris: Hatier, 1975).

ON: Opera News, New York, 1936.

OQE: Quaintance Eaton, Opera, a Pictorial Guide (New York: Abaris Books, 1980).

PBR: Mario Pasi, Le Ballet; repertoire de 1581 à nos jours, ed. Antoine Livo, trans. René Cecatty, Nathalie Castagnié, Dominique Dètallante (Paris: Editions Demoël, 1981).

PBSW: Pierre Brunel and Stéphane Wolff, L'Opéra (Paris: Bordas, 1980).

PGB: Claude Baignères, Petit guide de l'auditeur de musique: ballets d'hier et d'aujourd'hui (Paris: Plon, 1954).

PJ: Arthur Pougin, Un ténor de l'Opéra au XVIIIe siècle: Pierre Jélyotte et les chanteurs de son temps (Paris: Librairie Fischbacher, 1905).

PM: Parmenia Migel, The Ballerinas from the Court of Louis XIV to Pavlova (New York: The Macmillan Co., 1972).

PY: Peter Yates, Twentieth Century Music (New York: Pantheon Books, 1967).

RBP: Ivor Guest, The Romantic Ballet in Paris (Middletown, Conn.: Wesleyan University Press, 1966).

RC: Rodolfo Celletti, Le grandi voci (Roma: Istituto per la collaborazione culturale, 1964).

RCB: Donald Brook, Six Great Russian Composers; Their Lives and Works (London: Rockliff, 1947).

RdM: Revue de musicologie, 74 vols., 1922.

RHCM: Revue d'histoire et de critique musicales, 1904.

RLVB: Robert Lawrence, The Victor Book of Ballets and Ballet Music (New York: Simon and Schuster, 1950).

RM: Revue musicale, Paris, 1927.

RMI: Rivista musicale italiana, 1894-1932, 1936-43, 1946-55.

RNI: Francoise Reiss, Nijinsky ou la grâce: sa vie, son esthétique et sa psychologie (Plan de la Tour, Var: Editions d'aujourd'hui, 1980).

SDLD: Saisons de la danse, Paris, 16 vols. 1967.

SIMG: Sammelbände der internationalen Musikgesellschaft, 1899.

SS: Riccardo Mezzanotte, ed., The Simon and Schuster Book of the Ballet (New York: Simon and Schuster, 1980).

SSBO: Riccardo Mezzanotte, ed., The Simon and Schuster Book of the Opera (New York: Simon and Schuster, 1978).

SST: Charles Séchan, Souvenirs d'un homme de théâtre, 1831-1855, ed. Adolphe Badin (Paris: Calmann Lévy, 1893).

Stoullig: Edmond Stoullig, Les Annales du théâtre et de la musique````1875-1916 (Paris: Charpentier, 1876-96; Ollendorff, 1897-1918).

SW: Stéphane Wolff, L'Opéra au Palais Garnier, 1875-1962 (Paris: L'Entr'acte, 1962).

TDB: The Decca Book of Ballet, ed. David Drew (London: Frederick Muller Limited, 1958).

Thieme: Hugo Paul Thieme, Bibliographie de la littérature française de 1800 à 1930, 3 vols. (Paris: E. Droz, 1933).

Thompson: The International Cyclopedia of Music and Musicians, ed. Oscar Thompson, 6th ed., ed. Nicholas Slonimsky (New York: Dodd, Mead, & Co., 1949).

Thurner: A. Thurner, Les Reines du chant (Paris: A. Hennuyer, n.d.).

TWT: David Ewen, The World of Twentieth-Century Music (Englewood Cliffs, N.J.: Prentice-Hall, 1968).

VBO: Léandre Vaillat, Ballets de l'Opéra de Paris (Paris: Compagnie française des arts graphiques, 1943).

VfMw: Vierteljahrsschrift für Musikwissenschaft, 1885.

VOP: Léandre Vaillat, Ballets de l'Opéra de Paris; Ballets dans les opéras, nouveaux ballets (Paris: Compagnie française des arts graphiques, 1947).

Wks: Charles Beaumont Wicks, The Parisian Stage, 1800-1850, 3 vols. (University, Alabama: University of Alabama Press, 1950-61).

WLC: William L. Crosten, French Grand Opera, An Art and a Business (New York: King's Crown Press, 1948).

WMRS: William Mann, Richard Strauss: a Critical Study of the Operas (London: Cassell, 1964).

WOC: Stéphane Wolff, Un Demi-siècle d'opéra-comique, 2 vols. (Paris: André Bonne, 1953).

WT: Walter Terry, Great Male Dancers of the Ballet (Garden City, N.Y.: Anchor Press-Doubleday, 1978).

WWO: Maria F. Rich, Who's Who in Opera (New York: Arno Press, 1976).

XXJ: Odette Joyeux, Le XXe Siecle de la danse (Paris: Hachette, 1981).

XYZ: X.Y.Z. pseud. T. Faucon, Le Nouvel Opéra (Paris: Michel Lévy frères, 1875).

ZfMw: Zeitschrift für Musikwissenschaft, Leipzig, 1918-35.

ZIMG: Zeitschrift der internationalen Musikgesellschaft, 1899-1913.

The Paris Opéra

A

Abel, by Rudolphe Kreutzer, was also entitled La Mort d'Abel (see eighteenth-century volume for Kreutzer). It was revived in 1823, but it had its world premier at the Royal Academy of Music in its original form of three acts on 23 March 1810. As a pre-1815 composition, it is discussed in the eighteenth-century volume.

Abott, Bessie Pickens (b. 1878, Riverside, N.Y.; d. 9 February 1919, New York City), an American vocalist, sometimes billed as Bessie-Abott in France, sang operettas in New York and London until Jean de Reszké* heard her and urged her to train for the operatic stage. She went to Paris to study under Victor Capoul, Jacques Bouhy,* and Mathilde Marchese. Finally, on 9 December 1901, she made her debut as a soprano at the Opéra in Charles Gounod's* Romeo et Juliette.* She was cast next as La Voix de l'Oiseau in Siegried,* a role she created on 31 December 1901. She remained in the French capital until 1905, and she was back in New York at the Metropolitan Opera by 1906. She returned to Europe before her retirement in 1911, but she was never again billed at the Opéra.

BIBLIOGRAPHY: EFC 174; ICM 3; KRJ 1-2; W. H. Seltsam, Metropolitan Opera Annals (New York: H. W. Wilson Co., 1947), 154; SW 190-91, 202.

Achard, Leon (b. 16 February 1831, Lyon; d. July 1905, Paris), French Tenor, pursued his academic studies at the collège Henri IV and obtained a license to practice law in 1852. As a child he had learned the rudiments of music, and he decided now to enroll at the Conservatoire to improve his knowledge of this art that continued to interest him. His teacher was Bordogni, and he won first prize in comic opera in 1854 despite being obliged to work in a law office. His success encouraged him to sign a contract with the Théâtre-Lyrique, where he made his theatrical debut as a tenor on 9 October 1854, in a minor work by Baron François Gevaert. The public applauded his performance, and he went on to do a number of roles that secured his position at the theatre.

His career was interrupted unexpectedly at this point by the death of his father in 1856, but he was able to secure another contract to sing at the opera house in Lyon directed by M. Halanzier Dufresnoy. After a successful engagement in this city, he was invited by M. Emile Perrin to appear at the Opéra-Comique, where he made his debut on 4 October 1862 in the popular La Dame blanche. Not yet satisfied with his professional attainments, Achard went to Milan at this time to perfect his knowledge of Italian repertory. He did Marchetti's Romeo e Giulietta and the Italian version of Manon in Italy, and word of his accomplishments abroad reached M. Halanzier, now director of the Opéra. M. Halanzier-Dufresnoy, director of the Opéra since 1871, was currently in need of a tenor to sing Yorick in La Coupe du roi de Thulé,* and he invited Achard back to Paris to create this role on 10 January 1873 in the Le Peletier* opera house.

At the Opéra, Achard went on to sing Vasco da Gama in L'Africaine* and Raoul in Les Huguenots* during the remainder of 1873. Later he was billed in the title-role in Faust* as Don Ottavio in Don Juan* in 1874, and as Fernand in La Favorite* in 1875.

Achard was named professor at the Conservatoire in 1887.

BIBLIOGRAPHY: DBF I, 294 Fétis Suppl. I, 3-4; GE I, 376-77; Lajarte II, 244-46; Lermina 11; Martin 9; A. P., "Nécrologie...Léon Achard," Le Ménestrel 71 (1905), 232; PBSW 170; SW 26, 75, 88-89, 118; XYZ 193-96.

Ackté, Aïno (b. 23 April 1876, Helsinki; d. 8 August 1944, Nummala, Finland), French soprano by training, studied voice first with her mother and then at the Conservatoire under Duvernoy, Girodet, and Paul Vidal.* After completing her studies, she accepted a contract with the Opéra and appeared in her debut as Marguerite in Charles Gounod's* Faust* on 8 October 1897. She made a favorable impression upon spectators with her dramatic soprano voice, and her contract was renewed. She sang Juliette in Roméo et Juliette* in 1897 and Richard Wagner's* famous heroines of Lohengrin* and Tannhaüser* Elsa in 1898 and Elisabeth in 1899. She executed the title-roles of Hellé* in 1900 and Thäis* in 1910.

In the first six or seven years of her affiliation with the Paris Opéra, she created a half dozen roles performed for the first time at the Garnier Palace* in a world or local premiere. Her two world premieres included Herwine in La Cloche du Rhin* on 8 June 1898 and Tisbé in Orsola* on 21 May 1902. She brought to the Opéra for their initial performances at the Garnier opera house three compositions: she did Benjamin of Joseph* on 26 May 1899, Nedda of Paillasse* on 14 December 1902, and Margyane of La Statue* on 6 March 1903. Her Alceste of 11 November 1900 was also the first time that Christoph Willibald Gluck's heroine was heard in the present Paris opera house (see eighteenth-century volume for Gluck).

Mlle Ackté acquired an enviable reputation with her classical and Wagnerian repertory, and she was invited to appear in many of the leading opera houses of the world. She traveled to Stockholm, Dresden, and Copenhagen as well as to Covent Garden and the Metropolitan Opera between 1903 and 1905. After her marriage to her countryman, Heikki Renvall, she retired from the stage to write her memoirs and to become director of the Helsinki Opera on the eve of World War II.

BIBLIOGRAPHY: EFC 171; ICM 8; KRJ 2; PBSW 170; J. Scarry, "Northern light," Opera 40 (May 1976), 24-25; SW 31, 63, 88, 111, 127-28, 135, 164, 168, 191, 204, 206, 209.

Adam, Adolphe-Charles (b. 24 July 1803, Paris; d. 3 May 1856, Paris) a French composer, began his schooling by studying literature at the Lycée Napoléon, but his lack of interest in this program persuaded his father to allow him to leave school to take private lessons in music. He proved to have an innate gift for the piano and organ, and he was soon playing these instruments. Riche instructed him in harmony and counterpoint, and he began to write airs, duets, and even scenes that attracted the attention of François-Adrien Boïeldieu, who decided to introduce him into the intricacies of composition (see eighteenth-century volume for Boïeldieu). The two musicians became close friends, and their common gift for harmony fostered the development of similar styles in the writings of teacher and student alike.

After placing second in one of the contests in composition held by the Academy of Fine Arts, Adam turned to creating scores for the theatre without really giving too much thought to the serious aspect of his task, and he remained content at first with the writing of popular vaudevilles and the creation of variations for the piano on passages from such popular operas as <u>La Muette de Portici</u>,* <u>Le Comte Ory</u>,* and <u>Guillaume Tell</u>.*

<u>Pierre et Catherine</u> was his first title for the musical theatre, and he staged it in one act at the Opéra-Comique in February 1829. <u>Danilowa</u> followed at the same theatre in three acts in April 1830. Emboldened by his success, Adam now wrote too hastily, and he produced five pieces for the stage in 1831 and 1832. But, on 17 September 1833, he saw his greatest success to date, <u>Le Proscrit</u>, billed at Opéra-Comique. After another four compositions, Adam had an enthusiastically applauded score played at the Opéra-Comique on 13 October 1836, <u>Le Postillon de Longjumeau</u>: "Oh! oh! oh! oh! qu'il était beau, Le Postillon de Longjumeau!"

Adam continued to contribute to the repertory of the troupe of the Opéra-Comique now at the Salle des Nouveautés in the place de la Bourse between 1832 and 1840, and he gave them <u>Le Brasseur de Preston</u> (1838) and four other titles before they moved into the second Favart Theatre in 1840. But he had also been hoping to hear his music at the Opéra itself, and he had already turned to composing scores for ballets to realize this ambition. He had set Filippo Taglioni's <u>La Fille du Danube</u>* for the Opéra on 21 September 1836, and he then did the music for this theatre again with his greatest hits to date, <u>Giselle</u>,* on 28 June 1841 and <u>La Jolie Fille de Gand</u>* on 22 June 1842 (see eighteenth-century volume for Taglioni). He was still writing for the Opéra-Comique, and he did one grand ballet for performance at St. Petersburg and another for the London stage. But he was also well entrenched at the Opéra at this time, and he did the score for no fewer than eight librettos here between 1844 and 1856: Richard en Palestine* of 7 October 1844, Le Diable à quatre* of 11 August 1845, La Bouquetière* of 31 May 1847, Griséldis* of 16 February 1848, Le Fanal* of 24 December 1849, Les Nations* of 6 August 1851, Orfa* of 29 December 1852, and Le Corsaire* of 23 January 1856. He also collaborated with Clemenceau de Saint-Julien* on La Filleule des fées* of 1849 besides writing a cantata for the ball given by the National Guard in honor of the duchess of Orléans in June 1837. His second cantata was La Crimée (1855), for which Emile Pacin did the words.

But all did not go smoothly for the prolific composer during this period of his life, because he had fallen into a quarrel with Alexandre Basset, the new director of the Opéra-Comique, and he could no longer expect his work to be given at this theatre. He decided to open his own theatre, therefore, and he managed to obtain a license to run the new Théâtre National in 1847. Matters went poorly from the start and ended in total disaster with the Revolution of 1848. Adam lost everything that he had and more besides. His 80,000 francs in personal savings were wiped out, and he owed another 70,000 francs for which he was sued. He managed to emerge from this calamity with only 2,400 francs annual income as professor of composition at the Conservatory.

A man of courage, Adam began to compose again when he found the stage of the Opéra-Comique open to him once more. In addition to the 1848-56 titles at the Opéra just noted, Adam did Le Farfadet (1852) for the Opéra-Comique, La Poupée de Nuremberg (1852) and Si J'étais Roi (1852) for the Théâtre-Lyrique, Le Sourd (1853) for the Opéra-Comique, La Faridondaine (1853) for the Porte Saint-Martin theatre, Le Roi des Halles (1853) for the Théâtre-Lyrique, Le Houzard de Berchiny (1855) for the Opéra-Comique, Falstaff (1856) for the Théâtre-Lyrique, and a number of other lesser titles. As if this were not enough, Adam added to his labors by writing for the Paris newspapers from time to time.

Adam had been decorated with the Cross of the Legion of Honor in 1836, and he had been elected to the Institute in 1844. Yet these honors and

his success on the boards of the principal theatres of the French capital had been nullified in his eyes by his one calamitous error in trying to be a business man as well as an artist of the theatre. After the blow of this failure he literally worked himself to death. He came home from the Opéra on the evening of 2 May 1856, and he was found dead in bed the following morning. His notes on his own life and music were published posthumously under the title of <u>Souvenirs d'un musicien</u> (1857). Today he is remembered almost exclusively for his greatest and most enduring hit, <u>Le Châlet</u> (1834).
BIBLIOGRAPHY: Adolphe Adam, <u>Souvenirs d'un musicien</u> (Paris: Calmann-Lévy, 1884); idem, <u>Derniers souvenirs d'un musicien</u> (Paris: Michel Lévy, 1859); DBF I, 429-31; EGC 9-10; Fétis I, 14-16; Jacques François Fromental Elie Halévy, <u>Souvenirs et portraits</u> (Paris: Michel Lévy frères, 1861), 275-306; Hut 140-43; Lajarte II, 154, 168, 171, 177, 179, 185, 187, 204-5, 209, 211, 219, 252-53; PBSW 170; Arthur Pougin, <u>Adolphe Adam</u> (Paris: G. Charpentier, 1877).

Adams, Suzanne (b. 28 November 1872, Cambridge, Mass.; d. 5 February 1953, London), soprano, studied voice under Mathilde Marchesi and Jacques Bouhy* before making her debut as a soprano in Juliette at the Opéra on 9 January 1895. Her career at the Opéra was relatively brief despite the success which she won as Charles Gounod's* heroine, because she left the company after appearing as Gilda in <u>Rigoletto</u>* in 1895 and as Marguerite in <u>Faust</u>* in 1896. She was invited to Convent Garden in 1898-1906, and she sang at the Metropolitan Opera in 1898-1903. She retired from the operatic stage in 1906 despite the enthusiasm she inspired in audiences as a highly skilled coloratura soprano.
BIBLIOGRAPHY: EFC 170; ICM 15; KRJ 3; <u>Musical America</u> 73 (July 1953), 19; SW 88; 183, 191.

Adiny, Ada (b. 1855, Boston; d. 1924, Dieppe), Soprano, <u>nèe</u> Adele Chapman, studied voice in Paris under Pauline Viardot-Garcia* and Giovanni Sbrighi. She sang in Italy, the United States, Germany, and Poland before coming to the Paris Opéra for the first time on May 1887 as Chiméne in <u>Le Cid</u>.*

Mlle Adiny remained at the Garnier Palace* until she left France to fill an engagement at La Scala in Milan during 1893. The first interval of five or six years during which she performed at the Opéra saw her sing the title-role of Aïda,* Valentine of Les Huguenots,* Sélika of L'Africaine,* and Dona Anna of Don Juan* during the year of her Paris debut. The following year, 1888, she was cast as Brunehilde in Sigurd* and as Rachel in La Juive.* She did Catherine d'Aragon in Camille Saint-Saëns'* Henry VIII* in 1889. The last part that she added to her repertory during this time was Dolorès of Patrie!* in 1891. She created a single role at the Garnier opera house, the duchess d'Estampes in Ascanio* on 21 March 1890.

Mlle Adiny appeared at the Opéra in the later years of her career, but she never felt the need of expanding her repertory further because she had already mastered the coloratura parts and the Wagnerian roles essential to the success of a soprano at the turn of the century. She had appeared in the premiere of La Walkyrie* at La Scala in Milan during 1893, and she had done the Italian versions of Sigurd, Patrie!, Le Cid, and La Navarraise during her 1894-95 engagement at this same theatre.

BIBLIOGRAPHY: EFC 159; ICM 16; KRJ 3; Martin 10; H. Moréno, "Débuts de Mlle Adiny à l'Opéra," Le Ménestrel 53 (8 May 1887), 180; SW 26, 29, 42, 62, 74, 112, 117, 130, 171, 203.

Aelia et Mysis was billed as a pantomimic ballet in two acts with a score by Henri Potier* and a libretto and choreography by Joseph Mazilier,* Cambon, Thierry, and Despléchin created its sets. It had its premiere at the Imperial Academy of Music on 21 September 1853, but audiences were not impressed by it, and it had to be dropped from the repertory after its 13th performance on 4 January 1854.

The ballet is set in Ostium at the villa of the Roman consul Messala. Aelia has just emerged from her bath, and the mime Scurra tries to amuse her, but his attempts in this direction are useless. Her father Messala asks her why she is so downcast when she is about to marry Prince Tigrane. He orders his lictors to spread Tigrane's presents before her, but she remains disinterested because she is in love with the

Greek poet and mime Euclio. The leader of the Asiatic company comes to greet her but begins to have misgivings about his prince's choice of a bride; Messala assures him that his daughter is only temporarily indisposed. When Messala is left alone with his daughter, he reproaches her for her indifference; she replies that he cannot expect her to be enthusiastic as well as obedient. Crafty Scurra suggests that Euclio be summoned to amuse her, and Messala agrees. The magician Mysis calls for Euclio, who enters with a company of mimes, dancers, acrobats, and other entertainers. Aelia displays a lively interest in him, and Scurra whispers to him that Messala's daughter is in love with him. Scurra orders everybody to leave so that his friend and ex pupil Euclio may amuse Aelia. Mysis refuses to heed this command; she accuses Euclio of preferring Aelia to her. He persuades her to leave, however, and the poet takes advantage of being alone with Aelia to declare his love to her. He urges her not to become the bride of an Asiatic prince who will take her from Rome. Mysis is eavesdropping on this conversation and swears to Euclio that she will denounce him to Messala unless Euclio leaves with her for Thessaly.

A fanfare of trumpets announces Tigrane's arrival for the wedding. A procession of Vestals led by the high priestess Samnio enters, and Messala gives the order for Scurra to pour a welcoming libation. The amphora has not been filled, and trembling Scurra drops it. Messala is furious over this evil omen, and he orders his negligent slave killed, but the high priestess commutes his sentence. Euclio tells Scurra that he is glad to see him alive and ready to help him. The attelana begins.

Vulcan (Scurra) strikes a rock and his troop of Cyclops emerge to help him in his quest for a wife. He prays to Jupiter, who drops a handful of flowers into the sea, and Venus (Aelia) emerges from the watery depths surrounded by Graces and Pleasures. Eros is in her company and presents her to Vulcan, who leads his bride into his grotto. Mischievous Eros decides to stir up trouble, and he shoots an arrow into the air. It hits Mars (Euclio), who enters with his troop of Amazons. The god of war falls passionately in love with Venus, and they embrace with great fervor.

Tigrane is so upset by this spectacle that he rises to object to the subject treated in the attelana, and Messala stops the show. Mysis is so angry that she reveals the secret of Aelia's love for the poet to her father. Enraged, Messala orders his lictors to execute Euclio, but Aelia declares that she will marry no one except the man she loves. Scurra helps the poet escape from the lictors; he throws himself into the sea to avoid capture, torture, and execution. Messala directs the Vestals to escort his daughter back to their temple.

The second act presents Aelia performing the usual duties of a novice in the grove surrounding the temple of Vesta. She is speaking with her aunt, the high priestess Samnio, when Mysis enters Vesta's enclave to report that Messala wishes his daughter to take her final vows before sunset. Aelia replies that she is still engaged to Euclio, but Mysis counters that he is dead. Samnio suggests that they wait until evening, when Vesta may offer a solution. The novices urge Mysis to dance for them, and, while they are watching her perform, Scurra shoots an arrow with a message attached to it: "Euclio lives." Aged Gorgo tells her youthful charges to stop their dancing and to leave the novice to her prayers. Alone, Aelia sees Euclio enter the enclosure by means of a rope ladder. Scurra follows him. Suddenly they realize that they are on dangerous ground. They rush to escape, but Mysis has cut the ladder. Euclio is about to stab her, when Aelia intervenes to explain that Mysis destroyed their means of escape because she is in love with him. Grateful Mysis is moved by Aelia's generosity and hides the men. Darkness falls, and the initiation rites for Aelia begin. Mysis orders the torch-bearers to dance in the hope that they will become too interested in themselves to notice Euclio and Scurra. The ruse fails, and Samnio discovers the intruders. Aelia rushes to Euclio and vows that they will perish together. Samnio summons the lictors, and the two men are condemned to die in the raging flames that angry Vesta has prepared for them. Aelia consents to join the Vestals if the culprits are spared, and the flames disappear. She escorts her lover and his faithful teacher from the temple under the protection of the sacred bough, and she then returns to the foot of Vesta's altar to die.

The score of Aelia et Mysis was correct, but it was uninspired and did not attain to any lyric heights. The male roles were filled by Lucien Petipa* (Euclio), Louis Mérante* (Tigrane), Lenfant (Messala, and Francisque Berthier* (Scurra). The female parts were created by Mme Olimpia Priora* (Aelia), Mme Guy Stephan (Mysis), Mlle Louise Marquet* (Samnio), and Mlle Aline (Gorgo).

BIBLIOGRAPHY: Chouquet 413; Léon Escudier, "Académie Impériale de Musique: Aelia et Mysis," FM 17 (25 September 1853), 309-10; Ivor Guest, The Ballet of the Second Empire (London: Pitman Publishing, 1974), 70-73, 258; Lajarte II, 213-214.

Affre, Augustarello (b 23 October 1858, St. Chinian; d. 27 December 1931, Cagness-sur-Mer), tenor, took his first lessons in voice in Toulouse and completed his studies at the Conservatoire in Paris. Encouraged by Pierre Gailhard,* director of the Paris Opéra, the tenor made his debut at the Garnier opera house as Edgard in Lucie de Lammermoor* on 22 January 1890. The same year he sang Léopold in La Juive,* the title-role in Camille Saint-Saëns'* Ascanio,* the duke in Rigoletto,* Fernand in La Favorite,* and Charles Gounod's* Roméo. In 1891, he was cast as Laërte in Hamlet,* Don Gomez in Henry VIII,* and Lohengrin. His third year on the stage of the Opéra saw him perform as Ruodi in Guillaume Tell,* Jean in Le Prophète,* Shahabarim in Salammbô,* Raoul in Les Huguenots,* and Tybalt in Roméo et Juliette.* Although he had reached the status of a house tenor by now, Affré's activities at the Opéra diminished after 1892 as far as presenting new roles was concerned, and he learned no new parts for public performance in Paris until he sang Rhadamès in 1895, Faust in 1896, and Samson in 1898. Subsequently, he was cast as Hercule in Astarte* (1901), Vasco in L'Africaine* (1902), the protagonist of Ernest Reyer's* Sigurd* (1905), Renaud in the 1905 revival of Christoph Willibald Gluck's Armide, and Nour-Eddin in the 1907 run of Thamara* (see eighteenth-century volume for Gluck and Armide).

Affré created the role of Un Prisonnier in Le Mage* by Jules Massenet* on 16 March 1891, and he did Sélim in La Statue* for its initial production at the Garnier Palace* on 6 March 1903. He sang

Belmont for the premiere of Un Enlèvement au sérail for its premiere at the new opera house on 1 December 1903 (see eighteenth-century volume for Un Enlèvement au sérail). Finally, on 6 June 1906, he sang Polyeucte in Leconte's cantata entitled Le Gloire de Corneille and produced to mark the tercentenary of the dramatist's death.

M. Affré had strong feelings of gratitude toward Pierre Gailhard of the Opéra, and he was never tempted to leave, despite his occasional engagements elsewhere. His success in Paris confirmed the wisdom of this decision. When M. Gailhard left the directorship of the Opéra at the end of 1907, however, M. Affré felt free to leave the theatre where he had made his debut nearly 20 years previously. He sang in San Francisco in 1911, New Orleans in 1912, and Havana in 1913. He entertained Allied soldiers during World War I, but retired after the Armistice.

BIBLIOGRAPHY: ICM 24; KRJ 3-4; H. Moréno, "Les Débuts du tenor Affré à l'Opéra," Le Ménestrel 56 (26 January 1890), 26-27; PBSW 170; SW 26, 29, 41-43, 79,88, 90, 106, 110, 112, 116, 131, 135, 137-38, 182, 190-91, 198, 203-4, 209, 367.

L'Africaine is an opera in five acts with music by Giacomo Meyerbeer* and a libretto by Eugène Scribe.* The composer was already dead at the time of the premiere of L'Africaine on Friday, 28 April 1865, and his work did not enjoy the usual benefit of the careful revisions he was in the habit of making during rehearsals to improve the quality of his compositions on the stage. The opera was a success from the start, however, and it was almost the only piece billed at the Imperial Academy of Music between 28 April and 1 November 1865. It returned 11,000 or 12,000 francs to the box office constantly during its first year at the theatre, while other programs were producing half this amount. It enjoyed new casts in 1867 and 1872; it reached its hundredth performance at the Le Peletire* opera house as early as 9 March 1866; it was billed on 225 dates before it was produced at the present opera house in Paris. In all, it was given 484 times by the Opéra before it was dropped from the repertory on 8 November 1902. Subsequently, it was mounted in Paris for the last time at the Gaîté-Lyrique in 1918. It managed to achieve this impressive record, although it was not staged in the French capital between 1894 and 1902 because its sets were destroyed in the warehouse fire of 6 January 1894. Yet the extent of its success was evident from the start. It had its premieres in London, Berlin, Brussels, and New York the same year that it had its world premiere in Paris.

The curtain rises on L'Africaine at the moment that Don Diégo is wishing that his daughter might marry Don Pédro, although she has been waiting two years for her beloved Vasco to return from his voyages of discovery. Don Pédro explains to her that Diaz' fleet, in which Vasco is sailing, has been destroyed by a hurricane off Africa, and he has been lost. The royal council meets to deliberate over future plans for exploration, and it is announced that a survivor wishes to speak of Diaz' fate and fleet. Don Diégo and Don Pédro are astonished to learn that the petitioner is Vasco da Gama (I, 1-3), who asks for a ship to sail around La Tempête cape. He guarantees wealth for his king and asks only for the chance to win glory for himself (I, 4). He presents two men named Sélika and Nélusko, whom he has picked up at sea; he argues that they are not from Africa, but from still undiscovered land that he would like to find. Don Pédro, Don Diégo, and the Grand Inquisitor lead the opposition to Vasco's plan, and it is rejected. Vasco remonstrates so angrily that an anathema is placed upon his head (I, 5-7).

The second act is also set in Lisbon, where Vasco is now a prisoner in an Inquisition dungeon with his two slaves. Sélika is moved by his plight, but Nélusko tries to slay him because he is a Christian. A queen in her own land, Sélika feeds her white master and reveals that she made the passage from east to west around La Tempête cape. Vasco is overjoyed to learn of the existence of inhabited islands off the coast of the continent, and he throws him arms around Sélika in his exuberance just as Don Pédro and Inès enter the cell (II, 1-3). Inès announces that she has brought Vasco his liberty, but her disdain is so evident that he feels impelled to give her Sélika and Nélusko to prove that they are only slaves to him. Sélika is crestfallen; Nélusko is indignant. Don Pédro announces that he has been chosen by the king to circumnavigate Africa. Vasco is furious, but Nélusko is exultant and offers to serve as Don Pédro's guide. The final blow for Vasco is the revelation that Don Pédro and Inès are now man and wife (II, 4).

Don Pédro's vessel has rounded the cape at the start of the third act, but he has lost his other ships, and Don Alvar suspects the pilot, who is Nélusko. Don Pédro believes that he is the first explorer to enter the new ocean, but a sail is sighted ahead. The wind rises; Nélusko warns of a storm and gives the order to head north. He sings with joy at the sight of the fierce tempest. A Portuguese craft approaches and lowers a boat (III, 1-2). Vasco boards Don Pédro's vessel to warn him of a reef ahead and the savages ready to salvage his wrecked craft (III, 3). Don Pédro greets his advice with sarcasm and refuses to believe him; he accuses him of trying to separate him from Inès. Vasco draws his sword, and Pédro calls for his marines. Vasco is about to be executed, when Don Pédro's ship runs onto the reef. Nélusko calls for his friends to board and to pillage the wreck (III, 4-6).

Sélika is returned to her throne, and all Christians except Vasco have been slain. He beholds the New World where he finds himself now and asks to return to his ship before he is sacrificed (IV, 1-3). Sélika saves his life by swearing that he is her husband and by forcing Nélusko to corroborate her assertion. The high priest reminds them that Brahman law dictates that this union is still in force, and Vasco swears his love for Sélika (IV, 4-6). Suddenly, Inès appears, and Sélika orders Nélusko to place her and Vasco on the latter's ship. They are to sail away and read Sélika's letter once they are out of sight of land (V, 1-2). A second Dido, Sélika goes to a grove of poisonous trees to dream of Vasco and heaven before dying in Nélusko's arms (V, 3-4).

The music of <u>L'Africaine</u> made an outstanding impression in its day, and there is scarcely any limit to the passages that might be recalled. Yet almost any list of its memorable moments would include Inès romance, "Adieu, rives du Tage" (I, 1); Selika's lullaby, "Sur mes genoux, fils du soliel" (II, 1); Nélusko's air, "Fille des rois, à toi l'hommage" (II, 2); the sailors' prayer, "O grand saint Dominique" (III, 1); and Nélusko's ballade, "Adamastor, roi des vagues profondes" (III, 2). Nor should the following high points be forgotten: the septet without accompaniment closing the second act; Sélika and the female chorus singing "Le rapide et léger navire" (III, 1); the Indian march in the coronation scene led by the high priest of Brahma (IV, 1); and the famous "air du mancenillier" sung by Sélika before her death (V, 3).

The roles of Vasco and Nélusko were created by Emilio Naudin* and Jean-Baptiste Faure,* respectively, with Mme Marie Sass* as Sélika and Mlle Marie Battu* as Inès. The choreography was provided by Louis Mérante,* and the ballet in the fourth act was danced originally by Mlle Marquet* and M. Cornet. The artists who filled the principal parts in L'Africaine for its last representation at the Opéra on 8 November 1902 were M. Affré* (Vasco), M. Noté* (Nélusko, Mme Lucienne Bréval* (Sélika), and Mme Marguerite de Noce (Inès).

BIBLIOGRAPHY: Neil Cole Arvin, Eugène Scribe and the French Theatre, 1815-60 (Cambridge: Harvard University Press, 1924), 210; Henri Blaze de Bury, Meyerbeer et son temps (Paris: Lévy Frères, 1865), 312-90; Chouquet 421-22; Henri de Curzon, Meyerbeer (Paris: Renouard, n.d.), 79-91; DDO I, 11-15; Christhard Frese, Dramaturgie der grossen Opern Giacomo Meyerbeers (Berlin-Lichterfelde: Robert Lienau, 1970), 218-67; JB 152-53; KCOB 743-48; Lajarte II, 237-38; OQE 157-58; SW, 25-26.

Agussol, Charlotte-Marie (b. 29 November 1863, Toulon; d. ?), vocalist, won second prizes in singing and in opéra-comique at the Paris Conservatoire in 1887 and made her debut at the Opéra as Urbain in Les Huguenots* on 19 September 1888. She enjoyed a relatively successful career at this theatre, where she created a half dozen parts over the next score of years:

Role	Opera	Premiere
Stéfano	Roméo et Juliette* (Gounod)	28 November 1888
Waltraute	La Walkyrie*	12 May 1893
Une Jeune Fille	Joseph*	26 May 1899
Ascagne	La Prise de Troie*	15 November 1899

Une Etoile	La Catalane*	24 May 1907
Une Voix	Le Lac des Aulnes*	25 November 1907

Mlle Agussol was cast in another 16 roles including Jenny in Guillaume Tell,* Siebel in Faust,* and Inès in La Favorite,* which she sang during her first year at the Garnier Palace.* Her strong soprano voice made her a likely choice for Wagnerian operas, although she went on to perform in only three other Wagnerian parts: the shepherd in Tannhäuser,* Ortlinde in La Walkyrie,* and the voice of the bird in Siegfried.* Her other assignments were the priestess in Aïda* and Colombe in Ascanio* during 1890 as well as one of the neophytes in Le Prophète* and three parts in Thaïs*: Crobyle (1896), Myrtale (1901), and the dancer la Charmeuse (1907). She appeared as Beltis in Le Fils de l'étoile* in 1904 and as a Plaisir in Armide during 1905 (see eighteenth-century volume for Armide). The remaining roles that she filled were Fatime in Zaïre* (1890) and Hilda in Sigurd* (1891).

BIBLIOGRAPHY: EFC 161; SW 41, 57, 127, 176-77, 189-91, 224-26.

Aïda is an opera in four acts and seven tableaux with a score by Giuseppe Verdi.* Its libretto was derived from a short sketch by Egyptologist Mariette Bey that Camille Du Locle* and Charles Nuitter* put into verse. This French poem was translated subsequently into Italian by Antonio Ghislanzoni, to whom Verdi and Giuseppina Strepponi made numerous suggestions. The work was commissioned by Ismaïl Pacha, viceroy of Egypt, who wished to produce it for the inauguration of the new opera house in Cairo, and it was given in the Italian version at this theatre on 24 December 1871.

The original French version of Aïda had its first billing at the Théâtre de la Monnaie in Brussels on 15 January 1877, and its Paris premiere took place on 1 August 1878 at the Théâtre Lyrique Ventadour because Verdi did not wish his work to be produced at the Opéra at this time. It was not until 22 March 1880 that the opera was mounted on the stage of the National Academy of Music. Louis Mérante* was in charge of the ballet in the second act, and Daran, Rubé, Chapéron, Chéret, J. B. Levastre, the elder

Levastre, and Carpézat all worked on the sets, while the costumes were designed by Eugène Locaste with technical assistance from the Egyptologist Maspero. Sax manufactured wind instruments especially for this premiere. The following year, on 15 October 1881, Aïda was on the bill, when the Garnier Palace* was illuminated with electricity for the first time.

The opera opens in the place of the king of Memphis, where Ramphis reveals to Rhadamès that Ethiopia is invading Egypt and that Isis has selected the leader of the Egyptian forces (I, 1). Alone, Rhadamès wishes that he were this leader and could lay his glory at Aïda's feet (I, 2). Amnéris asks him whether love as well as ambition does not prompt his hopes for the leadership of the army (I, 3). Aïda appears, and jealous Amnéris concludes that it is this slave girl whom Rhadamès loves. Aïda protests that it is the coming war, not love, that makes her nervous, but Amnéris is not deceived (I, 4). The king receives a message from the south. The Ethiopians are attacking Thebes with Amonasro at their head. In an aside, Aïda reveals that the latter general is her father, and the Egyptian king announces that Isis has chosen Rhadamès to lead the forces of Egypt. Aïda endures her dilemma alone, but Rhadamès declares his joy over his generalship to all present (I, 5.). When she is alone, Aïda analyzes the opposing aspects of her situation: a lover who may slay her father, and a father who may kill her lover (I, 6). The act closes with the second tableau presenting the dance and chorus of the priestesses in the temple of Vulcan, where the ceremony to inaugurate Rhadamès' leadership is held.

Amnéris is in her apartment, where she is preparing to appear at the triumphal feast. Aïda enters, and Amnéris asks her why she grieves. The slave replies that she mourns for her family. Crafty Amnéris tells her that Rhadamés is dead. Aïda cannot conceal her love for the general, and Amnéris is now certain that Aïda is her rival. She confesses to Aïda that Rhadamès is alive and accuses her of dissembling. Desperate, Aïda defies Amnéris, and the latter threatens the slave girl with death. Their quarrel is interrupted by the return of the Egyptian forces to the city (II, 1-2). The scene shifts to the throne room, where the king presides over the triumph following his victory. He hails the return of Rhadamès, who keeps gazing fondly at Aïda until Amnéris realizes that he loves her. Her conclusion is confirmed, when he frees his prisoners despite opposition from the priests. Ramphis suggests that the enemy will rise again, if their liberty is restored, but Rhadamès reminds the king and court that he has slain their leader Amonasro. He is believed because only Aïda has recognized her father among the prisoners. The king gives Amnéris' hand in marriage to Rhadamès, and the people acclaim their leader's wisdom. Only Aïda and Rhadamès feel betrayed by events (II, 3-4).

The moon is shining on the Nile and on the temple of Isis, where Ramphis, Amnéris, and a few veiled women have come to pray to the goddess before Amnéris' wedding (III, 1). Aïda enters to keep a rendezvous with Rhadamès, who has something to tell her (III, 2), but it is her father Amonasro who appears first. He knows that she is about to meet Rhadamès, and he convinces her to wrest from him the location of his army so that he can use this information to tactical advantage (III, 3). Rhadamès protests his love to Aïda, but she accuses him of lying to her because he allows the king, his ministers, and his daughters to dictate his actions. He reveals to her that a second battle with Ethiopa is inevitable. Thus, it is patriotism, not love for Amnéris, that dictates his movements and decisions. She suggests that they flee together, and he accepts her suggestion. She inquires about the route that they will follow to avoid his army, and he reveals that his forces will be at Napata (III, 4). Amonasro steps from the shadows and identifies himself. Rhadamès is filled with remorse because he has betrayed Egypt, but Amonasro insists that he and Aïda join forces with him (III, 5). Amnéris steps through the doorway of the temple; she sees Aïda with Rhadamès. She calls the guards, and they capture the fugitives before they can escape (III, 6).

Amnéris is in the royal palace, where she is trying to devise a plan to save Rhadamès. She has the guards bring him into her presence, but he refuses to speak in his own behalf. She informs him that Amonasro is dead and that Aïda has escaped. She promises him a pardon if he will renounce Aïda, but he rejects her offer (IV, 1-2). Amnéris regrets having called the guards to arrest

Rhadamès, and the priests enter to conduct his trial. He refuses to speak and is sentenced to be buried alive in the temple. Amnéris leaves in desperation (IV, 3).

The second tableau of the last act presents an upper stage depicting the interior of Vulcan's temple, while a lower stage represents a crypt. Rhadamès is entombed in the lower setting, which the priests are sealing. He is wondering where Aïda has gone, when she appears before him to explain that she anticipated his sentence and slipped into his tomb. They accept their fate, and Amnéris enters the temple of Vulcan to mourn the death of Rhadamès and to prostrate herself on his tomb (IV, 4).

Aïda was a resounding triumph in every opera house in Europe where it was billed, and it soon became a part of the international repertory. In Paris, it had phenomenal success in Italian at the Ventadour* theatre, and it has enjoyed at least 666 presentations in Italian and in French at the Opéra between the time of it premiere and 12 February 1968. Nearly every artist of note has been cast in it. At its premiere, the roles of the female characters were filled by Gabrielle Krauss* (Aïda), Rosine Block* (Amnéris), and Jenny Howe (La Grande Prêtresse). The male parts were created by Henri Sellier* (Rhadamès), Victor Maurel* (Amonasro), and Menu (the king). Subsequently the part of Aïda has been sung by such artists as Ada Adiny* (1887), Eva Duffranne* (1887), Marcelle Demougeot* (1903), Félia Litvinne* (1908), Maria Kousnietzoff* (1913), Germaine Lubin (1917), Jeanne Bonavia (1926), Marjorie Lawrence (1933), Renata Tebaldi (1959) (see twentieth-century volume for Lubin, Lawrence, and Tebald). Germaine Hoerner became especially associated with the role of Aïda on account of her appearances in this part between 1939 and 1952, but José Luccioni sang Rhadamès even more frequently between 1933 and 1952 (see twentieth-century volume for Hoerner and Luccioni). Other noteworthies to be cast in this part include Jean de Reské* (1887), Albert Alvarez* (1895), and, at the Châtelet, Enrico Caruso* (1910).

BIBLIOGRAPHY: Franco Abbiati, Giuseppe Verdi, 4 vols. (Milan: Ricordi, 1959) III, 406-10, 413-15, 456-59, 485-87, 647-49, 565-61; L'Avant-scène 4 (July-August 1976), 1-129; Michel Boctor, Le Centenaire de l'opéra "Aïda" (Alexandria: Les

Cahiers d'Alexandrie, 1972); Ferruccio Bonavia, Verdi (London: Dennis Dobson Ltd., 1947), 88-97; France-Yvonne Bril, Verdi (Paris: Hachette, 1972), 74-78; Andrea della Corte, Le opere de Giuseppe Verdi: Aïda (Milano: Bottega de poesia, 1923); Frederick J. Crowest, Verdi: Man and Musician (London: John Milne, 1978), 167-77, 241-47; DDO I, 17-23; Filippo Filippi, Musica e musicisti (Milano: G. Brigola, 1876), 319-90; Carlo Gatti, Verdi, the Man and His Music (New York: G. P. Putnam's Sons, 1955), 222-53; idem, Verdi (Milano: Edizioni "Alpes," 1931), 189-258; "Genesi dell' Aïda con documentazione inedita a cura di Saleh Abdoun," Quaderni dell'Istituto di Studi Verdinai 4 (11 December 1972), 1-185; Vincent Godefroy, The Dramatic Genius of Verdi (London: Victor Gollancz Ltd., 1977), II, 173-216; "M. Halanzier et Aïda, L'Art musical 14 (24 June 1875), 193-94; Paul Hume, Verdi, the Man and His Music (New York: E. P. Dutton and Metropolitan Opera Guild, 1977), 95-104; D. Humphreys, Verdi: Force of Destiny (New York: Henry Holt, 1948), 210-26, 243; Dyneley Hussey, Verdi (London: J. M. Dent & Sons, 1973), 170-99; Adolphe Jullien, Musiciens d'aujourd'hui (Paris: Librairie de l'art, 1892), 119-27; KCOB 629-45; LOA 179-80; George Martin, Verdi, His Music, Life and Times (New York: Dodd, Mead and Co., 1963), 446-60, 511-12; MCDE II, 1090-91, 1249-50; Albertine Morin-Labrecque, Verdi et ses opéras (Montréal: Les Editions de l'étoile, 1945), 26-27; MPPA 273-79; OEN I, 134-53; OQE 416-22; Pierre Petit, Verdi, trans. Patrick Bowles (London: John Calder, 1962), 127-36; Edward Prime-Stevenson, Long-haired Iopas (Florence: The Italian Mail, 1927), 145-72; Max de Schauensee, The Collector's Verdi and Puccini (Philadelphia: J. B. Lippincott, 1962), 74-81; William Kelly Simpson, "At the Source: Auguste Mariette," ON 40, no. 17 (6 March 1976), 32-34; Stoullig VI (1880), 15-24; SW 27-30; Thompson 26, 2102; Francis Toye, Giuseppe Verdi; His Life and Works (New York: Alfred A. Knopf, 1946), 345-59; Giuseppi Verdi, Aïda (New York: Watts, 1970); Verdi's "Aïda," ed. and trans. Hans Busch (Minneapolis: University of Minnesota Press, 1978); Joseph Wechsberg, Verdi (New York: G. P. Putnam's Sons, 1974), 143-53, 195-96; Franz Werfel and Paul Stefan, Verdi: the Man and His Letters, trans. Edward Downes (New York: L. B. Fischer, 1942), 353-54.

Aimon, Pamphile-Léopold-François (b. 4 October 1779, Vaucluse; d. 2 February 1866, Paris), composer, received his first music lessons from his father and went on to head the orchestra at the Marseilles Theatre in 1796. He applied himself to the study of the major scores of German and Italian composers during his sojourn in this southern city and then left for Paris in 1817 to seek his fortune as a composer.

Aimon's first task was to set Jean Bouilly's* Les Jeux floraux* for performance at the Opéra on 16 November 1818. This was to be his only contribution to the Royal Academy of Music, and it failed. Aimon accepted an invitation to lead the orchestra at the Gymnase dramatique in 1821, therefore, and he wrote some very popular vaudeville airs here. He moved to the Comédie-Française in 1822 to fill the post of orchestra leader left vacant here by Baudron's retirement. Finally, he decided to leave this theatre after a few years to compose at his leisure. He did a number of recital pieces for the violin, clarinet, bassoon, piano, and other reed or string instruments, but his major efforts were scores for Jouy's Velléda and three other works for the Opéra entitled Abufar, Alcide et Omphale, Les Chérusques as well as Martinelli's Les Deux Figaros for the Opéra-Comique. None of these five compositions was ever produced.

Aimon was also the author of four studies on music including a treatise on harmony. These writings were on the more elementary aspects of music and grew out of Aimon's resolution to renounce his theatrical ambitions that had proven so fruitless and to remain content with teaching.

BIBLIOGRAPHY: DBF I, 1023; Fétis I, 42-43; Lajarte II, 93, 113, 258.

Aladin Ou La Lampe Merveilleuse was billed at the Opéra as a fairy tale opera in five acts with a score started by Nicolò Isouard and completed by Ange-Marie Benincori (see eighteenth-century volume for Isouard). The latter composer wrote the march in B flat of the first act, the second and third scenes of the second act, and the last three acts. The score included parts for the harmonica and the ophicleide. Charles Etienne* created the libretto, and Pierre Gardel was responsible for the choreography (see eighteenth-century volume for Gardel). Appropriately enough, illuminating gas was used for the first time at the Opéra for Aladin, which had its premiere at this theatre on 6 February 1822. It proved a very popular composition, perhaps because 170,000 francs had been spent on its production. It was mounted every year between 1822 and 1831 and was not dropped until after its 145th presentation on 22 February 1830. It was mounted on 53 programs in 1822 alone.

The opera opens with the fisherman Aladin living in a simple hut with his sister Zarine and his mother, Thémire. It is daybreak, and he is dreaming of his beloved Princess Almasie when his mother awakens him to tend to his nets. Thémire insists that her son must be mad to think of a princess whom no one can see until her wedding day. Zarine reminds him that King Timorkan has already asked for her hand in marriage. She is convinced that her brother has lost his sanity when he insists that he sees the princess every day. He explains that he passes close to her gardens in his fishing boat to sing to her (I, 1-2). The cádi informs Thémire that her house must be evacuated because it is to be demolished lest King Timorkan be obliged to pass around it on his way to the palace. She and her daughter are complaining about being displaced, when Aladin returns to announce that happiness is within their grasp. He has rescued a stranger at sea, and the grateful man has presented him with a lamp endowed with incredible powers. He illustrates his meaning by pressing a spring on the lamp. Celestial music is heard; an invisible chorus offers to do his bidding; Ismenor appears with his genii to explain to Aladin that it was he who was drowning in his human form when Aladin pulled him from the sea. Grateful, he vows to serve him in every way possible as long as Aladin possesses the lamp and keeps it lighted at night (I, 3-5). Aladin's first wish is for rich garb to enable him to present himself at court. The Cádi returns to destroy Thémire's home, but the genii stops him with flaming swords (I, 6-8). Aladin directs the cádi to announce his arrival in court to ask for the princess' hand, and he orders the genii to construct a sumptuous palace to serve as his residence (I, 9).

The setting changes to the royal palace, where Almasie confides to Zulime that she is unhappy over her imminent marriage to Timorkan, who has threatened war if she does not become his bride (II, 1-2). The bloodthirsty king pledges to make the entire world subservient to Almasie, and he assures her that he will slay her enemies to the last man, but she asks to be spared these violent boasts (II, 3). The cádi, dressed in silk and jewels, announces Aladin's arrival, and desperate Almasie takes hope, while Timorkan becomes enraged at the prospect of having a rival. He vows to crush him and his army (II, 4-6). Aladin evades Almasie's questions about his provenance, but he assures her of his love for her and reveals that it was he who disguised himself as a fisherman to sing to her. He calls upon his genii to drive Timorkan from Almasie's country, and the princess declares a victory celebration to take place as soon as he returns to court (II, 7-8).

The third act is set in Aladin's palace, where his mother Thémire longs for the peaceful days she used to spend in her humble abode by the sea. Aladin's triumph is proclaimed with shouts of joy, and preparations begin for his marriage to Almasie. Timorkan is forgiven and granted the freedom of the palace (III, 1-3), but he is humiliated by his defeat and refuses to be treated with pity. A band of shadowy spirits assure him that his moment of revenge is at hand, and they invite him to the underworld (III, 4). The bridal couple attend a celebration featuring singing and dancing (III, 5).

The fourth act is set in the wedding chamber, where the cádi informs Aladin that he cannot remove his bride's veil until daylight. The law of the land forbids it, but the groom is certain of Almasie's beauty although she has worn a veil since childhood. He places his precious lamp upon a tripod, and Thémire presents Almasie to him (IV, 1-3). Aladin asks Almasie to unveil so that he can hear her speak, and his lamp flares up as if to support Almasie's protest that his request is illegal. She demands that the lamp be removed, but he refuses lest he break its charm, and she walks toward the door. Afraid of losing her, Aladin extinguishes the lamp and loses his title to it. The shadowy spirits appear with Timorkan and transfer the lamp and its powers to the rejected suitor. Aladin's palace disappears (IV, 4).

The fifth act opens in Timorkan's palace of bronze, where bewildered Almasie does not understand what has happened. Ismenor informs her that she is in Timorkan's power, and he adds that Aladin must die. He suggests to Almasie that she try to recover control of the lamp. She agrees with him and decides that she may have more success by pretending to love her captor. She begins by apologizing to Timorkan for having been foolish enough to believe that she could love Aladin. She follows this ploy with an admission of her interest in him. Deceived, Timorkan assures her that they will be married without delay, and he commands his soldiers to recognize their queen (V, 1-3). The cádi is amazed by Almasie's fickle heart and reports her words and actions to disillusioned Aladin, who welcomes his execution as a solution to his painful predicament. Ismenor enters to assure him that his situation is about to improve (V, 4-6). The scene shifts to a palace of light, where Almasie is seated on a throne with Zarine and Thémire as her attendants. She has managed to put Timorkan to sleep with a secret potion, and she has stolen his lamp. Aladin receives a crown from resourceful Almasie, and the opera ends in a joyous celebration in honor of Aladin's restored bride and lamp (V, 7).

The score was not an unusual piece of work, but it found favor with audiences in a number of places, especially in act 3, scene 5, where Zarine sang "Venez, charmantes bayadères." The role of Aladin was sung by Nourrit père and fils with the other male roles created by Dérivis (Timorkan), Dabadie (the cádi), and Bonel (a genius). The female parts were created by Mlles Grassari (Almasie), Reine (Zuline), Paulin (Thémire), Jawurek (Zarine), and Caroline Lépi (Ismenor). The action was set in Hormuz in Persia.

BIBLIOGRAPHY: Chouquet 390; DDO I, 24; Lajarte II, 100-101; Moniteur universel 39 (8 February 1822), 185.

Alaffre, Benjamin (b. 1803, Paulhan; d. ?) was a professor on the faculty of the lycée at Toulouse and the author of two French grammar books published in 1839 and 1854 that continued to enjoy reprintings for nearly 40 years. He composed a tribute to Dante for the Jeux Floraux held in the city where he taught. Ricordi entrusted him with the task of translating Giuseppe Verdi's* Luisa Miller into French without any apparent hesitation, but Verdi had not been consulted, and he was dismayed to learn of his representative's seemingly casual selection of a translator for his opera. Alaffre's French version Louise Miller* was his only contribution to the Opéra.

BIBLIOGRAPHY: Franco Abbiati, Giuseppe Verdi, 4 vols. (Milan: G. Ricordi, 1959) II, 156, 161, 180, 184, 186; Catalogue général des livres imprimés de la Bibliothèque Nationale, (Paris: Catin, 1924) I, 439-40; DBF I 1064.

Alary, Jules (b. 1814, Milan; d. 17 April 1891, Paris), composer, was born of French parents in Italy and studied music at the Conservatory in Milan. His first work entitled Rosamonda was mounted initially on 10 June 1840 at Florence, although he had been in Paris since 1835. In the French capital, he made a reputation for himself in certain exclusive and aristocratic circles by writing pieces for private concerts. later he gave public concerts in Paris and in London and included his own works on the programs, especially his popular barcarolle entitled Le Lac de Como.

All these activities were quite pleasant, but time was passing, and Alary had not yet produced the great dramatic work that the public was expecting him to create, although he did evoke admiration with his oratorio, La Rédemption. His less serious contribution to the stage was his Le Tre Nozze performed at the Théâtre-Italien. His publications included a number of ariettas, but his only work for the Opéra was La Voix humaine* done with Anne-Honoré-Joseph Duveyrier* and dropped shortly after its premiere on 30 December 1861.

BIBLIOGRAPHY: DBF I, 1127; Fétis I, 46; Lajarte II, 232.

Albers, Henri (b. Amsterdam, 1 February 1866; d. Paris, 12 September 1926), French singer, made his debut as a baritone in Anvers and went on to sing in other provincial cities of France before appearing in Monte Carlo and London. In 1898, he joined a troupe featuring Emma Calvé,* Nellie Melba,* and the Reszke* brothers, and he appeared with these international stars in the opera houses of New York, New Orleans, and San Francisco.

The experienced baritone returned to Europe after his North American appearances to sing Zurga in Les Pêcheurs de perles on 26 October 1899 at the Opéra-Comique, and he was heard again in the French capital on 1 July 1908, when he was cast in the part of Wolfram in Tannhäuser* at the Garnier palace.* This same year, 1908, he sang Athanaël in Thaïs* on the same stage, and he created the part of André Thorel in Thérèse,* when the second act of this work by Jules Massenet* was staged for a gala at the Garnier on 10 December 1911.

Yet it was at the Opéra-Comique that Albers was billed most constantly. Here, he sang a number of parts, including Escamillo in Carmen,* Golaud in Pelléas et Mélisande,* Scarpia in Tosca, and Albert in Werther* besides creating the title-role of Macbeth and the parts of Tonio in Paillasse* and Kurwenal in Tristan et Isolde* (see twentieth-century volume for Tosca).

BIBLIOGRAPHY: KRJ 6-7; PBSW 170; SW 210; WOC 280.

Alboni, Marietta (b. 6 March 1826, Castello; d. 23 June 1894, d'Avray), vocalist, exhibited a precocious interest in languages and music, and her parents arranged for her to study these subjects in her native village and Bologna. Her intelligence and enthusiasm for music aroused Gioucchino Rossini's* interest in her, and he helped her to learn the contralto roles in his work. She made her debut as Maffeo Orsini in Lucrezia Borgia in 1843 and then moved on to La Scala to appear in Domenico Gaetano Donizetti's* La Favorita. She created enough interest at this latter theatre to have her contract renewed for four seasons.

She left her native country for the first time to appear in Vienna, St. Petersburg, and Hamburg in 1845. In Germany, she also gave concerts at Leipzig and Dresden before undertaking an excursion to Hungary. She then stopped in Rome long enough to sing during the 1847 carnival season and to appear as Arsace in Rossini's Semiramide before making her first trip to England. At this time, Jenny Lind was the principal attraction of the singing world, and it seemed unlikely that a relatively unknown Italian contralto could challenge her position. Yet although the Swedish nightingale was already enjoying undisputed success at another theatre, Alboni challenged her supremacy with her own programs, and she was soon singing to large audiences at Covent Garden.

Mlle Alboni had now attained the status of an international star, but she felt that her credits would remain incomplete as long as she did not perform in Paris. Her next public appearances were in the French capital, therefore, where she opened with a series of three concerts before singing the role of Arsace again at the Italian theatre. Her triumph in this part was followed by a second success in La Cenerentola, but her efforts as Malcolm in La Donna del lago failed to persuade her audiences that her voice was suited for this robust part. Yet it was agreed by spectators and critics alike that her performance was more than competent, and it was the Revolution of 1848 rather than any diminution of her vocal powers that brought the first phase of Alboni's Paris career to a halt.

Like many other artists, she went to England and Belgium to avoid the violence of 1848 in Paris, but she returned to the Théâtre Italien the following year. She added L'Italiana in Algeri and La Gazza-Ladra to her Paris offerings, and then, in 1850, she went on a tour that took her to Geneva, Lyon, Marseilles, and Bordeaux, where she performed in French. After doing Charles VI, La Favorite,* La Reine de Chypre, and La Fille du régiment in the provinces, she undertook the parts of Odette in Charles VI* and the title-role in Zerline* as well as Fidès in Le Prophète* in the French capital. Daniel Auber* created the part of Zerline for her, but she was quite successful in all these works, because she had learned finally that an opera is not merely an opportunity to concertize in costume, but rather a dramatic presentation demanding stage presence and a capacity to act.

Alboni continued her career with a tour of Spain and a series of appearances in North and South America. Her visit to the United States in 1852 was especially rewarding, and she did not retire from the theatre until the death of her husband, Count Pepoli, in 1866. She settled down in Paris, where she married an officer in the French army in 1877.

BIBLIOGRAPHY: Chouquet 411-12; Ellen Clayton, Queens of Song (Freeport, N.Y.: Books for Libraries Press, reprint of 1865 ed.), 439-50; DBF I, 1279; DEO 13; Escudier, "L'Alboni," FM 10 (29

August 1847), 285-86; EFC 143; EZF 126-28; Fétis I, 56-57; GE I 1185; ICM 30; Herman Klein, Great Women-Singers of My Time (Freeport, N.Y.: Books for Libraries Press, 1968), 156-61; Lajarte II, 172, 209; Léon, "Mlle Alboni à l'Opéra," FM 10 (17 October 1847), 341-42; Edward B. Marks, They All Had Glamour (Westport, Conn.: Greenwood Press, 1944), 138-41; PBSW 170; Henry Pleasants, The Great Singers (New York: Simon and Schuster, 1966), 223-24; Arthur Pougin, Marietta Alboni (Paris: Plon-Nourrit, 1912); Alphonse Royer, Histoire de l'Opéra (Paris: Bachelin-Deflorenne, 1875), 163; N. Slonimsky, "Musical Oddities," Etude 73 (5 June 1955), 5; Thurner 218-24.

Alfred Le Grand was billed as a pantomime ballet in three acts with choreography by Jean Aumer and music by Wincelas Robert, count de Gallenberg* (see eighteenth-century volume for Aumer). Every effort was made to secure success for this work. A complete military band was featured on the stage; the hero made a valiant stand on a bridge; three striking and expensive sets were provided by Pierre Cicéri.* Yet the composition enjoyed only 14 performances during its first run at the Opéra from its premiere on 18 September 1822 until 17 February 1823. It was revived for another seven presentations between 23 June and 24 September 1824, and it was billed on another four dates in 1825-26. It had its 25th and last production on 4 September 1826.

The ballet opens in Altheney near Dénulf's farm and within sight of Count Edelbert's castle. The villagers have gathered to select the most virtuous maiden of the region, but they return to their homes after the completion of preparations for the celebration. Alfred and his page Oliver enter disguised and in flight before the approaching Danes (I, 1-3). Oliver knocks at Dénulf's door, and Bertha gives the fugitives food and drink, but her mother scolds her and the page, when the latter kisses Bertha's hand in gratitude (I, 4-6). The father thinks that he recognizes his king in the stranger, but he dismisses this notion, when "Wulf" asks to remain on his farm as a cowherd (I, 7). Alfred reveals his identity to his former warrior because of the latter's loyalty and generosity, but the women in the household are excluded from their secret. Mme Dénulf accepts the new cowherd more easily, however, when she hears the melodious music he creates upon his harp. Bertha and Oliver dance (I, 8-9), but they are interrupted by the music and the laughter of the villagers returning to the celebration. Bertha wins the contest for the most virtuous maid, but none of the swains can win her hand by hitting the falcon tied to the top of a tree, although Adelmo comes closest to carrying off the prize. Alfred asks permission to become a contestant, and he scores a perfect performance. Adelmo and Mme Dénulf are upset, but the king relinquishes his claim to Bertha's hand (I, 10). The Danes announce that anyone aiding Alfred will be executed, and Alswith rushes into the village to seek help in rescuing her father from the enemy. Alfred leads the armed villagers to the attack (I, 11-13).

The scene shifts to the count's castle, where Alfred returns Count Edelbert to his daughter Alswith. She cares for the king's wounds, and he reveals to Oliver his love for their hostess (II, 1-3). Alswith regrets that she can never admit her love for a lowly cowherd, but he refrains from disclosing his identity. The count enters with Alswith's fiance Odun, whose jealousy is aroused immediately. Alfred reassures him that his feelings for Alswith are only sentiments of gratitude (II, 4-6), but he declares his love to her as soon as they are alone. She suggests that Alfred improve his station in life by becoming a warrior. A banquet is held to hail Odun's victory over the enemy (II, 7-9). Oliver announces that the Danes are pursuing Alfred, and Dénulf adds that they have put his farm and the village to the torch. A portrait of Alfred in the banquet hall suggests to the count that his humble guest is the king, and Alfred admits his identity. The Saxons swear to follow him into battle (II, 10-11).

The Danish soldiers bring the count before their leader Gothrun, and the prisoner is attacked on account of his defiant attitude (III, 1-2). Gothrun offers the count his freedom if he will espouse the Danish cause, but he rejects the offer (III, 3). Dénulf enters disguised as a Dane and manages to liberate Alswith and her father (III, 4-5). The Danish camp falls into complete chaos on account of Gothrun's absence; Alfred and Oliver mingle with the enemy to add to the confusion (III, 6-7). Gothrun returns and orders the two strangers from his camp. The Saxons attack immediately, and their unyielding valor wins them complete victory (III, 8-10). Count Edelbert and his daughter rejoin the Saxon army, and a triumphal march announces Alfred's return to his throne. The Saxon king grants total pardon to the Danes, and they swear fealty to him. Alfred crowns Alswith and asks her to share his throne forever (III, 11).

The large cast of Alfred le Grand was headed by M. Albert in the title-role with the other male parts filled by Milon (Count Edelbert), Mérante (Gothrun), Aumer (Dénulf), Coulon (Adelmo), Mont-Joie (Odun). Mlle Bigottini was cast as Oliver. The three important female roles were assigned to Mme Anatole (Alswith), Mme Elie (Mme Denulf), and Mlle Julie Aumer (Bertha).

BIBLIOGRAPHY: Chouquet 390; Lajarte II, 102-3; Moniteur Universel 262 (19 September 1822), 1558; ibid. 263 (20 September 1822), 1562; RBP 43-46; Wks II, 3081.

Ali-Baba was an opera in four acts and a prologue with a score by Luigi Cherubini and words by Eugène Scribe* and Anne-Honoré-Joseph Duveyrier Méles.* Jean Coralli* was the choreographer (see eighteenth-century volume for Cherubini). The work was written for the Opéra-Comique originally, but its authors revised it and took it to the Opéra for its premiere on 22 July 1833. It was not successful, probably because it was largely a reworking of an old 1793 composition entitled Koukourgi by Duveyrier's father. After its first performance, it was repeated on the evenings of 24, 26, 31 July 1833 before being withdrawn for changes designed to make it more acceptable. It was then returned to the stage on 11 September 1833 for another six presentations, but it had to be dropped from the repertory after its tenth billing on Christmas 1833.

The prologue was written as part of the main intrigue and is set in a forest where Nadir laments being unable to wed Délie, whose avaricious father has pledged her hand in marriage to his wealthy rival, Aboul-Hassan. Suddenly, desolate Nadir sees 40 thieves emerging from a cave in a rock that opens at the command of "Sésame!" The brigands leave, and Nadir enters their secret vault by pronouncing the magic word (sc. 1-2). He steals their wealth and transports his newly acquired riches to Ali-Baba's home to convince the latter that his marriage to Délie can bring him greater wealth than Aboul-Hassan has ever seen (I, 1-3). Speechless, Ali beholds Nadir's priceless caravan. He recovers long enough to award his daughter's hand to him, but he retracts this hasty decision as soon as he remembers that Aboul-Hassan is head of customs and can confiscate his smuggled stores of coffee. Nadir persuades him to change his mind once again by tripling the sum he will offer for Délie. The young couple rejoice over their success, but Hassan claims his bride, and fearsome Ali must surrender Délie to him (I, 4-7).

Nadir bribes Hassan to forget Ali's coffee and daughter, and slaves from all quarters of the world dance at the Délie-Nadir wedding. Ali insists upon knowing the source of his son-in-law's sudden wealth, and Nadir tells him the secret of "Sésame!" on condition that he never go to the magic rock (II, 1-4). When Ali is transporting his coffee to his warehouse in Erzeroum for safekeeping, Délie is kidnapped, and Ali disappears. Nadir believes that Aboul-Hassan is responsible and mobilizes a force to rescue his beloved and her father (II, 5-6).

At the start of the third act, the thieves decide to leave their quarters to plunder Ali-Baba's home because their last caravan raid brought them only coffee and a slave girl called Délie. Ali-Baba enters their camp shortly after their departure, but he has dropped his memorandum with "Sésame!" written on it, and he cannot reopen the rock before the outlaws' return because the magic word has escaped from his memory (III, 1-4). The thieves discover him and prepare to kill him despite Délie's pleas for mercy (III, 5-6), but Calaf recognizes him and his daughter, and he suggests that they will return a handsome ransom. They ride off to Erzeroum to execute this plan (III, 7).

Nadir is blaming Aboul-Hassan for Délie's disappearance, when she and her father ride up to Ali's stronghold with Ours-Kan and Calaf disguised as merchants. The two bandits dismiss everybody except Délie, Ali, and Nadir. Délie exits to prepare supper; Ali and Ours-Kan leave to settle the matter of the ransom; Nadir remains in the custody of Calaf, but he forces the thief to reveal to him the true identity of Ours-Kan (IV, 1-5). Morgiane reports to Nadir that their servants have been dismissed and that 40 trespassing brigands are hiding in sacks in Ali's warehouse (IV, 6). Ours-Kan returns to order a banquet and dancing before his men emerge from their hiding places to seize Ali's wealth. Aboul-Hassan's soldiers enter at the last moment to impound and to burn Ali's illegal coffee to which the torch is put without the customs officers observing the outlaws hidden in it (IV, 7-8).

The principal roles in Ali-Baba were sung by Nourrit as Nadir, Levasseur as Ali-Baba, and Mme Damoreau as Délie. The work also enjoyed sets by Cicéri, Cambon, and Philastre.

It will be recalled that the now aged Cherubini* had written a successful La Bacchanale for his Achille à Scyros (I, 9) in 1804. He repeated this composition in a revised form in the divertissement of the last act of Ali-Baba (see eighteenth-century volume for divertissement).

BIBLIOGRAPHY: *Edward Bellasis, Cherubini: Memorials Illustrative of His Life (New York: Da Capo Press, 1971), 250-57; Charles de Boigne, Petits Mémoires de l'Opéra (Paris: Librairie Nouvelle, 1857), 74-75; Chouquet 397; DDO I, 33; Richard Hohenemser, Luigi Cherubini: sein Leben und seine Werke (Wiesbaden: Dr. Martin Sändig, 1969), 472-82; Lajarte II, 146; Moniteur universel 204 (23 July 1833), 1870; ibid. 205 (24 July 1833), 1876; M. Quatrelles L'Epine, Cherubini: notes et documents inédits (Paris: Fischbacher, 1913), 121; Wks III, 14; WLC 63, 89.*

Aline, Reine De Golconde was a pantomime-ballet in three acts with choreography by Jean Aumer and music by Pierre Berton and Pierre Monsigny and newly arranged by Gustave Dugazon (see eighteenth-century volume for Aumer, Berton, and Monsigny). Not to be confused with Michel-Jean Sedaine's heroic ballet bearing the same title, Aumer's composition had its premiere on 1 October 1823, and it was successful enough to enjoy 19 performances before the end of the year (see eighteenth-century volume for Sedaine). It was retained in the repertory and was mounted on another 29 dates between 1824 and 1826. Its 48th and final presentation took place on 28 April 1826.

The ballet opens in the royal palace with Osmin greeting his wife Zélie and his son Nadir. This affectionate family scene is interrupted by the arrival of queen Aline and her escort. She dismisses her guards and distributes presents to her retinue, but she ignores Sigiskar, when he proposes marriage to her (I, 1-2). Osmin and Zélie sing a ballad describing the queen's past happiness with Saint-Phar. She orders all her attendants except Zélie to leave so that she can show her a picture of the village where she knew Saint-Phar (I, 3-4). The arrival of the French ambassador is announced, and the queen greets him only to discover that he is Saint-Phar. Zélie recognizes him from the picture she has just seen, but she remains silent. Sigiskar is puzzled by the strange effect the ambassador seems to produce upon the two women (I, 5-6).

The setting changes to an exotic Asiatic garden, where Aline and Zélie appear in each other's garments to test Saint-Phar's love for the queen. Osmin cannot identify them correctly on account of their veils, but Aline takes the added precaution of directing her servants and retinue to obey Zélie (II, 1-4). Saint-Phar mistakes Zélie for the queen, and Zélie responds by exerting her wiles and charms upon him. He pays no attention to her, however, because he has eyes only for her companion, who disappears suddenly (II, 5-6). When Aline returns, he tries to speak with her but is put to sleep under a shower of poppies. He is carried back to the village, and Aline is overjoyed, although Sigiskar is enraged by the "queen's" advances to the ambassador. He persuades his friends to join his conspiracy to dethrone Aline and to kill Saint-Phar (II, 7-8).

Zélie and Osmin are waiting for Saint-Phar to awaken, while peasants dressed as inhabitants of Provence dance a ronde in the village decorated to look like Saint-Phar's native hamlet. When he opens his eyes, he recognizes the place of his birth and early years. He recalls his happy days here with Aline. He calls her by name (III, 1-2). Aline appears, and he recognizes her. They embrace (III, 3). The natives of Golconde continue to execute Provençal dances to sustain the illusion, but Sigiskar and his accomplices put the village to the torch (III, 4-5). Saint-Phar mobilizes his grenadiers for a counterattack, and his victory inspires a lavish celebration in honor of the queen. Sigiskar refuses to ask for a pardon, and Aline ignores Saint-Phar's plea to forgive him. Saint-Phar proves his continuing fidelity to Aline by refusing to take the queen's hand, because he is unaware of her true identity (III, 6-7). Zélie leads him to the queen finally, and he recognizes her as Aline. She throws herself into his arms and offers to share her throne with him. He agrees. The ballet ends in a sumptuous celebration (III, 8-9).

Mme Emilie Bigottini scored another triumph as Aline, and the other female roles were filled by Mme Lise Noblet (Zélie) and Mlle Bertrand (Nadir). The principal male parts were danced by Louis Montjoie (Saint-Phar), Paul (Osmin), Jean Aumer (Sigiskar) (see eighteenth-century volume for Bigottini, Montjoie, and Aumer).

BIBLIOGRAPHY: AEM I, 1802-12; Adolphe Boschot, Chez les musiciens (Paris: Plon, 1922), 23-52; CB 44-45; Chouquet 391; DDO I, 334; P. Hédouin, Notice historique sur Monsigny (Paris: Au Magasin de musique de la lyre moderne, 1821), 1-28; Lajarte II, 106; Moniteur universel 276 (3 October 1823), 1170; Arthur Pougin, Monsigny et son temps (Paris: Fischbacher, 1908); RBP 49-52; Désiré R. Rochette, Notice historique sur la vie et les ouvrages de M. Berton (Paris: 1846), 41-42; Wks II, 3087.

Alizard, Adolphe-Joseph-Louis (b. 29 December 1814, Paris; d. January 1850, Marseilles), vocalist, persuaded his mother to allow him to pursue a musical career instead of becoming a teacher. When he went to Beauvais with her, therefore, he studied under the direction of Victor Magnien. The latter sent his pupil to Paris to study violin with Urhan, but his new teacher was so impressed with his voice that they arranged for him to enter the Conservatoire so that he might study singing under Banderali. Two years after his admission to the Conservatoire, in 1836, young Alizard was awarded first prize in singing.

The management of the Opéra learned of his talents immediately and offered him a contract. He accepted and made his debut as a bass in the role of Saint-Bris in Les Huguenots* on 23 June 1837. He enjoyed a moderate success and took Massol's place as Fieramosca in Benvenuto Cellini* in January 1839. He appeared in a minor part at the premiere of La Vendetta* on 11 September 1839 and sang friar Benoist in Le Drapier* on 8 January 1840. When he was billed as the hermit in Le Freischütz* on 7 June 1841, he was obliged to admit himself that he would never be given a major rôle at the Opéra because the public refused to accept his deep bass voice emanating from his peculiarly shaped and overly short body.

As first step toward a more satisfactory career, Alizard went to Brussels for two years, where he tried to become a baritone. His attempts to master the baritone repertory of the Opéra led to ruinous results, however, and he was advised to take a vacation in Italy so that he might profit by a warmer climate in his efforts to restore his bronchial tubes. He was back in Paris in 1846, and he had every reason to believe that he was healed. He sang Roger in Jérusalem* on 26 November 1847, Nugnes in L'Apparition* on 16 June 1848, and Lucifer in L'Eden* on 25 August 1848. then, in October 1848, Alizard was stricken once again. This time the blow was more crushing, because it was his larynx that was afflicted. He went to the midi to regain his health for the second time, but it was too late, and he was dead within a period of months.

BIBLIOGRAPHY: Chouquet 401-403, 409; DBF II, 74-75; E., "Rentrée d'Alizard à l'Opéra," FM 10 (18 April 1847), EZF 128-29; Fétis I, 69-70; GE II, 241-42; Lajarte I, 158, 187; SW 101, 118.

Alvarex, Albert (b. 1861, Bordeaux; d. 26 February 1933, Nice) was a French tenor whose true name was Albert-Raymond Gourron. After serving in the army as a bandmaster, he went to Paris in 1883 to study under Martini. He made his debut in Ghent and toured the provinces before appearing on the stage of the Opéra for the first time as Faust on 14 March 1892, a role he repeated for the 1,000th presentation of Charles Gounod's* opera on 14 December 1894.

The young tenor made a favorable impression upon the public in his first performance at the Opéra, and management retained him to appear in a number of important title-roles in works currently enjoying a surge of popularity. He sang the parts of Roméo, Lohengrin, and Tannhäuser in the 100th presentations of these compositions: Roméo et Juliette* on 29 October 1892, Lohengrin* on 28 april 1894, and Tannhäuser* on 11 January 1901. He was also cast as Camille Saint-Saëns'* Samson in 1893, Louis Reyer's* Sigurd in 1896, and Giuseppe Verdi's* Othello in 1903.

In addition to the title-roles he sang between 1892 and 1903, Alvarex learned another ten parts for programs at the Opéra in the 1893-1906 interval. After appearing as Siegmund in La Walkyrie* in 1893, he did Rhadamès in Aïda* (1895), Fernand in La Favorite* (1896), Raoul in Les Huguenots* (1897), and Jean in Le Prophéte* (1898). In 1900, he was billed as Karloo in Patrie!* and Don Rodrigue in Le Cid.* After his engagements at the Metropolitan in New York for the seasons of 1901-1902 and 1902-1903, he was selected to portray Manrique in Le Trouvère* for the premiere of this opera at the Garnier Palace* on 31 May 1904. Finally, he was cast as Canio in Paillasse* and as Mathô in Salammbô* in 1906.

Yet this was not the entire extent of Alvarez' repertory at Paris, because he created no fewer than ten roles at the Garnier opera house before his retirement. He was the first to sing Nicias in Jules Massenet's* Thaïs* (16 March 1894), Mirko in Augusta Holmes'* La Montagne noire* (8 February 1895), Mérowig in Saint-Saëns' Frédégonde* (18 December 1895), Jean in Victor Duvernoy's* Hellé* (24 April 1896), and Guillaume in Alfred Bruneau's* Messidor* (19 February 1897). He was selected to be the first Walther at the Garnier theatre on the occasion of the initial production there of Les Maîtres Chanteurs de Nuremberg* on 10 November 1897 and the first Tristan as well, when Tristan et Isolde* was given its premiere at the Opéra on 11 December 1904. And he created three other roles in this period between these two Wagnerian assignments; Gautier in La Burgonde* on 23 December 1898, Hercule in Astarté* on 15 February 1901, and Bar-Kokéba in Le Fils de l'etoile* on 17 April 1904.

Alvarez also appeared at the Opéra-Comique in 1902 to sing Don José in Carmen* and des Grieux in Manon.*

BIBLIOGRAPHY: ICM 38; KRJ 11; Martin 14; PBSW 170; SW 28, 43, 53, 62, 85, 89, 96, 100, 111, 116, 135, 139, 148, 151, 165, 168, 171, 178, 190, 194, 198, 203, 206, 208, 215, 217, 226; WOC II, 280.

L'Ame en Peine was offered as a fantastic opera in two acts with music by Friedrich von Flotow,* a libretto by Jules Saint-Georges,* and choreography by Jean Coralli.* Thierry created the sets for the first act; Cicéri* and Rubé provided them for the second act. The opera had its premiere at the

Royal Academy of Music in Paris on 29 June 1846, and it enjoyed a satisfactory measure of success principally on account of the melodic quality of the score. It was billed on 25 dates at the Opéra the year of its first presentation there, and it was mounted again on another dozen programs during 1847. It reached its 41st performance on 6 September 1849, and its first act was staged separately on 12 and 16 November 1849. It was dropped finally after its 49th billing at the Opéra on 3 April 1850, when it was presented with Stella.*

The opera is set in a wooded valley of Styrie, where Frantz' cabin is located. A hunt is in progress (I, 1), and the hunters knock at Frantz' door, where his young cousin Paola explains that her guardian has gone to the neighboring village to meet the countess de Rosenthal (I, 2). Alone, Paola wonders in her turn why Leopold is so late in arriving, but her beloved appears at last to explain that he has been called to the colors. He pledges his love to her and gives her a ring before leaving for the army (I, 3-4). Paola has been selected to receive the countess because she is her foster sister, and Frantz reveals his love for his ward Paola as soon as she has left (I, 5-5). The villagers gather to receive the countess, who is returning to her native village after the death of the count whom her father had selected to be her husband, despite her love for Léopold. The seneschal of the manor instructs Ulrich to watch for the countess' arrival from the storm bridge, but Frantz countermands the order because the timbers of the bridge have rotted and are about to collapse (I, 7). The countess enters with her retinue and is greeted by Frantz, Paola, and the villagers, who toast her return. She promises Frantz to speak to Paola of his love for her, and she experiences a renewed love for Léopold. She enters Frantz' humble abode, but Paola contrives to wait outside for Léopold so that she may greet him on his way to the frontier. She decides to watch for him from the flood bridge, and the villagers gather to waltz by the light of the moon (I, 8-10). A loud noise is heard in the ravine, but the dancers pay no attention to it until Paola's absence is noticed. Search parties are formed, and Frantz returns with her scarf and the announcement that Paola is dead. He faints with grief, and

Léopold's regiment is heard marching off into the distance (I, 11).

The scene shifts to the Rosenthal castle two years later with the abbey of Sainte-Irène visible through the trees. The villagers are preparing to celebrate the marriage of the countess and Léopold, and Frantz enters insane from the untimely death of Paola and believing that the festivities are being organized to welcome her back to her village. The seneschal reminds the villagers that the wedding is being held on Sainte-Irène's day, when the souls of dead lovers come back to earth but speak only to the living who continue to love them. The villagers reject this incredible tale, but the seneschal insists that they will know that a dead lover has arrived among them, when the bells of the abbey toll, and a bright flame dances across the heather and through the woods. These signs will reveal that the troubled soul of a lover is searching for a prayer or a kind thought to relieve his misery (II, 1-2). Léopold expresses his regrets over Paola's death, and she enters, but he does not see her. The countess greets him joyously, and she and Léopold pledge their undying love to each other. They are about to exchange rings, when the outraged soul exchanges her own ring for the countess' wedding band. Saddened, the soul laments that no one on earth loves her. Frantz enters and sees her immediately. Paola realizes that he alone loves her. Surprised and alarmed, she disappears into the flowers (I, 3-5). Frantz is overcome with grief on account of her disappearance; he reveals to Léopold how Paola died for her love for a faithless soldier. She climbed to the flood bridge to bid him farewell and fell to her death. Léopold admits that he was the departing soldier, and the shock of learning the identity of his successful rival restores Frantz' sanity. He is about to shoot Léopold when Paola's soul reappears and intervenes. She persuades Frantz to put down his rifle, and she forgives Léopold for his short memory (II, 6-8). Léopold and the countess enter the chapel for their wedding ceremony, and Paola's soul points to heaven, where she and dying Frantz will be united in eternal love (II, 9-13).

The score of <u>L'Ame en peine</u> made a favorable impression upon audiences, and the music for Frantz' romance, "Depuis le jour, j'ai paré ma chaumière" (II, 1), was used again in Vincenzo Bellini's* Norma with different words a decade later at the Théâtre-Lyrique. The two female parts of the opera were filled by Mlle Dobré (the countess) and Mlle Maria Nau* (Paola), and the male roles were created by Paul Barroilhet* (Frantz), Italo Gardoni* (Léopold), Brémond (the seneschal), and Koenig (a peasant).

BIBLIOGRAPHY: AEM IV, 433-37; Castil-Blaze, "L'Ame en peine à l'Academie royale de musique," FM 9 (5 July 1846), 210-11; Chouquet 408; DDO I, 43; Rosa Rosine Flotow, Friedrich von Flotow's Leben (Leipzig: Breitkopf und Hartel, 1892), 102-11; Karl Maria Klob, Beitrage zur Geschicte der deutschen komischen Oper (Berlin: Harmonie, 1903), 87-88; Lajarte II, 183.

Ancelot, Jacques-Arsène-François-Polycarpe (b. February 1794, Le Harve; d. 7 September 1854, Paris), librettist, obeyed his father's wishes by consenting to study literature and followed his uncle's example by obtaining employment in the Navy Department. Young Ancelot's official travels took him to Paris ultimately, and he profited from his presence in the capital to read his Warbeck to the Comédie-Française in 1816. His tragedy was accepted but never produced. Undaunted, the dramatist returned to his desk and wrote Louis IX, which he submitted to the actors three years later. They accepted and produced it in 1819; Louis XVIII was so pleased with him that he granted him a pension of 2,000 francs and a title. After this success, Ancelot had other works accepted more easily, especially Fiesque (1824) and L'Homme du monde (1827), mounted at the Odéon. He was rewarded for his energetic use of his talents with the post of librarian at the Arsenal library, and he was admitted to the Legion of Honor.

The happy course of events in Ancelot's life was interrupted by the Revolution of 1830, however, and the playwright found himself obliged to write for a living because he was now deprived of his previous sources of income. He turned to composing skits and vaudevilles and accepted the position of director of the Vaudeville Theatre in 1842, although he had been elected to the French Academy in the previous year. His connection with the Vaudeville Theatre pushed him deeply into debt unfortunately, and it was not until the change in government in 1848 that his lot improved. He was now sent to Rome and to Venice to help settle certain affairs relative to authors' and publishers' rights in the international book trade. Later, in 1852, he represented the French Academy at the unveiling of the statues of deceased members of this group in Amiens and Le Havre. Also, he continued to be active at the Comédie-Française until 1848 in addition to contributing to journals like La Foudre and Le Réveil. He completed a successful novel entitled Une Fortune mystérieuse in 1853.

Yet Ancelot made only a single contribution to the Opéra in the course of all this literary activity. He had collaborated with Pierre Guiraud* and Alexandre Soumet* on the libretto of Pharamond* of 10 June 1825 for which François Boïeldieu and two other composers had created the score (see eighteenth-century volume for Boïeldieu). Although he was only 31 years old at the time of the premiere of Pharamond, Ancelot never returned to the Opéra.

BIBLIOGRAPHY: DBF II, 792-94; Henri-Alexandre Frère, Ancelot, sa vie et ses oeuvres (Rouen: A. Le Brument, 1862); Lajarte II, 111-12; Joseph Morlent, Ancelot devant ses concitoyens, notice biographique (Paris: Jullien, 1855); SST 186.

Anne, Théodore (b. 7 April 1797, Rouen; d. 12 August 1869, Paris), librettist, was an uncompromising legitimist, and his strong political convictions exercised an irresistible influence upon his literary views. He was editor of La France and theatre critic for L'Union and his opinions as a journalist involved him in at least one duel. As a creative writer, he was of romantic persuasion and preferred subjects related in some way to the national patrimony of France, and his first efforts as an author were clearly in the realm of history with such titles as Eloge historique du duc de Berry (1820) or Mémoire sur l'intérieur du palais de Charles X (1831). His novels dealt with cognate subjects albeit in fiction: La Baronne et le prince and L'Homme au masque d'acier (1852).

As might be expected, Anne's political position aided the acceptance of his plays by theatres operating with the permission of the Restoration government, and he also had little trouble having his works produced by nearly all the troupes in Paris throughout the Second Empire. He collaborated at first with Dartois, Desaugiers, and Théaulon before La Chambre rouge (1852) was billed at the Gaîté. L'Enfant du régiment (1854) was given at the Ambigu, which also mounted L'Espion du grand monde (1856) that he did with Jules Saint-Georges.* His two contributions to the Opéra were Le Guérillero* of 1842 and Marie Stuart* of 1844 besides the words for Emile Paladilhe's* Ivan IV, the cantata that won the Prix de Rome in 1860.

BIBLIOGRAPHY: DBF II, 1308-9; Lajarte II, 170, 178, 191, 257.

L'Anneau du Nibelung called Der Ring des Nibelungen in the original German and Ring of the Nibelung in English, is the collective name of the famous trilogy by Richard Wagner.* Also designated as a tetralogy, it is composed of a prologue and three self-sufficient music dramas produced separately as well as together. The entire work was staged as a unit for the first time in Bayreuth during August 1876, and it had its English premiere at Covent Garden in London on 5, 6, 8, 9 May 1882. Also, it was staged at the Metropolitan Opera in New York on 4, 5, 8, 11 March 1889.

Yet it was not until June 1911 that it was heard at the Garnier opera house, where the prologue L'Or du Rhin* was mounted on 11 June with the dramas following on 11 June (La Walkyrie*), 13 June (Siegfried*), and 15 June (Le Crépuscule des dieux*). The first day saw Mme Maty as Fricka and Jean-François Delmas* as Wotan. Mmes Lucienne Bréval* and Grandjean filled the role of Brunnhilde during the next three performances, while Laurent Swolfs was cast as Siegmund on 11 June. Charles Dalmorès sang Siegfried on 13 June with Delmas now in the part of Wotan. Finally, on 15 June, Ernest Van Dyck* appeared as Siegfried with Henri Danges* and André Gresse* as Gunther and Hagen, respectively.

Three more presentations of the entire L'Anneau du Nibelung took place at the Opéra during June 1911 and June 1912, but 43 years passed before it was returned to this stage for the fifth and sixth times in May 1955. The seventh and eighth performances of the trilogy in its entirety took place at the Opéra, during May 1957.

The orchestra directors who have shared in these eight productions of Wagner's masterpiece have included Félix Weingartner,* André Messager,* and Hans Knappertsbusch (see twentieth-century volume for Knappertsbusch).

BIBLIOGRAPHY: Richard Aldrich, A Guide to "The Ring of the Nibelung," the trilogy of Richard Wagner (Boston: O. Ditson Co., 1905); L'Avant-scene 30 (November-December 1980), 166-67; ibid 6-7 (November-December 1976), 1-215; Ramsden Balmforth, Drama, Music-Drama and Religion as Illustrated by Wagner's "Ring of the Nibelung" and "Parsifal" (London: The Yearbook Press, 1913); Paul Bekker, Richard Wagner, His Life and Work, trans. M. M. Bozman (Westport, Conn.: Greenwood Press, 1971), 219-84; Louise Brink, Women Characters in Richard Wagner, a Study in "The Ring of the Nibelung" (New York: Nervous and Mental Disease Publishing Co., 1924); Aylmer Buesst, The "Nibelung's Ring": an Act by Act Guide to Plot and Music (London: George Bell & Sons, 1932); Clyde Robert Bulla, The Ring and the Fire (New York: Crowell, 1962); Alice Leighton Cleather and Basil Grump, "The Ring of the Nibelung": an Interpretation Embodying Wagner's Own Explanations (London: Methuen, 1911); idem, The Ring of the Nebelung (New York: G. Schirmer, 1903); John Culshaw, "Ring" Resounding (New York: Viking Press, 1967); A.E.F. Dickinson, The Musical Design of the "Ring" (London: Oxford University Press, 1926); Robert Donington, Wagner's "Ring" and Its Symbols (London: Faber and Faber, 1974); Henry T. Finck, Wagner and His Works (New York: Greenwood Press, 1968), 326-75; Leo Fremgen, Richard Wagner heute (Heusenstamm: Orion-Heimreiter-Verlag, 1977), 137-47, 174-78, 186-94; Victor Gollanez, The "Ring" at Bayreuth (London: Gollanez, 1966); Léon Guichard, La Musique et less lettres en France au temps de Wagnerisme (Paris: Presses Universitaires de France, 1963), 253; Gertrude Henderson, "The Ring of the Nibelung" (New York: A. A. Knopf, 1932); Ernest Hutcheson, A Musical Guide to the Richard Wagner "Ring of the Nibelung" (New York: Simon and Schuster, 1940); Emerich Kastner, Wagner-Catalog (Hilversum: Frits Knuf, 1966), 55-64; KCOB 253-60; Gustave Kobbé, How to Understand Wagner's "Ring": Story Analysis, Motives (London: W. Reeves, 1916); idem, Wagner's Music Dramas Analyzed (New York: G. Schirmer, 1904); Henry-Louis de La Grange, "News . . .

France . . . Paris," Opera 6 (1955), 514-19; Katherine A. W. Layton, The "Nibelung" of Wagner, University Studies, vol. 3, no. 4 (Urbana-Champaign, Illinois: University of Illinois Press, 1909); L. Archier Leroy, Wagner's Music Drama of the "Ring" (London: N. Douglas, 1925); Hans Mayer, Richard Wagner (Zurich: Belser Verlag, 1978), 158-69; MCDE 1124-31; OQE 472-74; PBSW 59-60, 160-62, 205; Detta, Petzet, and Michael Petzet, Die Richard Wagner-Buhne Konig Ludwigs II (Munchen: Prestel-Verlag, 1970), 182-263; Walter Panofsky, Wagner: A Pictorial Biography (London: Thames and Hudson, 1963), 84-99; Guy de Pourtalès, Richard Wagner: The Story of an Artist (Westport, Conn.: Greenwood Press, 1972), 186-203; Fridol Riedel, "Der Ring des Nibelungen" (Leipzig: M. Beck, 1942); Special Ring issue, ON 39, no. 15 (February-June 1975); O. de S., Paris-Munich et retour: le cycle wagnérien en 1893 (Paris: J. Lievens, 1894); Gustave Samazevilh, "Souvenirs sur l'Anneau des Nibelung," L'Opéra de Paris 11 (1955), 42-44; SSBO 267-76; SW 34-36; Edward M. Terry, A Richard Wagner Dictionary (Westport Conn.: Greenwood Press, 1971), 107-24, 131; Thompson 1558, 2212; Charles Vincens, Wagner et le Wagnérisme au point de vue français (Paris; Fischbacher, 1902), 12-17; Richard Wagner, Der Ring des Nibelungen (Leipzig: H. Fikentscher, 187-); Curt von Westernhagen, The Forging of the "Ring," trans. Arnold Whittal and Mary Whittal (New York: Cambridge University Press, 1976); Hans von Wolzogen, Guide to the "Nibelung Ring": a Thematic Key (New York: G. Schirmer, 1895).

L'Apparition was an opera in two acts and three tableaux with a score by François Benoist* and a libretto by Germain Delavigne.* It had its world premiere on 16 June 1848 at the Opéra, then called the Théâtre de la Nation.

The opera opens in a grotto in Spain, where Béatrix is telling fortunes to a group of peasants. An impostor, she makes a pretense of calling her demons from hell, and, when she declares that she sees the fallen angel running toward her, the peasants scatter in fear (I, 1). Alone, she laughs, and Clara de Torellas enters. Béatrix is overjoyed to see her visitor because she had reason to believe her to be dead. Clara reveals that she has sworn to take vengeance on the French soldier Roger, whom she used to love;

she explains that she will never forgive him for failing to appear at the church for their wedding or for her funeral staged to allay his fears of retaliation. Béatrix agrees that Roger must die, and Clara reveals that they will have their opportunity for revenge when the Frenchman comes to the village in the evening to see the wandering ghosts of Torellas. She notes finally that she is going to ask Alvar for help (I, 2-3). Clara has no difficulty in persuading Alvar to do her bidding, because he loves her, and she insists that he is to slay Roger, even if she appears to change her mind at the last moment (I, 4). The French contingent of soldiers arrives in the village; Clara and Alvar swear before Béatrix that they will honor their agreement to marry after Roger's death (I, 5).

The setting changes to the village square, where the populace is toasting Pédro for his prowess in the bullring. The matador thanks the crowd; a ballet provides an interlude. Roger appears with his officers but refuses to share in the celebration on account of his grief over Clara's death. Fargy assures Roger that he could not have explained his absence from his own wedding because he was on a military mission and pledged to secrecy. Fargy then tries to find quarters for Roger and himself, but no one will offer them hospitality (I, 6-7). Béatrix identifies Roger for Alvar, and Nugnes announces that they can billet themselves at the Torellas castle, but he cautions Roger not to accept lodging there on account of the ghosts. He repeats the false story of how the baron defied these spectres, and his defiance resulted in Clara's death. Béatrix warns the soldiers that Clara now appears with a glass of wine in her hand to laugh and to sing with any intruders. The latter are found dead the following day. Béatrix and Alvar vow that Roger will see Clara and die, and the French officers leave for Torellas (I, 8).

The second act is laid in the castle, where the servants light the fireplace and set the torches in place. Nugnes the muleteer is filled with foreboding, but his companions persuade him to remain with them. Roger is certain that he will not see Clara because she is dead; Fargy and Nugnes decide to look in the kitchen for something to eat (II, 1-2). Alone, Roger calls upon the ghost of Clara so that he may explain his absence at their wedding. Fargy and the muleteer return with food. They sit down to dine and congratulate themselves for having found champagne. Their spirits rise, and they toast the baron and his squire; midnight sounds, and they toast Clara. She appears in the gallery above them and ask why they have called her. Puzzled Fargy recalls that he attended her funeral; Roger gives thanks that his prayers have been answered; Nugnes is certain that the walls of the castle are about to collapse upon his shoulders. Roger dares to drink with her, and Clara orders his companions to leave (III, 3-5).

Clara informs Roger that her thirst for vengeance has destroyed her love for him, and he replies that his duty to his country forced him to be absent from their wedding. He declares his undying love for her, and her desire for vengeance begins to waver. She declares that she is going to return to her tomb, and he threatens suicide to be with her in death. His words convince her of his sincerity, and she confesses her undying love for him. She admits that she is alive, and Roger is beside himself with joy. Suddenly, Clara hears Alvar and his henchmen, and she urges Roger to flee, but he refuses to leave her. She admits that she has plotted for his death (III, 6). Alvar ignores Clara's prayers not to attack Roger, and Clara seizes a torch to present herself to Roger's assailants as the ghost of Torellas. They kneel before her in total fear. Trumpets sound an alarm, and it is announced that French troops are storming the castle. Roger instructs his troops to stop fighting, and the Spanish guerrillas accept the peace (II, 7-9).

The work was a failure largely on account of its improbable and poorly constructed libretto, and because it relied too heavily on ghosts in Gothic castles and alternately living or dead spectres. It had to be withdrawn after its third presentation on 21 June 1848, when it failed to return more than 1,367 francs 9 <u>centimes</u> to the box office. On the other hand, its score provoked favorable comment, although it was heard on only three occasions. The outstanding passage in the music was the quartet, "Quoi! c'est Clara, c'est elle!" (II, 5), but spectators applauded at three other intervals as well: the duet by Roger and Fargy, "Nous restons dans ce vieux manoir" (II, 1); Roger's solo, "Ah! que Dieu me la rende en ce

triste séjour" (II, 3); Roger's "Toi qui vois tout du haut des cieux" (II, 6). The male parts in the opera were created by M. Placide Poultier* (Roger), Paul Barroilhet* (Fargy), Portchaut (Alvar), Adolphe Alizard* (Nugnes), Joseph Barbot* (Pédro, matador), and Koenig (officer). The female roles were filled for the first time by Mlles Masson (Clara de Torellas) and Courtot (Béatrix).
BIBLIOGRAPHY: Chouquet 409; DDO I, 67; EDS II, 261-62; Lajarte II, 188.

Arago, Etienne-Vincent (b. 1802, Estagel; d. 1892, Paris) was a theatre director and writer, but his involvement in politics was so complete and continuous that his activities as an artist have been forgotten. In 1829, he was director of the Vaudeville theatre, and he had to sell his unique art collection in 1871 to pay off the debts he incurred when this theatre burned down in 1838. The second disaster of his life was the verdict condemning him to deportation in 1849. He returned to France in 1859 after a general amnesty was declared by the government, and, a relentless Republican, he found freedom finally with the establishment of the Third Republic. He was named archivist of the School of Fine Arts in 1878 and curator of the Luxembourg museum in 1879.

Arago wrote countless skits, light comedies, and vaudevilles besides publishing essays, pamphlets, and poetry, but his contribution to the Opéra was minimal. He helped Jean Bayard* with the libretto of Le Démon de la nuit* of 1851. If he is remembered for any single piece of work, it is probably his Les Aristocraties, a comedy in five acts that he wrote alone for staging at the Comédie-Française on 29 October 1847.
BIBLIOGRAPHY: DBF III, 203-4; GE III, 522-23; Lajarte II, 207-8.

Arbell, Lucy (b. September 1882; d. 1947), vocalist, née Georgette Wallace, made her operatic debut at the Garnier palace* as Dalila in Samson et Dalila* by Camille Saint-Saëns* on 23 October 1903. She was well received by the public and cast successively as Amnéris (Aïda*) and Madeleine (Rigoletto*) in 1904, Uta (Sigurd*) in 1905, and Fricka (La Walkyrie*) in 1909.

Miss Arbell came to be associated with Jules Massenet's* works, however, because she created parts at the Garnier in the following three compositions by this composer:

Role	**Opera**	**Premiere**
Perséphone	Ariane*	28 October 1906
Queen Amahelli	Bacchus*	2 May 1909
Posthumia	Roma*	24 April 1912

She was likewise scheduled to perform in Les Chansons du bois d'amaranthe by Massenet, but this piece was never produced at the Opéra after its audition of 24 December 1907.

The contralto had created the role of Posthumia at the world premiere of Roma in Monte Carlo on 17 February 1912. She had already sung the first Dulinée at this same Monte Carlo opera house, when management there had produced Massenet's Don Quichotte* on 19 February 1910, and her greatest success on this stage was in the female lead of Thérèse* as early as 7 February 1907. She brought this latter part to the Opéra-Comique on 19 May 1911. Finally, in 1913, she was billed into the Gaîté to sing Colombe in Panurge (1913) before her premature retirement and her exclusively charitable works for the orphanage known as the "Orphelinat des Arts."

BIBLIOGRAPHY: EDS I, 784; EFC 176; Jules Massenet, My Recollections, trans. H. Villiers Barnett (Westport, Conn.: Greenwood Press, 1970), 244-77, 298; SW 38-39, 44-45, 76, 210, 362.

Arensky, Anthony Stepanovich (b. 11 August 1861, Novgorad; d. 25 February 1906, Terioki, Finland), composer, was born into a musical family, and his parents sent him to study with Zikke and Nikolav Rimsky-Korsakov* at the Conservatory in St. Petersburg. He distinguished himself as a student, and he was named to the faculty of the Conservatory at Moscow in 1882. A dozen years later, in 1894, he became director of the Imperial Chapel in St. Petersburg.

Arensky wrote sacred music for the most part, but he also composed songs, symphonies, and a cluster of pieces for the theatre, although only a few of his compositions found their way to the stage of the Opéra in Paris. He and Serge Taneiev* did the prelude for the ballet Cléopâtre* produced at the Garnier Palace* in 1910 after its world premiere at the Châtelet theatre the previous year. His music was also included in Les Orientales* which Serge Diaghilev's Ballets russes* presented for the first time at the Opéra on 25 June 1910.

None of Arensky's three operas has ever been billed at the Garnier Palace.

BIBLIOGRAPHY: BBD 52; EDS 804-5; Grove I, 194-95.

Ariane was an opera in five acts with a score by Jules Massenet,* a libretto by Catulle Mendès, and choreography by Joseph Hansen.* Pierre Gailhard* was in charge of the first production of this work at the Opéra for which Bétout had designed the costumes. The sets were done by Jambon and Bailly (a. 1, 2, 5) and Amable (a. 3, 4). The composition had its world premiere at the Garnier Palace* on 28 October 1906, and it was revived in a production by Pierre Chéreau on 21 February 1937 with new sets and costumes by Souverbie (see twentieth-century volume for Chéreau).

The opera opens in Crete before the infamous labyrinth, where Thésée's sailors are listening to the sirens' song. Pirithoüs upraids the sailors for their idle ways, and he regrets that he has not been allowed to share in the fight against the Minotaur. He orders his men tied to the masts of the ships. Ariane enters pale, wan, and bemoaning her love. She goes to the door of the labyrinth and predicts Thésée's victory. She explains to Phèdre that she has fallen love with Thésée, whom she is trying to protect from the savage Minotaur. She has given him a thread to mark his passage into and out of the maze. Phèdre is shocked that her sister has betrayed her gods, her country, and her father, but Ariane's only excuse is her love for Thésée. The Athenians within the labyrinth call for help against the monster attacking them, and Thésée slays the beast. The intended sacrificial victims escape through the bronze door, and Thésée attributes his success to Ariane. Phèdre falls in love with him at first sight. Ariane consents to leave Crete with Thésée, who agrees that Phèdre may accompany them to Athens (a. 1).

The second act transpires in a galley bound for Greece. Ariane and Thésée profess their undying love for each other, and Phèdre cannot understand why she is troubled. A storm erupts; Phèdre wonders whether she has not prayed for it in the hope that all hands would perish. The storm abates quickly, however, but the pilot, Phéréklos, announces that he has lost his way during the excitement. He adds that they are bearing down on Naxos, and Thésée grants permission for the ship to stop over at this island. The sirens sing a welcoming song (a. 2).

It is dawn, and the Greeks have settled in an ancient palace adorned with figures of Cypris, Eros, the three Graces, and other divinities related to Venus. Thésée is awakened by the sound of Phèdre's horn in the forest. He refuses to admit that she attracts him, but he is tempted to move toward the forest. Pirithoüs asks him where he is going; he observes that Thésée has been idle for four months. Thésée agrees to leave Naxos but refuses to set a date for the departure of the fleet. Ariane enters weeping because she is aware that Thésée loves her no longer. She asks Phèdre to speak to him in her behalf. Phèdre agrees, and she reminds Thésée that her sister has given up everything for him, but he answers that he is consumed by another passion: his love for Phèdre. She objects that he is an ungrateful wretch and asserts that she despises him. He insists that she loves him until she falls into his arms. Ariane comes upon them, and Phèdre is ashamed of her own infamy, when her sister faints. Ariane is carried to her bed, where she remains until nightfall, when Pirithoüs tells her that Phèdre has died beneath the weight of a statue of Adonis that she was trying to destroy. Her body is brought to the palace. Ariane notices the depth of Thésée grief, and she prays to Cypris for aid. The goddess descends from the frieze in the palace to ask her what she wishes. She begs for Phèdre's return to life, and she offers to take her sister's place in hell. Cypris agrees and gives her the three Graces as guides (a. 3).

The fourth act shifts to the underworld, where Perséphone is regretting her lost beauty until her attention is diverted by a balletic duel between the three Graces and the three Furies. Ariane asks Perséphone for the return of Phèdre to earth. The queen of hell refuses her request until Ariane shows her the roses that she has brought to her. Persuaded, Perséphone permits an interview between the two sisters, but Phèdre refuses to leave until Ariane recalls that their destinies demand Phèdre's return to the living (a. 4).

The last act opens with the announcement that the Amazons are attacking Athens. Pirithoüs remains undisturbed by the news, because Thésée is too occupied with the fate of Ariane and Phèdre to worry about Athens. When Thésée does learn of the peril to his city, he remains indifferent. Suddenly, Ariane appears with Phèdre. Thésée is so impressed that Ariane went to hell to restore Phèdre to him that he swears his love for Ariane has been reborn out of his admiration for her. Phèdre is so grateful for her sister's generous action that she returns Thésée to her. Ariane climbs up to the palace; Thésée and Phèdre remain behind to assure each other that they will not fall in love again. Their old passion overtakes them, however, and they put their arms around each other as they walk toward the ships. They keep swearing that they will never fall in love. Ariane looks back and sees them sailing away in fond embrace. Finally, she descends into the sea to join the sirens and their world of lost illusions (a. 5).

Ariane was not one of Massenet's most popular operas, but it was billed at the Garnier Palace on 75 dates before it was dropped from the repertory after its last performance there on 27 August 1937. The female roles were filled at the premiere of the work in Paris by Lucienne Bréval* (Ariane), Louise Grandjean (Phèdre), Lucy Arbell* (Perséphone), and Marcelle Demougeot* (Cyris). The principal male parts were created by Lucien Muratore* (Thésée), Jean-François Delmas* (Pirithoüs), and Henri Stamler (Phéréklos).

BIBLIOGRAPHY: *P. Bertrand, "Reprise d'Ariane de Massenet," Le Ménestrel 99, no. 9 (26 February 1937), 69-70; Amédéi Boutarel, "Ariane; introduction à l'opéra de Massenet," Le Ménestrel 72 (1906), 317-19, 325-26 ff; Charles Bouvet, Massenet (Paris: Librairie Renouard, 1929), 104-6; René Brancour, Massenet (Paris: Félix Alcan, 1922), 111-13; José Bruyr, Massenet, musicien de la belle époque (Lyon: Editions et imprimeries du Sud-est, 1964), 103-6, 109; H. t. Finck, Massenet and His Operas (New York: John Lane Co., 1910), 209-14; James Harding, Massenet (New York: St. Martin's Press, 1970), 162-66; Demar Irvine,*

Massenet: a Chronicle of His Life and Times (Seattle: the author, 1974), 306-12; Jules Massenet, My Recollections, trans. H. Villiers Barnett (Westport, Conn.: Greenwood Press, 1970), 244-52, 267; Louis Schneider, Massenet: l'homme, le musicien (Paris: L. Carteret, 1908) 281-87; Stoullig XXXII (1906), 12-20; SW 38-39.

Artot, Désirée (b. 21 July 1835, Paris; d. 3 April 1907, Berlin), vocalist, studied voice under the direction of Pauline Viardot-Garcia* and started her career by appearing in concert in Belgium, Holland, and England. She came to the attention of Giacomo Meyerbeer* before long, and he arranged for her to make her theatrical debut at the Opéra in Paris, where she appeared first as Fidès in Le Prophète* in February 1858. Her interpretation of this role was greeted with great enthusiasm by French audiences, but she left Paris almost immediately for a series of successful appearances in Germany, England, and Russia. She returned to Paris to teach after her retirement from the stage in 1887, but she seems to have preferred living in Berlin, where she had been idolized in her younger days as a soprano and mezzo-soprano.
BIBLIOGRAPHY: EFC 147; KRJ 21-22.

Ascanio was an opera in five acts and seven tableaux that had its world premiere in a Pierre Gailhard* production at the Opéra on 21 March 1890. Camille Saint-Saëns* composed its score, and the libretto was the work of Louis Gallet, who based his text on a play entitled Benvenuto Cellini that Paul Meurice and Auguste Vacquerie had written for the Porte Saint-Martin theatre in 1852. Joseph Hansen* provided its choreography. Its sets were designed by the teams of Lavastre and Carpazat (tabl. 1, 2, 4, 5, 7) and Rubé, Chapéron, Marcel Jambon* (tabl. 3, 6), while Charles Bianchini created its costumes.

The original play was an overly complicated composition in the romantic style, and its involved intrigue persisted into the lyric version of the drama. Thus, the forward course of the action was not always easy to follow, although its evolvement provided interesting moments for the composer to exploit musically.

The opera opens in the Paris studio of Benvenuto Cellini, where the master directs his students to prepare to welcome the king (I, 1).

Cellini questions his apprentice Ascanio about a love letter that he has received (I, 2), while jealous Scozzone reproves the sculptor for not having chosen her to serve as the model for his statue of Hébé. She adds that Ascanio is in danger because he is in love with the duchess d'Etampes, mistress of the king (I, 3). François 1er, the duchess d'Etampes, and the royal retinue arrive. The duchess purchases a bracelet made by Ascanio, and she asks him to put it on her arm. The king gives the Grand-Nesle mansion to Cellini so that the artist may have ample room to work, and Ascanio rejoices over the prospect of being so close to the duchess. François 1er directs Cellini to organize a festive program to entertain Charles V during his imminent visit to Fontainebleau (I, 4).

The second tableau starts with worshipers entering the Grand-Nesle chapel, while a cluster of students continues to drink at a nearby tavern. D'Orbec assures d'Estourville that he must vacate Grand-Nesle in favor of Cellini, but d'Estourville answers that he will not relinquish his residence to a common locksmith (II, tabl. 2, 1-4). Cellini appears, and d'Estourville denies him entrance to his new quarters. Cellini enters the tavern, and d'Estourville tries to persuade the duchess d'Etampes to come to his aid, while Scozzone begs the king's mistress not to lead Ascanio into danger. At this moment, Ascanio emerges from the chapel to speak with the duchess, but Cellini interrupts their rendez-vous lest they be discovered (II, tabl. 2, 5-7). The provost arrives with an eviction order for d'Estourville. Cellini tries not to become angry with obdurate d'Estourville, because he is in love with his daughter Colombe, but he finally mounts a frontal attack on Grand-Nesle when his students arrive (II, tabl. 2, 8-10).

Cellini is now installed in Grand-Nesle, where Scozzone is singing to lighten the apprentices' tasks (II, tabl. 3, 1-2). The master dismisses his workers, and Scozzone returns to the studio to reproach him for spurning her in favor of Colombe. Ascanio enters with a letter from the king. Cellini shows him the statue of Hébé. Ascanio realizes that it is a likeness of Colombe, and that his master has fallen in love with her (II, tabl. 3, 3-5). A symphony is heard at Colombe's house nearby, and Scozzone explains to

Cellini that Colombe d'Estourville and the count d'Orbec are to be married in a week. Cellini is crushed, and he receives a second blow when he opens the letter from the king and learns that he has been banished from the royal presence (II, tabl. 3, 6).

The action shifts to the Louvre, where the duchess d'Etampes advises François 1er to seize Charles V, while he is in their power. He agrees. Ascanio delivers the jewelry that the duchess has ordered. He launches into a sudden and spirited description of his great passion for an unattainable beauty, and the duchess is charmed by his words until Colombe enters. She then realizes that Ascanio is in love with Colombe d'Estourville, not her. She swears to punish the happy couple (II, tabl. 4, 1-4).

The third act opens with the <u>divertissement</u> supposed to honor Charles V (see eighteenth-century volume for divertissement). François 1er gives Cellini three days to finish his Jupiter, and he promises the duchess that the celebration at Fontainebleau will close with the marriage of Colombe and d'Orbec (III, 1-2).

The scene returns to Cellini's studio, where Pagolo tells the duchess and Scozzone that Cellini and Ascanio hope to kidnap Colombe to prevent her marriage to d'Orbec. They plan to carry her in a reliquary to a convent. The duchess insists that the kidnappers must take Colombe to the Louvre, where she will die because a person can live only a few hours in the reliquary (IV, 1-2). Cellini enters, and Scozzone boasts that she knows about his scheme to kidnap Colombe. She asks him whether he knows that Colombe is in love with Ascanio, who returns to the studio while helping Colombe to escape from her family. Cellini is shocked to hear Colombe confess her love to Ascanio, but he assures the lovers that he will ask the king to permit them to marry. The royal guards knock at the door; Colombe hides in the reliquary (IV, 3-4). D'Orbec demands the return of his fiancee and the arrest of Cellini. The artist tells the guards that he has a reliquary to deliver to a convent for the queen, but it is agreed that Scozzone will deliver it. Cellini orders his apprentices to prepare to cast Jupiter (IV, 5).

The duchess d'Etampes approaches the reliquary in the Louvre to verify that it contains the body of Colombe. She reaches into it and feels and icy hand. A curtain parts, and Cellini's magnificent Jupiter is seen surrounded by an admiring throng. The king orders the sculptor to ask for whatever favor he might wish, and he grants the sculptor's request that Colombe and Ascanio be allowed to marry. The duchess is speechless to see Colombe. The reliquary is opened. Scozzone is in it. Cellini cannot restrain his tears (V, 1-2).

It must not have been easy to compose a score for this involved libretto filled with exposition, and Ascanio was not one of Saint-Saëns' more admirable achievements. Yet there were moments in the music that were touching: Cellini's "Enfants, je ne vous en veux pas"; the king's madrigal, "Adieu, beauté ma vie"; Colombe's ballad, "Mon coeur est sous la pierre." Also, the work was popular enough to justify its revival in 1921 and to enjoy 41 presentations at the Opéra before it was dropped from the repertory after 19 December 1921.

The male roles in Ascanio were created by Jean Lassalle* (Benvenuto Cellini), Emile Cossira (Ascanio), Paul Plançon* (François 1er), Eugène Bataille (Charles V), Gallois (d'Estourville), and Téqui (d'Orbec). The female parts were sung for the first time by Ada Adiny* (duchess d'Etampes), Emma Eames* (Colombe), and Rosa Bosman (Scozzone).

BIBLIOGRAPHY: Emile Baumann, L'oeuvre de Camille Saint-Saëns (Paris: Ollendorff, 1923), 439-40; Camille Bellaigue, "Ascanio, opéra en 5 actes," in his L'Année musicale, octobre 1889 à octobre 1890 (Paris: Librairie Charles Delagrave, 1891), 112-34; Paul Bertrand, "Opéra . . . reprise d'Ascanio," Le Ménestrel 83, no. 46 (18 November 1921), 450-51; Jean Bonnerot, C. Saint-Saëns: sa vie et son oeuvre (Paris: A. Durand & fils, 1914), 135-36, 138; Arthur Dandelot, La Vie et l'oeuvre de Saint-Saëns (Paris: Editions Dandelot, 1930), 118-23; DDO I, 85; René Dumesnil, La Musique contemporaine en France (Paris: Armand Colin, 1930) I, 12-15 and II, 64-65; Arthur Hervey, Saint-Saëns (Freeport, N.Y.: Books for Libraries Press, 1969), 64-68; Adolphe Jullien, Musiciens d'aujourd'hui (Paris: Librairie de l'art, 1892), 322-31; Watson Lyle, Camille Saint-Saëns: His Life and Art (New York: E. P. Dutton, 1923), 166-68; Charles Malherbe, Notice sur "Ascanio" (Paris: Librairie Fischbacher, 1890);

Antoine F. Marmontel, Virtuoses contemporains (Paris: Heugel et fils, 1882), 14-28; Otto Neitzel, Camille Saint-Saëns (Berlin: Harmonie, 1899), 42-51; Georges Servières, La Musique Française moderne (Paris: Havard, 1897), 285-404; Stoullig XVI (1890), 3-12; SW 42; Thompson 1604-8.

Aspasie et Périclès was an opera in a single act with a libretto by Jean Viennet,* a score by Etienna Méhul's nephew Louis Daussoigne-Méhul* and choreography by Pierre Gardel (see eighteenth-century volume for Méhul and Gardel). It was produced at the Royal Academy of Music for the first time on 17 July 1820, but it did not prove very popular and had to be dropped after its 17th performance on 28 March 1821.

The opera opens with Périclès confiding to Euripide that he would like to lead the Athenian army against the Spartans. He adds that he is unhappy over the prospect of leaving Aspasie, however, and Euripide urges him to remain in Athens long enough to celebrate Aspasie's birthday and perhaps to marry her (sc. 1). Cléon informs Périclès that Aspasie awaits him (sc. 2-3) and then vows to punish Aspasie for spurning his love. Similarly, he complains that Périclès overshadows him constantly in public life, and he decides to accuse Périclès of favoring the subversive sect of sophists (sc. 4). Périclès assures Aspasie that his campaign against the Spartans will be his last military adventure (sc. 5), and Euripide enters with his friends to celebrate her birthday. She thanks them for their gifts (sc. 6), and Alcibiade assures her that Périclès will be victorious in the impending struggle. A ballet forms to support the celebration (sc. 7).

Socrate reports that Aspasie has been denounced as a blasphemer and heretic. He explains that the people have called for her condemnation and that the judges are about to consider her case. Aspasie suspects Cléon of this treachery, but she will not permit Périclès to defend her because she insists that he be ready to sail with the army. Périclès refuses to allow her to become a victim of Cléon's jealous hatred, and he leaves for the tribunal (sc. 9). A noise offstage suggests that a verdict has been reached, and a chorus of Athenians calls for the punishment of the enemies of Pallas. Aspasie confronts

Cléon, but he denies that he wishes her harm and offers to help her in her struggle to vindicate herself. She replies that she has a competent defender, and he suggests that she await the outcome of events in his palace (sc. 10-12). Euripide announces that Périclès offered such an eloquent plea that he moved the judges to tears and persuaded Aspasie's accusers to reveal that Cléon was the instigator of the entire affair. Aspasie assures Cléon that she was certain that he was the author of the conspiracy against her, and he is so enraged that he orders his men to take Aspasie to his palace (sc. 13). Périclès orders Cléon's servants to relinquish her. He refers to her as his wife and announces that Cléon has been sentenced to exile. He suggests finally that it is time to celebrate his marriage to Aspasie (sc. 14-15).

The part of Aspasie and her companion Léonide were filled by Mlles Grassary and Reine, respectively, while Alcibiade as a child was done by Mlle Caroline. The male roles were assigned to Prosper Dérivis* (Périclès), Lafeuillade (Cléon), Eloy (Euripide), Bonnel (Socrate), and Pouilley (Hermippus, Cléon's friend) according to the printed libretto. Chouquet lists Adolphe Nourrit doing Périclès and Dérivis as Cléon.

BIBLIOGRAPHY: Chouquet 389; DDO I, 96; EDS IV, 211; Lajarte II, 96; *__Moniteur universel__* *198 (16 July 1820), 1022; ibid. 201 (19 July 1820), 1034; Wks II, 3195.*

Astarté is an opera in four acts and five tableaux with a libretto by Louis de Gramont, a score by Xavier Leroux,* and choreography by Joseph Hansen.* It had its world premiere at the Garnier Palace* on 15 February 1901 in a production by Pierre Gailhard.* Its sets were created by Marcel Jambon* and Marcel Bailly (a. 1, 2), Amable (a. 3), and Carpezat (a. 4, tabl. 1, 2). Charles Bianchini designed its costumes, and Claude Paul Taffanel* was at the desk for its initial presentation.

The opera opens before the palace of Hercule, who has convoked his warriors to suppress Astarté's growing ambition. This evil goddess, he explains, wishes to extend her sway, and Omphale, queen of Lydia, is her latest acquisition. Hercule's men swear to follow their leader against Omphale's forces (I, 103), but Déjanire emerges from her house to ask them whether or not they are being moved by their desire to see the beautiful and infamous queen. Hercule asserts that his intentions are noble, but he refuses to promise his wife that he will avoid looking at the queen (I, 4). He collects his weapons and bids his wife farewell (I, 5-6).

Iole comes out of the temple of Vesta to tell Déjanire that she has been warned to watch over her master lest he be sacrificed on Astarté's altar. She adds that they can protect him only with a magic talisman. Déjanire explains that the centaur Nessus has given her a magic robe that will make Hercule forget whoever tries to steal his love. She suggests that they persuade Hercule to wear this garment. Iole volunteers to take the robe to Hercule (I, 7), and Déjanire prays for her husband (I, 8).

The second act shifts to Sorde, where Astarté's high priest Phur declares that Hercule will meet a fearsome death because he has offended Vesta. He explains that the only condition to his certain destruction is that the followers of Astarté must abet the evil desire that has alienated Vesta from him. Astarté's followers rejoice and prepare to defend their stronghold (II, 1). Hercule's men camp before the walls of Sorde, while their leader prepares his strategy, but the women of the city greet them with open arms and amphoras of wine. The soldiers succumb to the enemy's wiles and enter the city with the women (II, 2).

Hercule enters a public square in Sorde, where music, song, and laughter are heard, and an altar to Astarté is visible. Phur tells him that Omphale is in the adjacent palace and ready to surrender. Omphale appears, and Hercule vows to sacrifice her to vesta, but her beauty overcomes him. She dares him to slay her, but he cannot summon the courage to destroy her, and he claims her charms as a victor. She rejects him. He lays his weapons at her feet and swears to do her will in all things, but his willingness to sacrifice his glory to her beauty does not win her hand. He must also abjure Vesta for Astarté and prostrate himself at her feet before her people and his soldiers. He agrees and swears allegiance to Astarté. Phur gives Omphale a potion for Hercule. He drinks it, and it makes him fall into a deep sleep. Omphale and her subjects rejoice. Hercule awakens at nightfall. He has forgotten Déjanire, his promises to her, and all other aspects of his prior life. He throws himself into Omphale's arms (III, 1).

Cléanthis and Omphale's attendants are weaving a wedding robe for Hercule, but, while Phur exhorts them to complete it, Omphale orders them to undo at night their work of the previous day. Phur plans to murder Hercule during the wedding ceremony, and he suspects that Omphale is responsible for the delay in completing the garment because she loves Hercule (IV, 1-2). He asserts to Hercule that only marriage to Omphale in the temple of Astarté will keep Omphale faithful to him (IV, 3). Accordingly, Hercule proposes marriage to Omphale, but she tries to convince him that it would be more prudent for him to return to Déjanire than to incur the wrath of Astarté by marrying her. This argument means nothing to Hercule, of course, because he has forgotten Déjanire, and he leaves Omphale with the warning that she must marry him or perish (IV, 4).

Iole enters with Nessus' tunic, which will supposedly return Hercule to Déjanire, and Omphale sees in the garment a solution to her dilemma. She will not have to doom Hercule to the fate that Astarté has prepared for him, and Hercule will not condemn her to the fate that he has reserved for her if he forgets her for Déjanire (IV, 5-6). But Hercule enters in agony. The tunic is burning into his body, and he cannot remove it without tearing his flesh. He swears to destroy Omphale's palace, and he sets it afire with burning fragments of the dreadful garment. Finally, he falls dead. Omphale remains beside the dead hero to sing the glory of the flames that will cleanse her of her sinful passion before she sails for Lesbos and the temple of Astarté (IV, 7).

The work was never popular enough to be accepted into the international repertory, but Paris audiences supported it until 11 November 1901, when it was dropped after its 23rd billing at the Opéra. Its principal female roles were created by Meyrianne Héglon (Omphale), Louise Grandjean (Déjanire), and Jeanne Hatto* (Iole) with Albert Alvarez* (Hercule) and Jean-François Delmas* (Phur) in the male parts. The corps de ballet was led at its Garnier premiere by Mlles Ixart, Carré, Couat, Barbier.

BIBLIOGRAPHY: EDS VI, 1415-16; Arthur Pougin, "Première Représentation d' Astarté à l'Opéra," Le Ménestrel 67 (17 February 1901), 50-51; Stoullig XXVII (1901), 4-9; SW 43.

Astolphe et Joconde ou les Coureurs d'aventures was a pantomime ballet in two acts with music by Louis Hérold* and choreography by Jean Aumer who based his scenario on a comic opera by Charles Etienne (see eighteenth-century volume for Aumer and Etienne). Pierre Cicéri created the sets. A popular work in its time, it had its premiere at the Royal Academy of Music on 29 January 1827, and it enjoyed 29 presentations during its first year at the Opéra. It was billed for a total of 50 performances before it was dropped from the repertory on 30 August 1831.

The complicated ballet opens with Mathilde and Edile in the drawing room of a castle in Provence, where they are preparing gifts for their suitors, a scarf and a locket. Astolphe and Joconde appear before the two ladies, and Astolphe offers Mathilde a diadem as a pledge of his love, but he also presents Edile with a bracelet. Joconde is jealous, but Edile assures him of her love; Mathilde dismisses Astolphe's actions as mere caprice. The guests offer their congratulations to Countess Mathilde on her approaching marriage to Astolphe, and the wedding celebration starts. Joconde becomes jealous of the attention paid to Edile by Prince Astolphe, who tells his guest that the festivities are over so that he may speak privately with Edile. Joconde objects, and the ladies retire. Astolphe then asks Joconde to win Mathilde's love because he fears that she is marrying him only through obedience to her family. Joconde yields to the prince's wishes on condition that Astolphe refrain from courting Edile. The two women overhear this conversation, and they decide to turn their knowledge of it to their own advantage. Edile pretends to weep and complains to Astolphe of Joconde's jealousy; she assures Astolphe that she has never loved Joconde. Astolphe throws himself at her feet and declares his love for her; she responds by reminding him of his love for Mathilde, and he asserts that he has forgotten the countess for her. Edile appears convinced, and Astolphe grasps the locket that she was preparing for Joconde. She runs away, and the prince leaves. Edile then returns to tell

Mathilde of her lover's perfidy, however, and the countess determines to seek revenge. She flirts with Joconde, who forgets Edile and declares his love to the countess. She gives him the scarf she had intended to present to Astolphe. She leaves, and Astolphe enters to explain to Joconde that Edile loves him. Joconde believes that Astolphe is deceiving him, but he is convinced ultimately and is overcome by surprise. When he recovers, he assures his master that Mathilde does not love him. The two men realize the inconstancy of the two women and decide to return their presents. Mathilde and Edile run to the arms of their suitors as if nothing has happened. Martial music is heard; the knights enter dressed in armor. Astolphe and Joconde announce that they will not appear in the tournament because they are leaving to fight the Infidels. Mathilde and Edile try to dissuade them and then decide that there is something strange about their plan. The two women follow the two crusaders to satisfy their curiosity.

The second act shifts to a rural scene, where Jeannette is spinning before her door. Lucas declares his love to her, and the couple executes a pas de deux. Lucas leaves after the dance, and Astolphe and Joconde enter dressed as troubadours. They sing of Jeannette's beauty, and they argue over the privilege of being the first to dance with her, but she runs into her house. The sheriff now leads the villagers in a parade preparatory to the Feast of the Rose.

At the celebration, Jeannette dances with the troubadours until Edile and Mathilde appear disguised as gypsies. Night falls, and the sheriff orders the celebrants to return to their homes. Mathilde leaves with Jeannette, and the other "gypsy" scolds Joconde. Joconde gives the gypsy a purse and asks her help in making Jeannette fall in love with him, and Edile vows to punish him for his fickle ways. Astolphe and Joconde keep a rendez-vous with Jeannette, who has been persuaded to conspire with Mathilde and Edile by pretending to be interested in both troubadours. Astolphe gives her Mathilde's scarf, and Joconde presents her with Edile's locket. When they ask Jeannette to reveal which of them she prefers, she promises to disclose her choice later. The bailiff sees them near Jeannette's house, and he overhears them talking of kidnapping her. Jealous, he rushes off for help; the troubadours leave for their appointed meeting with Jeannette; Lucas enters to serenade Jeannette, and she rushes into his arms. Astolphe sees the couple embrace, and he thinks that Jeannette has chosen Joconde; Joconde comes upon the same scene, and he is certain that she prefers Astolphe. Finally, Astolphe grows impatient waiting for "Joconde" to rejoin him and he screams at him to hurry. Lucas is puzzled; Jeannette is amused. The two lovers disappear, and the two troubadours collide in the darkness. They argue over Jeannette and accuse each other of lying because they do not yet understand what has happened. They make so much noise near Jeannette's house that the jealous bailiff arrests them, and Mathilde and Edile are delighted with the havoc that they have managed to create.

The sheriff feels free now to declare his love to Jeannette, and she does not discourage him, because he can prevent her from winning the contest at the village fair. Astolphe and Joconde escape from prison, however, and they hear Jeannette tell Lucas that the two troubadours who tried to seduce her were in the trees near her house when she and Lucas were together the previous night. Lucas laughs; Astolphe and Joconde are speechless but recover in time to threaten Jeannette with reporting her revelation to the sheriff. She runs away, and the sheriff is about to arrest Astolphe again, when he receives a letter revealing that the countess Mathilde is arriving to crown the winner of the Feast of the Rose. Mathilde enters, and the troubadours try to hide, but the countess asks that the troubadours be brought before her. She "recognizes" Prince Astolphe, and the dazed sheriff issues an order for the arrest of the gypsies. Astolphe and Joconde realize at last that Mathilde and Edile have tricked them. A celebration in honor of the Feast of the Rose follows a complete reconciliation among the characters, and Prince Astolphe crowns Jeannette the winner of the contest. He invites all present to continue the festivities at his castle.

The male roles were filled by François Albert (Astolphe), Paul l'<u>aérien</u> (Joconde), Jean Aumer (the sheriff), and Ferdinand (Lucas). The female parts were assigned to Mme Constance Anatole (Mathilde), Mlle Lise Noblet* (Edile), Mme Pauline

Montessu* (Jeannette) (see eighteenth-century volume for Albert, Aumer, and Anatole).

BIBLIOGRAPHY: *Adolphe Adam,* Souvenirs d'un musicien *(Paris: Calmann Lévy, 1884), 27-38; AEM VI, 250-59; H. Blaze de Bury,* Musiciens du passé, du présent et de l'avenir *(Paris: Calmann Lévy, 1881), 197-214; idem,* Musiciens contemporains *(Paris: Michel Lévy frères, 1856), 165-68; CB 44-45; Chouquet 392; Benoît J. -B. Jouvin,* Hérold, sa vie et ses oeuvres *(Paris: Au Ménestrel, 1868), 150; Lajarte II, 125;* Moniteur universel *31 (31 January 1827), 136; Arthur Pougin,* Hérold *(Paris: Henri Laurens, 1906), 79; RBP 68-70; Wks II, 3198.*

L'Attaque du Moulin was a lyric drama in four acts with a score by Alfred Bruneau* and a libretto by Louis Gallet based upon Emile Zola's story by the same name. It had its world premiere on 23 November 1898, when the company of the Opéra-Comique presented it in the Châtelet theatre with sets by Marcel Jambon* and costumes by Thomas. Léon Carvalho* was in charge of production.

The action of the drama is set in the courtyard of a mill, where Marcelline is supervising preparations for the betrothal party of Françoise and Dominique (I, 1). The father of the prospective bride reminds Marcelline that she did not approve of Dominique at first because he was a stranger. She recalls that Merlier and all the other villagers had a low opinion of the groom until he proved that he was ambitious and tireless. Merlier admits that he was also suspicious of the stranger until his recent behavior changed his mind (I, 2).

The guests welcome Dominique with a song, and Dominique assures the gathering that he will cherish and protect Françoise, who agrees to become his wife. The banquet is about to begin when a drummer announces that war has begun. All healthy males are to report to city hall. Merlier proposes a toast to the soldiers of France, and Dominique assures Françoise that he is exempt from military service because he is from Flanders (I, 3-5).

The second act depicts the villagers defending the mill under the leadership of an army captain, who announces that it is time to retreat because they have stopped the German advance for the requisite five hours. Left alone with Françoise and Dominique, Merlier regrets the impending loss of his mill. The enemy fills the courtyard (II, 1-2), and the invading captain threatens to execute Dominique because he has fought for the French army without being a citizen of France. Merlier defends him successfully, but the enemy officer condemns him to death because he will not guide the Germans through the forest (II, 3-4). Françoise tells him of a secret exit that will enable him to escape (II, 5).

A sentinel is standing near a willow tree beside the mill where Dominique is imprisoned. Marcelline engages the guard in conversation (III, 1-4), while Dominique tries to escape. The sentry sees him, and Dominique is obliged to kill him. The Germans discover their comrade's body, and the captain orders Merlier to return Dominique for punishment or to suffer the consequences. Françoise offers herself in place of Dominique or her father, but the captain insists that she give him her father or her sweetheart (III, 5-6).

It is dawn, and the courtyard is under military guard. Françoise and Marcelline hear French infantry approaching. Suddenly, Dominique appears (IV, 1). Françoise and Dominique sit down by the well to talk, but the enemy captain does not notice them when he enters with Merlier. He tells his prisoner that he will be shot on the spot if the French attack (IV, 2-4). Merlier charges Marcelline to inform Françoise that he is no longer a prisoner; he assures Dominique that he is free. Deceived, Françoise rejoices that war no longer threatens the mill and its inhabitants. The French forces are heard again, and Dominique runs to tell them that they can recapture the mill with their superior numbers (IV, 5). Merlier begins to recall Françoise's childhood, and his sentimental monologue arouses her suspicions. The French attack the mill, and the enemy captain pushes Merlier offstage. The French soldiers rush in with shouts of victory, but shots are heard in the wings, and it is too late to rescue Merlier (III, 6-7).

This work was well received by the public, and it was billed on 53 dates by the Opéra-Comique after this company revived it for its 40th presentation at the Favart Theatre on 25 March 1922. It was also staged at the Gaïté Lyrique on 16 December 1907 with Nelly Martyl (Françoise), Marie Delna (Marceline), Henri Albers (Merlier), and Gaston Dubois (Dominique) in the cast. The same roles had been created in 1893 by Mme Georgette Leblanc making her debut at the Opéra-Comique as Françoise, Mme Maria Delna* (Françoise), Max Bouvier (Merlier), and Edmond Vergnet* (Dominique).

L'Attaque de moulin was never taken to the Garnier Palace.*

BIBLIOGRAPHY: Etienne Destranges, "L'Attaque de moulin": étude analytique et thématique (Paris: Fischbacher, 1901), 9-43; René Dumesnil, La Musique contemporaine en France (Paris: Armand Colin, 1930) I, 172-73 and 11, 57-60; Hugues Imbert, Médaillons contemporains (Paris: Fischbacher, 1903), 81-90; Paul Landormy, Histoire de la musique (Paris: Delaplane, 1920), 376-77; MSRL 35-36; WOC 25-26.

Auber, Daniel-François-Esprit (b. 29 January 1782, Caen; d. 11 May 1871, Paris, composer, was born into a family of comfortable means, and his parents planned to educate him in business and in music so that he might have a comfortable and pleasant life. He went to London to learn the secrets of commercial success, but he was not impressed by the prospect of being a merchant or broker, and he returned to Paris to enjoy a more lively existence in the capital. He became quite popular before long on account of his gift for producing lighter romances or songs like his Bonjour! and he attracted the attention of more serious musicians with his compositions for piano, violin, and violoncello. The pieces he created for the cellist Lamare prompted his friends to suggest that a brilliant future was in store for the witty young man from Normandy, who also did a dramatic work for the Doyen amateur group in Paris and then a second piece for private production at the prince de Chamay's private theatre in Belgium.

These limited experiences with the stage were enough to convince Auber that he should improve his knowledge of composition if he wished to achieve any real measure of success in the musical theatre, and he arranged to study under Luigi Cherubini (see eighteenth-century volume for Cherubini). In 1813, he had his first professional work produced for the general public, Le Séjour militaire, given at the Feydeau Theatre. It was not the success that Auber was seeking, and he seemed about to suppress his ambitions for a career in the musical theatre when his father's death obliged him to earn his own living, and he turned to the stage for the resolution of his predicament. The Opéra-Comique accepted his *Le Testament et les Billets-doux* in 1819, but the spectators failed to respond favorably once again. Auber could not retreat now, however, and his *La Bergère châtelaine* at the Opéra-Comique in 1820 vindicated his persistence and justified earlier assertions that a successful future awaited him.

After Auber did his fourth work, *Emma* (1821), for the Opéra-Comique, he had the good fortune to team up with Eugéne Scribe* as his librettist, and the two men in collaboration went on to produce no fewer than 30 works for the Opéra-Comique alone between 1823 and 1864. All seven compositions Auber had billed at the Opéra were also done jointly with Scribe: *La Muette de Portici** of 1828, *Le Dieu et la bayadère** of 1830, *Le Philtre** of 1831, *Le Serment** of 1832, *Le Lac des fées** of 1839, *L'Enfant prodigue** of 1850, *Zerline** of 1851 all given initially at the Opéra. *Marco Spada** and *Le Cheval de bronze*,* both heard for the first time at the Opéra in 1857, had had the premieres of their original versions at the Opéra-Comique in 1852 and 1835, respectively.

The last sixty years of Auber's life can be said to have been passed at his desk in Paris, and the only important incidents of his later years that might be recalled here in addition to the productions of his compositions are his election to membership in the French Academy in 1829 and his appointment as director of the Conservatoire by Louis-Philippe in 1842. Auber refused to leave Paris during the siege of the capital in the Franco-Prussian War, and, at his death in the spring of 1871, it was already evident that the French theatre had lost its last great creator of comic opera scores. it is agreed today that Auber's talents as a musician made him the peer of François Boïeldieu, Louis Hérold,* and Adolphe Adam* in his chosen field (see eighteenth-century volume for Boïeldieu). His titles for the Opéra-Comique included *Le Séjour militaire* (1813), *Le Testament et les billets-doux* (1819), *La Bergère châtelaine* (1820), *Emma* (1821), *Leicester* (1823), *La Neige* (1823), *Le Concert à la cour* (1824), *Leocadie* (1824), *Le Maçon* (1825), *Le Timide* (1826), *La Financée* (1829), *Fra Diavolo* (1830), *La Marquise de Brinvilliers* (1831), *Lestocq* (1834), *Le Cheval de bronze* (1835), *Actéon* (1836), *Les*

Chaperons blancs (1836), L'Ambassadrice (1836), La Domino noir (1837), Zanetta (1840), Les Diamants de la couronne (1841), Le Duc d'Olonne (1842), La Part du diable (1843), La Sirène (1844), La Barcarolle (1845), Haydée (1847), Marco Spada (1852), Jenny Bell (1855), Manon Lescaut (1856), La Circassienne (1861), La Fiancée du roi de Garbe (1864), Le Premier Jour de bonheur (1868), and Rêve d'amour (1869).

Auber may have been an officer in the Legion of Honor, an occupant of a chair at the French Academy, director of the Conservatoire, and chapelmaster for Louis-Philippe and Napoleon III, but his greatest distinction remains his position as one of the great nineteenth-century contributors of scores to the Opéra-Comique with Le Philtre or Le Dieu et la Bayadère and to the Opéra as well with La Muette de Portici.* It was this last work, it will be remembered, that set off the uprising in Belgium leading to the expulsion of the Dutch from this country and to the subsequent liberty of its inhabitants.

BIBLIOGRAPHY: Jules Carlez, L'Oeuvre d'Auber (Caen: Le Blanc-Hardel, 1874); Henri Delaborde, Institut de France. Académie des beaux-arts. Eloge d'Auber (Paris: Firmin-Didot, 1875); Fétis I, 162-64; GC 14-16; HBM 143-64; Benoît Jouvin, D.-F.-E. Auber, sa vie et ses oeuvres (Paris: Heugel, 1864); Lajarte II, 106, 129, 136, 138, 144-45, 159, 206, 209, 222-23, 253-54, 258; Charles Théodore Malherbe, Auber: Biographie critique (Paris: H. Laurens, 1911); PBSW 170; Arthur Pougin, Auber, ses commencements, les origines de sa carrière (Paris; Pottier de Lalaine, 1873); Julien Tiersot, "Auber," RM 14 (1933), 265-78.

Augier, Emile (b. 17 September 1820, Valence; d. 26 October 1889, Croissy), dramatist and librettist, began his studies in the schools of his native city and then went to Paris to finish his academic education at the lycée Louis-le-Grand. Although the young man had no deep convictions about pursuing a career before the bar, his father continued to encourage him to become a lawyer. Accordingly, he entered law school in 1840 but had more real interest in his first play submitted to the company of the Ambigu-Comique this same year. His work was rejected. Yet Emile persisted, and his La Ciguë was accepted at the Odéon on 13 May 1844.

After this initial success, the apprentice playwright refused to be thwarted in his ambition to write plays, and he became one of the most celebrated dramatists of his age. Augier himself observed once with a smile that his biography was his bibliography, but his appraisal of his activities was an exaggeration. He accepted the post of librarian for the duke d'Aumale in 1846; he became editor of Le Spectateur républicain in 1848; he ran in the elections of 1852 at Bordeaux and was elected to the General Council of this city by a large majority. He entered the French senate in 1870. It was his literary accomplishments, however, that were responsible for his holding the rank of commander in the Legion of Honor (1868), to which he had been elected in 1850. He became a member of the French Academy in 1857.

Augier's writings were destined almost exclusively for the theatre and included about 30 social comedies dealing with problems related to marriage, money, business, and prostitution. Le Gendre de Monsieur Poirier and Le Fils de Giboyer were among his most successful and enduring compositions. His contribution to he Opéra was minimal and included only the libretto for Sapho* of 1851.

BIBLIOGRAPHY: H. Gaillard de Champris, Emile Augier et la comédie sociale (Paris: Grasset, 1910); DBF IV, 540-42; Lajarte II, 208; C. Lecigne, Emile Augier (Arras: Sueur-Charrvey, 1901); P. Morillot, Emile Augier (Grenoble: A. Gratier, 1901); Hippolyte Parigot, Emile Augier (Paris: Lecène, Oudin et Cie., 1890).

Auguez, Numa (b. 1847, Saleux; d. 27 January 1903, Paris), vocalist, was known to audiences in Italy and in Paris, where he made his debut at the Le Peletier* opera house on 7 July 1873 as Maurevert in Les Huguenots.* He sang Albert in La Juive* for the program given to inaugurate the Garnier Palace* on 5 January 1875 after appearing as one of the bishops and the Grand Brahmin of L'Africaine* in 1873 and one of the knights in Robert le Diable* during 1874 in the rue le Peletier.

After the opening of the Garnier Palace, Auguez was billed as Leuthold in the first production of Guillaume Tell* at the new theatre on 26 February 1875. This same year, 1875, he was cast at the Opéra as one of the grave diggers in Hamlet* and as Mazetto of Don Juan.* He did Wagner in Faust,* the officer in Le Prophète,* and le Bar du Duc of Auguste Mermet's* Jeanne d'Arc* in 1876; he appeared during 1877 as Albert in Robert le Diable, Melchtal in Guillaume Tell, Mathisen and Oberthal of Le Prophète, and Cosse and Saint-Bris of Les Huguenots. His last additions to his Garnier repertory were made in 1879, when he was billed as Nélusko in L'Africaine, Valentin in Faust, and Pietro in La Muette de Portici.* His only two creations at the Opéra were Un Chef in Le Roi de Lahore* on 27 April 1877 and Néarque in Polyeucte* on 7 October 1878.

M. Auguez' full and powerful voice ranged from bass to baritone in the course of his career, and his flexibility made him an invaluable addition to the company of the Opéra, where he performed for more than a dozen years.

BIBLIOGRAPHY: EDS I, 1134; SW 25, 89, 106, 109, 118, 125, 153, 175, 185-86; Thompson 81.

Aveline, Albert (b. 1883, Paris; d. 3 February 1968, Anvières) dancer, entered the ballet school of the Paris Opéra at age 11 in 1894. He joined the corps de ballet at the Garnier Palace* after completing his studies, and he won public approval almost immediately with his performance in a pas de cinq from Joseph Hansen's* La Ronde des saisons* in 1905. Subsequently he was promoted so quickly through the ranks of the balletic hierarchy that he was given the title of primo ballerino assoluto in 1908.

The young star went on to establish himself as one of the great dancers of the first half of the twentieth century, and he appeared with such stars as Carlotta Zambelli* and Olga Spessivtzeva in some of the most enthusiastically applauded performance staged at the Opéra in the decades before and after World War I. His repertory was varied and provided ample proof of the dancer's versatility and capability. He appeared in the premiers of the following ballets on the dates indicated besides filling roles in revivals of Les Deux Pigeons* (Tzigane in 1912, 1935), Javotte* (Jean in 1915), and Giselle (Albert in 1924):

Role	Ballet	Premiere
Sylvain	España	3 May 1911
Bacchus	Les Bacchantes	30 September 1912
Lycas	Philotis	18 February 1914
Hansli	Hansli le bossu	20 June 1914
Danseur	Une Fête chez La Pouplinière	25 May 1916
	La Favorite divertissement	24 May 1917
	Le Cobzar	27 June 1917
Styrax	Cydalise et le chèvre-pied	15 January 1923
Pas de deux	La Nocturne des amoureuses	20 January 1923
L'Excentrique	Impressions de Music-Hall	6 April 1927
Le Petit Homme noir	Le Diable dans le beffroi	3 June 1927
	Soirée romantique	27 November 1934

Aveline had become balletmaster at the Opéra in 1913, and his interest in choreography was accordingly stimulated, but he did not have time to pursue this aspect of his art until he decided to retire from the stage in 1934. Ultimately he revised or created choreography for a dozen compositions in addition to providing new dances for Lalo's Namouna (1935), the Nutcracker Suite (Trépak, 1938), Tannhaüser (Bacchanale, 1939), and Jules Massenet's* Le Cid (1942):

Ballet	Premier
La Grisi	21 June 1935
Un Baiser pour rien	15 June 1936
Elvire+	8 February 1937

Fête champêtre	8 February 1938
Ballet blanc	8 February 1938
Vie et lumière	8 February 1938
Les Santons	18 November 1938
Le Festin de l'araignée	1 May 1939
Jeux d'enfants	16 July 1941
La grande jatte	12 July 1950
"Ball." de l'Aiglon	15 May 1953
La "Trag." de Salomé	15 December 1953

*Elvire was performed by the company at the Théâtre des Champs-Elysées.

Aveline also composed the choreography for the first two ballets in Jean-Philippe Rameau's Les Indes galantes in the 1952 revival of the work (see eighteenth-century volume for Rameau and Les Indes galantes).

Aveline taught at the ballet school attached to the Opéra during his later years.

BIBLIOGRAPHY: CB 546-52; CDB 23; CODB 33; EDB 37; EDS I, 1174-75; SW 241-44, 254-55, 260, 267, 271, 273, 276-78, 283-85, 288, 290, 300, 302, 312, 322, 325, 332-33, 337.

B

Bacchanale is the name of the wild and riotous celebration, and it is for this reason that this name was chosen as the title for the ballet in Camille Saint-Saëns'* Samson et Dalila* when this passage in the last tableau of the opera was excerpted from the longer work for separate performance. Bacchanale was performed apart from its parent work for the first and only time at the Garnier Palace* on 18 November 1911 in choreography by Léo Staats.* Léa Piron and M. Guillemin starred in it on this occasion, but the work was not repeated by itself, doubtlessly because the thousand or so billings that the opera has enjoyed at the Opéra and other French theatres have provided ample opportunity for the public to see and hear Saint-Saëns' ballet.
BIBLIOGRAPHY: CODB 35; Grace Robert, The Borzoi Book of Ballets (New York: Alfred A. Knopf, 1946), 33-35; SW 241.

Les Bacchantes was billed as a ballet in two acts and three tableaux based upon Euripides with a score by Alfred Bruneau* and words by its composer in conjunction with Félix Naquet. It had its world premiere at the Opéra in Paris on 30 September 1912 with sets by Mouveau and costumes by Pinchon. Yvan Clustine did its choreography.

The ballet is set in a public square adjacent to the temple of Cérès in Thebes, where a procession of the priests and priestesses of this goddess stops in astonishment upon hearing strange music. A crowd of Thebans gathers in the square

(I, 1-2), and Bacchus enters with his entourage of colorfully dressed dancers from various regions of the Orient. He announces that he is establishing his cult and its dances in Thebes. Five dancers explain and illustrate five of the new dances. Myrrhine presents a sixth dance, while Lamia and Erinna sing accompaniments (I, 3). Trumpets announce the return of Penthée and his army to Thebes. Angry, he demands to know why he finds his city filled with Asiatic dancers. Bacchus defies him. Penthée orders Bacchus' arrest, and the Bacchantes implore him to be less severe. He refuses to listen to their plea, and the Thebans protest their ruler's attitude, but Penthée has Bacchus cast into chains (I, 4).

The second tableau presents Bacchus about to be cast into the dungeon of Penthée's castle. Myrrhine and her companions bribe the guards to release their prisoner, but Bacchus cautions them against committing a dishonorable act (II, 1). Penthée questions the god about his background, and the latter asserts that he has come to Thebes to deliver its citizens from the pain and woe of life with wine, dancing, and sleep. The king demands to know the rites of this new cult, but Bacchus assures him that he could not understand the divine nature of his religion. Penthée insists, and the followers of Bacchus dance for him, but he falls into a rage and breaks Myrrhine's goblet. Myrrhine tries to divert him with a seductive dance, and he succumbs to her charms, but he refuses to pardon Bacchus. A storm erupts, and the prison crumbles. Penthée draws his sword to prevent his prisoner from escaping, but Bacchus eludes him. The Thebans rejoice over Bacchus' deliverance (II, 2-3).

The last tableau depicts Cithéron, where a group of Bacchantes are drinking and relaxing, while their companions are hunting in the distance (II, 1 bis). Fauns emerge from the forest to join the Bacchantes. The huntresses dance to the music furnished by their company, and Bacchus is covered with flowers by his followers. Myrrhine leads her companions in a dance, and Penthée joins the festivities disguised as a Bacchant. Myrrhine recognizes him, and she invites him to drink to Bacchus. He refuses. Bacchus asks him to join his followers, but he finds that he is too clumsy to dance. Bacchus condemns him to death for having offended heaven. The Bacchantes execute a frenzied dance, and they obey Bacchus' order. Penthée is dead at the feet of Bacchus, who now ascends victorious into the sky (II, 2-3 bis).

Mlle Carlotta Zambelli* danced the part of Myrrhine with Yvan Clustine* as Penthée and Albert Aveline* as Bacchus. The singing roles of Lamia and Erinna were filled by Alice Dauman and Lyse Charny, respectively. Bruneau's work was reasonably successful after its premiere as a companion piece to Salomé on 30 October 1912. It was mounted on eight dates during November 1912 and on two occasions during December 1912. It was then billed on seven dates in 1913, and it was revived in 1914 for another two performances on 20 and 30 March. It was dropped from the repertory permanently after this 20th production on 20 March 1914.

BIBLIOGRAPHY: BOP 153; René Dumesnil, La Musique contemporaine en France (Paris: Armand Colin, 1930) I, 172-73 and II, 57-60; "Opéra . . . Les Bacchantes . . . première représentation," Le Ménestrel 78 (2 November 1912), 346-47; Stoullig XXXVIII (1912), 24-28; SW 241; Thompson 249.

Bacchus was presented as an opera in four acts and seven tableaux with a libretto by Catulle Mendès and a score by Jules Massenet.* Its choreography was created by Léo Staats.* Pinchon did the costuming, and the sets were designed by Amable and Cioccari (a. 1; a. 3, tabl. 1); Rochette and Landrin (a. 2, 4); and Mouveau and Demoget (a. 3, table. 2). It had its world premiere at the Opéra on 2 May 1909, but it failed to arouse the interest of audiences, and it had to be dropped from the repertory after its sixth performance on 19 May 1909.

The curtain rises on Bacchus to disclose Perséphone wondering whether Ariane is among the living or the dead until her companions from act 4 of Ariane* assure Perséphone that she has not yet descended to the underworld. Perséphone consults Clotho about Ariane's destiny on earth, and she replies that Ariane is on an isle with Bacchus, who has called upon his devine powers to assume the appearance of Thésée. Antéros appears to the accompaniment of thunder; he has decreed that Ariane will follow Bacchus to the Orient. The ceiling of hell becomes transparent, and Ariane is seen through an oceanic haze. She is disembarking on foreign soil with regal authority (a. 1).

The first tableau of the second act moves to Nepal in the Indian country of the Sakias. The priest Ramavaçou and his four disciples are comtemplating Buddha beside a pond filled with lilies and shaded by a fig tree. They are welcoming mendicants to their community when they hear the singing of a drunken crowd. Silène is celebrating the grape and its vine; Mahouda insists that he has been drinking red water before he falls asleep on the wayside. Amahelli tells Ramavaçou that the drunken invaders have destroyed his dominions; he calls upon his compatriots to annihilate the bestial enemy. The priest decides that he will call upon the powerful anthropoids of the Himalayas to eradicate them.

Bacchus' followers fall to planting vines in their new country, and his warriors gather to protect their gains. Bacchus enters with Ariane, and a pantomime is enacted to celebrate his victory, while the royal couple declare their mutual love with Ariane still believing that Bacchus is Thésée. The attack by the anthropoids begins, and the noises of a frightful battle are heard nearby (a. 2, tabl. 1).

The forces of Bacchus have been defeated, and Queen Amahelli hears weeping. It is Ariane beginning to realize what has happened. She discovers Bacchus, whom she revives, and he stands up in all his celectial might and beauty to question Zeus about the meaning of his defeat. Amahelli falls in love with him; the priest wishes to slay him. Queen Amahelli decides that he is to be kept a prisoner. She orders Ariane's death, however, when she learns that she is the prisoner's wife (a. 2, tabl. 2).

The setting moves to the palace of the Sakias, where Bacchus appears for judgment. The priest asks him to divulge his name and country, and he answers in riddles. Finally, he declares that he has been charged to bring the joy of wine to the world, and the priest observes that he has been given a most ignoble task. They argue, and the priest threatens him with execution. Queen Amahelli orders everybody to leave, especially the priest, and she throws herself at Bacchus' feet. He asks her to dismiss her morose priests and to free his Bacchantes; she agrees. Bacchus asks her to rescue Ariane and to order a celebration for her; she is willing. Bacchus requests too much, however, when he asks Amahelli to be Ariane's servant. Amahelli realizes that Ariane is Bacchus' wife. When Ariane enters to throw herself into Bacchus' arms, Amahelli loses her patience and condemns her rival to death. Yet when Ariane displays her willingness to die for Bacchus, Amahelli agrees to Bacchus' demands (a. 3, tabl. 1).

The third act closes with the initiation rites into the Dionysiac mysteries and the induction of Buddhist nuns and warriors into the company of Bacchus (a. 3, table. 2).

The fourth act returns to the Sakias' palace, where Ariane urges Amahelli to take heart. The anthropoids are crushed, and Bacchus is about to return. Amahelli replies that it has been foretold that Bacchus is to die at the stake in the morning. Amahelli adds quietly that the execution is certain unless Zeus agrees that a less important maiden be substituted for him. Ariane recognizes the allusion to herself, and again she rejoices that she is able to die for her "spouse-king." A funeral procession meets Ariane, and a priestess gives her a knife to ease her pain. Suddenly, Amahelli vents her jealous rage on Ariane, but it is not long before Bacchus returns to ask her where Ariane has gone (a. 4, table. 1). He notices the stake in the distance, where Ariane has stabbed herself when the fire was lighted at her feet. He runs to the temple of Zeus for justice. A storm gathers, and the lightning kills Amahelli. Ariane rises into the heavens (a. 4, tabl. 2).

The principal female roles of Bacchus were filled at the premiere of the work by Lucienne Bréval* (Ariane) and Lucy Arbell* (queen Amahelli), while the male parts were created by Lucien Muratore* (Bacchus), Léon Gresse* (the priest), Marcelin Duclos (Silène), and Triadou (Mahouda). M. Muratore had already sung Thésée in Jules Massenet's Ariane, and his starring in both roles strengthen the illusion in Bacchus that Bacchus had disguised himself as Thésée to win Ariane's love.

BIBLIOGRAPHY: "Bacchus," Le Ménestrel 75 (8 May 1909), 147-48, 153-54, 161-62ff; Charles Bouvet, Massenet (Paris: Librairie Renouard, 1929), 109-11; René Brancour, Massenet (Paris: Félix Alcan, 1922), 113-16; Henry T. Finck, Massenet and His Operas (New York: John Lane Co., 1910), 217-20; James Harding, Massenet (New York: St. Martin's

Press, 1970) 174-78; D. Irvine, Massenet: a Chronicle of His Life and Times (Seattle: the author, 1974), 321-23; Jules Massenet, My Recollections, trans. H. Villiers Barnett (Westport, Conn.: Greenwood Press, 1970), 267-73; PBSW 206; SW 38-39, 44-45.

Bacchus was a ballet in three acts and five tableaux with a score by Victor Alphonse Duvernoy,* a libretto by Georges Hartmenn and Joseph Hansen,* and choreography by Hansen. It had its world premiere at the Garnier Palace* on 26 November 1902, and Paul Vidal* was at the desk for its first performance. Its sets were designed by Amable, Moisson, Jambon, Brandt, and Rabuteau. Charles Bianchini created its costumes.

The ballet begins in the main square of Ayodhia, capital of the first kings of Hindustan. A magnificent temple is situated at the end of a wide terrace in front of the royal palace. Darsatha, king of India, has invited Sakouni, king of the mountains, and a host of neighboring princes to gamble with him on the terrace, while they watch the bayadères dance. The High Brahman and his priestesses are on their way to the temple to pray for the safety of their country, when the young priestess Yadma gazes at the king. He summons her into his presence to ask her to become his queen, but she reminds him that he should be at the head of his armies and defending his country. He is angered by her insolence and orders her arrest (I, tabl. 1, sc. 1-2). The holy man Le Mouni indicates that the enemy can be repulsed only by the virgin in the temple, who proves to be Yadma. Le Mouni frees her from her chains with a sacred gesture, and he commissions her to cast a spell over the enemy king and to poison him (I, tabl. 1, sc. 3-4).

Darsatha's defeated and fleeing soldiers rush into the square followed by victorious Bacchus, his soldiers, and his bacchants. Yadma looks at Bacchus and recognizes the warrior of her dreams. Alert Le Mouni reminds her of her vow to poison him (I, tabl. 1, sc. 5).

The scene shifts to the interior of Bacchus' tent at the gates of the city. It is siesta time, and Bacchus is sleeping. His attendants are dancing around him in silence, and hushed Indian slaves are bringing gifts from conquered Darsatha (I, tabl. 2, sc. 1). Yadma enters disguised as a dancing girl and accompanied by slaves carrying an amphora of wine. Bacchus awakens and is captivated by her. He dismisses everybody but Yadma despite Silène's warnings (I, tabl. 2, sc. 2). She pours a cup of the fatal wine, but she asks him not to drink it until she has concluded her dancing. She executes three dances, and Bacchus seizes the cup. Alarmed, Yadma knocks the cup from his hands. She declares her love to him and admits her previous intent to poison him. Bacchus takes her into his arms and swears his undying love to her, while Silène orders the dancers to perform (I, tabl. 2, sc. 3-4).

It is dawn in Bacchus' camp at the foot of the Himalaya mountains, and Bacchus invites Darsatha to a banquet for Yadma. The king is desperate when he realizes that Yadma and Bacchus are in love, but Le Mouni assures him that he and his men will be able to capture the lovers after sunset. Yadma and Bacchus mount their thrones (II, tabl. 1, sc. 1-2) to witness a divertissement portraying the birth of the vine (II, tabl. 1, sc. 3) (see eighteenth-century volume for divertissement). The sun sets after the dance, and Le Mouni's soldiers attack and disperse Bacchus' guards. Darsatha, Sakouni, and the princes seize Bacchus, while Le Mouni captures Yadma. Bacchus and his men regroup, however, and they rescue Yadma (II, tabl. 1, sc. 4).

Le Mouni has thrown Yadma into a deep ravine to die. Sakouni comes upon her while returning to his mountain kingdom, but he remembers her treachery and leaves her to her plight. Desperate, Yadma prays to Venus, and she finds Bacchus. The reunited lovers sing a hymn to honor the goddess (III, tabl. 1, sc. 1).

The scene returns to Bacchus' camp. The captured Indian soldiers are about to be punished, but Yadma forgives them. The rejoicing Indians acclaim her and Bacchus, and Erigone leads the god's merry retinue in a dance and orgy that end in the apotheosis of Bacchus and his generous queen (III, tabl. 2, sc. 1-2).

The ballet was not too well received by Paris audiences despite the care and money put into its production. It enjoyed only 13 performances. MM. Ladam (Darsatha) and Vanara (Le Mouni) were cast in the two male roles of the ballet, and Bacchus was danced by Mlle L. Mante in travesty. The

other important female roles were filled by Mlles Zambelli* (Erigone), Sandrini (Yadma).
BIBLIOGRAPHY: *H. Moréno, "Première Représentation de Bacchus à l'Opéra," Le Ménestrel 68 (30 November 1902), 378-79; Stoullig XXVIII (1902), 18-21; SW 241; VBO 42; VOP 82, 88.*

Bachelet, Alfred (b. 26 February 1864, Paris; d. 10 February 1944, Nancy), composer, studied music at the Paris Conservatoire as a young man, and his cantata Cléopâtre won the Prix de Rome at this institution in 1890. He showed an early interest in composing for the stage, and he attracted the attention of the public for the first time with his lyric drama Scémo,* mounted at the Opéra on 6 May 1914. After World War I, M. Bachelet returned to the theatre with two titles. Quand la cloche sonnera* was performed at the Opéra-Comique on 6 November 1922, when it enjoyed the first of its 60 performances in the rue Favart; Un Jardin sur l'Oronte had eleven billings at the Garnier Palace* between 3 November 1932 and 26 February 1934 (see twentieth-century volume for Un Jardin sur l'Oronte).

Bachelet was well liked by audiences for his full use of the orchestra and the colorful idiom that always enlivened his productions. It is not by coincidence that one of his most striking compositions for orchestra is his musical setting for one of Le Conte de Lisle's Indian poems on a Vedic legend.

The composer was conductor at the Opéra during the 1914-18 period, and, in 1919, he succeeded Ropartz as director of the Conservatoire in Nancy. Also, he did the musical arranging for the ballet called Une Fête chez La Pouplinière in which music by Jean-Philippe Rameau, Christoph Gluck, Egide-Romuald Duni, and Giovanni Pergolesi was used (see twentieth-century volume for Une Fête chez La Pouplinière and the eighteenth-century volume for Rameau Gluck, Duni, and Pergolesi). This work had its premiere at the Opéra on 25 May 1916, when Bachelet was conductor at this theatre.
BIBLIOGRAPHY: BBD 81; EDS I, 1220-21; ELM I, 330; Grove I, 339; PBSW 171.

Badet, Régina (b. 1876, Bordeaux; d. November 1949, Bordeaux), dancer, was only ten years old at the time of her admission into the corps de ballet of the Grand Theatre in her native city. Also, she was 15 when she was rewarded with the rank of premier sujet at this same opera house in 1891. Yet she was already attracted to the legitimate stage even at this early point in her career despite her success as a dancer, and she enrolled at the Bordeaux Conservatoire to study acting. She decided to attempt to carve out a career for herself as an actress after only a few months of study, and she traveled to Paris to make her debut in the capital on the stage of the Châtelet Theatre. She was not yet satisfied with her progress, however, and she returned to Bordeaux to dance at the Grand once again. Finally, in 1905, she was offered a contract to dance at the Opéra-Comique. Here, she starred in such works as Léo Delibes'* Lakmé (1905), Georges' Miarka (1905), and Camille Erlanger's* Aphrodite (1906).

Yet she was still consumed with the desire to become an actress, and she followed the suggestion of Andrée Mégard to try drama once again. She appeared in Pierre Louys' La Femme et le pantin and was successful enough in her role to decide to renounce dancing. She was never again booked at the National Lyric Theatres, although she was billed in Jean Cuvelier's* operetta Sapho (1912) at the Théâtre des Capucines. She spent most of her time entertaining Allied troops and making films during and after World War I. In all, she had performed only once at the Opéra, when she had appeared at the Garnier Palace* as a guest artist to dance the flamenca in Carmen* for a gala program on 27 December 1907.

BIBLIOGRAPHY: EDS I, 1235-36; SW 55, 149.

Bakst, Léon (b. 10 May 1866, Grodno; d. 28 December 1924, Paris), né Lev Rosenberg, was one of the artist founders of The World of Art, a Russian periodical published by Serge Diaghilev* in 1899. A friend of the Russian impresario from his early days, Bakst was one of the original artists with the Ballets russes, and he became quite famous shortly after the arrival of this dance company in Paris during the spring of 1909. His exotic sets and costumes were done in the manner of Aubry Beardsley and featured brilliant reds, blues, greens, and golds. This quasi-Persian style soon set a worldwide fashion, and Cartier began to set emeralds alongside sapphires, while fashionable Parisians donned blouses, scarves, and boots worthy of The Arabian Nights.

Bakst provided sets and/or costumes for the following ballets produced at the Opéra by Diaghilev:

Ballets	**Premiere**
Carnaval	4 June 1910
Schéhérazade	4 June 1910
Cléopâtre	11 June 1910
Spectre de la rose	11 December 1911
La Légende de Joseph	14 May 1914
Les Femmes de bonne humeur	27 December 1919
Thamar	25 January 1920
Prélude à l'après-midi d'un faune	23 May 1922

The artist also created the sets and costumes used by Mme Ida Rubinstein in her production of Le Martyr de Saint-Sebastien at the Opéra on 17 June 1922.

BIBLIOGRAPHY: CODB 37; HAZ 17-20; PBSW 171; SW 250, 255, 276-77, 294, 313-14, 324, 326-27, 331.

Balfe, Michael William, DIT Balph, Michel-Guillaume (b. 15 May 1808, Dublin; d. 20 October 1870, Rowney Abbey, Herts), librettist, took lessons on the violin as a child and was introduced to the British public as a violinist in 1817. He went to London after his father's death in 1823 and became acquainted with Count Mazzara in 1825. He accompanied the count to Rome, where he continued to study his instrument. A few years later, he journeyed to Paris and met Gioacchino Rossini,* who heard him sing with the Italian Opera in the French capital. He made his Paris debut as a vocalist in the role of Figaro, but his health started to fail, and he returned to Italy and a new patron, Count Sampieri.

Balfe started to write now, and his first opera was I Rivali di sè stessi (1829). He married Lina Rosa at this time and continued to sing, but he was back in England by 1833. He went to Paris again in 1843-44 long enough to compose Le Puits d'amour (1843) and Les Quatre Fils Aymon (1844) for the Opéra-Comique with librettos by Eugène Scribe* and Jules Saint-Georges.* Then, in 1845, he set L'Etoile de Séville* for performance at the Opéra on 17 December 1845. This was his last composition for the Paris theatres, although a French version of his Bohemian Girl (1843) was billed at the Théâtre-Lyrique in 1869. He was accepted into the Legion of Honor during the Second Empire and visited France several times before his death.

BIBLIOGRAPHY: William Barrett, Balfe: His Life and Work (London: Remington, 1882); DNB I, 964-67; Fétis Suppl. I, 39; Lajarte II, 179-80, 192; PBSW 171.

Ballets russes was a company dedicated to the propagation of Russian ballet; it grew out of an exhibition of Russian painting and sculpture that Serge Diaghilev* organized for the Paris Salon d'Automne of 1906. This 1906 affair was so successful that the gifted entrepreneur undertook a second project of a similar nature, although he devoted this second season in Paris during 1908 to Russian music and the accomplishments of such musicians and composers as Piotr Tchaikovsky,* Nikolay Rimsky-Korsakov,* Sergei Rachmaninov, Félia Litvinne,* Feodor Chaliapin,* Alexander Borodin,* Modest Mussorgsky,* Alexander Scriabin, and Fëdor Glinka. It is difficult to imagine the success enjoyed by the Paris introduction of Chaliapin in Boris Godounov* or of Arthur Nikisch conducting Tchaikowsky, but the operatic program of 1908 at the Opéra had included the Paris premiere of Boris Godounov with Chaliapin on 19 May, and 27; 450 francs 95 centimes, had been left at the box office on these two occasions. Mussorgsky's opera was billed on another five dates in 1908 with equally happy results at the box office between 21 May and 4 June, when the public bought 128,847 francs 95 centimes worth of tickets.

If Diaghilev had promoted two tremendous successes in 1906 and 1908, he was now faced with the problem of achieving a third triumph for 1909, and he resolved the difficulty by choosing an art form that would incorporate painting, design, music, and the dance: the ballet. He arrived at his basic conviction that the authors of ballets should place equal stress upon the choreography, sets, and the score in the production of their work. Also, at this time, Diaghilev was learning the truth of the old adage that success breeds success, and his recent box office triumphs in Berlin and in Venice as well as in Paris were winning imperial aid for his 1909 venture: a generous cash subsidy, the use of the Hermitage Theatre for rehearsals, a gifted cluster of artists including Léon Bakst* and Alexander Benóis,* the services of N. N. Tcherepine (the ballet conductor at the Mariinsky Theatre), and the talents of the critic V. Svetlov. His corps de ballet counted among its membership Mikhail Fokine,* Anna Pavlova,* Tamara Karsavina,* Vaslav Nijinsky,* Jean Coralli,* and Mikhail Mordkin.* He was able to secure the services of singers like Chaliapin, Smirnov, and Lipkovska.

Yet there were obstacles set in Diaghilev's way, especially when his patron, the grand duke Vladimir Alexandrovitch died, or when the impresario managed to offend Kshesinskaya. Still, nothing halted the march of the Ballets russes to Paris, and Diaghilev opened his first season with his company in Paris on 19 May 1909 at the Châtelet Theatre. "Triumph" and "success" were the most modest words used to describe the miracle that the magician Diaghilev achieved on this evening. Thirty years later, for example, Louis Gillet likened the first performances of the Ballets russes to a mirage. The troupe came into being with great éclat and much flattery, and one of the most eloquent of these compliments was the rapidity with which Diaghilev's company was invited to perform at the Opéra. Here, at the Garnier, they presented the second and third acts of Boris Godounov, Le Festin* and Les Sylphides.* Mlles Anna Pavolva and Tamara Karsavina starred with Nijinsky and Léonide Massine. Spectators left 35,108 francs at the box office on this evening of 19 June 1909. The program was so well received that the Russian visitors were called upon to present the program for a gala at the Opéra on 26 June 1909. They offered Le Vieil Aigle* with Feodor Chaliapin as the Khan Asvab and Danses russes starring Mlle Pavlova and M. Mordkin in choreography by Mikhail Fokine.

Diaghilev returned to St. Petersburg after the 1909 season to prepare his 1910 programs, and the first two important developments to which he had to adjust his company were the loss of Anna Pavlova, who had resigned from the troupe, and the acquisition of Igor Stravinsky,* who was to write the music for eight pieces to be used by Diaghilev. When the impresario arrived in the French capital in the spring of 1910, it became obvious within a week that his new season would surpass anything that he already had done. His new conductor, Gabriel Pierné,* was performing effectively; he had a half-dozen new productions including the luminous Schéhérazade* for which Bakst had done magnificent sets, and a revised Giselle,* in which Mme Karsavina proved to be a successful substitute for Anna Pavlova, who was originally scheduled to partner Nijinsky. the full 1910 schedule of a dozen programs by the Ballets russes at the Opéra included nine titles of which six were new additions to the repertory. They were billed on the following dates in June:

Ballet	Dates
Le Carnaval	June 4, 7, 9, 25, 28, 30
Schéhérazade	June 4, 7, 9, 11, 14, 16, 21, 23
Le Festin	June 4, 7, 9
Danses polovtsiennes	June 7, 9
Cléopâtre	June 11, 14, 16
Les Sylphides	June 11, 14, 16
Giselle	June 18, 21, 23
L'Oiseau de feu	June 25, 28, 30
Les Orientales	June 25, 28, 30

Success had come so constantly and so unreservedly to the Ballets russes that Diaghilev found himself facing an almost preposterous problem at the start of 1911. His competitors were becoming more and more envious of his theatrical accomplishments and importance, and they were beginning to launch schemes to undermine his ambition to place his Ballets russes on a permanent footing instead of relying upon seasonal improvisations. He found himself opposed by the grand duke Serge Mikhailovitch, who was trying to restore Teliakovsky as the director of the Imperial Theatres. He lost the services of his popular star, Nijinsky. Yet opportunity was still waiting during the season of 1911, and Diaghilev decided to establish independent headquarters for his company in Monte Carlo. Plans were formulated immediately to have the team of Stravinsky, Benóis, and Fokine complete Pétrouchka,* while Vaudoyer, Weber, Bakst, and Fokine were to conclude Le Spectre de la rose.* The company spent so much time in England in response to an invitation to participate in the coronation celebration, however, that the Ballets russes appeared at the Opéra at the end of the year to mount the following works:

Ballet	Dates
Le Carnaval	December 24
Les Sylphides	December 24, 31
Le Spectre de la rose	December 24, 31
Schéhérazade	December 24, 31
L'Oiseau de feu	December 31
Les Danses polovtsiennes	December 31

The months immediately before World War I saw Diaghilev veer away from nationalistic Russian topics and turn toward works that dealt with a subject that offered the opportunity for modern experimentation or restated legends and themes derived from classic antiquity. Also, the impresario did not take his works to the Opéra in 1912-13 because he had contracted for his company to appear in London, Berlin, Budapest, and Vienna as well as at the Champs-Elysées theatre in Paris. This lack of time to offer a season at the Garnier Palace* in 1912-13 did not destroy the friendship between Jacques Rouché at the Opéra and Serge Diaghilev, however, and the Ballets russes returned to the Garnier in 1914 to present compositions on ten separate occasions between 14 May and 6 June 1914:

Ballet	Dates
La Légende de Joseph	May 14, 17, 19, 21; June 4, 6
Les Papillons	May 14, 17, 19
Schéhérazade	May 14, 17, 19, 21
Pétrouchka	May 21, 24
Le Coq d'or	May 24, 26, 28
Le Rossiginol	May 26, 28
Cléopâtre	June 2, 4, 6
Midas	June 2

The Ballets russes then came back to the Opéra on 29 December 1915 to offer Schéhérazade, L'Oiseau de feu, La Princesse enchantée, Le Soleil de nuit, Mélodies russes, and Danses polovtsiennes before the creation of Parade by Cocteau-Satie-Picasso-Massine at the Châtelet Theatre in Paris on 18 May 1917.

The end of the war found the personnel of the Ballet russes more or less scattered and still suffering from the opprobium that had been the lot of Russians in Western Europe since the defection of the Bolshevik government from the Allied cause during World War I. Eventually, however, the company was able to reunite for a year of performances in London and Manchester starting in December 1919, and they had ample time to organize their programs for their first postwar appearances at the Opéra. La Boutique fantasque and Le Tricorne were given their premieres in this London season, and several important changes were about to influence the work of the company. Pablo Picasso was now an active member of the group of painters that included Bakst, André Derain, and Henri Matisse. Massine was about to have an argument with Diaghilev and leave the troupe. Sergei Prokofiev was on the point of becoming the leading musician of the company. More importantly, the company and its leader were fired with fresh enthusiasm, when they left England for Paris to fill two contracts at the Garnier Theatre after an absence of four years.

The first series of performances at the Opéra by the Ballet russes after the war began on Christmas Eve 1919 and ran until 16 February 1920:

Ballet	Dates
Pétrouchka	Dec. 24; Jan. 22, 27
La Boutique fantasque	Dec. 24, 30; Jan. 22, 25, 29
Danses polovtsiennes	Dec. 24, 27; Jan. 25, 31
Carnaval	Dec. 27; Jan. 21, 31
Les Femmes de bonne humeur	Dec. 27, 30; Jan. 20, 27
Soleil de nuit	Dec. 30; Jan. 22, 29; Feb. 3
Contes russes	Jan. 20, 23; Feb. 2, 7
Les Papillons	Jan. 23, 29
Le Tricorne	Jan. 23, 27, 31; Feb. 3, 10, 16
Thamar	Jan. 25; Feb. 2
Le Chant du rossignol	Feb. 2, 5, 7, 10, 16
Les Sylphides	Feb. 3, 7

The company now returned to Monte Carlo in February 1920 to prepare for the coming Paris season by readying Pulcinella, Astuce feminine and the new version of Le Sacre du printemps. This second Paris season after only three months gave no evidence that the popularity of the Ballets russes was diminishing at the Opéra, even if Massine was no longer a member of the company. The spring 1920 season lasted from 8 May until 4 June:

Ballet	Dates
Les Sylphides	May 8, 17, 26
Les Femmes de bonne humeur	May 8, 30
Pétrouchka	May 8, 18, 22; June 1
La Boutique fantasque	May 13, 20, 30; June 2

Le Tricorne	May 13, 20, 29
Danses polovtsiennes	May 13, 22, 25, 27
Contes russes	May 15, 25
Pulcinella	May 15, 17, 18, 20, 25
Soleil de nuit	May 15
Schéhérazade	May 17, 26, 31
Le Chant du rossignol	May 18
L'Oiseau de feu	May 22, 26; June 4
Austuce féminine	May 27, 29; June 1, 2, 4
Parade	May 30

The Ballets russes appeared once again at the Opéra in May and June 1922, when they staged 16 programs composed of three or four titles apiece. As in previous years, Diaghilev's company had new works to stage, and the first among them was Le Mariage de la belle au bois dormant. As indicated titularly, this composition was an extract from La Belle au bois dormant, which was not given in its entirety at the Opéra until 27 September 1954. Mlle Trefilova danced the part of the princess opposite Vladimirov as Prince Charming in this ballet that enjoyed nine presentations. Le Renard was billed as a "ballet burlesque" with Mme Nijinska as "le renard" and Iszikowsky as "le Coq" in all of its five performances at the Garnier. Prélude à l'après-midi d'um faune was based upon Mallarmé's poem and, offered as a "tableau chorégraphique," it had a stormy premiere at the Châtelet Theatre on 29 May 1912. Nijinska executed the part of "le Faune" in 1922; this role would be done later by Serge Lifar in 1922, 1927, 1954. Mme Nijinska also danced the lead in Le Sacre de printemps for the 1922 season of the Ballets russes at the Opéra. The company presented 16 programs at the Garnier in this 1922 season lasting from 18 May until 13 June:

Ballet	Dates
Carnaval	May 18, 20, 25; June 1, 7
Le Mariage de la Belle au bois dormant	May 18, 22, 23, 25, 31; June 1, 2, 9, 13
Le Renard	May 18, 20, 23; June 1, 6
Danses polovtsiennes	May 18, 22, 25; June 1, 6
Le Spectre de la rose	May 20, 25, 31; June 8
Pétrouchka	May 20, 22, 27; June 2, 3, 8, 12
Prélude à l'après-midi d'un faune	May 23, 27, 31; June 8
Soleil de nuit	May 23, 27
Le Sacre du printemps	May 27; June 3, 13
Schéhérazade	May 31; June 7, 9
Contes russes	June 2, 6, 12
Mavra	June 3, 6, 7, 8, 9, 12, 13

The Ballet russes returned to the Opéra in 1927 after an absence of five years to perform on only two dates, but they produced two new works during their brief 1927 stay at the Garnier: Prokofiev's Pas d'acier and Henri Sauguet's La Chatte. The full schedule of 1927 programs by Diaghilev's company at the opera included:

Ballet	Dates
Pas d'acier	December 27
La Chatte	December 27, 29
L'Oiseau de feu	December 27, 29
Prélude à l'après-midi d'un faune	December 29
Danses polovtsiennes	December 29

The company was back at the Garnier for two more brief periods at the end of 1928 and at the start of 1929, when they danced choreography by George Balanchine for the first time at the Opéra in Les Dieux mendiants and Apollon Musagète. The troupe managed to mount 14 performances on the four dates that constituted this Paris 1928-29 engagement.

Ballet	**Dates**
Le Chant du rossignol	Dec. 20, 27
Les Dieux mendiants	Dec. 20, 27; Jan. 3
La Chatte	Dec. 20; Jan. 3
Soleil de nuit	Dec. 20
L'Oiseau de feu	Dec. 24; Jan 3
Apollon Musagète	Dec. 24; Jan. 3
Pétrouchka	Dec. 24, 27

After these January 1929 performances, Diaghilev started to prepare for the spring season of 1929, and his work kept him and Serge Lifar shuttling back and forth between Monte Carlo and Paris. Finally, it was decided that he and his new ballet master would direct the spring season of 1929 in Paris from the Hotel Scribe. The troup performed at the Théâtre Sarah Bernhardt, but they were not scheduled to dance at the Opéra in late 1929, however, and Diaghilev left France for Germany and England before going on vacation in Venice to recover his health and strength. Unfortunately, his physical condition deteriorated despite the efforts of his friends and doctors. The impresario and his company ceased to exist on the morning of 19 April 1929.

BIBLIOGRAPHY: ACPM 296; CODB 50-51; Collab., "Les Ballet russes de Serge de Diaghilev," RM special issue (1 December 1930), bibliography on 106-12; Gilberte Courmand, "Diaghilev et les peintres," SDLD (January 1972), 22-24; HAZ 40-50; André-Philippe Hersin, "Hommage à Diaghilev," SDLD (February 1973), 2-3; Serge Lifar, Serge Diaghilev: His Life, His Work, His Legend New York: Da Capo Press, 1976; idem, Histoire du ballet russe depuis les origines jusqu'à nos jours

(Paris: Éditions Nagel, 1950), 197-251; Olga Maynard, "Diaghilev and the Ballets russes," *Dance Magazine* *45, no. 3 (March 1971), 50-56; Pierre Michaut, "Souvenir de Diaghilev,"* *RM* *182 (March 1938), 161-72; André Schaikevitch, "Diaghilev,"* *SDLD* *(January 1972), 16-21; Shaeffner, "Théâtre Sarah-Bernhardt: Ballets russes,"* *Le Ménestrel* *89, no. 23 (June 1927), 257-58; TDB 10-15, 518-19; XXJ 89-940.*

Le Bal masqué is the title given to the ballet in Daniel Auber's Gustave III, when this segment of the opera is performed separately. It was produced apart from its parent work for the first time on 27 April 1834 with choreography by Filippo Taglioni (see eighteenth-century volume for Taglioni). It became very popular in its own right, and it was billed at the theatre in the rue Le Peletier* and at the Garnier Palace* on 69 dates during the nineteenth century. It was produced for the last time at the Opéra on 29 January 1877, when it became part of a program designed to honor Daniel Auber.* Mlle Laura Fonta* and Louis Mérante* filled the roles of the married man and the married woman on this occasion. These two parts were created originally by Pauline Montessu* and Joseph Mazilier.*
BIBLIOGRAPHY: AEM 13, 1426-63; DDO I, 537; EDS IX, 1572-84; Lajarte II, 145-46; SW 243.

Balochi, Ballochi, or Balloco, Louis (b. 1766, Verceil; d. April 1832, Paris), librettist, studied at Pisa and earned a doctorate in jurisprudence at the university in this city in 1786. He gave up the practice of law in favor of poetry, however, and started his literary career in 1802 with a translation of a composition by Legouvé entitled Il Merito delle donne. He came to Paris this same year as writer and director for the Théâtre-Italien and remained with this troupe for a score of years. Apparently subject to periods of depression after the death of his wife, he left the company only to fall victim to cholera while still living in the French capital. When he was working for the Italians, he had found time to write librettoes for Le Siège de Corinthe* of 1826 with Alexandre Soumet* and for Moïse* of 1827 with Victor Jouy (see eighteenth-century volume for Jouy). His literary production also included a number of dramas written in Italian but published

at Paris: I Virtuosi ambulanti (1807), Penelope (1815), Il Viaggio a Reims (1825), and Roberto il Diavolo imitated from Robert le Diable.* His cantata on the death of Domenico Cimarosa was never set to music.
BIBLIOGRAPHY: Bibliothèque universelle des romans II, 689; Lajarte II, 123, 125.

Banville, Théodore de (b. 14 March 1823, Moulins; d. 13 March 1891, Moulins), librettist, was sent to Paris at the age of seven, and he liked to create the impression later in life that he was a native of the capital. His father planned to send him to law school, but he had already fallen under the influence of Victor Hugo* and Théophile Gautier,* and he was accordingly resolved to become a poet and leader in the current Bohemian revolt against materialism. He published his two most famous collections of verse in the forties, Cariatides and Stalactites, and he became a contributor at the same time to such lively periodicals as Le Corsaire, Le Pamphlet, and Le Pouvoir. He discovered his favorite writer and personal idol, Charles Baudelaire, during this 1842-56 period, when he made his lone and slight contribution to the Opéra, the ode for the divertissement of 1851 entitled Les Nations* (see eighteenth-century volume for divertissement).
BIBLIOGRAPHY: DBF V, 80-84; Lajarte II, 209.

Les Barbares was a lyric tragedy in three acts with a score by Camille Saint-Saëns* and a libretto by Victorien Sardou* and P.-B. Gheusi. Marcel Jambon* and Marcel Bailly created its sets; Charles Bianchini designed its costumes. Joseph Hansen* was in charge of its choreography. It had its world premiere in Paris at the National Academy of Music on 20 October 1901.

The curtain rises during the prologue to disclose the ancient theatre of Orange, where Scaurus outlines the basic situation from which the opera evolves. Three hundred thousand Germans have been driven southward from the shores of the Baltic by a raging hurricane; the Roman legions are fleeing before them, and the invaders are free to invest the cities in their path. One of the centers they have seized is Orange, where a young Vestal will stop their violence and liberate her city by giving herself to the enemy in an apparent betrayal of her vows.

The first act is set in the Roman theatre of Orange, where a crowd of women and children have come to seek protection against the Germans in the Vestals' temple. A choir is offering prayers, and the Vestal Floria assures the people that Vesta has promised to protect them, although the lookout reports that Euryale will not be able to repulse the invaders. Livie's confidence is not shaken, and she is certain that her husband Euryale and Scaurus will protect them. Floria, Livia, and the choir continue to pray to Vesta; the lookout climbs to the top of the wall to observe the battle, and Floria sees the death of Scaurus or Euryale in Vesta's flame, and the lookout announces that the latter has fallen. Moments later, wounded Scaurus appears at the entrance to the temple (I, 1) to return Euryale's body to Livie. He urges the women to flee with the Lares, while the men return to battle. Livie asks the identity of the barbarian who has killed her husband, but he cannot answer her question (I, 2). Livie swears to find him and to slay him. The Vestals lead grieving Livie away, and Floria urges the women and children present to remain under the protection of Vesta in the temple. The lookout announces that the Germans have seized the city (I, 3).

The barbarians, led by Hildibrath, rush into the temple screaming for blood and shouting the praises of Odin and Thor. They are about to massacre the women and children, but they refrain from violence when their leader Marcomir appears. He gives them the women to enslave or murder, and he orders Vesta's altar overturned. The sacred fire leaps into the air at a sign from Floria, however, and Hildibrath and Marcomir recognize the flame as Thor. Marcomir is amazed at Floria's power to command the gods. She reveals her name and position as a Vestal, and the Germans call for her death. Marcomir orders them into the street and proclaims the theatre a holy place to be entered only on pain of death. Marcomir and Floria gaze at each other as the curtain falls (I, 4).

Moonlight illuminates the interior of the theatre, where Livie is longing to identify her husband's killer. Floria tells her to be grateful to Vesta for being alive, but she responds that it was Venus who bent Marcomir's will to do her bidding and protect them. Suddenly, they hear steps (II, 1). It is Scaurus come to lead them to the safety of the new Roman army that is forming. Livie refuses to leave the place where Euryale was slain; Floria will not abandon Vesta (II, 2). Hildibrath enters with his soldiers; they are seeking Scaurus. He emerges from the darkness to surrender and is thrown into chains. Hildibrath adds that Scaurus will be executed in Marcomir's presence. Floria calls for the German leader, and Marcomir enters. Floria asks for Scaurus' deliverance. Scaurus insults and defies Marcomir, but the German frees him. Everyone leaves except Floria, who is detained by Marcomir (II, 3-4). He wishes to tell her that he has granted her wish because he loves her. He warns her that his soldiers will return to carnage as soon as they begin to drink again. Only he can stop them. She is indignant at the implications of his threats, but he tells her openly that she must give herself to him. He insists, and she agrees finally to save her compatriots. He orders Hildibrath to forbid the soldiers to drink and to be ready to leave Orange in the morning. Vesta's fire goes out, but Marcomir suggests that she can now serve Freia, goddess of youth and love. The act ends in a passionate duet when Floria discovers that she loves Marcomir (II, 5).

It is morning, and Hildibrath is giving orders for the soldiers' departure. A chorus of Gallo-Romans reflects the surprise and feelings of joy abroad in the city. The Germans disappear in the distance, and a ballet of thanksgiving is danced in the theatre (III, 1). After the dance, Floria enters radiant, and she confesses to the townspeople that she has left Vesta to become Marcomir's wife. The crowd is outraged, but Scaurus points out that her decision has saved them and their homes. The enlightened citizenry pays homage to their heroine.

Floria announces her plans to follow Marcomir, who returns Orange to its inhabitants because they have given her to him. Livie asks to accompany Floria in her new life, and Floria agrees. Livie requests a moment to collect some ashes from a funeral pyre, and Marcomir inquires about the identity of the deceased. Floria tries to avoid trouble by answering simply that the dead man was Livie's husband. Marcomir insists upon knowing his name, however, and Floria exclaims, "Euryale!". Marcomir tells her to be quiet because it was he who slew the consul in battle. Livie returns with the javelin that slew her husband, and Floria tries to discourage her from leaving Orange. Livie grows suspicious, and she resorts to a trick. She admits that she will never forgive the man who struck her beloved in the back. Marcomir protests that he struck him in the heart. Her suspicions confirmed by her ruse, Livie slays Marcomir with his own javelin. Floria cannot support the sight of her dead groom, but Livie smiles in triumph (III, 2-3).

Critics felt that the score of Les Barbares was cold and colorless and that the work added nothing to Saint-Saëns' reputation as a composer. Yet it was agreed that there were passages that redeemed the work to some degree; for example, the symphonic introduction to the first act and the "Divinité libératrice" at the start of the third act. The tragedy was billed at the Garnier Palace* on 27 dates between the time of its premiere there on 20 October 1901 and 15 December 1902. Extracts from it were offered on 19 June 1913, 22 April 1914, and finally twice in the curtailed 1914-15 season, when it had a certain progaganda value. The principal female roles were created by Mmes Jeanne Hatto* (Floria) and Meyrianne Héglon (Livie). The male parts were sung for the first time by Albert Vaguet* (Marcomir), Jean-François Delmas* (Scaurus), and Riddez (Hildibrath).

BIBLIOGRAPHY: Emile Baumann, L'Oeuvre de Camille Saint-Saëns (Paris: Ollendorff, 1923), 459-62; Jean Bonnerot, C. Saint-Saëns: sa vie et son oeuvre (Paris: A. Durand et fils, 1914), 164-67; Arthur Dandelot, La Vie et l'Oeuvre de Saint-Saëns (Paris: Editions Dandelot, 1930), 185-88; DDO II, 1189-90; René Dumesnil, La Musique contemporaine en France (Paris: Armand Colin, 1930) I, 12-15 and II, 64-66; James Harding, Saint-Saëns and His Circle (London: Chapman & Hall, 1965), 204-5; Arthur Hervey, Saint-Saëns (Freeport, N.Y.: Books for Libraries Press, 1969), 69-70; Watson Lyle, Camille Saint-Saëns: His Life and Art (New York: E. P. Dutton, 1923), 169-70; PBSW 206; Arthur Pougin, "Première Représentation des Barbares à l'Opéra," Le Mânestrel 67 (27 October 1901), 338-39; Georges Servières, La Musique françoise moderne (Paris: Havard, 1897), 285-404; Stoullig XXVII (1901), 20-27; SW 46; Thompson 1604-7.

Barbier, Henri-Auguste (b. 29 April 1805, Paris; d. 13 February 1882, Nice), librettist, studied law upon completion of his studies at the lycée Henri IV, but his publication of a historical novel entitled Les Mauvais Garçons (1830 with Alphonse Royer* indicated more exactly the directions that his ambition was to follow. After the revolution of 1830, he wrote a satire for the Revue de Paris assailing the false friends of liberty and making him famous for his uninhibited attack upon these self-proclaimed heroes of the barricades.

The sudden yet complete success that had come to Barbier for writing a single piece in the satiric vein led him to continue in this same genre, and his compositions treated subjects as diverse as crushing poverty, the Napoleonic myth, or the laws governing the press. These juvenalian poems composed between 1830 and 1835 were published as Iambes et Poèmes in 1836. They were Barbier's only enduring success except for the libretto that he wrote with Léon de Wailly for Hector Berlioz'* Benvenuto Cellini* of 1837. He gave up satire after 1840, but he continued to write and produced verse, short stories, translations, and especially memoirs. He was elected to the French Academy in 1869 and joined the Legion of Honor in 1878, but he never captured the public's eye or heart again, and he never attempted to write another line for the Opéra after 1837.

BIBLIOGRAPHY: DBF V, 318-19; Lajarte II, 158; Hector Berlioz, Memoirs, trans. and ed. David Cairns (New York: Knopf, 1969), 131, 242-46, 527.

Barbier, Jules (b. 8 March 1825, Paris; d. 16 January 1901, Paris), librettist, began to write for the theatre at age 13; he had his La Voix de la France produced in 1838. He had scarcely finished his schooling, moreover, when he gave L'Ombre de Molière to the Comédie-Française, and he never stopped writing for the theatres of Paris as long as he could pick up a pen. It would be an extremely onerous task to present a complete list of all the dramatic pieces that he did alone or in collaboration for the Paris theatres of his day, but it is necessary to note that the best known of his titles for the legitimate theatre were Le Poète (1847) and Le Dernier des adieux (1851) for the Comédie-Française; Graziella (1849) for the Gymnase; Voyage autour d'une jolie femme (1856) for the Vaudeville; Le Maître de la maison (1866) and La Loterie du mariage (1868), in which Sarah Bernhardt made her debut, for the Odéon; and La Fille du maudit (1866), Cora (1866), and Un Retour de jeunesse (1877) for the Ambigu.

If his titles for French actors of the time seem numerous, a list of his total works for the singers of his day is incredible not only on account of the quantity of items in it, but also because it includes so many of the top hits at the Opéra-Comique and the Opéra. The following are his most memorable works for the former theatre: Galathée (1852), Les Noces de Jeannette (1853), Les Saisons (1855) with Michel Carré* as his colibrettist for music by Victor Massé;* Faust (1859), Philémon et Baucis (1860), Roméo et Juliette (1867) again with Carré but for Charles Gounod;* Psyché (1857) and Mignon (1866) with Carré; Le Pardon de Ploërmel (1859) for Giacomo Meyerbeer* and La Statue for Ernest Reyer,* both with his regular collaborator. His Les Contes d'Hoffmann (1881) proved to be one of the most popular pieces offered at the temporary branch of the Opéra-Comique opened in Biarritz during the first World War. Barbier did not have as many compositions with their premieres at the Opéra, but some of his Opéra-Comique compositions like Faust were booked into the more prestigious theatre later. In fact, his La Reine de Saba* of 1862, his Hamlet* of 1868, his Polyeucte* of 1878, and his Françoise de Rimini* of 1882 were his only operas having their initial presentations at the Opéra, although two ballets to which he had contributed his time and talents were performed for the first time at the larger theatre: Sylvia* of 1876 and La Tempête* of 1889.

This uninterrupted writing for the theatre would have consumed the strength of any average mortal, but Barbier still found the energy to publish three volumes of poetry and a French mass, and all these activities were recognized by his colleagues who named him president of the dramatic writers' society in France. He was elected to the Legion of Honor in 1880, and, after the fire of 1887 at the Opéra-Comique, he was selected to be interim director of the company until order could be restored in the affairs of the corporation.

BIBLIOGRAPHY: Pierre Brunel and Stéphane Wolff, L'Opéra (Paris: Bordas, 1980), 171; DBF V, 331-32; Lajarte II, 233, 242-43, 248.

Le Barbier de Séville, entitled Il Barbiere de Siviglia in Italian and The Barber of Seville in English, was offered originally as a "melodramma buffo" in two acts with a score by Gioacchino Rossini* and a libretto by Cesare Sterbini based upon the comedy by Pierre Beaumarchais (see eighteenth-century volume for Beaumarchais). It had its world premiere at the Teatro Argentina on 20 February 1816. It was billed at the Park Theatre in New York on 3 May 1819, and it was given initially in Paris in Italian at the Théâtre Italien on 26 October 1819. It was offered to the public in French for the first time at the Grand opera house in Lyon on 19 September 1821 in a version prepared by François-Joseph Blaze.* The work was staged next in Paris at the Odéon on 6 May 1824, and its first act reached Le Peletier* opera house in the French capital on 14 January 1828 on the occasion of a gala program that also included Rossini's Semiramide.* Le Barbier de Séville was rehearsed at the Opéra-Comique in 1834, but its performance at this theatre was forbidden at this time because the Comique was not permitted to offer works in translation. It was not until 8 November 1884 that Rossini's masterpiece was admitted into the repertory at the Opéra-Comique. Subsequently Le Barbier de Séville was to enjoy 532 performances here between 8 November 1884 and 7 March 1943. Meanwhile it also became part of the repertory at the Théâtre National de l'Opéra on 18 May 1933, when Fanny Heldy sang Rosine with Léon Ponzio as Figaro. If one counts the four presentations of Le Barbier de Séville by the Monte Carlo Company at the Opéra in 1912, Rossini's work has been billed at the Garnier Palace* on 45 dates between 1912 and 1972.

The intrigue of Le Barbier de Séville develops from Dr. Bartholo's desire to marry his wealthy ward, Rosine, although she is in love with hansdome Count Almaviva, who uses Figaro's talents to thwart her guardian's selfish plan.

The opera opens in a street in Seville, where Count Almaviva is serenading Rosine in the predawn darkness. The musicians play long and lively, but Rosine fails to appear on her balcony. The count remains on the scene until he hears someone approaching. The intruder proves to be Figaro, the barber of Seville and factotum of the city where he plies his trade. The count recognizes him and is aware of his ability to help lovers of every age and station. He charges the barber with arranging matters so that he may speak with Rosine, and he explains further that he must assume the name of Lindoro in this affair because he does not wish Rosine to be overly impressed or intimidated by his rank.

Rosine appears on her balcony at last, but her greedy and suspicious guardian joins her immediately. She manages to drop a letter to the count, and he picks it up without delay. Bartholo rushes to retrieve it, but he cannot find it. The count is obliged to hide, but he overhears the doctor inform his servants that he intends to wed Rosine this very day. He also cautions his domestics that no one is to enter his house except his ward's music teacher, Don Bazile. The doctor disappears down the street, but Rosine is still on the balcony, and the count follows Figaro's suggestion to sing a love song to her. She reacts with enthusiasm to his serenade which declares her suitor to be a poor and humble student named Lindoro. The encouraged count assures Figaro that he will be well rewarded for whatever help he can provide in getting him into Dr. Bartholo's house, and resourceful Figaro recalls that a regiment is about to arrive in town. He suggests that the count dress as a soldier and get himself billeted in Dr. Bartholo's home (I).

The scene shifts to a room in Dr. Bartholo's house, where Rosine is reading a note from Lindoro. She leaves when her crabbed guardian and the music teacher Bazile enter. The two old men reveal their suspicion that the mysterious serenader is Count Almaviva, and they decide to scuttle his suit for Rosine's hand by besmirching his character with false and malicious gossip. Rosine returns with Figaro, who informs the incredulous girl that her guardian intends to marry her. Also, he notes that the young man she saw beneath her balcony is madly in love with her. Impatient to speak with her suitor, she entrusts Figaro with a letter addressed to Lindoro.

Bartholo suspects that his rebellious ward is exchanging love letters with the count through Figaro, and he questions her about the ink on her fingers, a recently sharpened quill, and a missing sheet of writing paper. Rosine is quick with evasive answers, and the old man can only respond with empty threats. Suddenly there is a knock on the door. It is a drunken soldier come to claim his quarters. Rosine recognizes her suitor, but Bartholo asserts that he is exempt from the burden of billeting soldiers. He summons the military police to enforce his allegation, but the surprised soldiers fail to arrest the intruder when he reveals his true identity to them.

The ruse of the drunken soldier fails, but Figaro is able to hit upon another plan, and the count presents himself at Bartholo's door as Don Alonzo, a music teacher. He explains that he has come to give Rosine her music lesson because Don Bazile is ill. Dr. Bartholo is suspicious as always, but the count sweeps away his doubts by pretending to be his ally. He gives him Rosine's letter to Lindoro. He explains that he found the letter at the inn where Count Almaviva is staying, and he volunteers to persuade Rosine that the count is deceiving her. The beguiled and gullible doctor is delighted.

Figaro arrives at Bartholo's house to shave the doctor. He steals a key to the house when he is procuring some fresh linen. Matters seem to be progressing well for the conspirators until Don Bazile appears on the scene, but the count saves the day by persuading Dr. Bartholo to get rid of Bazile by convincing him that he is ill. The count enforces the doctor's gloomy prognosis with a timely bribe, and bewildered Bazile leaves for home and his bed. The lovers are now free to plan their elopement, while the barber splatters soap into Dr. Bartholo's eyes. The old man comes to realize finally that he has been duped, but the happy conspirators laugh at him and leave him to his frustration.

Yet Dr. Bartholo refuses to surrender. He shows Rosine the note stating that her adorable Lindoro is about to hand her over to Count Almaviva. She becomes furious and agrees to marry her guardian and to betray Lindoro and Figaro to the police. Figaro and the count return to Dr. Bartholo's house, however, and she reproaches them for their treachery. Yet all is forgiven when the smiling count reveals his identity. Don Bazile enters with a notary and a marriage broker for the Rosine-Bartholo wedding, but the count and Rosine have already signed their marriage contract. When

Dr. Bartholo returns, he finds himself obliged to accept the marriage of his wealthy ward and happy Count Almaviva (II).

A number of international stars have filled the part of Rosine at the Opéra, and among them may be mentioned Mmes Laure Cinthie-Damoreau* (1828), Julie Dorus-Gras* (1831), Angiolina Bosio* (1853), Supervia (1930), and Heldy (1933). Almaviva has been sung by Adolphe Nourrit* (1828), Gilbert Duprez* (1841), and Villabella (1933, 1936). MM. Henri Dabadie* (1828), Tamburini (1837), Paul Barroilhet* (1841), and Léon Ponzi (1930-36) have been cast as Figaro. More recently, Le Barbier de Séville has been revived at the Garnier Palace in 1969 in a P. Ethuin production, and G. Rivoli has supervised its presentation in 1971-72. The role of Rosine has been sung on these occasions by M. Mesplé (1969, 1971-72), C. Eda-Pierre (1969, 1972), and J. Berbié (1971), and the title-part has been filled by M. Trempont (1969), Y. Bisson (1969, 1972), R. Massard (1969, 1971), and C. Calès ((1972). R. Soyer (1969, 1971) and J. Van Dam (1971, 1972) have become associated in our day with the part of Bazile, while C. Clavensy (1969) and F. Voutsinos (1971, 1972) have been cast most frequently as Bartholo.

BIBLIOGRAPHY: AB I, 41-43; AEM II, 950-51, 974; L'Avant-scène 37 (November-December 1981), 3-171; Arnaldo Fraccaroli, Rossini (Verona: A. Mondadori, 1941), 121-37; JB 97-101; Kobbé 400-410; MCDE II, 805-9; MSRL 194-96; OEN I, 34-74; OQE 297-300; PBSW 53-54, 109-10, 206; SSBO 131-34; Stendhal, Life of Rossini, trans. Richard N. Coe (New York: The Orion Press, 1970), 176-200; SW 47-48; Thompson 145, 1872-78; Francis Toye, Rossini, a Study in Tragi-Comedy (New York: Alfred A. Knopf, 1947), 43-51; Herbert Weinstock, Rossini, a Biography (New York: Alfred A. Knopf, 1968), 53-63; WOC 26-27.

Barbot, Joseph-Théodore-Désiré (b. 12 April 1824, Toulouse; d. 1 January 1897, Paris), vocalist, started his singing career at the cathedral in Toulouse, but he left his native city to pursue his musical studies at the Paris Conservatoire on 25 March 1843. His program included the study of voice under the direction of Garcia and Morin as well as courses with Moreau-Sainti (opéra-comique) and Michelot (opera).

Barbot made his debut at the Opéra in Robert le Diable* in 1848, and his performance as Raimbaut induced management at the opera house in the rue Le Peletier* to accept him into the cast of François Benoist's* ill-starred L'Apparition* on 16 June 1848. the tenor now left the Opéra to accept a contract with the Théâtre Royal de la Monnaie in 1850, and, in Brussels, he made his debut in Thomas' Songe d'une nuit d'été. Yet he was back in Paris by 1856 to sing at the Opéra-Comique in such standard works of the repertory as La Dame blanche, and Grétry's Richard Coeur de Lion, Fra Diavolo, and Les Montenegrins by the close of 1858.

The Théâtre Lyrique was preparing to stage the world premiere of Charles Gounod's* Faust* at this time, and Barbot was chosen to fill the part of the protagonist. His performance won high personal praise from Gounod, but, curiously enough, Barbot decided at this point in his career to dedicate his efforts to the execution of the Italian repertory. He retired from the stage to accept a chair at the Conservatoire in Paris in 1875.

BIBLIOGRAPHY: EDS I, 1484; Lajarte II, 188; SW 84, 184-86.

Barbot, Mme R. (b. 27 April 1830), vocalist, née Caroline Douvry, studied with Delsarte and her tenor husband, Joseph-Théodore-Désiré Barbot.* She made her debut at the Paris Opéra as Valentine in Les Huguenots* on 1 December 1858, but she left the troupe in the rue Le Peletier* to fill contracts in Bologna (1860), Rome, Milan, and St. Petersburg (1862).

The soprano went to Russia because Giuseppe Verdi* had invited her to appear there as Leonora in La Forza del destino after he had received favorable reports on her performances at the Opéra in his Les Vêpres siciliennes.* She was also cast with great success at St. Petersburg in Il Ballo in maschera, Gioacchino Rossini's* Otello, and Faust, but little is known of her immediate subsequent theatrical activity except that she sang in Thomas' Hamlet at Montpellier during 1870.

Ultimately, however, she appeared again at the Paris Opéra in 1877 to sing Fidès in Le Prophète* and to add another six parts to her Paris repertory in the following half-dozen or so years: Edwige in Guillaume Tell* (1878), Queen

Gertrude in Hamlet* (1878), Dame Ragonde in Le Comte Ory* (1881), Amnéris in Aïda* (1881), and Dame Marthe in Mefistofele* (1883). She was also cast as Virgile for the world premiere of Thomas' Françoise de Rimini* at the Opéra on 14 April 1882. She signed what was apparently her last theatrical contract with Monnaie in Brussels in 1885, and it was not long before chroniclers of the lyric theatre in Europe lost track of her stage activities, if she continued to be active after 1885.
BIBLIOGRAPHY: EDS I, 1484-85; EFC 151-52; Lajarte II, 218; SW 27-30, 99, 105-6, 108-9, 115-17, 177-79.

Barrez, Hippolyte (b. 28 November 1795, Paris; d. December 1868, Paris), dancer, received his first instruction in ballet from Antoine Coulon.* Although his teacher held the rank of premier danseur at the Opéra, Barrez left Paris to tour the provinces. He had engagements at Lyon and Bordeaux, where he was very successful, and he was offered the position of premier danseur at the Grand Theatre in the latter city. He accepted and remained at the Grand for six years.

News of Barrez' accomplishments reached Paris before long, and the Opéra exercised its right to direct him to appear on the stage of the Royal Academy of Music. The dancer obeyed the directive and made his debut at the Opéra on 31 August 1821 in Le Jugement de Pâris.* If Barrez showed little talent for anything but the dance itself, and if his physical appearance left something to be desired, his powerful and precise style persuaded audiences to accept him. He became director of dance at the Opéra after he stopped performing, and his tenure at the theatre lasted for 30 years.

The premieres in which Barrez appeared included L'Ile des pirates* of 1835; Le Diable boiteux* of 1836; La Tarentule* of 1839; Le Diable amoureux* of 1840, in which he did Hortensius; and La Péri* of 1843, in which he filled the role of Roucem.
BIBLIOGRAPHY: CB 114, 137; Chouquet 399; GE V, 489; Lajarte II, 151, 154, 160, 163-64, 173.

Barroilhet, Paul (b. 22 September 1810, Bayonne; d. 2 April 1871, Paris), vocalist, decided to forego a business career in favor of music despite his father's opposition, and he entered the

Conservatoire in Paris at age 18. After two years of study with Banderali, the young man failed to distinquish himself in academic competition, and he emigrated to Italy in the hope of finding acceptance in another country because he knew that the Opéra was not interested in him. He took lessons from Panizza in Milano, and he accepted engagements in third-rate theatres in Genoa, Verona, Trieste, and other cities until he obtained a contract to appear at the opera house in Palermo during 1835.

Barroilhet was unexpectedly successful in Sicily, and he was invited to Rome, where he attracted so much attention that Domenico Donizetti wrote L'Assedio di Calais for him. The baritone was enjoying stardom, when tragedy threatened. His larynx became too weak to allow him to perform. He went to Naples to rest, and he was in this city when Adolphe Nourrit* met his sad fate in a hotel there. Barroilhet decided that it was now time for him to return to France.

As soon as he arrived in Paris, the Opéra offered him a contract which he accepted. Donizetti was in Paris at the time and inevitably aware of this development in Barroilhet's career, and he wrote the baritone part of King Alfonso IX in La Favorite* for him. The singer's voice had recovered, and he received a tumultuous ovation at his Paris début in this role on 2 December 1840, when 8,996.70 francs were left at the box office.

Barroilhet remained at the Opéra until 1847, when he left the company on account of a quarrel with management over his salary. In these seven years, he appeared in eight other premieres in the following roles: Lusignan of La Reine de Chypre* in 1841; the title-part of Charles VI* and Le Camoens of Dom Sébastien, roi du Portugal* in 1843; Mirobolante of La Lazzarone,* Iago of Othello,* and Murray of Marie Stuart* in 1844; Asthon of Lucie de Lammermoor* and Frantz of L'Ame en peine* in 1846.

The baritone spent the remainder of his singing years appearing in concerts and performing at local theatres in the provinces of France, but he dropped dead in Paris, while he was playing dominoes in the Café de la Régence.

BIBLIOGRAPHY: Chouquet 403-7; DBF V, 617-18; Escudier, "Paul Barroilhet", FM 4 (7 March 1841), 73-75; EZF 135-36; Fétis I, 254; GE V, 504; Lajarte II, 164-65, 169, 172, 174-78, 180-81, 183;

Léon, "Débuts de Barroilhet", FM 10 (19 September 1847), 310; Arthur Pougin, "Barroilhet," Le Ménestrel 38 (25 February 1872), 101; Alphonse Royer, Histoire de l'Opéra (Paris: Bachelin-Deflorenne, 1875), 168; SW 89, 136, 180.

Bartet, Jean (b. 13 December 1862, Gurs, Basses-Pyrénées; d. ?), vocalist, won a second prize in opera and the first prize in singing at the Conservatoire in 1893. A student of M. Barbot and M. Giraudet, he made his debut as Nélusko in L'Africaine* on 6 November 1893. He spent about 15 years at the Opéra, and he appeared in the premieres of seven works during this time in the following roles:

Role	Opera	Premiere
Kothner	Les Maîtres Chanteurs	10 November 1897
Hatto	La Cloche du Rhine	8 June 1898
Berik	La Borgonde	23 December 1898
The Catechist	Briséis	4 May 1899
Markhoël	Lancelot	7 February 1900
The Duke	Orsola	21 May 1902
Kaloum-Barouck	La Statue	6 March 1903

M. Bartet performed in at least ten parts during the first few years of his stay at the Opéra, although he did not sing his first new role until 1897. These initial compositions in which he was cast were Faust* (Valentin) in 1893; Thaïs* (Athanaël) and Djelma* (Raim) in 1894; La Montagne noire* (Alsar), Tannhäuser* (Wolfram), and Sigurd* (Gunther) in 1895; Sigurd (the High Priest), La Favorite* (Alphonse), Don Juan (Mazetto), and Walkyrie* (Wotan) in 1896. He did another 17 parts before leaving the Opéra, including Amonasro in Aïda* Telramund in Lohengrin,* Mathias in Messidor,* and the High Priest in Samson et Dalila* during 1897. The range of his versatile and rich voice won him not only the baritone parts of Matthiesen (Le Prophète*), Nevers (Les Huguenots*), and Hamilcar (Salammbô*), but also such parts regularly assigned to a bass as Narr-

Havas (Salammbô), Mazetto (Don Juan), and Count Capulet (Roméo et Juliette*).
BIBLIOGRAPHY: SW 52-54, 63, 133, 139-40, 164, 204.

Bassi, Amadeo (b. 29 July 1874, Montespertoli; d. 15 January 1949, Florence), Italian tenor, sang in guest appearances on nearly every prestigious operatic stage in Europe and the United States. He was billed as the duke in Rigoletto* on 7 April 1913 at the Opéra almost immediately after Enrico Caruso* had appeared in this role in Paris, and, the same year, he portrayed Rhadamès in Aïda.*

In 1916, Bassi was billed at the Garnier Palace* on two programs apparently designed to bring some variety to the war-weary audiences of the time. He appeared as Grieux in the fourth act of Giacomo Puccini's* Manon Lescaut on 12 March, and, on 16 March, he did Dick Johnson in the second act of La Fanciulla del West and Manrico in II Trovatore.

Bassi's postwar commitments never permitted him to return to the Opéra after 1916, although his youthful and brilliant tenor voice enabled him to sing in public until 1940. He had appeared once at the Opéra-Comique to sing Mario of La Tosca on 5 June 1913.
BIBLIOGRAPHY: ICM 133; KRJ 29; SW 29, 96, 141, 182, 217; WOC II, 283.

Battu, Marie (b. 1840, Paris; d. 1870, Paris), vocalist, was the daughter of Pantaléon Battu, second concertmaster at the Opéra, and she was accordingly raised in a cultured and musical milieu. She studied voice under Gilbert-Louis Duprez* and made her debut at the Théâtre-Italien on 12 January as Amina in La Sonnambula. Her career at this opera house was quite successful and won her the reputation of being able to manage the difficult roles in the Italian repertory. After singing Gilda, Zerlina, and Despina with complete competence and confidence, the soprano was advised by her director Giocchino Rossini* to accept a contract at the Opéra.

Mlle Battu made her debut at the Imperial Theatre of the Opéra in a revival of Moïse on 7 December 1864. Her authentic voice, natural stage presence, and flawless technique won her prompt applause at the French opera house in the rue Le Peletier,* and, on 28 April 1865, she confirmed the validity of the spectators' previous approval of her work by her creation of the role of Inès in L'Africaine.*

Receipts at the box office for Giacomo Meyerbeer's* work remained between 10,000 and 13,000 francs for the 11 consectuive performances it enjoyed after its premiere. On 27 May, receipts rose to the almost incredible figure of 14,041.50 francs.

Subsequently Mlle Battu was cast as Zerline in the 100th presentation of Don Juan* and as Mathilde in Guillaume Tell* in 1866; once again she appeared as Zerline in the 500th production at the Opéra of Rossini's work on 22 May 1868, and, in this same year, as Marguerite de Valois in Les Huguenots.* But her greatest triumphs came to her for her interpretations of Sélika in L'Africaine in 1867 and of Lilia in the 1868 revival of Herculanum.* Here, she proved herself to be the peer of Mmes Pauline Gueymard* and Marie-Constance Sass,* who had created these roles. Fétis had presided over the rehearsals of Meyerbeer's last work, and he had said of her that she was "in the first rank of the singers of our time." Yet she left the Opéra at the very summit of her career to tour with a company devoted exclusively to the music of her beloved master, Rossini. Her last two theatrical engagements were with the Théâtre de la Monnaie in Brussels and the Opéra-Comique in Paris.

BIBLIOGRAPHY: Chouquet 417, 421-22; EFC 149; Fétis Suppl. I, 55-56; GE V, 844-45; Lajarte II, 147-48, 226; H. de Pène, "Notre Italie: Mlle Battu," FM (1 February 1863), 29-30; SW 25-26, 73, 105, 116.

Bayard, Jean-François-Alfred (b. 20 March 1796, Charolles; d. 19 February 1853, Paris), librettist, was supposed to pursue a career before the bar but showed neither interest nor aptitude in this subject, while he was a clerk in the office of Guyonnet-Merville. Eugène Scribe* had started his aborted study of the law with the same attorney, and this common experience of sharing in the same sort of failure in the same office seems to have induced Bayard and Scribe to become collaborators after the former had written his intitial text for the theatre, and vaudeville entitled Promenade à Vaucluse. Later, Bayard married Scribe's niece and went on to contribute texts to the Palais-Royal, the Vaudeville, the Variétés, and especially the Gymnase. His most resounding successes included Christine ou la reine de seize ans (Gymnase, 1828), Les Premières Armes de Richelieu (Palais-Royal, 1839), and above all Le Gamin de Paris (Gymnase, 1836), which enjoyed more than 200 performances before being dropped. He had other titles billed at the Comédie-Française, but he did only a single work for the Opéra. Le Démon de la nuit* of 1851, for which he wrote the libretto with Etienne-Vincent Arago.*

BIBLIOGRAPHY: DBF V, 993; Lajarte II, 207-8; Ch. Lénient, La Comédie en France au XIXe *siècle (Paris: Hachette, 1898), 157-83.*

Bazin, François-Emmanuel-Joseph (b. 4 September 1816, Marseille; d. 2 July 1878, Paris), composer, enrolled at the Conservatoire in Paris to study composition under Berton and Jacques Halévy* and to take other courses with Dourlen, Lecoupey, and Benoît. After two years, he won numerous prizes in the contests of 1836 and 1837. His cantata earned second place at the Institut in 1839 and first place the next year. He did not feel that his education was complete by 1840, however, and he continued his studies in Rome until 1843. Named to a professorship at the conservatoire upon his return to Paris, he started to compose shorter pieces for the Opéra-Comique in 1846 with Le Trompette de Monsieur le Prince. His most successful work at this theatre was his Maître Pathelin (1856) with a book by Leuven and F. Langlé that remained in the repertory for 15 years. After two more hits with Les Désespérés (1859) and Le Voyage en Chine (1865), he was elected to the Academy of Fine Arts on 5 April 1873. His only work heard at the Opéra had been his cantata Loyse de Montfort sung on 7 october 1840 with words by Emile Deschamps* and Emile Pacin.

BIBLIOGRAPHY: DBF V, 1024; Henri Delaborde, Institut de France. Académie des beaux-arts. Funérailles de M.F. Bazin (Paris: Firmin-Didot, 1878); Fétis I, 281; Lajarte II, 257.

Beauchet, or Bauchet, Magloire (b. ?; d. 17 May 1875, Paris) made his debut as a dancer at the Opéra in the premiere of Stella* on 22 February 1850. He never reached the status of a major figure in the rue Le Peletier,* but he seems to have been called upon without hesitation whenever a porteur with special talent was needed to assist one of the leading ballerinas of the company. He executed a pas de deux in Vert-Vert* with Adeline Plunkett* at the premiere of this ballet on 24 November 1851, and he did a second pas de deux with Marie Guy Stéphan* in Aelia et Mysis* on 21 September 1853. He also helped Francesca Cerrito* with the famous mirror scene in Gemma* on 31 May 1854 before dancing a pas de deux with Fanny Génat in the first act of La Sylphide* during its revival in 1858. At this time, he appeared in a series of divertissements produced in conjunction with the staging of Zerline* on 16 May 1851, La Fronde* on 2 May 1853, Sainte-Claire* on 27 September 1855, and Sémiramis* on 9 July 1860 (see eighteenth-century volume for divertissement). He was given parts to dance in Jovita* (1853), Les Elfes* (1856), and Le Cheval de bronze* (1857) during the same interval. Beauchet was more a workhorse than a star despite whatever ability he might have had. As late as 20 November 1861, he danced the fisherman Momolo in L'Etoile de Messine.* He retired shortly after this last assignment.

BIBLIOGRAPHY: CB 205-8, 377-82; Ivor Guest, The Ballet of the Second Empire (Middletown, Conn.: Wesleyan University Press, 1974), 12, 60, 71, 81, 132, 135, 172, 260-61; Lajarte II, 205-6, 215, 220, 223-24.

Beaugrand, Léontine (b. 26 April 1842, Paris; d. 27 May 1925, Paris), ballerina, was enrolled at age eight in the dancing school attached to the Opéra. She studied with Mme Dominique, Henri Mathieu, and subsequently with Marie Taglioni.* As a result of her association with Taglioni, she made her debut as one of the ethereal sylphides in the corps de ballet during the 1858 revival of La Sylphide.* On 9 July 1860, she danced in the divertissement of Sémiramis* at the premiere of this work, and, on 26 November 1860, she performed in a short écot that Taglioni had choreographed for the second act of Le Papillon* (see eighteenth-century volume for divertissement).

Mlle Beaugrand worked hard without complaining about the modest roles being assigned to her, and, perhaps on account of her quiet cooperation, she was scheduled to perform in the divertissement of Moïse* on 28 December 1863. It was at this moment that Taglioni rewarded her protégée's patience and gave her private lessons to help her with the title-role of Diavolina.* She performed in this composition for the first time on 27 November 1864, and the critics were most enthusiastic about her work. Théophile Gautier* spoke of "the new sparkle" that she brought to the stage, a comment that the poet might have made with tongue in cheek because the star of the evening had brought real champagne to the theatre to drink during the wedding feast on stage. Her next assignment was to dance in the divertissement of Don Juan* with a new orchestration by Daniel Auber.* She did a variation tacquetée in this revival of Mozart's opera on 2 April 1866, and her execution of this pas was so effective that it came to be known as "Beaugrand's variation."

Beaugrand was still a star of the second magnitude at the Opéra, but it was almost inevitable that she should win a part in Léo Delibes'* new ballet, La Source,* which had its premiere on 12 November 1866. Her role was minor, one of the two French dancers, but she rehearsed faithfully and was applauded for the exquisite performance that she achieved. In fact, the presentation was delayed momentarily by the applause showered upon her. Critics called her pas in the second act a masterpiece of precision, and they pointed to the grace of her pointes and tacquetés despite the lack of sweep in her role.

La Beaugrand danced next in the divertissement of Don Carlos* on 11 March 1867, and she appeared before Alexander II, tsar of Russia, on 4 June 1867 as Zulmé in Giselle.* After Angelina Fioretti* left the Opéra in 1870, Beaugrand succeeded her as Hélène in the divertissement now inserted in the last act of Faust.* Yet after all this service to the company since 1858, she was overlooked when it came time to cast Coppélia.* Yet there might have been some justification for this seeming neglect because she was given the female lead opposite Louis Mérante* in the divertissement of Le Freischütz.* Carl Maria Von Weber's* opera was the companion piece for Coppélia on the program of 25 March 1870, the date of the first performance of Coppélia.

After the end of hostilities in the war against Germany, Beaugrand returned to the Opéra to dance in the divestissement of L'Esclave* on 17

July 1874. This performance took place in the temporary Ventadour* opera house, but it would be only a relatively short time before the Garnier Palace* would open, and Beaugrand would become one of the relatively few dancers to appear on all three stages. She danced La Folie in Le Bal masqué* from Gustave III* on 29 January 1877, and she was next chosen to do la Carmencita in Fandango* on 26 November 1877. It was not until just before her retirement that she was selected to present Swanilda in Coppélia on 10 November 1879.

Mlle Beaugrand was appearing in La Fête du printemps from Ambroise Thomas'* Hamlet,* when she decided to leave the theatre permanently after her 21 April 1880 performance because she could no longer tolerate the intrigue and machinations transpiring behind the scenes at the Opéra. Her career had lasted for a score of years, and her dancing had never ceased to prompt critics to express their delight with her ability to create the illusion of flight on the stage. The famous poet Sully Prud'homme sang her praises constantly because he considered her performances and example of the perfection that he sought in his art.

BIBLIOGRAPHY; ACD 65; CD 294, 488-89; CODB 60; DBF V, 1088; EDS II, 102-3; EZF 138-39; Ivor Guest, The Ballet of the Second Empire (Middletown, Conn.: Wesleyan University Press, 1974), 132, 143, 187, 205, 211, 214, 217, 223, 226-29, 234-36; Lajarte II, 125-26, 240-41, 244-47; Parmenia Migel, The Ballerinas from the Court of Louis XIV to Pavlova (New York: The Macmillan Co., 1972), 234, 238-39, 241-42; SW 109, 243, 258, 275; XYZ 307-10.

Beauvais, Laure (b. 28 October 1869, Paris; d. ?), vocalist, was a student of Crosti, Mangin, and Taskin at the Conservatoire in her native city, where she won second prize in Opéra-Comique in 1893. She made her professional debut at the Opéra as Albine in Thaïs* at the world premiere of Jules Massenet's* composiiton on 16 March 1894, the day that Sybil Sanderson* gave her first performance at the theatre in the title-part of the same work. Mlle Beauvais had an adaptable voice that allowed her to fill roles assigned to sopranos or contraltos, and she went on to sing the following parts in the initial representations of five other pieces at the Opéra:

Role	Opera	Premiere
Myrrha	Hellé*	24 April 1896
Hécube	La Prise de Troie	15 November 1899
Une Vieille	L'Etranger*	1 December 1903
La Servante	Le Fils de l'étoile*	17 April 1904
Térésa	La Catalane*	24 May 1907

One of the curious features of Mlle Beauvais' operatic career was the ease and frequency with which she switched roles in the same work apparently without stopping to catch her breath. She sang both Rossweisse and Siegrune in La Walkyrie* in 1894, admittedly not a great demonstration of versatility even if she did go on to appear as Grimguerde in the same work during 1907. Yet at the same time she performed first as Marthe (1894) and then as Siebel (1895) while doing both Gertrude and Stefano in Roméo et Juliette* in 1894. In 1897, she was cast as Johanna, Madeleine, and the countess in Rigoletto.*

Mlle Beauvais also appeared at the Opéra as Ourvaci (Djelma*), Taanach (Salammbô*), and Myrtale (Thaïs) in 1894 and as the High Priestess in Aïda* as well as the shepherd in Tannhäuser* and Inès in La Favorite* during 1896. After filling the part of Magdelaine of Les Maîtres Chanteurs* in 1898, she was cast for parts in Le Bourgeois Gentilhomme, La Burgonde,* and Joseph* during 1899, but these assignments constituted her last appearances at the Opéra.

BIBLIOGRAPHY: EFC 169-70; SW 27-29, 57, 72, 81-82, 96, 111, 139-40, 176-77, 181-84, 193-94, 208-9, 224-26.

Beeth, Lola (b. 23 November 1864, Cracow; d. 18 March 1940, Berlin), vocalist, studied with Pauline Viardot-Garcia* in Paris, but her busy schedules in Berlin (1882-88) and Vienna (1885-95) kept her from the Opéra until 1892, when she made her Paris debut as Elsa in Lohengrin* on 31 October. Her only other guest appearance at the Garnier Palace* was as Vénus in Tannhäuser* in 1895.

BIBLIOGRAPHY: EFC 166; ICM 146; KRJ 33; SW 135, 207.

Beethoven, Ludwig van (b. 15 December 1770, Bonn; d. 26 March 1827, Vienna) showed a precocious interest in music, and his father gave him his first lessons on the piano, organ, and violin before entrusting him to Christian Neefe, who taught him the rules of composition. The youth learned quickly and was soon placed in the court orchestra of the elector, who sent him to Vienna to continue his studies with Wolfgang Amdeus Mozart (see eighteenth-century volume for Mozart).

The young musician had to leave Vienna almost immediately to return home on account of his mother's serious illness, however, and he decided to improve his academic background by enrolling at the University of Bonn to study literature and philosophy.

Ultimately Beethoven found himself an orphan at age 22, and, left to his own devices, he returned to Vienna to work with Franz Joseph Hydn and Antoine Salieri (see eighteenth-century volume for Haydn and Salieri). Now protected by Count Waldstein, he moved in the best social circles of the Austrian capital, where the wealthy members of the court lionized him and applauded his prowess at the piano. He did embark upon a trip to Germany and to Poland, but the favors showered upon him in Vienna induced him to stay in the Austrian capital for the remainder of his life. Here his admirers included the members of the Brunswick family, Prince Lobkowitz, Archduke Rodolphe, and other members of nobility as well as his fellow musicians. He spent his time organizing concerts, composing, and amassing a personal fortune to recompoense him for the deafness that began to strike him in 1798-1800.

Beethoven never visited Paris, and his influence was slight at the Opéra. His only opera, Fidélio* which had had its world premiere in Vienna on 20 November 1805, did not find its way to the French capital until it was booked into the Théâtre Lyrique de l'Odéon in 1825. It was then produced at the salle Favart (1831), the Théâtre-Italien (1852), the Théâtre-Lyrique (1860), and the Opéra-Comique (1898) before the Royal Opera Company of the Hague presented it at the Opéra for the first time on 15 February 1926. It was not produced by the company of the Garnier Palace* until 13 January 1937, when this troupe performed it at the Champs-Elysées Theatre.

Serge Lifar made his debut at the Opéra on 30 December 1929 in a ballet entitled Les Créatures de Promethée, which employed the music of Beethoven's work by the same title, and the ballet Prière by Lifar called upon the second movement of the composer's Seventh Symphony for its score (see twentieth-century volume for Lifar). Later Beethoven's Thirty-three Variations on a Waltz by Diabelli (1823) was also adopted for the score of the ballet called Variations on a Simple theme, which Brian MacDonald brought to the Opéra on 30 April 1974.

BIBLIOGRAPHY: AEM I, 1509-65; BBD 126-32; Paul Bekker, Beethoven (New York: Dutton, 1925); John N. Burk, The Life and Works of Beethoven (New York: Random House, 1943; CBCM 288-338; EDS II, 140-46; EGC 29-34; ELM I, 365-78; JB 110-12; KOH 80-87; MCDE I, 65-105; MM 162-207; MOTO 154-87; NEO 67; PBSW 171; Robert Haven Schauffler, Beethoven: the Man Who Fired Music (New York: Tudor, 1947); Leo Schrade, Beethoven in France (New Haven: Yale University Press, 1942); A. W. Thayer, The Life of Ludwig van Beethoven, 3 vols. (London: Centaur, 1960); Thompson 147-59.

La Belle au bois dormant was a fairyland ballet with music by Louis-Joseph Hérold,* a libretto by Eugène Scribe,* and choreography by Jean Louis Aumer (see eighteenth-century volume for Aumer). It had its premiere at the Opéra on 27 April 1829 and was given annually between 1829 and 1838 for a total of 77 performances before it was dropped from the repertory on 23 March 1838. Its first run extended from 27 April to 19 August 1829, and it was billed on 28 dates during these four months. It is not to be confused with Michel Carafa de Colobrano's work by the same title that failed in 1825.

The ballet begins in the typically romantic setting of a gothic hall, where the princess' page Arthur is disconsolate over the marriage of Princess Iseult and his rival, Prince Gannelor. The feast celebrating the imminent wedding is interrupted by the arrival of the fairy Nabote, who is angry at not having received an invitation to the festivities. She transforms the flowers on a table into reptiles spitting fire, and Iseult rushes to Arthur for protection. Apparently satisfied with the guests' terror, Nabote orders the ball to begin, but she freezes everybody to the floor at the height of the dancing to dance alone, then with one and later with two partners (I, 1-2). The guests leave at last, and Tiphaine tries to console Arthur, but Nabote frightens them away (I, 3-5). The fairy now reveals to Gannelor and the duke de Montfort that the latter's daughter Iseult loves her page Arthur, and she persuades them to witness a tender reunion of the two lovers (I, 6-7). Gannelor orders Arthur's execution but then spares him on condition that he go into exile and that Iseult marry him immediately (I, 8). She agrees, and her servants smuggle Arthur to her room. She stabs herself in despair and has to be carried to her quarters. The duke and Gannelor beg Nabote to save her life. The fairy agrees, but Iseult is to sleep for a century and marry the man who awakens her. Nabote smiles over her latest act of mischief and disappears (I, 9-11).

The second act opens a hundred years later with Bobi telling Marguerite and Gombault the story of Iseult and her long sleep. She warns Gombault not to enter the castle where Iseult is supposed to be sleeping and which is guarded by an array of monsters. Gombault wishes to find a wealthy husband for his daughter Marguerite, and he refuses to give her hand to humble Gérard unless he can enter the castle to seize the wealth piled up inside this formidable fortress (II, 1-2). The fairy Nabote presents him with a horn that will allow him to overcome all obstacles by blowing it (II, 3-4). He makes his way past evil spirits, threatening monsters, and seductive nymphs to reach the château by virtue of his magic horn (II, 5-7). Gérard finds the inhabitants of the château silent, motionless, and in attendance upon Iseult. Puzzled, he blows his horn, and Iseult awakens (III, 1-2). Gombault and all the villagers enter the château, because the spell is broken, and Gérard rejoices to see his beloved Marguerite again. These two lovers are about to wed, when Nabote reappears to remind Iseult that she must fulfill the oracle by marrying Gérard. The latter refuses to acquiesce, but Nabote threatens to turn him into a toad or a green monkey. Margurite urges him to avoid this metamorphosis by becoming Iseult's husband (III, 3-4). Iseult is bewailing her fate, when Arthur emerges from his coffin to declare his deathless love to Iseult. Nabote enters with Gérard to make him propose to Iseult (III, 5-6). Nabote leaves for a moment, and Arthur and Gérard agree to marry their intended brides despite Nabote's wishes to the contrary. Arthur puts Iseult's wedding veil on Marguerite, and he is married to her. When the fairy finds that she has been tricked, she vows to take vengeance for this deception. Arthur and Iseult explain that she is now powerless because the oracle has not been betrayed. The good genius suppresses Nabote's powers and leaves for four lovers to their happy fates (III, 7-10).

Composed originally in four acts, Aumer's La Belle au bois dormant owed at least some of its success to its first cast that included Mmes Marie Taglioni,* Lise Noblet,* and Amélie Legallois,* and MM. François Decombe Albert,* Louis Mérante,* and Louis Montjoye (see eighteenth-century volume for Albert and Montjoye).

BIBLIOGRAPHY: CB 44-45; Chouquet 394; GMSM 162-85, 187; B. Jouvin, Hérold, sa vie et ses oeuvres (Paris: Heugel, 1868), 150; Lajarte I, 133; PBR 140; Arthur Pougin, Hérold (Paris: Renouard, n.d.), 79; Moniteur universel 66 (7 March 1825), 332; ibid. 118 (28 April 1829), 633; Germaine Prudhommeau, "La Belle au bois dormant: naissance d'un chef-d'oeuvre," Danser I (April 1983), 52-55; RBP 91-92; Wks II, 8; WLC 60.

La Belle au bois dormant by Piotr Ilyitch Tchaikovsky* and Marius Petipa* is discussed in the twentieth-century volume.

La Belle Hélène was an opera-bouffe in three acts with a score by Jacques Offenbach* and a libretto by the team of Henri de Meilhac* and Ludovic Halévy. It had its world premiere at the Théâtre des Variétés on 17 December 1864, and it enjoyed a complete success with its unexpected anachronisms and burlesque exaggerations. Its raucous and irreverent tone precluded production at the Opéra, but management at the Garnier Palace* did not feel averse after World War II to staging the ballet that the opera inspired Marcel Archard and Robert Manuel to compose for musical adaptation by Louis Aubert and Manuel Rosenthal (see twentieth-century volume for Aubert and Rosenthal). This second work was also entitled La Belle Hélène, and it had its premiere at the Paris opera house in choreography by John Cranko. Vertès created its sets and costumes, and it had its premiere at the Garnier Palace on 6 April 1955.

The opera begins in a public square in Sparta, where the augur Calchas is complaining about the cheap offerings left for the gods at the temple. Hélène enters and talks with Calchas about how she may thwart the prophecy that she will abandon her husband Ménélas to run away with Paris. They arrive at no solution, and Hélène enters the temple. Paris appears in shepherd's garb. He reveals his identity to Calchas and relates the story of how Vénus has promised Hélène to him because he declared Vénus to be more beautiful than Minerve and Junon. Calchas obeys Vénus' instructions to point out Hélène to Paris when she leaves the temple. The Greek queen is attracted to the shepherd immediately, and she declares her love to him while assuring him that she will see him at the coming tournament of wit.

King Ménélas enters with Achille and the two Ajax come to compete in the tournament. Achille tries first to compose a poem using prescribed rhymes, but he and his comrades reveal a lack of literary talent. Paris carries off the prize, of course, and he identifies himself. Ménélas invites him to dinner, but Calchas intervenes with the announcement that Jupiter wishes Ménélas to spend a month in the mountains of Crete. The king is puzzled, but he bids farewell to Hélène. Paris is overjoyed (a. 1).

The second act opens in Hélène's apartments, where the queen reveals her fears that she may succumb to Paris' charms. She resolves to dress modestly to avoid trouble, but Calchas assures her that a few expensive offerings to the gods will protect her virtue. She falls asleep, and she believes that she is still dreaming when she awakens to find Paris before her. He is dressed as a slave. She asks him whether Vénus is more beautiful than she, and he admits that the goddess' charms were enhanced by her kisses. Suddenly, Ménélas appears in his traveling clothes and carrying his umbrella. Hélène realizes that she is not dreaming. The king is outraged to find his wife with a slave, but he recognizes Paris before long. He calls for aid, and his dinner guests respond to his cries. They remind him that husbands should always announce their premature return home lest they find reason to be upset.

Hélène urges her Trojan idol to depart from Greece before harm befalls him (a. 2).

The scene moves to the fashionable seaside resort of Nauplie, where Oreste, Achille, and the other Greeks are dancing, singing, and drinking. Hélène informs Ménélas that he is annoying her by following her wherever she goes, and she threatens him with giving him good reason to suspect her infidelity. Agamemnon and Calchas announce that an epidemic of irresponsible love is sweeping across the country because the Greeks have defied Vénus by demeaning Paris. The grand augur of Vénus arrives on a golden galley and orders the Greeks to be gay and lively as befits his mistress; he informs the Greeks that the time has come for their queen to take a short trip with him on Vénus' galley. Ménélas informs Hélène that she must embark for Cythère to satisfy Vénus, and the goddess' grand augur whispers to Hélène that he is Paris. Delighted, she agrees to sail with him. Defiant Paris proclaims his identity from the deck of his ship at the last moment, and a chorus of patriot Greeks swears to avenge Ménélas' sullied honor (a. 3).

There is no precise record of the popularity that the opera enjoyed at the Variétés or of the money it returned to the box office at this theatre, but the ballet was billed on a dozen dates at the Opéra between 6 April 1955 and 21 March 1956. The leading male roles in the opera were filled by MM. Dupuis (Paris), Kopp (Ménélas), and Grenier (Calchas) with Mme Schneider as Hélène. The ballerinas in the subsequent ballet included Mlles Chauviré (Hélène) and Claude Bessy (Vénus) appearing alongside MM. Renault (Paris), Bozzoni (Agamemnon), and Blanc (Calchas).

BIBLIOGRAPHY: René Brancour, Offenbach (Paris: Henri Laurens, 1929), 51-68; Jacques Brindejont-Offenbach, Offenbach, mon grand-père (Paris: Plon, 1940), 30-37, 65-66, 192-93; CODB 65; DDO I, 139-41; Alain Decaux, Offenbach, roi du Second Empire (Paris: Perrin, 1975) 197-220, 234-35; Jean Gourret, Histoire de l'Opéra-Comique (Paris: Les Publications universitaires, 1978), 169-70; Anton Henseler, Jakob Offenbach (Berlin-Schöneberg: Max Hesses Verlag, 1930), 112, 291-98; KCOB 801-5; Siegfried Kracauer, Orpheus in Paris (New York: Alfred A. Knopf, 1938), 243-50, 333-34, 342-44; idem, Jacques Offenbach ou le secret du Second Empire (Paris: Bernard Grasset, 1937),

263-71; Paul LeFlem, "La Belle Hélène," L'Opera de Paris II (1955), 30-37; Arthur Moss and E. Marvel, Cancan and Barcarolle (New York: Exposition Press, 1954), 172-79, 279; Richard Northcutt, Jacques Offenbach: a Sketch of His Life and a Record of His Operas (London: The Press Printers, 1917), 40; SW 245; Thompson 1277-78.

La Belle Hélène, a ballet by Marcel Achard and Robert Manuel, is discussed in the twentieth-century volume.

Bellini, Vincenzo (b. 1 November 1802, Catania; d. 23 September 1835, Puteaux), composer, was not an especially studious youth, but his musical talents were evident enough to win him a scholarship at the Royal Conservatory in Naples, although his father was not eager to have him pursue a career in music. Nicolas-Antoine Zingarelli was in charge of the Conservatory, which Bellini entered in 1819, but where he did not distinguish himself until his last year there at the time of Barbaia's visit to the school in 1825 (see eighteenth-century volume for Zingarelli). Barbaia managed La Scala at Milan and the San Carlo at Naples as well as a cluster of lesser known theatres, and he was so delighted upon hearing Bellini's opera Adelson e Salvina that he asked for and produced the composer's Bianca e Gernando at the San Carlo on 30 March 1826. Barbaia had already presented Bellini's cantata Ismène and, with the added success of Bianca e Gernando, he was sure that he had found in Bellini what he was seeking, a composer to replace Gioacchino Rossini* and his endlessly imitated style, which had to be replaced if the public's interest was to be sustained. Thus, Barbaia urged his prospective star, only 29 years old, to do his third opera for La Scala. One of the great tenors of the time, Rubini, sang the simple airs that Bellini wrote for the new piece entitled Il Pirata, which was performed for the carnaval of 1827. The work was an international as well as a local success.

Two years later, Bellini's La Straniera was mounted at La Scala on 14 February 1829. As in the case of Il Pirata, Bellini enjoyed the sympathetic and competent service of the librettist Romani for La Straniera, but he seemed now to have lost some of his initial impact. Zaïra failed at the opening of the new theatre in Parma in 1829. Bellini's fortunes changed almost immediately, however, and he enjoyed his great successes with I Capuletti ed i Montecchi at the La Fenice Theatre in Venice in 1830 and with La Sonnambula at the Carcano Theatre in Milan in 1831. The latter composition was so fail-safe with audiences that the role of the heroine came to be the favorite part of singers making their debuts. Norma* was then brought out within a year, on 26 December 1831, at La Scala with the composer directing. As if he knew that he had now produced his masterpeices, Bellini wrote nothing in 1832 and wended his way south to Sicily for a vacation and the cheers of his countrymen.

But he was only 30 years old and had no plans for retirement. He gave Beatrice di Tenda at the Fenice Theatre in 1833. Then, in 1833, he moved on to London and Paris. The Théâtre des Italiens welcomed his presence in the latter city and requested him to do a piece that would disrupt the monotony of their now Rossini-dominated repertory. He accepted the invitation and composed I Puritani for them. It was produced on 25 January 1835, but the effort to finish this opera along with the rigouous French climate undermined his health, and he was dead before the end of the year.

Bellini's only contributions to the Paris Opéra were the first three acts of Roméo et Juliette* billed on 7 September 1859 and Norma, given initially at the Garnier palace* by the troupe of the Communal Theatre of Florence on 11 June 1935. It had been performed previously in Paris at the Théâtre des Italiens (1835) and the Théâtre-Lyrique (1883).

BIBLIOGRAPHY: Bio. univ. III, 585-88; L. Cambi, Bellini (Milano: A. Mondadori, 1938); Giuseppe Tito De Angelis, Vincenzo Bellini: la vita, l'uomo, l'artista (Brescia: Editrice Ancora, 1935); EGC 34-37; Arnaldo Fraccaroli, Bellini (Verona: A. Mondadori, 1942); JB 132-43; Lajarte II, 226; G. G. Mezzatesta, Vincenzo Bellini nella vita e nelle opere (Palermo: L. Hachette et Cie, 1935); Gino Monaldi, Vincenzo Bellini (Milano: Sonzogno, 1935); Leslie Orrey, Bellini (London: J. M. Dent and Son Ltd., 1969); Arthur Pougin, Bellini, sa vie et ses oeuvres (Paris: Quaderni de la Sinossi, 1868); Calcedonio Reina, Il cigno catenese: Bellini (Catania: Etna, 1935); Ottavio Tiby, Vincenzo Bellini (Turin: Edizioni Arione, 1938); SW 157; Herbert Weinstock, Vincenzo

Bellini: His Life and His Operas (New York: Alfred A. Knopf, 1971).

Belval, Jules-Bernard Gaffiot DIT (b. 2 June 1819, La Fère; d. 15 September 1879, Paris), vocalist, entered the Conservatoire in Paris in 1843. His impressive personal appearance and rich bass voice set him apart immediately, and he began his successful career at Anvers in 1846. He continued to appear in the provinces and accepted engagements in Holland and Belgium before making his debut at the Opéra on 7 September 1855 as Marcel in Les Huguenots.* He remained with the company until his retirement from the Paris stage in 1876, when he traveled abroad for a few engagements before his death at age 60.

At the Opéra, Belval's early career took place in the rue Le Peletier,* where he sang a number of roles that included Bertram in Robert le Diable,* Balthazer in La Favorite,* Cardinal Brogni in La Juive,* Walter in Guillaume Tell,* and Zacharie in Le Prophète.* He created four roles in the following works:

Role	Opera	Premiere
Solimon	La Reine de Saba*	28 February 1862
Turpin	Roland à Roncevaux*	3 October 1864
Don Pèdro	L'Africaine*	28 April 1865
The king	Hamlet*	9 March 1868

The program for the inauguration of the Garnier Palace* on 5 January 1875 included Belval as Cardinal Brogni in the presentation of the first two acts of Halévy's composition. Belval's daughter sang Eudoxie on this occasion.

If Belval was not a great singer, he was a competent and durable performer who was sure of his craft as an actor and as a singer. He did not retire from the Opéra until 1876 and thereby served the theatre for more than a score of years.
BIBLIOGRAPHY: Chouquet 420-23; DBF V, 1391-92; GE VI, 114; Lajarte II, 150, 204, 233-34, 238; SW 25, 108, 129.

Belval, Maria Gaffiot DITE (b. 1853, Gand; d. ?), vocalist, studied piano with Le Coupey and harmony under Savard at the Paris Conservatoire, but she became interested in the theatre and made her debut at the Théâtre-Italien on 7 October 1873 in Don Pasquale. She moved over to the Opéra for the following season, when she sang Marguerite de Valois on 14 October 1874. She was cast as Isabelle in Robert le Diable* this same year and helped to inaugurate the Garnier Palace* by singing Eudoxie there in La Juive* on 5 January 1875. She preferred the Italians' repertory, however, and she never returned to the Opéra after filling the role of Mathilde in Guillaume Tell* on 26 February 1875.

BIBLIOGRAPHY: DBF V, 1392; EFC 152; GE VI, 114; Lajarte II, 149-50; H. Moréno, "Reprise de Robert le Diable; débuts de Mlle Belval et du tenor Vergnet," Le Ménestrel 40 (6 September 1874), 315; Moréno, "Reprise des Huguenots et débuts de Mlle Belval à l'Opéra-Ventadour," Le Ménestrel 40 (24 May 1874), 195; SW 105-6, 115-16, 129-33, 184-85.

Benincori, Ange-Marie (b. 18 March 1779, Brescia; d. 30 December 1821, Belleville), composer, received musical instruction on the violin from Rolla when he was only a child, and his progress was so rapid that he gave his first public concert at age seven. The duke of Parma was so impressed by the young artist's performance that he hired Cimarosa and other famous violinists to instruct him. After composing a mass for his benefactor, Benincori journeyed to Spain and to Germany before settling in Paris in 1803. He gave lessons to support himself and wrote three comic operas for the Feydeau theatre: Les Parents d'un jour (1815), La Promesse de mariage (1818), Les Epoux indiscrets (1819). His skills were manifest in these compositions, and he was selected to complete the score of Nicolò Isouard's unfinished Aladin ou la lampe merveilleuse* of 1822 for which he did portions of the first two acts and all the last three acts (see eighteenth-century volume for Isouard). He was visiting his father-in-law Gersin, the dramatist, when he died only a few weeks before the premiere of his work. He left a number of non theatrical works including a symphony, a half-dozen pieces for the violin, and several trios. His operas Galathée (1804) and Hésione (1807) were never performed.

BIBLIOGRAPHY: Bio. univ. III, 633; Lajarte II, 100-101, 114.

Benois, Alexandre Nicolaievich (b. 3 May 1870, St. Petersburg; d. 9 February 1960, Paris), artist, was captivated by the theatre even as a child, when he was taken to fairs to see the puppet shows in his native city that featured the masked characters of Russian folklore. At age 13, he discovered ballet, the dancer Marie Petipa, and Coppélia,* and eventually he came to know Serge Diaghilev,* who asked him to help create the sets for Sylvia* with Léon Bakst* and Serov. When Diaghilev took his exposition of Russian art to the Grand palais in Paris, Benois was commissioned to draw up the catalogue for the show. In it, he included a brief history of Russian art.

The success of Diaghilev's Paris exposition in 1906 induced the impresario to bring Boris Godounov* to the French capital, and Benois now helped to create the sets for the production of Modest Mussorgsky's* masterpiece in 1908. When Diaghilev's Ballets russes* opened at the Théâtre du Châtelet the following year on 19 May 1909, the scenery designers for his troupe were Benois, Bakst, and Nicholas Roerich.

Benois and Diaghilev fell to arguing on many occasions after the formation of the Ballets russes, but the disputes between the two men did not prevent the artist from supplying the sets for five ballets produced by the company at the Opéra:

Ballet	**Premiere**
Les Sylphides*	19 June 1909
Le Festin*	19 June 1909
Giselle*	18 June 1910
Pétrouchka*	13 June 1911
Le Rossignol*	26 May 1914

When Benois was not employing his talents for the benefit of the Ballets russes, he was busy filling commissions for Mme Ida Rubinstein, for whom he did sets and costumes used in the production of the following three ballets at the Opéra: La Bien-Aimée, 22 November 1928; Les Noces de Psyché et de l'Amour, 22 November 1928; and, La

Valse, 23 May 1929. Benois' Memoirs were published in English in 1960.
BIBLIOGRAPHY: CODB 66; SW 191-92, 245-46, 277, 301, 311, 328-29, 335.

Benoist, François (b. 10 September 1794, Nantes; d. 3 may 1878, Paris), composer, took his first lessons in music and piano in his native city before continuing his studies at the Conservatoire in Paris under the direction of Charles Catel and Adolphe Adam (see eighteenth-century volume for Catel). He won first prizes for harmony and piano during his 1811-14 residence at th Conservatoire, where his composition for the cantata Enone earned him the prix de Rome in 1815.

After three years in Italy at the expense of the French government, he returned to France to become organist of the royal chapel upon the death of Nicolas Séjan on 16 March 1819. He was named professor of organ at the Conservatoire this same year and held this position until 1872. He was named chorusmaster at the Opéra in 1840.

Benoist's first work for the lyric theatre was Félix et Léonore billed at the Feydeau in 1821. He wrote nothing else for the musical stage until 1839, when he did the music for the first act of La Gipsy.* The success of this composition might have encouraged him to collaborate on the score of Le Diable amoureux,* for which he did the music of the first and third acts. This 1840 pantomime-ballet was even more successful than La Gipsy, and Benoist scored his two 1848 works without benefit of collaborators, but neither his opera L'Apparition* nor his ballet Nisida* inspired much enthusiasm among spectators. His final contribution to the repertory of the Opéra was Pâquerette* of 1851.

Benoist's authorship also includes a requiem and a dozen volumes of pieces for the organ; he is remembered more as a teacher and organist than as a composer of ballets or operas on account of his 53 year tenure at the Conservatoire.

Benoist was elected to the Legion of Honor on 18 November 1851.
BIBLIOGRAPHY: Fétis I, 347 and Suppl. I, 69-70; HAZ 62-64; Lajarte II, 158, 163, 188, 207; Wks 4678, 6276, 6494, 8512, 9811, 11660.

Benvenuto Cellini is an opera written in two acts with a score by Hector Berlioz* and a libretto by

Auguste Barbier* and Léon de Wailly* based upon Cellini's autobiography. The work was three years in the writing, and it had its world premiere at the Opéra on 10 September 1838 after going through an exceptionally long period of 29 rehearsals because Berlioz's music presented so many problems to the musicians. It enjoyed three consecutive performances on 10, 12, 14 September 1838; it was mounted again on 11 January 1839, when it brought only 2,947 francs, 10 centimes to the box office. Its first act was produced alone on 20 February and 8, 17 March 1839, but it had to be dropped, and this untimely failure closed the doors of the Opéra to Berlioz.

The poor showing made by Benvenuto Cellini was doubtlessly aided and abetted by Berlioz' insistence upon composing his score according to his own convictions and taste in musical matters, but circumstances also seemed to conspire toward its lack of success. The press, led by the critic Joseph Mainzer, voiced doubts and even hostility toward the opera even before the public had a chance to hear it; the tenor Gilbert Duprez* was not only a mediocre actor, but he caught cold before the scheduled premiere that was already being placed in jeopardy by the imminence of the leading lady's departure from the Opéra. Also, there had existed a cabal against the composition from the start, and its adversaries managed to reduce the spectators and receipts far below normal expectations. The house was only half full as early as the second presentation. Gradually, however, it was admitted that Benvenuto Cellini had merit, and it was fairly successful in London (1853), Hanover (1879), and Vienna (1911) before it was returned to Paris in 1911, when it was billed at the Champs-Elysées Theatre.

The opera is set in Rome during carnival season, and it opens at eventide in the apartments of the papal treasurer Balducci, who is preparing to leave for the Vatican. He finishes dressing and is inveighing against Cellini when a bouquet flies through the window--from Cellini, of course. Balducci assures his daughter Teresa that this Florentine blackguard will never be his son-in-law (I, 1). Balducci leaves, and Cellini knocks at the door. Teresa asserts that he and she may never wed because her father has forbidden her to see him (I, 2-3). Fieramosca enters with flowers for Teresa, but he sees her with Cellini and hides in the bedroom. Cellini does not see the intruder, and he tells Teresa to be outside the opera house on Mardi Gras evening. Here, she is to take the arm of the monk in the brown habit who will pass next to her. He will be accompanied by a penitent in white. The two men in religious garb will be Cellini and his student Ascanio prepared to escort her to Florence and to happiness.

Fieramosca overhears this plan (I, 4), of course, but Balducci returns home suddenly and demands to know why Teresa is still up. Cellini has time to escape because Balducci goes directly to his daughter's bedroom, where he finds Fieramosca. Surprised Teresa and Balducci call upon their neighbors to help them to capture the intruder. They threaten to tie Fieramosca up and to leave him in the fountain all night, but he eludes his pursuers (I, 5-7).

The second tableau represents the Piazza Colonna at the corner of the Corso, where Cellini and his comrades are drinking and singing. The waiter refuses to continue to serve them because their bill is already too large. Ascanio arrives with a sack of silver and reminds his master that the money comes to them in payment for the statue that must be cast by morning. When the innkeeper sees the money, he is again ready to serve them, but Cellini calls a halt to the drinking to seek vengeance against Balducci for the insufficient payments he has allowed for the statue ordered by the church. The company decides to make a fool of the papal treasurer at Cassandro's carnaval show near the opera house (I, 8-10). Fieramosca appears suddenly in the background and asks Pompeo to help him convince Balducci that his intentions were honorable when Teresa's father apprehended him in his daughter's bedroom. Also, he wishes to save Teresa from a spurious kidnapping plot, but he is too old to embark upon such a strenuous adventure without help. Shrewd Pompeo suggests that he and Fieramosca don monks' habits and run off with unsuspecting Teresa before Cellini arrives at the opera house (I, 11-12).

The third tableau starts with the arrival of Balducci and Teresa in the Piazza Colonna. Cassandro's show begins, and, when the curtain parts, the spectators see a figure of Balducci representing Midas. The raucous spectators identify the papal treasurer immediately, and humiliated Balducci is furious. Cellini and Fieramosca locate Teresa. Balducci rushes at the stage; disguised Cellini and Fieramosca likewise dressed as monks make their way through the confusion to perplexed Teresa. Cellini draws his sword and slays Fieramosca's accomplice during the turmoil. Cellini is arrested, but the carnival candles are extinguished to signal the start of Lent, and Cellini escapes in the darkness. Ascanio whisks Teresa away from her father and Fieramosca. Balducci sees Fieramosca in his religious habit; he mistakes him for Pompeo's murderer; he seizes him and calls for his arrest (I, 13).

Teresa and Ascanio are in Cellini's studio at dawn. They are praying for Cellini's safe return when he appears in the doorway. The artist orders Ascanio to forget their plans for the statue of Perseus and to fetch a horse so that they may escape. Teresa and Cellini are counting their blessings when Ascanio returns to warn Cellini that he has seen Fieramosca and Balducci approaching the studio. Teresa has scarcely enough time to hide behind the mould of Perseus (II, 1-4). Balducci calls for his daughter, and she emerges from her hiding place. Her appearance causes a quarrel between the claimants for her hand, but the entrance of Cardinal Salviati restores peace. The cardinal accuses Cellini of taking money without finishing his work. He threatens to allow another artist to fill the commission. Cellini is furious. The cardinal orders the sculptor's arrest, but Cellini leaps upon his scaffold and threatens to smash the matrix of his work. He will finish his masterpiece, only if he receives a plenary indulgence, Teresa's hand in marriage, and time to complete his statue. The cardinal agrees but vows to hang him, if his work is not complete by nightfall (II, 5-6).

Cellini is melting metal for his Perseus, when Fieramosca enters with two assassins. He challenges Cellini to fight the brigands, and the sculptor accepts. Teresa rushes in to tell him that her father has betrayed them, and she begs Cellini not to risk his life, but he leaves with Ascanio after telling her that Fieramosca has challenged his honor (II, 6-13).

Cellini's helpers threaten to leave their jobs because their master seems unwilling to share their labors. Teresa is trying to convince them to remain with Cellini, when Fieramosca enters. She accuses him of slaying the artist. The workers seize him, and gold spills from his pockets. He tries to lure the apprentices from their tasks with promises of higher pay, but they ignore his offers (II, 14-16). Cellini returns and upbraids Fieramosca for refusing to fight. He gives him an apron and forces him to work. The cardinal and Balducci enter the studio to verify Cellini's success or failure (II, 17-19).

The workers and spectators gather in the Coliseum, where the foundry is installed. Fieramosca calls for more metal. Another batch of bronze is needed, and Cellini is obliged to throw his already finished masterpieces into the seething cauldron. Finally, the cauldron cracks, and the hot metal is made to flow into the mould. A stunning Perseus is the result of Cellini's labors. Happy, Balducci gives his daughter's hand in marriage to the successful artist, and the pleased cardinal forgives his sins. The opera closes with a laudium of art and beauty (II, 20).

The two female roles in the opera were filled at the Paris premiere by Mme Julie Dorus-Gras* as Teresa and Mme Rosine Stoltz* in travesty as Ascanio. The male parts were created by Duprez (Cellini), Prosper Dérivis* (Balducci), Massol (Cardinal Salviati). The striking passages in the score include the overture of ten minutes duration; Cellini's declaration of love to Teresa, "O Teresa, vous que j'aime" (I, 2); and his andante aria while casting his statue (II, 20). Teresa holds the spotlight with her <u>cavatina</u> inspired by Cellini's bouquet (I, 1).

BIBLIOGRAPHY: Michael Ayrton, <u>Berlioz, a Singular Obsession</u> (London: British Broadcasting Corp., 1969), 44-46; Claude Baillif, <u>Berlioz</u> (Paris: Su Seuil, 1968), 125-26; Henry Barraud, <u>Hector Berlioz</u> (Paris: Costard, 1955), 108-16; Jacques Barzun, <u>Berlioz and the Romantic Century</u> (New York: Columbia University Press, 1969) I, 289-308; idem, <u>Berlioz and His Century</u> (New York: Meridian Books, 1956), 158-60, 166, 170-80, 281-82, 290-92; idem, <u>Le Crépuscule d'un romantique</u> (Paris: Plon, 1913), 298-300, 305, 315; "<u>Benvenuto Cellini</u>," <u>ON</u> 37 (July 1972), 26-27; "<u>Benvenuto Cellini</u>," <u>Neue Zeitschrift fur musik</u> 133 (July 1972), 394-96; Adolphe Boschot, <u>Le Crépuscule d'un romantique</u> (Paris: Plon, 1950), 164, 172, 182, 262; idem, <u>Un Romantique sous</u>

Louis-Philippe: Hector Berlioz, 1831-1842 (Paris: plon, 1908), 257, 263, 325, 329, 339-40, 397-98, 401, 404, 409, 412-50; Chouquet 401; Léon Constantin, Berlioz (Paris: Sequana, 1934) 139-45; DDO I, 213; Suzanne Demarquez, Hector Berlioz Paris: Seghers, 1969), 38-39, 95-99; A.E.F. Dickinson, The Music of Berlioz (New York: St. Martin's Press, 1973), 179-91; John H. Elliot, Berlioz (London: J. M. Dent and Sons, 1967), 153-54; Jacques Feschotte, Berlioz: la vie, l'oeuvre (Paris: La Colombe, 1951), 105-7; Yves Hucher and Jacqueline Morini, Berlioz (Paris: Hachette, 1969), 46-47; JB 153-58; Adolphe Jullien, Hector Berlioz, sa vie et ses oeuvres (Paris: La Librairie de l'Art, 1888), 109-32; KCOB 757-64; Lajarte II, 158; J. M. "Première Représentation de Benvenuto Cellini," FM 1 (16 September 1838), 1-5; Paul-Marie Masson, Berlioz (Paris: Félix Alcan, 1923), 118-20, 173-80; MCDE I, 122, 130-31; Moniteur universel 255 (12 September 1838), 2192; PBSW 57, 124, 207; C. Pitt, "Cellini Returns to l'Opéra," Opera 23 (July 1972), 641-43; Guy de Pourtalès, L'Europe romantique (Paris; Gallimard, 1949), 783-87; Jacques Gabriel Prod'homme, "Les Deux Benvenuto Cellini de Berlioz," SIMG 14 (1912-1913), 449-60; idem, Victor Berlioz, 1803-1869 (Paris; Delagrave, 1905), 179-96; Earnest Reyer, Notes de musique (Paris: Charpentier, 1875), 340-41; Victor Seroff, Hector Berlioz (New York: The Macmillan Co., 1967), 78, 80, 131; Arthur Smolian, "Benvenuto Cellini" par Hector Berlioz (Leipzig: H. Seemann, 1900); SSBO 184-85; Thompson 167, 2109; W. J. Turner, Berlioz: the Man and His Work (New York: Vienna House, 1934), 185-86, 191-92, 207-12, 276-79; Tom S. Wotton, Hector Berlioz (Freeport, N.Y.: Books for Libraries Press, 1970), 146-47.

Beretta, Caterina (b. 8 December 1839, Milan; d. January 1911, Milan) dancer, was born into a theatrical family and studied at the ballet school associated with La Scala. She was a student of Augusto Hus, and she seemed well enough prepared to take advantage of an opportunity that came to her from Paris when she was only 16 years old. Crosnier was director of the Opéra at this time, and he wished to find and to prepare a younger dancer to fill Carolina Rosati's* place at a later date. Accordingly, he offered Mlle Beretta a contract for three years.

The director wished to have an idea of his protégée's ability and potential, of course, and he revived Le Diable à quatre* for her. Inevitably and unfortunately, audiences compared the younger and inexperienced Beretta with the established star, Carlotta Grisi,* in the role of Mazourka, and the fledgling suffered greatly by this comparison. Critics agreed that she was strong, too strong, and they complained that her figure was too solid and muscular to give the necessary illusion of feminine lightness. Yet audiences and journalists alike were quick to admit that her technique was flawless, even astounding.

Apparently Crosnier could not decide upon the fate of his future star from her execution of this single role, because he now gave her the part of L'Automne in the divertissement of Giuseppe Verde's* Les Vêpres siciliennes,* created on 13 June 1855 before the emperor and empress of France (see eighteenth-century volume for divertissement). The result was a disaster. Saint-Victor likened her to "a little female clown" trying to be an athlete, and Jouvin described her as a "goose girl who has learned to dance." Her lucrative contract was broken. She sued, however, and the courts ruled in her favor. She continued to appear at the theatre in the rue Le Peletier,* despite the action taken against her, and she went so far as to create a part in the premiere of Sainte-Claire* on 27 September 1855. Finally, she left the Opéra of her own accord in January 1957.

Mlle Beretta's experiences in France had no apparent effect upon her subsequent career. She returned to Italy to dance at La Scala in Milan, Il Regio in Turin, La Fenice in Venice, and the Teatro pagliano in Florence. She made successful appearances in Austria and Russia before returning to La Scala to teach.

BIBLIOGRAPHY: CODB 67; EDS II, 278-79; Ivor Guest, The Ballet of the Second Empire (Middletown, Conn.: Wesleyan University Press, 1974), 92-93, 255, 260.

Berlioz, Louis-Hector (b. 11 December 1803, La Côte-Saint-André; d. 8 March 1869, Paris), composer, came to Paris in 1821 to study medicine and to follow in his father's footsteps as a physician, but a visit to the Opéra one evening to hear Les Danaïdes made such an impression upon him that he returned to the theatre the following week to attend a performance of Etienne Méhul's Stratonice* and Louis Persuis' Nina (see eighteenth-century volume for Les Danaïdes, Mehul, Persuis, and Nina). He was troubled by the fact that his personal inclinations continued to push him to the rue Le Peletier,* while his filial duty directed that he give his entire attention to his medical studies. He discovered next that the library at the Conservatoire was open to the public, and he took even more time from the anatomy laboratory to plunge into the scores of Christoph Willibald Gluck (see eighteenth-century volume for Gluck). The inevitable split with his family was not long in coming because his father would not tolerate his wasting his time over music. Berlioz renounced medicine, however, and he was obliged to seek employment as a chorister in the Gymnase Theatre after his father cut off his allowance.

The young man lived in the barest of rooms and ate the cheapest of foods while he was studying at the Conservatoire and making his first attempts at composition. He wrote a mass that was executed at the Church of Saint-Roch in 1824, but this affair resulted in a fiasco. Undismayed, he went on to do the Waverly and Les Francs juges overtures in 1827 after a reconciliation with his father, and he redeemed his failure at Saint-Roch with a successful presentation of his mass in 1827 with Henri Valentino conducting.

If the 1820s were a time of hunger, study, and exploration for Berlioz, the 1830s were no less a desperate struggle for him despite the first real success that he achieved during this period of his life. He won the Prix de Rome competition in 1830 with his cantata La Mort de Sardanapale. After his return from Rome, he met and married the singer Henriette Smithson in 1833, but this union did not withstand the strain of two different temperaments, and the couple were separated in 1840. In the meantime, the added responsibility of a wife obliged Berlioz to write for journals devoted to music, especially La Gazette musicale in which he proclaimed his old preferences for Gluck and Wolfgang Amadeus Mozart while attacking Gioacchino Rossini* and his compatriots (see eighteenth-century volume for Mozart). His achievements during the decade included the completion of La Symphonie fantastique, which was rehearsed in an uproar in May 1830 and given a successful premiere the following December (see twentieth-century volume for Léonide Massine's choreographic adaption of La Symphonie fantastique). His Harold en Italie, written at the request of Niccolò Paganini, was performed initially at the Conservatoire on 23 November 1834; the Grande Messe des morts was heard for the first time in the Invalides at the funeral of General Damrémont in 1837.

Benvenuto Cellini* was a failure at the Opéra in 1838 and had to be dropped after 29 rehearsals and four billings. Berlioz' only other contribution to the Opéra would be his collaboration with Emilien Pacini on the libretto for the French version of Carl Maria von Weber's* Der Freischütz (see Le Freischütz) on 7 June 1841, although his works of an operatic nature would be posted at this theatre after his death. But a happy event took place in December 1838, when he received a letter from Paganini informing him that he, Paganini, would be most happy if Berlioz would accept from him a subsidy of 20,000 francs so that he might be free to compose music instead of being obliged to write articles for extra income. Berlioz was overjoyed and set about immediately to devote all his energy to a symphony with a chorus, soloists, and choral recitative. Roméo et Juliette was finished in seven months and given at the Conservatoire on 24 November 1839.

The third phase of Berlioz' career was an interval of travel and continuing creativity. He had been named curator of the Conservatoire in 1839, but he refused to be tied to a desk and journeyed to Germany (1843), Austria (1845), and Russia (1847). He found that his works met with greater enthusiasm outside than inside France, and he was able to earn some money by performing them in various cities of these countries, especially Germany. His additions to his bibliography in this same period included the Symphoni funèbre et triumphale (1840) composed for the anniversary of Louis-Philippe's advent to power. One of his finest lyric pieces written in 1846, La Damnation de Faust,* was given to a half-empty house at the Opéra-Comique, which Berlioz had rented for 1,600 francs. It was his depleted bank account that induced him to make the Russian trip the following year.

The last score of years of Berlioz' life was a time of bitter and even dreadful experiences for him. His second wife, Marie Recio, died on 13 June 1862; his son Louis, who was in the navy succumbed to yellow fever in Havana in June 1867. His physical condition was becoming more and more painful, and he had to keep increasing his intake of laudanum. But before he reached the point of being unable or unwilling to continue in his work, he finished his L'Enfance du Christ for presentation in the Salle Herz on 10 December 1854. this oratorio was applauded and received a good press, but the treatment extended to Les Troyens was a scandal matched only by the barbaric reaction of Paris theatregoers to Tannhäuser* in 1861 (see twentieth-century volume for Les Troyens). The last three acts were staged at the Théâtre-Lyrique under the title of Les Troyens à Carthage on 4 November 1863 with Carvalho imposing all sorts of abridgments and revisions lest the audience laugh. The first part of Les Troyens had to wait until 28 January 1891 to be staged at Nice as La Prise de Troie. The opera in its entirety had its premiere outside France, in Karlsruhe, on 6 February 1890, and it was not brought to Paris until 10 June 1921. Berlioz' last title for the theatre, Béatrice et Bénédict, was given in Germany, in Baden, on 9 August 1862.

Berlioz spent his last years journeying to southern France, Austria, and Switzerland. He undertook another trip to Russia in 1867-68, but it was his last effort. Finally, he had to take to his bed in Paris after a fall in Monte-Carlo, and he lapsed into a coma before he died with his mother-in-law and Mme Charton-Demeur at his bedside. The latter had created the role of Didon at the Théâtre-Lyrique only five years previously.

BIBLIOGRAPHY: AB 1-35, 85-94; AWL 110-44; Henry Barraud, Hector Berlioz (Paris: Costard, 1955); Jacques Barzun, Berlioz and the Romantic Century, 2 vols. (Boston: Little & Brown, 1950); Hector Berlioz, Memoirs, ed. David Cairns (New York: Alfred Knopf, 1969); Emmanuel Bondeville, "Berlioz ou le combat d'un romatique indépendant," L'Opéra de Paris 8 (195?), 26-30; BOP 187, 205, 220, 246; Adolphe Boschot, Hector Berlioz, une vie romantique (Paris: Plon, 1951); idem, Histoire d'un romantique: Hector Berlioz (Paris: Plon, 1950); DBF VI, 26-27; DGM 165-94; EGC 37-42; Alfred Ernst, L'Oeuvre dramatique de Berlioz

(Paris: Lévy, 1884); M. Esaudier, Arthur Pougin, E. Eryer, "Berlioz (mort et funeraillès)," FM 33 (14 March 1869), 72-79; J. Feschotte, Hector Berlioz (Paris: La Colombe, 1951); GIR 170-75; G. Guillemot-Magitot, Hector Berlioz (Paris: Hatier, 1958); Cecil Hopkinson, A Bibliography of the Works of Hector Berlioz (Edinburgh: 1951); HUT 102-5; JB 153-65; Gerard Mannoni, "Berlioz et la danse," SDLD 125 (10 June 1980), 38-39; MM 338-73; MPPA 331-68; MSRL 19-23; PBSW 56-58, 61, 172; G. de Pourtalès, Berlioz et l'Europe romantique (Paris: Gallimard, 1939); J. Rousselot, La Vie passionnée de Berlioz (Paris: Seghers, 1962); SSBO 184-85, 206-8, 210, 238-40, 242; Julien Tiersot, "Hector Berlioz and Richard Wagner," MQ 3 (1917), 453-92.

Berthier, Francisque Garnier (b. 1813, Lyons; d. 27 December 1875, Paris), dancer, held the position of régisseur de la danse at the Opéra from 1855 until his retirement in 1867, but his obligation to maintain discipline in the corps de ballet did not diminish the affection in which his charges held him. When he married his deaf and mute financée in 1857, most of the dancers under his direction attended his wedding party because they considered him a colleague rather than a heartless disciplinarian.

Berthier achieved a reputation as a performer because of his skill in depicting comic roles, but he appears to have been quite capable of handling any assignment that management might give him. He created more than a dozen parts between 1848 and 1861, during which time he was active as a mime and dancer, and it was probably his ability to portray this variety of characters that prevented him from being chosen for leading parts. In 1848, he represented Jacobus in Griseldis,* Don Oscar in Nisida,* and the Burgomeister in La Vivandière.* He did Sergeant Bridoux in Pâquerette* and the hero's guardian in Vert-Vert* in 1851. After filling the role of Loki in Orfa* on 29 December 1852, he performed as Mére Simon in La Fille mal gardée* and as Scurra in Aelia et Mysis* in 1853 before executing a comic pas de deux in Jovita* with Mme Dominique on 11 November of this same year. The last five characters he created at the Opéra included Babinella in La Fonti* of 1855, Isaac in Le Corsaire* of 1856, Patimate in Le Papillon* of 1860, the sergeant in Graziosa* and

Jacopon in L'Etoile de Messine* of 1861. He was cast as Gurn in the 1852 and 1858 revivals of La Sylphide.* His last two appearances before retirment were as Bridoux in Diavolina* on 6 July 1863 and as Gros-Guillaume in Le Roi d'Yvetot* on 28 December 1865.
BIBLIOGRAPHY: Ivor Guest, The Ballet of the Second Empire (Middletown, Conn.: Wesleyan University Press, 1974), 6, 34, 40, 42, 54, 59, 62, 67, 69-71, 76, 87, 98, 108, 132, 141, 167, 172, 190, 254, 257; Lajarte II, 210-12, 219-20, 222-23, 231-32, 234-35.

Bertin, Louise-Angélique (b. 15 February 1805, Les Roches; d. 1877, Les Roches), composer, tried her hand at painting before becoming interested in music. She had a contralto voice that led her to turn to dramatic music, but she had never studied harmony or counterpoint despite her ability to play the piano. She learned to write airs, duets, and overtures simply by attempting to compose them without preliminary training, and she managed gradually to put her ideas into more or less acceptable musical form. She approached the process and problems of orchestration in the same fashion. Finally she could boast that she had created an opera in three acts, Guy Mannering. Her friends were inclined to be skeptical, and they raised a stage in a greenhouse to see how this incredible creation would sound with an orchestra and before an audience. The production was limited, but the spectators on hand pronounced it a success. Mlle Bertin then determined to set a libretto by Eugène Scribe,* Le Loup garou. It was billed at the Feydeau Theatre on 10 March 1827. Strangely enough, it was selected for performance in some of the provincial theatres of France after its short run in Paris. Encouraged and refusing to acknowledge limits to her creative ability, the composer embarked next upon a Faust that was mounted eventually at the Favart Theatre on 8 March 1831.

Mlle Bertin crowned her career with an opera in five acts rehearsed under the title of Notre-Dame de Paris but billed as La Esméralda* with a libretto by Victor Hugo* himself. It was given at the Opéra on 18 November 1836 but failed, and Mlle Bertin seems to have withdrawn to her native village of Les Roches a few miles outside Paris. Strangely enough, Hector Berlioz* said that her musical talent was "more intellectual than instinctive." The author of Les Troyens* knew her and her work because her father founded and owned Le Journal des débats for which he wrote, and he had asked him to supervise the rehearsals of La Esméralda.

BIBLIOGRAPHY: Victor Berlioz, Mémoires, ed. David Cairns (New York: Knopf, 1969), 241-42, 316-22, 530-31, 560, 596; DBF VI, 247; Fétis I, 384; GE VI, 456; Lajarte II, 155; LXIX II, 621; Wks, 4713, 8960.

Betly was an opera in two acts with a score by Domenico Gaetano Donizetti* and a libretto that was a translation by Hippolyte Lucas* of the original Italian words by Donizetti, who had based his work on the libretto of Le Châlet written by Eugène Scribe* and Anne-Honoré-Joseph Duveyrier.* Ultimately, the story had its source in the comedy of Goethe entitled Jeri und Baetely. Betly was one of Donizetti's least successful compositions. It had its premiere on 27 December 1853 on a gala program given for the benefit of the elder Lepeintre, a member of the company at the Opéra. It had to be dropped after its fifth performance on 11 January 1854.

The opera opens with a chorus of fishermen and women celebrating the return of their famous compatriot and naval captain Franz (I, 1), while André expresses his delight with his beloved Betly's arrival in the village (I, 2). André asks Betly's guardian Léonard to press his suit for Betly's hand in marriage, but Léonard discloses that he prefers a more prestigious husband like Franz for his ward (I, 3-4). Léonard then tells Betly of his plans for her, but she replies that she prefers her freedom to marriage (I, 5-6). André declares his love to her, but she makes light of his serious attitude toward marriage. He insists so strongly upon his love for her that she is moved to pity and tells him to look elsewhere for a bride (I, 7). Léonard arrives on leave and greets his joyous friends before entering his uncle's house to fetch some wine to celebrate his homecoming. Léonard tries to persuade Betly that Franz is no longer a boisterous youth, and André attempts to convince her that the captain has not outgrown his former ways. Betly finds him charming and attractive; he considers her to be most graceful and attractive. The company sits down to dine (I, 8-9).

Franz begins to drink and to sing with his friend, but Betly loses patience with this carousing. His uncle tries in vain to moderate his behavior, but he sings of the loves of a sailor and boasts that he sails from conquest to conquest. Léonard despairs; Betly leaves with André (II, 1-2). Léonard upraids his nephew for offending his future wife and threatens to disinherit him. Franz is reluctant to surrender his freedom even for his uncle's fortune, and he suggests that Betly may refuse to marry him (II, 3). André enters to fall asleep after drinking so much wine, and Betly hears him describe in his sleep how much he loves her. She is moved by his obvious sincerity and awakens him, but she is frightened away by Franz' approaching footsteps (II, 4). Franz decides to frighten André, and he threatens to kill him if he tries to steal Betly from him. He orders André to tell Betly that she should marry him, Franz, and André appears frightened into complying with Franz's extravagant commands and threats (II, 6). Betly takes the situation seriously and informs Léonard that his nephew is threatening to kill André. Léonard urges her to restore peace by marrying Franz, but she answers that André is her choice for a husband. Léonard complains that his old age will never be cheered by the presence of small children, and Franz grasps this opportunity to present to him his wife and his young children dressed as sailors. Betly agrees to marry André, and happiness reigns in the village (II, 7-8).

The four roles of Betly were filled by Morelli (Franz), Boulo (André) Coulon* (Léonard), and Mme Bosio* (Betly).

BIBLIOGRAPHY: *William Ashbrook, Donizetti (London: Cassell, 1965), 190-92, 487; Guglielmo Barblan, L'Opera de Donizetti nell'età romantica (Bergamo: Banca mutua popolare de Bergamo, 1948), 137-39; Lea Bossi, Donizetti (Brescia: La Scuola, 1956), 159-62; Chouquet 414; DDO I, 151; Marie Escudier, "Betly, de Donizetti," FM 18 (1 January 1854), 5; A. Fraccardi, Donizetti (Verona: A. Mondadori, 1945) 215-16; Jacques François Fromental Eli Halévy, Souvenirs et portraits (Paris: Michel Lévy frères, 1861), 225-26; Angelo Geddo, Donizetti: l'uomo, le musiche (Bergamo: Edizioni della rotonda, 1956), 57-58; Lajarte II,*

215-16; Herbert Weinstock, Donizetti and the World of Opera (New York: Pantheon Books, 1963), 148, 188, 222, 351-52; Guido Zavadini, Donizetti (Bergamo: Instituto italiano d'artigrafiche, 1948), 62-66.

Betty was a pantomime ballet in two acts with a score by Ambroise Thomas* and a book by Joseph Mazilier.* The latter choreographed his own scenario, and the sets were created by Pierre Cicéri,* Rubé, Despléchin, Diéterle, Séchan, Philastre, and Cambon. It was produced for the first time at the Royal Academy of Music on 10 July 1846. The work was suggested by Alexandre Duval's La Jeunesse de Henri IV.

The ballet transpires in and around London toward the end of the reign of Charles I, and the first scene presents a court page about to disguise himself as an ordinary citizen to keep a rendez-vous with a commoner (I, 1). After Edouard's departure from the royal palace, Count Rochester enters with Lady Clara, who refuses to believe assertions of his love for her. She suggests that she might listen to his proposals of marriage if he stopped consorting with women of easy virtue and tried to provide a proper example for Charles to follow (I, 2). Lady Clara assures Princess Cathérine du Portugal, Prince Charles's wife, that she has convinced Rochester to abandon his dissolute ways (I, 3).

Rochester berates Edouard when he returns from his rendez-vous, but the page explains that he is truly in love with a charming girl who appears to return his love. She is the daughter of a retired naval officer who runs the Grand-Amiral tavern, and he gives her dancing lessons every morning. Rochester decides that this situation has possibilities, and he orders two sailor suits (I, 4). King Charles returns from the hunt and hurries through the task of signing documents demanding his signature because he is tired (I, 5). Princess Cathérine reminds him sarcastically that it would be a great favor to her if he could take time from his work to attend her ball in the evening (I, 6). Prince Charles begins to feel troubled about having neglected Cathérine, but Rochester undermines his good intentions by telling him about the pretty lass in the Grand-Amiral tavern. They agree to don their sailor suits to visit her (I, 7).

The second tableau of the first act is set outside the tavern on the banks of the Thames, where the proprietor Coop and his daughter Betty are stopping quarrels and awaiting the arrival of a ship. Betty is overjoyed to see her dancing master Edouard, and he rehearses her in steps that she will execute for the approaching sailors. A merry party marks the disembarkation. Charles arrives on the scene with Rochester, and nervous Edouard recognizes them. He tries to leave, but Rochester prevents him from escaping by threatening to expose him to Charles. The prince notices that Edouard appears upset, and he tells Rochester to amuse him while he dances with Betty. Charles sits down to drink with Coop, but he drops his purse unwittingly when he pulls out his handkerchief. Edouard retrieves it on the sly. The customers leave at the sound of the ship's bell, but Charles and Rochester insist upon remaining in the tavern. Coop reminds them that he must close. Rochester chooses this moment to depart unnoticed and to leave Charles without money and at the mercy of Edouard. Coop presents the bill to the prince who looks in vain for his purse. Heated words are exchanged. Charles offers Coop his watch as a pledge of payment. Coop cannot understand how a commoner can own a gold watch encrusted with diamonds. Edouard points to the royal crest engraved upon it and suggests that it was stolen from the king. Coop agrees and refuses to part with it. Charles is seized and held prisoner pending the arrival of the police (I, 1-2 bis).

Coop is detaining Charles in the tavern, and Betty is trying to console him. He offers Edouard a precious ring if he will help him to escape and to avoid the executioner's axe. Edouard accepts the bribe, and the two lovers lower him from the window. Coop enters with the police; Betty faints; Edouard runs off to the royal palace (II, 1-4).

Edouard arrives at the palace, where the ball is about to begin. He is followed by Rochester, who describes Charles' misfortunes to an amused Lady Clara. Edouard is tired from his escapade, and he falls asleep in a chair, while Lady Clara and Rochester hide behind a colonnade to await developments. Charles enters through a secret door, and he is quite happy to have escaped public notice until he finds that he cannot enter the room because the sleeping page is blocking his path with his chair. Edouard wakes up suddenly with a shout of alarm, however, and Lady Clara comes running to his aid. She is surprised to find Charles in a sailor's suit, but she seizes the opportunity to have him sign a petition from Princess Cathérine. He rushes to his room to change his costume for the ball, but he pauses long enough to scold Rochester for having left him without funds. Rochester and Lady Clara tell Cathérine about the king's nocturnal adventures; she thanks them calmly and gives the signal for the ball to start (II, 1-3 bis).

Charles enters the ballroom, and Princess Cathérine asks him slyly why he seems so angry with Rochester, but he assures her that he has no quarrel with the count. Edouard informs Rochester that Betty and Coop have a watch to return to Charles, and Rochester relays the information to the king loudly enough for Princess Cathérine to hear. Trapped, Charles can only deny losing a watch, and he gives orders that the tavern keeper and his daughter are to be denied access to the ballroom. Cathérine countermands this directive. The page ushers Betty and her father across the ballroom. Coop is disturbed by the resemblance between the page and his daughter's dancing master. He is speechless when he is presented to Rochester, who looks like the identical twin of the sailor in his tavern. Betty tries to extricate her father from his embarrassment by describing the situation to Charles, but he looks like the other sailor, and she loses her composure. Finally, Princess Cathérine interrupts the farce to admit that the whole affair was a hoax designed to bring Charles to his senses. The prince realizes what has happened, and he forgives Rochester and Edouard. A total reconciliation is reached at last, therefore, and Charles gives his blessing to the marriage of his page and Betty (II, 4-5 bis).

The ballet was only moderately successful because it was felt that the scenario was a series of scenes "hastily arranged" to provide a vehicle for the premiere performance of Mlle Sofia Fuoco* at the Opéra. Yet the ballerina herself was praised for her dancing, and audiences applauded her for her vivacity, elevation, and precision. Betty was dropped from the repertory after its 27th presentation on 11 February 1848. The other

female roles were filled by Mlles Maria (Edouard), Célestine Emarot* (Cathérine du Portugal), and Pierson (Lady Clara). The three male parts were danced by Lucien Petipa* (Charles), Jean Coralli* (Rochester), and, Mazilier (Coop).
BIBLIOGRAPHY: CB 190-96; Chouquet 408; Escudier, "Betty," FM 9 (12 July 1846), 218 and (19 July 1846), 229; Lajarte II, 183-84; RBP 255-57.

Biletta, Emmanuel (b. 20 December 1825, Casal; d. November 1890), composer, learned piano from his father and was able to play in public by the time that he was 14 years old. He continued his studies with Joaquin Turina and was given professional guidance by Gioacchino Rossini.* He had written masses and several other nontheatrical compositions before he did his first opera, Marco Visconti, which was never produced, but he left Bologna for England via Paris before long to do ballets and White Magic for production in London. He returned to the continent to produce his next opera at Parma, L'Abbazia di Kelso (1853), and it was then that he moved to the French capital long enough to do La Rose de Florence* in 1858, a work that was sung in Italian at Florence in 1875. This was his only contribution to the Opéra. Biletta never took time to publish his collected works, which include a profusion of overtures, madrigals, and selections for the piano, as well as an uncounted quantity of pieces for one, two, three, or four voices.
BIBLIOGRAPHY: Fétis Suppl. I, 90; GE VI, 832; Lajarte II, 221.

Birch, Charlotte, née Pfeiffer (b. 23 June 1800, Stuttgart; d. 25 August 1868, Berlin), playwright, was also known as Birch-Pfeiffer and Birchpfeiffer. She moved to Munich in 1806 with her father, who served with the Bavarian government in this city until he became blind in 1809. Charlotte began to read Schiller and the classics aloud to him, and this activity gave her a precocious interest in the theatre. In 1813, she made her debut as an actress at age 13 on the stage of the Isarthor Theatre in Munich as Princess Thermutis in Peter Lindpaintner's Mosis Errettung. She managed to gain parental consent to embark upon a theatrical career only through the intervention of King Max Joseph.

The young actress inspired enthusiasm at court and in public theatres, and she advanced quickly to the rank of star. She modeled her artistry after Sophie Schroëder and made a reputation for herself by playing such characters as Sappho, Medea, and Marie Stuart. She married the Danish writer Christian Andreas Birch in 1825.

Now at the height of her powers, Charlotte undertook successful tours that included appearances in Prague, Stuttgart, Karlsruhe, Mannheim, Darmstadt, Vienna, Hanover, Berlin, Dresden, and Hamburg. She broke her ties to Munich to accept invitations as a guest star in Danzig, Riga, and St. Petersburg. She left Russia in 1827 to go to Prague, Danzig, Leipzig, and Vienna. Then, after 1830, she was billed in Pest, Breslau, and Berlin before returning to Munich. She used this latter city once more as her base to travel to Amsterdam, Hamburg, Berlin, but she then took over the management of the Zurich Theatre until 1843. She spent the last years of her life as the replacement for Amalie Wolff at the Royal Theatre of Berlin.

Unfortunately, Birchpfeiffer lacked the charm and grace necessary to becoming a great actress, although she possessed the energy to appear on so many stages of Europe. She won more enduring fame as a playwright than as an actress, and her literary production included a large number of original compositions in addition to the short stories she adapted to the stage. She produced as well a series of compositions for the theatre based upon the writings of Van der Velde, Walter Scott, Victor Hugo,* Georges Sand, and Auerbach. The roles she created for the actors in her plays were vital with emotion and endowed with color. In all, she created at least a hundred scripts for the theatre, but nearly all of them except Dorf und Stadt, Der Grille, and Die Waise aus Lowood have disappeared from the repertory.

Known as Mme Birch-Pfeiffer in France, Charlotte's only contribution to the Paris Opéra was the Russian legend that she had used in one of her works and that the Belgian poet Gustave Oppelt* had adapted to the French operatic stage under the title of Sainte-Claire* in 1855.

BIBLIOGRAPHY: Allgemeine deutsche Biographie (Leipzig: Duncker u. Humblot, 1875) II, 654-56; Chouquet 415; DDO II, 1001-2; Lajarte II, 218-19.

Bis, Hippolyte-Louis-Florent (b. 29 August 1789, Douai; d. 3 March 1855, Paris), librettist, began his public career by circulating pamphlets denouncing the Bourbon dynasty in 1816. This act of subversion took place in Lille, but it had national repercussions that were laid to rest by Bis' appointment to the Ministry of Finances in 1819. After his arrival in the capital, Bis had leisure time and set about to have his Attila performed at the Odéon in 1822. The tragedy was suppressed because of political allusions in its text, but his Blanche d'Aquitaine encountered no difficulties and was accepted and performed by the Comédie-Française on 29 October 1829. Yet it was not these two tragedies in five acts but his libretto for Guillaume Tell* that won the admiration of the public for him.

After the success of Gioacchino Rossini's* work in 1829, Bis enjoyed his second triumph with the Revolution of 1840. He entered the fray and created La Marseillaise du nord in praise of the bourgeois king, Louis-Philippe. His faction won, of course, and he was made head of the Ministry of Finances. He still had hopes for a success at the Comédie-Française, and he created Jeanne de Flandre for this company, but it failed completely. Bis never wrote another word for the theatre.

BIBLIOGRAPHY: DBF VI, 526-27; GE VI, 924-25; Lajarte II, 133; LXIX II, 768; Francis Toye, Rossini (New York: Knopf, 1947), 118-19; Herbert Weinstock, Rossini (New York: Knopf, 1968), 160-61; 508; Wks, 3204, 3317, 4363, 10259.

Bizet, Georges (b. 25 October 1838, Paris, d. 3 June 1875, Bougival), composer, gained admission to the Conservatory on 9 October 1848 with a precocious exhibition of skill at the piano, although he had not yet reached the required age of ten. When he was ten, he took first prize in solfeggio and captured the attention of Jacques Halévy.* Later, but before he was 17, Bizet met Charles Gounod* and published a piano reduction of La Nonne sanglante* besides an arrangement of Gounod's First Symphony in D. He started his own symphony entitled Roma on 29 October 1855. Bizet made a successful showing in the Prix de Rome competition in the spring of 1856 and followed this accomplishment by sharing with Charles Lecocq* a prize posted by Jacques Offenbach* for the best comic opera submitted to a jury specially selected for this occasion. The future author of Carmen* had become well enough known in the musical circles of Paris to be invited to the fashionable salons of the capital, and he was also confident enough now to enter the Prix de Rome competition for the second time in May 1857. He won first prize with his cantata Clovis et Clotilde on the second ballot.

Bizet left for Rome on 21 December 1857, and the course of his journey led him through Lyons, Arles, Marseille, Nice, and Florence before his arrival at the Villa Medici in Rome on 27 January 1858. The director of the French Imperial Academy here was the colorful Victor Schnetz, whose efforts to entertain his wards included dinners, recitals, and mascarades. The young musician busied himself in his new surroundings with long walks through the countryside, delightful evenings at the home of the Russian ambassador Kisseldef, and writing reassuring letters to his mother about his health, conduct, and studies.

His first musical effort in Rome was Don Procopio, an Opéra-bouffe. His work was adjudged a complete success by the Academy, but Bizet's joy was diminished by news of his mother's failing health and by the prospect of having to leave Rome. He petitioned the Minister of Fine Arts in Paris for permission to stay at the Villa Medici instead of passing his third year in Germany. His request was granted, and he set about to finish his ode-symphony Vasco de Gama that he did not complete until the spring of 1860.

Bizet was now obliged to leave Rome and his precious freedom, and he decided to take a tour of northern Italy on his way back to Paris. He arrived home at the end of September and found his mother more ill than he had imagined. He received a flattering report on his Vasco de Gama from the Academy and worked on La Guzla de l'Emir while helping Gounod with La Reine de Saba.* Then, on the morning of 8 September 1861, his mother died.

Bizet had not been entirely idle during this interval, however, and he was able to promise Carvalho* a new work, Les Pêcheurs de perles, when the latter was preparing programs for his new Théâtre-Lyrique. The composition was to have its premiere on 14 September 1863, but it was not given until a week later because of the illness of the star. Bizet's opera in three acts was applauded in the theatre, but the press seemed to resent Bizet's obvious youth when he appeared on stage to acknowledge the applause he had earned. The notices used such words as "feeble" or "Wagnerism" or "shrieking"; Jouvin stated sourly that there were "no pearls in the music." But Carvalho was enthusiastic and had enough faith in the composer's future to commission him to finish Ivan IV. Bizet withdrew to his newly acquired retreat a few miles from Paris and completed his appointed task only to learn that Ivan could not go into production. The Théâtre-Lyrique had no money, and Carvalho had been obliged to resign. These frustrating experiences with his work plunged Bizet into the gloomy depths, and he began to exhibit symptoms of a persectuion complex. His alarmed friends tried to cheer him up with kind words and attempted to distract him from his bellicose moodiness by having him meet personalities prominent on the political and social scene. Finally, he decided to quit Paris, and he took up permanent residence in his rural hideaway at Le Vésinet.

If Bizet thought that he had escaped from Paris completely, he was mistaken, because it was not long before Carvalho was knocking at his door with a new libretto based on a novel by Walter Scott and entitled La Jolie Fille de Perth. The style of the text was affected and almost beyond redemption, but the composer made the best of a bad poem and handed the completed work to Carvalho on 24 December 1866. Plans were made to schedule its premiere on 15 August 1867, the month when Paris is traditionally empty, but a series of unforeseen events delayed its first performance until 26 December. Bizet thought that he had a success at last, but La Jolie Fille de Perth had to be withdrawn after only 18 presentations, because Carvalho had moved his theatre to the place du Châtelet, a location removed from other theatrical activity and traffic. Bizet was disappointed, of course, and he started to complain of abscesses in his throat and pains in his chest.

Yet despite his health and his composing La Coupe du roi de Thulé for an Opéra contest, Bizet found time to marry Geneviève Halévy on 3 June 1869. He set about immediately to ponder over which of seven subjects he might develop into an opera so that he might support his modest family when war erupted. He served in the defense of

Paris and spent the period of the Commune uprising in Le Vésinet with his bride. The return of peace found him ready to accept Camille Du Locle's* commission to set Djamileh to words by Louis Gallet for the Opéra-Comique. A cast could not be found for the work, however, and Djamileh as well as Griséldis* were put off indefinitely. Bizet blamed "the Offenbach invasion" for his troubles and started on Clarissa Harlowe. Finally, in 1872, Djamileh went into rehearsal at the Opéra-Comique in March and opened on 22 May. Even now, Bizet did not have a success. The cast of Djamileh could not handle their roles, and this composition had to be dropped after only ten billings. Yet two events encouraged the composer in the summer of 1872. He was invited to write a piece for the Opéra; his son Jacques was born on 10 July.

But Carvalho had other plans for him, and he asked him to collaborate with Dudet on a new version of L'Arlésienne that was already being mounted as a play with background music. The project appealed to both men, and the premiere of the work took place at the Vaudeville Theatre on 1 October 1872. The public was not enthusiastic, however, and L'Arlésienne was dropped after a fortnight, although Bizet did manage to excerpt the famous suite from it and so obtain an overwhelming success on 10 November.

The composer knew that he had found his way despite the failure of L'Arlésienne, however, and he had already started on a new opera before the old one closed. It was called Carmen and was based upon a tale by Prosper Mérimée. Guilhen de Castro's medieval poem on Le Cid had distracted him momentarily, it is true, but Carmen was starting to take shape as early as the end of October 1873, when Bizet asked his collaborators, Gabriel Fauré* and Gallet, to confer with him about making it acceptable to Halanzier, director of the Opéra. But the Opéra promptly burned down on 28 October. It was decided to take the composition to the Opéra-Comique, therefore, and Gallie-Marié was offered the title role. Rehearsals were set for August 1874 and then delayed until October, an unfortunate postponement that upset Bizet, who was already witnessing the dissolution of his marriage. Carmen did not have its premiere until 13 March 1875, and then its realistic portrayal of low-class characters as well as its original music and surprising plot hindered its success in the middle-class Opéra-Comique, which was given more to happy endings and virtuous conduct on the stage.

The apparent failure of Carmen, the approaching end of his marriage, and the worsening condition of his throat left Bizet in a state of morbid desperation. He began to suffer from cruel headaches, and the abscesses spread to his mouth. He returned to Bougival on 28 May and foolishly indulged his passion for swimming in the Seine the following day. He was subsequently stricken with a fever and paralysis. A cardiac attack followed, and he grew steadily weaker until he lapsed into unconsciousness and died on 3 June 1875. Funeral services were held in the Church of La Trinité in Paris on 5 June, and Gounod delivered the eulogy. That night, Carmen was performed at the Opéra-Comique.

BIBLIOGRAPHY: Camille Bellaigue, Georges Bizet, sa vie et ses oeuvres (Paris: Delagrave, 1887); Martin Cooper, Georges Bizet (London: 1938); Mina Curtiss, Bizet and His World (New York: Alfred Knopf, 1958); DBF VI, 542; Winton Dean, Bizet (London: J. M. Dent & Sons, 1948); Marc Delmas, Georges Bizet (Paris: 1930); EGC 42-45; Hugues Imbert, Georges Bizet (Paris: P. Ollendorff, 1899); JB 241-48; KOH 156-64; Paul Charles René Landormy, Bizet (Paris: Gallimard, 1950); H. Malherbe, La vie et l'oeuvre de Georges Bizet (Paris: A. Michel, 1959); Gérard Mannoni, "Bizet et la danse," SDLD 111 (10 February 1979), 31-32; Archimède Montanelli, Giorgio Bizet, cenni biografici (Massa: E. Medici, 1893); MPPA 317-30; MSRL 23-26; NEO 83; Douglas Parker, Bizet (London: Routledge & Kegan Paul, 1951); PBSW 62, 172; Charles Pigot, Georges Bizet et son oeuvre, 2d ed. (Paris: Delagrave, 1911); Michel Poupet, "Gounod et Bizet," L'Avant-scène 41 (May-June), 106-17; RdM XXII (November 1938) devoted to Bizet; SSBO 237-38, 250, 258, 264-67, 270; Julien Tiersot, "Bizet and Spanish Music," MQ XIII (1927), 566-81. See also twentieth-century-volume entries for Jeux d'enfants and Le Palais de cristal.

Blache, Alexis, choreographer, studied under his father and succeeded him as balletmaster at Marseilles and Bordeaux after 1819. He wrote a number of ballets for the provincial stage; for

example, Les Amours d'automne and Les Lauriers d'Ibérie. His most popular composition was the burlesque pantomime entitled Les Meuniers, which was billed in Paris as well as in the provinces. After a short stay in the French capital, Blache fils left his native land to become balletmaster at the Imperial Theatre of St. Petersburg. None of his ballets was ever produced at the Opéra.
BIBLIOGRAPHY: CODB 75; GE VI, 981; Marian Hannah Winter, The Pre-Romantic Ballet (New York: Dance Horizons, 1974), 256, 258.

Blanche de Provence ou la Cour des fees was an opera in three acts and only 13 scenes with a score by Henri Berton, François Boïeldieu, Luigi Chérubini, Rodolphe Kreutzer, and Ferdinand Paër.* The libretto was the work of Marie-Emmanuel Théaulon* and de Rancé; the choreography was created by Pierre Gardel and Louis Jacques Milon (see eighteenth-century volume for Barton, Boïeldieu, Cherubini, Kreutzer, Gardel, and Milon). It was written to celebrate the birth and baptism of the duke de Bordeaux, and it had its world premiere at the Tuileries before the king on 1 May 1821. It was performed at the Royal Academy of Music on 3, 7, 9 May 1821 before it was dropped from the repertory.

The opera opens with the Genius of Evil threatining to drench the earth in blood, while the Genius of Good promises to oppose this heinous plan with every resource at her command. Alcine adds that the new born king, Henri, will assist her because his mother Blanche de Provence will lead him to the court of the Fairies, where he will learn the way of virtue (I, 1). A chorus sings the praises of the infant king destined to end the strife ravaging Provence, and Hermance announces Blanche's arrival with her son (I, 2-4). Blanche and her child enter a chariot surrounded by their dancing and singing subjects. Blanche urges her followers to accompany her to the woods of Ellidore, where Henri will receive gifts from the spirits dwelling there (I, 5).

The genius of evil is already in the forest waiting to ambush Henri, Blanche, and their retinue to preserve the powers of darkness. The infernal demons dance and evoke a terrifying storm. Blanche's subjects scatter, and she is left to wander through the darkness with her son. She prays for protection, and Alcine appears; the latter dissipates the darkness and repulses the demons (II, 1-2). Hermance and his soldiers enter to protect the king (II, 3).

The fairies of the entire universe arrive in magnificent chariots, and a throne appears among them. It is reserved for Alcine, who charges her subjects to watch over the young king (III, 1-2). She summons Henri and his mother to explain that the dark days of war and evil have passed; she explains to the assembly that it is time to pay homage to their monarch for restoring peace (III, 3). Alcine gives her blessing to the child and endows him with prudence, charity, justice, diligence, and a loving respect for the arts. The sylphids sing a lullaby over his cradle and foretell the glory of his reign (III, 4-5).

The role of Blanche de Provence was filled by Mme Rose Branchu with Mlle Gerard Grassari* as Alcine and Adolphe Nourrit* as Hermance (see eighteenth-century volume for Branchu). The lesser parts were done by Lays (un Troubadour), Prosper Dérivis* (un Citoyen), Bonel (Le Génie du Mal), and Mme Lebrun (une Sylphide) (see eighteenth-century volume for Lays). The most enduring piece in the score was Chérubini's lullaby sung by the chorus, "Dors, mon enfant." This finale of Blanche de Provence was heard in a number of concerts at the Paris Conservatoire long after the opera was forgotten.

BIBLIOGRAPHY: AEM II, 1170-82 and VI, 1781-83; Edward Bellasis, Cherubini: Memorials Illustrative of His Life and Work (New York: Da Capo Press, 1971), 190, 290-91; Chouquet 389; DDO I, 158; Richard Hohenemser, Luigi Cherubini: sein Leben und seine Werke (Leipzig: Breitkopf 7 Hartel, 1913), 451-52; Lajarte II, 99; Moniteur universel 125 (5 May 1821), 618; H. G. Sear, "Background for Cherubini," M&L 24 (1943), 15-25; Wks II, 3318.

Blasis, Carlo (b. 4 November 1799, Naples; d. 15 January 1878, Cernobbio), dancer, was taken as a baby from his native city to Marseille, where his father arranged for him to study dancing as soon as his age permitted him to take lessons. He made his debut as a dancer on a local stage at age 12 and then moved on to better known theatres in Aix, Avignon, Lyon, Toulouse. His family moved next to Bordeaux, where Jean Dauberval was at the Grand Theatre, and Carlo resumed his studies with him (see eighteenth-century volume for Dauberval). He performed in ballets reflecting the preferences of his teacher who had been formed in the tradition and tastes of the eighteenth-century, for example, Télémaque and Le Deserteur (see eighteenth-century volume for Télémaque and Le Deserteur). His talents were obvious, and his audiences were so enthusiastic that Blasis was invited to the Opéra.

In Paris, he performed in revivals of Miller's Télémaque and Le Jugement de Pâris as well as in Achille à Scyros usually as the partner of Mlle Gosselin or Mlle Amélie Legallois* (see eighteenth-century volume for Le Jugement de Pâris and Achille à Scyros). The young dancer received a good press, and he continued to study with Gardel but he became the object of professional jealousy, and his career in the French capital was cut short by intrigue. He left Paris to tour the provinces for a while before becoming premier danseur at La Scala and choreographer and soloist at the King's theatre in London. Ultimately, he became director of the Royal Academy of the Dance, where he was considered one of the most illustrious teachers of ballet in the world. Many of his students danced at the Opéra later, and he left many books and articles on the ballet, mime, drama, and dancing as a profession. His ideas still constitute the basic doctrine of classical ballet.

BIBLIOGRAPHY: ACD 72; CODB 76-77; EDB 67; Ivor Guest, The Ballet of the Second Empire (Middletown, Conn.: Wesleyan University Press, 1974), 74, 91, 93, 103, 188, 204, 262; idem, The Romantic Ballet in England (Middletown, Conn.: Wesleyan Univeristy Press, 1972), 34, 130-31; Lincoln Kirstein, Dance: a Short History of Classical Theatrical Dancing (New York: G. B. Putnam's Sons, 1935), 229-63; Lillian Moore "Blasis to Bournonville," D Mag 38 (February 1964), 52-53; idem, Artists of the Dance (New York: Thomas Y. Crowell Co., 1938), 147-54; Mark Edward Perugini, A Pageant of the Dance and Ballet (London: Jarrolds, 1946), 183-91, 269-70; Marian Hannah Winter, The Pre-Romantic Ballet (New York: Dance Horizons, 1974), 4, 5, 11, 175, 191, 246, 263.

Blau, Edouard (b. 1836; d. 1906, Paris), librettist, wrote the libretto used by Eugène Diaz* in his La Coupe du roi de Thulé,* which

Georges Bizet* also selected for his unproduced work of the same title. In 1885, he created the texts for Jules Massenet's* Le Cid* with L. Gallet and for Joncière's Le Chevalier Jean given without success at the Opéra-Comique. Edouard Lalo's* popular Le Roi d'Ys was a hit at this latter theatre in 1888 with a score set to his words, and the two following years saw him enjoy public approval with Massenet's Esclarmonde in 1889 at the Opéra-Comique and then suffer a rebuff with the failure at the Opéra of Zaïre* by La Nux in 1890. He supplied the libretto for Massenet's Werther* at Vienna on 16 February 1892, but this work was not sung in Paris until its first billing at the Opéra-Comique on 16 January 1893. Blau's original French text had already been used at Geneva on 27 December 1892.

BIBLIOGRAPHY: Chouquet 425; DDO II, 271-73; Winton Dean, "An Unfinished Opera by Bizet," M&L XXVIII (1947), 347-63; Lajarte II, 245-46; SW 62-63, 80-81, 187-88, 227.

Blaze, François-Joseph, DIT Castil-Blaze or Castil-Blaze père (b. 1 December 1784, Cavaillon; d. 11 December 1857, Paris), writer, studied law before entering the Conservatoire. He continued to use his legal training as a government inspector in Vaucluse until he decided to go to Paris to promote his French version of Wolfgang Amadeus Mozart's Don Juan* and to find a publisher for his De l'opéra en France (see eighteenth-century volume for Mozart). The latter work appeared in 1820 and was responsible for his appointment to the post of music critic for Le Journal des débats. His Dictionnaire de musique moderne was printed in two volumes a year later. Castil-Blaze expanded these two aspects of his writing to an almost incredible degree by writing for a cluster of journals featuring music news, history, or criticism and by composing an equal number of books devoted to the history of the French musical theatre. His work for the Opéra included his translations of Carl Maria von Weber's* Euryanthe* of 1831 and of Mozart's Don Juan produced finally in 1834.

BIBLIOGRAPHY: DBF VI, 658; Fétis I, 441-43; Lajarte II, 137-38, 147-48; LXIX II, 812-13; PBSW 172; Wks III, 238.

Bloch, André (b. 18 January 1873, Wissembourg, Alsace; d. 7 August 1960, Paris), composer, studied with Ernest Guiraud* and Jules Massenet* at the Paris Conservatoire, where he won the Premier Grand Prix de Rome in 1893. Subsequently, he became conductor of the orchestra at the American Conservatory in Fontainebleau. His only work for the Opéra was Broceliande.
BIBLIOGRAPHY: BBD 182-83; KT 53-62.

Bloch, Rosine (b. 1832, Bischheim, Bas-Rhin; d. 1891, Nice), singer, studied music under the direction of Battaille and Levasseur at the Paris Conservatoire. Her perfectly sculptured features and striking mezzo soprano voice won her an appointment to the Opéra, where she made her debut as Azucena in Le Trouvère* on 13 November 1865, but it became evident as time passed that her flawless beauty and voice lacked the human quality needed to make her a great singer.

She continued with success at the Le Peletier* theatre, however, and she was especially impressive in Herculanum* and La Favorite* as well as in the two parts she created in La Fiancée de Corinthe* and La Coupe du roi de Thulé.* She moved to the new opera house with the troupe in 1875 and sang Amnéris of Aïda* for the premiere of Giuseppe Verdi's* work there on 22 March 1880 before retiring. At the Garnier Palace*, she had also been billed as Léonore in La Favorite (1875), Fidès in Le Prophète* (1876), Catarina Cornaro in La Reine de Chypre* (1877), and Gertrude in Hamlet* (1878).
BIBLIOGRAPHY: DBF 6, 683-84; EFC 149; EZF 144-46; GE VI, 1142; Lajarte II, 164-65, 203-4, 246; SW 27, 89, 108-9, 177-78, 180.

La Bohème is an opera in four tableaux with a score by Giacomo Puccini* and a libretto by Giuseppe Giacosa and Luigi Illica* based upon Henry Murger's Scènes de la vie de bohème. It had its world premiere at the Teatro Regio in Turin on 1 February 1896. The following year it was produced in Alexandria, Moscow, Lisbon, Milan, Manchester (in English), Belrin (in German), Rio de Janeiro, London, Vienna, Los Angeles, and the Hague. In 1898, it was staged in Prague, Barcelona, Athens, and New York before having its Paris premiere on 13 June 1898 at the Théâtre-

Lyrique in the place du Châtelet, where the Opéra-Comique was performing after the destruction by fire of the salle Favart in 1887. Adolphe Maréchal (Rodolphe) and Julia Guiraudon (Mimi) headed the cast for this production of Puccini's work billed under the title of La Vie de Bohème. The work was taken by the Opéra-Comique to their new theatre in the place Boïeldieu on 11 January 1899, and the company went on to mount the work on 1,496 dates between 13 June 1898 and 2 April 1972. Its last production by the company saw Georges Liccioni as Rodolphe, Michel Dens as Marcel, Andrée Esposito as Mimi, and Hélia T'Hézan as Musette.

The opera opens in an attic on the Left Bank in Paris. It is cold, and Marcel is painting a canvas entitled The Passage through the Red Sea, while Rodolphe is writing. They decide to warm up the room by burning the latter's manuscript, and the philosopher Colline joins them with a load of books. Two delivery boys bring in wood, wine, food, and cigars purchased by the musician Schaunard, who has managed to earn some money. The four young men are enjoying themselves in these circumstances, when there is a knock on the door. It is the landlord looking for his rent. Fortunately his tenents have evidence of his conjugal infidelity, and they are able to counter his demands for money by threatening to expose his irregular behavior. They push him out of the room and decide to go to the café Momus to celebrate Christmas Eve. Rodolphe stays behind to finish an article. A second knock is heard. It is Mimi asking for help. She needs a match to light her candle. She enters the room and faints from exhaustion; Rodolphe revives her and lights her candle. She is about to leave, when she discovers that she has lost her key. Her candle blows out again. Rodolphe and she crawl around the room in their quest for her key, and they continue to grasp each other's hands. Rodolphe finds the key at least, but he slips it into his pocket. They give up their search to talk about their interests, hopes, and activities. Rodolphe's friends call up to him to hurry, and he puts his arm around Mimi. They admit their sudden love for each other and leave for the café Momus (tabl. 1).

The second act moves to the Latin Quarter, where the crowd is observing Christmas Eve. Screaming mothers are trying to control their hyperactive children; merchants are selling chestnuts, beer, coffee, dates, nougat, fish, oranges, candy. Rodolphe and Mimi continue to whisper words of love to each other, and they sit down with Rodolphe's companions to dine. Parpignol enters with his cart of toys, and the children renew their screams. The four men and Mimi are about to drink a toast, when Marcel's former sweetheart Musette enters with her present lover, old and wealthy Alcindor. They sit near the company of artists, and Musette tries to capture Marcel's attention. She goes so far as to throw a dish to the ground, but he continues to ignore her. Alcindor tries in vain to quiet her. She pretends that her feet hurt, and Alcindor falls victim to her ruse by rushing off to buy a new pair of shoes for her. While he is gone, Marcel succumbs to her charms, and they embrace. The waiter brings the two bills, and Musette assures him that Alcindor will pay, while she leaves with Marcel and the rest of the crowd following a parade (tabl. 2).

The third tableau moves to the place de la Barrière just before sunrise. Mimi enters in the cold and snow. She is looking for Marcel, who paints signs for the owner of a neighborhood café where he lives. The sun rises, and she comes upon him. She explains to him that he must help her because Rodolphe has just left her, although she knows that he still loves her. Rodolphe emerges from the café, where he has been sleeping, and Mimi hides behind a tree. Rodolphe explains to Marcel that Mimi is quite ill. Marcel tries in vain to prevent Mimi from overhearing this account of how sick she is, and her coughing betrays her presence. Rodolphe takes her in his arms, but she bids him farewell. Musette comes from the café, where she has been flirting with a stranger. She and Marcel begin to quarrel again, and she defies him by reminding him that she is not his wife. She announces that she is leaving him, but Mimi and Rodolphe decide to remain together until spring (tabl. 3).

The action returns to the attic of the first act, where Marcel tells Rodolphe that he has seen Musette and Mimi riding in splendid carriages and wearing expensive clothes. The four friends dine on a crust of bread and a bottle of water while joking about their impoverished style of life. They are dancing as if to celebrate their way of living, when Musette enters. She is followed by Mimi, whom they place on the bed. Musette tells them that Mimi wished to see Rodolphe because she had a premonition of dying. Musette directs Marcel to pawn her earrings to buy a bottle of cordial. She reminds him to fetch a doctor. Mimi asks for a muff to warm her hands, and Musette leaves with Marcel to find a muff. Colline decides to pawn his coat. Alone with Rodolphe, Mimi declares her love to him, and he assures her of his love for her. They recall their first meeting on Christmas Eve. Musette returns with a muff for Mimi; she begins to pray for the dying girl, and Marcel warms a cordial for her. Rodolphe hangs his coat over the window to keep the sun from shining into Mimi's eyes. He is about to give her the warm cordial, when he realizes that she is dead (tabl. 4).

After its run of 75 years at the Opéra-Comique, LaBohème was taken to the Opéra for its premiere at the Garnier Palace* on 23 November 1973. Gian Carlo Menotti was in charge of the production on this occasion, and Luigi Samaritani did its sets. The opera was staged at its new Paris home during 1973-75, 1977, and 1979. Jeannette Pilou, Katia Ricciarelli, Andréa Guiot, Mirella Freni, and Kiri Te Kanawa have been among the stars to fill the role of Mimi in this period, while the part of Rodolphe has been sung by Carlo Cossutta, Jean Dupouy, Placido Domingo, and Giacomo Aragall. At its Garnier premiere, the other parts of La Bohème were assigned to G. Meloni (Marcel), J. Bruno (Musette), Yves Bisson (Schaunard), José van Dam (Colline), M. Roux (Benoît), and J. Loreau (Alcindor). It should be added finally that a gala performance at the Opéra on 19 June 1910 saw the following stars gathered to do only the third act of Puccini's work: Enrico Caruso* (Rodolphe), Géraldine Farrar* (Mimi), Antonio Scotti (Marcel), and Bella Alten (Musette).

BIBLIOGRAPHY: Giuseppe Adami, Puccini (Milan: Fratelli Treves, 1938), 30-38; Dominique Amy, Giacomo Puccini (Paris: Seghers, 1970), 47-55, 104-14; L'Avant-scène 20 (March-April 1979), 4-137; A. Billeci, "La Bohème" di Giacomo Puccini: studio critico (Palermo: Besca, 1931); "La Bohème," l'Avant-scène, Opéra 20 (March-April, 1979), 1-137; Mosco Carner, Puccini: a Critical Biography (Old Woking, Surrey: Duckworth, 1974),

328-47; Claudio Casini, Giacomo Puccini (Turin: Utet, 1978), 184-203; DDO II, 1194; Jean-Louis Dutronc, "La Première Mimi à Paris: Julia Gueraudon," Opéra de Paris 5 (January 1983), 14; Louis C. Elson, Famous Composers and Their Works (Boston: J. B. Millet Co., 1900), 148; Dante del Fiorentino, Immortal Bohemian (New York: Crown Publishers, 1962), 80-88; Arnaldo Fraccaroli, La vita de Giacomo Puccini (Milan: G. Ricordi, 1925), 79-103; Guido M. Gatti, "The Work of Giacomo Puccini," MQ 14 (1928), 216-54; André Gauthier, Puccini (Paris: Du Seuil, 1961), 61-78; Edward Greenfield, Puccini: Keeper of the Seal (Tiptree, Essex: The Anchor Press, 1958), 33-46, 222-24; Henry W. Hart, Hart's Guide to the Opera "La Bohème," Music by Puccini (New York: The Hart Publishing Co., 1909); Cecil Hopkinson, A Bibliography of the Works of Giacomo Puccini, 1858-1924 (New York: Broude Brothers, 1968), 14-19; Stanley Jackson, Monsieur Butterfly: the Story of Giacomo Puccini (New York: Stein and Day, 1974), 59-69; KCOB 1157-65; Gaston Knosp, G. Puccini (Brussels: Schott frères, 1937), 65-81; H. Ludwig, "Der Exodus der Gefuehle: Puccini's La Bohème in der Grossen Oper von Paris," Opern Welt 1 (January 1974), 24; Giorgio Magri, Puccini et le sue rime (Milano: Giorgio Borletti, 1974), 326-29, 360-67; Gerard Mannoni, "La Nouvelle Mimi à Paris: Leona Mitchell," Opéra de Paris 5 January 1983), 15; George R. Marek, Puccini: a Biography (New York: Simon and Schuster, 1951), 136-78, 330-34, 363-67; Wolfgang Marggraf, Giacomo Puccini (Leipzig: Philipp Reclam, 1977), 55-77; Guido Marotti, Giacomo Puccini (Florence: Valecchi, 1949), 49-81; Olivier Merlin, "La Bohème vue par Menotti, à l'Opéra," Le Monde 27 November 1973, 27; Modern Drama and Opera: Reading Lists on the Works of Various Authors, ed. Frederick W. Faxon (Boston: The Boston Book Co., 1915), 215-17; MSRL 171-72; OCM 595-602; OEN II, 345-49; OQE 252-58; PBS 71-72, 246; Leonardo Pinzauti, Giacomo Puccini (Turin: Eri, 1975), 47-62, 186-88; idem, Puccini: una vita (Florence: Ballechi, 1974), 41-58; Giacomo Puccini, Letters, ed. Giuseppe Adami, trans. Ena Makin (New York: AMS Press, 1971), 82-83, 87-88, 106, 108, 110, 113-15, 118-19; G. Rothon, "Menotti Produces Bohème," Opera 25 (March 1974), 246-48; Claudio Sartori, Puccini (Milan: Nuova academia Editrice, 1958), 129-88, 255-57, 366-67; Vincent Seligman, Puccini Among

Friends (London: Macmillan & Co., 1938), 31-40; Enzo Siciliano, Puccini (Milan: Rizzoli, 1976), 111-59; Richard Specht, Giacomo Puccini: the Man, His Life, His Work, trans. Catherine Alison Phillips (Westport, Conn.: Greenwood Press, 1970), 126-51; SSBO 314-15, 320-22; SW 222-23; Thompson 203, 2110; Richard Valente, The Verismo of Giacomo Puccini (Ann Arbor, Mich.: Braun-Blumfield, 1971), 129-43; William Weaver, Puccini, the Man and His Music (New York: E. P. Dutton, 1977), 130-32; WOC 177.

Boito, Arrigo (b. 24 February 1842, Padua; d. 10 June 1918, Milan) was admitted to the Milan Conservatory at age 14, and his work here won him a scholarship enabling him to continue his studies in France and Germany. He returned to Italy to be caught up in the Garibaldi movement, but, in the meantime, he continued to work on his opera Mefistofele* designed to clarify and to win acceptance for the new ideas about the lyric theatre that his experiences in northern Europe had awakened in his mind. After working on his composition between 1866 and 1868, he produced it at La Scala on 5 March 1868. Mefistofele was given only three performances in Milan before it was withdrawn from the stage, and it seemed that Boito's work was a failure. He revised it over the next six or seven years, however, and it was brought back to the stage in Bologna during 1875, when it started on its successful career in the international repertory. Its second act was produced as early as 5 April 1883 at the Garnier Palace*, but it was given in its entirety at this same theatre for the first time on 9 May 1912.

It will be recalled that Boito's librettos for Verdi's Otello* and Falstaff* were likewise used at the Opéra in Paris.

BIBLIOGRAPHY: AEM II, 73-77; Ferdinando Ballo, Arrigo Boito (Turin: Edizioni Arione, 1938); BBD 195-96; A. Borriello, Mito, poesia e musica nel "Mefistofele" de Arrigo Boito (Naples: Guida, 1950); CBCM 599-602; EDS II, 701-6; EGC 50-52; ELM I, 424; John W. Klein, "Verdi and Boito," MQ 14 (1928), 158-71; idem, "Boito and His Two Operas," M&L VII (1926), 73-80; Adriano Lualdi, "Arrigo Boito, un'anima," RMI 25 (1918), 524-49; MSRL 28; Piero Nardi, Vita de Arrigo Boito (Milan: Mondadori, 1944); NEO 91; Luigi Pagano, "Arrigo Boito: L'artista," RMI 31 (1924), 199-234;

Raffaello de Rensis, Arrigo Boito (Florence: Sansoni, 1942); SSBO 250-51; Fausto Torrefranca "Arrigo Boito," MQ 6 (1920), 532-52; Massimiliano Vajro, Arrigo Boito (Brescia: La Scuola, 1955); Stefano Vittadini, Il primo libretto del "Mefistofele" de Arrigo Boito (Milan: Gli amici del museo teatrale alla Scala, 1938).

Bonnehée, Marc (b. 1828, Moumours, Basses-Pyrénеés; d. ?), vocalist, studied music at the Conservatoire in Paris, where he won first prize for grand opera in 1852 and first prize for singing in 1853. He made his debut at the Opéra on 16 December 1853, when the program consisted of La Favorite* and La Vivandière.* He remained with the company for nearly a score of years and sang in a number of roles besides appearing in the premiere performances in Paris of Les Vêpres siciliennes* on 13 June 1855, La Rose de Florence* on 10 November 1856, La Magicienne* on 17 March 1858, and Pierre de Médicis* on 9 march 1860. He sang Guy de Montfort, the duke, Stello, and Julien de Medícis, respectively, in these four compositions.
BIBLIOGRAPHY: Chouquet 415-18; EZF 146-47; Lajarte II, 218, 221, 224, 227; Lermina 182.

Borghi-Mamo, Adélaide (b. 9 August 1826, Bologna; d. 28 September 1901, Bologna), vocalist, made her debut at Urbino in 1846 and was invited by Colonel Ragani to come to the Théâtre-Italien in 1853. She remained at this theatre for three years and then accepted a contract to sing at the Opéra in 1856.

Endowed with a remarkable mezzo-soprano voice, she was as popular at the Imperial Theatre of the Opéra as she had been with the Italians. She made her debut as Fidès in Le Prophète,* which was revised for her on 17 September 1856, and receipts on days when Giacomo Meyerbeer's* work was billed increased immediately to the 10,000 franc level. La Favorite* was brought back to the stage for her on 24 November 1856, but the financial results were not as spectacular, although they remained at more than 8,000 francs for eight of the nine performances of Domenico Gaetano Donizetti's* work in 1856.

In 1857, E. Pacini's French version of Il Trovatore* had its Garnier palace* premiere on 12 January 1857, and Borghi-Mamo was cast as Azucéna.

One of the few truly successful works in French translation, Giuseppe Verdi's* text provided an excellent vehicle for the singer's third hit in four months at the Opéra. Her fourth role was Méluzine in Jacques Halévy's* La Magicienne* given its initial performance on 17 March 1858. This part and the role of Olympia in Herculanum* given its premiere on 4 March 1859, were Borghi-Mamo's last triumphs at the Opéra. The latter work was given on six consecutive programs between 4 and 15 April 1859 and earned more than 9,000 francs at each of these presentations.

The mezzo-soprano returned to the Théâtre-Italien in 1860, and she was never again billed at the Opéra. She went to London to make her début at Her Majesty's Theatre on 12 April 1860, and she went on to visit Russia, but she then returned to Italy and eventual retirement to Florence.

BIBLIOGRAPHY: Chouquet 416-17; EFC 146; Fétis Suppl. I, 110; GE VII, 409; ICM 210; Lajarte II, 221-22, 224-26; SW 90, 178, 216.

Boris Godounov, by Modeste Moussorgsky* and Nikolay Rimsky-Korsakov,* was based on the drama of the same name by Aleksander Pushkin. It had its world premiere in St. Petersburg in 1874, but it was not billed at the Opéra in Paris until 19 May 1908, when the troupe of the Imperial Opera of Moscow presented it at the Garnier Palace* in Russian but without the scene in the inn. A French version by Michel Delines was performed at the opera house in Lyons on 26 January 1913, and this text was used for its production at the Champs-Elysées Theatre in Paris on 22 May 1913. Louis Laloy completed the Delines translation only days after the Lyons premiere of the work, and it was this full version of the opera that was mounted at the Garnier on 8 March 1922, the date when a complete French text of Moussorgsky's work with revised instrumentation by Rimsky-Korsakov was created at the Opéra. The work itself was presented in a prologue, four acts, and nine tableaux; it was the eighth time that Moussorgsky's work had been billed at the Garnier in one form or another.

The prologue of the French version is composed of two tableaux, and the first of them opens with a crowd of peasants standing about in the courtyard of the Novodievitchi monastery. The police Exempt orders them to fall to their knees and to pray that the retired tsar will leave the monastery to resume his rule. The secretary of the Duma Tchelkalow reads a proclamation stating that the tsar will not return to his throne. The second tableau presents the square between the cathedral of the Assumption and the catherdral of Archangels. The people are kneeling, the bells are tolling, and Prince Chouiski wishes Boris Féodorovitch a long reign in a loud voice from the narthex of the cathedral. The people echo his sentiments, and Boris appears once again before his subjects. He will continue his reign. The carillons ring out, and the tsar returns to his palace with his children, Féodor and Xénia.

The first act opens in a cell of a monastery. Pimène is writing a book on national history based upon his personal experiences, and Grigori is asleep. He awakens and tells Pimène that he keeps having the same dream about falling from a tower, and Pimène advises him to pray to avoid troublesome dreams. Grigori voices the wish that he had had an exciting youth like Pimène, and his awareness of Pimène's extensive knowledge of the tsars prompts him to ask the older man about the age of the tsarevitch at his death. Pimène replies that he was Grigori' age when Boris killed him. Matins ring. Pimène leaves, but Grigori remains in the cell to ponder Boris' escape from justice (tabl. 3).

The scene shifts to an inn near the Lithuanian border, where two monks named Missail and Varlaam enter with Grigori disguised as a peasant and calling himself Dimitri. They ask for alms and wine, and Varlaam drinks until he falls asleep. Dimitri-Grigori asks the innkeeper where the road leads, and she verifies that it goes to Lithuania. She assures them that the border is only a day distant, but she warns them that Moscow has sent out word to arrest a fugitive making his way to Lithuania. At this moment, an officer and his patrol enter and ask Grigori to explain his presence. He assures them that he is from the region and is accompanying the monks on their quest for alms. The officer cannot read the warrant that he is carrying, and he hands it to Grigori, who reads it while changing the description of the fugitive to match Varlaam's appearance. The latter awakens from his stupor and reads the real description that fits Grigori, who pulls his knife and escapes through a window (tabl. 4).

The second act opens in Boris' apartments in Moscow, where Fédor is studying geography, and Xénia is reading with her governess. She is sad, because her fiance has died. Her governess tries to comfort her by singing alone or with the tsaravitch Féodor. Boris tries to restore Xénia's spirits and urges her to forget her worries. He reminds Féodor that he must work to prepare to rule a vast empire, and he confides to him that the power of his position has become for him a source of worry and misfortune. Alone now, Boris cannot sleep. He has visions of young Dimitri covered with blood. Prince Chouiski enters, and Boris denounces him as an intriguer, but the intruder is undeterred and tells Boris that a claimant to the throne has won the support of the pope and other important parties. His name is Dimitri, of course, and alarmed Boris orders the borders closed. He asks Chouiski whether he is certain that he saw the tsarevitch dead. The prince answers affirmatively and gives him the gruesome details to which he was a witness. Boris collapses under the weight of his troubled conscience (tabl. 5).

The third act transpires at the château of Sandomir in Poland. here, Marina Maichek dismisses her retinue to dwell upon the only trace of adventure in her life provided by Dimitri, who is trying to overthrow Boris. She decides to win the powerful lords of Poland over to his cause and to make herself empress of Russia by marrying Dimitri. Père Rangoni enters to urge her to charm Dimitri with all her feminine wiles so that the church will prosper in Russia. At first she refuses, but she cannot withstand his threats of condemnation, and she agrees to do his bidding (tabl. 6).

Dimitri serenades Marina Maichek from the park outside her window, and Père Rangoni assures him that she will see him shortly. Dimitri refuses to believe him, but Rangoni asserts that she is helplessly in love with him. Dimitri is so overjoyed to hear these words that he vows to make her empress. Père Rangoni has no idea that Dimitri is really Grigori, and he blesses Dimitri (Grigori) for this promise, but he suggests that he hide because her guests are coming into the park with her. The Polish nobles with Marina swear to overthrow Moscow, and they flatter their hostess extravagantly. Dimitri remains crushed in his hiding place, and he vows now to destroy Poland. Marina tells him that she treasures his love, however, and Grigori-Dimitri returns to the status of a fervent suitor until she reminds him that she will accept him only if she is tsarina. He informs her that he is planning to return to Moscow in the morning without her; he observes sarcastically that he will be amused to see her apologizing at his feet, when he has deposed and replaced Boris. She asks him to forgive her hasty words; she pleads that she meant only to describe her confidence in his future greatness. She calls him her king, and they embrace. The Polish nobles and the Jesuit are pleased with this turn of events (tabl. 7).

The scene is set in a clearing in the forest of Kromy, where a group of vagabonds tie up and abuse the Boyar Khroutchov. They taunt him because he was a favorite of "that thief Boris." They sing songs referring to Boris' crimes; Varlaam and Missail enter with the suggestion that they accept as their tsar the son of Ivan, Dimitri. Lovitzki and Tcherniakovski call for Dimitri to become emperor, but the anticlerical crowd drags them off into the woods. Dimitri's army arrives, and he promises to bring aid and relief to Russia. He continues on his way, and everybody except an idiot follows him. Left behind, the idiot grieves over the future of Russia (tabl. 8).

The Duma is convened in extraordinary session in the Kremlin to decide the fate of Dimitri-Grigori. He is not in custody, but all agree that he should die, and the suggested methods of execution are brutal beyond description. Prince Chouiski describes how Boris looked, when he saw him last: tortured, frightened, trembling, sweating, weeping. Boris enters the room. He is distraught, but he denies that he is a murderer and declares that Chouiski should be quartered for perjury. An aged stranger seeks admission to the room. It is Pimène. He describes how a blind shepherd told him to pray on the tomb of the tsarevitch Dimitri in Ouglitch. He followed these directions, and his sight was restored. It is evident, therefore, that Dimitri is dead. Boris calls for his son, and Féodor is brought into the room to comfort his father. The tsar tells his son to rule wisely, to suppress the revolt in Lithuania, and to take care of Xénia. He prays for forgiveness and dies.

Boris Godounoff proved very popular at the Opéra, where it enjoyed 251 performances between the time of its premiere and its last performance at the Opéra on 23 January 1970. The last eight of these presentations were given by the Bolshoi theatre Company. The artists of the National Academy of Music who helped create the opera at the Garnier Palace included Germaine Lubin (Marina), Ketty Lapeyrette (the innkeeper), Jeanne Montfort (Xénia's nurse), Yvonne Courso (Féodor), and Jeanne Laval (Xénia) (see twentieth-century volume for Lubin and Lapeyrette). The principal male roles were filled for the first time by Vanni Marcoux (Boris), John Sullivan (Dimitri), A. Huberty (Pimène), André Gresse* (Varlaam), and Henri Fabert* (Prince Chouisky) (see twentieth-century volume for Marcoux and Huberty).

It is a tribute to the theatricality of the work that it overcame early hostility or puzzlement to win acceptance as soon as audiences realized that the composition was to be viewed as a musical chronicle composed of acts and scenes making no claim to cohesive unity but being effective and valid each in its own right. The scenes that seem to have proved most popular in France are the military scene of the prologue, the inn scene of the first act, and the closing act after Boris' appearance.

BIBLIOGRAPHY: AB I, 95-100; Gerald Abraham, "Mussorgsky's Boris and Pushkin's," M&L 26 (1945), 31-38; Marie Olénine d'Alheim, Le legs de Moussorgski (Paris: Eugène Rey, 1908), 34-63; Pierre d'Alheim, Moussorgski (Paris: Mercure de France, 1896), 145-89; L'Avant-scéne 27-28 (May-August 1980), 1-250; Alfred E. Bacharach, The Lives of Great Composers (London: Gollancz, 1935), 380-85; Charles-Barzel, Moussorgsky (Paris: Emile-Paul frères, 1939), 59-67; Alexander Benois, Reminiscences of the Russian Ballet, trans. Mary Britnieva (London: Putnam, 1941), 267-70; M.-D. Calvocoressi, Moussorgsky (Paris: Félix Alcan, 1911), 188-208; DDO I, 163-64; Vladimir Fedorov, Moussorgsky (Paris: Renouard, 1935), 54-58, 75-108; Scott Goddard, "Editions of Boris Godunov," M&L (1929), 278-86; Robert Godet, "Les deux Boris," RM 3, no. 6 (1 April 1922), 1-17; A. Goléa, "Boris Godounov à l'Opéra de Paris," Musica

75 (June 1960), 20-23; Ratislav Hofmann, Moussorgski (Paris: editions du Courdrier, 1952), 181-220; JB 210-14; KCOB 888-900; Paul Le Flem, "Boris Godounov," L'Opéra de Paris VII (n.d.), 2-5; Marcel Marnet, Moussorgsky (Paris: Du Seuil, 1962), 105-30; MCDE II, 691-94; M. Montagu-Nathan, Moussorgsky (New York: Duffield and Co., 1917), 54-66; MSRL 138-40; Kurt Nilsson, Die Rimskij-Korssakoffsche Bearbeitung des "Boris Godounov" von Mussorgskij als Objekt der Vergleichenden Musikwissenschaft (Munster i W: Heinrich Buschmann, 1937); NMO 559-85; OEN I, 312-38; OQE 205-14; PBSW 67-69, 164; Arthur Pougin, "Opéra: Boris Godounow, opéra en trois actes," Le Ménestrel 74 (23 May 1908), 161-64; RCB 53-61, 66; Oskar von Riesemann, Moussorgsky, trans. paul England (Westport, Conn.: Greenwood Press, 1970), 181-222; SSBO 260-61, 263, 265-292; SW 50-52; Théâtre National de l'Opéra: Boris Godounow (Paris: 1908); The Musorgsky Reader (New York: Da Capo Press, 1970), 126-84; Thompson 2111-12; Vanni Marcoux, "Sur la mise en scene de Boris," L'Opéra de Paris VII (n.d.), 7-9; Emile Vuillermoz, "Boris Godounov à l'Opéra," RM 3, no. 6 (1 April 1922), 69-71; Mikhail O. Zetlin, The Five: the Evolution of the Russian School of Music (New York: International Universities Press, 1959), 194-224.

Borodin, Alexander (b. 12 November 1833, St. Petersburg; d. 27 February 1887, St. Petersburg), composer, was the illegitimate son of Prince Ghedeanov of Georgia and the wife of an army doctor. The boy received a splendid education with emphasis on music and foreign languages, and he wrote his first piece of music at age 14. In 1850, he entered the Academy of Medicine in St. Petersburg, where he showed an unusual interest in chemistry. He undertook a career related to chemistry, but he did not slight his music, and it was not long before he became one of the Great Five group formed to acknowledge Russian accomplishments in music.

Borodin became known as a composer especially because of his Prince Igor opera, from which the Danses Polovtsiennes* was extracted and presented in ballet form to Western Europe by Serge Diaghilev* and his Ballets russes.* This famous company brought this lively work to the Garnier Palace* on 7 June 1910, and it was followed by two other works featuring Borodin's music. Diaghilev used Borodin's music for the ballet Les Orientales on 11 June 1926; Mme Ida Rubinstein did likewise for her Nocturne performed at the Opéra on 29 November 1928.

Curiously enough, the opera Le Prince Igor has been given in the French version by Jules Ruelle at the Théâtre Royal de la Monnaie in Brussels (1924) and at the Grand Théâtre in Bordeaux (1927), but it has never been produced in its entirety at the Opéra. It had its first production in its entirety in Paris at the Opéra-Comique on 23 May 1932, when it was sung in Russian by the Russian Opera of Paris.

BIBLIOGRAPHY: AEM 11, 142-44; BBD 205-6; CAR 155-77, 501-2; CBCM 713-18; EDS 11, 850-52; EGC 53-56; ELM I, 430; Abraham Gerald, Borodin (London: Reeves, n.d.); MCDE I, 153-62; MSRL 29-31; NEO 98-99; OG 393-95; RCB 21-38, SSBO 299-300, 305-6; Thompson 212-14.

Bortniansky, Dimitri (b. 1751, Glukhov, Ukraine; d. 10 October 1825, St. Petersburg) is discussed in the twentieth-century volume.

Boschetti, Amina (b. 1836, Milan; d. 2 January 1881, Naples), dancer, was only nine years old, when she executed pas de deux and pas de quatre at La Scala in the ballet Lindor, and her success won her subsequent engagements in Turin, Florence, and Venice. Her first foreign tour was to the United Kingdom, where she performed for four years before accepting a contract at the San Carlo Theatre in Naples. Emile Perrin had become aware of her talents by this time, and he persuaded her to sign an agreement to dance at the Opéra after her sojourn in Naples.

At age 26 and at a salary of nearly 3,000 francs a month, Boschetti arrived in Paris and placed herself in the care of Adice, who set himself to the task of coaching her back into form after the recent illness she had had in Italy. He and his pupil exercised behind closed doors lest Parisians discover how heavy Boschetti had become, and the ballerine was able to start rehearsals for La Maschera* in the last weeks of 1863. This new ballet opened on 19 February 1864, and the combination of Rota's choreography and Boschetti's talents assured the acceptance of the work by Parisians, although the latter were inclined to think that the star was too stocky and inclined to overact.

Critics agreed that Boschetti's pointe work was impeccable, her elevation remarkable for a woman of her stature, and her strength beyond question, but Perrin was not too enthusiastic about her continuing at the theatre now that Martha Muravieva* had returned to Paris and was available for his future plans for the Opéra. Finally, Boschetti realized that she was being ignored intentionally when her name was omitted from the bill for a benefit program about to be held for the dramatic artists of the company. She complained, and she received billing for this occasion, but she was hissed and otherwise patently insulted during her performance. She sought satisfaction from M. Perrin, but neither explanations nor apologies were forthcoming. She packed her trunk and left the Opéra after her appearance in La Maschera on 30 May 1864. She enjoyed subsequent success in Belgium and Italy before her retirement from the stage in 1864. She was only 45 when she died of a heart attack.

BIBLIOGRAPHY: CB 280, 310-13; CODB 85; GE VI, 1016; Ivor Guest, The Ballet of the Second Empire (Middletown, Conn.: Wesleyan University Press, 1974), 181-91, 194-96, 204, 233-34; Lajarte II, 235; LXIX II, 1016.

Bosio, Angiolina (b. 22 August 1830, Turin; d. 13 April 1859, St. Petersburg), vocalist, was born into a theatrical family and studied music under Cataneo in Milan, where the impresario Barocchio offered her a contract at age 16 to appear in the Rè Theatre. She made her inconspicuous debut here in I Due Foscari before moving on to Verona, but it was her first engagement outside Italy in Denmark that won her any degree of popularity in Western Europe. She was flattered and offered every inducement to remain in Copenhagen, but eventually she had to quit the rigorous climate of this northern city, and she accepted a contract with the Circo Theatre in Madrid for 1847-48. It was at this time that she received an invitation to perform in the Italian Theatre in Paris, but she did not remain in the French capital very long, because she failed to impress audiences here and was free after the expiration of her agreement to join Marti's troupe for appearances in Havana, Philadelphia, New York, and Boston.

In 1851, Angiolina was back in Europe, where she married Xinda Velonis. She was tendered and accepted a contract next with the Royal Italian Opera in Rome, and she performed for the first time with this company on 15 June 1852 in L'Elisir d'Amore. As in Paris, she did not impress her audience, specifically because she followed Mme Michelle Viardot,* Mme Castellan, and Jenny Lind in the role of Adina. She sang next in Ernani, but her performance in this second work did little to enhance her reputation in her native land. Then, at the end of the season, her opportunity presented itself, when she was chosen to do Elvira in I Puritani after Temerlik fell ill, and la Grisi refused to stand in for her. At first, she seemed about to give another adequate but ordinary performance, but her second and third acts swept the spectators off their feet, and management rushed to offer her a flattering contract.

La Bosio was unquestionably a star of international standing now, and, in the spring of 1853, she did Gilda with the cast that presented Rigoletto* for the first time in England on 14 May in addition to interpreting Marguerita de Valois in Gli Ugonotti. But she also had an agreement to appear at the Paris Opéra in the rue Le Peletier* for 1852 and 1853. Here, she did the title-role of Giuseppe Verdi's Louise Miller* on 2 February 1853, Rosine in Le Barbier de Séville* on 9 December 1853, and the female lead in Domenica Gaetano Donizetti's Betly* on 27 December 1853. The Théâtre-Italien objected when she appeared in the French premiere of Gioacchino Rossini's* Il Barbiere di Seviglia,* but she was asked to return to this theatre in 1854 after a series of impressive performances at Rome, where she sang Le Comte Ory* among other works.

Mme Bosio had now traveled to nearly every country in Europe having an operatic stage, and she added Russia to her itinerary in 1855 by agreeing to sing at the Italian Theatre in St. Petersburg. She fell ill shortly after her arrival in this city, but she recovered and joined the artists to produce L'Etoile du nord on 4 January 1856 and La Traviata on October 1 1856. She then returned to Rome to repeat the role for which she was best known and most applauded, Violetta in La Traviata. She toured Europe again and started the season of 1858 in St. Petersburg as Violetta in a performance that won her a shower of jewels and other precious gifts. She was in England by May and opened her stay there at Covent Garden as Violetta. She returned to Russia in 1859, and the tsar named her his <u>première cantatrice</u> and presented her with another cluster of diamonds. Unfortunately, she caught cold one day during a ride through the city, and she lacked the strength to withstand the combination of her illness and the northern climate. She was dead in a matter of hours. All of St. Petersburg mourned her passing, and the German Opera company sang Mozart's <u>Requiem</u> at her funeral services in the Church of St. Caterine. her flower-covered casket was lowered into the ground in Saint Mary's cemetery.

BIBLIOGRAPHY: Chouquet 413-14 EFC 145; EZF 147; Fétis Suppl. I, 111-12; GE VII, 455-56; ICM 215; Lajarte II, 212-13, 215-16.

Bosquin (b. 29 September 1843, Deville-lès-Rouen; d. March 1909, Paris), vocalist, was very young when he was admitted to the Conservatoire in Paris to study voice and opera under the direction of Laget, Mocker, and Levasseur, but he distinguished himself by winning prizes in singing and the study of opera. He left school in 1865, and he began his career by traveling to different provincial opera houses until Carvalho* discovered him in Marseilles. The impresario booked him into the Théâtre Lyrique and other theatres, where he attracted attention with his interpretations of the male leads in <u>Martha</u> and <u>Les Noces de Figaro</u>. His success as Pylade in <u>Iphigénie en Aulide</u> finally won him a contract with the Opéra.

Bosquin made his debut at the Imperial Academy of Music in the rue Le Peletier* on 18 October 1869. When the company moved to the new Garnier Palace* after the war with Germany, he resumed his career on the stage of this opera house in the following roles.

Role	**Opera**
Léopold	<u>La Juive</u>*
Ruodi	<u>Guillaume Tell</u>*
Laërte	<u>Hamlet</u>*
Faust	<u>Faust</u>*

Octavio	Don Juan*
Alphonse	La Muette de Portici*
Raimbaut	Robert le Diable*

Bosquin made his debut at the salle Le Peletier as Fernand in La Favorite.* The only role that he created at the National Academy of Music was Sextus in Charles Gounod's* Polyeucte* on 7 October 1878.
BIBLIOGRAPHY: EZF 147-48; Henri Heugel, "Nécrologie . . . le ténor Bosquin," Le Ménestrel 75 (27 March 1909), 104; SW 75, 106, 109, 130, 152, 186.

Boudouresque, Auguste-Acanthe (b. 28 May 1835, Bastide-sur l'Hers, Ariège; d. 1905, Marseilles) singer, went to work for the railroad at Béziers before he moved to Marseilles in 1857 to become an inspector for the department of municipal street lighting in this city. He began to study at the Marseilles Conservatoire, where he won a prize for singing, but he continued to work and bought a café. On 5 September 1874, he was asked at the last moment to serve as a substitute on a program at the Valette Theatre. He was so successful as Silva in Ernani that he decided to apply for admission to the company of the Paris Opéra, where he was accepted on 1 January 1875.

Boudouresque made his debut at the Garnier Palace* as Cardinal Brogni in La Juive* on 10 April 1875, and he went on to create five parts at the premieres of the following works:

Role	Opera	Premiere
Timour	Le Roi de Lahore*	27 April 1877
Siméon	Polyeucte*	7 October 1878
Ramfis	Aïda*	22 March 1880
Le Légat	Henry VIII*	5 March 1883
Sparafucile	Rigoletto*	27 February 1885

The singer's rich bass voice made him especially eligible to fill roles demanding an authoritative presence on a political, social, or religious level, and he was cast as Melchtal and Walter in Guillaume Tell* and as Balthazar in La Favorite* during his first year with the Opéra. In 1876, he did Marcel in Les Huguenots* and Bertram in Robert le Diable.* After filling the part of Don Pédro in L'Africaine* (1877), he sang the role of the governor in Le Comte Ory* during 1880. His last assignment at the Opéra was Le Chant du départ, which he did for the first time at the Garnier Palace on 14 July 1883. He made several trips abroad and to provincial opera houses in France after his retirement from the Opéra, when he also devoted himself to the painting of marine scenes.

BIBLIOGRAPHY: DBF VI, 1267; EZF 148-49; Lermina 190-91; SW 25-30, 64-65, 89-90, 105-7, 111-12, 175, 181-84, 186-87.

Bouhy, Jacques (b. 18 June 1848, Pépinster, Belgium; d. 1929, Brussels), vocalist, studied organ, piano, and singing in Belgium and at the Paris Conservatoire, where he distinguished himself as a student of M. Victor Duvernoy* and M. Masset. He won first prize for opera at the latter institution and made his debut at the Opéra as Méphisto in Faust* in 1871. This same year, he sang the title-role of Erostrate* for the premiere of this work at the Le Peletier* theatre on 16 October in addition to appearing in the regular repertory. He transferred to the Opéra-Comique for the next five years and then accepted an engagement at the Théâtre-Lyrique, where he made his debut in Giralda on 12 October 1876.

Bouhy was in New York between 1885 and 1889, and the municipal government there commissioned him in 1886 to establish a municipal conservatory of music. His other engagements abroad included appearances at the Théâtre Italien in St. Petersburg and Covent Garden in London.

The baritone was back in Paris in 1890 to perform at the Eden Theatre, but he returned to the Opéra in May 1892. Previously, he had filled the roles of Alphonse in La Favorite* and had done the title-part in Hamlet* during 1878, and, in 1879, he had sung Méphisto in Faust and Don Juan. Also, he had been invited to contribute to the programs of the Pasdeloup and Colonne concerts.

BIBLIOGRAPHY: H. Moréno, "Reprise d"Hamlet à l'Opéra; le baryton Bouhy et Mlle Daram," Le

Ménestrel 44 (18 August 1878), 297-98; idem, "Début de M. Bouhy à l'Opéra," Le Ménestrel 44 (21 July 1878), 266; E. de Seyn, Dictionnaire biographique des sciences, des lettres et des arts en Belgique (Brussels: Editions L'Avenir, 1935) I, 81; SW 73-75, 84-89.

Bouilly, Jean-Nicolas (b. 24 January 1763, Tours; d. 17 October 1842, Paris), librettist, was raised by his father-in-law, who planned a career in law for him. A trip to Paris and introductions into the salons of Mme Necker and Mme de Staël induced Bouilly to turn to literature, however, and he was fortunate enough to have André Grétry write a score for his Pierre le Grand (1790) (See eighteenth-century volume for Grétry). He went on to do a number of plays and operas for the Paris stage including Deux Journées (1801) set for the Opéra-Comique by Luigi Cherubini.* His failure of 1818 entitled Les Jeux floraux* and provided with a score by Léopold Aimon was his only composition for the Opéra. Etienne Méhul, Nicolas Dalayrac, François Boïeldieu, and Daniel Auber* did the music for other pieces by Bouilly, who also wrote novels and memoirs besides the textbooks he composed for the schools of France during and even after his tenure on the Committee of Public Education (see eighteenth-century volume for Méhul, Dalayrae, and Boïeldieu). His last tutorial work was Contes offerts aux Enfants de France, a book he did at the request of the duchess de Berry for the count de Chambord and his sister.

BIBLIOGRAPHY: Chouquet, 388; DBF VI, 1333; E. Mercier Dupaty, Discours prononcé . . . en recevant M. Bouilly, membre de la Légion d'honneur . . . 27 Novembre 1837 (Paris: Mme de La Combe, n.d.); Lajarte II, 93; Ernest Legouvé, Jean-Nicolas Bouilly (Paris: Ducessois, 1842); LXIX II, 1086; Wks III, 239.

Boulanger, Ernest-Henri-Alexandre (b. 16 September 1815, Paris; d. 14 April 1900, Paris) was the son of the popular singer Mme Marie-Julie Halligner Boulanger and a violinist in the royal chapel. He was admitted to the Conservatoire in 1830 and studied solfeggio under Valentin Akan, counterpoint under Jacques Halévy,* and dramatic style with Jean-François Lesueur (see eighteenth-century volume for Lesueur). He won first prize in the 1835 competition for composition with his cantata Achille and continued his studies in Italy on a government subsidy until 1839. His first work was based on a libretto by Eugène Scribe,* Le Diable à l'école billed at the Opéra-Comique on 17 January 1842. This success was followed by the comic operas entitled Les Deux Bergères on 3 February 1843, Une Voix of 28 May 1845, and La Cachette of August 1847, all billed at the Opéra-Comique, where his most successful composition was the amusing Les Sabots de la marquise of 29 September 1854. Jules Barbier* and Michel Carré* did the libretto for this last work in a single act. Boulanger did a ballet entitled Zara for the Opéra, but it was never produced there, and management accepted and staged his opera in one act called Le Docteur Magnus* of 1864 by way of compensating him for his disappointment. Boulanger was professor of voice at the Conservatoire from 1871 to 1894.

BIBLIOGRAPHY: DBF VI, 1346 (after Marie-Julienne Hallinguer Boulanger); Fétis II, 41; Lajarte II, 236; LXIX II, 1089; Wks 7222, 8341, 8499, 14031, 14081.

La Bouquetière was an opera in a single act with music by Adolphe Adam* and words by Hippolyte Lucas.* It was based upon a vaudeville entitled Mes derniers vingt sous by Marie-Emmanuel Théaulon* and Ramond, which had had its premiere at the Gymnase Dramatique on 6 November 1824, and it featured scenery representing old Paris created by Thierry. Lucas' work enjoyed 22 performances at the Royal Academy of Music between its world premiere there on 31 May 1847 and 21 December 1849. It was revived on 27 January 1851 for another nine showings. It was dropped from repertory after its 31st billing at the Opéra on 6 February 1852.

The opera opens in the flower market of Paris in 1780 with a chorus of flower girls trying to sell their wares amidst a deafening din of their own making. The inspector warns them to be quiet and to behave like ladies. Finally, he has to order them not to speak (s. 1-2). Nanette enters singing of the importance of her merchandise to lovers. The inspector is so enchanted by her song and so captivated by her charms that he forgets to direct her to be quiet. He proposes marriage to her, but he is interrupted by a fracas in an adjacent gambling house. The florists forget themselves immediately and harass their customers who complain loudly about the shouting and the pushing of the flower girls. Nanette leaves to make up a special bouquet for a young man who stops at her stall every morning (sc. 3). The inspector orders his men to arrest the flower vendors and the unruly gamblers (sc. 4). Alone, the inspector cannot find Nanette, and he runs off to rescue her because he believes that she has been led off to jail with the other prisoners (sc. 5). The vicomte de Courtenai refuses to feel sorry for himself, although he has lost all his money in the gambling house; he decides to spend the remainder of his days in some modest retreat or in the army. He has twenty sous left, however, and he resolves to buy a lottery ticket before he faces poverty (sc. 6).

Nanette returns with the vicomte's bouquet, but he explains that he cannot pay for it. She is pleased to find that he is as poor as she is now, and they begin to feel a strong sympathy for each other. He gives her his lottery ticket to cancel his debt to her, and he leaves to enlist in the army (sc. 7). Nanette realizes that she has fallen in love with him (sc. 8). The inspector returns to the market; he is delighted to have eliminated Nanette's business competition and is deluded into thinking that she has a renewed interest in him until she asks him to close the recruiting office across the square to save her handsome young friend from the army. Inevitably, he refuses (sc. 9). The vicomte returns wearing the insignia of a recruit; he assures Nanette and the inspector of his future fame and glory as a warrior. Nanette is unhappy over his imminent departure, but the inspector makes no secret of his joy (sc. 11) and begins to propose marriage to Nanette. The fanfare announcing the lottery drawing drowns out his voice, and the lottery employees ask him to pick the number. He agrees reluctantly and draws Nanette's number (sc. 12-13). The vicomte rejoins the other conscripts about to leave the city, and he hears of Nanette's good fortune. She rushes up to him to explain that he is free because she has redeemed his enlistment papers. She offers him the lottery money, but he protests that he would lose it at the gaming tables. When he reveals finally that he is the vicomte de Courtenai, the inspector explains that the police are looking for him because his rich uncle in India has died and left him an estate worth millions. He agrees now to accept the lottery money and lead a quiet life if Nanette will be his bride. She acccepts his offer to the joy of everyone except the inspector (sc. 14-16).

The most striking passage in Adam's lively score was the overture, although at least five other portions of the music captured the attention of audiences: Nanette's couplets (sc. 3) and solo (sc. 8); the trio by Nanette, the vicomte, and the inspector (sc. 10); the lottery music (sc. 12); the chorus of enlistees (sc. 15). The principal roles were filled by Mlle Maria Nau* (the flower vendor), Ponchard fils (the vicomte), and Brémond (the inspector).

BIBLIOGRAPHY: AEM I, 76-77; Chouquet 408-9; DDO I, 167; Escudier, "La Bouquetière," FM 10 (6 June 1847), 189; Lajarte II, 185; Arthur Pougin, Adolphe Adam: sa vie, sa carrière, ses mémoires artistiques (Genève: Minkoff reprint, 1973), 188-89, 274; Wks II, 4930.

Bournonville, August (b. 21 August 1805, Copenhagen; d. 30 November 1879, Copenhagen) choreographer, received his first instruction in ballet from his father, a former colleague of the Auguste Vestris and Pierre Gardel (see eighteenth-century volume for Vestris and Gardel). He showed promise and was sent to Paris in 1820 to continue his studies with Jean-François Coulon and Auguste Vestris (see eighteenth-century volume for Coulon). In 1824, he continued his preparation for the stage with Pierre Gardel. After his graduation in 1826 from the ballet school associated with the Opéra, he was accepted into the corps de ballet of the company, but he remained in Paris only a brief time before returning to Copenhagen.

The young dancer resided in Denmark for the next 18 years of his career, although he traveled to Vienna once during this time. The first thing that he did upon his return to his native city was to introduce Jean Aumer's La Somnambule and Gardel's Paul et Virginie to his compatriots (see eighteenth-century volume for Aumer and Paul et Virginie). He realized quickly that Danish audiences considered ballet a decadent form of art, however, and he turned to subjects drawn from the national tradition to overcome this apathy when he began to create his own works. He was highly successful with this strategy and managed to bring large and enthusiastic audiences to the Royal Theatre with the 40 ballets, numerous divertissements, countless dances and curtain-raisers that he choreographed over the years (see eighteenth-century volume for divertissement).

A dispute in 1861 and 1862 with the director of the Royal Theatre induced Bournonville to leave Denmark for Sweden, but this episode had relatively little influence upon his authorship as a whole. His creations are rooted in Scandinavian lore, manners, and values, but his style was the result of his French training and was lodged in the balletic tradition extending from Noverre to Mikhail Fokine.* The choreography of his works is expressive, and the dancing in his ballets is always dramatically motivated. One of the striking differences between his ballets and the compositions of his contemporaries on the Continent, however, was the dominance in his pieces of the male dancers who had been reduced to the status of catchers on account of the growing popularity of such stars as Marie Taglioni* and Franzeska Elssler.*

BIBLIOGRAPHY: ACPM 151; Erik Aschengreen, "Auguste Bournonville," SDLD 118 (10 November 1979), 16-19; idem, "Auguste Bournonville, fiche technique," SDLD 118 (10 November 1979), 21; idem, "August Bournonville and the Romantic Ballet in Denmark," trans. Patricia N. McAndrew, Dance Perspectives 58 (summer 1974), 33-52; L'Avant-Scène, Ballet-Danse 6 (May-September 1981), 80-102; Auguste Bournonville, My Theatre Life, trans. Patricia N. McAndrew (Middletown, Conn.: Wesleyan Unitersity Press, 1979); idem, "Souvenir de ton père," D Mag 41, no. 5 (May 1967), 50-54; Erik Bruhn and Lillian Moore, Bournonville and Ballet Technique (New York: Macmillan, 1961); CODB 87; Margaret Crosland, Ballet Carnaval (New York: Arco, 1955), 12; Jean-Claude Diénis, "Festival Bournonville," SDLD 120 (10 January 1980), 7-12; EDB 72; EDS II, 925-28; GE VII, 808-9; Henry Godfrey, Iris M. Fanger, Selma Jeanne Cohen, David Vaughan, Rose Anne Thom, "The Bournonville Centenary, 1879-1979," D Mag 53 (November 1979), 67-82; Flemming Hjorth, "Augusta Bournonville: A life in Paris, 1846," D Mag 41, no. 6 (June 1967), 59-61 and 41, no. 7 (July 1967), 22-23; Flemming

Hjorth and Erik Aschengreen, "Bournonville Revisited; Excerpts from Letters," D Mag 41, no. 7 (July 1967), 22-23; LXIX II, 1136; Lillian Moore, "Bournonville's London Spring," New York Public Library Bulletin 69 (November 1965), 565-88; Kirsten Ralov, The Bournonville School (New York: Audience Arts, Marcel Dekker, 1979); RBP 63-64; Walter Terry, The King's Ballet Master (New York: Dodd, Mead & Co., 1979); Tobi-Tobias, "August Bournonville Centenary: The Festival in Copenhagen," D mag 54, no. 3 (March 1980), 58-65; T. G. Veale, "Debut Examination of August Bournonville," D mag 30 (August 1956), 36-37.

Bourgault-Ducoudray, Louis (b. 2 February 1840, Nantes; d. 4 July 1910, Vernouillet, Seine-et-Oise), composer, intended to pursue a career as a lawyer because his family had strong connections with the government of the Second Empire, but his interest in music led him to enter the Conservatoire in Paris. Here, he studied under Ambroise Thomas,* and, in 1862, he won first prize in composition for his cantata entitled Louise de Mézières. He became known to Parisians in 1868, when his Stabat Mater was heard at the Church of Saint-Eustache in Paris, and in 1874, when two of his compositions were included on programs organized by the Concerts Populaires.

Yet the theatre had a strong influence upon Bourgault-Ducoudray, and he wrote two operas called Michel Colomb (1887) and Bretagne (1892) besides his Thamara* in three acts performed initially at the Opéra on 28 December 1891. His music was also used in the scores of two ballets named Danses de jadis et de naquère* and Danses grecques,* performed at the Garnier Palace* on 22 September 1900 and 5 June 1901, respectively. His interest in the music of Greece induced the composer to write two monographs on the subject and to compile an anthology of Greek songs. He lectured on the history of music at the Conservatoire in Paris after 1878.

BIBLIOGRAPHY: EDS II, 921; ELM I, 435; Gringoire (pseud.) L'Oeuvre de L.-A. Bourgault-Ducoudray (Nantes: R. Guist'hau, 1898); Grove I, 845.

Bozzachi, Giuseppina (b. 23 November 1853, Milano; d. 23 November 1873, Paris), dancer, called attention to her agility and lightness of foot as early as 1857 when she was observed at age four imitating the airy grace of the angels on the walls of the San Paolo church in her native city. It was decided the following year that she should take dancing lessons, and it was not long before Amina Boschetti* of La Scala opera house noticed her precocity. The famous prima ballerina had agreed at this time to appear on the stage of the Paris Opéra, and the Bozzachi family followed her to the French capital, where Giuseppina took lessons with Mme Dominique. She appeared in an audition before Emile Perrin and Charles Saint-Léon* in 1868 at age 15. After winning a contract for six years on condition that she not perform in public before 1870, she returned to her work with renewed energy. The death of her father was a severe blow to her, but she was able to continue her lessons because the Italian Benefit Society of Paris augmented her salary and paid for her tuition.

Perrin had been director of the Opéra since 1868; he was planning to stage a new ballet to be created by Saint-Léon, Charles Nuitter,* and Léo Delibes,* the trio that had been responsible for the success of La Source* in 1866. Perrin was a skilled businessman by now, of course, and he knew that he should have a ballerina of the calibre of Adèle Grantzow* to dance in the leading role of the projected work. Plans were accordingly made for the recent star of Giselle,* and Néméa* to do the female lead in Coppélia,* and she was scheduled to appear at the opera house to begin rehearsals on 22 July 1867. Unfortunately, there were delays, and Adèle Grantzow fell ill in the summer of 1869, when it was thought that it would be possible at last to mount the new composition. She could not honor her commitment to create Swanhilda in Delibes' new work, and the situation seemed hopeless, when Perrin and Saint-Léon found the solution to their problem in the young dancer from Italy in Mme Dominique's class only a stone's throw from the theatre in the rue Le Peletier.* Any likelihood that Adèle Grantzow would recover in time to dance in Coppélia was eliminated when she injured her foot severely during a performance in St. Petersburg.

Giuseppina Bozzachi danced in the dress rehearsals of 21 and 22 May 1870 and in the premiere of 25 May 1870, which was also the date of Napoleon III's last visit to the Imperial Academy of Music. Her debut was an enormous success, and the spectators' enthusiasm was so overwhelming that the excited ballerina of 16 forgot to bow in the direction of the box where the emperor and the empress were applauding. The press was excellent the following day, and Giuseppina seemed well on her way to a series of triumphs. Management was optimistic about her future and offered her a new contract that doubled her initial salary of 6,000 francs. She danced Swanhilda on 14 programs before the eruption of the Franco-Prussian War on 19 July 1870. The Opéra remained open, however, and Coppélia was kept in the repertory until 31 August. Then fate intervened, and Saint-Léon dropped dead on 2 September, while the Germans gained total control of Paris on 18 September. Parisians were starving by November, the month when Mlle Bozzachi's health cracked, and she had to be put to bed. A victim of starvation as well as of fatigue, she succumbed to smallpox on her 17 birthday, 23 November 1870, and her funeral mass was held two days later at the church of Saint-Eugène. Perrin, Nuitter, and even aged Daniel Auber* were in attendance. Interment was in the Montmartre Cemetery, where the legend "Star of the Opera" was inscribed on the wooden cross marking her grave.

BIBLIOGRAPHY: ACD 78; "A propos de Coppélia: une étoile de seize ans, Giuseppina Bozzachi," Opéra 24, 32-33; Chouquet 424; CODB 89; EDB 73; EZF 149-50; Ivor Guest, The Ballet of the Second Empire (Middletown, Conn.: Wesleyan University Press, 1974), 230-31, 233-35, 241-42, 244-49, 251-53; edem, "Birth of Coppélia," D Mag 32 (February 1958), 52-53; idem, "Coppélia 1870," Ballet 2 (December 1946), 41-46; Serge Jouhet "La Première Swanilda: Giuseppina Bozzachi," Opéra de Paris II (1 October 1983), 33-34; Lajarte II, 244-45; Lillian Moore, Artists of the Dance (New York: Thomas Y. Crowell, 1938), 145-46; Arthur Pougin, "Nécrologie musicale: Giuseppina Bozzachi," Le Ménestrel 38 (10 March 1872), 117.

Brahms, Johannes (b. 7 may 1833, Hamburg; d. 3 April 1897, Vienna). For his music at the Opéra, see the twentieth-century volume.

Bréval, Lucienne (b. 4 November 1869, Berlin; d. 15 August 1935, Paris), vocalist, whose true name was Berthe-Agnès-Lisette Schilling, was a soprano of Swiss parentage who became a French citizen by reason of her long association with the Opéra and her lengthy residence in Paris. After studying at the Conservatoire in Geneva, she came to the French capital to continue her studies at the Conservatoire here under the guidance of Victor Warot,* Louis Obin,* and Alfred Giraudet.* She won first prize for opera in 1890 and made her debut on 20 January 1892 at the Opéra in Giacomo Meyerbeer's* L'Africaine.* She would sing the role of Sélika at the 484th and last presentation of this work a decade later on 8 November 1902. In fact, her career at the Opéra lasted for nearly 30 years. It was interrupted by a London engagement in 1899, and she took time on 20 November 1901 to create the title-role in Jules Massenet's Grisélidis* at the Opéra-Comique. She also created the heroine of Gabriel Fauré's Pénélope at Monte-Carlo on 4 March 1913 besides appearing in its Paris premiere at the Champs-Elysées theatre on 10 May 1913 (see twentieth-century volume for Pénélope).

Yet it was the Opéra that she considered her professional home, and her activities at the Garnier Palace* testify to the plausibility of this conviction. In the first place, she created a dozen roles in French and Wagnerian compositions at this opera house. She sang Brunnhilde at the French premiere of La Walkyrie* on 12 May 1893 and appeared in the 100th and 200th performances of this composition on 13 March 1899 and 10 December 1910, respectively. She did Eva for the premiere in Paris of Les Maîtres Chanteurs de Nuremberg* on 10 November 1897 and Kundry for the initial Paris production of Parsifal* on 4 January 1912. She executed Yamina in La Montagne noire* (8 February 1895), Brunnhilda in Frédégonde* (14 December 1895), Marguerite in La Damnation de Faust* (as an oratorio, 21 February 1897), and Hilda in La Burgonde* (23 December 1898). She performed as Vita in the premiere of L'Etranger* on 1 December 1903 and in its 1916 revival. The three remaining parts she sang for the first time before World War I included Séphora in Le Fils de l'étoile* on 17 April 1904, the heroine of Massenet's Ariane* on 28 October 1906, and Guilhen in Fervaal* on 31 December 1912. After the war, her only creation was Salomé in Mariotte's lyric tragedy of the same name that was mounted for the first time on 2 July 1919.

The three decades between 1892 and 1919 saw Lucienne Bréval in an uncounted number of performances because she assumed the status of a house soprano almost immediatley after her debut. The roles in which the public accepted her with the greatest warmth and enthusiasm included Jemmy in Guillaume Tell* (1892), Vénus in Tannhäuser* (1895), Valentine in Les Huguenots* (1897, 1903), Chimène in Le Cid* (1900), Cathérine d'Aragon in Henry VIII* (1903), Brunehilde in Sigurd* (1905) and Siegfried* (1912), La Crépuscule des dieux* (1912), Phèdre in Hippolyte et Aricie (1908), Dolorès in Patrie!* (1916), and the title-parts in Aïda* (1895), Salammbô* (1899), and Armide (1905) (see eighteenth-century for Hippolyte et Aricie and Armide). It should also be recalled that Mlle Bréval had created the title-role of Massenet's Grisélidis* at the Opéra-Comique in her debut at this theatre on 20 November 1901. She sang the part of the heroine of Christoph Willibald Gluck's Iphigénie en Aulide for the first time at this theatre on 18 December 1907 in addition to appearing there as Lady Macbeth in Macbeth,* Carmen, and Pénélope in Fauré's work (see eighteenth-century volume for Gluck and Iphigénie en Aulide). She enjoyed the distinction of having created this last role at Monte Carlo on 4 March 1913.

BIBLIOGRAPHY: APD 192; DBF VII, 257; EFC 165-66; ICM 236; KRJ 58; Martin 56; H. Moréno, "Débuts de Mlle Bréval à l'Opéra," Le Ménestrel 58 (24 January 1892), 27; PBSW 173; RC 98-99; SW 28, 39, 41, 53, 62, 67-69, 81-82, 91, 96, 100, 106, 112, 115-16, 139, 151, 169, 171, 193-94, 202-3, 206, 225, 295; WOC II, 29, 95, 109, 139, 240.

Brézilia was a ballet in a single act with a score by count de Gallenberg. Its book and choreography were created by Filippo Taglioni, and its sets were designed by Philastre and Cambon (see eighteenth-century volume for Taglioni). It had its world premiere at the Opéra on 8 April 1835, when it was included on a program given for the benefit of Mlle Marie Taglioni.*

The curtain rises on the ballet to disclose a rampart of high rocks surrounding an isolated forest in America. It is dawn, and Zamore scales the cliff to discover a number of hammocks in which young women are sleeping. He recovers from his surprise long enough to kiss one of them named

Brézilia. Awakened suddenly, she blows her horn (sc. 1-2), and Zamore is obliged to hide in a thicket. The queen of the colony orders her subjects to find the intruder, while Brézilia remains on watch in the clearing (sc. 3-4). Zamore emerges from the undergrowth to present himself to Brézilia, who warns him that he is in mortal danger. The young man ignores her advice, but she shows him a papyrus declaring that it is the duty of the inhabitants of the region to hate all men.

The queen returns to camp, and fearsome Brézilia urges Zamore to hide because she has fallen in love with him. Méloé sees him disappearing into his hiding place, but she dismisses this incident and suggests that the company go hunting (sc. 5-7). The women depart, and Zamore leaves his shelter to rejoin Brézilia on the heights. He declares his love to her, but she obeys the law of her tribe and dismisses him. He promises to leave if she will admit her love for him (sc. 8-9). Méloé overhears their conversation; she blows her horn. Zamore finds himself surrounded by the women, and the queen condemns him to death, but the tribe persuades her to commute his sentence to slavery for life. The women compete in matches of skill, grace, and agility to see which of them will have Zamore in their service. Brézilia wins the contest, but she manumits her prisoner. Méloé accuses her of treason and warns the queen that he may escape as long as he is alive. She takes Brézilia and Zamore into custody with the consent of the queen, but Zamore becomes angry and seizes his club. He begins to run away with Brézilia, and the latter's friends join him. The queen tries to slay Brézilia with her bow, but Zamore intercepts the arrow. He tries to establish peace by inviting the queen and Méloé to join forces with Brézilia and him, but they refuse his offer. The two lovers leave with their friends. The queen and Méloé remain behind to nurse their anger and jealousy (sc. 10).

Also called Brésilia or Brézila, the ballet was not very popular, and it had to be withdrawn after only five presentations. The single male role was created by Joseph Mazilier,* and the other parts were filled for the first time by Mlles Marie Taglioni* (Brézilia), Amélie Legallois (the queen), Pauline Leroux (Méloé), Yolande Marie

Duvernay* (Mazila), Fitzjames (Alzire), Bernard (Darina), Forster (Zalpha), and Mme Alexis-Dupont (Zilia).
BIBLIOGRAPHY: Chouquet 398; Lajarte II, 151; Moniteur universel 117 (27 April 1835), 976; RBP 139-400.

Brifaut, Charles (b. 15 February 1781, Dijon; d. 5 June 1857), Paris), librettist, was raised as an orphan by two abbots and went to Paris as soon as possible to embark upon a literary career. He made the acquaintance of the actor Saint-Prix in the capital, and his new friend introduced him to other theatre personalities including the critic Geoffroy. His first composition was the tragedy Jane Gray that Talma read to Napoleon at Fontainebleau, but the emperor found certain passages politically unacceptable, and the work was suppressed. Like all men of letters at this time, Brifaut now wrote a poem celebrating the marriage of Marie-Louise and Napoleon before he undertook the work that was to prove his greatest and last success, Ninus II. After the triumphant premiere of this tragedy at the Comédie-Française in 1813, the playwright was rewarded with a professorship in history at the Conservatoire. His good fortune continued into the Restoration, and he frequented all the fashionable salons of Paris under Louis XVIII. He was elected to the French Academy in 1826. The only two contributions made by Brifaut to Opéra repertory were given during the first years of the new Bourbon rule. He collaborated with Joseph Dieulafoy,* on the librettos of Les Dieux Rivaux* in 1816 and of Olympie* in 1819.
BIBLIOGRAPHY: Charles Brifaut, Lettres inédites . . . à J.-M. Frontin (Dijon: Darantière, 1885); DBF VII, 309-10; Lajarte II, 88-89, 94-95; LXIX II, 1266-67; Charles-Emile Poisot, Notice sur Charles Brifaut . . . lue à l'Académie de Dijon (Dijon: Marie, 1859); Sainte-Beuve, Causeries du lundi (Paris: Garnier, 1925) XV, 322-26.

Briséis was a lyric drama in three acts with a score by Emmanuel Chabrier* and a libretto by Ephraim Mikhaël and Catulle Mendès. Marcel Jambon* and Marcel Bailly created the sets. It was heard at the Concerts Lamoureux in Paris on 31 January 1893, when its first act was given in concert. It had its world premiere at the Garnier

Palace* on 4 May 1899; it was revived in 1916, but it did not arouse much interest and had to be dropped after its 11th billing on 21 November 1916.

Only the first act of Briséis was ever produced at the Opéra, and the action of this initial version of the opera was distributed in such a way that the act seemed to constitute a unit unto itself. In the original and unfinished text, the curtain rises to disclose an empty sea, although the crew of Hylas' ship can be heard singing in the distance. When the vessel appears in the moonlight, it becomes evident that Hylas is headed for Briséis' home on the beach. He lands and serenades her. She comes to her terrace, and he throws her a bouquet. She asks him whether he has decided not to leave home, and he explains that he has come to bid her farewell once again. He reminds her that her parents are very wealthy and demand that her husband also be rich. Thus, he assures her, he is facing the perils of the sea only to amass enough wealth to win her hand. Briséis voices her misgivings about his voyage and suggests that he may succumb to the charms of some Asiatic beauty. Troubled, they swear eternal love to each other. The crew reminds its captain that it is time to weigh anchor; Briséis and Jylas say farewell to each other, and the sailors resume their singing. Left alone, Briséis wonders for a moment whether Hylas will remain faithful to her, but she rejects this disturbing possibility and picks up her sweetheart's flowers. She sits down on a garden bench to dream about her wedding day (I, 1-2).

Briséis' ailing mother Thanastô enters worn and haggard. She protests that she is dying, and her daughter begs her not to entertain this dismal notion. Thanastô ignores her daughter's request and prays to God to spare her, and Strakolès announces that Thanastô is addressing herself to the new god of the Christians. Briséis begs her mother to come to her senses, and Strakolès warns her to be careful of demons, but Thanastô retorts that her only regret is that Briséis has not yet become a Christian. Her servants help her into the house, while Briséis is expressing her willingness to die to save her mother's life. Thanostô promises her daughter that she will not forget her words (I, 3).

Briséis and the servants are praying to Apollon, when the catechist appears on the dunes. He is dressed in white and holding a cross. He prays for Thanastô's recovery, and Strakolès warns Briséis and the servants that the catechist is a priest of the new religion that worships a sad and jealous god. The catechist retorts that his Christ was a man of clemency and love who saved mankind. Briséis wishes to know whether her mother will survive, and the catechist assures her that her mother will be saved, if her survival is Briséis' wish. Also, she must accept baptism. Frightened Briséis hesitates, and he adds that they will go to a holy place, where she will live in a community of Christian women. The servants condemn this suggestion, and Briséis refuses to renounce her love for Hylas in favor of a love for Christ. She accuses the catechist of being a liar, but her mother returns to confirm the catechist's words and to bid her daughter to follow him. Ultimately Briséis agrees to depart with the catechist because she has sworn to surrender her life to save her mother. Thanastô sings a hymn of triumph when the catechist and her daughter disappear over the dunes (I, 4-5).

The later and completed version of the opera presents the return of Hylas to Corinth. He has lost his ship and cargo, and he comes upon his sweetheart at the moment of her baptism. She is torn between her vow of fidelity to him and her dedication of her virginity to God, but she promises to marry Hylas (II, 1-5). The prospective groom returns to his home to await Briséis and their wedding, but a funeral procession passes his house, and his bride fails to appear (III, 1-2). Night falls, and a spectre in white addresses him. It is Briséis, who informs him that he must rejoin her in her sepulcher if he would remain with her in eternal love (III, 3). The final tableau shifts to the cemetery, where Thanastô opens her daughter's tomb only to find Briséis and Hylas side by side among the flowers. Strakolès reminds her that she cannot undo the forces of fate (III, 4).

The title-role of Briséis was created by Mme Berthet in 1899 and was sung by Mmes Yvonne Gall* and Madeleine Bugg* in 1916. The other artistes to perform in its premiere were Mme Alba Chrétien-Vaguet* (Thanastô), Albert Baguet* (Hylas), Jean Bartet* (the catechist), and Fournets (Strakolès).

BIBLIOGRAPHY: *René Martineau,* *__Emmanuel Chabrier__* *(Paris: Dorbon Aîné, 1910), 114-24; Rollo Myers,* *__Emmanuel Chabrier and His Circle__* *(London: J. M. Dent & Sons, 1969), 109-18; Francis Poulenc,* *__Emmanuel Chabrier and His Circle__* *(Teaneck, N.J.: Fairleigh Dickinson University Press, 1970), 109-19; Frédéric Robert,* *__Emmanuel Chabrier, l'homme et son oeuvre__* *(Paris: Seghers, 1970), 124-29; Stoullig XXV (1899), 8-9; SW 52-53;* *__Théâtre National de l'Opéra-Comique: Exposition Emmanuel Chabrier en commémoration du centenaire de sa naissance__* *(Paris: Pathé-Marconi, 1941), 41-42; Yvonne Tienot,* *__Chabrier par lui-même et par ses intimes__* *(Paris: Henry Lemoine, 1965), 101-7.*

Bruneau, Alfred (b. 3 March 1857, Paris; d. 15 June 1934, Paris), composer, studied with Jules Massenet* at the Conservatoire in Paris. He played in the Pasdeloup Orchestra, and his cantata entitled Geneviève de Paris won a Prix de Rome for him, but his interests were directed almost exclusively toward the theatre. He wrote a three-act opera entitled Kérim for the Théâtre du Château d'Eau in the spring of 1887, and he went on to devote most of his time and energy to the composition of works for the stage.

Bruneau contributed the following six titles to the repertory of the Opéra-Comique in the 30 years between 1891 and 1920:

Work	**Premiere**
Le Rêve, lyric drama, 4a.	18 June 1891
L'Attaque du moulin, lyric drama, 4a.	23 November 1893
L'Ouragen, lyric drama, 4a.	29 April 1901
L'Enfant Roi, lyric drama, 3a.	3 March 1905
Les Quatre Journées, lyric tale, 4a.	25 December 1916
Le Roi Candaule, lyric comedy, 5a.	1 December 1920

After World War I, Bruneau's veristic operas lost their popularity, and he turned to a more sentimental type of composition because he realized that his Zola-inspired works were out of date. The following catalogue of his works produced at the Opéra reflects this post-1920 trend away from naturalism:

Work	Premiere
Messidor, lyric drama, 4a.	19 February 1897
Les Bacchantes, ballet, 2a.	30 September 1912
L'Ouragan, lyric drama, 4a.	17 February 1916
Le Jardin du paradis, lyric tale, 4a.	29 October 1923
Virginie, lyric comedy, 3a.	6 January 1931

Thus, Bruneau wrote 11 pieces shown at three lyric theatres in Paris between 1887 and 1931: the Château d'Eau, the Opéra-Comique, and the Opéra. Half of these works were in four acts, most of them were inspired by Emile Zola, and only one of them was a ballet. Also, one of them, L'Ouragan, was billed at two of the composer's preferred theatres. The Opéra-Comique seems to have been the theatre favored by Bruneau, if only to a slight degree.

BIBLIOGRAPHY: AEM II, 403-5; BBD 244-45; Adolphe Boschot, La Vie et les oeuvres d'Alfred Bruneau (Paris: Fasquelle, 1937); EDS II, 1194-96; ELM I, 456; Grove I, 980-81; Jean-Max Guieu, Le Théâtre lyrique d'Emile Zola (Paris: Fischbacher, 1983); Arthur Hervey, Masters of French Music (Plainview, N.Y.: Books for Libraries Press, 1976), 223-52; MSRL 35-36; NEO 104-5.

Bugg, Madeleine (b. 1894?, Rheims; d. 1936, Paris), vocalist, studied under Guillamat at the Conservatoire in Paris and made her debut as a soprano on 29 November 1913 at the Opéra. She sang Thaïs on this occasion, and she was cast as Marguerite in Faust* this same year. She did not perform in any new roles during 1914, but in 1915 she made her first appearance as la belle Gabrielle in L'Offrande à la liberté and as L'Infante in Le Cid.* She executed three roles in 1916: Rafaëla in Patrie!,* Mathilde in Guillaume Tell,* and the protagonist of Briséis.* After the war, she sang Desdémone in Othello* and Marguerite in La Damnation de Faust* in 1919.

Mme Bugg created eight roles during her tenure at the Garnier Palace* beginning with one of the Filles-fleurs in Parsifal* at the Paris premiere of the French version of Richard Wagner's* work on 4 January 1914. She sang Cérès at the premiere of Mademoiselle de Nantes on 9 December 1915. At the first presentation of Les Virtuosi de Mazarin on 6 January 1916, she performed as one of the singers, and she did Jeannine in L'Ouragan on 17 February 1916. Her last four creations in the French capital included one of the singers in Une Fête chez la Pouplinière on 25 May 1916, the title-role of Rebecca on 25 May 1918, and, after the war, Vénus in Camille Saint-Saëns'* Hélène on 20 June 1919, and l'Enfant in Raynaldo Hahn's Fête triomphale of 14 July 1919 (see twentieth-century volume for L'Ouragan, Une Fête chez la Pouplinière, Rebecca, Hélène, and Fêtè triomphale).

The gifted soprano sang for six years at the Opéra, and she went on to appear in Barcelona and Lisbon in 1920 and in Rome during 1921. She traveled to South America in 1924 before returning to Italy and La Scala the same year. She did guest appearances in Marseilles, Toulouse, and Bordeaux before dropping out of sight about 1926-27. Then, in 1936, a Paris physician was about to do a dissection of a cadaver, when he recognized the corpse. It was the missing singer carrying papers under another name.

BIBLIOGRAPHY: EFC 189; KRJ 62-63; SW 53, 62, 69, 86, 110, 161, 165-66, 169, 171, 179, 295, 338, 365.

Burat de Gurgy, Edmond (b. 1809, Le Gers; d. 5 March 1840, Paris), librettist, left home to seek his fortune in Paris after the publication of two novels, La Prima Donna et le garçon boucher (1831) and Le Lit de camp (1832). He completed a third novel entitled Paillasse (1834) in the capital and collaborated on the composition of several comedies including Le Fils de Figaro (1835) and Deux Filles de l'air (1840). He did his only piece for the Opéra with Adolphe Nourrit,* Le Diable boiteux* of 1836.

BIBLIOGRAPHY: DBF VII, 678; Lajarte II, 154.

Burgmuller, Frédéric (b. 1804, Ratisbonne; d. ?), composer, studied music in his native city and then went to Cassel to study composition under Louis Spohr. He left for Paris after attracting the attention of the public in Germany by playing a piano concerto of his own composition there in 1832. He gave lessons on the piano in the French capital to support himself because his principal ambition was to remain there to write for the piano and for the stage. He did the score for La Péri* in 1843 and for one of the acts of Lady Henriette* in 1844. He disappeared from the operatic scene after the production of this second work, but he continued to publish a large number of light pieces for the piano.

BIBLIOGRAPHY: Edwin Binney, Les Ballets de Théophile Gautier (Paris: Nizet, 1965), 119; Fétis II, 117; Lajarte II, 173-74; LXIX II, 1424.

La Burgonde is an opera in four acts and five tableaux with a score by Paul Antonin Vidal* and a libretto by Emile Bergerat and Camille de Sainte-Croix. Joseph Hansen* created its choreography. It had its world premiere at the Garnier Palace* on 23 December 1898, when M. Claude Paul Taffanel* was at the desk, and M. Claudius Blanc directed the chorus. Its sets were furnished by the team of MM. Marcel Jambon* and Marcel Bailly (a. 1, 2, 3) and M. Carpezat (a. 4). Charles Bianchini designed its costumes.

The opera opens in a clearing in a forest of Orléanais. The tents and chariots of Attila's warriors are visible through the underbrush along with the areas reserved for their horses and cattle. The tents of Attila and his wives are pitched to the right. The tents of Hagen and Gautier stand on the left. It is the end of night, and a trace of dawn pierces the leaves.

Hagen emerges from his tent and is lamenting Atilla's tyranny, when Zerkan reports to him that his father, the king of Worms, is dead. He adds that his people are waiting for him to lead them in revolt against Attila and his Huns. Hagen reminds Zerkan that he, Ilda la Burgonde, and Gautier of Aquitaine are hostages. Thus, they must remain peaceful as part of the truce guaranteeing their regions from harm. He adds that Gautier of Aquitaine and he have become rivals for the hand of Ilda la Burgonde, and Zerkan promises him to help him win her affections in return for his pledge to free his subjects (I, tabl. 1, sc. 1).

Attila appears on the scene. Bérikh and Gautier d'Aquitaine return to camp with an ample supply of meat, and Hagen asks Ilda to marry him before Attila's assembled retinue. She does not answer him, and Attila commands her to speak. She remains silent. Angry Attila dismisses her and tells Hagen to return to Worms to rule his people (I, tabl. 1, sc. 2-4). Attila orders his subjects to celebrate the morning hunt (I, tabl. 1, sc. 5-6).

The scene changes to an enclosure in a corner of the camp where Gautier is waiting for Ilda. She appears and describes her fear of Attila, whom she detests. He suggests that they flee from the camp on the morrow during the festival, and he explains that they can encourage Attila to drink too much wine. He adds that they can always kill themselves if their plan to lead Aquitaine in revolt fails. She agrees (I, tabl. 2, sc. 1). Pyrrha, Attila's favorite, offers her help in making the lovers' plans succeed, and Zerkan overhears the trio's plans to deceive Attila (I, tabl. 2, sc. 3-4).

Attila's guests toast Gautier, the Scythian Sword, and the fields of Magog, and his warriors dance in honor of their fallen compatriots (II, tabl. 1, sc. 1-2). Zerkan plays the fool for Attila's amusement, and Attila's slaves entertain him with a ballet. Attila becomes so interested in the dance that Pyrrha decides that it is time for Ilda and Gautier to flee. Ilda leaves (II, tabl. 1, sc. 3-4). The dancing girls in Attila's retinue execute a ballet celebrating war, wine, and love. Drunken Attila mistakes Ruth for Ilda, but Zerkan points out to him that la Burgonde has disappeared. He flies into a rage when he learns that Ilda and Gautier have vanished, and he swears to have vengeance for this apparent treachery. Pyrrha snatches his sword, and he faints from anger, frustration, and drunkeness (II, tabl. 1, sc. 5). An unknown knight appears on horseback and demands 20 men to secure the return of the fugitives. Revived Attila accepts this sudden guarantee of success (II, tabl. 1, sc. 6-7).

The women of Arverne are lamenting the damage that the Huns have inflicted upon their country, and they manage to cross the Dordogne, but Ilda and Gautier arrive on the scene too late to join them. Gautier assures his sweetheart that he will find a way out of their predicament, and he begins to make a raft of logs and vines to cross the river into Aquitaine (III, tabl. 1, sc. 1-2). All goes well until Bérikh and his Black Horde of Huns enter and capture the lovers (III, tabl. 1, sc. 3-4).

The setting moves to Attila's wooden palace in Pannonie, where the disconsolate leader of the Huns is awaiting the appearance of Bérikh, the Unknown Knight, and Ilda. Pyrrha and the other women of his retinue are upset by Attila's dejected air, but the return of the Unknown Knight revives his spirits (IV, tabl. 1, sc. 1-3). He convenes his court to confront his prisoners and their captors, and the Unknown Knight unmasks himself. He is Hagen. He reminds Attila that he has kept his promise, and, he observes, it is now time for Attila to uphold his end of the bargain by granting him his wish. He would have Ilda as his bride. Ilda and Gautier protest, and Attila refuses the supplicant's request. He dismisses Pyrrha and makes Ilda the keeper of his sword, but he orders Gautier's execution. Ilda offers to become Attila's bride if he will free Gautier, but he refuses to listen to her plea (IV, tabl. 1, sc. 4). Gautier is led away to be prepared for execution (IV, tabl. 1, sc. 5-6). Angry Hagen repents his betrayal of Gautier and Ilda, and he decides to seek vengeance. The executioners set dry wood around the stake prepared for Gautier, and Attila gives Ilda his sword. Hagen rushes onto the scene of execution. He kills two guards and cuts Gautier's bonds. Gautier seizes a pike, but the other guards slay Hagen (IV, tabl. 2, sc. 7-8). Pyrrha helps Gautier to escape, and Ilda strikes Attila with his own sword. Attila's warriors arrive on the scene, but Gautier repulses them by raising Attila's Scythian Sword, which they are hesitant to confront. Pyrrha asks dying Attila to forgive her. Ilda and Gautier flee to Aquitaine for the second time (IV, table, 2, sc. 9-11).

La Burgonde was not well received by spectators, and it was dropped after its 11th performance on 25 June 1899. The leading female roles had been filled at its premiere by Lucienne Bréval* (Ilda), Meyrianne Héglon (Pyrrha), and A. Sauvaget (Ruth), while the male parts were sung initially by Albert Alvarez* (Gautier), Jean-

François Delmas* (Attila), Jean Noté* (Hagen), Albert Baguet* (Zerkan), and Jean Bartet* (Bérikh). The personnel of the ballet included Mlles Hirsch, Lobstein, Sallé, Girodier, and Hoquante.
BIBLIOGRAPHY: *SW 53-54.*

Büsser, Paul-Henri (b. 16 January 1872, Toulouse; d. 30 December 1973, Paris), French composer and conductor, began his musical education in the choir of the Toulouse catherdral. His manifest talents persuaded his parents to support his studies at the School of Religious Music and the Conservatoire in Paris. Charles Gounod* became interested in the young man's impressive musical ability, and he arranged for him to serve as organist in St. Cloud in 1892.

Büsser won the coveted Prix de Rome in 1893, and, after his return to France from Italy, he accepted the position of conductor at the Théâtre du Château d'Eau in 1900. Two years later, in 1902, he became musical director at the Opéra-Comique, where he made his debut on 16 September 1902 with Le Roi d'Ys. He was selected to conduct the orchestra at the Opéra-Comique for the world premiere of Le Cor fleuri on 10 May 1904, and he would also be at the desk for several presentations of Les Noces corinthiennes, for which he had done the score, but which would not have its world premiere at the Comique until 10 May 1922. He had also contributed Daphnis et Chloé (1897) and La Pie borgne (1929) to the repertory at the Favart Theatre.

In the meantime, however, M. Büsser presided at revivals of Christoph Willibad Gluck's Iphigénie en Touride and Orphée, Xavier Leroux'* La Reine Fiamette, Henri Rabaud's La Fille de Roland,* and Charles Gounod's* Le Médecin malgre lui (see eighteenth-century volume for Gluck, Iphigénie en Tauride and Orphée). He terminated his tenure at the Opéra-Comique in 1905, when he was asked to assume the directorship of the orchestra at the Opéra.

The conductor made his debut as leader of the orchestra at the Garnier Palace* with a performance of Gluck's Armide on 18 April 1906, and, during the course of his long career there, he presided over revivals of Thamara* in 1907, Rigoletto* in 1915, Patrie!* in 1916, Hamlet* and Roma* in 1917, Les Huguenots* in 1920, Le

Tourvère* in 1923, Giselle* in 1924 and Paillasse* in 1931 (see eithteenth-century volume for Armide). His responsibilities at the Opéra also included leading the orchestra at the Garnier premieres of nine operatic works presented on the following dates:

Title	Composer	Date
Le Sortilège	A. Gailhard	29 January 1913
Graziella	J. Mazellier	6 April 1916
Miguela	Theo. Dubois	18 May 1916
La Mégère apprivoisée	Ch. Silver	30 January 1922
Miarka	Al. Georges	16 January 1925
La Traviata	Verdi	24 December 1926
Persée et Andromède	J. Ibert	15 May 1929
La Vision de Mona	L. Dumas	15 October 1931
Les Noces corinthiennes	H. Büsser	22 April 1949

The conductor likewise proved the musical direction for a number of ballets danced intitally at the Opéra on the dates indicated:

Title	Composer	Date
Philotis	Ph. Gaubert	18 February 1914
Carême prenant	various	16 April 1916
La Favorite	Donizetti	24 May 1917
Le Cobzar	Mme Ferrari	27 June 1917
Taglioni chez Musette	extracts	4 May 1920
Le Rêve de la marquise	Mozart	11 May 1921
Petite Suite	Debussy	24 March 1922
Ascanio	Saint-Saëns	28 June 1922

La Nocturne des amoureuses	A. Fijan	20 January 1923
Laurenza	Franz Schubert	24 January 1924
Siang-Sing	G. Huë	19 March 1924
Soir de fête	Leo Delibes	30 June 1925
Le Rustre imprudent	L. Lambert	7 December 1931

M. Büsser had already presented his La Ronde des saisons* at the Opéra on 22 December 1905.

The conductor-composer's long service to the national lyric theatres was rewarded. He was asked to join the faculty at the Conservatoire, where he taught voice as early as 1904, and where he was invited to teach composition in 1931. He was elected to the French Academy in 1938.

BIBLIOGRAPHY: AEM II 527-32; EDS II, 1407-8; ELM I, 167; SW 104, 148-49, 155, 174, 204, 212-13, 224, 240, 255, 294, 302, 311, 318, 321, 324-25, 518; WOC 5, 121, 127, 133, 149, 334-35.

C

Calvé, Emma (b. 15 August 1858, Décazeville; d. 6 January 1942, Millau), vocalist, née Rosa Calvet, possessed a voice that ranged from A below middle C to E above high C, and she was accordingly a soprano and mezzo-soprano simultaneously. As if these gifts were insufficient, she followed technical advice offered her by the castrato Mustafa to increase her range even more. Thus, she could sing almost any role, and, in Le Mariage de Figaro* alone, she was named at different times to fill the parts of Cherubino, Susanna, and the countess.

Yet it can almost be said that Emma Calvé's ambition was to be an actress as well as a vocalist, because she studied declamation from Victor Maurel* and followed Eleanora Duse from city to city to learn her stage technique. She was too intelligent to neglect her voice, of course, and her teachers in this area included Marie Miolan-Carvalho,* Rosina Laborde, and especially Mathilde Marchesi.

As might be imagined, Calvé's repertory was extensive. It included the traditional parts of Lucia, Amina, Pamina, Marguerite, Juliette, Carmen, Ophélie, and Mascagni's Santuzza. Yet, despite her vocal capacity, she lacked time to do much else besides these roles because she did them so well that audiences insisted upon her repeating them. The demand for her to perform Carmen, Ophélie, and Santuzza was especially heavy, almost unrelenting, in fact, and it was her interpretation of La Vega's heroine that won her an international reputation and a contract at the Opéra-

Comique. Then, when she was cast for Carmen, she abandoned Galli-Marié's costume for a mantón de Manila and ignored her predecessor's dances in favor of el bracear style of dancing found among the gypsies of Seville. Her taste for realism was so marked that in some quarters, especially in London and New York, spectators protested that her portrayal of Georges Bizet's gitana was too lurid.

If Mlle Calvé was one of the most applauded vocalists of her time, she appeared only once at the Paris Opéra, where she did Ophélie in Ambroise Thomas'* Hamlet* on 29 May 1899. She would have appeared more frequently at the Garnier Palace* if she had not had highly profitable contracts at the Opéra-Comique and at the Gaîté and if she had not spent so much time abroad in New York, Madrid, and St. Petersburg. At the Opéra-Comique alone, she created Louise de la Vallière in Reynaldo Hahn's* La Carmélite (1902), Anita in La Navarraise* (1895), Leila in Les Pêcheurs de perles (1893) and Fany Legrand in Sapho* (1897). She was in revivals of Les Noces de Figaro (1886) as the countess and of La Flûte enchantée (1886) as Pamina (see eighteenth-century volume for Les Noces de Figaro and La Flute enchantée). She was selected to fill the title role at the 1,000th representation of Carmen on 23 December 1904.

BIBLIOGRAPHY: APD 206; Emma Clavé, sous tous les ciels j'ai chanté (Paris: Plon, 1940); idem, My Life, tans. Rosamond Gilder (New York: D. Appleton, 1922); idem, My Faborite French Songs (Boston: Oliver Ditson Co., 1915); Gladys Davidson, Opera Biographies (London: Laurie, 1955), 40-42; DBF VII, 929-30; EFC 173; David Ewen, Living Musicians (New York: H. W. Wilson Co., 1940), 71; GIR 128-32; ICM 275; Herman Klein, Great Women-Singers of My Time (Freeport, N.Y.: Books for Libraries Press, 1968), 149-55; KRJ 67-68; G. Odell, "Famous Precedent," Musical America 73 (1 December 1953), 10; Henry Pleasants, The Great Singers (New York: Simon and Schuster, 1966), 303-8; SW 110, 154; Desmond Shawe-Taylor, "A Gallery of Great Singers . . . Emma Calvé," Opera 6 (1955), 220-23; A. Wisner, Emma Calvé, Her Artistic Life (New York: 1902); WOC II, 241; Peggy Wood, "I remember Emma," ON 35, no. 15 (6 February 1971), 26-29.

Campagnola, Léon (b. 8 February 1875, Marseilles; d. 11 January 1955, Paris), vocalist, studied at

Marseilles and Paris before making his debut at the Opéra as Charles Gounod's* Roméo on 2 June 1910. He joined the Opéra-Comique in 1913 and remained in the French capital for the remainder of his career except for excursions to Chicago, Milan, and London. He bid farewell to the stage in Brussels in 1919 and returned to Paris to teach and to paint. His well disciplined tenor voice evoked applause especially in works by Georges Bizet* and Gounod.

His stay at the Paris Opéra extended from 1910 to 1913, and his first year at the Garnier Palace* saw him do the duke in Rigoletto* and the title-role in Faust* as well as Roméo. In 1911, he sang David in Les Maîtres Chanteurs de Nuremberg* and Armel in Gwendoline.* His only creation at the Opéra was Gennaro in Les Joyaux de la Madone,* which had its premiere at the Garnier opera house on 12 September 1913.

BIBLIOGRAPHY: KRJ 68; SW 88, 108, 128, 139, 183, 191.

Les Caprices de Cupidon is discussed in the twentieth-century volume.

Carafa de Colobrano, Michel-Henri-François-Vincent Aloys-Paul, DIT Carafa (b. 17 November 1787, Naples; d. 26 July 1872, Paris), composer, was born the second son of the prince de Colobrano, duke of Alvito. A relative of Admiral Caraccioli, he entered military service and was taken prisoner by the French at the battle of Campo-Tenese in 1806, but Jean-Paul Marat took an interest in him, and young Carafa became a citizen of France as well as a member of Marat's staff. He took part in the expedition to Sicily, where he became a captain, and his contribution to the French cause during the Russian campaign under Napoleon earned him additional honors that included membership in the Legion of Honor.

Carafa began his career as a composer in Naples, where a group of amateurs had staged his first opera II Fantasma as early as 1802. He went on to have works accepted by professional troupes in this same city as well as in Milan and Venice before taking up his permanent residence in Paris. Here, in the French capital, his Jeanne d'Arc in three acts was staged at the Opéra-Comique in 1821. After three more compositions by him were performed at this same theatre between 1822 and

1824, he had his first title posted at the Opéra on 2 March 1825, La Belle au bois dormant* in three acts. He then returned to the Opéra-Comique with Sangarido (1827), Masaniello (1827), La Violette (1828), and Jenny (1829). The Théâtre-Italien produced Le Nozze de Lammermoor in 1829, and the Opéra-Comique staged L'Auberge d'Auray in 1830, but Carafa went back to the Opéra with his ballet in three acts entitled L'Orgie* and gave its premiere there on 18 July 1831. His last work for the Opéra was Nathalie ou la laitière suisse* of 1832 that he did with Adalbert Gyrowetz,* but the Opéra-Comique staged another five compositions that he completed between 1831 and 1838.

Carafa's authorship also included more than a dozen Italian operas produced in the theatres of Naples, Milan, Venice, and Rome between 1811 and 1824 besides his collaborations entitled La Marquise de Brinvilliers and Les Premiers Pas (1847), the airs and recitatives done at Gioacchino Rossini's* request for Méry's translation of Sémiramis (1860), masses, contatas, and compositions for different instruments.

The composer was honored with election to the Academy of Fine Arts in 1837 to fill the vacancy left by Lesueur, and he was appointed director of the school for military music in 1838 (see eighteenth-century volume for Jean-François Lesueur). His professorship in composition at the Conservatoire dated from 1840, and he enjoyed tenure in this position until 1858.

BIBLIOGRAPHY: *François-Emmanuel-Joseph Bazin, Institut de France. Académie des beaux-arts. Notice sur Carafa . . . lue dans la séance du 5 novembre 1873 (Paris: Didot frères, 1873); La Grande Encyclopédie (Paris: Soc. anon. de la Grande Encyclopédie, n.d.) IX, 276-77; Fétis II, 183 and Suppl. I, 151-52; HUT 139-40; Lajarte II, 109-10, 114, 139, 145; PBSW 174.*

Carlini, Oreste (b. ?: d. ?), composer, was known only by the few operas he composed in a sparse musical career spread over a period of more than 25 years. His first work entitled La Gioventù di Enrico V was staged with some success at Naples in 1821, but his I Sposi fugitivi was not produced until 1833. The following year, he arrived in Paris and became known in the French capital after the presentation of his ballet, Chao-Kang. He worked with Casimir Gide* on the score of L'Ile

des pirates* billed at the Opéra in 1835. He returned to Italy to give Solimanno II at Milan in 1844 and Ildegonda at Florence in 1847.
BIBLIOGRAPHY: Fétis II, 192; Lajarte II, 151.

Carmen was a comic opera in four acts with a libretto by Henri Meilhac* and Ludovic Halévy* based upon Prosper Mérimée's story bearing the same title. Georges Bizet* created the score. It was produced for the first time on 3 March 1875 at the Opéra-Comique after a relatively long period of salary negotiations with Mme Marié-Galli, who agreed finally to sing the title-role. Paul Lévy DIT Lhérie filled the part of Don José with Deloffre leading the orchestra. Rehearsals started in the autumn of 1874, and, after 11 November, the artists went through their parts together nearly every weekday until the end of the year. Yet the librettists had no fewer than four compositions in performance at this time, and they were on hand to help matters along on only three occasions before 1 January 1874. They were not especially impressed by Carmen, moreover, and Meilhac was opposed to a woman's death furnishing the conclusion for a comic opera, while Halévy felt obliged to add some farcical nonsense to the composition by introducing El Dancairo and El Remendado. Nor were Bizet's spirits lifted by the belittling remarks made about his music by the director of the Opéra, du Locle. Also, arguments arose with the orchestra and singers over the music, and the troupe was filled with the pervasive fear that a dismal failure was in store for everybody connected with the production.

The curtain rises at the start of Carmen to disclose a troop of soldiers about to go off duty in Seville and assuring Micaela that Don José will arrive with the next guard (I, 1). She does not wait for Don José, but the latter's friends inform him of her inquiry into his whereabouts (I, 2). The soldiers pass their time looking at the pretty girls going to work in the cigar factory, and Carmen enters to flirt with the young men in general and disinterested Don José in particular. She gives him a flower and enters the factory (I, 3-6) before Micaela returns to deliver to him a letter, some money, and a kiss from his mother. He resolves to suppress the disturbing thoughts about Carmen that are troubling his mind and to limit his affections to Micaela. He is about to discard Carmen's flower when a fight erupts in the factory. Carmen stabs one of her coworkers (I, 7-8). She is arrested but persuades Don José to loosen her bonds so that she can push him to the ground and escape before they cross the bridge. She promises to meet him at Lilas Pastia's inn near the ramparts of the city (I, 9-11).

The second act moves to the inn filled with gypsies, smugglers, and some of the soldiers of the first act engaged in dancing and drinking. Carmen learns that José has been thrown into the guardhouse for allowing her to escape. The toreador Escamillo enters to inject new enthusiasm into the gathering and to flirt with Carmen (II, 1-2). Pastia closes his inn; the smugglers El Doncairo and El Remendado urge Carmen to join them in a projected venture that promises to show a handsome profit. She refuses because she has promised to wait for Don José. He enters and Carmen is dancing for him when the call to return to the barracks is sounded. Don José insists that he must heed this summons despite his love for her. Unconvinced and angered by his refusal to accompany her into the mountains, she denounces and dismisses him (II, 3-4). Don José's commanding officer enters and strikes him in a fit of jealousy, however, and he attacks his superior, who is now held captive by the smugglers. Don José has sealed his own fate, and he has no choice except to leave for the highlands with Carmen and the brigands (II, 5).

The third act presents the bustling camp of the smugglers, where Don José is wondering what his mother might think of his predicament. Carmen derides his misgivings and reads the cards to learn that tragedy and death await her (III, 1-2). The smugglers prepare to cross the frontier with their contraband, and the girls' role in this operation is to distract the border watch with their seductive charms (III, 3). Micaela appears on the edge of the camp looking for Don José, and Escamillo enters in search of his beloved Carmen. He explains to Don José that she had a lover but has tired of him. They are about to fight, but Carmen and her comrades intervene. Don José is disenchanted finally with Carmen and his life of banditry, but he agrees to leave with Micaela only after he learns that his mother is about to die (III, 4-5).

The concluding act transpires at the entrance to the bullring in Seville, where Carmen's friends reveal that Don José is still at large and that Carmen is with her new lover, the toreador Escamillo. The latter greets Carmen on his way to the arena, and Don José's presence in the crowd is disclosed (IV, 1). Suddenly, Don José confronts Carmen and suggests that they flee together to a distant place. She rejects his proposal and declares her love for Escamillo. The crowd cheers the latter's triumph in the ring, and Carmen exults over his success. She continues to declare her love for her champion and throws Don José's ring into the dirt. Don José cannot restrain himself and stabs her. He throws himself on the ground near her body as the curtain falls on his last expression of love for her (IV, 2).

It is possible to compile a rather lengthy catalogue of favorite passages from Carmen, but any list, long or short, would have to include the habanera, "L'Amour est une oiseau rebelle" (I, 5; the seguidilla, "Près des remparts de Séville" (I, 10; the toreador song, "Votre toast, je peux vous le rendre" (II, 2); and the card trio, "Mêlons! Coupons!" (III, 2).

The first night audience on 3 March 1875 was composed of writers, singers, music publishers, critics of almost every stripe, and boulevardiers waiting to see just how shocking the new work would prove. The first act was an unqualified success, but the last portion of the second act saw Carmen begin to inspire less and less enthusiasm. It was obvious by the end of the performance that Bizet had another failure, and the composer left the theatre to walk the streets of Paris until daybreak. After he had had time to recover from his disappointment, he returned to his troupe to shore up the weak spots in the production. The work seemed to gain new momentum and fresh spirit subsequently despite the bad press that the libretto had received. Strangely enough, critics had appeared to ignore the score for the most part. In retrospect, the critics' appraisals appear quite superfluous and irrelevant when it is recalled that Bizet's work went on to enjoy productions in at least a dozen languages including Bulgarian, Chinese, Japanese, and English. In Paris, the Opéra-Comique celebrated the centenary of Bizet's birth in 1938 with the 2,271st presentation of Carmen. In all, Bizet's work was mounted 2,942 times at the Opéra-Comique before the closing of this theatre. Also, its second act was given at the Opéra for a gala performance on 11 November 1900, and it was sung in its entirety for a second gala in this same theatre on 29 December 1907. Finally, it was provided with recitatives by Ernest Guiraud* for its true premiere at the Opéra on 10 November 1959 with General de Gaulle in attendance. Bizet's Carmen had become so taken for granted by this time, moreover, that its 3,000th performance in Paris on 10 January 1960 passed unnoticed.

BIBLIOGRAPHY: L'Avant-scène 26 (March-April 1980), 1-166; Camille Bellaigue, Promenades lyriques (Paris: Nouvelle Librairie National, 1924), 46-62; Andre Boll, "Carmen et ses d'écorateurs," L'Opéra de Paris 10 (1954), 59-63; Hugo Daffner, Friedrich Nietzches Rundglossen zu Bizets "Carmen" (Regensburg: Bosse, 1938); Winton Dean, "Carmen: An Attempt at a True Evaluation," MR 7 (1946), 209-20; DDO I, 199-201; Charles Gaudier, "Carmen" de Bizet: Etude historique et critique, analyse musicale (Paris: Mellottée, 1922); Edgar Istel, Bizet und "Carmen" (Stuttgart: Engelhorn, 1927); JB 242-48; KCOB 834-47; Henry Malherbe, Carmen (Paris: Michel, 1951); MSRL 24-26; OEN I, 239-96; OQE 40-45; Julien Tiersot, "Bizet an Spanish Music," MQ 13 (1927), 566-81; SW 55.

Le Carnaval, entitled Carnival in English, is a ballet in a single act with an argument by Michel Fokine* and a score by Robert Schumann.* Léon Bakst* created its scenery and costumes. It had its world premiere on 5 March 1910 at a ball in Pavlova Hall in St. Petersburg. It enjoyed its initial performance in a theatre on 20 May 1910 in Berlin at the Western theatre, but it was not brought to Paris until Serge Diaghilev's* Ballets russes* produced it at the Opéra on 4 June 1910 in choreography by Michel Fokine.

The curtain rises on the so-called "preamble" of Le Carnaval, with three girls rushing across the stage and their partners in pursuit. They are followed by other couples who execute a waltz before the entrance of Charina and Estrella.

After the introduction of these characters, Pierrot enters as if in search of somebody. Happy Arlequin mocks him, and Pierrot leaves the stage to six couples and Eusébius, who awaits his beloved Estrella. Florestan wins Estrella's attention, however, and Eusebius executes a happy pas de deux with Chiarina. Frustrated Pierrot tries in vain to court Papillon.

Columbine refuses to elope with Arlequin, and pompous Pantalon comes in to read a note. Columbine places her hands over his eyes, and Arlequin seizes the missive. Disappointed Pantalon leaves, and Arlequin tears up the note with a flourish and a pirouette. Arlequin is victorious once again.

Columbine tries to comfort Pantalon, but Arlequin enters. The trio execute a pas de trois until Pantalon is rejected by his partners, and Arlequin performs a pas seul. Guests enter to dance and to congratulate Columbine and Arlequin. Pantalon is forgiven with a kiss by Columbine. Yet incorrigible Arlequin cannot refrain from producing a discordant note by tying Pierrot and Pantalon together. The company gathers around Columbine and Arlequin, and poor Pantalon and Pierrot can only accept their rival's victory.

The ballet featured a slight intrigue and a predominantly joyous mood, and its ebullient tune endeared it to audiences, although it was never exceedingly popular in Paris, where it was withdrawn after its 13th representation at the Garnier Palace.* It was performed on seven dates by the Ballets russes at the Opéra between 4 June 1910 and 24 December 1911. After World War I, it was revived for another six programs by Diaghilev's company between 27 December 1919 and 7 June 1922. The various roles were created at the Opéra by Mlles Lopoukhova (Columbine), Véra Fokina* (Chiarina), Piltz (Estrella), and Bronislava Nijinska* (Papillon) alongside MM. Michel Fokine (Arlequin), Orlov (Pantalon), Scherer (Eusébius), Boulgakov (Pierrot), and Vassiliew (Floristan).

BIBLIOGRAPHY: ACD 86; Arsène Alexandre, Jean Cocteau, eds., The Decorative Art of Léon Bakst, trans. Harry Melville (New York: Benjamin Blom, 1971), 47-48, pl. 60-61; BB 51-53; BK 38; Richard Buckle, Nijinsky (New York: Simon and Schuster, 1971), 132-35; CB 571-75; Mary Clarke and David Vaughan, The Encyclopedia of Dance and Ballet (New York: G. P. Putnam's Sons, 1977), 80; CODB 106-7; Michel Fokine, Memoirs of a Ballet Master, trans. Vitale Fokine (Boston: Little, Brown and Co., 1961), 99-100, 134-37; GBAL 97-99; HAZ 78-79;

Boris Kochno, Diaghilev and the Ballets Russes, trans. Adrienne Foulke (New York & Evanston: Harper & Row, 1970), 38-44; LOB 130-31; "Opéra . . . Saison russe au ballet: Carnaval," Le Ménestrel 76 (11 June 1910), 186-87; PBR 158; RLVB 92-94; SS 160-63; SW 250; TDB 467-68.

Le Carnaval de Venise ou la constance à Lépreuve was offered as a pantomime ballet in two acts with music by Louis-Luc Persuis and Rodolphe Kreutzer and choreography by Louis-Jacques Milon (see eighteenth-century volume for Persuis, Kreutzer, and Milon). It had its premiere on 22 February 1816 and was applauded enthusiastically. It enjoyed 22 performances before it was reduced to a single act in 1817. It was produced subsequently every year until 1830. It was mounted on 149 dates in the 1816-30 interval. It was revived on 5 January 1833 for another four presentations during this year, and it was mounted twice in 1838 for a grand total of 156 productions before it was dropped from the repertory.

The ballet begins in a living room overlooking Saint Mark's square in Venice, where the countess Vittoria is trying on costumes for a masquerade part. Don Carlos is heard serenading the countess, whom he has not seen unmasked, but to whom he is attracted on account of her gracious manner and stunning figure. The maid Angelina opens the door for him and his valet Fabricio, and the two men declare their love to the two masked women, who admit their love to their Spanish visitors. The lovers agree on signals to enable them to recognize each other at the ball (I, 1-3).

The action shifts to a ballroom with a canal visible through a large window. The countess, dressed as a gypsy, steps from her gondola and stops Don Carlos to tell his fortune. She asserts that he loves and serenades a masked woman who is really quite ugly. He does not believe her and suspects her identity; he gives her the prearranged signal, but she ignores it (I, 4-5). Angelina tries to play the same trick on Fabricio, but he replies that he has forgotten his ugly sweetheart of former days, and Angelina thrashes him with her staff (I, 6). The countess enters the ballroom in her original costume representing La Folie, and she arouses universal admiration because she is unmasked. Angelina is her companion and represents L'Amour, who directs an arrow at Don Carlos and Fabricio. The ball ends with a pas de quatre executed by the principal characters. Don Carlos tries to escape from La Folie, but Fabricio surrenders to L'Amour (I, 7). Four masked men kidnap Don Carlos, and a fifth brigand challenges Fabricio to a duel. His assailant proves to be L'Amour, who locks him in a gondola before departing with the countess in a marine procession that closes the act (I, 8-11).

The second act shifts to a sumptuous salon, where Don Carlos' four kidnappers give him food and drink, while the countess Vittoria prepares to test her suitor (II, 1-2). She appears in her original gypsy costume, but Don Carlos ignores her. At a wave of her hand, a crowd of servants and guests convene to salute Don Carlos and the gypsy. She unmasks. This display of wealth and beauty fails to persuade Don Carlos to betray his first love. The guests depart after a lavish entertainment and ball (II, 3-5). The hostess proposes to her guest, when they are alone, and she pretends to faint in despair after he rejects her proposal. He repeats his determination to remain faithful, and his apparently furious captor has him locked into a room lest he run off to his beloved (II, 7).

The setting changes to the gardens around Vittoria's château, where frightened Fabricio finds himself under heavy guard. An officer pretends to recognize him as the new master of the château, however, and he is induced to dress for an interview with the mistress of the château. An aged crone enters to sing to him of love and to fall into his arms, but he tries to avoid her. She threatens him with her crutch, and he locks himself in a summer house in the garden (II, 8-9). Angelina takes off her cron's costume, and the countess appears in the garb she wore at the start of the ballet. She orders Don Carlos freed and retires. Fabricio and his master decide to flee now that flight is possible, but Vittoria and Angelina reappear to reveal their true identity, and the lovers are reconciled. The countess' vassals band together to celebrate this happy ending (II, 10-11).

Mlle Emilie Bigottini (the countess) and Mme Courtin (Angelina) filled the female roles with Albert as Don Carlos and Ferdinand as Fabricio (see eighteenth-century volume for Bigottini). One passage in the score of Le Carnaval de Venise

has been remembered: the theme in 6/8 time for which Niccolò Paganini wrote the first variations. Paganini gave concerts at the Opéra in two years (1831, 1833), when the ballet was being produced.
BIBLIOGRAPHY: AEM VII, 1781-83 and X, 1102-3; CB 6; Chouquet 387; Lajarte II, 86-87; Wks II, 3447.

Caron, Rose Lucille, *née* Meuniez (b. 17 November 1857, Monerville; d. 9 April 1930, Paris), was an operatic soprano. She studied at the Conservatoire in Paris between 1880 and 1882 and made her debut by creating Brunehilde in the premiere of Louis Reyer's* *Sigurd** at the Théâtre Royal de la Monnaie in Brussels on 7 January 1884. She made her Paris debut at the Opéra in the first performance of Reyer's same work in the French capital on 12 June 1885. She created six other roles at the Garnier Palace* during her tenure there: Elsa in *Lohengrin** on 16 September 1891, a part she repeated at the hundredth performance of this work on 28 April 1894; the heroine of *Salammbô** on 16 may 1892; Sieglinde in *La Walkyrie** on 12 May 1893; the heroines of *Djelma** and *Hellé** on 25 May 1894 and 24 April, respectively; and Desdémone in *Othello** on 10 October 1894.

Aside from the parts that she was the first to sing at the Opéra, Mlle Caron was billed as Rachel in *La Juive** in 1885-86, and, in 1886 and 1893, as Chimène in *Le Cid*.* In 1886, she performed as Valentine in *Les Huguenots*,* Cathérine in *Henry VIII*,* Marguerite in *Faust** and Agathe in *Le Freischütz*.* She did Donna Anna in *Don Juan** in 1896 and appeared in *L'Apothéose de Beethoven* of 1909.

Mlle Caron joined the company of the Opéra-Comique in 1898, and she joined the faculty of the Conservatoire in 1902. Later, she resigned from this position to give lessons privately and to appear in concert.
BIBLIOGRAPHY: APD 213; Adolphe Boschot, La Musique et la Vie (Paris: Plon, 1931), 183-90; Henri de Curzon, Ernest Reyer; sa vie et ses oeuvres, 1823-1909 (Paris: Perrin, 1924), 53-54, 59-60; idem, Croquis d'artistes (Paris: Fischbacher, 1898), 129-40; DBF VII, 1204; EFC 101-4; ICM 288; KRJ 72; Martin 72; PBSW 174; Erik de Solenière, Rose Caron, monographie critique (Paris: Bibliothèque d'art et de "la Critique,"

1896); SW, 62, 72, 74, 101, 111-12, 130, 134-35, 165, 202-3, 225, 361; WOC II, 242.

Carpeaux, Jean-Baptiste (b. 14 may 1827, Valenciennes; d. 12 October 1875, Courbevoie), French sculptor and painter, began his studies privately under the direction of the architect J. -B. Bernard, but, in 1838, he moved to Paris to enroll at the Royal School of Design and Mathematics. His first years in the French capital were filled with hardship, but he managed to survive by creating plaster models for merchants dealing in cheap bronze figures. He obtained his first serious commission in 1843 from M. L. Hollande, who requested him to make models of bas-reliefs with which this wealthy gentleman was planning to decorate his home. The following year, 1844, Carpeaux was admitted to the Ecole des Beaux-Arts.

Carpeaux now received other commissions and did original works that drew attention to his talent. He won two Prix de Rome, moreover, and he made his debut at the Salon in 1853 with a large plaster bas-relief entitled La Soumission d'Abd-el'Kadar. Napoleon III was so attracted to this work that he asked Capellaro to execute a duplicate of it in marble. It was at this time that Carpeaux won the Premier Grand Prix de Rome that carried with it the opportunity to study in Rome.

In Italy, Carpeaux did a number of pieces that won critical approval: L'Enfant boudeur (1856), La Rieuse (1857), La Pêcheur à la coquille (1858). Also, he began his Ugolin et ses enfants, inspired by the famous passage in Dante's Inferno, and he was allowed to remain in Italy until 1862 to finish this group, which would be cast in bronze and placed in the Tuileries gardens.

The sculptor returned to France in 1862, and it was not long before he was presented at court. He had never received a sufficient classical education, and his manners were not impeccable, but his personality as a creative artist stood him in good stead. He was asked to execute busts of Empress Eugénie and Princess Mathilde, and it became stylish to have Carpeaux do a bust or protrait of at least one member of a family. His greatest artistic success at this time was his statue of the imperial prince with his dog Nero, a work that carried the day at the Salon of 1866.

Also, the piece that would make Carpeaux' work visible to all Paris had already been begun, because the artist had received in 1865 the order to do the statue entitled La Musique destined to grace the opera house that Charles Garnier was building. E. Guillaume had won the commission for the piece called La Danse, and, after a few months, the two artists agreed to exchange subjects. Carpeaux was ready to unveil his masterpiece before the public on 27 July 1869. The newspapers condemned his work as immoral, even lecherous, and some critics noted that its five figures unbalanced the entire façade of the opera house. One group of outraged citizens directed another sculptur to do a second composition to restore the honor of France, but the Franco-Prussian War intervened, and the matter came to an abrupt end.

Carpeaux fell seriously ill in 1873, and he felt obliged to enter a sanatorium in 1874. His financial situation worsened too, and he had to be helped in his time of need by his friends who included Alexandre Dumas fils, the playwright; Bruno Chérier, the painter; Prince Stirby, his English patron who tried to make him comfortable at Nice, when the end was obviously close at hand.

Carpeaux finished a bust of Charles Garnier in 1869. This work is now in the Louvre with Carpeaux' bust of his wife in her wedding dress.

BIBLIOGRAPHY: E. Benezit, Dictionnaire critique et documentaire des peintres, sculpteurs, dessinateurs et graveurs (Paris: Grund, 1976), II, 542-43; DBF VII, 1209-11; Martine Kahane, "Les Lieux de la danse: L'Opéra de Paris," SDLD 129 (10 December 1980), 38-40; Petite Encyclopédie de l'Opéra de Paris (Paris: Le Théâtre national de l'Opéra, 1978), 55-59.

Carré, Marguerite (b. 1880, Cabourg; d. 1947, Paris), French soprano, was the daughter of the director of the Graslin Theatre in Nantes, where she made her theatrical debut as Mimi of La Vie de Bohème in 1899. She enjoyed her first appearance at the Opéra-Comique in this same role in 1902. Subsequently she became the wife of M. Giraud, director of the Opéra-Comique.

Mme Carré remained at the Opéra-Comique, where she created such roles as Jacqueline of Fortunio (1907) and Hélène of Le Mariage de Télémaque (1910) besides singing Mimi once again for the hundredth performance of Puccini's work at this theatre on 4 March 1903.

Yet Mme Carré's almost continuous activity at the Opéra-Comique did not prevent her from filling engagements at the Opéra, where she made her debut in the premiere of Le Vieil Aigle* on the occasion of a benefit gala there on 26 June 1909. She was chosen to fill this part at the Garnier Palace* because she had sung it in the world premiere of Raoul Gungsbourg's* work at Monte-Carlo six months previously. She sang the title-role of Thaïs* at the Opéra on 21 May 1916.
BIBLIOGRAPHY: Pierre Brunel and Stéphane Wolff, L'Opéra (Paris: Bordas, 1980), 174; EFC 191; SW 391; WOC 177.

Carré, Michel-Florentin (b. 21 October 1822, Besançon; d. 27 June 1872, Paris), librettist, came to Paris in 1840 to study painting and to write poetry incidentally, but he became involved in the musical theatre by collaborating with Jules Barbier* on the writing of librettos. He was likewise responsible for countless vaudevilles and comedies of no enduring value. He and Barbier did the poems for four compositions billed at the Opéra-Comique during the first decade of their partnership: Galatée (1852), Les Noces de Jeannette (1853), Les Sabots de la marquise (1854), and Gioacchino Meyerbeer's* Le Pardon de Ploërmel (1859). He also worked on librettos with Pierre Cormon* for Quentin Durward (1858) and with Hippolyte Lucas* for Lalla-Roukh (1862). But in 1859, he and Jules Barbier had supplied the words for Chalres Gounod's* Faust,* which was mounted at the Théâtre-Lyrique, and he was to be henceforth employed to work on the poems to be used by the leading composers of his day: François Boïeldieu's Le Chevalier Lubin (1866); Gounod's La Colombe (1860), Philémon et Baucis* (1860), Mireille (1864), and Roméo et Juliette* (1867); Jacques Offenbach's* Les Contes d'Hoffman*; Ambroise Thomas'* Mignon (1866); Bizet's Les Pêcheurs de perles (1863); Louis Reyer's* La Statue* (1861); and Camille Saint-Saëns'* Le Timbre d'argent (1877) (see eighteenth-century volume for Boïeldieu). Gounod's Faust was moved to the Opéra on 3 March 1869, of course, but Carré had four other titles posted there as well: Gounod's La Reine de Saba* of 1862 with Jules Barbier*; Ernest Boulanger's* Le Docteur Magnus* of 1864 with Cormon; Ambroise Thomas' Hamlet* of 1868 with Jules Barbier again; and Ambroise

Thomas' Françoise de Rimini* of 1882 with Jules Barbier. Carré's version of Fidélio was performed at the Opéra-Comique in 1898, and his text for Les Noces de Figaro was used at the Théâtre-Lyrique on 8 may 1858 and revived in 1936 at the Porte St.-Martin theatre by the troupe of the Opéra-Comique. *BIBLIOGRAPHY: DBF VII, 1230; GE IX, 535; Lajarte II, 233, 236, 242-43; LXIX III, 416.*

Carrère-Xanrof, Marguerite (b. 1869, Bordeaux; d. ?), vocalist, studied under the direction of Pierre-François Wartel* and Mmes Lheriter, Marie Krauss,* and Rosine Laborde. She made her operatic debut in Les Huguenots* at the Grand Théâtre in Marseilles in 1889 and then accepted an engagement at the Théâtre de la Monnaie in Brussesl for 1889-92. The range of her repertory and her talents as a performer won her admission to the Opéra, where she made her debut as Marguerite in Faust* on 24 June 1893. Her only creation was Guerhilde in La Walkyrie* on 12 May 1893, but her repertory included the following parts in the works indicated:

Role	**Opera, Year**
La Reine	Les Huguenots, 1892
Eudoxie	La Juive, 1892
Isabelle	Robert le Diable
Berthe	Le Prophète, 1892
Juliette	Roméo et Juliette, 1893
Sieglinde	La Walkyrie, 1894
Helmwigue	La Walkyrie, 1895
Vénus	Tannäuser, 1895
Urbain	Les Huguenots, 1897
Zerline	Don Juan, 1897
Hélène	Messidor, 1897
Briséis	Briséis, 1899

Benjamin	Joseph, 1899
Thaïs	Thaïs, 1901
Iole	Astarté, 1901
Stéfano	Roméo et Juliette, 1901

M. Léon Fourneau DIT Xanrof composed light pieces for the smaller theatres in Paris.
BIBLIOGRAPHY: EFC 166; SW 43, 52-53, 74, 116, 127, 129-31, 148, 177-79, 189-91, 205-9, 224-26.

Caruso, Enrico (b. 25 February 1873, Naples; d. 2 August 1921, Naples), tenor, studied under Guglielmo Vergine and made his debut at the Bellini Theatre in his native city in 1894. By 1900, he had sung there the tenor roles in Umberto Giordano's* Fedora,* Francesco Gilèa's Adriana Lecouvreur, and Alberto Franchetti's Germania, but he did not acquire an international reputation until he filled his brilliant engagement at Monte Carlo, where he sang with Nellie Melba* in La Bohème.* He went on to appear in Rigoletto* in London and the United States (1903), and, within a decade, he had made his name familiar to opera-goers throughout the world. He was the first Italian tenor to have his voice put on records, moreover, and this development brought his powerful voice to countless thousands of people who had never been inside an opera house.

At the Metropolitan Opera in New York, Caruso was billed in close to 40 roles, but his Paris repertory was by no means as vast because he spent comparatively little time in the French capital. He sang the duke in Rigoletto on 11 June 1908 at the Opéra on a gala program that began with La Marseillaise. In a second gala, he appeared on 19 June 1910 with the Metropolitan Opera Company of New York to sing Rodolphe in La Bohème and the title-part in Faust.* Lastly, he did Dick Johnson in Giacomo Puccini's* La Fille du Far-West* on 16 May 1912 with the Monte Carlo Opera Company. These three programs constituted Caruso's entire experience with the Paris Opéra.
BIBLIOGRAPHY: "A Century of Caruso," ON 37 (24 February 1973), 45-50; AEM II, 874-76; APD 214; Dorothy Caruso, Enrico Caruso, His Life and Death (New York: Simon and Schuster, 1945); GIR 138-43; ICM 291; Samuel Jackson, Caruso (New York: Stein

and Day, 1972); Pierre Van Renselaer Key, Enrico Caruso, a Biography (New York: Vienna House, 1972; KRJ 73-74; Jean Pierre Mouchon, Enrico Caruso: His Life and Voice (Paris: Editions Ophrys, 1974); Henry Pleasants, The Great Singers (New York: Simon and Schuster, 1966), 285-89, 294-98; RC 134-58; SW 95, 182; Thomas Russell Ybarra, Caruso: the Man of Naples and the Voice of Gold (New York: Harcourt Brace, 1953).

Carvalho, Caroline Félix-Miolan, DITE Mme Miolan-Carvalho (b. 31 December 1827, Marseilles; d. 10 July 1895, Puys, Seine-Inférieure), vocalist, was brought to Paris by her mother after the death of her father so that she might study voice. After taking private lessons, she was admitted to the Conservatoire to study under Gilbert-Louis Duprez.* She made such an excellent record here that Duprez recommended her to the management of the Opéra after her graduation in 1847. She sang parts in the first act of Lucie de Lammermoor* and in the trio of the second act of La Juive* at the Duprez benefit program for his retirement on 14 December 1849, but she was rewarded with a contract to appear at the Opéra-Comique, not the Opéra.

At the Opéra-Comique, she had a singularly successful engagement, and, after marrying one of her colleagues there, M. Léon Carvaille* DIT Carvalho, she moved on to the Théâtre-Lyrique. The lightness of her soprano voice and her versatility had won for her an enviable reputation at the Opéra-Comique, and these same qualities made her the toast of Paris at this second theatre. She did Chérubin in the French version of Les Noces de Figaro by Jules Barbier* and Michel Carré* on 8 May 1858, and she sang Marguerite in the world premiere of Charles Gounod's* Faust* on 19 March 1859 (see eighteenth-century volume for Les Noces de Figaro). Her next triumph at the Théâtre-Lyrique was as Pamina in La Flûte enchantée in its French version by Nuitter and Beaumont on 23 February 1865 (see eighteenth-century volume for La Flûte enchantée). She was cast as Zerline in the François-Joseph Blaze* and Deschamps translation of Don Juan on 8 may 1866 and as Juliette in Roméo et Juliette* on 27 April 1867 (see eighteenth-century volume for Don Juan).

News of Mme Carvalho's outstanding success in the French capital spread throughout the musical world, but she was invited to London first, and her appearances here became annual events of three months duration. She was likewise asked to sing in Berlin, St. Petersburg, and Brussels before her retirement in 1885.

Her first summons to the Opéra came in 1869, and she was acclaimed as usual here by Paris audiences. She did not create any roles in new operas during this stay at the opera house in the rue Le Peletier,* but her success was no less extraordinary in already known and established works. When she returned to the Opéra for her second engagement, however, the company had already moved into the new Garnier Palace,* and Mme Carvalho had the distinction of bringing three characters to its stage for the first time. She sang Ophélie in the initial staging of Hamlet* at the Opéra on 31 March 1875, and she did Marguerite de Valois of Les Hugenots* in the first production of this composition at the new opera house. Finally, on 6 September 1875, she appeared as Marguerite in Faust* at its Garnier premiere.

BIBLIOGRAPHY: Alfred Bablot d'Olbreuse, "Nouvelles diverses: Mme Carvalho," AM 14 (1 April 1875), 110; idem, "Reprise de Don Juan," FM 33 (12 December 1869), 389-91; idem, "Début de Mme Carvalho et représentation solennelle à l'Opéra," AM 9 (3 December 1868), 3-4; idem, "Mme Carvalho et le théâtre de Marseille," AM 3 (16 April 1863), 156-57; Gustave Bertrand, "Les Débuts de Mme Carvalho à l'Opéra," Le Ménestrel 35 (29 November 1868), 419-20; Alfred Bruneau, Musiques de Russie et musiciens de France (Paris: Charpentier, 1903), 232-37; Henri de Curzon, Croquis d'artistes (Paris: Fischbacher, 1898), 23-36; DBF VII, 1286; EFC 149-51; M. Escudier, "Début de Mme Carvalho dans Les Huguenots," FM 32 (29 November 1868), 373-74; idem, "Théâtre Imperial de l'Opéra: début de Mme Carvalho dans Les Hugenots," FM 32 (29 November 1868), 373-74; EZF 155-59; Fétis Suppl. I, 155-57; GE IX, 634; Henri Heugel, "Mme Carvalho," Le Ménestrel 61 (14 July 1895), 218-19; ICM 292; B. Jouvin, "Silhouettes et portraits d'artistes, Mme Miolan-Carvalho," Le Ménestral 36 (14 February 1869), 83-84; Lajarte II, 133-34, 147-48, 153, 242; Lermina 254, 1015; Martin 75; Arthur Pougin, "Mme Carvalho née Caroline Félix-Miolan," Le Ménestrel 44 (2 December 1877), 2; "Représentation au bénéfice de Mme Miolan-Carvalho," Le Ménestrel 26 (29 May 1859), 201-2;

E. A. Spoll, Mme Carvalho, notes et souvenirs (Paris: Librairie des bibliophiles, 1885); SW 74, 84-85, 97, 116, 156; Thurner 232-40.

Carvalho, Léon Carvaille DIT (b. 1825, Port-Louis; d. 26 December 1897, Paris), French theatre manager, started his theatrical career as a bass at the Opéra-Comique on 2 June 1849, when he filled the part of Scapin in Gilles Ravisseur. He left the Opéra-Comique in 1855 to assume the duties of director at the Théâtre-Lyrique, and, in 1870, he undertook the direction of the Théâtre Khédival in Cairo to supervise the world premiere of Aïda* there in 1871.

M. Carvalho left North Africa to return to Paris after the initial staging of Aïda because he had been offered the post of director at the Vaudeville Theatre, where his first efforts were devoted to the production of L'Arlésienne. Then, in 1875, he became assistant stage manager at the Opéra. Thus, he had a hand in the special program celebrating the opening of the Garnier Palace* under the directorship of M. Halanzier on 5 January 1875.

In 1876, M. Carvalho became director of the Opéra-Comique, an office that he filled with outstanding success, although fate intervened to bring disaster into his life. The Opéra-Comique caught fire backstage during the performance of 25 May 1887, and no one took the precaution of lowering the curtain. The lights went out immediately; exits were blocked; panic seized the spectators. Ninety-five bodies were recovered from the debris, and no one was able to establish the numer of those injured. M. Carvalho found himself the object of public indignation, and he was sentenced to three months in prison in addition to losing his personal fortune.

Ultimately, in 1891, M. Carvalho was acquitted of any wrongdoing in reference to the conflagration of 1887, and he returned to his position as director of the theatre in the rue Favart. He held this post until his death in 1897, and it was generally agreed that he had made the Opéra-Comique one of the more interesting theatres in France. He had dared to enlarge the repertory at this theatre by billing for the first time such works as La Flûte enchantée (1897), Le Barbier de Séville (1884), and Don Juan (1896). He produced such "old faithfuls" as L'Etoile du nord, La Dame Blanche, and Le Postillon de Longjumeau in addition to introducing Paris audiences to Jacques Offenbach's* Les Contes d'Hoffmann (1881), Léo Delibes'* Lakmé (1883), and Jules Massenet's* Manon (1884).

BIBLIOGRAPHY: Pierre Brunel and Stéphane Wolff, L'Opéra (Paris: Bordas, 1980), 174; Jean Gourret, Histoire de l'Opéra-Comique (Paris: Publications universitaires, 1978), 155-60, 166-71.

Casse-Noisette, called Nutcracker in English, is discussed under its French title in the twentieth-century volume.

La Catalane is a lyric drama in four acts with a libretto based upon Angel de Guimerá'a Terra Beixa, Paul Ferrier and Louis Tiercelin wrote its libretto, and its score was composed by Fernand Le Borne. Joseph Hansen* established its choreography. It had its world premiere at the Garnier Palace* on 24 May 1907 with costumes by Bétout and sets by Amable and Cioccari. Paul Vidal* was at the desk for the premiere of the work.

The opera opens on a plateau in the mountains, where Andrès lives. He is waving to Anita, whom he is planning to marry, and he looks longingly at the rugged landscape that he must leave on the morrow. He enters his cabin to sleep (a. 1).

The scene changes to the countryside near Anita's mill, where workers are going to the fields, and women are doing their laundry in a stream. Blas is counting the sacks that are being brought to the mill, and he is informing the farmers that the shepherd Andrès is going to wed Anita. Everybody agrees that he is a good choice because he is so ignorant, but Agnès warns them to be careful of what they say about him (II, 1). Andrès tells everybody how happy he is to have a mill and a wife. Gaspar and Pépa assure him that his bride is beautiful; he answers that he has prayed for a long time for a perfect wife, and the bystanders laugh. Blas, Gaspar, and Mateo call him a fool under their breath (II, 2). Miguel enters. He is the master of the region, and Andrès thanks him for arranging his marriage with the miller girl. Ironically, Miguel assures him that it is his pleasure, and Blas assures the master that everything has been settled. Miguel cautions Blass that there must be no error, and he tells him that everybody must keep his lips sealed. Miguel orders the bride and groom to be in the chapel within the hour (II, 3). Anita begs Miguel not to press her marriage to Andrès, and Miguel assures her that he loves her. He explains that he is having her marry Andrès only because the shepherd is so gullible and easily deceived. It is Andrès, he explains, who will allow him to continue to love her (II, 4). The villagers gather to escort the bride and groom to church, and Miguel assures Blas that Andrès will cause no trouble (II, 5).

The wedding feast is in full swing at the inn. Andrès assures his bride that he loves her, and he grasps her around the waist to kiss her. She is upset and tells him that she will never love him. Startled, he begins to wonder why she has married him (III, 1-3). He asks Agnès why some people laugh at him, whereas other villagers appear to be sorry for him. She holds his hand in sympathy, and Anita becomes jealous despite her apparent lack of interest in Andrès (III, 4). Anita and Agnès argue, and Anita quarrels with Miquel. She declares that she is ashamed of herself, and she accuses him of leading her into dishonor. He insists upon meeting her later, but she asserts that she refuses to be either the mistress of the master or the wife of the servant. She tells him that she despises him, but Miguel ignores her anger and promises to knock at the door of her mill when she turns off her light (III, 5-6).

Anita is in her mill, where she is beginning to realize that Andrès did not know that he was marrying her to promote his master's pleasure. She vows to be faithful to deceived Andrès, but she decides not to tell him of her sinful intentions. She hears voices and believes that Andrès has returned home (IV, 1), but it is Anita come to warn her that Andrès and Blas have had a fight, when the latter told Andrès to ask Anita whether it is true that she has a lover. She admits her guilt and asks forgiveness, but he announces that he is returning to the mountains. She begs him not to leave and threatens to return to her lover if he abandons her. He loses his temper and stabs her. She is not mortally wounded, but he is still thirsty for revenge and extinguishes the light to lure her lover to the mill (IV, 3). Miguel enters the room only to realize that he has been trapped.

He defies Andrès, however, and he reminds him that he is the master and in love with Anita. Andrès chokes him to death (IV, 4), and he offers his arm to Anita with the suggestion that they leave their valley of tears for the mountains (IV, 5).

La Catalane did not arouse much enthusiasm in Paris despite the colorful spectacle and dancing that it presented, and it had to be dropped after its ninth performance on 25 December 1907. The leading male roles in the opera were created by Lucien Muratore* (Andrès) and Jean-François Delmas* (Miguel) with Louise Grandjean in the part of Anita. The dances were executed by the corps de ballet of the Opéra headed by Mlles Carlotta Zambelli,* Beauvais, G. Covat, Meunier and M. Cléret.

BIBLIOGRAPHY: AEM 8, 415-16; Stoullig XXXIII (1907), 13-16; SW 57.

Cavalieri, Lina (b. 25 December 1874, Rome; d. 8 February 1944, Florence), was a soprano who studied in Paris under the direction of Mariani-Masi. After her debut in Lisbon as Nedda in December 1908, she sang in the opera houses of Italy, France, Poland, Russia, England, and the United States (1906, 1909-10).

Cavalieri was most effective in such French roles as Thaïs, Manon, and Hérodiade, but her constant traveling limited her appearances at the Paris Opéra. She made her professional debut at the Garnier Palace* in the part of Thaïs on 17 June 1907, but her repertory here never went beyond Princess Fedora, which she executed for the premiere of Umberto Giordano's* work at the Opéra on 20 October 1910 and Stéphana of Sibéria,* which she sang on 9 June 1911.

The soprano was killed near Florence during an American air raid near the end of World War II in Europe.

BIBLIOGRAPHY: EFC 178; ICM 299; KRJ 75-76; SW 90-91, 201, 208.

Cave, Hygin-Auguste (b. 24 December 1794, Doudeville; d. 30 March 1852, Paris), librettist, was involved more in administration than in purely musical matters pertaining to the theatre, and he established his literary reputation with a political satire entitled Les Soirées de Neuilly, which he published prudently in 1827 under the pseudonym of Fougeray. He also collaborated on Le

Globe, and the views he dared to express won him the favor of the new government after the Revolution of 1830. He was made director of Fine Arts at the Institut and was put in charge of theatres under the Minister of State. He wrote vaudevilles and occasional comedies, but he also had a ballet executed at the Opéra, La Tentation* of 1832, for which he and Charles Duponchel* composed the libretto.

BIBLIOGRAPHY: DBF VII, 1501-2; GE IX, 965; Lajarte II, 143; LXIX III, 645.

Cendrillon was billed as a fairy-tale ballet in three acts with a score by Ferdinand Sor* and a libretto and choreography by Albert Decombe (see eighteenth-century volume for Decombe). It had its world premiere at the Royal Academy of Music on 3 March 1823 and is not to be confused with later ballets based upon the Cinderella story. Its sets were designed by Pierre Cicéri.*

The curtain rises on the ballet to reveal a gothic room with a large fireplace where Cendrillon has been asleep. She is busy with her morning chores, while her sisters sleep, but she takes time to play an air on a harp and to dance around the furniture. When the other members of her family appear, she rushes to prepare breakfast with tears in her eyes because her henpecked father is afraid to greet her with a kiss. When the baroness is looking the other way, however, the baron manages to reasure his child by squeezing her hand affectionately (I, 1-2). The fairy Mélise knocks at the door in disguise to ask for a morsel of food, and the baroness dismisses her, but Cendrillon manages to give her something to eat. A royal page appears at the door; he has an invitiation to the prince's ball for Clorinde and Tisbé but not for Cendrillon (I, 3-4). Cendrillon is disappointed until she reads a legend over the fireplace telling her that his generous heart will quarantee her happiness (I, 5-6). Her stepsisters order Cendrillon to put the finishing touches on their toilettes, and the baron leaves with his wife and stepdaughters for the ball, but his own daughter remains by the fireplace. Mélise reappears. She dresses Cendrillon in a magnificent gown so that she may attend the ball and arouse envy in her step-sisters' hearts. The fairy warns the girl to leave the royal palace before midnight, and she conjures up a carriage drawn by a pair of unicorns to take her to the ball (I, 7-9).

The second act opens with preparations for the ball. Prince Ramir complains to his friend Olivier that he suffers the pangs of love without knowing whom he loves. Mélise is his guardian fairy as well, and she assures him that he will find the girl he loves before the day is done (II, 1-3). The guests start to arrive, and Cendrillon's stepsisters entertain the possibility that one of them may marry the prince. Ramir scrutinizes his guests, but he cannot detect the girl of his dreams until Cendrillon arrives with her retinue. The happy couple dance together, and the prince proposes marriage. Cendrillon is about to accept his proposal, when midnight begins to strike (II, 4-7). She rushes from the ballroom but loses her slipper in the gardens. Ramir resolves to look for his fugitive love by trying to find the girl whose foot fits the slipper that his guards have found (II, 8-11).

The third act returns to the baron's home, where Cendrillon is sweeping the floor and thinking of the prince. The sisters are sick with disappointment and complaining of their ailments, when the royal page and herald arrive with the announcement that the prince will marry the girl whose foot fits a slipper that he has. The sisters forget their afflictions immediately and begin to prepare for the journey to court. Cendrillon is aware that she has lost her slipper on the previous day, and she rejoices secretly. Mélise warns Cendrillon that she must present herself for the trial in her everyday clothes (III, 1-5).

The setting shifts to the royal gardens, where a throne has been installed. Ramir is worrying about the efficacy of his plan to find his love with the slipper, when Clorinde and Tisbé arrive only to be rejected (III, 6-8). Cendrillon enters with Mélise, and her stepmother rebukes her for her impertinence. Cendrillon is about to depart in tears, when the prince (III, 9) orders her to remain for the test. The slipper is brought before the throne, and Cendrillon's foot proves to be a perfect size for it. She is proclaimed wife of the prince, who cannot understand how a girl in dirty rags has become his princess. He explains his predicament to Mélise, and the fairy transforms Cendrillon into the girl whom he knew at the ball. He is jubilant and accpets Cendrillon as his bride. They give thanks to Mélise, who marries them with the wish that they will celebrate their marriage in joy (III, 10-11).

The ballet enjoyed a resounding success at the Opéra, where it remained in the repertory until 24 November 1930. It enjoyed more than a hundred performences at the Opéra during the seven years that it was billed there. The male parts were created by MM. François Decombe* (the prince), Louis F. Gosselin* (Olivier), Louis Mérante* (the baron), Ferdinand (Page), Lenoir (herald), and Romain (master of ceremonies) (see eighteenth-century volume for Albert). The female roles were filled initially by Mmes Emilie Bigottini (Cendrillon), Elie (the baroness), Anatole (Clorinde) and Mlles Gaillet (Mélise), Fanny Bias (Tisbé) (see eighteenth-century volume for Bigottini).

BIBLIOGRAPHY: BB 60-62; Chouquet 390; GBGB 49-65; HAZ 84-85; Lajarte II, 104; PBR 90, 147, 241; RBP 47-49; RLVB 107-10.

La Cenerentola by Gioacchino Rossini* is called Cendrillon in French and Cinderella in English. It is discussed in the twentieth-century volume under La Cenerentola.

Cerrito, Francesca Teresa Giuseppa Raffaela DIT Fanny (b. 11 May 1817, Naples; d. 6 May 1909, Paris), ballerina, began to study dancing in early childhood and enjoyed a successful debut in her native city despite pessimistic predictions about her future career. After winning approval in Italian and Austrian theatres, she appeared on the London stage in 1840. She created the major roles in Jules Perrot's* ballets at Her Majesty's Theatre in Haymarket, where she met her future husband, Arthur Saint-Léon.* It was during this interval of her life that the English director Benjamin Lumley had the happy idea of assembling in the spectacular Pas de quatre the four greatest dancers of the moment: Marie Taglioni,* Caronne Grisi,* Lucina Grahn,* and Fanny Cerrito. The production was billed on 12 July 1845 after disputes over the artists' order of appearance were settled on the principle that age should take precedence over beauty. In the meantime, Cerito and Saint-Léon had been married at the Batignolles church in Paris on 17 April 1845 after the pastor of Saint Roch had refused to unite them in matrimony because they were associated with the theatre.

As partners on the stage, Arthur Saint-Léon and his bride were now inspiring constant applause in England, and they prepared confidently for a triumph in Paris during the summer season of 1847. The husband established contact with Charles Duponchel* at the Opéra to indicate his choice of the ballet Alma for which he, Perrot, and Prosper Dider Deshayes* had done the choreography; he indicated that he considered this work a most suitable vehicle for his wife's talents. The couple arrived in the French capital during the early days of September with their revision of Alma, to which they had given the title of La Fille de marbre.*

Rehersals began in earnest and the premiere of the new composition was scheduled for 20 October 1847. Receipts at the box office were above average for Saint-Léon's work, and the spectators applauded the performance with enthusiasm, but critics were not always certain about the efficacy of Fanny Saint-Léon's technique despite the obvious appeal of her charms. It was in all probability the variety of her movements, her indifference at times toward the traditional manner of executing certain steps, and her preference for vivacity over correctness that upset the critics to some degree. One reporter complained of her "turned-up toes"; another journalist regretted that her knees sagged. Yet the bourgeois king was pleased and gave Cerrito an expensive bracelet, while rewarding Saint-Léon with a purse of 3,000 francs.

Cerrito and Saint-Léon were back in Paris in September 1848 after another series of appearances in London for the British impresario Lumley. They danced at the Opéra in La Fille de marbre on 6, 9, 13 October and then created the roles of Kathi and Hans in the premiere of La Vivandière* on 20 October. Saint-Léon had written the choreography, but critics were unkind towards his work and the manner in which he executed it, but his wife was praised for the effectiveness of her technique and the impressions she created with her steps.

The second production at the Opéra in 1848-49 by Saint-Léon was also a hurried affair. Le Violin du diable* was given its premiere on 19

January 1849, only three months after the billing of La Vivandière. Saint-Léon as Urbain danced the violinist in love with Hélène de Vardack (Cerrito). The popular appeal of the production lay in Saint-Léon's effectiveness as choreographer, dancer, and violinist, and critics compared him to Niccolò Paganini because they could think of no male dancer whom his dancing suggested. Yet Saint-Léon's relentless enemy in the press, Charles Maurice, was not at a loss for words. He complained of the choreographer's misplaced and asymmetrical head, his ill-shapen legs, and his too obvious paunch.

The married couple began a third season in Paris on Christmas eve 1849 with a presentation of Le Violin du diable booked as the companion piece for Le Fanal,* which was enjoying its premiere on this same date. Once again, however, the choreographer was preparing a new work in haste, and he managed to have Stella* ready for its initial production at the Opéra on 22 February 1850. It was a ballet designed to serve specifically as a vehicle for the talents of its author and his wife, who danced Gennaro and Stella. It served its purpose well, and the spectators applauded the performers rather than the composition. Théophile Gautier* had nothing but kind words for Saint-Léon who, he said, was called the "india-rubber man" for good reason in England. He was impressed equally by Cerrito's grace and verve. There were accusations of plagiarism directed against Saint-Léon as its author, but these charges created neither scandal nor suits, and, after a summer vacation in the country, the husband and wife team returned to the rue Le Peletier* to revive Le Violin du diable on 11 September 1850. Also, a choreographer was needed for La Pâquerette* upon which Théophile Gautier and the chef du chant François Benoist* were collaborating.

The new ballet Pâquerette was given its premiere on 15 January 1851, and at least one critic dismissed its libretto as ridiculous and even stupid by reason of its demands upon the credibility of spectators. Gautier himself admitted the truth of some of the charges but reminded his detractors that the story was evolved to afford an opportunity to present the talents of Fanny Cerrito (Pâquerette) and her husband (François) in a most advantageous light. The poet's argument was tenuous, and the work had to be dropped, even if it did enjoy the support of M. and Mme Saint-Léon.

The couple left Paris for Madrid in March 1851, but they returned to the French capital in June. Fanny continued on to London without her husband, who remained at the Opéra. Their marriage had run its course.

But Fanny Cerrito prayed for a return engagement at the Opéra and promised to donate a silver chalice to the chapel of the Blessed Virgin at Notre-Dame de Lorette. Her prayers were answered in October 1852 after 18 months, and she kept her word. Her new contract called for a monthly salary of 3,000 francs, and she was to dance for eight months in each of the ensuing two years. Her first ballet was Orfa,* arranged by Josepher Mazilier* and given its premiere on 29 December 1852. Critics noticed that she had grown slightly heavier, but her public was still faithful and appreciative of her efforts. Her star was setting, however, because management was beginning to welcome new names like Mathilde Besson, Olimpia Priora,* Marie Guy-Stéphan,* and especially Carolina Rosati.* She had to protest to win a part in a divertissement to be given at the Hôtel de Ville, although she did win the title-role in Gemma,* which had its premiere on 31 May 1854 (see eighteenth-century volume for divertissement). She was acclaimed for her performance, and she was honored for 20 years of success at the Opéra, but the work was danced only nine times. Her contract was renewed nevertheless, and she did Fenella in La Muette de Portici* on 13 December 1854, but she was falling into disputes with the new director, Crosnier, who had replaced Nestor Roqueplan. Her big quarrel was over a benefit performance in her behalf, a matter that she continued to discuss with Alphonse Royer* after Crosnier's departure from the Opéra. Ultimately, she was given 6,000 francs without a benefit program, and her ties with the Opéra were severed permanently in 1855.

Fanny Cerrito went to Russia after settling accounts with the Opéra, but she suffered a severe shock when her costume caught fire for a moment on the stage in Moscow. This alarming experience did not prevent her from keeping an engagement in London during the summer of 1856, but it contributed in some degree to her decision to retire from the theatre in the summer of 1856. Paris still had a hold on her, however, and she took up residence here in 1857. She elected to remain incognita and preferred to live by herself, but she was recognized from time to time by tourists from England or by her neighbors. She died at the age of 92 on 6 May 1909 at her home in the rue Théry.

BIBLIOGRAPHY: Chouquet 409-12, 414; CODB 111, Margaret Crosland, Ballet Carnaval (New York: Arco, 1955), 14; DBF VIII, 68; EDB 83; EZF 159-60; Ivor Guest, Fanny Cerrito: the Life of a Romantic Ballerina (London: Dance Books Ltd., 1974); idem, The Romantic Ballet in England: Its Development, Fulfillment and Decline (Middletown, Conn.: Wesleyan University Press, 1972), 76-82; idem, "Triumphs of Fanny Cerrito," D Mag 30 (November 1956), 44-45; Lajarte II, 186-87, 188-90, 206-7, 211-12, 216; André Levinson, Ballet romantique (Paris: Editions du Trianon, 1929), 18-27; Parmenia Migel, The Ballerinas from the Court of Louis XV to Pavlova (New York: Macmillan, 1972), 208-22; Lillian Moore, Artists of the Dance (New York: Thomas Y. Crowell Co., 1938), 136-46; Mark E. Perugini, A Pageant of the Dance and Ballet (London: Jarrolds, 1946), 205-8; SS 111-12, 122-23; Walter Terry, Star Performance (New York: Doubleday, 1954), 81-83.

Chabrier, Alexis Emmanuel (b. 18 January 1841, Ambert, Puy-de-Dôme; d. 13 September 1894, Paris), composer, showed an early interest in music, but his father would not permit him to pursue a career in the arts, and he went to Paris to study law at age 17. He graduated with a degree and was appointed to a position with the government in 1862, but he continued his musical studies quietly and as an avocation. Finally, after nearly a score of years with the Department of the Interior, he resigned his post to pursue his career in music.

Chabrier's first two works for the theatre had been two operettas entitled L'Etoile (1877) and L'Education manquée (1879), but it was his rhapsody España (1843) that made his name known whereveer music was played in France. Unfortunately, however, the composer's hopes for success in the theatre were now shattered by two unexpected events. His Gwendoline* disappeared from the stage of the Théâtre de la Monnaie in Brussels after only two performances in 1886, when this theatre had to close on account of bankruptcy; Le Roi malgré lui seemed headed for success at the Opéra-Comique in 1887, but this theatre burned down after the third presentation of this work. Also, it was now too late in the composer's life for him to be encouraged by the rivival of Gwendoline at the Opéra on 27 December 1893. The production of Albert Carré's revision of Le Roi malgré lui would not take place at the Opéra-Comique until 6 November 1929. As for his Briséis,* he did not live to finish it, and only its first act was given posthumously at the Opéra on 4 May 1899.

More recently, Chabrier's España inspired Jane Catulle-Mendès' ballet España,* which was given its world premiere at the Opéra on 3 May 1911. His music was heard again at the Garnier on 10 May 1952, when his Bourrée fantasque was played as the score for the ballet of the same name presented by the New York City Ballet.

Strangely enough, none of Chabrier's works for the lyric theatre has had its world premiere at the Opéra, and only one of them was staged there before his death. The following catalogue provides the dates when Chabrier's four compositions were heard at the Garnier Palace* for the first time in one form or another.

Work	Premiere
Gwendoline, opera, 3a	27 December 1893
Briséis, lyric drama, unfinished 1a.	4 May 1899
España, ballet, 1a	3 May 1911
Bourrée fantasque, ballet, 3 parts	10 May 1952

BIBLIOGRAPHY: AB I, 53-60; AEM II, 1004-7; BBD 300-301; CBCM 816-20; René Dumesnil, La Musique contemporaine en France (Paris: Armand Colin, 1930) I, 17-18 and II, 73-75; EDS III, 470-72; EGC 80-82; ELM I, 507; Grove II, 148-49; NEO 132; SSBO 292-93; 295, 359.

Chaillou Des Barres, Claude-Etienne (b. 6 June 1784, Beaumont-la-Ferrière; d. 22 August 1857, Paris), librettist, was more involved in political

affairs than in musical matters. He was appointed to the staff of the Council of State in 1805 and married Marguerite-Nicole Nompère de Champagny, daughter of the duke of Cadore, in 1806. He was transferred to the position of intendant of Lower Silesia after the war with Prussia, and the competency of his administration won him the Grand Cross of Civil Merit from the king of Bavaria. After his return to France in 1808, he was given an appointment with the Department of Roads and Bridges before becoming prefect of Ardèche in 1810. The Bourbons' return to power in 1815 obliged him to turn to literary pursuits, and he did the libretto for the Lasthénie* of 1823. He continued to write essays of a historical and economic sort besides founding several journals, but he did only Lasthénie for the musical theatre.
BIBLIOGRAPHY: DBF VIII, 179; GE X, 207; Lajarte II, 105; LXIX III, 834.

Chaliapin, Feodor Ivanovich (b. 13 February 1873, Kazan; d. 12 April 1938, Paris) was doubtlessly the most colorful bass of his generation because of his preoccupation with makeup and costume as well as with his voice. He was of peasant stock and had little academic or musical education before he joined a provincial opera company in 1890 and received some training from Oussatoff in Tiflis in 1892. He was invited to St. Petersburg in 1894, but he did not have an opportunity to sing leading bass parts in Russian operas until he joined Mamontoff's private company in Moscow in 1896.

Chaliapin had already appeared outside Russia at La Scala in Milan (1901, 1904) and in New York (1907), when he arrived in Paris to make his debut at the Garnier Palace* on 19 May 1908 in the title-role of Boris Godounov* with the Imperial Opéra of Moscow. On 26 June 1909, the date of his next engagement at the Opéra, he performed in the part of the Khan Asvab in Raoul Gungsbourg's* Le Vieil Aigle* for a benefit gala. He was back in Paris for the third time in 1912 to do the lead in Boïto's Mefistofele* at the Opéra on 9 May and to sing Bazile in Le Barbier de Séville* on 19 May. Lastly, on 3 July 1924, he filled the part of Dosiféi in the closing production of La Khovantchina at the theatre (see twentieth-century volume for La Khovantchina.

Chaliapin's activities at the Paris Opéra, therefore, were a relatively minor aspect of his career. As elsewhere, however, all his efforts on the stage of the Garnier were directed toward creating the precise illusion that he felt was necessary for the effectiveness of his performance, even if his actions might violate the cannons of good taste. An individualist to the core, he could not accept the Communist regime of his native land and decided in 1922 to live in exile.

BIBLIOGRAPHY: ADI 13-22; APD 222-23; Renée B. Fisher, Musical Prodigies (New York: Association Press, 1973), 59-60; Michel Georges-Michel, Gens de théâtre que j'ai connus, 1900-40 (New York: Brentano's, n.d.), 185-94; GIR 147-55; ICM 304-5; KRJ 78-79; Henry Pleasants, The Great Singers (New York: Simon and Schuster, 1966), 319-26; Fedor Ivanovich Shaliapin, Shaliapin: an Autobiography as Told to Maxim Gorky, with Supp. Correspondence and Notes, ed. and trans. Nina Froud and James Hanley (White Lion: 1976); idem, Man and Mask: Forty Years in the Life of a Singer, trans. Phyllis Megroz (Westport, Conn.: Greenwood Press, 1970); RC 159-66; SW 48, 50, 132, 147, 223; Mary Fitch Watkins, Behind the Scenes at the Opera (New York: Frederick A. Stokes Co., 1925), 287-300.

Chapuy, Alfred (b. 29 August 1829, Bastide; d. 2 June 1871, Brussels), dancer, danced at the Opéra between 1855 and 1866. His talents won him the role of Pietro in Graziosa* on 25 March 1861, and the short run of this ballet left him free in time to dance Don Raphaël in L'Etoile de Messine* the following fall on 20 November 1861. The next winter he appeared in the divertissement of Charles Gounod's* La Reine de Saba* on 28 February 1862 (see eighteenth-century volume for divertissement). Zina Mérante* was quite popular with the public at this time, and he had the distinction of serving as her partner for a pas de deux in the first act of Giselle* during the 8 May 1863 revival of this almost perennial ballet. His last part at the Opéra was Istwann in Néméa*; he shared in a pas de cinq with Martha Muravieva as his partner in the first act of this composition produced initially on 22 April 1864.

Alfred Chapuy was married to a former dancer, Louise Monnier, and their daughter Marguerite enjoyed the distinction of creating the role of

Micaela in Georges Bizet's <u>Carmen</u>* at the Opéra-Comique on 3 March 1875.
BIBLIOGRAPHY: CB 351, 369; Ivor Guest, <u>The Ballet of the Second Empire</u> (Middletown, Conn.: Wesleyan University Press, 1974), 23, 149-50, 167, 172, 183, 199, 257, 259, 261, 264; Lajarte II, 220, 232-34, 236-37.

Charles VI was an opera in five acts with a libretto by Casimir Delavigne* and Germain Delavigne.* Jacques-François Halévy* composed its score, and Joseph Mazilier* created the choreography. The sets were done by Cambon, Deterle, Despléchin, Philastre, and Séchan. The opera had its premiere at the Royal Academy of Music on 15 March 1843, and it was billed on 30 dates before the end of the year. It went on to enjoy another 21 presentations between 1844 and 1848, and it was mounted with revisions for the first time on 4 October 1847. It was seen on another two occasions in 1850, but it was dropped after the second of these two stagings on 25 September. It had been produced 53 times before disappearing from the repertory.

The opera begins in a modest farm house, the abode of an old soldier called Raymond and his daughter Odette. The latter warns her father not to speak so loudly about avenging the French defeat by the English while she is preparing to enter the service of the king of France (I, 1). Queen Isabelle interviews Odette and explains to her that she must humor the mad and dying king, and she notices that Odette is wearing an expensive locket. Odette is obliged to tell her that it is a persent from a certain Charles, who comes to see her on the farm. The queen replies that he must be taken prisoner because he is English (I, 2-4). Odette cannot believe the queen, and, when Charles appears, she questions him. He is evasive. She tells him to admit that he is the dauphin. Overwhelmed, Odette warns him that the English are about to seize him if he steps outside the cabin. He escapes through a window (I, 5).

At the English court, treasonous Queen Isabelle sings a villanelle by the poet Alain Chartier and then explains to Bedford that she has drawn up a decree transmitting the French crown to the young English king. She assures him that Charles VI will sign it, and the courtiers leave the hall to sit down at the banquet table (II, 1).

Charles VI enters alone, hungry, and mad; he recalls happier days an weeps (II, 2). Odette tries to help him and begins to play cards with him because he regains his sanity from time to time when he is absorbed in this pastime. He takes all the tricks until he is stopped by a queen, but he wins the hand finally by drawing a king (II, 3). Queen Isabelle and Bedfort dismiss Odette, and the queen gives Charles VI the decree to sign, but he demurs and asks to see Odette. Isabelle promises him that he and Odette may play cards for as long as they wish, if he signs the treaty. Duped, he affixes his signature to the document. Odette returns with the other courtiers, and Isabelle announces that peace has been established because the king has agreed that young Lancastre is to inherit the French throne. Charles VI asks Odette to cut the cards (II, 4-6).

The third act returns to Raymond's humble dwelling, where a chorus of students toasts the dauphin. Raymond is angered by the plot to surrender France to the English, and he resolves to fight. He leads the students in a patriotic song and accepts them into the growing army. The dauphin and his father enter, and the chorus wishes Charles VI a speedy recovery before leaving him in Odette's care (III, 1-3). Odette tries to make the king understand that the dauphin is his son and that he is the victim of an intrigue hatched by the queen. Charles recognizes his son at last and gives thanks to heaven for his restored memory (III, 4). Raymond announces that Isabelle wishes the king and Odette to return to her court at the hôtel Saint-Paul for a celebration in honor of Charles VI. Raymond adds that it has been arranged for the king to crown Lancastre on this occasion. Charles VI is on the point of refusing the invitation when the dauphin persuades him to return to Paris so that they may take vengeance upon Isabelle and her accomplices. The dauphin reveals his plans to attack the English at midnight (III, 5). The scene changes to Paris, where Isabelle, Charles VI, Odette, and Raymond are gathered on the steps of the hôtel Saint-Paul. Lancastre and Bedfort enter with their pages and squires. Bedfort orders Charles to recognize Lancastre with the kiss of peace, but the king objects. The people rush forward to protect him, but they are repelled by English pikes (III, 6).

Odette and Charles VI are now prisoners, and she ponders her king's fate until a voice exhorts her to die for him (IV, 1). Isabelle shows the king the treaty that he has signed, but he burns the document as a dishonorable act born of madness. He assures Bedfort and Isabelle that he has recovered his reason and sees through their vile deceptions (IV, 2). Isabelle assures her companion that she will remedy the situation (IV, 3). Tired, Charles falls asleep and sees the spectres of former kings of France who have been murdered. They dance around his bed and warn him that he is about to join them (IV, 4).

The fifth act opens with a group of French soldiers singing before their campfire and waiting to attack at midnight. Raymond and Odette come down the Seine in a skiff. Raymond announces that all is lost because Charles VI has lapsed back into his madness, while the dauphin has been captured. Lancastre will receive the oriflamme on the morrow at Saint-Denis. Odette suggests that they invade Paris and seize this standard before it is desecrated. The army follows Odette, and the setting shifts to the interior of Saint-Denis, where Charles in his madness is ordering his son to renounce his right to the throne. He presents the oriflamme to Bedfort, but Odette intervenes, and the French leaders call upon the English to surrender. They refuse, but Charles VI is able to prevent a struggle, and he recovers his anity long enough to transmit his crown to his son. Word reaches Saint-Denis that fighting has begun outside the walls of the city. Dying Charles and his faithful followers vow that the English will never rule in France (V, 1-4).

The principal male roles of <u>Charles VI</u> were created by Paul Barroilhet* (the king), Gilbert Duprez* (the dauphin), Canaple (the duke de Bedfort), Nicolas Levasseur* (Raymond), and Placide Poultier* (Gontran). The parts of Isabelle de Bavière and Odette were filled by Mme Julie Dorus-Gras* and Mlle Rosine Stolz,* respectively. The score offered a number of touching or stirring passages including the duet by Odette and Isabelle, "Respect à ce roi qui succombe" (I, 4); the dauphin's declaration to Odette, "En respect mon amour se change" (I, 6); and his query to her in the same scene, "Gentille Odette, eh quoi? ton coeur palpite" (I, 6). The most moving moment in the second act was probably Odette's romance sung to Charles VI in his madness, "Ah! qu'un ciel sans nuage" (II, 3). Odette's ballade to the king, "Chaque soir Jeanne sur la plage," was yet another of her effective moments. The patriotic vein was exploited successfully in "La France a l'horreur du servage" (III, 1) and in "A minuit" (V, 1) sung by Gontran and the chorus. The king had at least two major triumphs in the score: his recitative alone on the stage in act two, scene one, "J'ai faim . . . Que font-ils donc?" and his duet with Odette in the scene where they play cards, "A la victoire où nous courons" (II, 3).

BIBLIOGRAPHY: AEM V, 1341-48; Chouquet 404-5; DDO I, 222-24; EDS VI, 107-9; Léon Halévy, F. Halévy, sa vie et ses oeuvres (Paris: Heugel et Cie, 1863), 36-39; Lajarte II, 172-73; H. Moréno, "Semaine théâtrale: reprise de Charles VI," Le Ménestrel 37 (10 April 1870), 146-47; Wks III, 7539.

Charpentier, Gustave (b. 25 June 1860, Dieuze; d. 18 February 1956, Paris), French composer, was encouraged by his father and godfather to study music, and, when the advancing Germans forced his family to flee to Tourcoing in 1870, he continued his studies there and became a member of the municipal band. His apparent talent and strong interest in music impressed his friends, especially the owner of the Lille spinning-mill where he had gone to work in 1875. M. Albert Lorthiois financed his studies at the Lille Conservatoire. Charpentier's continuing success as a student and a performer over a period of six years in Lille now prompted the citizens of this city to finance his enrollment at the Conservatoire in Paris in 1881.

In the French capital, the young musician displayed a taste for the unfettered life of a student in Montmartre, and his refusal to bow to discipline soon set him in conflict with his professors, especially M. Massart. Charpentier's obligation to serve in the army put an end to these conflicts, however, and he returned to the Conservatoire in 1885 to complete his studies under the direction of Jules Massenet.* Finally, in 1887, he surprised his fellow-students and the faculty at the Conservatoire by winning the Prix de Rome.

Charpentier found the rules of conduct demanded of Prix de Rome students as bothersome as regulations at the Conservatoire, but he was not totally distracted and started on a work called <u>Louise</u>* besides finishing a symphony drama entitled <u>La Vie du poète</u>.

The student returned to Paris in 1890. He was enthusiastic about his <u>Louise</u>, for which he had completed the libretto, and he read his text to friends who advised him to inject more lyricism and less realism into his poem. He set to work and had a revised version ready to submit to editors by 1896. In the meantime, his <u>La Vie du poète</u> had been heard at the Garnier Palace* on 17 June 1892 with Edouard Colonne* at the desk.

Various producers were now offering to stage <u>Louise</u> in condensed or abbreviated form, but Charpentier rejected these opportunities until Albert Carré accepted the "musical novel" for presentation without abridgment at the Opéra-Comique on 2 February 1900. It would enjoy nearly a thousand performances at this theatre during the next fifty years, and M. Carré would keep begging the composer for another work in the vein of <u>Louise</u>. Finally, the successful author announced in 1912 that his next composition was ready to go into production. He took his manuscript down from Montmartre to the rue Favart, where Albert Carré, Georges Ricou, and the orchestra leader Albert Wolff examined the test without delay. Unfortunately, these men could see immediately that it was uneven in tone, riddled with obscurity, and even marred by incredible immaturity. Embarrassed, they knew equally as well that they had to stage this disappointing work, and they presented it to the Paris public on 4 June 1913. Ill-starred <u>Julien</u> had to be withdrawn after its 20th billing at the Opéra-Comique.

After 1913, none of Charpentier's announced plans for the theatre came to fruition. His lyric drama entitled <u>L'Amour du Faubourg</u> had remained unperformed. Only his friends came to know anything of his <u>Orphée</u>, although M. Delmas has reported that this work has been completed.

BIBLIOGRAPHY: AEM II, 1103-7; BBD 305; Pierre Brunel and Stéphane Wolff, <u>L'Opéra</u>, (Paris: Bordas, 1980), 175; J. Bruyr, "La Vie montmartroise de Gustave Charpentier," <u>Musica</u> 75 (1960), 39; DEC 127-32; Marc Delmas, <u>Gustave Charpentier et le lyrisme français</u> (Paris: Delagrave, 1931); EDS III, 545-48; ELM I, 524; Jean Gourret, <u>Histoire de l'Opéra-Comique</u> (Paris: Publications *universitaires, 1978), 187-88; Grove II, 186-87; K. O'Donnell Hoover, "Gustave Charpentier," MQ 15 (1939), 334; NEO 133; SW 378; L. Vauxcelles, "Enquête avec Gustave Charpentier," Figaro 23 October 1900; WOC 108.*

Chélard, Hippolyte-André-Jean-Baptiste (b. 1 February 1789, Paris; d. 12 February 1861, Weimar), composer, was admitted to the Conservatoire in 1803 to study violin, but he added harmony and composition with Dourlen and François Gossec to his program. He won the Prix de Rome competition in 1811 and passed his three years at Rome under the tutelage of Nicolas Zingarelli and the abbot Baini. Giovanni Paisiello became interested in him at Naples and staged his opéra bouffe entitled La Casa de vendere in 1815 (see eighteenth-century volume for Gossec, Zingarelli, and Paisiello).

Chélard returned to Paris in 1816 and joined the orchestra of the Opéra as a violinist besides giving lessons on this instrument. Prompted by his previous success in Naples, he did the score for Macbeth* by Roger de l'Isle and Auguste Hix. This tragedy in three acts was a complete failure on 29 June 1827, but Chélard refused to believe that his work had been rejected due to its shortcomings, and he went to Germany to induce the baron de Poissl to stage his revised composition. The German version with Mlle Schechner, Mme Sigl-Vespermann, and Pellegrini was applauded and taken to several other cities for performance, but it was never rescheduled in Paris.

Chélard was now honored for his efforts and success by being named to the position of chapel-master for the king of Bavaria, but his Paris failure still bothered him, and he returned to the French capital in 1829 to mount his comic opera, La Table et le logement (1830). This work proved to be his second failure in France and had to be withdrawn after only two or three billings. But the composer was still unwilling to admit total failure in his native city and readied Minuit in three acts for the Ventadour theatre. Unfortunately, the Revolution of 1830 erupted and left Chélard bankrupt and distraught. He tried to recoup his fortune in Munich, where he gave a German version of his latest work at court in June 1831. It was condemned as a very mediocre piece.

Yet he refused to surrender to bad fortune even now, and he managed finally to grasp elusive success with a German translation of La Table et le logement and a revival of a mass that he had already played at the Church of Saint-Roch. Confident, he summond his family to Germany and gave up all plans for returning to Paris. He went to England in 1822-23 to mount his L'Etudiant in English, and he scored another German libretto before he went to Weimar in 1836. Franz Liszt* replaced him a few years later, but, except for a short journey to Paris in 1852, Chélard chose to remain in Weimar for his retirement. His only contribution to the Paris Opéra, therefore, had been his unsuccessful Macbeth in 1827.

BIBLIOGRAPHY: DBF VIII, 968-69; Fétis II, 257-59; GE X, 1011; Lajarte II, 128; LXIX III, 1121.

Chenal, Marthe (b. 28 August 1881, Saint-Maurice; d. 29 January 1947, Paris), French soprano née Marie Louise Anthelme, started her formal musical education at the Conservatoire in Paris, but she interrupted her studies at this institution in 1901, when she decided to perform at the Moulin-Rouge. She returned to the Conservatoire before long to complete her formal training successfully, however, and, in 1905, she was invited to appear on the stage of the Opéra. Here, she made her debut as Brunnhilde in Sigurd* on 13 December 1905.

The soprano was quite successful at the Garnier Palace*, where she filled the following roles between 1906 and 1919.

Role	Opera	Year
Annette	Le Freischütz	1906
Elisabeth	Tannhäuser	1906
Ariane	Ariane	1907
Marguerite	Faust	1907
Armide	Armide	1910
Iphigénie	Iphigénie en Tauride	1916
Thaïs	Thaïs	1917

Marguerite	La Damnation	1917
Monna Vanna	Monna Vanna	1918
Salammbô	Salammbô	1919

She also created the parts indicated below, when the following compositions had their premieres at the Opéra:

Role	Opera	Premiere
Alix	Le Miracle	30 December 1910
Nymphe	Icare	19 December 1911
Bellone	La Forêt sacrée	5 February 1916
Graziella	Graziella	6 April 1916
Jeanne	Jeanne d'Arc	24 November 1917
Reine de Paris	Intermède	1 April 1919
La Gloire	Fête triomphale	14 July 1919
Rosario	Goyescas	17 December 1919
Catherina	La Mégère apprivoisée	30 January 1922

After World War I, Mme Chenal also appeared at the Opéra-Comique and the Gaîté-Lyrique, and her lively personality brought applause on every occasion, but contemporary audiences were especially moved by her interpretation of Tosca, Carmen, and Le Jongleur de Notre-Dame. It was almost inevitable that she be the artiste chosen to sing the Marseillaise at the Opéra on 11 November 1918.

BIBLIOGRAPHY: APD 225; Pierre Brunel and Stéphane Wolff, L'Opéra (Paris: Bordas, 1980), 175; DBF VIII, 975-76; ICM 317; KRJ 80; SW 39, 41, 88, 102, 123, 193, 203, 207, 209; WOC 243-44.

Le Cheval de bronze was an opera ballet in four acts with music by Daniel Auber,* a libretto by Eugène Scribe,* and choreography by Lucien Petipa.* It had its premiere at the Imperial Academy of Music on 21 September 1857 and enjoyed a score of performances before it was dropped from the repertory on 22 November 1858. It had been quite successful at the Opéra-Comique, but the recitatives added to it to make it acceptable to the Opéra slowed its pace, and the public regretted the loss of the liveliness it had had in 1835 before its transformation.

The curtain rises at the start of Le Cheval de bronze with Tchin-Kao rejoicing because his daughter Péki is about to wed the mandarin Tsing-Sing, who wishes to escape from the tyranny of his wife Tao-Jin (I, 1-2). The latter appears with Tsing-Sing's three other wives and informs her husband that he has been selected to serve as the constant companion of the imperial prince on his visit to their province. He must postpone his marriage to Péki because his duties begin immediately (I, 3-5). The prince announces that his trip is exclusively for pleasure, and he enjoys a rich repast and dancing girls before telling Tsing-Sing that he is looking for the girl of his dreams. The prince knows immediately that Tao-Jin is not the girl he seeks, and he finds out before long that Péki is not the bride of whom he dreams. Tao-Jin swears to have revenge as soon as she learns that her aged husband Tsing-Sing plans to take a fifth wife (I, 6-8). Disconsolate, Péki tells the prince that she loves poor Yanko, who has disappeared into the sky on a steed of bronze that flies off whenever he has a rider. Yanko returns suddenly, but he cannot divulge the nature of his adventures without suffering the death penalty (I, 9-12). The prince wishes Péki and Yanko to wed, and he is so curious about the bronze horse's celestial excursions that he orders Tsing-Sing to mount the statue with him (I, 9-13). In the meantime, Tchin-Kao has selected a rich merchant to be Péki's husband, but she suggests to Yanko that they elope. Tao-Jin supports their plan and promises them refuge in her palace (II, 1-6). Tsing-Sing returns from his travels aloft but refuses to describe his trip for Tao-Jin (II, 7-8). Tchin-Kao finds Tsing-Sing asleep in his house and decides to announce that the dinner he planned for the merchant Mouja-Ya is for Tsing-Sing; Péki tells Yanko to leave and prepares to disguise herself (II, 9-11). Tchin-Kao tries to awaken Tsing-Sing with music but discovers that he has turned into a statue because he has spoken of his trip on the bronze horse in his sleep. Yanko suffers the same fate after explaining the reason for Tsing-Sing's death. Péki determines to solve the mystery of the bronze horse and leaves to ride him (II, 12-14).

The scene shifts to the heavenly sphere, where Stella is happy over the prospect of her libration from her celectial prison by the prince. Her rescuer must remain with her for an entire day, however, or else he will be returned to earth. Péki arrives attired in male costume to find the bracelet that will break the spell cast over Yanko, but Lo-Mangli tells her that only women can remain in his land because all men succumb to the temptation to kiss one of its inhabitants and must be returned to earth forthwith. Stella enters with the prince at her heels, and he kisses her despite her protests. Accordingly, he is whisked away to earth (III, 1-4). Péki withstands all female blandishments and wiles for a day, of course, and she is able to return to earth with Stella and her bracelet (III, 5-8).

Tsing-Sing and Yanko are still wooden statues honored by the people as totems. Tao-Jin mourns her husband's death; Tchin-Kao wonders about Péki's fate. The latter appears with Stella to restore the statues to life with the charmed bracelet after making certain that Yanko and she are free to wed (IV, 1-4).

The score of Le Cheval de bronze was not extraordinary by any means, but there were at least three passages in the music that earned applause: Péki's ballade, "Là-bas, sur ce rocher sauvage" (I, 9); Péki's couplets, "Quand on est fille, hélas" (II, 3); the duet by Tao-Jin and Tsing-Sing, "Ah! ciel, en croirai-je mes yeux" (II, 7). The female parts were sung by Mlles Dussy (Péki), Moreau-Sainti (Tao-Jin), and Delille (Stella) opposite Obin (Tchin-kao), Marié (Tsing-Sing), Sapin (Yang), and Boulo (Yanko).

BIBLIOGRAPHY: Neil Cole Arvin, Eugène Scribe and the French Theatre, 1815-60 (Cambridge: Harvard University Press, 1924), 184; Chouquet 417; DDO I, 229; Lajarte II 223-24; Charles Malherbe, Auber (Paris: Renouard, n.d.) 44-45; Moniteur universal 270 (27 September 1857), 1059; SS 254.

Chopin, Frédéric (b. 1 March 1810, Zelazowa-Wola, near Warsaw; d. 17 October 1849, Paris), composer, showed signs of being a prodigy at age seven, and he gave his first public concert when he was nine.

Subsequently he entered the Conservatory in Warsaw to study harmony and composition, but his piano professors could teach him nothing that he did not already know.

It was not long before Chopin's reputation as a musician radiated from Warsaw to the other capitals of Europe, and, in 1829, he was applauded wildly at two concerts he gave in Vienna. Then, in 1830, he settled in Paris, where he was lionized by the upper crust of society. Fame, fortune, and the famous love affair with George Sand followed, but, after a winter spent with his mistress on the isle of Majorca in a dank, deserted, and delapidated monastery, Chopin's health began to deteriorate. He returned to the French capital eventaually, but he fell mortally ill after his last two concerts in London and Paris. He died the following year in his apartment on the place Vendôme.

Chopin's music was written almost exclusively for piano, and none of his compositions was planned as a ballet score. Yet choreographers have found his works ideally suited to their purposes in many instances. His music has been heard at the Opéra on numerous occasions, when it has served as the score for the following ballets:

Ballet	**Premiere**
Les Sylphides	19 June 1909
Suite de danses	23 June 1913
La Nuit ensorcelée	12 November 1925
Feuilles d'automne	24 November 1925
Soirée romantique	27 November 1934
La Mort du cygne	10 December 1948
Suite romantique	12 March 1958
Valse	9 June 1958

BIBLIOGRAPHY: AEM II, 1218-30; BBD 315-17; CBCM 491-507; CODB 118; DGM 197-252; EGC 89-93; ELM I, 533-42; Arthur Hedley, Chopin (New York: Collier, 1962); James Gibbons Huneker, Chopin, the Man and His Music (New York: Scribner's, 1900); MCDE I,

223-41; Gerard Mannoni, "Chopin et la danse," SDLD (10 November 1979), 38-39; MM 314-17; John F. Porte, Chopin: the Composer and His Music (New York: Scribner's 1935); Thompson 324-32; Herbert Weinstock, Chopin (New York: Knopf, 1949).

Choron, Alexandre-Etienne (b. 1772, Caen; d. 1834, Paris), teacher, devoted most of his time to teaching music and to promoting the cause of music in France, but he found time to write a number of methods books and treatises on his favorite topics. He served as director of the Opéra in 1816-17, and he founded the Conservatoire de Musique Classique et Religieuse that enjoyed undisputed prominence between 1817 and 1830. His most famous students included Duprez and Pierre Dietsch.* His most popular composition was entitled La Sentinelle.

BIBLIOGRAPHY: Alexandre Bisson et Théodore de Lajarte, Petite encyclopédie musicale (Paris: A. Hennuyer, 1884) II, 149.

Chrétien-Vaguet, Alba (b. 8 March 1872, Paris; d. ?), singer, studied piano at the Conservatoire in her native city and made her debut as a soprano at the Théâtre de la Monnaie as Alice in Robert le Diable* on 7 September 1891. She remained in Belgium for a year and then accepted a contract with the Opéra, where she made her Paris debut as Alice in the 31 July 1893 production of Robert le Diable.

Mme Chrétien-Vaguet created no more than two roles at the Garnier Palace,* the title-part of Déidamie* (1893) and Thanasto of Brisésis* (1899), and she appeared in only six other works at this theatre, but the parts that she did enabled her to furnish ample evidence of the fine quality of her soprano voice: Valentine in Les Huguenots,* Brunhilde in La Walkyrie,* Elsa in Lohengrin,* in 1893; the title-role of Djelma* in 1894 and Brunehilde in Sigurd* in 1895; and Ortrude in Lohengrin* in 1900.

The soprano was the wife of Albert Vaguet,* who retired from the stage to teach at Pau in 1903 after an accident.

BIBLIOGRAPHY: KRJ 451; SW 70, 72, 115-18, 134-36, 202-3, 224-26.

Cicéri, Pierre-Luc-Charles (b. 17 August 1782, Saint-Cloud; d. 22 August 1868, Saint-Chéron,

Seine-et-Oise), French artist and decorator, had an outstanding tenor voice as a young man, but an accident prevented him from pursuing a career in the lyric theatre, and he turned to studying art in the studio of the architect Bellanger. His first task as a professional artist was the decoration of Sèvres china, but he was soon called upon to restore the theatre in Cassel and to do the decorations for the coronation of Charles X.

After 1827, the painter did some watercolors that are among the holdings of the Louvre and the museum at Angers, but a greater responsibility came to him when he was appointed to serve as chief decorator at the Opéra. He was quite successful in his work for the theatre, and his sets for a number of works drew applause: Armide, La Muette de Partici,* Semiramis,* La Vestale, and Robert la Diable,* (see eighteenth-century volume for Armide and La Vestale). Also, he did the costumes for a number of these compositions, and the quality of his work may be said to have contributed stongly to the formation and spread of romantic taste.

If his sets for operas were abundant, his contribution to the staging of ballets after the exile of Napoleon I was no less impressive. His initial effort in this area was to provide the decor and costumes for Charles Didelot's Flore et Zéphire (1815) (see eighteenth-century volume for Didelot and Flore et Zéphire). He collaborated with a number of other artists on a series of such works as Jacques Halévy's* Manon Lescaut* and Michel Carafa's* L'Orgie,* but he was often the only painter to furnish the sets for ballets, as he did for the following:

Composer	**Ballet**	**Premiere**
Gustave Dugazon*	Les Financés de Caserte	17 September 1817
Jean Schneitzhoeffer*	Proserpine	18 February 1818
Jean Schneitzhoeffer	Le Séducteur au village	3 June 1818
Gustave Dugazon	Aline	1 October 1823
Louis Hérold*	La Fille mal gardée	17 November 1828

Louis Hérold*	La Belle au bois dormant	27 April 1829
Adalbert Gyrowetz*	Nathalie	7 November 1832

Cicéri was frequently one of a team of artists who furnished sets for the Opéra between 1820 and 1847. His collaborators on ballet scenery included Desplechin, Séchan, Philastre, Cambon, and Diéterle, and his joint efforts amounted to a score of compositions choreographed by such stars as Charles Saint-Léon,* Joseph Mazilier,* and Lucien and Marius Petipa.*

BIBLIOGRAPHY: BOP 304-11; DBF VIII, 1307-8; SST 6-12; WLC 59-63, 70, 121.

Le Cid is an opera in four acts and ten tableaux based upon the poem of Guilhen de Castro and the tragi-comedy of the same title by Pierre Corneille. Its score was composed by Jules Massenet,* and its libretto was written by the team of Louis Gallet, d'Ennery, and Edouard Blau.* It had its world premiere at the Opéra on 30 November 1885 in a production by Pedro Gailhard* with choreography for the divertissement established by Louis Mérante* (see eighteenth-century volume for divertissement). The costumes were designed by Count Lepic, and the sets were created by Carpezat (tabl. 1, 2), Robecchi and Amable (tabl. 3, 4), Rubé, Chaperon, Marcel Jambon* (tabl. 5, 6, 7, 8), J.-B. Lavastre (tabl. 9, 10).

The opera opens in count de Gormas' home, and his guests are discussing the kings' decision to make young Rodrigue a knight. Don Arias notes that the king is ready to name a tutor for the young prince, and everybody agrees that this honor must fall to the count (I, tabl. 1, sc. 1-2). Chimène rejoices over her father's acceptance of Rodrigue as his future son-in-law, but she is alarmed to learn that the Infante loves Rodrique despite her royal rank. The Infante reassures her that she cannot wed Rodrigue, a humble knight (I, tabl. 1, sc. 3).

The scene shifts to the interior of the cathedral of Burgos, where the people are giving thanks to their king and St. James for the defeat of the Moors. The king knights Rodrigue; he announces that Rodrigue's father, Don Diègue, is his choice for his son's tutor. The count is thunderstruck and insulted. The count and Don Diègue quarrel in the same terms in which they argue in Corneille's Le Cid, and the result is the same. Don Gormas challenges Don Diègue to a duel (I, tabl. 2, sc. 1-3). Like his Cornelian prototype, Don Diègue laments his old age and charges his son to sustain the family name on the field of honor. Don Rodrigue agrees to do his father's bidding (I, tabl. 2, sc. 4-5).

The setting moves to the street by the count's house, where Rodrigue challenges his fiancée's father to a duel. The count does not take the youth seriously at first, but Rodrigue leaves him no choice. They must fight (II, tabl. 1, sc. 1-2). Rodrigue slays the count. Chimène swears vengeance. No one will identify her father's assailant, and she realizes suddenly that it is Rodrigue who has slain her father (II, tabl. 3, sc. 3-4).

The people are dancing in the public square of Burgos. After the ballet (II, tabl. 4, sc. 1), Chimène throws herself at the king's feet and begs for justice. Don Diègue defends his son; the crowd splits into two factions according to their loyalties. Suddenly, a Moorish envoy enters with a declaration of war from his master, Boabdil. Don Rodrigue begs to lead the Spanish army against the infidels, and Chimène objects, but the king accepts Rodrigue's offer. Rodrigue reminds Chimène that his death in battle will serve Spain and her (II, tabl. 4, sc. 2-3).

Chimène is lamenting her predicament in her bedroom, when Don Rodrigue appears before her to declare his love and to assure her that he plans to die in the coming campaign. She is overcome by the prospect of his death and begs him to protect himself. Finally, she must declare her love to him to persuade him to survive. Rodrigue understands her at last and departs fully determined to return victorious and alive (III, tabl. 1, sc. 1-3).

The setting moves to the Spanish camp, where Don Rodrigue is ordering some of his soldiers to stop carousing and to prepare to continue the struggle against the Moors in the morning. Some of his men object that they have already been defeated, and he orders them to retreat to Grenada (III, tabl. 2, sc. 1-2).

Rodrigue laments the possibility of losing Chimène and the war, but St. James reassures him in a vision (III, tabl. 3, sc. 1). Dawn breaks, and Rodrigue announces to his soldiers that victory awaits them (III, tabl. 4, sc. 1).

The retreating Spaniards have reached Grenada, where they tell Don Diègue that his son is dead. The Infante faints, and Chimène reveals the depth of her grief in an anguished confession of her continuing love for the slain hero. The king enters to tell the Infante and Chimène that Don Rodrigue is alive and victorious (IV, tabl. 1, sc. 1-3).

The court and the people acclaim Don Rodrigue as a national hero under his new Moorish title, Le Cid. The king asks him to name his reward, and he looks at Chimène, but she insists that she prefers justice. The king promises her that she will not be disappointed because he plans to keep his promise to satisfy her request. Chimène protests against this decision, and Rodrigue offers to stab himself. Chimène cannot withstand these repeated offers of justice, and she throws herself into Don Rodrigue's arms. The king gives his blessing to their union, and the throng hails the Cid (IV, tabl. 2, sc. 1).

Massenet did not attend the opening night of Le Cid at the Opéra because he felt obliged to go to the Opéra-Comique on this evening, but he was aware from the start that his new work was a success. In fact, it has been produced at the Opéra on 152 dates, and it remained in the repertory at the Garnier Palace* until 24 November 1919. Its score aroused enthusiasm from the start with its proper tone, especially the chorus by the people and Rodrigue's invocation to his sword, "O noble lame étincelante!" in the first act, Chimène's "De cet affreux combat, O jours de première tendresse," and Rodrigue's vision of St. James in the third act. The two female roles were created by Fidès Devriès* (Chimène) and Rose Bosman (l'Infante). The leading male parts were sung for the first time at the Garnier Palace by Jean de Reszke* making his debut at the Opéra as Don Rodrigue, Edouard de Reszke* (Don Diègue), Pol Plançon* (the count), Léon Melchissedec* (the king). The divertissement was danced by Louis Mérante,* Mlles Rosita Mauri,* Mélanie Hirsch, and Keller, with the ballet of the Opéra. Later, the role of Chimène was sung by such stars as Rose

Caron,* Lucienne Bréval,* and Jeanne Bourdon, while Albert Saléza,* Albert Alvarez,* Paul Franz,* and Léon Laffitte* were cast as Don Rodrigue. Jean-François Delmas* appeared frequently as Don Diègue after 1900, and René Fournets sang Don Gormas (the count) on many occasions before 1900.

Le Cid had its North American debut in New Orleans at the French Opera House on 23 February 1890, and it was produced in New York at the Metropolitan Opera House on 12 February 1897.

BIBLIOGRAPHY: *Charles Bouvet, Massenet (Paris: Henri Laurens, 1929), 72-75; René Brancour, Massenet (Paris: Félix Alcan, 1922), 87-92; José Bruyr, Massenet, musicien de la belle époque (Lyon: Eise, 1964), 52-54; DDO I, 237-39; René Dumesnil, La Musique contemporaine en France (Paris: Armand Colin, 1930) I, 66-70; Henry T. Finck, Massenet and His Operas (New York: John Lane Co., 1910), 164-70; James Harding, Massenet (London: J. M. Dent & Sons, 1970), 33, 81-84, 117, 135, 142, 175, 204-5; Arthur Hervey, Masters of French Music (Boston: Milford House, 1973), 173-206; Demar Irvine, Massenet: a Chronicle of His Life and Times (Seattle: Demar Irvine, 1974), 177-95; Adolphe Jullien, Musiciens d'aujourd'hui (Paris: Librairie de l'Art, 1894) I, 416-24; Jules Massenet, My Recollections, 1848-1912 (Westport, Conn.: Greenwood Press, 1970), 148-60; Modern Drama and Opera: Reading Lists on the Works of Various Authors, ed. Frederick W. Faxon (Boston: The Boston Book Co., 1915), 186-87; H. Moréno, "Mme Bosman dans Le Cid," Le Ménestrel 52 (27 December 1885), 27; Albertine Morin-Labrecque, Jules Massenet et ses opéras (Montréal: éditions de l'étoile, 1914), 25-26; Arthur Pougin, Massenet (Paris: Fischbacher, 1914), 94-96; idem, "Le Cid, opéra en 4 actes et 10 tableaux," Le Ménestrel 52 (6 December 1885), 1-4; Louis Schneider, Massenet: l'homme, le musicien (Paris: L. Cartaret, 1908), 110-24; Georges Servières, La Musique française moderne (Paris: Havard, 1897), 117-220; Eugène de Solenière, Massenet: étude critique et documentaire (Paris: Bibliothèque d'art de la critique, 1897), 31-36; SSBO 290; Stoullig XI (1885), 48-55 and XXVI (1900), 7-9; SW 62-63; Thompson 338, 2120-21.*

Le Cid is a title designating the divertissement in Jules Massenet's* opera as well as the opera

itself, when this section of the longer work is performed alone (see eighteenth-century volume for divertissement). It was given separately from its matrix work for the first time at the Garnier Palace* on 15 July 1900. Louis Mérante* provided its choreography, and Massenet's original music was retained. Mlle Carlotta Zambelli* starred on this occasion alongside the younger Vasquez. Rosita Mauri* and Louis Mérante had headed the corps de ballet at the world premiere of Le Cid at the Garnier Palace 15 years previously on 30 November 1885. The opera was quite popular and enjoyed revivals in 1900, 1905, and 1919, and there was little reason for producing extracts from it, but the divertissement representing a fiesta in Burgos was staged by itself in 1917, 1942, and 1944 for a total of 17 performances. Also, F. Ambroisiny and Albert Aveline* were interested enough in these extra stagings of Massenet's divertissement at the start of the second act to create new choreography for it.
BIBLIOGRAPHY: DDO I, 238-39; SW 254.

Cinthie-Damoreau, Laure, née Montalant (b. 6 February 1801, Paris; d. 25 February 1863, Paris), vocalist, studied piano and harmony at the Conservatoire before she had reached her 14th birthday, and her progress was so remarkable that Plantade agreed to give her singing lessons to complete her musical education. When the Conservatoire was forced to close on account of the Bourbons' return to power, her professor continued her lessons privately because it was becoming more and more evident to him that his young student possessed unusual talents.

Mlle Montalant started her career by appearing in concerts that attracted the attention of a few connoisseurs, but it was not until the reopening of the Italian theatre in 1819 that she found an opportunity to appear before audiences by changing her name to Cinti and making her debut in Paris as Lilla in La Cosa rara. Her success was unique because if Italian singers might inspire applause at the Opéra, it was contrary to precedent for a French artist to win approval at the Italian theatre. Encouraged, therefore, Laure Cinthie resolved to study hard, and she began by memorizing roles and scores. Her zeal was rewarded before long, when she was chosen to sing

Cherubino in Le Nozze de Figaro with Garcia and the directress of the company, Mme Catalani.

The young star wished to perform at the Opéra, however, although it was Mlle Naldi who seemed to be favored by the great violinist Viotti, now director of both the Italian and the French opera houses. While she was awaiting her opportunity, she was offered a contract in 1822 to appear at the King's Theatre in London. She made new friends and money in England; she grew more confident and mature. Yet she still had the Opéra on her mind and returned to Paris after the expiration of her British agreement. Her French contract was renewed at the Italians' theatre, and she was obliged to mark time once again. She was now cast in Il Barbiere de Seviglia, Il Matrimonio segreto, Romeo e Giulietta, and Don Giovanni. Finally, in late 1824, Gioacchino Rossini* arrived in Paris to manage the Italian opera house, and he had with him Mosè in Egitto, containing a part written especially for her. The work was not a success, but its composer managed to persuade Louis Persuis and François Habeneck* to replace lyric tragedy with more Italianate compositions in the rue Le Peletier (see eighteenth-century volume for Persuis). The directors of the Opéra decided to add to their company a vocalist familiar with Italian works and able to perform in the French language. They agreed that la Cinti was ideal for their purposes, and she was nominated to create Pamyra in Le Siège de Corinthe* on 9 October 1826 with Adolphe Nourrit* as Néoclès. The work was a resounding success, and it was now obvious that la Cinti was on the verge of a brilliant career. She was cast next as Anaï in the French version of Rossini's Moïse,* which was billed for the first time on 26 March 1827, and she was also chosen for the female lead in Hippolyte Chélard's* Macbeth,* given its premiere on 29 June 1827. Then, incredibly, a quarrel arose between la Cinti and management, and she left the Opéra in the summer of 1827 to appear in Brussels. She married M. Damoreau in Belgium.

When Mme Cinti-Damoreau returned to her native city, she resumed her appearances at the Opéra without appearing to give a second thought to the recent dispute in which she had been involved. The roles that she created at this time included Elvire in La Muette de Portici* and La Comtesse in Le Comte Ory* of 1828, Mathilde in

Guillaume Tell* of 1829, Ninka in Le Dieu et la Bayadère* of 1830, Térézine in Le Philtre* and Isabelle in Robert le Diable* of 1831, Marie in Le Serment* of 1832, and Zerline in Don Juan* of 1834. This task of learning and executing eight new roles between 1828 and 1834 as well as performing in works already in the repertory did not prevent her from accepting a contract to travel to England with Niccolas Levasseur* and Nourrit in the summer of 1832. Also, she undertook still another excursion across the Channel the following year to appear in Tancredi and Don Giovanni. If she did nothing new at the Opéra in 1833, it was only because she was ill at this time and could not return to the Paris stage until the autumn of 1834.

Laure Cinthie-Damoreau continued to perform subsequently at the Opéra, the Opéra-Comique (1836-42), or in the provinces, and she made a trip to St. Petersburg, but she retired from the theatre after her return from Russia in 1843. She continued to appear in public as a concert artist, however, and she visited New York, Boston, Philadelphia, and New Orleans in this capacity during 1843. She was professor of singing at the Conservatoire between 1834 and 1856 before going into retirement and living quietly in Paris until her death at age 62.

BIBLIOGRAPHY: Paul Bernard, "Académie imperiale de musique: Guillaume Tell; débuts de Mme Marie Cinti-Damoreau," Le Ménestrel 29 (20 July 1862), 265-66; Chouquet 392-98; Ellen Clayton, Queens of Song (Freeport, N.Y.: Books for Libraries Press, reprint of 1865 edition), 221-27; DBF VIII, 1315-16; EFC 141; M. Escudier, "Nécrologie: Mme Cinti-Damoreau," FM 27 (1 March 1863), 64-65; Escudier frères, Etudes biographiques sur les chanteurs contemporains (Paris: Just Tessier, 1840), 207-29; EZF 171-73; Fétis II, 419-20; P. A. Fiorentino, "Laure Cinti-Damoreau, notice biographique," Le Ménestrel 30 (25 October 1863; 1, 8, 15, 22, 29 November 1863), 373 etc.; GE XI, 421; Jacques Gheusi, "Les Créateurs de Moïse à l'Opéra de Paris en 1827," Opéra de Paris 11 (1 October 1983), 20-21; GIR 44-46; J.-L. Heugel, "Mort de Mme Cinti-Damoreau," Le Ménestrel 30 (1 March 1863), 99-100; ICM 402; Lajarte II, 124-41, 144, 147-48; Amédé Le Froid de Méreaux, Variétés littéraires et musicales (Paris: Calmann Lévy, 1878), 169-77; "Mort de Mme Damoreau-Cinti," AM 3 (5 March 1863),

105-7; PBSW 176; SW 64, 73, 152, 184; Thurner 113-18.

Clapisson, Antonin-Louis (b. 15 September 1808, Naples; d. 20 March 1866, Paris), composer, was born at Naples into a family attached to the service of King Joachim Murat, but he returned to France in 1815 and entered the Conservatoire in 1830. He studied violin under François Habeneck,* who arranged for him to play second violin in the Opéra orchestra because of his competency with this instrument.

Clapisson's first dramatic composition was La Figurante (1838), staged at the Opéra-Comique. He did nearly a dozen titles for this theatre between 1838 and 1856 including his hits La Perruche (1840), Gibby la Cornemuse (1846), and Sylphe (1855). Most of these works slipped quickly and quietly into oblivion due to dull librettos, although it must be admitted that Clapisson's music was not always of the first order. It was in this interval that the composer did his only score for the Opéra, Jeanne la folle* of 1848.

The lack of success from which most of his works suffered had a discouraging effect upon Clapisson, but his spirits revived when he was named to the Institut; he produced one of his finest pieces shortly thereafter, La Fanchonette billed at the Théâtre-Lyrique in 1856. Mme Caroline Carvalho* enjoyed an enormous success in this work, and its author was inspired to go on by giving Margot to the same theatre in 1857 and Les Trois Nicolas to the Opéra-Comique in 1858.

BIBLIOGRAPHY: DBF VIII, 1355; Fétis II, 311; GE XI, 538-39; Lajarte II, 189, 192; LXIX IV, 383-84.

Clari ou la promesse de mariage was billed as a pantomime ballet in three acts with music by Rodolphe Kreutzer and choreography by Louis-Jacques Milon (see eighteenth-century volume for Kreutzer and Milon). It had its premiere at the Royal Academy of Music on 19 June 1820, and it was given on 93 dates in the following 12 years before it was dropped from the repertory after its performance on 11 March 1831. It was not seen very often between 1826 and 1831, however, because it enjoyed only 16 of its 93 presentations in this six-year period.

The ballet opens in a sumptuous apartment decorated with costly furniture and adjoining

Clari's bedroom. A second door leads to the duke de Mevilla's apartments. Errand boys are delivering packages, and Betti's curiosity prompts her to examine the duke's latest purchases for Clari (I, 1). Germano tries to embrace Betti, but the duke enters and is upset to hear Betti relate that Clari appears quite unhappy, especially when she mentions marriage in any context. He promises to finance the wedding of Germano and Betti, if they will help him to discover and to eliminate the cause of Clari's depression. He places his portrait on Clari's dressing table and leaves (I, 2-4).

Clari is happy to receive the duke's gifts, but she is troubled to think of her father's anger over her way of life after being seduced and kidnapped by the duke, who refuses to marry her (I, 5-6). She speaks of marriage when the duke returns, and he assures her of the sincerity of his lvoe (I, 7). A group of traveling players arrives, and the duke hires them to entertain at a party he is planning for Clari. He orders Germano to take care of the details, and Germano is so pleased with his management of this affair that he dons a cloak and plumed hat. A young actress mistakes him for the duke on account of his superior air, and he takes advantage of her error to embrace her. Betti discovers them, separates them, and exposes Germano as an impostor but she forgives him, when he swears to play no more tricks on pretty girls (I, 8-10). The guests arrive, the music begins, and Clari appears in her most elegant finery. The act closes with an interval of dancing followed by a banquet (I, 11).

The players present <u>L'Heureuse Distinée</u>, which depicts Adina seduced and kidnapped by a nobleman who refuses to marry her. Clari is so overcome by the similarity between the drama and her life that she loses control of her emotions and faints. The embarrassed duke has her taken to her apartment (II, 1-5). Distraught, she asks him to marry her, but he refuses. She attempts suicide, but the duke prevents her from killing herself, and she locks herself in her room (II, 6-7). The remoreful duke orders Betti to tell Clari that he will marry her, but Betti falls asleep before she can deliver the message, and Clari escapes from the château in her old peasant clothes (II, 8-11). Betti awakens in the morning to find Clari gone, and the frantic duke tries to decide what he should do to win Clari back (II, 10-12).

The last act is set on a farm, where Simonetta and Simeone are about to lunch, Matturino invites the old man to the wedding party of his daughter and Paolo, but Simonetta warns him that Simeone shuns all such events since his daughter's departure from home (III, 1-2). Clari arrives but is recognized only by her mother, who forgives her and warns her that her father will not be easily placated (III, 3-5). Simonetta hides Clari in a thicket, and the villagers begin to dance while awaiting the mayor's arrival for the wedding ceremony. Simeone congratulates Matturino, and his tears reveal the depth of his feelings toward his own child. Left alone, Simeone and Simonetta ponder their predicaments, and Simonetta tries to console her husband. Clari cannot support the situation any longer, and she rushes from her hiding place. Simeone is inexorable and berates his daughter for dishonoring her family. The weeping mother tries to reconcile her husband and her child in vain; Simeone orders Clari to leave (III, 6-8). The duke enters with Clari, whom he has met on the road. Simeone reaches for his rifle. Clari faints. Matturino tries to calm Simeone. Overwhelmed by the unhappiness he has brought to Clari and her family, the duke vows to right the wrongs he has done. He shows Simeone his written promise to Clari to marry her and bestows dowries upon Giulietta and Paolo besides endorsing the marriage of Betti and Germano. The duke invites the villagers to share in his joy, and they celebrate with an entertainment that concludes the ballet (III, 9).

The roles of Simeone and his wife were filled by Milon and Mlle Saulnier, and the part of Clari was the occasion of another triumph for Mme Emilie Bigottini. François Decombe Albert and Ferdinand were applauded as the duke and his valet Germano. Betti was done by Mme Courtin. Louis-François Mérante appeared as the head of the traveling troupe of players that included Mlles Bias, Coulon, and Marie Delisle as dancers (see eighteenth-century volume for Bigottini, Albert, Mérante, and Delisle). None of the music of Clari proved memorable. Its appeal was lodged principally in its libretto which was ahead of its time and skirted situations that were to be developed 30 or 40 years later by Emile Augier* and Dumas fils in the realistic theatre. It would not be until 1864 that La Traviata was given in French in Paris.

BIBLIOGRAPHY: AEM VII, 1781-83; CB 6; Chouquet 389; Lajarte II, 95-96; RBP 34-36; Wks II, 3566.

Cléopâtre was a ballet billed as a "mimodrame" in a single act based upon Aleksander Pushkin for which Mikhail Fokine* created the choreography and established the stage groupings. The work was created at the Châtelet Theatre on 8 June 1909 during the first season of Serge Diaghilev's* Ballets russes* in Paris, and Léon Bakst* provided its costumes and sets. Its music was composed by Anthony Arensky* and Serge Taneiev* (the prelude), Nikolay Rimsky-Korsakov* (Cléopâtre's entrance scene). Feodor Glinka (Cléopâtre's "veil dance"), Alexander Glazunov* (the orgy), Modest Mussorksy* (finale). Bakst's spectacular set for the ballet was destroyed by fire in South America in 1917, but Diaghilev commissioned Robert Delaunay to provide new sets in July 1918.

The curtain rises upon the ballet to disclose a typically Bakst set with monumental columns supporting an Egyptian temple and framing a view of the Nile in a breathtaking sunset. Ta-hor enters to keep a rendez-vous with her lover Amoun, and they celebrate their reunion in a dance. A group of slaves enters with a sarcophagus from which a figure arises wrapped in differently colored strips of gauze. It is Cléopâtre, who has enshrouded herself in bandages to protect her beauty from the sun, wind, and sand. Her slaves remove the wrappings one by one with movements suitable to the exigencies of their task. The queen herself removes the twelfth and last bandage to reveal her azure hair and golden jewels. She moves to her couch, where she reclines under the watchful eye of her jealous and doting slave.

Fascinated Amoun begins to succumb to Cléopâtre's exotic charm. Ta-hor is watching him steadily, when he begins to move toward the queen, and she pulls him away from the temptress. The lovers leave, but, almost immediately, an arrow lands at Cléopâtre's feet. Amoun is returned to the court with his bow in his hand. The slave girl communicates the message on the arrow to the queen. It is a declaration of love from Amoun to Cléopâtre, who announces to her suitor that he may pass the night with her if he swallows poison in the morning. He accepts her offer, and his spurned sweetheart upbraids him without mercy before disappearing into the desert.

The queen welcomes Amoun to her couch, and royal attendants protect the ardent couple from public gaze, while appropriate music by Glinka and Glazounov suggests their self-indulgence and prompts and orgy among the courtiers. Yet the night ends, and the fatal cup is extended to Amoun. He drinks the potion and falls dead. Cléopâtre looks at the corpse with obscene delight and leaves. Ta-hor returns in the growing light of dawn to throw herself upon her lover's body and to kiss him farewell (a. 1).

The work was not truly a ballet because no one danced in a balletic fashion during its performance, but it was so successful at the Châtelet in 1909 that it was accepted without hesitation for billing at the Opéra in 1910. In the latter theatre, it was included on three of the twelve programs that the Ballets russes presented there in 1910 between 4 and 30 June: 11, 14, 16 June 1910. In all, it was mounted on seven occasions at the Garnier Palace* with its other four presentations taking place on 1 July 1910 and 2, 4, 6 June 1914. The three female roles in Cléopâtre were created by Ida Rubinstein (Cléopâtre), Anna Pavlova* (Ta-hor), and Tamara Karsavina* (the slave) with the male parts filled by Fokine (Amoun), Boulgakov (high priest), and Vaslav Nijinsky* (slave). Karsavina was also cast as Cléopâtre in 1914; Fokine danced Amoun at the Châtelet in 1909 and at the Opéra in 1910, 1914.

BIBLIOGRAPHY: Arsène Alexandre, Jean Cocteau eds., The Decorative Art of Léon Bakst, trans. Harry Melrill (New York: Benjamin Blom, 1971), 25-28, pl. 17-23; BB 63-65; Alexandre Benois, Reminiscences of the Russian Ballet, trans. Mary Britnieva (London: Putnam, 1947), 294-98; BK 32-37; Richard Buckle, Nijinsky (New York: Simon and Schuster, 1971), 101-4; Michel Fokine, Memoirs of a Ballet Master, trans. Vitale Fokine, (Boston: Little, Brown, and Co., 1961), 121-28, 138, 141-46, 147-48; HAZ 94-95; PBR 124, 157; SW 255; CB 567-71.

La Cloche du Rhin is an opera in three acts with a score by Samuel Rousseau and a libretto by G. Montorgueil and P.-B. Gheusi. It had its world premiere at the National Academy of Music on 8 June 1898 in a production by Lapissida with sets by Amable, and costumes by Charles Bianchini.

The opera opens with the German people gathered together to pray to Herta for victory in the coming struggle against th Christians. Herman confesses his exasperation over the constant praying for bloody triumphs, because he sees his formerly invincible forces reduced to this last stronghold of old Germany in a castle overlooking the Rhine. Hatto tells his grandson Konrad that it is his responsibility now to preserve his heritage and to protect his country, and Konrad assures Hatto that he will survive. Hatto has heard the cloister bell on the Rhine ring out the prophecy of his death just as it had predicted the passing of his son. Liba and Konrad do not hear the bell, however, and Liba assures him that her magic will protect him (I, 1-2).

The German warriors return to the castle with the food and clothing that they have pillaged. Also, they present the captive Hervine to Hatto. Liba calls for the Christian virgin to be sacrificed on their altars, and Konrad notices her lack of fear. She is questioned and discloses that she comes from the cloister in the valley, where she passes the days in prayer to the one and true God. Furious Liba reminds her that the only god is Wotan, but Hervine ignores her. She tells Hatto that she has come to tell him that the bell in her monastery has neither rope nor clapper, but it is a diligent messenger of the truth. Tonight, she adds, the bell has sounded for him. He must repent or be damned for all eternity. Confident Hatto assures her that he has led a warrior's life pleasing to Wotan, and he condemns her to serve as a sacrifice on the German altars. Konrad intercedes for her, but Hatto draws his sword to slay her, and she consigns herself into God's hands. He lifts his weapon, but he cannot move his arm. The bell rings, and Hatto begins to choke in his own blood. Hervine prays for him, but he dies. Liba assures Hervine that she will die (I, 3).

The German warriors enter the castle. They are weary and defeated, and the people wish to know why they have lost favor with the gods. Liba retorts that they are displeased because Konrad is a weakling and has not yet wet his sword with enemy blood. Herman calls for his compatriots to make one more effort on the field of battle (II,

1). Konrad orders Herman to keep his place and to remain quiet. Herman answers that the gods must be appeased with the rivers of blood, but Konrad argues that God rejects cruelty and bloodshed. He calls for Hervine's release, and Liba accuses him of falling in love with his prisoner (II, 2). He frees her, and she asks for permission to return to her cloister. He begs her to remain and to become his wife, and she rejects him with the comment that his clemency was only a ruse. He insists even more strongly, and she begs for death. Liba, the soldiers, and the people enter in a frenzy (II, 3) to protest that their leader's apathy has opened the way to victory for the enemy. The Christians have climbed the walls, and they demand that Konrad lead them in their last effort. He remains unmoved until he learns that the Christian king demands Hervine. Angered by this development, he calls for his shield, sword, and spear. He ignores Hervine's protests and promises to burn and to throw into the Rhine the clock in her monastery (II, 4). The women and old men move onto the balcony to watch the battle in the valley. The Germans have victory within their grasp, but Hervine prays for the Christians, and the tide of battle turns against Konrad. Liba beseaches Odin to come to the defense of his warriors, but her prayers fail. She blames Hervine publicly for the Germans' defeat, and the people throw her from the battlements (II, 5). The sky glows red in the night, and Herman reports that Konrad has won the battle and put the monastery to the torch. Also, he has thrown the bell into the Rhine. Konrad asks for Hervine, and Liba tells him that she is dead.

The third act shifts to a forest on the edge of the Rhine. A gigantic oak and a stone altar are visible in the night. Konrad is searching for Hervine to tell her that he has discarded his sword and crown. He disappears, and the Germans enter to offer a sacrifice. Liba is preparing for the ritual, when Konrad returns to the clearing (III, 1-2). He seizes Liba's knife when she is about to use it at the altar. She pretends not to know him and denies that he can be the bold grandson of Hatto. She adds that Konrad would never weep over a woman, and he responds by destroying the articles used in the German rite. The people call for his death and slay him by the altar. Liba orders her followers to throw his body to the wolves and to abandon the desecrated grove. Liba and Herman disappear into the shadows. A ghostly Konrad enters to the sound of the monastery bell; he has visions of Hervine. He calls to her, and she appears as an illumination from the Rhine. She calls upon him to accompany her to paradise and eternal happiness together (III, 3-5).

La Cloche du Rhine was Rousseau's most prestigious composition for the theatre, but it never attained to any impressive degree of popularity, and it had to be dropped from the repertory on 19 November 1898 after its ninth presentation at the Garnier Palace. The two principal female roles were filled by Mmes Aïno Ackté* (Hervine) and Meyrianne Héglon (Liba). The male parts were created by Albert Vaguet* (Konrad), Jean Noté* (Herman), and Jean Bartet* (Hatto). Mme Eva Dufranne* also sang Liba.

BIBLIOGRAPHY: DDO II, 1205; Arthur Pougin, "Première Représentation de La Cloche du Rhin à l'Opéra," Le Ménestrel 64 (12 June 1898), 186-88; Stoullig XXIII (1897), 39, 41 and XXIV (1898), 12-17; SW 63.

Le Cobzar was a lyric drama in three acts with a score by Mmc Cabrielle Ferrari* and a libretto that resulted from a collaboration between Mme Hélène Vacaresco and Paul Milliet. It had its world premiere at the Monte Carlo opera house on 16 February 1909, and it was brought to the stage of the National Academy of Music on 30 March 1912 with choreography by Ivan Clustine, sets by Rochette and Landrin, and costumes by Pinchon. Le Cobzar is a popular bard in Rumania who plays a cobza, a sort of fat mandolin.

The drama of Le Cobzar begins at eventide in Rumania during harvest time, when the colorfully dressed workers are returning to their homes from the fields to the accompaniment of local songs. Nédelia and Viorica regret that there will be no dancing because the bard Stan left with a gypsy a year previously and never returned to the village. Ill-tempered Pradéa comes back to his house and orders the two girls to fetch some water. Iana is singing and spinning, and he reprimands her next. A young shepherd rushes into the yard to tell Pradéa that his harvesters are complaining because there is no cobzar for the harvest dance. Iana wonders whether Stan is dead, and her husband scolds her again because she preferred the singing poet to him before their marriage. Pradéa threatens to attack Stan with his knife if he ever sees him again. He leaves, and Iana leans sadly against the well. She breaks her spindle, a sign of bad luck. She tells her friend Nédelia of her misfortune, and Nédelia warns her that her heart will be broken before the night is done. She confesses that she has no heart because Stan stole it when he ran away with his gypsy.

Iana is weeping over her predicament when she hears the sound of laughter, and Stan enters the courtyard with a crowd of peasants. The young girls wonder what Pradéa and Iana will say. The harvesters call for him to play, but he remains with his arms crossed on his chest. Eventually he begins to perform, and the onlookers sit down in a circle at his feet to listen. Iana is surprised to see him, and she offers him a drink. The crowd rises to its feet and dances a ballet featuring the Hora and Sarba of Ploesti. The dancers drag Stan away into the night, but a gypsy girl remains alone in the yard. She knows that her husband Stan loves Iana, and she vows to have revenge on her through Pradéa before the night is done (a. 1).

It is still dark, and Stan returns to Pradéa's yard. Iana senses his presence and emerges from the house. He tells her that he has returned to ask her forgiveness, but she refuses to listen to his plea, although she admits that she had never forgotten him. Stan protests his burning love for her, and she admits that she is unhappy in her marriage. He suggests that they run away together, and they fall into each other's arms. He feels weak; Iana leaves to get him a glass of wine. Stan detects his wife in a thicket. She is laughing at him. He realizes that she has gained control of him with her magic potions and had made him return to Iana to incur Pradéa's jealous anger. She boasts that she has already warned Pradéa of what is happening behind his back. Stan is unable to control his temper. He runs after her and kills her.

Iana returns with wine for Stan, who urges her to flee with him. He tells her that he has killed his gypsy wife because she betrayed them to Pradéa. Iana hesitates to leave, and Stan explains that he can now be sent to the salt mines. He begins to see the mines in his imagination and to hear the criminals there calling for him to join him. Iana now urges him to run away without delay, but he cannot move. They begin to leave at last, but Pradéa blocks their way. He refuses to slay Stan because he prefers to know that he is in the mines, while Iana is with him. He laughs at the lovers. Stan attacks Pradéa, who overcomes him, but Iana buries Pradéa's knife in his back. She throws herself into Stan's arms when the crowd comes upon them standing over Pradéa's corpse. Iana declares that she and Stan will be together now, wherever they are (a. 2).

This production by Paul Stuart was not especially well liked by Parisians, and it had to be dropped after its sixth performance on 4 May 1912. The female roles were filled at its premiere by Jeanne Hatto* (Iana), Ketty Lapeyrette* (the gypsy girl), Mme Goulancourt (Nédelia), and Mme Dubois-Lauger (Viorica). The male parts were created by Lucien Muratore* (Stan) and Jean Noté* (Pradéa). The ballet was led by Mlle Aida Boni.

BIBLIOGRAPHY: Stoullig XXXVIII (1912), 6-11; SW 63.

Cohen, Jules (b. 2 November 1835), Marseilles; d. 13 January 1901, Paris), composer, studied music at the Conservatoire in Paris, where he distinguished himself by winning a seemingly endless array of prizes. Later, he served on the faculty of this venerable institution for 35 years. He remained at the Opéra as chorusmaster for two decades.

M. Cohen's work for the theatre includes opéras comiques, an opera entitled Les Bleuets for the Théâtre-Lyrique, choruses for stagings of Athalie, Esther, and Molière's Psyché at the Comédie-Française, but his only contribution to programs at the Opéra was his cantata, Terre, éclaire-toi. This illuminating exhortation for the earth to light up was sung at the Garnier Palace* on 15 October 1881 on the occasion of the Electrical Fair.

BIBLIIOGRAPHY: BBD 335; EDS III, 1040; Groves II, 366.

Colonne, Edouard (b. 23 July 1838, Bordeaux; d. 28 March 1910, Paris), French violinist and conductor, was born into a musical family, and his precocious interest in music was encouraged accordingly. He studied several instruments as a boy, but he went on to specialize in the violin under the guidance of Boudoin in his native city. His progress was rapid, and his family agreed that he should continue his studies at the Conservatoire in Paris, where he enrolled in 1857. Here, he studied violin with Sauzay and composition with Thomas. He won first prize for his work with the violin in 1863.

M. Colonne played violin in the orchestra of the Théâtre-Lyrique before he was appointed first violinist with the orchestra at the Opéra in 1858. Yet his work in the pits of these two theatres did not diminish his interest in concert appearances, and he became a member of the Lamoureux Quartet and the Concerts Populaires organizations. Finally, in 1873, he helped to found the Concert National group that played in the Odéon Theatre before shifting to the Châtelet Theatre in 1874. The Concert National fell upon hard times before long, but M. Colonne persisted by organizing his Association Artistque. This new group became well known for its presentations of Hector Berlioz'* La Damnation de Faust,* and its reputation was widespread especially after its presentations of the ten concerts that it was selected to give at the Trocadéro during the Exposition Universelle of 1878. Subsequent engagements took the successful orchestra leader on tour in Spain, Portugal, England, Germany, and Russia, and the Concerts Colonne became important events in the musical life of Paris.

Yet despite this activity as a concert artist, the conductor found time during one period of his life to lead the orchestra at the Garnier palace,* where he made his debut with Lohengrin* on 22 January 1892. He stood up throughout this performance of Richard Wagner's* work, and this innovative approach to directing was readily adopted by subsequent conductors. While he was at the Opéra, he also provided the musical direction for the revival of Le Prophète* in 1892 and for the hundredth performance of Charles Gounod's* Roméo et Juliette* on 29 October 1892. This same year, he was at the desk for the gala celebration of the Gioacchino Rossini* centenary at the Garnier palace on 29 February 1892, when Guillaume Tell* was presented.

Colonne conducted for no fewer than three premiere performances during his brief tenure at the Opéra:

Title	Composer	Date
Salammbô*	Louis Reyer*	16 May 1892
Samson et Delila*	Camille Saint-Saëns*	23 November 1892
La Walkürie*	Richard Wagner	12 May 1893

Colonne and his orchestra had introduced the public to the music of Samson et Dalila for the first time on 26 march 1875, when they had played the score of the first act of Saint-Saëns' opera at the Concerts Colonne in Paris.
BIBLIOGRAPHY: AB II 80-87; APD 236; GIR 204-9; SW 106, 190, 193, 196-97, 224-25.

La Comédie-Française has been the foremost government subsidized theatre devoted to the production of legitimate drama since its establishment by Louis XIV in 1680, and it has been involved with the Opéra from time to time since its inception. Several titles in its classical repertory had been billed at the Opéra between 1815 and 1914, and the administrative officers of the two companies entered into close collaboration for the presentations of works like Le Bourgeois Gentilhomme, which employ a musical score as well as a written text.

The Opéra and the Comédie-Française have also become involved with each other when one of these institutions has fallen victim to circustances beyond its control. A close collaboration was almost mandatory, for example, when the fire of 8 January 1900 rendered the actors' theatre completely useless, and they had to work out a system with the artistes at the Opéra until they could be returned to their own facility. On this occasion, the Opéra and the Comédie-Française established and adhered to their intertwining schedules with a minimum of friction, and the Journal de l'Opéra records that the actors presented 13 programs on eight days at the Opéra in March and April 1900:

Date	Work	Author
11 March 1900		
Matinée	Andromaque	Jean Racine
	Le Malade imaginaire	Molière
Evening	Le Bourgeois Gentilhomme	Molière
13 March 1900		
Matinée	Andromaque	Jean Racine
	Le Malade imaginaire	Molière
Evening	Le Bourgeois Gentilhomme	Molière
15 March 1900	Les Plaideurs	Jean Racine
18 March 1900		
Matinée	Oedipe roi (trans., J. Lacroix)	Sophocles
Evening	Tartuffe	Molière
20 March 1900	Oedipe roi (trans., J. Lacroix)	Sophocles
24 March 1900	Oedipe roi (trans., J. Lacroix)	Sophocles
25 March 1900		
Matinée	Oedipe roi (trans., J. Lacroix)	Sophocles
Evening	Phèdre	Jean Racine
	Les Femmes savantes	Molière
26 April 1900		
Matinée	Horace	Pierre Corneille
	Les Plaideurs	Jean Racine
Evening	Le Dépit amoureux	Molière
	Oedipe roi (trans., J. Lacroix)	Sophocles

After the preformance of Horace on 26 April 1900, Jules Clarétie of the Comédie-Française presented a bronze bust of Molière to Pierre Gailhard,* director of the Opéra.

The companies of the two theatres collaborated in an even more intimate manner in the summer of 1900, when the two troupes combined their talents to assure the success of five programs. The minister of Public Education and the Fine Arts sponsored the first of these galas on 15 July 1900 with the Comédie-Française contributing the fourth act of Jean Racine's Bérénice and the fifth act of Victor Hugo's* Ruy Blas to the program. The extracts offered by the Opéra included the overture of Giacomo Meyerbeer's* Les Huguenots,* the first tableau of the third act of Ernest Reyer's* Sigurd,* the second act of Charles Gounod's* Faust* and the ballet from Jules Massenet's* Le Cid.* The Marseillaise concluded the gala. The collaboration between the Opéra and the Comédie-Française on 22 July 1900 was not as lengthy, probably because it was mounted in the Salle des Fêtes Theatre, which was constructed for the World Fair held in Paris at the close of the nineteenth century. On this occasion, the actors staged only the first act of Molière's Monsieur de Pourceaugnac, while the artistes of the Opéra presented the second act of Gioacchino Rossini's* Guillaume Tell* and the dancers executed the ballet from Le Cid by Jules Massenet. The following week, on 29 July 1900, the two troupes were back at the Garnier Palace* to stage a gala sponsored once again by the minister of Public Education and the Fine Arts. This program featured three selections from the repertory of the Comédie-Française: the act of Psyché by Corneille, Molière, and Quinault; La Coupe enchantée by La Fontaine and Champmeslé; the fifth act of Louis XI by Casimir Delavigne.* The Opéra contributed the overture to Tannhäuser,* the prologue and the first act of Charles Gounod's Roméo et Juliette,* and Pierre Vidal's* ballet La Maladetta* choreographed by Joseph Hansen.*

The first of two galas in August 1900 was arranged as a benefit performance for the armed services of France. This program of 11 August 1900 presented the overture and second act of Guillaume Tell as well as La Maldetta, while the Comédie-Française supplemented these offerings with a presentation of the second act of La Tour d'Auvergne, a drama in five acts by Charles Raymond and Lucien Cressonnois. The following day, 12 August 1900, the Opéra contributed the prelude to Alphonse Daudet's L'Arlésienne with incidental music by Georges Bizet* and the second act of Charles Gounod's Roméo et Juliette, while the Comédie-Française appeared in the third act of Molière's Les Femmes savantes and the second act of Hamlet.

The International Congress of Railroads was honored at galas on 27 and 29 September 1900, and M. Leygues, minister of Public Education and the Fine Arts, sponsored still another special program on 11 November 1900, but the Comédie-Française did not contribute its talents to these events. Additional instances of borrowings by the Opéra from the repertory of the Comédie-Française will be found in Appendix II of this volume.

BIBLIOGRAPHY: SW 343, 345, 347, 350-52, 354-57.

Le Comte De Carmagnola, with a score by Ambroise Thomas* and a libretto by Eugène Scribe,* was billed as an opera in two acts. It was a failure and had to be dropped after its eighth performance on 20 August 1841. It had had its premiere at the Opéra on 19 April 1841 and appears to have been withdrawn for revision after its third presentation on 23 April because it was not returned to the stage until 23 June 1841.

The libretto opens with Governor Castruccio of Brescia and his wife Lucrezia enjoying the pleasures of peace until they learn that Carmagnola has slipped into their city to court an unidentified beauty (I, 1-2). Nizza, Castruccio's gardener, asks her master for protection against her father's plan to select for her a husband of his choice, although she loves a younger man who serenades her nightly. Castruccio does not relpy because he is occupied with posting a reward for Carmagnola's capture. Nizza hands a bouquet for Lucrezia to Castruccio, who finds in the flowers a letter from Carmagnola announcing that he will not leave Brescia before he has won Lucrezia's love despite her husband (I, 3). Two strangers enter the governor's gardens after dark, and they provoke each other to a duel. Then, suddenly, they realize that they are unknown in Brescia and that one of them could collect 6,000 écus by denouncing the other as Carmagnola. Stenio wins the distinction of impersonating Carmagnola and being put to death (I, 4). Bronzino rings the alarm. Ripardo says he knows Carmagnola and vouches for the identity of the prisoner. All present are astonished at this development, not only Bronzino and Stenio, but also Nizza, who recognizes the captive as the man who has been serenading her (I, 5).

As a visiting Spanish dignitary who has identified Carmagnola, Ripardo is shown the prison and learns of its secret tunnels. He defends Carmagnola before Castruccio and reveals in an aside to the audience that he is the famous condottiere, not a Spanish lord; he promises to help Stenio in other asides (II, 1-3). Jubliant Stenio tells Nizza to take heart, and he reassures her of his love. Castruccio orders the prisoner's death inmmediately, and Ripardo goes off to comfort Lucrezia (II, 4-7). The monks escorting the condemned man to the gallows discard their robes and level their muskets at Castruccio and his guards. They hail Ripardo-Carmagnola as their chief, and the latter wishes Nizza and Stenio good luck. He announces that he is now ready to leave Brescia because Lucrezia has smiled upon him at last (II, 8).

This curious opera celebrating the valor and adulterous love of an outlaw was not successful, but it offered at least four passages that seem to have evoked some enthusiasm among spectators: Nizza's romance beginning "De la grande tour de la ville" and the ensemble singing "Ah! grand Dieu! quelle audace" both in act 1, scene 3, as well as the trio "Bravant le sort qui m'est contraire" by Stenio, Ripardo, and Castruccio in act 2, scene 3, and the Nizza-Stenio duet in act 2, scene 5.

The cast included Prosper Dérivis* in the title-role and Ferdinand Prévôt as the governor with Mlle Dobré as his wife. Mme Julie Dorus-Gras* sang Nizza. Pierre Cicéri* did the sets.

BIBLIOGRAPHY: Chouquet, 403; DDO I, 257; Lajarte II, 166; Wks III, 43.

Le Comte Ory was a comic opera in two acts given at the Opéra on 20 August 1828 with music by Giacchino Rossini* and a libretto by the team of Eugène Scribe* and Charles Delestre-Poirson.* Its score was based upon the music the composer had already written for Il Viaggio a Reims performed at the Italians' theatre on 19 June 1825 to celebrate the coronation of Charles X at Rheims. Its libretto was derived from a short vaudeville that Scribe and Delestre-Poirson had written in 1817.

The first of the two acts of Le Comte Ory opens with Raimbaud sharing in the execution of the count's tricks and practical jokes, and he is telling the inhabitants of Formoutiers that the hermit who has arrived in their midst will cure their ills. He assures Dame Ragonde especially that the hermit will help the countess de Formoutier recover from th eailment that continues to plague her (sc. 1-2). Ory enters disguised as a hermit; he promises to give special attention to the young girls of the region and to the wives whose husbands are away on the crusade to the Holy Land (sc. 3). Ory's tutor and page arrive in search of their master, and the page discloses his ardent interest in the countess, his cousin (sc. 4-6). The "hermit" surprises his page by addressing him as Isolier, and the latter is so impressed that he reveals his feelings for the countess to Ory. He goes on to complain that his cousin will see no visitors until her husband returns to France, and he discloses his plan to enter her castle disguised as a pilgrim. He pleads that his suit would be helped if the hermit would explain to her that she must be more loving if she wants to recover from her affliction. Ory decides to use the page's plot to win the countess' affections (sc. 7). Encouraged to be more affectionate by the hermit, the countess admits her love for the page Isolier. The hermit thwarts the latter by tricking the countess into allowing him to come into the castle (sc. 8), but the count's tutor enters to reveal his true identity and to announce that the crusade is finished. The finale of the act features Ory's confusion and the wives' rejoicing (sc. 9).

At the start of the second act, the countess decries the wickedness of Count Ory, but her attendants protest that they are now safe inside the castle. A group of 14 women pilgrims drenched by the rain enters to seek shelter for the night. Ragonde and her companions fail to recognize Ory in the disguise suggested to him earlier by Isolier (sc. 1-2). Pretending to be disturbed and frightened, the count kisses his hostess' hand in gratitude for rescuing "her" from "cruel Ory." He suggests that Ory loves the countess, moreover, but she breaks off the interview so that the suffering pilgrims may eat. Raimbaud, who had hidden himself in the cellar of the castle, joins his fellows at the table with a selection of fine wine (sc. 3-5). The guests drink to the health of their host and hostess (sc. 6-7), and the countess congratulates herself on her charitable works when Isolier enters to announce the crusaders' return. He horrifies the countess and Dame Ragonde with his disclosure that the 14 pilgrims are Ory and his companions (sc. 8-9). Disguised as Sister Colette now, the wily count enters the countess' darkened room and declares his love to his page Isolier, whom he mistakes for his hostess (sc. 10). Exposed, he asks the countess to forgive his deception, and he leaves the castle with his companions at the moment of the crusaders' return (sc. 11).

Although this complicated plot might suggest that it alone was responsible for whatever success Le Comte Ory enjoyed, the truth of the matter is that the appeal of the work was more in its music than in the comedy promoted by its intrigue. Audiences were especially quick to applaud the count's cavatina, "Que les destins prospères" (I, 3) and the aria for bass sung by the count's guardian, "Veiller sans cesse" (I, 4). The knight's chorus, "Noble châtelaine" (II, 1), and the duo by the count and countess, "Ah! quel respect, Madame" (II, 3), as well as the knights' drinking song, "Partageons son butin" (II, 6), supported the second half of the composition.

Le Comte Ory was quite successful for everybody connected with it, although Rossini's enemies kept insisting that it was a mediocrity. It reached its 100th presentation at the Opéra on 29 August 1831 and enjoyed 433 performances at this theatre before it was dropped from the repertory in 1884. It was revived in 1853 to help celebrate the marriage of Napoleon III and Eugénie, but its most recent presentation in Paris was at the Théâtre des Nations in 1958 under the direction of Vittorio Gui. Le Comte Ory was sung in French in Belgium (1829), New York (1831), London (1849), Germany (1863). It has also been presented in German, Polish, Russian, and Italian, despite the general lack of interest shown in it in Italy. It might be noted finally that Le Comte Ory was Rossini's only French comic opera, although it was described variously from time to time as an opera or an opera buffa (see seventeenth-century volume for opera buffa.

BIBLIOGRAPHY: Fedele d'Amico, L'Opera teatrale di Gioacchino Rossini (Rome: Elia, 1974), 247-57; Alexis Azevedo, G. Rossini, sa vie et ses oeuvres (Paris: Heugel, 1864), 263-72; Jean-louis Caussou, Gioacchino Rossini (Paris: Seghers, 1967), 125-26; Chouquet 394; DDO I, 258; James Harding, Rossini (New York: Thomas Y. Crowell Co., 1972), 59-61; HUT 79-80; JB 103; KCOB 431-34;

Adolphe Kohut, Rossini (Leipzig: Philipp Reclam, n.d.), 69, Lajarte II, 131-32; Arturo Lancellotti, Gioacchino Rossini (Rome: Fratelli Palombi, 1942) 90; LOA 190-92 Moniteur universel 234 (21 August 1828), 1357 and 235 (22 August 1828), 1362; MSRL 197; OQE 303-4; Jacques Gabriel Prod'homme, "Rossini and His Works in France," MQ 17 (1931), 110-37; Giuseppe Radiciotti, Gioacchino Rossini: vita documentata, opere ed influenza su l'arte (Tivoli: Artigrafiche Majella di Aldo Chicca, 1928) II, 87-96; Luigi Rognoni, Gioacchino Rossini (Turin: Edizion: Radiotelevisione italiana, 1968), 209-17; Gino Roncaglio, Rossini l'Olimpico (Milan: Fratelli Bocco, 1953), 452-64; SSBO 155, 158; SW, 64-65; Francis Toye, Rossini: a Study in Tragi-Comedy (New York: Norton, 1963), 133-37; Herbert Weinstock, Rossini: a Biography (London: Oxford University Press, 1968), 158-60, 505-7; Roberto Zanetti, Gioacchino Rossini (Milan: G. Ricordi, 1971), 61-62.

Les Contes d'Hoffmann, by Jacques Offenbach* is discussed in the twentieth-century volume.

Coppélia is a ballet in two acts and three tableaux with a scenario by Charles Nuitter* and Charles Saint-Léon* set to music by Léo Delibes* and using choreography by Saint-Léon until Joseph Hansen* (1896), Ambroisiny (1916), and Albert Aveline* (1936) provided it with new choreography for subsequent revivals. It had its world premiere at the Le Peletier* opera house on 25 May 1870, and it reached its 300th and 400th performances at the Opéra on 22 April 1911 and 12 August 1920, respectively. The Opéra produced it for the 700th time on 22 April 1951 in Geneva. It was revived for another score of billings between 2 July and 31 December 1966, and its undiminished popularity led to its being mounted on another 44 dates between 1 January 1967 and 5 January 1971.

The ballet opens on a public square in Galicia, where a young girl emerges from her house to make way to Coppélius' home. A second girl is visible through the window of the latter's residence. She is thought to be Coppélius' daughter, and she is seen every morning reading a book while seated in a chair. She disappears later in the day, and the young men of the city have never been able to meet her because Coppélius opens his door to no one. Swanilda is curious about her because she suspects that her fiance Frantz is attracted to her. At this very moment, moreover, Frantz enters on his way to visit Swanilda. She hides to spy upon his actions, and he sends a kiss to Coppélius' supposed daughter. She appears to wave to him, and Swanilda is furious, but she pretends to have seen nothing. She chases a butterfly, which is caught and killed by Franz, and she scolds him for his cruelty and then for his fickle ways.

The burgomaster enters to announce that the lord of the manor has given the city a clock and that a celebration is to be held on the morrow. The young people rejoice but are frightened suddenly by the reddish light and sudden noise emanating from Coppélius' house. the burgomaster asks Swanilda whether she and Frantz will wed during the coming festival, and she answers him with a stalk of wheat. She holds the stalk to her ear and then to Frantz' ear; she asks whether he can hear the wheat tell him how unfaithful he is. He answers that he hears nothing, and she repeats the trick with one of his friends, who agrees that he hears the wheat whisper of Franz' faithless ways. Swanilda breaks the stalk to indicate to her sweetheart that she has broken her engagement to him. He leaves, and she dances away with her friends, while the tables are set out for the festival.

Everybody leaves the square because it is late, but Coppélius leaves his house and disappears into the darkness. Swanilda finds the key to his door; she and her friends enter his house. Frantz returns with a ladder in the hope that he can persuade Coppélius' daughter to elope with him, but the old man returns to look for his key and frightens the youth away.

The first tableau of the second act presents Coppélius' shop filled with tools, materials, and a group of mechanical figures that the old man had created: a bearded Persian, a Moor who plays the cymbals, a Chinaman with a dulcimer. The hesitant intruders see Coppélia seated in her chair and reading. Swanilda speaks to her and discovers that her pretty rival is an automaton. She laughs to think of Frantz' predicament, and the emboldened girls set the figures in motion. Coppélius returns in a rage, and the unwelcome guests take to their heels except for Swanilda. She hides behind a curtain. Coppélius turns to examining his creations for possible damage, when Frantz appears at one of the windows on his ladder. Coppélius hides until Frantz is in the room, and then he seizes him. Unpredictably, however, the toymaker asks Frantz to share a drink with him. He plies him with wine until he falls asleep. Coppélius sees an opportunity to attempt an experiment whereby he might bring Coppélia to life. He does not know that Swanilda has taken Coppélia's place and donned her costume, however, and it is really Swanilda whom he has placed beside the sleeping youth. Accordingly, he opens his book of magic and starts to engage in conjurations. He makes magnetic passes over Frantz' forehead and chest as if to transfer his animation to his automaton. Suddenly, "Coppélia" stands up and walks; her face becomes animated and fleshly; her gait is lighter and easier. She dances and achieves full expression in all her being. Coppélius is beside himself with joy. But "Coppélia" is human and therefore curious and destructive. She wishes to taste the liquor in Frantz' bottle, and her creator has to smash it on the floor. She desires to know the secrets of his book, and he has to close it without an explanation. She asks about the other figures, especially Frantz, whose sword she wields carelessly and dangerously. Coppélius gives her a mantilla that prompts her to execute a Spanish dance. She picks up a Scottish scarf and falls into a jig. Overly energetic, she keeps moving through the room and breaking nearly everything within reach. The ruckus awakens Frantz, and Coppélius hides "Coppélia" behind the curtains. He tries to chase Franz from his house, but "Coppélia" escapes from her hiding place to start the figures in motion and to run off with Frantz. Coppélius falls exhausted into a chair.

The tableau of the second act presents the festival of the clock that the popes have blessed. Swanilda and Frantz are reconciled, and they join the couples to be married at the celebration. Coppélius demands payment for the damage done to his creations and his shop, and the lord of the manor reimburses him. The festivities begin with the waltz of the hours from dawn through the time of work, from war to peace. When all is calm, the games and pleasures of the evening hours begin.

Mlle Giuseppina Bozzachi* was the third nomination for the role of Coppélia, but her performance in Saint-Léon work at the age of 15 or 16 constituted one of the great balletic triumphs of the century. The male roles were filled by E. Fiocre (Frantz), Dauty (Coppélius), Cornet (Le Bourgmestre), and Louis François Mérante* (Le Seigneur). The score was lively, elegant, and pleasant; it featured a waltz acting as a preface to the second act. The last tableau was suppressed after 1872. Cambon had created the sets for this scene and the first tableau. The set for Coppélius' shop had been the work of Despléchin and Lavastre.

BIBLIOGRAPHY: ACD 109-10; AEM III, 126-34; anon., "A propos de Coppélia: une étoile de seize ans, Giuseppina Bozzachi," Opéra 24 (1965), 32-33; L'Avant-scène, Ballet Danse 4 (November 1980-January 1981), 2-97; Gustave Bertrand, "Première Représentation de Coppélia," Le Ménestrel 37 (29 May 1870), 203-4; Bernadette Bonis, "Six Swanilda au miroir," L'Opéra de Paris 11 (1 October 1983), 34-36; Ilona Borska, Coppelia (New York: Watts, 1971); Adolphe Boschot, La Musique et la vie (Paris: Plon, 1931), 97; CB 483-89; Chouquet 424; Warren Chappell, Coppelia (New York: A. A. Knopf, 1965); Henri de Curzon, Léo Delibes: sa vie et ses oeuvres, 1836-1892 (Paris: G. Legouix, 1926), 101-16; EDS IV, 391-94; GBAL 130-143; GBGB 75-92; GMSM 80-101, 188; Ivor Guest, The Ballet of the Second Empire (Middletown, Conn.: Wesleyan University Press, 1974), 229-53; HAZ 99-101; André-Philippe Hersun, "Coppélia à l'Opéra," SDLD 109 (10 December 1978), 10; Pierre Lacotte, "Fidèle à Coppélia," 11 (1 October 1983), 32; Lajarte II, 244-45; PBR 131; Ralph, "Théâtre impérial de l'Opéra: reprise du Freyschutz, Coppélia," AM 10 (2 June 1870), 209-10; SS 133-135; SW 258-59.

Le Coq d'or was billed in Paris as a "story-fable-opera" in three tableaux. Its libretto by Vladimir Ivanovitch Bielsky was based upon a composition by Alexander Pushkin, and its score was the work of Nikolay Rimsky-Korsakov.* It had its world premiere at the Imperial Opera of Moscow on 7 October 1909, and it was performed at the Garnier Palace* for the first time on 24 May 1914 by Serge Diaghilev's* Ballets russes* in a presentation wherein a singer and a dancer interpreted the same role. Michel Fokine was in charge of choreography on this occasion, and Mlle

Nathalie Gontcharova created both the sets and the costumes. Pierre Monteaux conducted the orchestra. The work was taken into the repertory of the Opéra on 12 May 1927 with a French libretto by Calvocoressi and choreography by Albert Aveline*; its sets and costumes were designed by Alexandre Benois.* It had already been produced at Drury Lane in London on 15 July 1914 and at the Metropolitan Opera in New York on 6 March 1918.

The opera opens in the throne room of King Dodon, who has called a meeting of his advisers to consider ways of resisting invasions of his kingdom on the southern steppes of Russia. His sons Gvidon and Aphron offer suggestions, but their proposals are rejected in favor of the aged astrologer's plan to place a golden cockerel upon an upraised lance. The young rooster will see an approaching enemy and will give warning of the imminent peril by crowing. King Dodon is delighted with this solution to his problems because it leaves him free to enjoy games, entertainments, and good food. He promises to grant to the astrologer whatever request he may make, and his attendant Amelfa arranges his bed so that he may have a nap after dining.

The entire kingdom is soon asleep except for the noonday files, but, suddenly, the cockerel crows, trumpets sound, and horses whinny. The people rush for their arms, and Polkan arouses Dodon with the news that the enemy is advancing. The soldiers are about to march out to face the foe, when princes Gvidon and Aphron refuse to fight because life in their father's army is unpleasant. King Dodon forces them to depart, however, and he returns to bed. The cockerel crows again, but the king does not awaken. None of his guards dares to disturb him, but Polkan upsets him with the announcement that the veterans are needed to repel a second invastion because the regular soldiers are occupied elsewhere. Dodon decides to lead his forces. His breastplate is too small, his shield is rusty, and his sword seems too heavy, but his aides help him into his saddle, and he rides off to meet the foe (a. 1).

In the second act, the stage represents a battlefield at night strewn with corpses and more ghastly by the troubled light of the moon. Prince Gvidon and Prince Aphron are among the casualties. King Dodon's army comes upon the scene, and the aged monarch stumbles over the bodies of his sons.

He swears to punish his enemies, and the rising sun reveals a tent upon the adjacent mountainside. Suspicious, General Polkan advances upon it with a contingent of artillery, but the men panic and abandon their piece. A beautiful young woman wearing a white turban and a dress of red silk emerges from the tent. She is the queen of Chemakha. She explains to Dodon that she has come to conquer his country with her smiles, words, and beauty. She persuades Dodon and Polkan to drink a toast with her. They discuss less serious subjects until the queen demands that the general be dismissed, and Dodon complies immediately. She assures him that she has a beautiful body and skin as resplendent as dew, and the flustered king assures the queen that a slight touch of liver trouble is the only source of discomfort for him. She sings to cure his ailment and invites him into her tent. He accepts her invitation and asserts that he is not as old as he looks. He tries to sing to her, but his voice cracks. She compliments him and describes her native land in terms that reduce her aide to tears. He offers to banish her sadness, and she smothers him with gratitude. Finally, she asks him to dance, and he removes his armor, but he insists that the bystanders leave. They form a circle about the king and queen, however, and the queen teaches Dodon to dance in a scene recalling Molière's M. Jourdain and his dancing master. A series of pirouettes leaves the king breathless, but he is able to offer his partner his entire kingdom for one of her smiles. He assures her that she will have everything except a white blackbird. He will even behead General Polkan for her. She accepts his offer, and they break camp (a. 2).

The third act is set in the street before the palace, where the cockerel stands on its high perch in the sunlight. Amelfa announces that Dodon has saved a young princess from a dragon, and the triumphal procession begins with the passing of the royal guard and Queen Chemakha's curious retinue of one-eyed creatures, dwarfs, and giant Ethiopians. The king and queen appear next. He is wan and pale; she is nervious and brusque, but the populace hails the royal couple with enthusiasm. The astrologer enters; he and the queen stare at each other. Finally the astrologer presents his request to the king: the queen of Chemakha. She is amused, but th king is dismayed.

Dodon refuses the petition; the astrologer insists; the king knocks him over the head with his sceptre and kills him. Clouds cover the sun; thunder rolls across the sky. The queen laughs until Dodon tries to kiss her. Angry, she promises him that she will have nothing to do with him and that his rule is about to end. The cockerel crows and leaves his perch. He pecks at the king and kills him with his beak. The sky darkens again; the queen and the cockerel disappear, although her laughter is heard above the tumult. The people mourn this sad state of affairs, which has left them without their king, their promised queen, and the golden cockerel (a. 3).

The opera was popular in Paris, where it enjoyed 61 presentations before it was dropped from the repertory after its performance on 24 May 1947. Its 1914 premiere in Russian at the Garnier had seen two artistes well known to Parisians in the cast: Tamara Karsavina* and E. Ceccheti danced the queen and the astrologer, respectively. The French version of 1927 presented Gabrielle Ritter-Ciampi (the queen) and Andrée Marilliet (the golden cockerel) in the leading female roles with the principal male parts filled by Albert Huberty (Dodon), Edmond Rambaud (the astrologer), Grommen (Polkan), Madlen (Gvidon), and Charles Guyard (Aphron) (see twentieth-century volume for Ritter-Ciampi and Huberty).

BIBLIOGRAPHY: Gerald Abraham, Rimsky-Gorsakov: a Short Biography (London: Duckworth, 1976), 120-27; BK 99; HAZ 101-2; Rostislav-Michel Hofmann, Rimski Korsakov, sa vie, son oeuvre (Paris: Flammarion, 1958), 218-27; KCOB 947-53; Markevitch, Rimsky-Korsakov (Paris: editions Rieder, 1934), 77-83; MCDE 789, 791-92, 796; MSRL 192; NMO 102-16; OQE 292-93; Nikolai-Andreyevich Rimsky-Korsakov, My Musical Life, trans. Judah A. Joffe (London: Eulenburg Books, 1974), 435, 439-49, 452, 456-61; SS 179-80; SSBO 348-49, 353, 355; SW 65-66; Nikolai van Gilse van der Pals, PBR 177; N. A. Rimsky-Korssakow Opernschaffen (Leipzig: W. Bessel & Co., 1929), 641-91.

Coralli, or Coraly, Jean (b. 1779, Paris; d. 1 May 1854, Paris) was a gifted dancer and choreographer who started his career with surprising success at Vienna and Marseilles before filling engagements in Spain and Italy. His effectiveness as an artist and his experience abroad led to an invitation for him to become balletmaster at the Porte St.-Martin Theatre, and he held this position from 1824 to 1830. He wrote a number of pantomime ballets for this Paris theatre during his tenure here, and his better-known compositions included Les Ruses espagnoles, Monsieur de Pourceaugnac, Gulliver, La Visite à Bedlam, and Léocadie.

His continuing effectiveness as balletmaster and his fecundity as a choreographer induced the management of the Opéra in 1830 to ask him to join the company of the Royal Academy of Music. He accepted the offer and became balletmaster at the more prestigious theatre conjointly with Taglioni at first and with Joseph Mazillier* later. He was the author and producer of eight ballets during his 1830-44 tenure in the rue Le Peletier*: L'Orgie* of 1831, La Tempête* of 1834, Le Diable boiteux* of 1836, La Tarantule* of 1839, Giselle* of 1841. La Péri* of 1843, Eucharis* of 1844, and Ozaï* of 1847. Similarly, he did the ballets or divertissements for Ali Baba* (1833), Stradella* (1837), Le Lac des fées* (1839) (see eighteenth-century volume for divertissement).

BIBLIOGRAPHY: ACPM 226-27; BCS 205; CB 137-80; Chouquet 390-401, 403, 405, 408; CODB 132; DBF IX, 585; EDB 95; GE XII, 921; Lajarte II, 139, 146, 149, 154-56, 159-60, 173, 176, 185; SS 100-101, 104-8, 112-13.

Cormon, Pierre-Etienne Piestre DIT Eugène (b. 5 May 1810, Lyon; d. 7 March 1903, Paris), librettist, deluged the theatres with his manuscripts between 1832 and 1880; he had roughly 150 works published, but no one has yet undertaken a full description of his authorship that includes unpublished as well as published dramas and comedies written mostly in collaboration.

Cormon was an administrator of the Vaudeville Theatre and director of the Opéra for a short time. His only contribution to the repertory of the Opéra was the help he gave Michel Carré* on the composition of the libretto for Le Docteur Magnus* of 1864. He shared in three hits at the Opéra-Comique: Le Chien du jardinier (1855), for which he did a witty libretto with Joseph Philippe Lockroy; Quentin Durward (1858), for which he wrote the words with Michel Carré; Les Dragons de Villars (1868) again with Lockroy.

BIBLIOGRAPHY: *DBF* IX, 662; *GE* XII, 976-77; Lajarte II, 236; *LXIX* V, 145.

Le Corsaire was a pantomime ballet in three acts and five tableaux with a score by Adolphe Adam,* a libretto by Jules-Henri de Saint-Georges* and Joseph Mazilier,* and choreography by Mazilier alone. Its sets were created by Despléchin, Cambon, Thierry, and Martin, and its machinery was designed by Sacré. The ballet was suggested but not heavily influenced by Lord Byron's poem of the same title. It had its premiere at the Imperial Theatre of the Opéra on 23 January 1856, and the presence of Napoleon along with the enthusiasm shown for the work by his empress helped Mazilier's composition to win quick acceptance by the public. Adam's lively score and Carolina Rosati's success as Médora along with the loud applause she received during the second and third acts especially removed all doubts about the future of the ballet, and it enjoyed 50 billings at the Opéra between 23 January and 30 December 1856. It was selected for eight programs in 1857 and mounted on five dates in 1858, when the second tableau of the first act was given separately on 1 May. Le Corsaire was not brought back to the stage until 21 October 1868, when the empress requested that it be performed again at the Opéra. It was produced another ten times before it was finally dropped after its 78th staging at the Opéra on 23 November 1868. The ballet had been performed in London at Her Majesty's Theatre as early as 8 July 1856 with Rosati herself and several other members of the original Paris cast performing, and it was taken to the Bolshoï Theatre in St. Petersburg in January 1858.

The composition begins in a slave-market in Andrinople, where the Greek girl Médora throws a bouguet to Conrad from the balcony of the slave-dealer's house (I, 1-2). Médora descends into the market to flirt with Conrad, while her uncle, Isaac, is examining his slaves (I, 3). The dissolute and aged pasha of Cos enters to restock his harem; he finds only Médora who suits his fancy, and Isaac cannot refuse the large price he offers for his niece. She is angry and fearful, but Conrad assures her with a nod of his head that he and his corsairs will protect her. He throws money to the slave girls, who begin to dance with his crew, and, at a prearranged signal, his men kidnap the girls and Isaac. Conrad makes good his promise to resuce Médora from the pasha (I, 4).

The second tableau presents Conrad's subterranean palace filled with gold, jewels, and silks. The pirate leader offers his treasures to Médora on condition that she become queen of his outlaw empire, and she accepts his offer if he will renounce piracy. He accepts her demands (I, 1-2 bis). Conrad assembles his court to watch Médora lead his newly acquired slaves in a fan dance. After the performance, Conrad grants Médora's wish that he free his slaves, but his captain Birbanto objects until Conrad forces his will upon him (I, 3-4 bis). Angered by his defeat, Birbanto and his men persuade Isaac to buy back his niece. At first Isaac protested that he was bankrupt, but Birbanto then found a fortune hidden in his clothes. Still puzzled, however, Isaac does not know how Birbanto can separate Médora from Conrad until the pirate pours a soporific on a bouquet and puts Conrad's outer sentinel to sleep by persuading him to smell the flowers (I, 5). Conrad finishes his meal, and a slave hands Médora a bouquet for the table. Conrad smells the flowers and falls asleep; six masked men enter to kidnap Médora. She defends herself and stabs Birbanto, and she leaves a note in Conrad's hands during the confusion, but Birbanto's men recover their wits and kidnap her (I, 6).

The second act shifts to the pasha's palace on Cos, where the favorite Zulméa has just emerged from her bath (II, 1). The odalisques show their scorn for Zulméa and their preference for her rival Gulnare; they break into open revolt by surrounding the eunuch in a dance of mockery (II, 2). Sayd-Pasha enters still furious over events at Adrinople, and he threatens to execute his entire harem if they continue to complain and to argue. Only Gulnare refuses to be intimidated and she dances her way back into her master's favor. He throws his handerchief at her feet, but she picks it up and throws it to another odalisque. The handkerchief continues on its way around the harem until it falls into the hands of an aged negress. The pasha is outraged, but Gulnare runs away, and the pasha's anger is interrupted by the announcement that a slave dealer is at the door. Isaac enters with Médora, and Zuléma observes jealously the passion with which the pasha views the stranger. Isaac sells her to the pasha; she attempts to stab Isaac; the pasha laughs (II, 3-4). Gulnare and Médora join forces to oppose the pasha, who tries in vain to win over his new acquisition with jewels and silks (II, 5).

Pilgrims on their way to Mecca beg the pasha for hospitality, and the pasha tells their aged leader that they are welcome if his harem does not bother them. The holy man is obliged to witness ballets led by Gulnare and then by Médora, who recognizes him as her lover. Night falls, however, and the pasha orders his eunuchs to escort Médora to his quarters. Conrad throws aside his disguise, draws his sword, and sounds his horn. His crew appears, and he promises to save Gulnare as well as Médora. The latter recognizes Birbanto as her kidnapper and accuses him before Conrad. She verifies her accusation by pointing to the wound on Birbanto's arm, and the culprit can only admit his guilt. Conrad is about to execute him on the spot, but the two women intercede, and the pirate flees (II, 6). Gulnare is thanking Conrad for his kindness, when Birbanto returns with the pasha's men and kidnaps Médora for the second time. Conrad rushes after her, but he falls into an ambush and is captured. The pasha orders his execution (II, 7).

The third act opens with the pasha holding court. He gives Médora the choice of marrying him or of witnessing her lover's death. She refuses to choose, and the pasha confronts her with Conrad in chains. He leaves them alone in the hope that they will decide to spare Conrad the pain of death, but Conrad insists upon death before dishonor, and Médora swears to follow him to the grave (III, 1-3). Grateful Gulnare overhears them and explains to them a way to save their lives (III, 4). When the pasha returns, Médora announces that she will yield to him to save Conrad. Sayd frees his prisoner, who assures Médora that he will return to rescue her at midnight. The pasha orders preparations for his marriage to begin; the wedding march is heard; Gulnare enters in Médora's bridal gown and veil. The pasha slips a ring upon the bride's finger and leads her to his apartments (III, 5-7). He is awaiting his wedding night when his bride is led to his quarters. The pasha removes her veil. It is Médora, but she is awaiting her deliverance by Conrad, and she tries to invent reasons for delay. She begins to dance. She pretends to be afraid of the pasha's knife and pistols. She dances again but now pretends to be playing a game by binding the pasha's hands with her veil. He is amused, although he suspects that she is tying the knot too tightly. Midnight sounds, Conrad appears, and the lovers escape. The pasha cannot sound the alarm until it is too late. Sayd looks through the open window and sees a pirate ship leave port. Gulnare enters to assure Sayd that he has not lost his bride. She holds up her hand to display the wedding ring on her finger (III, 8-10).

The last tableau depicts the pirate ship in the doldrums with Médora and Conrad on the bridge. He distributes gold to his men as a reward for their assistance; he breaks open a cask of rum. The Greek girls on board celebrate the occasion by dancing. Suddenly a storm arises and strikes the ship in all its fury; lightning hits the vessel. The pirates kneel and pray for help, but God shows no mercy toward these men who have lived by the sword, and all hands disappear into the depths (III, 1 bis).

The storm subsides, and a last piece of flotsam is seen drifting in the moonlight. Médora and Conrad are clinging to it, and the wind is blowing them toward a lighthouse. They reach shore and fall to their knees to pray. No one has ever seen the pirate again.

One of the most picturesque spectacles offered by the ballet was the fan dance in which the members of the corps du ballet elaborated a series of configurations holding peacock feathers. The most dramatic moment was doubtlessly the scene in which the large pirates' ship plunged to the bottom of the sea to the accompaniment of lightning and thunder. Other impressive spectacles were offered by the colorful bazaar of Andrianople, the exotic cave of the corsair, and the harem of the pasha. The male roles were filled by Domenico Segarelli* (Conrad), François Dauty (the pasha), Francisque Berthier* (Isaac), Fuchs (Birbanto), Petit and Cornet (eunuchs). The female parts were created by Mme Carolina Rosati (Médora), Mlle Louise Marquet (Zulméa), Mlle Claudina Couqui (Gulnare), Mlle Aline (the negress).

BIBLIOGRAPHY: *ACD 111; AEM I, 76-77; CB 208-18; Chouquet 415-16; CODB 133; Léon Escudier, "Théâtre Impérial de l'Opéra: Le Corsaire," FM 20 (27 January 1856), 25-26; GBAL 143-44; Ivor Guest, The Ballet of the Second Empire (Middletown, Conn.:*

Wesleyan University Press, 1974), 96-102, 224-26, 258; Lajarte II, 219-20; Moniteur universel 27 (27 January 1856), 105-6; PBR 122; Arthur Pougin, Adolphe Adam: sa vie, sa carrière, ses mémoires artistiques (Geneva: Minkoff reprint, 1973), 231-34, 254, 275; SS 93, 123.

Courderc, Joseph-Antoine-Charles (b. 1810; d. 1875) was a house tenor for the Opéra-Comique, where he enjoyed considerable success in such standard compositions as Le Chalet, in which he created the role of Daniel on 25 September 1834, and Le Domino noir on 2 December 1837, in which he sang Horace for the first time. He lost the ability to hit higher notes midway through his career, and he moved to the baritone roles of the repertory without much personal loss. He was cast in this range for Quentin Durward and Le Voyage de Chine as well as being chosen to fill the baritone part of Jean in the very popular Les Noces de Jeannette, which had its world premiere at the Opéra-Comique on 4 February 1853.

Couderc was appointed to the faculty of the Paris Conservatoire in 1865 as professor of comic opera, but he was not interested in the academic aspect of music and decided to retire at a relatively early date.

BIBLIOGRAPHY: Alexandre Bisson and Théodore de Lajarte, Petite encyclopédie musicale (Paris: A. Hennuyer, 1884) II, 152; WOC 129.

Coulon, Antoine (b. 1796, Paris; d. 1849), dancer, studied ballet with his father, Jean-François, and made his debut at the Opéra in the divertissement of Anacréon, and his performances were so effective that he was cast next in the male lead of Paul et Virginie, but it was not until the 1817 revival of Fernand Cortez that he began to play an important part in the production of ballets at the Opéra (see eighteenth-century volume for Jean-François Coulon, Anacréon, Paul et Virginie, and Fernand Cortez). He was named premier sujet on 1 April 1823.

Coulon had danced in the first presentations of La Servante justifiée* on 30 September 1818 and of Olympie* on 22 December 1819, but these two assignments were only the start of his career. He went on to appear in another eight premieres before he left the Opéra in 1830:

Opera	**Premiere**
Clari	19 June 1820
La Mort du Tasse	7 February 1821
Aladin	6 February 1822
Alfred le Grand	18 September 1822
Verdôme en Espagne	5 December 1823
La Belle au bois dormant	2 March 1825
Moïse	26 March 1827
La Muette de Portici	29 February 1828

The ballerino went to London for a dozen series of appearances between 1821 and 1844 and he became director of the ballet at Her Majesty's Theatre in 1844 besides dancing there from time to time.

BIBLIOGRAPHY: CODB 134; GE XIII, 50-51; EDS III, 1636; Ivor Guest, The Romantic Ballet in England (Middletown, Conn.: Wesleyan university Press, 1972), 33, 52-53, 73, 85, 96-97, 102-3; Lajarte II, 32-33, 93-97, 100-103, 106-7, 109-10, 125-26, 129-30.

La Coupe du roi de Thulé was presented as an opera in three acts and four tableaux with a score by Eugène Diaz,* words by L. Gallet and Edouard Blau,* and choreography by Mérante.* The team of Cambon, Chapéron, Displéchin fils, Lavastre, and Rubé created the sets for this remarkable production. It had its world premiere at the National Theatre of the Opéra on 10 January 1873, and it proved popular enough to enjoy a score of presentations during its first year at the Opéra. Unfortunately, the composition was never revived because its score was lost in the fire that destroyed the Le Peletier* opera house on 28 October 1873.

The opera opens with the court of Thulé discussing the condition of the king (I, 1-2), who is dying of unrequited love for Myrrha (I, 3). The court jester mocks the mourners for their concern, but he is warned that he does not amuse Myrrha or Angus. The courtiers leave (I, 4), and

Paddock observes that he alone mourns the king sincerely; his friend Yorick refuses to leave Thulé on his advice because he cannot endure separation from Myrrha. Paddock urges him to declare his love to Myrrha so that her inevitable rejection of him for Angus will prompt him to help destroy her (I, 5-6). Myrrha enters on Angus' arm, and Yorick presents her with a pearl. Paddock asks Angus not to disturb the dying king, and Angus boasts that he will hold the royal sceptre before long. Myrrha reminds him that possession of the golden bowl, not of a sceptre, signifies the holding of power in Thulé. Harold announces that the king is about to die and send for Paddock. Myrrha assures angry Angus that a court jester cannot supplant him, but Paddock reappears with the bowl (I, 7-9) to announce the death of the king. He informs the courtiers that he has been charged to name the new recipient of the bowl, and he throws the bowl into the sea. Myrrha announces that she will wed the man who recovers this precious talisman (I, 10), and Yorick leaves to retrieve it despite Paddock's warnings (I, 11).

The scene shifts to the bottom of the sea, where the queen of the sirens reveals her love for the fisherman Yorick (II, 1-3). One of the sirens presents Claribel with the golden bowl of Thulé, which she has found on the floor of the sea, and she calms the waters for the fisherman who is descending to her realm (II, 4-5). Her retinue entertains him with their dancing, and he explains that he wishes to gain possession of the bowl to win the love of Myrrha. Claribel reminds him that love is not eternal on earth, and she hints at her affection for him by revealing that it was she who cast pearls in his path. Claribel is determined that he will live but not love Myrrha (II, 6), and she arranges for Yorick to behold the palace of Thulé, where Angus and Myrrha are declaring their undying love for each other. Yorick does not believe his eyes and ears, and he insists upon his love for Myrrha. The queen of the sirens releases him to return to earth. When he wishes to return to her, he is to drink thrice from the golden bowl (II, 7-8).

Paddock is in the arms room of the royal palace, where he is rejoicing over the friction and discontent he has aroused. He is happy that Yorick is dead, because he does not wish his friend to suffer useless torment. The members of the council argue over a method of selecting a new king, and Paddock aggravates the situation by suggesting that Angus is the only worthy candidate. The council decides to leave the nomination to the peopl, but Myrrha insists that she and Angus be named. Yorick appears with the bowl, however, and he calls upon Myrrha to keep her promise (III, 1-3). He gives her the bowl and recognizes her as his queen, but she hands it to Angus and claims him as her king. Yorick is speechless (III, 4-5), but he admits that Claribel was right. When the bowl comes back to him to toast the new rulers, he hails "a distant queen." A storm breaks out; he calls for the death of Myrrha and Angus; the palace and the throne crumble in ruins, and the royal couple are killed in the catastrophe. The storm abates, and Claribel arrives with her retinue to escort Yorick back to her "blue palace" (III, 6-9).

The principal male roles were filled by Léon Achard* (Yorick), Jean-Baptiste Faure* (Paddock), Bataille (Angus), and Gaspard (Harold) with Pauline Gueymard* as Myrrha and Rosine Bloch* as Claribel.

BIBLIOGRAPHY: Gustave Bertrand, "Première représentation à l'Opéra de la Coupe du roi de Thulé," Le Ménestrel 39 (12 January 1873), 51-52; Guy de Charnace, Musique et musiciens (Paris: Lethielleux, 1874) I, 231-43; Chouquet 425; "Concours du Grand Opéra: La Coupe du roi de Thulé," Le Ménestrel 36 (28 November 1869), 412-13; DDO I, 271-73; Lajarte II, 245-46; Wks IV, 15992.

Cousinou, Robert (b. 1888; d. 1958, Paris), vocalist, spent the 1918-20 interval of his life with the Metropolitan Opera Company and at Covent Garden, but otherwise he was at the Opéra almost continuously from 1913 until 1928. In this period of 15 years, he sang no fewer than 20 different roles at the Garnier Palace* in addition to creating another five parts performed at the Opéra for the first time in this span of time.

After his debut as Geywhir in Fervaal* on 9 June 1913, he was heard in another four parts before the end of the year: Hérault in Lohengrin,* Valentin in Faust,* Maurevert in Les Huguenots,* and Gaucher d'Arcourt in Le Miracle.* He did Mercutio in Roméo et Juliette* in 1914 and

Jonas in Patrie!* in 1915, but 1916 saw him cast in four roles: Iago in Othello,* Le Roi in Le Cid,* Ossian in Le Sommeil d'Ossian, and Le Catéchiste in Briséis.* He performed the title-role in Hamlet* in 1917, Athanaël in Thaïs* in 1918, and his first two postwar billings were the protagonist of Rigoletto* and Le Grand Prêtre of Samson et Dalila* in 1920. He portrayed the beggar in Ascanio* in 1921, and, in 1923, Beckmesser of Les Maîtres Chanteurs de Nuremberg* and Dosiféi of La Khovantchina. His last two assignments at the Opéra, not including the parts he created, were d'Orbel in La Traviata in 1927 and Sharpless in Madame Butterfly in 1928 (see twentieth-century volume for La Kovantchina, La Traviata and Madame Butterfly).

Consinou did one of the two "chevaliers" in Parsifal,* when Richard Wagner's* work was brought to the stage of the Opéra for the first time on 4 January 1914, and he sang the male voice in Carême Prenant for its world premiere on 16 April 1916. He executed Ramiro in the Garnier premiere of L'Heure espagnole on 5 December 1921, and he was cast as the marquis de Saluces in Grisélidis* for its initial production there on 29 November 1922. When Turandot was given its Paris premiere on 29 March 1928, he sang Ping (see twentieth-century volume for Carême Prenant, L'Heure espagnole, and Túrandot).

It is obvious that M. Cousinou gave the National Academy of Music a full measure of faithful and efficient service, and that his rich and well disciplined voice came to be accepted as an almost inevitable ingredient of a successful evening at the Opéra.

Although M. Cousinou's appearances at the Opéra-Comique have been forgotten, he made his debut there as Gad in Joseph on 11 January 1912. Also, he sang Alfio of Gavalleria rusticana there as a younger man.

BIBLIOGRAPHY: KRJ 90; PBSW 176; SW 42, 53, 63, 91, 104, 110, 114, 132, 140, 150, 164, 166, 169, 184, 188, 197, 208, 213, 220, 250; WOC II, 290.

Le Crépuscule des dieux, known originally in Germany as Gotterdämmerung, is a musical drama in a prologue, three acts, and seven tableaux written as the third act and third day of L'Anneau du Nibelung.* Richard Wagner* created its libretto and score, and it had its world premiere at

Bayreuth on 17 August 1876 in the complete framework of all four days of Wagner's composition. It was given subsequently at London (1882), New York (1888), and Brussels (1901) before it was heard in Paris for the first time at the Château-d'Eau Theatre on 17 May 1902. It had its 1901 premiere in Brussels in a French translation by Alfred Ernst, and this same text was used in Paris at the Château-d'Eau Theatre. Finally, on 23 October 1908, the Ernst version was used at the Garnier Palace* for the first time in a Paul Stuart production with costumes by Pinchon and sets by Carpézat (Prologue; a. 1, tabl. 1), Dubosq and Belluot (a. 1, tabl. 2; a. 3), Marcel Bailly and Marcel Jambon* (a. 2).

The translation of Wagner's German libretto into the French language did not affect the order or the nature of events and music in the original composition. The prelude is set upon the Walkyries' rock, where the three Norns are singing and spinning out the golden thread of fate. The thread breaks, however, and they realize that the end of Valhalla is at hand. They tie themselves to each other with the thread and vanish into the earth. Wotan demands a new spear. It is recalled that Loge will put Valhalla to the torch when two conditions are fulfilled. The curse of the ring no longer hangs over God and the world; the Rheingold has been returned to the daughters of the Rhine. In the meantime, Wotan and the gods are awaiting the end. When dawn breaks, Siegfried enters fully armed with Brunnhilde. He is about to set out in search of new adventures on earth, and she gives him her horse Grane. Grateful, he presents her with the famous ring that Albéric made from the gold that he stole from the Rhine daughters. They swear their undying love to each other, and Siegfried descends into the valley (prol.).

The first act begins in the hall of the Gibichungs near the Rhine. Hagen is urging Gunther to wed Brunnhilde despite her love for Siegfried, whom he would like to marry to his sister Gutrune. He is aware that only Siegfried can penetrate the protective fire surrounding Brunnhilde, but he has a solution for his problem. He will trick the hero into drinking a potion of forgetfulness (I, 1). Siegfried arrives at the hall, where he drinks the magic draught. He forgets Brunnhilde and falls in love with Gutrune.

He enters into a solemn pact of brotherhood with Gunther, and he promises that he will go to Brunnhilde to persuade her to become Gunther's wife because the latter cannot walk through the fire with immunity (I, 2).

The setting moves back to the Walkyrie's rock, where Brunnhilde is dreaming about her ring. Her sister Waltraute arrives to tell her that their father Wotan sits in Valhalla motionless, dreaming, and waiting for his ravens to return. He has told Waltraute that gods and men alike will remain under a curse until she, Brunnhilde, returns the ring to the Rhine daughters. Waltraute begs Brunnhilde to restore the ring to its rightful owners and thereby release the world from its troubles. Brunnhilde refuses to part with Siegfried's gift to her, even if it means the destruction of Valhalla. Despairing Waltraute rides away. At sunset, Siegfried appears and crosses the fiery threshold. The powers of his helmet have allowed him to assume the appearance of Gunther, and alarmed Brunnhilde believes that she has been betrayed. Siegfried-Gunther asks her to become his wife. She threatens him with her ring and repulses his advances. He is too strong, however, and she cannot prevent him from seizing her ring and forcing her into the cave (I, 3).

The second act returns to the hall of the Gibichungs. It is night. Albéric makes Hagen swear that he will slay Siegfried and retrieve the golden ring. Hagen promises to do his father's bidding (II, 1). Siegfried assures Gutrune and Hagen that he has Brunnhilde in his power. He explains that she and Gunther are on their way to the hall. Siegfried and Gutrune leave to prepare a reception for the prospective bride and groom (II, 2); Hagen orders his vassals to arrange for the wedding ceremony and sacrifices (II, 3). When Siegfried appears with Gutrune, Brunnhilde is so downcast and perplexed that her demeanor arouses anxiety. Her perplexity turns to anger, however, because Siegfried is calm and self-possessed when he refers to her as Gunther's bride and to himself as Gutrune's husband. Brunnhilde now sees the ring upon his finger, and she announces that she has been deceived and betrayed. Crafty Hagen leads Gunther and Brunnhilde to believe that Siegfried has dishonored Gunther; he convinces them that Siegfried must be slain during the hunt on the following day. Then he, Hagen, will come into possession of the ring (II, 4-5).

The daughters of the Rhine are swimming in circles and lamenting the loss of the Rheingold. They greet Siefgried cheerfully and ask for his ring. He ignores their request, and they warn him of imminent doom if he retains it. He dismisses their gloomy prediction, and they leave (III, 1). Hagen and Gunther appear on the heights with their vassals, and the hunters begin to dine. Hagen hands Siegfried a drink that restores him memory, and Siegfried tells his companions of the time when he grew up with Mime, slew the dragon Fafner, and forged his sword Notung; he relates how he came to understand the birds and was able to acquire the ring and Tarnhelm. Suddenly, two ravens appear, and Hagen plunges his spear into Siegfried's back. The wounded hero remembers Brunnhilde and dies; Gunther's vassals place his body upon a shield and carry him away to the accompaniment of death music (III, 2).

The last tableau represents the hall of the Gibichungs, where Gutrune awaits Siegfried until Gunther appears with Siegfried's body. Hagen tells her that he was slain by a wild boar, but Gunther reveals the truth. Hagen objects that he was avenging his honor, but Gunther curses him, and they fight. Gunther is killed, and Brunnhilde enters when Hagen claims the ring. Gutrune asserts that Brunnhilde's slanderous remarks about Siegfried were the cause of his death. Brunnhilde silences her accuser with scorn and orders a funeral pyre built for her dead husband on the banks of the Rhine. She takes the ring from his finger, and his body is placed upon the pyre. She lights it and rides Grane into the flames. The waters of the Rhine rise, and the daughters of the river reach out and retrieve the ring. Frantic Hagen leaps into the rushing water to seize the precious object, but two of the daughters drag him down into the depths. The pyre has been extinguished by the swollen Rhine, but a fiery glare grows brighter in the sky. The palace of Valhalla is aflame, and the gods disappear in the conflagration.

The three principal female roles of the opera were created at the Garnier Palce by Louise Grandjean (Brunnhilde), Rose Féart (Gutrune), and Ketty Lapeyrette* (Waltraute), and the daughters of the Rhine were represented by Yvonne Gall,*

Antoinette Laute-Brun,* and Ketty Lapyrette. Marie Charbonnel, Caro-Lucas, and Alice Baron were cast as the Norns. The four male parts were sung initially at the Opéra by Ernst Van Dyck* (Siegfried), and Dinh Gilly* (Gunther), Marcelin Duclos (Albéric), and Jean-François Delmas* (Hagen). Brunnhilde of Gotterdämmerung especially has attracted an impressive cluster of stars in Paris: Mmes Félia Litvinne* (1909), Lucienne Bréval* (1912), Borgo (1912), Marcelle Demougeot* (1925), Bunlet (1928), Leider (1931), Marjorie Lawrence (1933), Helena Braun (1950), Flagstadt (1950), Moedl (1955), Varnay (1957), and Grob-Prandl (1962). Le Crépuscule des dieux has proved to be the least popular of the ten compositions by Wagner that have won a place for themselves in the Garnier repertory.

BIBLIOGRAPHY: The Authentic Librettos of the Wagner Operas (New York: Crown Publishers, 1938), 246-306; L'Avant-scène 13-14 (January-February 1978), 1-199; Paul Bekker, Richard Wagner, His Life and Work, trans. M. M. Bozman (Westport, Conn.: Greenwood Press, 1971), 245-46, 258-62, 268-81; Alice Leighton Cleather and Basil Crump, The Ring of the Nibelung (New York: G. Schirmer, 1903), 98-131; John Culshaw, Ring Resounding (New York: The Viking Press, 1967), 167-214; DDO I, 276-78; Robert Donington, Wagner's "Ring" and Its Symbols (London: Faber and Faber, 1963), 217-73; Henry T. Finck, Wagner and His Works (New York: Greenwood Press, 1968), 355-67; Carl Friedrich Glasenapp, Wagner-Encyklopadie (Hildesheim, New York: Georg Olms Verlag, 1977), 65-66, 255-58; Léon Guichard, La Musique et les lettres en France au temps de Wagnérisme (Paris: Presses universitaires de France, 1963), 255, 257-58; Emerich Kastner, Wagner-Catalog (Hilversum: Frits Knuf, 1966), 94-97; KCOB 301-16; MCDE II, 1105-6, 1126-28; MSRL 263-65; OQE 490-96; PBSW 59-60, 90, 161, 164; Richard Pohl, Richard Wagner (Leipzig: Bernhard Schlicke, 1883), 174-85; Arthur Paugin, "Opéra: Le Crepuscule des dieux, drame musical . . ., "Le Ménistrel 74 (31 October 1908), 346-48; Guy de Portalès, Richard Wagner, the Story of an Artist (Westport, Conn.: Greenwood Press, 1972), 318-25; Robert Raphael, Richard Wagner (New York: Twayne Publishers, 1969), 65-72; SSBO 271-75; SW 224-26; Edward M. Terry, A Richard Wagner Dictionary (Westport, Conn.: Greenwood Press, 1971), 120-24; Thompson 681, 2153-54; Curt von

Westernhagen, The Forging of the "Ring" (Cambridge: Cambridge University Press, 1976), 179-240.

Croiza, Claire (b. 14 September 1882, Paris; d. 27 May 1946, Paris), French mezzo-soprano, made her theatrical debut in Nancy in 1905, and, in 1906, she joined the company at the Théâtre de la Monnaie in Brussels, where her first role was the female lead in Camille Saint-Saëns'* Samson et Dalila.* She remained with this theatre for the next two decades, but her increasing repertory and obvious talents won her contracts with other theatres and warm praise from critics.

Mme Croiza was invited to sing Dalila at the Opéra in Paris as early as 26 August 1908, but her only other billing at the Garnier palace* was as one of the singers in Les Vertuosi de Mazarin on 6 January 1916. She was also cast as Charlotte in Jules Massenet's* Werther,* Orphée in Christoph Willibald Gluck's Orphée, and Pénélope in Gabriel Fauré's* Pénélope at the Opéra-Comique, where she made her debut as the heroine of Doret's La Tisseuse d'orties at the world premiere of this lyric drama on 29 November 1926 (see eighteenth-century volume for Gluck).

Later in life, the soprano served on the faculties of the École Normale and the Conservatoire in Paris.

BIBLIOGRAPHY: APD 246; EFC 181; SW 338, 396; WOC 133, 139, 170, 181, 246.

Cruvelli, Johanne Sophie Charlotte (b. 12 March 1826, Bielefeld, Germany; d. 6 November 1907, Monte Carlo), vocalist, changed her name from Crüwell because her repertory as a singer was predominantly Italian. Her father was an amateur trombonist, and her mother was a vocalist, and her musical education was limited to what she learned from her parents. Accordingly, she lacked discipline and technique despite the unbridled admiration she inspired in audiences overwhelmed by the natural beauty of her soprano voice.

She made her theatrical debut in Venice during the carnaval season of 1847, and she created such a favorable impression on Italian musical circles that she was invited to sing in London during 1848. Unfortunately, she chose to sing Susanna in Le Nozze de Figaro, while Jenny Lind was appearing in the same role, and her performance suffered by comparison. She returned to Italy after this slight rebuff and then accepted an invitation to come to Paris, where she had already been billed in several concerts. She appeared in Ernani at the Théâtre-Italien and created a surge of enthusiasum in the French capital with her magnificent stage presence and untamed voice. After a second trip to England, she was asked to sing at the Opéra for the incredible salary of 100,000 francs per year.

The publicity that Cruvelli was receiving and the excitement that she was causing had reached almost ridiculous proportions by the time that she made her debut at the Imperial Academy of Music on 16 January 1854 as Valentine in Les Huguenots.* While other works had been returning 4,000 to 6,000 francs to the box office at this time, Les Huguenots with Cruvelli was earning 8,000 to 9,000 francs, although it had been in the repertory since 1836. The largest returns were counted on 27 February, when 9,505.75 francs were left at the box office. After this first wild excitement had subsided, however, it became apparent that Mlle Cruvelli was more a personality than an artist of genius, and a contrary reaction began to prevail. Yet she had a contract and was cast as Julia in a revival of La Vestale on 17 March 1854, and she was billed again in Les Huguenots on 20 November 1854 (see eighteenth-century volume for La Vestale). The following year, on 13 June, she had the opportunity to sing the lead in the sort of work in which she felt more at east, Les Vêpres siciliennes.* At its premiere, it drew only 7,391.56 francs, but, as word of Mlle Cruvelli's improved performance as Hélène spread, receipts climbed as high as 10,570.93 francs in the first run of ten consecutive billings that Giuseppe Verdi's* work enjoyed by 4 July 1854.

Les Vêpres siciliennes was the last opera in which Mlle Cruvelli appeared because she married Count Vigier the following winter and retired from the theatre.

BIBLIOGRAPHY: Chouquet 415; Ellen Clayton, Queens of Song (Freeport, N.Y.: Books for Libraries Press, reprint of 1865 edition), 483-90; EFC 145-46; EZF 169-70; Fétis II, 402; GE XIII, 524; ICM 393; Lajarte II, 218; "Nécrologie: Sophie Cruvelli," FM 32 (9 August 1868), 252; PBSW 171; SW 222; Thurner 225-31.

Cucchi, Claudina (b. 6 March 1834, Monza; 8 March 1913, Milan), dancer, studied ballet at the school attached to La Scala opera house. She was graduated from here in 1853 but continued her studies under the direction of Carlo Blasis,* director of the dance academy at La Scala. She became interested in Count Carlo Locatelli at the very start of her career, and she traveled to Paris with him in 1855.

Once in the French capital, Mlle Cucchi became associated with the Opéra and made her debut there as La Primavera in the divertissement of Les Vêpres siciliennes* at the premiere of Giuseppe Verdi's* work in Paris on 13 June 1855 (see eighteenth-century volume for divertissement). Her blonde hair and delicate features along with her lively performance won her critical acclaim, although her name was spelled incorrectly more often than not: Mlle Couqui.

The ballerina's second and last role at the Imperial Academy of Music was Gulnare, a concubine in Joseph Mazilier's* Le Corsaire,* which had its world premiere at the Opéra on 23 January 1856.

La Cucchi left Paris at this point in her career to remain at the Hofoper in Vienna for the next ten years. She visited Berlin and London in 1860, and she was billed into Prague, Budapest, Hamburg, and St. Petersburg in 1865. She grew quite heavy and was obliged to give up dancing wih the passage of time, however, and she ended her days in poverty despite her marriage to Baron Zemo. Mlle Cucchi has left a book entitled Venti anni di palcoscenico (1904), but it is more an apologia pro sua vita than a bona fide autobiography.

BIBLIOGRAPHY: ACD 122; CB 208-18, 262; CODB 138; EDS III, 1784-85; Ivor Guest, The Ballet of the Second Empire (Middletown, Conn.: Wesleyan University Press, 1974), 93, 98, 255, 260; Lajarte II, 220.

Cuvelier de Trie, Jean-Guillaume-Auguste (b. 15 January 1766, Boulogne-sur-Mer; d. 25 May 1821, Paris), writer, studied in Paris and became a lawyer in his native town. It was not long before he took an active interest in the political events of the Revolution, however, and he took up residence in Paris during 1790. In the capital, he was chosen to represent the new government in the western provinces. Subsequently he was transferred to the office of public education.

The rise of Napoleon saw Cuvelier de Trie join the military forces, and he was attached to the corps of interpreters being mobilized for the planned invasion of England. When this campaign was canceled, he was assigned to the early campaigns in Prussia and Poland. He fell ill finally and resigned from the army to devote himself to literary pursuits.

As an author, Cuvelier de Trie proved to be quite prolific, but only a few of his creations earned the sustained admiration of the public. The libretto he wrote for Manuel Garcia's* La Mort du Tasse* was among the more successful texts he composed for the theatre, however, and it enjoyed 23 billings at the Opéra after its world premiere there on 7 February 1821. He was also the author of the poem for Alexandre Piccinni's Alcibiade solitaire, which had been a disastrous failure on 8 March 1814 (see eighteenth-century volume for Piccinni and Alcibiade solitaire).

BIBLIOGRAPHY: DBF IX, 1433-34; Lajarte II, 83, 97.

D

Dabadie, Henri Bernard (b. 1798, Southern France; d. 1856, Paris), French baritone, entered the Conservatoire in 1818 and was subsequently accepted as a student at the Opéra. He made his debut at the Royal Academy of Music in the Montansier opera house in the present rue de Richelieu on 12 December 1819 as Cinna in La Vestale (see eighteenth-century volume for Montansier Theatre and La Vestale).

After his first appearance on the stage of the Opéra, Dabadie was named to act as François Lays' replacement in January 1821, and, when the latter performer retired, Dabadie became head of the baritone section at the theatre (see eighteenth-century volume of Lays). He had an important and successful career at the Opéra until his retirement in 1836, when he went to Italy for a tour of the famous opera houses of this country. He returned subsequently to France to enjoy his retirement in his native land.

Dabadie contributed to the creation of seven operas during the first six years of his association with the Paris Opéra. He was cast as the governor in La Mort du Tasse* on 7 February 1821, as Le Cadi in Aladin* on 6 February 1822, and as Virginius in Virginie* on 11 June 1823. He performed as Lopez in Vendôme en Espagne* on 5 December 1823, and he was billed as Isorin in Ipsiboé* on 31 March 1824. His sixth assignment at the Opéra was the part of Sénéchal at the initial production of La Belle au bois dormant* on 2 March 1825. The spring of this same year, on 29

May 1825, he presented Théomir in Pharamond* for the first time.

Dabadie's last ten years at the Opéra were even more demanding than his 1821-26 period at the theatre. He appeared in revivals of works that continued to interest the public, and he shared in the staging of programs presenting additions to the repertory. He sang Pharaon in Moïse* first mounted on 26 March 1827, and he was named to do Duncan for the premiere of Macbeth* on 29 June 1827. He had the distinction of creating one of the roles in the spectacular La Muette de Portici,* when he performed as Pietro on 29 February 1828. Although this work by Daniel Auber* would be popular enough to reach 100 presentations by 23 April 1830, management undertook to offer Le Comte Ory* to the public on 20 August 1828, and Dabadie was selected to do Raimbaud in this composition. But his greatest moment came when Gioacchino Rossini* wrote Guillaume Tell* for him and his baritone voice. He did the title-role in this work at its premiere, of course, on 3 August 1829 in the Peletier* opera house with his wife as Jemmy. On 15 March 1830, he created Le Senechal in François Ier à Chambord,* and, on 6 April 1831, he appeared in the part of Lysiart in the unsuccessful French version of Carl Maria von Weber's* Euryanthe.* The last roles that the baritone created at the Opéra were Joli-Coeur of Le Philtre* on 20 June 1831, captain Jean of La Tentation* on 1 October 1832, Dehorn of Gustave III* on 27 February 1833, Ours-Kan of Ali-Baba* on 22 July 1833, Masetto of Don Juan* on 10 March 1834, and Ruggerio of La Juive* on 23 February 1835.

Dabadie and his wife Louise had appeared on the scene as the romantic movement was cresting, and he possessed the talents, energy, and discipline necessary to take advantage of the opportunities at hand. It is curious that the importance of his contributions to the musical accomplishments of his day have not yet been measured more precisely.

BIBLIOGRAPHY: Chouquet 389-99; DBF IX, 1455; EZF 170; Fétis II, 410; Jacques Gheusi, "Les Créateurs de Moïse à l'Opéra de Paris en 1827, "Opéra de Paris" (1 October 1983), 18-19; Lajarte II, 97, 104-7, 125-26, 128-30, 133-34, 138-39, 144, 147-48; SW 64, 105, 152; WLC 37.

Dabadie, Louise-Zulmé, née Leroux (b. 20 March 1804, Paris; d. 21 November 1871, Paris), French soprano, was admitted into the Conservatoire on 9 July 1814 to study voice at age ten under the direction of Plantade. A successful student, she was offered a contract at the Opéra and made her debut as a soprano on 31 January 1821 as Antigone in Oedipe à Colone (see eighteenth-century volume for Oedipe à Colone). Her agreement with the Royal Academy of Music was amended shortly thereafter to confer upon her the responsibility of substituting for ill or absent stars. It was not long before both Mme Rose Branchu and Mlle Gerard Grassari* failed to meet their performance schedules, and Mlle Leroux filled her assignment so satisfactorily that she was given Mme Branchu's position on the staff after this singer went into retirement (see eighteenth-century volume for Branchu).

Mlle Leroux married M. Dabadie in 1822, the year that she created the title-role of Reicha's Sapho* on 16 December 1822. Her next assignment for a premiere was L'Ange de la France in Pharamond* on 10 June 1825. She did no new parts in 1826, but, in 1827, she sang Lady Macbeth in Macbeth* on 29 June only a few months after she had done Sinaïde in Moïse* on 26 March. She did not do any additions to the repertory until she was billed as Mizaël in the first production as La Tentation* on 20 June 1832, and her last creation at the Opéra was Arvedson in Gustave III* on 27 February 1833.

The singer seemed happy and competent in her work when her voice started to lose its quality and strength. Her condition grew worse, probably because she did not stop to rest for a sufficiently long period of time, and she was forced into retirement in 1838.

BIBLIOGRAPHY: Chouquet, 390, 392-93, 395-97; DBF IX, 1455; EFC 140; EZF 171; Fétis II, 410; Jacques Gheusi, "Les Créaturs de Moïse à l'Opéra de Paris en 1827," Opéra de Paris" (1 October 1983), 21; Lajarte II, 125-26, 128, 143.

La Dame de Monsoreau was offered as a grand opera in a prologue and four acts divided into seven tableaux with a score by Gaston Salvayre* and a libretto by Auguste Maquet.* Mlle J. Subra provided the choreography, and Joseph Hansen* directed the ballet at the beginning of the third act. Charles Bianchini designed its costumes. The work had its premiere at the Opéra on 30 January 1888 with Auguste Vianesi at the desk. Maquet based his opera on the play by the same title that he had written with Alexandre Dumas.

The prologue presents Monsoreau as having aroused the anger of Diane de Méridor because he has accidentally slain this lady's pet doe. Accordingly, she has decided to reject his proposal of marriage, but Monsoreau has her brought by force to the estate of the duke d'Anjou, the disloyal brother of the king (prol., 1-3). Monsoreau now gains access to Diane's apartment to assure her of his good will by offering to return her to her father. Suddenly, the duke's footsteps are heard in the hall. Monsoreau throws Diane's veil into the castle moat so that the duke will believe that Diane has drowned herself (prol., 4). The duke enters the empty apartment and looks through the open window. He sees the veil on the water, and he believes that his fair prisoner is dead (prol., 5).

The first act begins at the wedding celebration of St. Luc in the hôtel de Montmorency, where the groom fears that a fight over the throne of France may erupt between the royalists and the duke d'Anjou's faction (I, 6). St. Luc presents his bride to the king, and the duke d'Anjou starts an argument immediately by insisting that Monsoreau, not Bussy, should be named leader of the Royal Hunt. Bussy refuses to be drawn into the quarrel because he has more urgent business. A crime has been committed against his friend, the baron of Méridor, whose daughter has been kidnapped. The duke d'Anjou insists that the missing girl is dead and that her father has gone mad (I, 7-9). The ball begins despite the news of this tragedy, although the guests are obviously on the edge of violence (I, 10).

Diane and Gertrude have entered their house in the rue St. Antoine, when the members of the royal faction appear in the street. Bussy enters and is obliged to stand alone in a duel against four opponents. He is wounded but able to escape into Diane's house. The duke's men are trying to break down the door when the bells of the Bastille sound the alarm. Bussy's assailants flee, but he falls unconscious from his wounds (I, 11).

The setting of the second act presents a vestibule and Diane's bedroom, where the baron's daughter is wondering where Gertrude has hidden the wounded stranger. She is thinking about his handsome features and courageous actions when Gertrude informs her that three men have entered the house. One of them is Monsoreau with the news that the duke d'Anjou knows that she is alive and plans to kidnap her. Also, he bears a letter from her father urging her to marry Monsoreau (II, 12-16). The duke knocks on her door at this instant, and Monsoreau explains that he can defend her only if she is his wife. She agrees to marry him (II, 17). They leave to find a priest just before Bussy enters in search of Diane. He is singing of his love for her when the sound of wedding music is heard in the oratory of the house. Bussy looks into the oratory in time to see Diane receive a ring from the priest, but he cannot identify the groom. He hides in a closet only to discover that Monsoreau is his successful rival. Diane expresses the desire to return to her father, but Monsoreau refuses to grant her wish. They argue, and she draws a dagger. She rushes into a closet, and he orders her to obey his commands. She threatens to kill herself. Bussy intervenes with a promise to help her, but Monsoreau leaves to keep an appointment with the duke, and Diane expresses her joy over learning that her new champion is Bussy D'Amboise, the most loyal knight in France (II, 18-19).

In the Louvre, the followers of the duke d'Anjou inform their leader that the League has decided that he is to be crowned king of France. He agrees to the plan and grants Bussy's request that the Diane-Monsoreau marriage be declared null and void (II, 20-23). Monsoreau laments over his troubled marriage, and the duke denounces him as a traitor and a liar. Monsoreau insists that he loves Diane, but the duke demands that he annul his marriage. Monsoreau reminds him that he cannot destroy what God has created, and he asserts that he will seek the support of the new king about to be chosen by the League. The duke admits defeat when he learns that he has not been selected by the League to rule France, and he is obliged to default on his promise to give Monsoreau's bride to Bussy. Inevitably, Bussy is amazed when the duke now presents Diane to the king as the countess de Monsoreau. He denounces the duke, and the duke orders his arrest (II, 24-26).

The third act opens at Dry Tree Crossroads, where Monsoreau is awaiting the signal to put the new king of France upon the throne, and the conspirators are singing their pact. The duke still has hopes of wearing the crown, and he is still thirsty for vengeance against Monsoreau (III, 27). A ballet of fools serves as an interlude before Bussy apologizes to Diane for having failed to protect her from the abuse showered upon her by her husband. She assures him of her gratitude, and they declare their mutual love to each other. The members of the League parage across the stage on their way to ambush the king (III, 28-29).

Bussy assures Diane that Monsoreau and the other members of the League have been discovered and condemned to death, but her page announces that Monsoreau has escaped from his captors (IV, 30-31). The fugitive breaks in upon the lovers, and his men kill the page and wound Bussy (IV, 32), who recovers the page's sword to slay Monsoreau (IV, 33) before dying of his wounds and leaving Diane disconsolate and alone (IV, 34).

These complications arising from the Wars of Religion in the sixteenth century apparently failed to interest audiences by 1888, and Salvayre's opera had to be withdrawn after its eighth performance on 30 January 1880. The male stars cast in this Pierre Gailhard* production included Jean de Reszké* (Bussy), Jean-François Delmas* (Monsoreau), Guillaume Ibos (duke d'Anjou), and Muratet (Saint Luc). The female roles were filled by Rosa Bosman (Diane), Mme Maret (Gertrude), and Mlle Canti as the page. The Ballet of Fools was headed by Mlle Subra alongside the elder Vasquez. The sets reflecting the historical scenes were elaborate and were created by Rubé, Marcel Jambon,* Chaperon (tabl. 1), Poisson (tabl. 2, 3), Carpezat (4, 7 tabl.), and Lavastre (tabl. 5, 6).

BIBLIOGRAPHY: *Camille Bellaigue, L'Année musicale: octobre 1887 à octobre 1888 (Paris: Delagrave, 1889), 39-56; Arthur Pougin, "Première Représentation de la Dame de Monsoreau à l'Opéra," Le Ménestrel 54 (5 February 1888), 43-44; Stoullig XI (1885), 3 and XIV (1888), 1-6.*

La Damnation de Faust was presented by its composer as a dramatic legend, and it has been offered to the public as an oratorio and as an opera. Hector Berlioz* composed its score and joined forces with Gandonnière to write its libretto based upon Goethe's Faust in its French translation by Gérard de Nerval. The work was created as an oratorio, and it was performed first in this form at the Opéra-Comique on 6 December 1846. In 1847-48, it was given again under the direction of Berlioz in St. Petersburg, Moscow, Riga, Berlin, and London. It was mounted on the stage in operatic form for the first time at the Casino Theatre in Monte Carlo on 18 February 1893. The adaptation to the stage was done by Raoul Gungsbourg,* and the leading roles were sung at Monte Carlo by Rose Caron* (Marguerita), Jean de Reszké* (Faust), and Maurice Renaud* (Méphistophélès). The work was then brought to the Garnier Palace* on 21 February 1897, but it was presented here as an oratorio at a Sunday concert. Finally, it reached Paris in Raoul Gungsbourg's adaptation on 7 May 1903, when it was produced at the Sarah Bernhardt Theatre. As an opera, it moved on to Brussels and New York in 1906, the year of its second performance as an oratorio at the Garnier. On 14 February 1908, it was produced as an opera in Rouen, and, ultimately, it reached the Garnier Palace as an opera on 10 June 1910. The opera returned 53,929 francs, 93 centimes, to the box office on its first three programs at the Opéra on 10, 13, and 17 June 1910.

The opera opens with Faust listening to peasants singing and dancing to celebrate the spring season on a plain in Hungry, while troops are marching off to war (sc. 1-3).

Faust is now alone in his study, where he declares himself to be quite bored and desperate. He decides to drink a cup of poison, but the strains of an Easter hymn strike his ears, and his mind turns to more cheerful thoughts. Also, Méphistophélès appears disguised as the spirit of life, and he offers Faust a life of joy and pleasure. Faust agrees to flee with him, and they arrive at a tavern in Leipzig, where students and soldiers are carousing. One of the revelers sings a song about the misadventures of a rat, and Brander asks for a more dignified song, a fugue. Méphistophélès congratulates the singers upon their performance, and he sings a ballad about the noble flea who invited all his friends and relatives to court. Faust finds this entertainment crude, and he suggests that Méphistophélès take him elsewhere (sc. 4-6). Méphistophélès leads him to a prairie by the Elbe River. Here, Faust falls asleep to a concert by the spirits of the earth and air. He sees Marguerita in his dreams, and the sylphs of the region present a ballet for him. He awakens, and Méphistophélès takes him to Marguerita in the company of a band of singers (sc. 7-8).

Faust is in Marguerita's bedroom, where he hides himself behind the curtains of her bed. She enters with a candle and absorbed by thoughts about her handsome lover, who has appeared to her in her dreams (sc. 9-11). In another room, Méphistophélès calls upon the spirits of unfaithful lovers to welcome another member to their group, and they execute a ballet for him. He sings a song for them before he leaves for Marguerita's room, where she recognizes Faust as the hero of her dreams. The lovers swear undying love to each other, and Marguerita falls into Faust's arms (sc. 12-13).

Méphistophélès warns the lovers that the vociferous neighbors are already awake and complaining to Marguerita's mother about the singing in her house. He assures them that they will be together during the coming evening, and Faust and Méphistophélès escape through the garden, where they hear the neighbors shouting to old lady Oppenheim that her daughter has a lover in the house (sc. 14).

Marguerita is singing of love and of her lover who has not yet returned to her arms (sc. 15); Faust is in a forest and singing the praises of nature. Méphistophélès tells him that Marguerita has been arrested for homicide because she is accused of having killed her mother, to whom Méphistophélès gave too much sleeping potion. Méphistophélès agrees to take Faust to her, if Faust will sign a contract to help him. Faust agrees and affixes his signature to his own condemnation (sc. 16-18). The two ride across the stormy sky on Méphistophélès' two black steeds until Méphistophélès has trapped Faust in a sulphurous gulf. They are in the abyss of hell, and Faust is consigned to the flames. Méphistophélès guarantees the custodians of the pit that Faust has agreed of his own free will to spend eternity in hell (sc. 19).

An epilogue presents earthlings asserting that nothing but the grinding of teeth and the suffering of souls was heard in hell after Faust's condemnation. Marguerita is summoned into paradise because her faults have been forgiven (epilogue).

La Damnation de Faust became quite popular in France, where it has been performed on 353 dates at the Garnier opera house with revivals in 1919, 1933, and 1950. Its score has aroused enthusiastic response, especially the three selections that have endured as concert pieces: the "Dance of the Will-o'-the-Wisps," "The Dance of the Sylphs," and the "Hungarian March" based upon a Hungarian folk theme. Other passages favored from the start by audiences are Méphistophélès' serenade, Marguerita's spinning song, and the race to the abyss near the conclusion of the opera. It is true that some critics were upset at first by Berlioz' unusual approach to opera in this work, but their objections were forgotten before long in the face of public acceptance of the composition. It was produced on a hundred occasions in concert form at the Châtelet Theatre alone.

The original cast at the Opéra included Louise Grandjean (Marguerita), Paul Franz* (Faust), Maurice Renaud* (Méphistophélès), and Joachim Cerdan (Brander). Berlioz' Marguerita has also been sung by Marcelle Demougeot,* Jeanne Bourdon, Madeleine Bugg,* Germaine Lubin, Jeanne Hatto,* Rita Gorr, and Régine Crespin (see twentieth-century volume for Lubin, Gorr, and Crespin). Robert Lassalle, José Luccioni, Léon Laffitte,* Georges Thill, and Raoul Jobin have been among the tenors billed as Faust (see twentieth-century volume for Luccioni, Thill, and Jobin). The baritones cast as Méphistophélès have included Marcel Journet,* Vanni Marcoux,* Beckmans, Etcheverry, Pernet, and Savignol (see twentieth-century volume for Etcheverry and Pernet).

BIBLIOGRAPHY: L'Avant-Scène 22 (July-August 1979), 1-88; Michael Ayrton, Berlioz, a Singular Obsession (London: British Broadcasting Corp., 1969), 50-52; Claude Baillif, Berlioz (Paris: Du Seuil, 1968) 117-18; Henry Barraud, Hector Berlioz (Paris: Costard, 1955), 140-44; Jacques Barzun, Berlioz and the Romantic Century (New York: Columbia University Press, 1969) I, 470-503; Idem, Berlioz and His Century (New York: Meridian Books, 1956), 75-78, 237-47; Camille Bellaigue, Promenades lyriques (Paris: Nouvelle Librairie

Nationale, 1924), 159-74; Adolphe Boschot, "L'Invocation à la nature et l'âme romantique," RM special no. 233 (1956), 79-86; idem, Le Crépuscule d'un romantique (Paris: Plon, 1950), 51, 55-57, 65, 73-76, 128, 189, 210-21, 262, 408; idem, "A propos du centenaire de La Damnation de Faust," RM 22 (February-March 1946), 11-14; idem, Le "Faust" de Berlioz (Paris: Plon, 1945); idem, Le "Faust" de Berlioz: étude sur "La Damnation de Faust" et sur l'âme romantique (Paris: Plon, 1945); idem, "Un Peu d'inédit sur la Damnation de Faust," Le Ménestrel 89, no. 10 (11 March 1927), 105-7; Raymond Bouyer, "L'Amour et son expression musicale chez Berlioz," Le Ménestrel 87, no. 13 (27 March 1925) 145-47; Léon Constantin, Berlioz (Paris: Editions Emile-Paul frères, 1934), 95-100, 214-29; DDO I, 293-94; Suzanne Demarquez, Hector Berlioz (Paris: Seghers, 1969), 109-19; Alan E. F. Dickinson, The Music of Berlioz (London: Faber and Faber, 1973), 63-79; John H. Elliot, Berlioz (London: J. M. Dent & Sons, 1967), 179-84; Gabriel Fauré, Opinions musicales (Paris: éditions Rieder, 1930), 2-3; Z Fekete, "Berlioz' Damnation at the Paris Opéra," Music News 41 (September 1949), 13; G. Ferchault, Faust: une légende et ses musiciens (Paris: Larousse, 1948), 46-73; Jacques Feschotte, Berlioz: la vie, l'oeuvre (Paris: La Colombe, 1951), 58-59, 83-94; A. Goléa, "La Damnation, une victoire remportée par le théâtre lyrique d'aujourd'hui," Musica 122 (May 1964), 18-22; Michel Guiomar, Le Masque et le fantasme (Paris: José Corti, 1970), 372-75; Emil Haraszt, Berlioz et la "Marche hongroise," (Paris: Revue Musicale, 1946); D.-E. Inghelbrecht, "Le Faust de Berlioz," RM 198 (1946), 11-19; Otto Jahn, Gesammelte Aufsätze über Musik (Leipzig: Breitkopf und Härtel, 1887), 87-94; Adolphe Jullien, Hector Berlioz, sa vie et ses oeuvres (Paris: La Librairie de l'Art, 1888), 182-98; Jacques Lonchampt, "La Damnation de Faust à l'Opéra de Lyon," Le Monde 6 February 1969, 19; Paul-Marie Masson, Berlioz (Paris: Félix Alcan, 1923), 158-66; MCDE 119, 128-29; Yves Hucher and Jacqueline Morini, Berlioz (Paris: Hachette, 1969), 27-28, 56-57; MSRL 20-21; Ernest Newman, Berlioz, Romantic and Classic, ed. Peter Heyworth (London: Victor Gollancz, 1972), 186-90; Arthur Pougin, "Semaine théâtrale: La Damnation de Faust, d'Hector Berlioz," Le Ménestrel 76 (18 June 1910), 194-95; Guy de Pourtalès, L'Europe *romantique* (Paris: Gallimard, 1949), 823-32; J.-G. Prodhomme, *Victor Berlioz, 1803-1869* (Paris: Delagrave, 1905), 272-84; Ernest Reyer, *Notes de musique* (Paris: Charpentier, 1875), 340-51; Julian Rushton, "The Genesis of Berlioz' *La Damnation de Faust*," *M&L* 56 (1975), 129-46; Camille Saint-Saëns, *Outspoken Essays on Music*, trans. Fred Rothwell (Freeport, N.Y.: Books for Libraries Press, 1969), 52-73; Marcel Schneider, "*La Damnation de Faust*," *L'Opéra de Paris* XXIII (n.d.), 20-26; Victor Seroff, *Hector Berlioz* (New York: The Macmillan Co., 1967), 45, 112-14, 116; SSBO 206-8, 210, Stoullig XXXVI (1910), 23-25; SW 68-70; Thompson 402, 2128-29; Julien Tiersot; "*La Damnation de Faust" de Berlioz* (Paris: P. Mellottée, 1924); W. J. Turner, *Berlioz: the Man and His Work* (New York: Vienna House, 1934), 242-44; Léandre Vaillet, "A propos de *la Damnation de Faust*," *Le Ménestrel* 95, no. 14 (7 April 1933), 151; Tom S. Wotton, *Hector Berlioz* (Freeport, N.Y.: Books for libraries Press, 1970), 67-68, 169-71, 179-81.

Dangès, Henri (b. 1872; d. 8 November 1958), singer, made his theatrical debut at the Opéra-Comique on 11 November 1898 in *Barnabé*. He was billed for the world premiere of Gustave Charpentier's* *Louise** at this same theatre on 2 February 1900, and he enjoyed immense popularity at the Opéra-Comique until he left this theatre to make his debut at the Opéra on 27 January 1908 in Valentin of *Faust*.* The production of Charles Gounod's* work was a special occasion, because it inaugurated the directorship of MM. Broussan and Messager. Eager to begin their tenure of office in a burst of glory, they had arranged for Carpezat (a. 1, 3), Amable (a. 1, 3), Ciocarri (a. 1, 3), Simas (a. 2), Jambon (a. 3), Bailly (a. 3), and Ronsin (a. 4, 5) to supply fresh sets and costuming. Léo Staats* was placed in charge of choreography. It was a distinct tribute to Dangès to invite him to assume the part of Valentin on this occasion that returned 20,014 francs, 25 centimes, to the box office.

After this auspicious beginning, Dangès was retained to sing Nevers of *Les Huguenots*,* Kurwenal of *Tristan et Isolde*,* Telramund of *Lohengrin*,* Wolfram of *Tannhäuser*,* Mercutio of *Roméo et Juliette*,* Athanaël of *Thaïs*,* and Gunther of *Le Crépuscule des dieux** the year of his debut at the Garnier Palace.* The following year, 1909, he was cast in only three parts: Hidraot of Armide, Gunther of Sigurd,* and the lead in Rigoletto* (see eighteenth-century volume for Armide). He was billed as the High Priest of Samson et Dalila,* Albéric of L'Or du Rhin,* and Méphisto of La Damnation de Faust* during 1910. The baritone added the 15th and 16th roles to his Garnier repertory in 1911, the title-part of Hamlet* and Iokanaan of Richard Strauss'* Salomé.* he did Guido of Monna Vanna* in 1912. Dangès' busy association with the Opéra also included three creations: Gaucher d'Arcourt in Le Miracle* on 30 December 1910; Gléby in Sibéria* on 9 June 1911; and Philoctète in Déjanire* on 22 November 1911.

BIBLIOGRAPHY: DBF X, 99; SW 41, 67, 70-71, 86, 110, 118, 135, 150, 162, 184, 191, 196, 198, 201, 207, 209, 215.

Danses de jadis et de naguère was presented first at the Trocadéro on 5 August 1900 for a celebration arranged by Pierre Gailhard,* director of the Opéra. The choreography was provided by Joseph Hansen,* and the artistes of the Comédie-Française and the Opéra assisted in its production. The music of Jean-Philippe Rameau, Hector Berlioz,* Léo Delibes,* Emmanuel Chabrier,* Edouard Lalo,* Ambroise Thomas,* Jules Massenet,* and Ernest Reyer,* and nearly a dozen other composers was used (see eighteenth-century volume for Rameau). M. Paul Vidal* directed the orchestra of the Opéra in the presentation of these musical selections.

The work was divided into four tableaux entitled Danses barbares, Danses grecques, Danses françaises, and Danses modernes. The argument for the first tableau was provided by Camille de Sainte-Croix; it starred Paul Mounet and Mlle Hirch. The scenarios for the second and third parts were created by P.-B. Gheusi and Auguste Dorchain, respectively. Mme Bertet and Mlle Sandrini headed the cast in the former tableau, and they were followed in the third entree by Mlles Désiré and Lobstein alongside M. Boucher. The concluding scene furnished by Louis de Gramont was executed by Mlles Brandes and Carlotta Zambelli* in the company of Mlle Sandrini.

The ballet was presented for the first time at the Garnier Palace* on 11 November 1900, and it

enjoyed a total of eight performances at the Trocadéro and the Opéra before it was dropped.
BIBLIOGRAPHY: AEM 8, 464-65; René Dumesnil, La Musique contemporaine en France (Paris: Armand Colin, 1930) I, 12-15 and II, 64-66; Henri Rebois, Les Grands Prix de Rome de musique (Paris: Firmin-Didot, 1932), 57-62; Gustave Samazeuilh, Musiciens de mon temps (Paris: Marcel Daubin, 1947), 33-36; SW 263.

Danses grecques was one of three ballets choreographed for the Garnier Palace* by Joseph Hansen* and using for its score a medley of extracts from his favorite composers' works. The music employed for Danses grecques was taken from compositions by Hector Berlioz,* Louis Bourgault-Ducoudray,* Victor Duvernoy,* Ernest Guiraud,* Paul Veronge de la Nux, Jules Massenet,* and Paul Vidal.*

The ballet had its world premiere at the Opéra on the gala program of 5 June 1901, but it was not well received by the public, and it was dropped from the repertory after its third billing. No male dancers were needed for the cast that included Mlles Barbire, Beauvais, Bouissavin, Carré, Carrelet, L. Couat, Meunier, Piodi, Régnier, Sandrini, and Viollat. Jean Bartet* supplied the vocal performance required for its production, and Edouard Mangin was at the desk during its brief run.
BIBLIOGRAPHY: EDS II, 921; SW 264.

Les Danses polovtsiennes is a ballet taken from the end of the second act of Alexandre Borodin's* opera entitled Le Prince Igor.* The ballet was performed as a separate entity for the first time by Serge Diaghilev's* Ballets russes* at the Châtelet Theatre in Paris on 19 May 1909. Its new choreography had been created by Mikhail Fokine* at Diaghilev's request. Diaghilev then staged the work at the Garnier Palace* for the first time on 7 June 1910 with the same choreography by Fokine and with the same costumes and set by Nicolas Roerich. The composition was billed at the Opéra on 26 dates before the corps de ballet of the Opéra executed it on 22 June 1949 with fresh choreography by Serge Lifar and Nicholas Zvereff (see twentieth-century volume for Lifar). Karinska did the costumes on this occasion, and Doboujinsky created its set.

The action of the ballet transpires in the Polovtsian camp during the twelfth century, and its argument is based upon the legends growing out of the struggle between the Russian, Prince Igor, and the invading Polovtsians, who have occupied the Don plain. Prince Igor has been taken prisoner with his son Vladimir in a one-sided battle, but their captor, the Khan Kontchak, is a generous and gracious host. He entertains his prisoners with Polovtsian dances executed by his soldiers, slaves, and other prisoners. The dancers wear the bright costumes of the Orient and accompany themselves with tambourines and other musical instruments to contribute to the frenzied and colorful climax of their performance.

The ballet opens with the warriors of the Polovtsian army asleep on the ground, while the women are awake and talking. The men rise to reveal their mottled clothing and painted faces. The women begin to dance slowly but in rhythm, and they form two concentric circles around a stranger dressed in scarlet and wearing pearls in her hair. The women disband, and the Polovtsian chief performs a wild and energetic dance that inspires his officers to follow his example. A group of warriors now imitate their actions on the field of battle, and they are followed by four more soldiers executing a pas de quatre. The maidens and warriors return en masse, and the chief bounds into their midst. The entire company accelerates its pace and ends its exhibition with a shout of triumph.

The ballet has been quite popular at the Opéra, where it enjoyed its hundredth performance on 11 July 1958. It has been given on nearly 150 occasions at the Opéra, and its last productions were part of the ballet programs organized for the spring of 1979. The leading roles in the first presentation of the ballet at the Garnier were created by Alexandra Federova (the young girl), Yekaterina Geltzer (the slave), and Vaslav Nijinsky* (the warrior). The first members of the corps de ballet of the Garnier to dance these same parts were Geneviève Guillot, Rita Thalia, and Alexandre Kalioujny. The cast for the May 1979 productions were headed by Fabrice Bourgeois (chief), Viviane Descoutures (the favorite), and Marie-Josée Redont (the young girl). Mikhail Fokine's choreography was restored and supervised

by Irina Gjebina, who also provided new choreography for the dance of the slaves.
BIBLIOGRAPHY: BB 182-84; BK 28; CB 560-64; Mary Clarke and David Vaughan, The Encyclopedia of Dance and Ballet (New York: G. P. Putnam's Sons, 1977), 283; CODB 425; Michel Fokine, Memoirs of a Ballet Master, trans. Vitale Fokine, ed. Anatole Chujoy (Boston: Little, Brown & Co., 1961), 147-51; HAZ 109-10; André-Philippe Hersin, "De Petipa à Taylor," SDLD 43 (10 May 1979), 6-9; Boris Kochno, Diaghilev and the Ballets russes, trans. Adrienne Foulke (New York & Evanston: Harper & Row, 1970), 28-29; André Levinson, Les Visages de la danse (Paris: Gresset, 1933), 46-49; LOB 28-29; LVD 121-22; "Opéra...Saison russe au ballet: Danses polovtsiannes," Le Ménestrel 76 (11 June 1910), 186-87; PGB 55-56; Maurice Pourchet, "The 1948-49 Ballet Season in Paris," The Ballet Annual 4 (1950), 119; Grace Robert, The Borzoi Book of Ballets (New York: Alfred A. Knopf, 1946), 239-42; RLVB 326-28; Stoullig XXXVI (1910), 20-21, 31; SW 264; TDB 409-10.

Danses russes was a suite of dances based upon music by various Russian composers with choreography by Michel Fokine.* It was presented on a gala program organized on 26 June 1909; its companion piece on this occasion was Le Vieil Aigle* by Raoul Gunsbourg.*

Danses russes was never accepted into the repertory at the Garnier Palace,* where it was staged on only one date. It featured a pas de deux by Anna Pavlova* and Mikhail Mordkin,* a mazurka by Mlle Wassilieva and M. Alexandreff, and a second pas de deux by Mlle Kschesinska and M. Légat. M. Paul Vidal* was at the desk for its single production at the Opéra.
BIBLIOGRAPHY: SW 265.

Daria was billed as a musical drama in two acts with a score by Georges Marty and a libretto by Aderer and Ephraim in collaboration. Marcel Bailly and Marcel Jambon* designed the sets, and Charles Bianchini created the costumes. Joseph Hansen* was responsible for the choreography of this Pierre Gailhard* production that had its world premiere at the National Academy of Music on 24 January 1905.

The opera begins on the estate of the Russian nobleman Boris. Ivan and Boris' mistress Daria are in the main room of the castle, where the former is telling Daria that he heard on his recent trip to Moscow that Boris is taking a wife within a month. A peasant by birth, Daria weeps from disappointment, and Ivan reminds her that nobles are fickle. Also of humble origins, Ivan adds that he is angry to see her treated in this fashion because he loves her, although she was willing to become Boris' mistress. She rejects his advances, and Boris' return to his estate convinces her that Ivan is a rogue (I, 1).

Boris enters surrounded by officials, servants, and the pope. He orders a celebration for the following day (I, 2), and Daria asks him whether he still loves her. He replies that she has been his happiness. His ambiguous answer renews her suspicions; she presses him to be more explicit, and he admits that he is marrying to replenish the family funds. He assures her that their affair is finished. The conversation ends in an explosion of threats and insults on both sides (I, 3-4). Boris loses control of his temper, and he orders his servants to scourge Daria until she bleeds. Ivan intervenes for her by reminding Boris that a powerful master must be a clement judge. Impatient Boris demands to know the reason for Ivan's concern. The latter replies that he cannot see her suffer. Boris suggests that if Ivan loves Daria so fervently, he should marry her. He calls for the pope to marry them. They are wed and leave for the forests of the Ukraine after Daria reminds Boris that he may not always be so powerful (I, 5).

The second act presents Daria and Ivan living in a cottage in a clearing in a Ukrainian forest, where Daria is singing a lullaby to her son. Ivan returns home with a group of woodcutters singing the praises of freedom and happiness. Daria assures Ivan that she is content in their forest home despite their lack of money (II, 1-2). A hunter knocks at the door and asks for Ivan the woodcutter because his master Boris has lost his way on a hunt and seeks shelter (II, 3). Daria is worried, but Ivan asserts that Boris cannot affect their lives now. She suggests that he may be intending to evict them from their home, but Ivan promises that he will never tolerate this assault upon their happiness.

Boris enters and greets his hosts; he invites them to share his brandy. Daria warns Ivan not to drink too heavily, and Ivan remarks upon the fine quality of the wine. Boris invites Daria to sit next to him; Ivan warns him not to be too friendly with his wife. Ivan begins to sing and to dance; Boris thinks that he is drunk and asks Daria for a kiss. She refuses. Ivan picks up an axe. Boris thinks that Ivan is quite drunk, when he continues to drink, but his drinking is more a pretense than real. Boris resumes making advances to Daria, but she assures him that she is happy without him, and Ivan appears to be unaware of what is transpiring. Boris confesses that he has come to the Ukraine expressly to assure her of his love. She replies that she is not impressed, even if she is only a woodcutter's wife. She insists that her only wish is to be with her family. Annoyed, he seizes her and throws his arms around her. Ivan arises from the floor and grabs Boris by the throat; he chokes him to death, while he and Daria sing to drown out his cries. They set fire to their cottage and walk slowly through the door (II, 4-5). They tell the sentry that they are going to sleep outside the house because their child keeps disturbing Boris. The guard is impressed by their concern over Boris' rest, and he allows them to continue on their way into the forest (II, 6).

Marty's work did not arouse much enthusiasm in Paris and had to be dropped after its eighth presentation on 11 March 1905. Mme Geneviève Vix* made her debut at the Garnier Palace* in the title-role of the opera at its premiere. The male parts were created by Jean-François Delmas* (Ivan), Charles Rousselière* (Boris), and Cabillot (the sentry).

BIBLIOGRAPHY: SW 70.

Dartoy, Marie-Marcelle (b. 6 February 1869, New Orleans; d. ?), vocalist, appeared in public first at Bordeaux as a singer of lighter songs and then at the Opéra in Paris, where she made her debut as Urbain in Les Huguenots* on 20 November 1888. She was cast subsequently as Siébel in Faust* in 1888, as Stéfano in Roméo et Juliette* in 1889, and as Inès in La Favorite* in 1890, but she did not return to the stage of the Garnier Palace* until 1893 to do Siegrune in La Walkyrie* and, once again, Urbain of Les Huguenots. After these last two appearances, Mlle Dartoy never sang again at the National Academy of Music.

BIBLIOGRAPHY: EFC 161; SW 190, 397.

Daussoigne-Méhul, Louis-Joseph (b. 10 June 1790, Givet; d. 10 March 1875, Liége), composer, was the nephew and then the adopted son of Etienne-Henri Méhul, who enrolled his ward in the Conservatoire in 1799 so that he might study piano with Adolphe-Charles Adam,* harmony with Charles Catel, and composition with Luigi Cherubini and Méhul himself (see eighteenth-century volume for Méhul, Catel, and Cherubini). He proved to be quite gifted and won the Prix de Rome competition in 1809. While he was at the Villa Medici, his uncle sent him the libretto of Robert Guiscard to set.

When the young musician returned to Paris, he had this opera in three acts as well as Le Faux Inquisiteur, Le Testament, and Les Amants corsaires completed and ready for rehearsal, but all his efforts proved fruitless. Finally, on 17 July 1820, his Aspasie et Périclès was given. it was not a success. He was commissioned next to convert the dialogues of Méhul's Stratonice* into recitatives so that this work might be performed at the Opéra in 1821, and he finished his uncle's Valentine de Milan for its premiere at the Feydeau Theatre on 28 November 1822. Les Deux Salem* was his second and last attempt to have a hit at the Opéra, but, like Aspasie, it aroused no enthusiasm. The failure of Les Deux Salem discouraged him, and he decided to give up theatrical music; he went to Liége to become director of the Conservatoire in this Belgain city, where César Franck* would be one of his students.

BIBLIOGRAPHY: DBF X, 303; GE XIII, 992-93; Lajarte II, 96, 108, 115; LXIX VI, 152.

David was an opera in three acts with a score by Auguste Mermet,* a libretto by Alexandre Soumet* and Félicien Mallefille,* and choreography by Jean Coralli.* It had its world premiere at the Royal Academy of Music in Paris on 3 June 1846. The sets were the work of Séchan, Diéterle, and Despléchin (a. 1, 3) and Pierre Cicéri* (a. 2).

The opera opens in the lush valley of the Térébinthe with shepherds singing of their good fortune and a chorus of women giving thanks for the blessings of peace (I, 1-2). David declares his love to Michol, who has misgivings about the future because she seems to bring misfortune wherever she goes. She warns him that she is the daughter of a cursed king who is the prey of

Satan; she reminds him that he is a simple shepherd unworthy of a princess. David resolves to become a mighty warrior (I, 3).

Saul complains that his subjects continue to shun him, and he warns that misfortune is about to strike again because the witch of Endor has approached the royal palace. He thinks that the moment has arrived when the unknown king will depose him. A voice calls to him (I, 4), and the witch appears on the heights. She warns Saul that his time has come. He, David, and Michol are terrified to receive this message of doom. Michol and David pray for protection, but Saul yields to his fears until David bolsters his spirits with a hymn addressed to God (I, 5-6). The king's son, Jonathas, announces that Goliath has issued a challenge to Israel. Saul will not allow Jonathas to fight the giant because the prince's death has been predicted by the witch, but he offers Michol's hand in marriage to whoever fights for Israel. David volunteers (I, 7).

The second act transpires before the tomb of Samuel in the ruins of Ramatha. Michol and her companions are praying for David, when Saul announces the shepherd's victory and directs Michol to prepare for her wedding (II, 1-2). The king denounces predictions of his demise and declares that he will destroy the witch while guaranteeing the succession to Jonathas. The witch appears and tries to withstand Saul, but the king forces her to summon Samuel from the realm of the dead. They enter his tomb. A troupe of Israelite warriors appears with the banners of victory. The high priest and a retinue of maidens are escorting David clothed in magnificent garments, and the triumphant warrior is flanked by Jonathas and Michol dressed as a bride. A ballet adds to the festive note III, 4), but flames begin to spurt from the tomb, and Saul is hurled from its entrance. He announces that Samuel has revealed that David is to be king of Israel. Outraged, he orders the youth's execution. The royal guards seize the shepherd despite objections by the high priest and the people (II, 5).

The last act is set on Mount Gelboë, where David bids farewell to his harp while awaiting execution (III, 1). Michol and Jonathas offer to help him to escape, and he accepts their suggestion so that he may serve Israel and spare them the pain of his death. He leaves wrapped in

Jonathas' cloak (III, 1-2), and Jonathas remains in his tent (III, 3). Saul enters with sword in hand. He mistakes his son for David and slays him. The priest and the witch enter with David to inform Saul that the shepherd has been named king of Israel. Saul rushes at the youthful monarch, but the witch deters him, and lightning strikes him dead. The high priest places his hands on David's head, and the people kneel before him in a final tableau (III, 4-5).

Some spectators felt that the libretto made too many changes in the original biblical version of the Saul story; for example, Saul and Jonathas were slain together in battle, and audiences did not support the opera beyond eight performances. The score of Mermet's first dramatic composition was not without effective moments, however, especially the march at the end of the overture, the duet beginning "Mon âme est enivrée" by Michol and David, and David's plaintive "Ma harpe, il faut te dire adieu!" The cast at the premiere included Mme Rosine Stoltz* (David), M. Brémond (Saul), Mlle Maria Nau* (Michol), M. Italo Gardoni* (Jonathas), Mlle Moisson (the witch), and M. F. Prévot (the high priest). The divertissements featured the dancing of Mmes Robert, Adeline Plunkett,* and Adèle Dumilâtre* (see eighteenth-century volume for divertissement).

BIBLIOGRAPHY: Chouquet 407-8; DDO I, 299; Lajarte II, 182.

David, Félicien-César (b. 13 April 1810, Cadenet; d. 29 August 1876, Saint-Germain-en-Laye), composer, was raised by his sister after the death of his father, who had given him music lessons at a very early age. A member of the Opéra orchestra heard him sing and urged him to study voice. David followed the advice of this enthusiastic oboe player and also wrote a few hymns and motets before he was 13. He completed his academic studies at the Jesuit school of Aix and then became chapelmaster at Saint-Sauveur in this same city. He did a relatively large number of compositions at this time, and a small income from his uncle permitted him to go to Paris to meet Luigi Cherubini, who had become interested in him through these works (see eighteenth-century volume for Cherubini). He was able to enroll in the Conservatoire, therefore, and he continued his studies under Benoist, Fétis, Millaud, and Reber.

The Orient attracted him after the termination of his work at the Conservatoire, and he left Marseille in 1833 to see Smyrna, Egypt, and the Holy Land. He traveled with his own piano.

When David returned to France in 1835, he published a collection of songs of Eastern inspiration, but they made little impression upon the public. Discouraged, the composer went to Isigny to rest a little and to compose two symphonies and a large number of other pieces that included 24 string quartets. The tenor Walter began to sing his songs at this time, and David found that he was becoming better known in Paris. He returned to the capital in 1841. His symphony-ode about the Near East, Moslems, and dancing girls entitled Le Désert was applauded in 1849, and his La Perle du Brésil was a success at the Théâtre-Lyrique in 1851. He had failed at the Opéra with L'Eden* in 1848, but now his growing confidence in himself persuaded him to try this prestigious theatre again with his Herculanum* in 1859. It was a complete and resounding success. Lalla Roukh was another triumph for its author at the Opéra-Comique in 1862 as was Le Saphir of 1865 at the same theatre.

David capitalized now on his good fortune by going on a tour of the principal cities of Germany, Vienna, Trieste, Genoa. After his return to Paris, he was selected to succeed Hector Berlioz* as librarian at the Conservatoire, and the Fine Arts division of the Institut awarded him a prize of 20,000 francs for the totality of his accomplishments in music. David's importance in the evolution of theatre music in the nineteenth century lay in his innovative addition of Oriental music to the repertory. It is easy to understand why Berlioz admired his gift for musical description and how David influenced the Charles Gounod* of La Reine de Saba* and the Léo Delibes* of Lakmé.* The delicate coloration and picturesque orchestration that distinguish his scores make him one of the important precursors of the Impressionist school.

BIBLIOGRAPHY: René Brancour, Félicien David (Paris: H. Laurens, 1908); DBF X, 346; GE XIII, 1002; Lajarte II, 189, 193, 225; LXIX VI, 165-66.

Debussy, Claude Achille (b. 22 August 1862, St.-Germain-en-Laye; d. 25 March 1918, Paris), composer, will always be remembered for providing the answer to Wagnerism in France with his impressionistic score for Pelléas et Mélisande.*

The young musician moved to Paris with his family after his father went bankrupt running a gift shop in Claude's native city. In the capital, the youth attended classes at the Conservatoire between 1873 and 1884; Durand, César Franck,* Guiraud,* and Jules Massenet* were among his professors. He won the Premier Grand Prix de Rome in 1884, and he was then engaged as the pianist of the baroness de Meck, whom he accompanied to Switzerland, Italy, and Russia. Debussy returned to Paris before long, and he remained in the capital for the rest of his life except for short concert tours in Austria, Russia, Italy, and Holland. Yet although he was a genuine Parisian, he did not pursue a social career or try to win immediate popularity with his skills as a pianist, because composition interested him almost exclusively now.

Debussy wrote two lyric works that were produced initially on Paris stages at the start of the century. His Pelléas et Mélisande was produced at the Opéra-Comique on 3 April 1902, and his Le Martyre de Saint-Sébastien had its world premiere at the Théâtre du Châtelet on 22 May 1911 (see twentieth-century volume for Le Martyre de Saint-Sébastien). Although Pelléas et Mélisande never made its way to the stage of the Opéra, other works by Debussy were offered at the Garnier Palace* on account of their appeal to theatregoers and because choreographers were attracted to his music. The following catalogue indicates the dates when his music was played for the first time at the Opéra. The names of the lyric dramas, ballets, or other types of composiiton for which his music served as the score are likewise provided:

Composition	Dancer	Premiere
Le Lys de la vie	Loïe Fuller	1 July 1920
Petite Suite	Pasmanik	24 March 1922
Prélude à l'après-midi d'un faune	Nijinsky	23 May 1922
Le Martyre de St. Sébastien	Fokine	17 June 1922

Fluorescences	Loïe Fuller	9 February 1938
Pas et lignes	Lifar	5 March 1958
Clair de lune	Lapaouri	8 June 1958
Jeux	Flindt	12 April 1973
Après-midi d'un faune	Jerome Robbins	3 October 1974

Pelléas et Mélisande was never staged at the Opéra because it was considered the "property" of the Opéra-Comique, where it was revived every four or five years for a total of approximately 350 performances between 1902 and 1952.

BIBLIOGRAPHY: AB II, 103-17; AEM III, 62-77; L'Avant-scène 11 (September-October 1977), 140-45; BBD 389-91; "Bibliographie sommaire de quelques musiciens français depuis 1900," RM 210 (January 1952), 208; CBCM 886-93; Maurice Dumesnil, Claude Debussy (New York: Washburn, 1940); EDS IV, 295-300; ELM I, 629-41; HAZ 112-13; Kathleen Hoover, "Quiet voluptuary," ON 27, no. 8 (29 December 1962), 8-13; JB 291-301; JV 177-79; KOH 174-83; KT 77-116; LD 57-89; Edward Lockspeiser, Debussy: His Life and Mind (New York: Macmillan & Co., 1965); MCDE I, 255-78; MIT 1-23, 42-53; MM 529-55; MMFM 61-101; NEO 169-70; PBSW 73-76, 124, 150, 153; PY 80-86; Leonid Sabaneev, "Claude Debussy," M&L 10 (1929), 1-34; Victor Seroff, Debussy: Musician of France (New York: Putnam & Sons, 1956); SSBO 332-33, 335-37, 356, 363-64; Oscar Thompson, Debussy, Man and Artist (New York: Dodd Mead, 1937); Thompson 413-24; TWT 195-211; Leon Vallas, Claude Debussy: His Life and Works (London: Oxford University Press, 1933).

Déidamie is an opera in two acts with a libretto by E. Noël, a score by Henri Maréchal,* and choreography by Joseph Hansen.* It was given initially at the National Academy of Music on 15 September 1893.

The opera opens in the place of King Lycomède of Scyros, where Déidamie is telling her sisters that she was happy as long as her husband Achille remained on Scyros disguised as a woman in accordance with the wishes of his mother Thétis. Now, however, he may have to leave home to fight the Trojans because the oracle has predicted that he alone will enter Troy victorious, and his life will be "bound to the exploits of the Greeks." She begs her sisters to hide him and to guard him (I, 1). Achille informs Déidamie that Greek ships have entered the harbor laden with gold and other valuables. Fearsome Déidamie tells her husband of her misgivings, but he reassures her that the Greeks in the harbor are simple merchants on a trading expedition (I, 2).

Ulysse and the Greek leaders enter disguised as merchants, and Ulysse orders the slaves to set down the bales of merchandise. He tells his companions that they must find Achille and drag him from his refuge; he places a sword among the jewels, perfumes, and priceless artifacts. The women of Scyros enter to inspect the offered goods, and Ulysse tells Déidamie to select adornments for herself. Disguised Achille notices the sword. He picks it up and brandishes it. Ulysse provikes him by suggesting that he lay the weapon aside to examine the perfumes. Achille loses his temper and is goaded into revealing his identity. Déidamie is filled with misgivings and berates Ulysse. She is in the midst of her tirade (I, 4), when Lycomède enters. Ulysse is a friend of Lycomède and presents himself to the king. He explains that he is executing an order for the gods. The Greeks lack a leader to help them to defeat the Trojans, and he has come to win Achille to their cause. Achille refuses to believe Ulysse, but Lycomède replies that it is fitting for his ward to do the will of the gods. It is decided that Achille will leave with the Greeks on the morrow, therefore, and Achille and Ulysse are reconciled. Déidamie prays to Vénus to help her to keep her husband with her (I, 5).

The second act is set in the gardens of the king dominated by a statue of Pallas with her spear and shield. A ballet centered about Pallas and a pas de deux begin the act. The dance ends, and Ulysse is wondering whether or not his trick has worked, and he prays to the goddess for help (II, 1-2). A company of young Greeks emerges from the palace to escort Ulysse to the celebration in the palace, and Achille enters with Déidamie. She is weeping and reproaching him for leaving her. Achille cannot withstand her tears and agrees to remain on Scyros. Ulysse returns to see them reunited and filled with joy; he realizes what has happened (II, 3-4). Achille tells Ulysse that he cannot accompany him to the shores of Troy, and Ulysse reminds him of the wrath of the gods. The sky darkens; a storm erupts (II, 5). A voice warns Achille that he will tarnish his name if he persists in his refusal to serve the Greeks. The sky lightens finally, and Déidamie and Achille become visible again. Ulysse has triumphed. Déidamie has consented to Achille's departure. He and Ulysse sail away to resume the siege of Troy (II, 6-8).

Déidamie was not greeted with enthusiasm by Paris audiences, and it had to be dropped from the repertory after its 12th performance on 12 May 1894, when it was produced as the second work on a program that included the premiere of Charles Lefebvre's* Djelma.* At the first presentation of Déidamie, Mme Alba Chrétien-Vaguet* created the title-part with the principal male roles filled by Albert Vaguet* (Achille), Maurice Renaud* (Ulysse), and Auguste Dubulle* (Lycomède). Mlles Gina Ottilini and Mathilda Sallé starred in the ballet.

BIBLIOGRAPHY: DDO I, 301; Stoullig XIX (1893), 25-34; SW 70; Thompson 1091-92.

Déjanire is a lyric tragedy in four acts with a score by Camille Saint-Saëns,* a libretto by Louis Gallet and Saint-Saëns, and choreography by Yvan Clustine. It was first presented as an ancient tragedy with singing at Béziers on 28 August 1898. It was then brought to the Odéon in Paris on 11 November 1898, and it was given its first presentation in its lyric form at the Monte Carlo opera house on 14 March 1911. Finally, it was billed initially at the Opéra on 22 November 1911 with sets by Rochette, Landrin, and Mouveau. Pinchon created its costumes on this occasion. The work is based upon Sophocles' Les Trachnyiennes and grew out of a plan to renew the great spectacles of antiquity by presenting them in open-air productions. The first production of Louis Gallet's tragedy at Béziers was attended by 15,000 persons.

The action begins in the courtyard of a palace in Oechalia, where a victory and wedding pyre is being prepared in honor of Hercule, who has completed his labors and captured Iole after slaying her father Eurytus. The Oechalians lament Iole's fate and wonder what will become of them. Hercule appears with Philoctète; he is complaining of Junon's insistence upon persecuting him by making him fall in love with Iole, although he is married to Déjanire. He directs Philoctète to tell Déjanire that he is going to marry again, but Phénice delivers a message to him from his wife. She has come to Oechalia to see him. Hercule bids her tell Déjanire to forget him because he loves another woman. Phénice predicts an evil fate for him and leaves, while Philoctète confesses his love for Iole after Hercule's departure. Iole begs Philoctète to protect her from Hercule. She declares her love to him and vows to pass the remainder of her life in the gynoeceum. The chorus describes the savage fury of Déjanire, and Philoctète tries in vain to diminish her anger (a. 1).

The scene shifts to the gynoeceum, where Iole explains to Déjanire that her projected marriage to Hercule is not her plan, and Hercule informs his wife that she must accept his marriage to Iole. Déjanire tells her husband that she is willing to return to Calydon if Iole will accompany her. Hercule refuses this proposition, and she vows that she will have revenge for his rejection of her love. Déjanire decides to remain in Oechalia, and Philoctète announces to Hercule that Iole will not marry him because he has slain her father. Hercule tries in vain to persuade Iole to change her mind, and he is speechless with rage when he discovers that Philoctète is his successful rival. He arrests him and wonders when Junon will grow tired of persecuting him (a. 2).

Déjanire explains to Phénice that she has decided to use her talisman, the secret shirt that Nessus gave to her with the assurance that it had the power to eliminate rivals for her fickle husband's heart. Iole begs Déjanire to help her because Hercule has arrested Philoctète. Déjanire rejoices to have an ally and discards her plan to use Nessus' shirt. She bids Hercule farewell and pretends to give her blessing to his marriage to Iole. Hercule is suspicious of her motives, and he intercepts Iole trying to flee with Déjanire. He offers her a choice of marriage to him or the death of Philoctète. Crushed Iole chooses marriage to her father's slayer, and Hercule orders the temple prepared for his wedding. Déjanire is about to rescue Iole, but the latter explains her predicament and her decision to Hercule's wife. Philoctète tells Iole that he is free; he upbraids her for her weakness. Déjanire decides that it is time to rely upon Nessus' talisman. Phénice warns her that the shirt is a trap, but Déjanire refuses to listen to her, and the chorus calls upon the god of love to rekindle Hercule's passion for Déjanire (a. 3).

A joyous crowd has gathered around the wedding pyre of the first act, and Hercule proclaims a day of games and dancing to celebrate his marriage to Iole. She presents the groom with his nuptial robe, and a divertissement prefaces the wedding ceremony (see eighteenth-century volume for divertissement). Hercule asks for the blessings of the gods and pours a libation, and the setting sun strikes his garment. He drops the sacrifical cup in pain, and when Nessus' fiery shirt burns into his flesh, Iole prays for him to be spared the torture being inflicted upon him, but he throws himself into the flaming pyre, where he is consumed. Déjanire stabs herself in grief (a. 4).

The work seemed to have lost its charm for the public, when it was brought to the stage of the Opéra in traditional operatic form. It had to be dropped after its 17th presentation on 2 July 1913. At the Garnier Palace,* Mmes Félia Litvinne* and Yvonne Gall* created the parts of Déjanire and Iole, respectively, with Lyse Charny as Phénice. The two important male parts were created by Lucien Muratore* (Hercule) and Henri Danges* (Philoctète). The divertissement was danced by Mlles Blanche Kerval, J. Delsaux, and Blanche and Suzanne Mante heading the corps de ballet of the Opéra.

BIBLIOGRAPHY: Jean Bonnerot, C. Saint-Saëns, 1835-1921; sa vie et son oeuvre (Paris: A. Durandet et fils, 1922), 166-69, 180, 188, 190, 192-97; DDO II, 1210; René Dumesnil, La Musique contemporaine en France (Paris: Armand Colin, 1930) I, 12-15 and II, 64-66; Gabriel Fauré, Opinions musicales (Paris: Rieder, 1930), 133-34; James Harding, Saint-Saëns and His Circle (London: Chapman & Hall, 1965), 196; Arthur Hervey, Saint-Saëns (Westport, Conn.: Greenwood Press, 1970), 75-77; Watson Lyle, Camille Saint-Saëns, His Life and Art (Westport, Conn.: Greenwood Press, 1970), 39-40; Modern Drama and Opera: Reading Lists on the Works of Various Authors, ed. Frederick W. Faxon (Boston: The Boston Book Co., 1915), 201; Otto Neitzel, Camille Saint-Saëns (Berlin:

Harmonie, 1899), 67-68; D. C. Parker, "Camille Saint-Saëns: a Critical Estimate," MQ 5 (1919), 561-77; A. Pougin, "Opéra . . . Déjanire," Le Ménestrel 77 (25 November 1911), 369-70; J.-G. Prod'homme, "Camille Saint-Saëns," MQ 8 (1922), 469-86; Georges Servières, La Musique française moderne (Paris: Havard, 1897), 285-404; Stoullig XXXVII (1911), 21-26; SW 71.

Delavigne, Jean-François Casimir (b. 4 April 1793, Le Havre; d. 11 December 1843, Lyon), librettist, pursued his academic studies in his native city and Paris. He began his career as a poet by writing a Dithyrambe sur la naissance du roi de Rome in 1811, which attracted Napoleon's attention and won him a modest position in the imperial government. When the emperor was defeated and overthrown in 1814-15, Delavigne published his Messéniennes which elicited Louis XVIII's approval and obtained for him the post of librarian at the Chancellery during the Restoration. After weathering the 1815 change in government, Delavigne turned to the theatre and enjoyed a complete success in 1819 at the Odéon with his tragedy, Les Vêpres siciliennes. He continued in the theatre with Les Comédiens (1820) and Le Paria (1821), but he lost his librarianship at the Chancellery only to be appointed to the same position in the household of the duke d'Orléans at the Palais-Royal. It was at this time in his life that he produced his best comedy, L'Ecole des vieillards (1823), and his well known Marino Faliero (1829).

The Revolution of 1830 could have only one effect on Delavigne, who had managed to win imperial and then royal favor under Napoleon and Louis XVIII. He had to suspend his plans for his future literary works to insure his position with the new government of Louis-Philippe. Accordingly, he wrote a "national march" entitled La Parisienne, and all Paris was humming it within a few days. He was safe once again and resumed his literary endeavors with a series of six tragedies and comedies but only one composition for the musical theatre, Charles VI* of 1843, for which he and his elder brother Germain did the words. This opera in five acts and his La Parisienne were the only works by Delavigne that were performed at the Opéra.

BIBLIOGRAPHY: Saint-Albin Berville, *Etude sur Casimir Delavigne* (Paris: F. Maltesta, 1858); Bio. Univ. X, 309-15; Paul-Antoine Cap, *Casimir Delavigne, éloge couronné par l'Académie royale . . . de Rouen en 1846* (Paris: Dubochet, 1847); DBF X, 756-57; Mme Marcelle Fauchier-Delavigne, *Casimir Delavigne intime* (Paris: Société française d'imprimerie et de librairie, 1907); Lajarte II, 172, 252; Edmond Sambuc, *Etude sur Casimir Delavigne* (Paris: L. Duc, 1893); Ferdinand Vuacheux, *Casimir Delavigne, étude biographe et littéraire* (Le Havre: Impr. du Commerce, 1893); Wks III, 248.

Delavigne, Germain (b. 1 February 1790, Giverny; d. 30 November 1868, Montmorency), librettist, was a younger brother of the well-known dramatist, Casimir Delavigne.* He attended the collège Saint-Barbe, where Eugène Scribe* was one of his schoolmates. The two youths formed a lifelong friendship that evolved into a partnership producing plays and opera librettos used by some of the leading composers of the time.

Although Germain Delavigne held a government position between 1831 and 1848, his literary productivity does not appear to have diminished after Louis Philippe's accession to the throne of France in 1830. Also, it will be observed from the following catalogue of the works in whose composition he shared that he collaborated with nearly all the important composers of the romantic movement at the Opéra:

Opera	Collaborator or Editor	Date
La Muette de Portici	D.-F.-E. Auber	29 February 1828
Robert le Diable	Giacomo Meyerbeer	21 November 1831
Charles VI	J.-F.-F.-E. Halévy	15 March 1843
L' Apparition	François Benoist	16 June 1848
La Nonne sanglante	Charles Gounod	18 October 1854

BIBLIOGRAPHY: DBF X 757-58; GE XIII, 1172; Lajarte II, 140-41, 172-73, 188, 217; Wks III, 248.

Deldevez, Ernest-Edouard-Marie (b. 31 May 1817, Paris; d. 5 November 1897, Paris) composer, enrolled as a student at the Conservatoire in 1825 to study under François Habeneck.* He won first prize for violin in 1833 and continued his musical studies with Jacques Halévy.* After winning another first prize in 1838, he published a collection of songs with piano accompaniment and enjoyed his first public success at his 1840 concert at the Conservatoire. The musical theatre tempted him at this point in his career, and he did the score for four ballets danced initially at the Opéra: Lady Henriette* of 1844 for which he did the score with Frédéric Burgmuller* and Friedrich Flotow*; Eucharis* of 1844 and Paquita* of 1846, which he set alone; Vert-Vert* of 1851, on which Jean-Baptiste Tolbecque* collaborated with him.

Habeneck was dead now, and Deldevez wrote a Messe de requiem (1853) in memory of his former teacher besides completing a number of other non-dramatic pieces including his Symphonie héroï-comique. This same year, 1853, he composed for a 15 February program at the Opéra his Cantate pour le mariage de l'Empereur. He devoted most of his time in his later years to the writing of his memoirs and to composing treatises on subjects of a musical nature. He had been promoted to leader of the Opéra orchestra in 1873 besides being named to a professorship at the Conservatoire.

BIBLIOGRAPHY: CB 183, 189, 197, 202-3; DBF X, 781-82; Ernest Marie Deldevez, Le Passé, à propos due présent, faisant suite à mes Mémoires (Paris: Chaix, 1892); idem, Mes Mémoires (Le Puy: Marchessou fils, 1890); GE XIII, 1176; Lajarte II, 174, 176, 181, 210, 253; Wks 9012, 10474, 11951.

Delestre-Poirson, Charles-Gaspard (b. 22 August 1790, Paris; d. 19 November 1859, Paris), librettist, started his literary career in the odic vein with a poem celebrating Napoleon's marriage in 1810, but he turned to writing for the theatre during the Restoration by entering into a very profitable contract with Eugène Scribe* whereby the latter was to offer his texts only to the Gymnase Theatre of which Poirson had become director in 1820. Since Scribe was not free to submit his works to other theatres if they were competitors of the Gymnase, both men became quite wealthy through this arrangement, which amounted to a monopoly on Scribe's formidable productivity for Poirson. The latter's second lucrative maneuver was to reduce to a single act his theatre works already given at the Comédie-Française in their original and longer form. Delestre-Poirson was rich and a member of the Legion of Honor by 1826.

Poirson's only contribution to the Opéra was the libretto he did with Scribe for Le Comte Ory* of 1828, but his collaboration with Scribe produced 14 titles for the Vaudeville Theatre, including such deservedly forgotten works as Les Montagnes russes (1816), Le Nouveau Pourceaugnac (1817), and Une Visite à Bedlam (1818).

BIBLIOGRAPHY: DBF X, 813; Lajarte II, 131; LXIX VI 351; Wks III, 248.

Delibes, Clément-Philibert-Léo (b. 21 February 1836, Saint-Germain-du-Val; d. 16 January 1891, Paris), composer, was an only son whose father died and left his family without resources. The boy and his mother came to Paris in 1848, and the future composer was fortunate enough to find a place in the choir of the Madeleine to help support his mother and himself. The quality of his voice called attention to his talents, and he was admitted to the Conservatoire to study under the direction of Bazin, Benoist, Adam, and Le Couppey.

The ambitious youth obtained a position as accompanist at the Théâtre Lyrique through Adolphe Adam* in 1853, and, exposed to theatrical activity now, he composed pieces for the theatre where he was employed and for the Bouffes-Parisiens. He enjoyed varying degrees of success during the following decade. Then, in 1863, he became accompanist at the Opéra and, in 1865, assistant chorusmaster there under Victor Massé.* He remained in this latter position until 1872, when he married Mlle Denain, previously and actress at the Comédie-Française.

After his marriage, Delibes received a commission to do a ballet for the Opéra with Léon Minkus.* This work was called La Source,* and it was greeted by the public with such enthusiasm that Delibes was asked to write a balletic piece to be added to Adam's Le Corsaire.* He displayed so much skill in executing this second commission that he was now given the truly major task of providing the entire score for Coppélia.* This composition proved to be still another extraordinary success for Delibes, and he was encouraged to go on to do additional pieces for the Opéra-Comique and the Opéra. The following summary charts his total activity at both these theatres:

Work	Premiere	Theatre
La Source	12 November 1866	Opéra
Valse	21 October 1867	Opéra
Coppélia	25 May 1870	Opéra
Le Roi l'a dit	24 May 1873	Opéra-Comique
Sylvia	14 June 1876	Opéra
Jean de Nivelle	8 March 1880	Opéra-Comique
Lakmé	14 April 1883	Opéra-Comique
Kassya	24 March 1893	Opéra-Comique
Soir de fête (from La Source)	30 June 1925	Opéra
Fluorescences (Pas des fleurs)	9 February 1938	Opéra

Lakmé was the work that crowned Delibes' career in a last burst of glory and assured him of a place among the great composers of his age. It enjoyed nearly 1300 performances at the Opéra-Comique by 1950.

BIBLIOGRAPHY: AEM III, 126-33; BBD 397; Adolphe Boschot, La Musique et la vie (Paris: Plon, 1931), 96-102; CB 354, 359, 373, 483, 488-89, 494-95; H. de Curzon, Léo Delibes, sa vie et ses oeuvres (Paris: Legouix, 1926); DBF X, 529-30; EDS IV, 391-94; GE XIII, 1186; Ernest Guiraud, Institut de France. Académie des beaux-arts. Notice sur la vie et les oeuvres de Léo Delibes (Paris: Firmin-Didot, 1892); Henri Heugel, "La Mort de Léo Delibes," Le Ménestrel 57 (18 January 1891), 17; Lajarte II, 240, 244, 248, 255; Paul Landormy, La Musique française de Franck à Debussy (Paris: Gallimard, 1943), 133-36; LXIX VI, 355; MSRL 53-55; Arthur Pougin, Musiciens du XIXe *siecle (Paris: Fischbacher, 1911); SS 130-35, 136-37; Thompson 431.*

Deligny, Eugène (b. 30 December 1816, Paris; d. March 1881, Paris), librettist, gave up his medical studies to pursue a career in the theatre. He became secretary of the Ambigu-Comique after his Le Fils du bravo and Hermann l'ivrogne were performed on the stage of this theatre in 1836. His La Porte secrète was also mounted here four years later in 1840. After composing a series of comedies and vaudevilles for the Variétés, he became general secretary of the Opéra and added the ballet of 1848 entitled Nisida* to the repertory of this company.

BIBLIOGRAPHY: DBF X, 835; GE XIII, 1187; Lajarte II, 188; Wks III, 248.

Delioux de Savignac, Charles (b. April 1830, Lorient; d. 1880, Paris), composer, was a child prodigy and still quite young at the time of his piano concerts before the French and English courts at the Tuileries and in London. He entered the Conservatoire in 1845 to study composition with Jacques Halévy,* and he counted piano pieces of Spanish inspiration among his many compositions for this instrument. His sole work for the Imperial Academy of Music was his Le Rhin allemand, a contata orchestrated by Léo Delibes* and given on 29 July 1870.

BIBLIOGRAPHY: DBF X, 838; Lajarte II, 255.

Delmas, Jean-François (b. 14 April 1861, Lyons; d. 27 September 1933, St. Alban de Montbel) was a bass and a pupil of Aubin and Bassine at the Conservatoire in Paris. Skilled in declamation and gesturing, he made his debut at the Opéra as St.-Bris in Les Huguenots* on 28 September 1886. He sang nearly a score of roles in the two decades after his first appearance at the Opéra, and these parts were in compositions based upon a wide variety of traditions. They included such diverse characterizations as Gaspard in Le Freischütz* (1886), Méphistophélès in Faust* (1887), Leporello in Don Juan (1887), Hagen in Siguard* (1891), Iago in Othello* (1894), and Thésée in Hippolyte et Aricie (1908) (see wighteenth-century volume for Don Juan and Hippolyte et Aricie).

Yet Delmas' greatest value to management was doubtlessly his ability to take a new role from a work being readied for its premiere and to learn it effectively and punctually. In fact, his creation of no fewer than 42 new parts at the Opéra must have set some sort of record for performers. The following chart provides the roles he created, the operas from which they come, and the date of their premieres. It will be observed that Delmas performed in four new compositions in 1901.

Role	**Opera**	**Premiere**
Monsoreau	La Dame de Monsoreau	30 January 1888
Capulet	Roméo et Juliette	28 November 1888
Orosmane	Zaïre	28 May 1890
Amrou	Le Mage	16 March 1891
The King	Lohengrin	16 September 1891
Narr' Havas	Salammbô	16 May 1892
Wotan	La Walkyrie	12 May 1892
Athanaël	Thaïs	16 March 1894
Gauthier	Hellé	24 April 1896
Mathias	Messidor	19 February 1897
Hans Sachs	Les Maîtres Chanteurs de Nuremberg	10 November 1897
Attila	La Burgonde	23 December 1898
Jacob	Joseph	26 May 1899
Phur	Astarte	15 February 1901
Duc de Guise	Le Roi de Paris	26 April 1901
Scaurus	Les Barbares	20 October 1901
Wotan	Siegfried	31 December 1901
L'Evêque	Orsola	21 May 1902
Tonio	Paillasse	14 December 1902

Arnigiad	*La Statue*	6 March 1903
L'Etranger	*L'Etranger*	1 December 1903
Akiba	*Le Fills de l'Etoile*	17 April 1904
Kurwenaal	*Tristan*	11 December 1904
Yvan	*Daria*	24 January 1905
Auguste	*La Gloire de Corneille*	6 June 1906
Périthoüs	*Ariane*	28 October 1906
Miguel	*La Catalane*	24 May 1907
Hagen	*Le Crépuscule des dieux*	23 October 1908
Marco	*Monna Vanna*	10 January 1909
Wotan	*L'Or du Rhin*	14 November 1909
Pierre	*La Forêt*	13 February 1910
Pierre Dupont	*Intermède*	10 December 1911
Dédale	*Icare*	19 December 1911
Fabius	*Roma*	24 April 1912
Argagard	*Fervaal*	31 December 1912
Gurnemanz	*Parsifal*	4 January 1914
Gervais	*Ouragan*	17 February 1916
Rubini	*Le Roman d'Estelle*	9 March 1916
Fonfrède	*Les Girondins*	26 March 1916
Jacques d'Arc	*Jeanne d'Arc*	24 November 1917
L'Ermite	*La Léfende de Saint Christophe*	6 June 1920
Malek	*Antar*	14 March 1921

Charlemagne	La Fille de Roland	27 October 1922
L'Empereur Phorcas	Esclarmonde	24 December 1923
Le Mendiant	Les Burgraves	24 February 1927

BIBLIOGRAPHY: ICM 436; KRJ 102-3; Martin 111; SW 37, 39, 43, 46, 53-54, 57, 66, 68, 70, 80, 82, 91, 95-96, 99, 102, 111, 118, 126-27, 133-34, 138-39, 148, 151, 162, 164, 166, 168-70, 187, 189, 190, 193, 201-2, 204, 208, 215, 225, 227, 318, 367, 369.

Delna, Marie (b. 3 April 1875, Paris; d. 24 July 1932, Paris) was a contralto whose stage name was an anagram of her true name, Ledan. A pupil of Rosine Laborde, she made her debut at the Opéra-Comique on 19 June 1892 as Didon in Hector Berlioz'* Les Troyens (see twentieth-century volume for Les Troyens). She remained with this company for six years and distinguished herself in the title-role of Benjamin Godard's La Vivandière on and after 1 April 1895. She was also popular as Carmen.

Mlle Delna left the Opéra-Comique to appear on the stage of the Opéra for the first time on 9 May 1898 as Fidès in Le Prophète,* a role she repeated for the 500th performance of Giacomo Meyerbeer's* work on 10 February 1899. This same year, 1899, she sang Dalila in Camille Saint-Saëns'* Samson et Dalila* and Léonore in Domenico Gaetano Donizetti's* La Favorite.* She was selected to sing Carmen on 11 November 1900, when the second act of Georges Bizet's* work was included in a gala program sponsored by the Ministry of Education and Fine Arts. While she was at the Opéra during the closing years of the nineteenth century, she created the roles of Cassandre in Berlioz' La Prise de Troie on 15 November 1899 and of Guinèvre in Victorin de Joncières' Lancelot* on 7 February 1900 (see twentieth-century volume for La Prise de Troie).

After her marriage to M.A.H. de Saône in 1903, the singer announced her retirement from the stage only to return to the Opéra-Comique to join the cast of Alfred Bruneau's* L'Attaque du moulin* before the end of the year. Also, she visited the United States in 1909-10 to fill an engagement with the Metropolitan Opera Company of New York.

She appeared at the Opéra again on 24 February 1916 to help stage the third act of Bruneau's L'Ouragan by singing the part of Marianne, but this contribution to the war effort could scarcely be construed as a return to the stage.

Some measure of Mlle Delna's activity at the Opéra-Comique may be deduced by recalling that she created the following nine parts at this theatre on the following dates:

Role	Opera	Date
Charlotte	Werther	16 January 1893
Marceline	L'Attaque du moulin	23 November 1893
Mrs. Quickly	Falstaff	18 April 1894
Marion	La Vivandière	1 April 1895
Orphée	Orphée	6 March 1896
Zerline	Don Juan	17 November 1896
Fée Grignotte	Hansel et Gretel	30 May 1900
Marianne	L'Ouragan	29 April 1901
Vieille Tili	La Lépreuse	7 February 1912

BIBLIOGRAPHY: APD 261; DBF X, 864-65; EFC 171-72; ICM 436; KRJ 102-3; Martin 112; PBSW 177; SW 55, 90, 133, 166, 176-78, 198; WOC 25, 62, 69-70, 90-91, 105, 133-34, 179, 181, 248.

Delrat (d. Toulon, November 1911), singer, made his debut as a baritone at the Le Peletier* opera house in the role of Maurevert in Les Huguenots* on 22 July 1871. He remained with the Opéra long enough to perform at the Garnier Palace,* where he sang for the 1875-76 season. He was cast in three roles during this latter interval: Melchtal in Guillaume Tell,* Albert in La Juive,* and a nobleman in Le Prophète.* He was in retirement from the theatre when he died.
BIBLIOGRAPHY: SW 116, 461.

Delrieu, Etienne-Joseph-Bernard (b. 1761, Rodez; d. 4 November 1836, Paris), dramatist, lived in Versailles until 1793, when he moved to Paris to serve the new government as head of the customs office in the French capital. He retained this position during the Empire, when he secured his reputation as a man of letters by writing poetry celebrating the birth of the king of Rome in 1811.

Delrieu was primarily a playwright, however, and his first work for the stage was Arsinoüs, a tragedy in three acts of 1791. He also wrote a series of comic operas beginning with Les Deux Lettres of 1796, and he made his only contribution to the repertory at the Opéra in 1822, when he supplied the libretto for Florestan, ou le conseil des dix.* Unfortunately this work was not a success, and Delrieu never wrote another text for this theatre. His numerous pieces for other theatres stood him in good stead, however, and his tragedies, comedies, and comic operas won him a pension of 2,000 francs under the Empire despite the accusations of plagiarism lodged against him.

BIBLIOGRAPHY: DBF X, 924-25, Lajarte II, 101-2.

Demeur, Anne Arsène (b. 5 March 1824, Sanjon; d. 30 November 1892, Paris), née Charton, was a French operatic soprano. She studied under Bizot in Bordeaux, where she made her debut in 1842, and she went on to perform in Brussels (1846) and London (1846-52) as well as at the Opéra-Comique in Paris during 1849 and 1853. After going on tours in Russia, Austria, and North and South America, she created the role of Béatrice in Hector Berlioz'* Béatrice et Bénédict at the Baden-Baden opera house on 9 August 1862. Her performance was so effective that Berlioz cast her in the part of Didon in the premiere of his Les Troyens à Carthage at the Théâtre Lyrique in Paris on 4 November 1863. Finally, when Berlioz' La Prise de Troie was performed at the Pasdeloup Concerts in 1879, she was called out of retirement to appear as Cassandre, although she was now 55 years old.

BIBLIOGRAPHY: Alexandre Bisson and Théodore de Lajarte, Petite Encyclopédie musicale (Paris: A. Hennuyer, 1882) II, 146; DDO I, 133-34; SW 218-19.

Le Démon de la nuit was an opera in two acts with a score by Jakob Rosenhain* and a libretto by Jean Bayard* and Etienne Arago.* It was based upon a popular 1836 vaudeville by Mlle Anaïs Fargueil and had its world premiere at the National Academy of Music on 17 March 1851.

The opera is set at the Danish court during the time of Louis XIII, and the action starts in the gardens of the royal palace, where a group of courtiers are celebrating youthful Frédéric's accession to the throne. When the maids of honor enter under the watchful eye of their governess, Mme Grommer, the baron asks which one of them has lost her scarf. No one admits having misplaced her scarf, and the baron suggests that the scarf was put on the terrace gate by "the demon of the night." A young officer named Edgard reveals that the king has announced a ball for the coming evening (I, 1-2). Alone with Edith, Mathilde reveals to her friend that the scarf in question belongs to her. She lost it when she was fleeing from "the demon of the night" who stole into her bedroom to serenade her. The "demon" begins to sing again at this moment. Mathilde and Edith call upon him in a duet, but he refuses to appear (I, 3).

The king enters with his retinue and asks Edgard to help him avoid a marriage to which he has already consented (I, 4). Edgard presents Mathilde to Frédéric, but he appears to ignore her. He dismisses his court (I, 5), and Edgard reveals to Frédéric that he is plannign to wed Mathilde. The astonished king refuses to grant his permission for their union, and he discloses that he has already chosen Edith to be Edgard's bride. Edgard rejects this arrangement. A quarrel ensues, and the angry king banishes Mathilde from his court. Suddenly, the king regrets his tyranny, and he agrees that Edgard and Mathilde may wed despite his secret love for the prospective bride (I, 6). Edgar proposes marriage to Mathilde with the explanation that he promised her dying father to become her husband, but she is scarcely swept off her feet by this proposal (I, 7). Mathilde feels obliged to accept the situation, however, because the baron announces that the court is to assemble in the chapel for the wedding, which the king will witness. Mathilde hears the voice of the "demon" once again, and she begs the king to excuse her from marrying Edgard. She declares that she is already wed, but only Edith realizes that Mathilde is being faithful to "the demon of the night." Mme Grommer wonders how Mathilde could have married in such complete secrecy (I, 8).

The second act shifts to the apartments of the maids of honor, who are listening to a chorus of officers (II, 1). Mathilde has been dismissed by the queen mother, but Edith assures her that her "demon" will help her. It is growing late, and Edith gives Mathilde a lamp to see her "demon" during the night; her other companions vow to watch over her and give her a bell to ring in the event that she needs help (II, 2-3). After Mathilde and the maids of honor have left the room, Frédéric climbs through the window. Mathilde returns to the darkened room and prays to her "demon" to help her; he answers her. Mathilde reaches for her lamp to see him, when the baron enters in search of Mme Grommer. He leaves quickly when he discovers that he has stumbled upon Mathilde, but it is too late. She believes that the baron is her "demon," and she is shocked to discover that he has grey hair and an uncertain step. Downcast Frédéric tries to convince her that all lovers are not young, and she notices his youthful voice. She realizes that she is speaking with a man of blood and flesh, and she concludes that he has come to seduce her. She rings the bell, and Frédéric flees, but the baron comes running into the room. When the maids of honor see him, they believe him to be the elusive "demon," and Mathilde is certain that the baron has been in her room from the beginning. She faints. The baron is perplexed. He will condemn himslef by remaining silent, but he will expose the king by offering explanations (II, 7-8). Edith and Edgard denounce him, and the latter draws his sword. The king arrives in time to prevent a duel between the baron and Edgard, however, and Edgard reproaches Frédéric for betraying his honor on the very evening that he has extricated him from an unwelcome marriage contract. The exultant king breaks out in song, the song of "the demon of the night" that Mathilde recognizes. He apologizes to Edgard and announces that Mathilde is to become his queen (II, 9-10).

Critics reacted kindly to Le Démon de la nuit on account of the score and the skill of the performers, but spectators rejected the work and its implausible plot. Thus, it had to be withdrawn from the repertory after only four performances despite a number of effective passages in the score, for example, the mixed chorus at the start of the second act, the aria for the soprano beginning "Sur cette terre je n'ai que lui," and the kings' "demon" song, "Ombre du mystère." The female roles were filled by Mme Laborde (Mathilde), Mme Maria Nau* (Edith), and Mme Printems (Mme de Grommer) with MM. Gustave Roger* (Frédéric), Brémont (the baron), and Marie (Edgard) in the male parts.

BIBLIOGRAPHY: Chouquet 441; DDO I, 306; Elise Kratt-Harveng, Jacques Rosenhain, Komponist und Pianist (Baden-Baden: Emil Sommermeyer, 1891), 14-16, 19, 21-23; Lajarte II, 207-8; Antoine F. Marmontel, Virtuoses contemporains (Paris: Heugel et fils 1882), 6-7, 11.

Demougeot, Marcelle (b. 8 June 1876, Dijon; d. 23 November 1931, Ste-Maxime-sur-Mer), vocalist, studied in her native city under the direction of Charles Laurent before going to Paris to become a pupil of Hettich at the Conservatoire.

She made her debut as a soprano at the Opéra as Dona Elvire of Don Juan on 17 October 1902. Her strong and brilliant voice was to make her the leading Wagnerian soprano in France during her time, and management showed no hesitancy about assigning important parts to her from the very beginning of her career. She sang Vénus in Tannhaüser,* the title-role of Aïda,* and Marguerite in Faust* in 1903. She did Léonore in Le Trouvère* and Brunehilde in La Walkyrie* the following year, and, in 1905, she was cast as Berthe in Le Prophetè,* as the heroine of Daria,* and as Lucinde in the revival of Christoph Willibald Gluck's Armide (see eighteenth-century volume for Gluck and Armide). Her only new assignment in 1906 was Valentine in Les Huguenots,* and she performed only Anita of La Catalane* in 1907.

The years just before World War I saw her billed as the heroine of Salammbô* and as Marguerite of La Damnation de Faust* in 1910, and as Chimenè in Le Cid* in 1911. She did three roles during 1912; the female leads of Déjanire* and Tristan et Isolde,* and Brunehilde in Siegfried.* She learned no new Wagnerian roles in 1913, when her efforts were centered around doing Floria in Les Barbares* and Guilhen in Fervaal.* Her theatrical activities did not stop with France preparing for total mobilization, and she appeared as Kundry in Parsifal* and Vita in L'Etranger* during 1914. She then went on to sing Catherine in Henry VIII* in 1915, Thanasta in Briséis* in 1916, and Bia in Prométhée in 1917 during the enforcement of Jacques Rouché's policy of sustaining the Opéra as generously as the conflict permitted. The only role that she added to Garnier repertory after 1918 was the duchess d'Etampes of Ascanio* in 1921.

She created seven roles during the years that she was associated with the Opéra, although she had taken extra time to fill other assignments at Monte Carlo, Nice, Strasbourg, and Bordeaux. She did Beltis in Le Fils d'Etoile* on 17 April 1904, a coryphée in La Gloire de Corneille on 6 June 1906, Cypris in Ariane* on 28 October 1906, Fricka in L'Or du Rhin* on 14 November 1909, Laurence in Les Girondins on 26 March 1916, and the heroines of Miguela and Hélène on 18 May 1916 and on 20 June 1919, respectively (see twentieth-century volume for Les Girondins, Miguela and Hélène).

BIBLIOGRAPHY: DBF X, 1005-6; EFC 174-75; KRJ 104; SW 29, 39, 42, 46, 52, 57, 62, 69-71, 75, 82, 88, 91, 96, 102, 110, 112, 117, 149, 162, 170, 178, 193, 202, 207, 215, 217, 367, 375.

Dereims, Etienne (b. 26 April 1845, Montpellier; d. ?), vocalist, was encouraged to attend the Paris Conservatoire, where he won the prize for opéra-comique in 1875. He made his theatrical debut this same year on 5 September at the Athénée Theatre as Almaviva in Le Barbier de Séville.* He toured the provinces in 1873-76 and filled an engagement in Barcelona during 1876-77 before returning to Paris to appear in the premiere of Cinq-Mars at the Opéra-Comique on 5 December 1877. The quality of his performance won him a contract to join the Opéra in 1879, and he remained with this company until 1885, when he went on a series of tours abroad.

M. Dereims made his debut at the Garnier Palace* in the title-role of Faust* on 5 December 1879. Subsequently he created three roles at the Opéra: Don Gomès of Henry VIII* on 5 March 1883, Gauthier in Tabarin* on 12 January 1885, and the duke of Mantua in Rigoletto* on 27 February 1885. His repertory at the Garnier Palace included the following nine parts written for tenors:

Role	**Opera and Year**
Fernand	La Favorite (1879)

The count	Le Comte Ory (1880)
Raimbaut	Robert le Diable (1881)
Ottavio	Don Juan (1881)
Rhadamès	Aïda (1882)
Manoël	Tribut de Zamora (1882)
Faust	Mefistofele (1883)
Vasco	L'Africaine (1883)
Phaon	Sapho (1884)

BIBLIOGRAPHY: SW 25-30, 111-12, 147, 181-82, 184-85, 198-99, 205, 213-14.

Dérivis, Prosper (b. 28 October 1808, Paris; d. ?), singer and the son of the singer Henri-Etienne Dérivis, entered the Conservatoire on 8 April 1829 (see eighteenth-century volume for Henri-Etienne Dérivis). He distinguished himself as a student of declamation and singing under the direction of Adolphe Nourrit* and Pellegrini, and he made his debut at the Opéra on 21 September 1831 as the protagonist of Gioacchino Rossini's* Moïse.* His powerful bass voice made him eligible for the roles of kings, prophets, philosophers, priests, and other types of seers, and he created Belzébuth in La Tentation,* which had its premiere on 20 June 1832.

He remained at the Opéra for nearly a decade and worked hard at perfecting his already admirable voice. He was cast as Thamar for the premiere of Ali-Baba* on 22 July 1833, and he was selected to do the commander in the first production of the French version of Don Juan* by François Blaze* and Deschamps* on 10 March 1834. He appeared as a herald for the world premiere of La Juive* on 23 February 1835, and he was the almost inevitable choice for the part of Nevers in the initial presentation of Les Huguenots* on 29 February 1836. His next five creations at the Opéra were the duke in Stradella* on 3 March 1837, Manfredi in Guido et Ginevra* on 5 March 1838, Barducci in Hector Berlioz's* Benvenuto Cellini on 3 September 1838, Cojuelo in La Xacarilla* on 28

October 1839, and Félix in Les Martyrs* on 10 April 1840.

Dérivis fils made a trip to Italy in 1840, but he was able to perform as Captain Albert in the presentation of the cantata entitled Loyse de Montfort sung first at the Institut and then at the Opéra on 7 October 1840. The following year, on 19 April 1841, he executed the title-role of Le Comte de Carmagnola* at its initial production. He then left the Opéra to visit Milan and Vienna in 1841-43 and Genoa, Trieste, and Parma in 1844. He was booked in Rome and Genoa again during 1845, but he returned to Paris in 1846. He appeared briefly at the Opéra, but he did not renew his association with management here.

BIBLIOGRAPHY: Chouquet 396-403; DBF X, 1135; EDS IV, 498-99; EZF 178; Fétis II, 483; HUT 108-9; Lajarte II, 143-44, 146-50, 152-53, 155-58, 161-63; PBSW 177; SW 73, 115-16, 129.

Derley, J. was the assumed name under which Count Roger de Sainte-Marie created the scenario for the ballet entitled Graziosa.* Staged during the boldest period of the Second Empire (1861) at the Opéra, this work generated a great deal of excitement because its librettist was a young, wealthy, and influential member of the Jockey Club that had hooted at Richard Wagner's* Tannhaüser* less than a fortnight previously. In fact, it was accepted and billed for production so quickly by management because of the latter's desire to calm the still belligerent members of the Jockey Club. Graziosa was "Derley's" only creation for the Opéra.

BIBLIOGRAPHY: CB 365-69; Chouquet 419; Ivor Guest, The Ballet of the Second Empire (London: Pitman Publishing, 1974), 164, 166-68, 180; Lajarte II, 231.

Desarbres, Nérée (b. 12 February 1822, Villefranche-sur-Saône; d. 16 July 1872, Lyon), writer, started his career in the theatre with a comedy entitled Madame Diogène (1852). He continued in this light vein with vaudevilles, operettas, and comedies of the calibre of Madame est de retour (1853) and Deux Femmes à gage (1854). These compositions and others that Desarbres wrote in this 1852-55 interval were very successful. Then, in June 1856, he was named secretary of the Opéra during the administration of Alphonse Royer*; he held this position until February 1863.

He wrote two more comedies during his tenure of seven years at the Opéra, but his only contribution to the repertory here was the poem he did for the 1862 cantata entitled La Fête de l'empereur. After the expiration of his term of office at the Imperial Academy of Music, he published two volumes that proved to be more entertaining than informative: Sept Ans à l'Opéra (1864) and Deux Siècles à l'Opéra (1868). He worked next on the words of La Servante à Nicolas (1861) for Erlanger and of Les Oreilles de Midas (1866) for F. Barbier. In 1866, he decided to go to Lyon, where he wrote Les Eaux de Bourbon-Lancy (1868) a few years before his death.

BIBLIOGRAPHY: DBF X, 1183; Fétis Suppl. I, 259; GE XIV, 203; Lajarte II, 255; LXIX VI, 519.

Desaugiers, Auguste-Félix (b. 1770, Fréjus; d. 1836, Paris), librettist, was the son of Marc-Antoine Désaugiers (see eighteenth-century volume for Marc-Antoine Desaugiers). He embarked upon a diplomatic career and was sent to Rome in 1791. His next assignment took him to Copenhagen in 1793. He remained in Denmark for more than 20 years and was retired with the rank of general consul by the government of Napoleon and Louis XVIII. After his retirement in 1815, he continued his literary activity, which had occupied his spare hours in foreign lands and furnished the words for cantatas that were part of the free programs at the Opéra on 25 August 1815 honoring Louis XVIII and on 4 November 1825 saluting Charles X. His principal effort was directed toward the composition of librettos that were never mounted at the Opéra except for Virginie* of 1823.

BIBLIOGRAPHY: DBF X, 1190-91; DDO II, 1149; Lajarte II, 104, 251; LXIX VI, 524; Wks 6048.

Deschamps de Saint-Amand, Anne-Louis-Frédéric-Emile (b. 20 February 1791, Bourges; d. 22 April 1871, Versailles), librettist, was assured an excellent education by his devoted father, who also obtained a government position for him at Vincennes. After the two sieges of this city at the end of the First Empire and the return of peace with the return of the Bourbons to the throne of France, Deschamps turned to literature and wrote a pair of hit comedies with H. de Latouche for the Odéon in 1818: Selmours and Le Tour de faveur. His success won him admission to the premier cénacle, the stronghold of romanticism, where he found himself on friendly terms with Nodier, Victor Hugo,* Alexandre Soumet,* and de Vigny.

Quick to react to his surroundings, Deschamps now founded the review Études françaises et étrangères and issued one of the three important manifestos of the romantic school in its pages in 1828 besides calling attention to the accomplishments of Goethe, Schiller, and Shakespeare. Letters were not his only interest, however, because he knew the romantic painters and their works as well as he knew his colleague's poems and plays. Yet music attracted him even more strongly, and he found time to write words for Gioacchino Rossini's* Ivanhoë and numerous romances in addition to contributing to the Opéra. He worked with François Blaze* on the French translation of Wolfgang Amadeus Mozart's Don Juan* in 1834 besides collaborating with Eugène Scribe* on the libretto of Giacomo Meyerbeer's* Les Huguenots* of 1836 (see eighteenth-century volume for Mozart). He did the libretto for Louis Niedermeyer's* Stradella* of 1837 with Emilien Pacini and supplied the poem for François Bazin's cantata entitled Loyse de Montfort that won the Prix de Rome competition in 1840. Finally, he did the words for Hector Berlioz'* symphony, Roméo et Juliette.

It is indeed surprising that Deschamps' activity and competency in letters, art, and music have not led to a greater interest in this energetic and informed figure who occupies such a prominent place on the well studied romantic scene.

BIBLIOGRAPHY: Eugène Bazin, Emile Deschamps (Paris: Sauton, 1873); DBF X, 1272-73; GE XIV, 225-26; G. Jean-Aubry, "A Romantic Dilletante: Emile Deschamps (1791-1871)," M&L 20 (1939), 250-65; Lajarte II, 147, 155, 257; LXIX VI, 538-39; Armand Putois, Académie de Mâcon. Séance publique du . . . 30 mars 1874. Notice sur Emile Deschamps (Mâcon: E. Protat, 1874); Achille Taphanel, Emile Deschamps à Versailles (Versailles: J. Aubert, 1911); idem, Notice sur Emile Deschamps (Paris: Lecoffre fils, 1872).

Deschamps-Jehin, Blanche (b. 18 August 1857, Lyons; d. June 1923, Paris), vocalist, studied voice in her native city and at the Paris Conservatoire before making her debut at the Théâtre de la Monnaie in the female lead of Mignon in 1879. After singing the part of the heroine in the world premiere of Hérodiade in Brussels on 19 December 1881, she returned to Paris to appear in a series of works at the Opéra-Comique that included Le Médecin malgré lui (1886) and Le Roi d'Ys (1888). She moved over to the Opéra for the Giacomo Meyerbeer* gala on 14 November 1891 to sing Fidès in Le Prophète* and the especially restored part of Catherine de Médicis in the fourth act of Les Huguenots.*

Deschamps-Jehin remained at the Opéra after the Meyerbeer centenary to do Léonore in La Favorite* in 1891 and Amnéris of Aïda,* Edwige of Guillaume Tell,* and Queen Marguerite of Hamlet* in 1892. The next year she appeared as Ortrude in Lohengrin,* Uta in Sigurd,* and Marthe in Faust.*

At the Opéra, she also created three parts: Fricka in La Walkyrie* on 12 May 1893, Véronique in Messidor* on 19 February 1897, and Dalila in Samson et Dalila* on 5 October 1898.

Mlle Deschamps became known as Deschamps-Jehin after her marriage in 1889 to the conductor Léon Jehin. She retired from the operatic stage in October 1902 after a performance at the Opéra-Comique. Her varied repertory and the range of her voice were the principal factors contributing to her success as a singer. Her creations at the Opéra-Comique included:

Role	Opera	Date
Margared	Le Roi d'Ys	7 May 1888
Mme de la Haltière	Cendrillon	24 May 1899
La Mère	Louise	2 February 1900
Mme Jolicoeur	La Troupe Jolicoeur	30 May 1902

BIBLIOGRAPHY: DBF X, 1269-70; EFC 164-65; GE XIV, 226; KRJ 106; Martin 118; PBSW 177; SW 29, 48, 85, 89, 106, 109, 113, 135, 148, 178, 197, 203, 225; WOC 42, 108, 152, 155, 174, 248.

Deshayes, Prosper Didier (b. 1760, ?; d. ?), composer, wrote operettas, ballets, and divertissements for the theatres of Paris in addition to writing two oratorios entitled Les Maccabées and Le Sacrifice de Jephté (see eighteenth-century volume for divertissement). His only contribution to the stage of the Opéra was the choreography he created for Zémire et Azor* by Jean-Madeleine Schneitzhoeffer,* which was performed in 1824.
BIBLIOGRAPHY: Lajarte II, 109; Riemann 187; Wks 6092.

Les Deux Pigeons is a ballet in two acts and three tableaux with a score by André Messager* and an argument by Henri Régnier in collaboration with Louis Mérante,* who also created the choreography. The scenario is based upon La Fontaine's poem by the same title. The work had its world premiere at the Opéra on 18 October 1886 with sets by the team of Rubé and Chaperon (a. 1) and Lavastre (a. 2). Charles Bianchini designed its costumes.

The ballet is set in a village square dominated by a pigeon cote with a roof of red tiles. The young pigeon Pépio is bored with his financee Gourouli, and he leaves her for a traveling gypsy. Gourouli accepts the advice of her mother Mikalia, and she follows the fugatives at a distance to be certain that no harm befalls her errant fiance (a. 1).

The scene shifts to a public square in a strange city, where the gypsies' tent is pitched outside an inn. Pépio is so occupied with his new love that a pickpocket steals his purse with ease. He is not deterred from pursuing his gypsy love, however, but a storm breaks out, and the gypsy girl takes flight. Left alone, Pépio despairs (a. 2, tabl. 1).

Pépio returns to the pigeon cote, where Gourouli forgives her wayward lover, and the two lovers are reconciled. They invite their friends to share their joy, and the curtain falls on a happy celebration (a. 2, tabl. 2).

The ballet was not well received by audiences at first, and the indifference shown toward it by such figures as Charles Gounod* did little to promote it. It was dropped after only a relatively few performances, therefore, but it was revived after Broussan and Messager became codirectors of the Opéra in 1910. The grace and lightness of the score apparently made a more favorable impression on the audiences of this later era, and the ballet was appreciated at its true worth. Subsequently, it was never really dropped from the repertory, and, during the first half of the twentieth century, it was billed at the Opéra on nearly 200 dates.

The cast selected for the creation of Les Deux Pigeons was headed by Rosita Mauri,* who had come to the Opéra on the recommendation of Gounod. Gourouli was one of her most successful roles, and she created a sensation in it by appearing as a blonde in the first act and as a brunette in the second act. The three other female parts were created by Mélanie Hirsch (Djali), Mlle Montaubry (Mikalia), and Mlle Monnier (the queen of the gypsies). Pépio was danced in travesty by Marie Sanlaville. Louis Mérante danced as the male gypsy.

There is an added historical interest to Les Deux Pigeons, because it was the first ballet that Messager created for the Opéra, and it was the last work for which Louis Mérante wrote the choreography before his death. Also, Les Deux Pigeons was the first ballet to be rehearsed at the Opéra to piano accompaniment; the violin and viola had served this purpose until 1886. Lastly, it might be added that Régnier was selected to write the scenario based upon La Fontaine because he was working on his great edition of the works of this poet for the celebrated Grands Ecrivains series.

BIBLIOGRAPHY: Camille Bellaigue, L'Année musicale: octobre 1886 à octobre 1887 (Paris: Delagrave, 1888), 1-7; BOP 135-37, 149; CB 508-12; CODB 156; Jean-Claude Diénes, "A l'Opéra, spectacle de l'Ecole de Danse," SDLD 124 (10 May 1980), 20; HAZ 118; LOB 83-84; H. Moréno, "Première Représentation du ballet les Deux Pigeons, à l'Opéra," Le Ménestrel 52 (24 October 1886), 377-78; "Opéra . . . Les Deux Pigeons, reprise," Le Ménestrel 78 (6 April 1912), 107-8; PGB 106-8; Stoullig XII (1886), 21-23; SW 267; VBO 35-40.

Les Deux Salem was billed as a fairy-tale opera in a single act with a score by Louis-Joseph Daussoigne-Méhul,* a libretto by Paulin de Lespinasse, and choreography by Pierre-Gabriel Gardel (see eighteenth-century volume for Gardel). It had its world premiere at the Royal Academy of Music on 12

July 1824, and it was composed in a single act with sets by Pierre Cicéri.*

The curtain rises on the opera to disclose the interior of a grotto cluttered with instruments and equipment used in physics, astronomy, and chemistry experiments. The sorcerer Thalamir is complaining that Salem's wife Zuléma remains indifferent toward him despite his use of occult powers to attract her. He decides to make one last effort to seduce her, however, and he hits upon the plan of disguising himself to look and to talk like her husband. He conjures up Zarès, the god of metamorphosis, and he summons his undines and salamanders. Zarès is shocked to learn why Thalamir seeks his services, but he is obliged to cooperate, although he can effect this transformation for one day only. Thalamir is also warned that he must not call upon his spirits for help during this time. He promises to abide by these conditions (sc. 1-2).

The setting shifts to a palace garden near Ispahan at dawn. Zuléma admits to Fatmé that she is worried by her husband's prolonged absence. She is singing a love song to while away the hours (sc. 3), when Thalamir presents himself to her in the guise of Salem. Zuléma greets him effusively, of course, and he orders a feast to be prepared. He directs Fatmé to invite the paupers of the city to the celebration as a sign of his contentment, but puzzled Zuléma asks him why he has to have a crowd around him on this occasion. They do not allow Thalamir's plans for the feast to interfere with their reunion, however, and they exchange vows of eternal love before falling into a fervent embrace (sc. 4-5).

Fatmé announces the start of the feast, and slaves lay lavish presents at Zuléma's feet. A ballet has just been executed to celebrate the return of Salem, when a caravan appears in the distance (sc. 6). It is Salem. He notices the festivities, of cource, but he believes that his wife has been preparing a celebration for his return. When he sees his double with his wife, he falls into a rage and asks the stranger to identify himself. Thalamir acts in identical fashion, and the onlookers can only wonder how it is possible for two Salems to be in the palace. They take sides, and the two Salem factions are about to fight, when the Cadi rushes in to stop the quarrel.

The Cadi tries to identify the true Salem by interviewing the two men and Zuléma, but he cannot arrive at a conclusion, and he orders his men to lock up the two "husbands" pending a more thorough investigation. everybody leaves but Fatmé, who remains by the two kiosks where the prisoners are incarcerated. Salem knows how to escape from his kiosk, and he begins to question Fatmé, who cannot understand how he has forgotten the fervor with which Zuléma kissed "him" only hours previously. Salem is beside himself with rage, but the Cadi returns, and he has to hide in his kiosk (sc. 7-10).

The Cadi has not been able to find a solution to the problem of the two Salems in the Coran, but he resolves to hand down a decision (sc. 11). The court convenes. Zuléma suggests to the Cadi that only her husband can sing her favorite love song, but both claimants pass this test. The Cadi remains puzzled. He announces finally that he will decide the case in a year. Salem reveals that he will leave Ispahan until the situation is settled, but Thalamir recalls that his disguise will last for 24 hours only, and he refuses to accept the postponement. He defies the Cadi and draws his dagger. Arrested, he calls upon his undines and salamanders for help. They chase the Cadi into one of the kiosks. Zarès appears to inform Thalamir that his powers have left him because he has called upon his spirits. Zarès and the salamanders whisk him away to hell (sc. 12-13). The Cadi returns to claim credit for a wise and just solution, while Zuléma and Salem fall into each other's arms (sc. 14).

The first presentation of Les Deux Salem was attended by the first claque in the history of the Opéra, but the evening of 12 July 1824 proved to be more unruly than historic. The claque became so noisy that an "anticlaque" group of spectators mobilized, and a savage fight ensued. The riot at the premiere might have contributed to the downfall of Daussoigne's work, which enjoyed only 13 performances before being dropped.

The three female roles were created by Mme Louise Dabadie* (Fatmé), Mme Grassari (Zuléma), and Mlle Sainville (Zarès). The basic idea of the opera was suggested by the similarity in appearance and voice between Adolphe Nourrit* (Thalamir) and his son (Salem). Prosper Dérivis* sang the part of the Cadi. It should be noted

also that the similarity between Plautus' The Menaechmi and Les Deux Salem has been observed.
BIBLIOGRAPHY: Chouquet 391; DDO I, 322; Lajarte II, 108-9.

Devriès, Fidès Adler (b. 22 April 1852, New Orleans; d. ?), vocalist, received her first lessons from her father and then went on to continue her studies under M. Duprez. She made her Paris debut at the Théâtre Lyrique as Rose-de-Mai in Le Val d'Andorre during 1869, and she moved on to the Opéra several years later for her initial appearance with this company at the Le Peletier* opera house as Marguerite in Faust on 3 November 1871. At the Le Peletier, she sang Isabelle in Robert le Diable* in 1871, Inès in L'Africaine* and Ophélie in Hamlet* during 1872, and Agathe in Le Freischütz* in 1873. When the company moved to their new and sumptuous quarters on the place de l'Opéra, she repeated these four roles, but she left the Garnier Palace* finally in 1874 only to return there to appear in the 200th presentation of Hamlet* on 21 February 1883.

Mlle Devriès withdrew from the Opéra at this point in her career to sing at the Théâtre-Italien in 1883-84, but she was induced once again to return to the Opéra to do the part of Chimène in Jules Massenet's* Le Cid at the premiere of this work on 30 November 1885. Finally, on 30 April 1887, she was selected to sing Elsa in the Paris premiere of Lohengrin* at the Eden Theatre. She went on a tour abroad after filling her engagement at the Eden, and she never again returned to the stage of the Opéra despite the opinion in Paris that her soprano voice was ideally suited to the execution of the Wagnerian and French works dominating the repertory in her day.
BIBLIOGRAPHY: Gustave Bertrand, "Une Nouvelle Ophélie, Mlle Fidès Devriès," Le Ménestrel 39 (8 December 1872), 11; EFC 151; EZF 180-82; SW 25-26, 62-63, 100-101, 108-9, 134-35, 184-85.

Devriès, Herman (b. 25 December 1858, New York; d. ?), vocalist, received his musical education in France and made his debut as a bass at the Opéra in Méru of Les Huguenots* on 5 August 1878. This same year he sang the roles of the centurion in Polyeucte* and of Wagner in Faust.* He filled seven parts in 1879, but none of them was challenging enough to make him feel enthusiastic about his future at the Opéra except perhaps for the chief in Le Roi de Lahore* and the bailiff in L'Africaine,* a man of the people and Albert in La Juive,* Maurevert in Les Huguenots,* Selva in La Muette de Portici,* and Polonius in Hamlet.* Whatever his final sentiments about his position at the Opéra might have been, however, he left the company for the Opéra-Comique after doing the part of the peasant in Le Prophète* in 1881, and he never returned to the theatre where he had started his career.

BIBLIOGRAPHY: Etude 67 (November 1949), 56; ECM, 447; Musical America 69 (September 1949), 42; N.Y. Times, 25 August 1949, 23; SW 152, 175, 187.

Le Diable amoureux was presented as a pantomime ballet in three acts and eight tableaux with music by François Benoist* (a. 1, a. 3) and Henri Reber* (a. 2), a libretto by Jules-Henri de Saint-Georges,* and choreography by Joseph Mazilier.* Philastre and Cambon created sets for it that elicited almost unreserved praise from the press. Mazilier's work had its premiere at the Royal Academy of Music on 23 September 1840, and it proved to be a reasonably popular composition. It was mounted in its entirety on 49 dates between 1840 and 1845, and it was not dropped from the repertory until 17 January 1845. Only its first act was performed with Richard en Palestine* on 9 October 1844. It was billed at Her Majesty's Theatre in London as early as 11 March 1841, when it was observed shrewdly that the ballet might benefit by being condensed.

A party is in progress in the gardens of Phoebée's country estate at the start of the ballet. Count Frédéric is pretending to give his undivided attention to his hostess and mistress, although he is fascinated by the peasant Lilia. Phoebée is not deceived and obliges him to remain with her, when he starts to compliment the younger girl. As soon as Phoebée moves among her guests, however, he strikes up a conversation with Lilia and her mother, Thérésine. He learns that he and Lilia played together as children; he is delighted and kisses Lilia's hand first as Phoebée appears (I, 1-2). Frédéric explains his actions to Phoebée, who suggests that he please the girl with a gift, not kisses, and he gives Lilia a ring (I, 3). Frédéric and his mistress begin to quarrel, and Phoebée assures him that she is going to become more interested in her other suitors. Old Hortensius congratulates his former student for breaking off relations with Phoebée (I, 4), but Frédéric loses his temper, when he sees her flirting with a group of men. He decides to forget his anger at the gaming table, and he loses his entire fortune. Only Lilia tries to help him by retrning his valuable ring and adding her few jewels and a gold cross to her donation. He keeps the cross but returns the other objects. Phoebée shows her resentment, tempers flare, and Hortensius drags Frédéric away before he becomes involved in a duel (I, 5).

The second tableau shifts to the count's old gothic tower, where Jenetta and Semplice open the door for him and Hortensius (I, 1-2 bis). The men decide to read instead of worrying about their predicament. Frédéric comes upon a manuscript giving directions on the ways to conjure up the devil, and he decides to follow them. A storm arises, and Belzébuth appears with Urielle, who is to be Frédéric's slave. Belzébuth transforms her into a page to serve her new master, and he disappears. Frédéric awakens after his sudden sleep, and he does not know what to think when he sees a page kneeling before him. He tests his new servant by ordering a sumptous meal, and his request is granted. It becomes obvious that Urielle is falling in love with her new master, moreover, because the page tries to kiss his hand (I, 3 bis). Hortensius and Frédéric dine well. Frédéric falls asleep; the page puts Hortensius to sleep. She changes from her page's uniform to more tempting garb and dances her way into Frédéric's dreams. When Frédéric awakens, Urielle disappears, and he has to arouse Hortensius to help him find the ethereal dancer. They come upon the page in a dresser drawer. The next morning, the page pays off Frédéric's clamoring creditors, and they sign receipts. The page converts their money into smoke and then confronts them with a sneer and their receipts when they claim their money again (I, 4-6).

At the start of the second act, Frédéric has acquired a palace where drinking, gambling, and dancing never cease. Hortensius is alarmed at Frédéric's new way of life. Frédéric flirts with his servant Janetta, and Urielle becomes jealous and arouses Simplicé's jealousy, but Frédéric discharges him. Angry, Urielle extinguishes the lights in the palace, and chaos ensues. She cannot separate Janette and Frédéric, and she decides to bring Phoebée to the palace. Phoebée joins the festivities, and the page tries to arouse Frédéric's jealousy by dancing with her. Frédéric is furious and stops the dancing (II, 1-3). Urielle is still helpless but angry, when her master dismisses her, but she is resourceful and makes Lilia appear in a mirror as Frédéric is embracing Phoebée. He notices her, but she disappears, and he leaves Phoebée to find her. Phoebée is humiliated and leaves (II, 4). Lilia reappears at the door with her mother, and Frédéric throws himself at her feet. Phoebée returns to see the count at her rival's feet and seizes a dagger to stab him. Lilia intervenes and receives the blow; she falls unconscious into Frédéric's arms. Semplicé goes in search of the police; Thérésine is overwhelmed with grief; Phoebée disappears. The bailiff enters and arrests Frédéric, but the page whisks him away, and the bailiff decides to imprison Semplicé (II, 5-8).

The fourth tableau depicts a beach where Bracaccio and his pirates have landed. Janetta and her friends return from fishing and dance with them before leaving. The pirates hide, and Lilia emerges from a nearby house. She is weak but alive and assisted by her mother and Hortensius. Frédéric enters looking for her, and, having found her, he asks her to be his wife. She agrees. They plan to wed immediately, but Urielle is aware of their plans. Phoebée enters, sees the page, and asks him about the count. The jealous page loses no time in telling her that Frédéric and Lilia are about to wed. Phoebée refuses to believe him, but he enables her to see her rival in her bridal veil. Phoebée is filled with rage and hires the pirates to kidnap Lilia (II, 1-6 bis). The page then pays them to kidnap Phoebée. Frédéric arrives to lead Lilia into the church (II, 7-8 bis), and Urielle advances in Lilia's gown and veil to take his arm. She grows more restless as she approaches the chapel, however, and Frédéric has to drag her to the altar. Suddenly, the sky darkens, and thunder rolls. The priest recoils in horror; the candles are extinguished; lightning strikes the bride. Frédéric recognizes Urielle, and everybody begins to search for Lilia. Simplicé recounts how she was kidnapped, and Urielle disappears into the earth (II, 9-10).

The start of the third act presents Belzébuth giving Urielle three days to deliver Frédéric to hell (III, 1), and the sixth tableau depicts a slave market and bazaar in Ispahan, where Bracaccio is selling Lilia and Phoebée. A European ship drops anchor in the harbor, and Frédéric comes ashore to examine the slaves. The count recognizes the two captives of the pirate leader, and he outbids all prospective purchasers (III, 2-5) until the grand vizier comes on the scene and takes an interest in Lilia. Frédéric is pushed to the limit of his resources and flies into a panic until he sees Urielle. He asks her for more money, but she ignores him, and Lilia is carried away by the vizier. Finally, Urielle tells Frédéric that he can have Lilia if she can have his soul. He is desperate and signs the pact that she offers him (III, 6-7). She tells him to delay the vizier, and she transforms herself into an exotic dancer. She conjures up her own music and attracts the vizier's attention. He wishes to buy her, but she tells him that only Frédéric can sell her. He asks the price, and Frédéric replies, "Lilia!" The bargain is struck. Frédéric takes Lilia to his ship; Urielle disappears as soon as she is placed in the vizier's caravan; the frustrated vizier buys Phoebée (III, 8-10).

The seventh tableau returns to the tower of the first act. It is the eve of the wedding of Lilia and the count, who reassures his bride that nothing can interfere with their plans (III, 1 bis). She retires. Midnight strikes, and Urielle appears with pact in hand. She orders him to follow her, but he asks her why she insists upon this outlandish contract being honored. She replies that her love for him will not permit her to allow him to marry another woman. She is leading him to hell when Lilia rushes from her room to save him. Frédéric explains to his bride that he must comply with the terms of the contract, but he adds that he intends to kill himself first. He attempts suicide, but Urielle stops him because she realizes suddenly that Lilia is the angel of good over whom the angel of evil can never triumph. She throws the contract into the fireplace, and Belzébuth takes her life from her. The count places Lilia's cross on Urielle's heart and flees with Lilia (III, 1-2 bis).

The last tableau represents hell, where Belzébuth is waiting for Urielle. A devil enters with her body, and the demons are about to throw themselves upon her when an angel appears and restores her to life. She protects herself with Lilia's cross until the vault of hell is split. Lilia and Frédéric are seen going to church for their wedding, and Urielle is lifted up into heaven (III, 1-2 ter).

The male roles in this intricate and lengthy ballet were filled by Mazilier (Frédéric), Hippolyte Barrez* (Hortensius), Montjoie (Belzébuth), Elie (Semplice, Le Grand Vizir), Simon (Bracaccio), Adice and Desplaces fils (pirates), L. Petit (priest), and Quériau (bailiff). The female parts were created by Mmes Lise Noblet* (Phoebée), Pauline Leroux (Urielle), N. Fitzjames (Lilia), Mazilier (Thérésine), Adèle Dumilâtre* (Janetta), and Roland (demon).

BIBLIOGRAPHY: CB 169-77; Chouquet 402; CODB 157; Escudier, "Le Diable amoureux, première représentation," FM 3 (27 September 1840), 349-51; Lajarte II, 163-64; RBP 192-96.

Le Diable a quatre, known in English as The Devil to Pay, was a pantomimic ballet in two acts with a scenario by Adolphe Leuven and Joseph Mazilier,* a score by Adolphe Adam,* and choreography by Mazilier. Pierre Cicéri* did the sets for the first act and the first tableau of the second act; Despléchin, Séchen, and Diéterle provided them for the last two tableaux. P. Lormier furnished its costumes. These sets and costumes were destroyed along with those of Tannhäuser* in the fire that destroyed the property warehouse in the rue Richer on 19 July 1891. The ballet had its world premiere at the Opéra in Paris on 11 August 1845. It was produced at the Princess Theatre in London this same year, but its New York premiere at the Broadway Theatre did not take place until 1848.

The ballet is set in Poland on the estate of Count Polinski, and the curtain rises to reveal the entrance to his castle, a pavillion, and a basket-weaver's humble abode. The master of the hunt announces that the count is about to give a hunting party, and it is also revealed that the porter of the castle and the countess' maid Yelva have decided to marry (I, 1-2). The count gives the happy couple a purse as a dowry, and he grants them permission to have a ball at the castle entrance to celebrate their engagement (I, 3). The count's guests arrive, and the hunt is about to begin when Yelva tells her master that the hunting horn has awakened the countess. She adds that her mistress is furious because she has been disturbed, and she refuses to allow the hunt to continue (I, 4-5). The countess scolds her husband, but he insists that the hunt will not be canceled. He informs his guests that they are invited to dine with the countess on the morrow to accept her apologies. The countess withdraws in a rage, and the hunt begins (I, 6).

The basket-weaver's wife, Mazourka, agrees to stop dancing long enough to weave a basket when her husband assures her that he will stop drinking and do his work (I, 7). Mazourki steals a drink from his bottle, however, but she is not deceived and throws down her work. Yet she is not angry. On the contrary, she laughs and throws down her work. They laugh and agree to allow each other to follow their own inclinations (I, 7). Yvan, Yelva, an old blind man, and other friends of the groom gather for the ball. Yvan invites Mazourki and Mazourka ot join the celebration, and they are delighted to have another opportunity to drink and to dance. The ball begins with the blind fiddler furnishing the music, and the count returns with his guests. The festivities are loud and joyous (I, 9) until the irate countess rushes in and breaks the old man's fiddle. The guests leave hurriedly; Yvan and Yelva follow their master into the castle (I, 10).

Mazourka emerges cautiously from her cabin to pay the fiddler for his services, and the grateful musician volunteers to read her palm. He predicts that she will be wealthy, powerful, and the mistress of the castle before her eyes. As for the countess, she will become Mazourki's wife. Mazourka protests that she loves her husband, but she agrees to accept her fate when she learns that she will be a countess only for a day. The old man transforms himself into a sorcerer and dresses Mazourka in rich raiment and jewels, while the sleeping countess is clothed in Mazourka's modest garb. Demons carry Mazourka into the castle (I, 11-12).

The setting changes to the interior of Mazourki's cabin filled with empty bottles and unfinished baskets. It is morning, and Mazourki awakens his "wife" who asks how she has come to sleep in such a lowly place, and he thinks that she has gone mad (II, 1). Yvan and Yelva invite him and his "wife" to their wedding, and they believe that "Mazourka" has lost her senses when she asks them to protect her against Mazourki. Outraged, the countess attacks Yelva, but the latter escapes with her fiance, and Mazourki chastises his "wife" for being insolent to Yelva and slapping him. He forgives her, however, and he allows her to dance before ordering her to help him dress for the coming wedding. The humiliated countess is furious to find herself performing this menial task. She manages to escape (II, 1-3).

The second tableau of the second act moves inside the castle, where Yelva approaches the "countess" filled with fear. Her "mistress" does not scold her. On the contrary, she displays every sign of benevolence toward her (II, 4-5). The count is delighted with the sudden display of cordiality and friendliness by his "wife"; he announces that he is going to give a ball (II, 6-7). A dancing-master tries to give lessons to the "countess," but the sorcerer intervenes, and Mazourka is able to forget her village dances long enough to execute a perfect waltz (II, 8).

The last tableau depicts the count and his "wife" receiving their guests. The "countess" is a most gracious hostess and obviously an expert dancer. At the height of the evening, however, the genuine countess forces her way into the ballroom. She is overwhelmed to see her counterpart so obviously at ease in her home and with her husband. Mazourki then forces his way into the castle to find his "wife" and to beat her until she learns to behave. Mazourka feels compassion for the countess and persuades the sorcerer to return the situation to its proper disposition, a piece of wizardry he performs to the delight of the count, Mazourki, their wives, and their guests (II, 9-12).

The ballet was extremely popular during the nineteenth century, and it was executed on 105 dates at the Opéra between 1845-1863. Mazilier created it especially for Carlotta Grisi,* who was followed in this part of Mazourka by Adèle Plunkett,* Caterina Beretta,* and Marie Petipa. The other female roles were filled by Mlle Maria (the countess), and by Mlle Célestine Emarot,* who made her debut at the Opéra as Yelva. The male parts were danced for the first time by MM. Petipa* (the count), Mazilier (Mazourki), Desplaces (Yvan), Elie (the fiddler), and Jean Coralli* (the dancing-master).

BIBLIOGRAPHY: CB 177-83; Camille Bellaigue, Notes brèves (Paris: C. Delagrave, 1914), 167-86; Chouquet 406-7; CODB 157; Marie Escudier, "Théâtre Impérial de l'Opéra: Reprise . . . du Diable à quatre," FM 26 (22 June 1862), 195; Ivor Guest, The Ballet of the Second Empire (Middletown, Conn.: Wesleyan University Press, 1974), 39, 45, 90, 92-93, 112, 124, 166, 176-77; Jacques François Fromental Elie Halévy, Souvenirs et portraits (Paris: Michel Lévy frères, 1861), 225, 254; Lajarte II, 179; RBP 246-50; SS 116.

Le Diable boiteux, inspired by Lesage's picaresque novel, was a pantomime ballet in three acts with a score by Casimir Gide,* a libretto by Edmond Burat de Gurgy* and Adolphe Nourrit,* and choreography by Jean Coralli.* The sets for its ten tableaux were created by Jules Diéterle, Feuchères, Séchan (tabl. 1, 2, 3, 9) and Cambon and Philastre (tabl. 4, 5, 6, 7, 10). It had its world premiere at the Royal Academy of Music on 1 June 1836, and it remained in the repertory until 26 February 1840, when it enjoyed its 65th presentation. The striking intrigue of the ballet, the colorful sets, and Franziska Elssler's* execution of her famous cachuca in the second act helped to make Le Diable boiteux a profitable work at the box office.

The first tableau presents the foyer of the Royal Theate in Madrid, where a masked ball is in progress, and where Cléophas is making Don Gilès and captain Bellaspada jealous of his success with their partners from whom he has received a ring, a rose, and a ribbon (I, 1). Cléophas then disguises himself in feminine attire, and he flirts with the two men. He unmasks and reveals that he has made fools of them; he seizes Don Gilès' sword and dares the captain to engage him. Don Gilès tries to have him arrested, but he escapes (I, 2-3).

The second tableau shifts to an alchemist's shop cluttered with supplies and apparatus. Cléophas lowers himself into the laboratory through a skylight and hears groans escaping from a jar. He breaks it, and the devil Asmodée appears and swears fealty to Cléophas for setting him free. The student tests him by asking to see the three women with whom he became involved at the ball. Asmodée opens the wall of the room to reveal the working girl Paquita, the dancer Florinde, and the young widow Dorothéa. Asmodée instills in each woman the desire to consult the alchemist, whose costume Cléophas dons (I, 4-5). Paquita arrives first to ask the alchemist whether or not she is loved by a young man who flirted with her at the ball. Cléophas is not interested in her, and he returns her ring while dismissing her (I, 6). Dona Dorothéa enters accompanied by her brother and Don Gilès; she wishes to know why she cannot sleep, and Cléophas tells her to take a husband, preferably the young man she met at the ball. She agrees with his precription and loses interest in Don Gilès when Cléophas proves the efficacy of his prescription by returning her ribbon (I, 7-8). The dancer Florinde is the last to present herself, and Cléophas reveals his identity to her. She asks for the rose he took from her at the ball, but Don Gilès returns at this moment, and Florinde pretends to faint. He sends Don Gilès for smelling salts and steals the key to Florinde's dressing room before she leaves (I, 9-10). Cléophas thanks Asmodée for his help (I, 11).

The third tableau represents a Moorish palace conjured up by Asmodée to help the poor student impress Dona Dorothéa and Florinde. Cléophas is surrounded by servants and all sorts of luxurious comfort and sumptuous food that he enjoys while watching a ballet of sylphids (I, 12).

The second act opens in the dance foyer at the Madrid opera house, where Asmodée replaces the balletmaster, and Cléophas watches the ballerinas practice (II, 1). Paquita seeks admission into the corps de ballet, but she fails in her audition. A group of Spanish noblemen enters to pay their ocmpliments to the ballerinas, and Florinde asks the balletmaster to give her a more impressive role. Asmodée refuses her request, and the call-bell summons the dancers to the stage. Paquita is left alone after Florinde and Cléophas ignore her. Asmodée is touched by her predicament and promises to help her (II, 2-5).

The fifth tableau depicts backstage at the opera house with Asmodée and Cléophas in the prompter's box. The ballet begins, but Florinde draws no applause. She pretends to sprain her foot; Don Gilès and Cléophas rush to her aid. Asmodée is satisfied with the revenge he has taken for poor Paquita (II, 6-10).

The sixth tableau reveals Florinde's hairdresser and maid waiting for her in her dressing room. Don Gilès tells them of Florinde's injury; the devil and the student hide in the balcony. Florinde is brought to her dressing room. Cléophas confronts her, and she is delighted to see him, when he reveals his identity, but he has to hide immediately on account of the approaching balletmaster and the return of Don Gilès with a doctor (II, 11-16). The physician assures Florinde and Don Gilès that the dancer has suffered no injury, and joyous Don Gilès declares his love for her. Cléophas loses patience and storms into the room from the balcony to berate the nobleman; he is stupefied. Florinde protests that the intruder is unknown to her; she suggests that he is her maid's lover. The devil enters laughing and pulls Cléophas from the room (II, 17).

The seventh tableau changes to Florinde's home, where the dancer's guests are toasting her. She performs the cachuca. The ceiling of the room rises to disclose Asmodée and Cléophas spying on the party; Cléophas is disillusioned to know how infrequently Florinde thinks of him. He throws back to her the rose that she gave him at the ball and disappears (II, 18-19).

The eighth tableau depicts a square in Madrid, where Dona Dorothéa lives. Cléophas is about to serenade her, and Asmodée plans to disillusion him once more. The widow appears on her balcony, and Don Gilès comes upon the scene. Florinde's maid enters to deliver a letter to Cléophas, but he tears it up angrily without reading it (III, 1-3). Don Gilès returns with the widow's brother Bellaspada, but Don Gilès' hopes for revenge are dashed when the captain approves Cléophas' request to marry his sister (III, 4). Asmodée plans to prove to the student that Dona Dorothéa and Bellaspada are interested only in his money, and, when Cléophas ignores Paquita to accept an invitation to dine with the widow, he abandons him in disgust (III, 5). Florinde disguised as an army officer challenges Cléophas to a duel, but Paquita intervenes and stops the quarrel. Florinde and Paquita join forces to punish Cléophas for his indifference, and they find an ally in Asmodée (III, 6-7).

The action moves into Dorothéa's home for the ninth tableau that revolves about an evening of gambling. Cléophas is greeted by the hostess, and Paquita enters next with the "officer" who delivers such a flowery and exaggerated declaration of love to Dorothéa that she is flattered into giving "him" Cléophas' ribbon (III, 8-9). Paquita and Cléophas surprise Dorothéa's new admirer proposing to her, and they beat a hasty retreat. The embarrassed hostess tries to welcome her guests calmly, and disgusted Cléophas walks into the gaming room, where the devil arranges for him to lose all his money. The widow and Bellaspada lose all interest in him (III, 10-11).

The last tableau offers a festival outside Madrid, where gypsies are drinking, dancing, and indulging in feats of strength. Cléophas sees and follows Dorothéa walking with Gilès, and he also comes upon Paquita and the "officer." He reminds the latter of their duel, but "he" requests a postponement, because "he" is too occupied with Paquita to fight. Asmodée enters and begins to tell fortunes. He assures Paquita that she will obtain what she seeks; he pulls the false mustache from Florinde's face to reveal her true identity; he announces that Cléophas is a penniless student. No one except Paquita is interested in Cléophas now. Asmodée gives him his bell to ring if he has need of him in the future. The student forgets his cares because he knows that his future is secure (III, 12-16).

The principal male parts were created by Hippolyte Barrez* (Asmodée), Joseph Mazilier* (Cléophas), Montjoie (Bellaspada), and Elie (Don Gilès) with Coralli as the hairdresser, L. Petit as the physician, and Châtillon as the balletmaster. The female roles were filled by Fanny Elssler (Florinde), Amélie Legallois* (Dona Dorothéa), Leroux (Paquita), and Roland (the maid).

BIBLIOGRAPHY: ACD 150; CB 114-22; Chouquet 399; CODB 157; GBAL 726-27; Lajarte II, 154; Moniteur universel 180 (28 June 1836), 1526; RBP 148-52; SS 100; Wks III, 8514.

Diaghilev, Serge Pavlovich (b. 31 March 1872, Nijni-Novgorod; d. 19 August 1929, Venice), impresario, was the first and only son of his mother who died in childbirth on the military reservation where his father was stationed. He remained motherless until his father married Hélène Panaeva in St. Petersburg, where Diaghilev began to study law in 1890. The young law student soon became a member of a circle of painters, musicians, and writers over whom Alexander Benois* and Léon Bakst* presided. Diaghilev grew more and more interested in the theatre at this time, and he helped to found the review Mir Iskousstva (The World of Art). Fate now intervened, when Prince Serge Volkonsky was named director of the Imperial Russian Theatres. Diaghilev had left law school in 1896, and, in 1899, he was free to accept Prince Volkonsky's invitation to become editor of Annual of the Imperial Theatres.

Unfortunately, Diaghilev soon found his good luck cut short by politics, and he was forbidden to hold any governmental post in Russia. He was undiscouraged and still interested in painting, however, and he decided to organize an exposition of French Impressionists. His plan was to schedule parallel soirées featuring music by Claude Debussy,* Paul Dukas,* and Maurice Ravel. Excited by the success of these undertakings, he made up his mind to go to Paris.

Diaghilev arrived in the French capital in 1906 to repeat his exposition, and, in 1907, he turned the tables in France by presenting five concerts of Russian music at the Opéra. The resounding success he achieved with these concerts in 1907 induced him to produce Boris Godounov* at the same theatre in 1908 with Feodor Chaliapin* in the title-role. The performances were in Russian and scheduled for 19, 21, 24, 31 May and 2, 4 June, and the inn scene was omitted. Receipts on the first night soared to 27,450 francs, 95 centimes, and the six performances earned a total of 156,298 francs, 90 centimes. Diaghilev was jubilant and fell to formulating new plans to bring Russia to France. He returned to Paris the following year, 1909, with a group of dancers whom he called the Ballets russes,* and whom he booked into the Théâtre du Châtelet on the banks of the Seine. The ballets they presented were:

Ballet	Composer	Premiere
Le Pavilion d'Armide	Tcherepnine	19 May 1909
Danses polovtsiennes	Alexander Borodin*	19 May 1909
Cléopâtre	Glinka	2 June 1909

The rest is history. Diaghilev was to travel throughout Europe and America with his troupe, whose dancing would revolutionize the art of ballet. His dancers included stars of the calibre of Pavlova, Rubinstein, Karsavina, Smirnova, Nijinska, Volinine, Spessivtseva. His costumes and stage sets were designed by such artists as Benois, Bakst, Larionov, Picasso. His scores were by Rimsky-Korsakov, Stravinsky, Reynaldo Hahn, Ravel, Debussy, Glazounov, Tchaikovky, Satie. Michel Fokine, Boris Ramanov, Léonide Masside provided his choreography.

BIBLIOGRAPHY: ACPM 296; "Around the World with the Russian Ballet: A previously Unpublished Interview with Serge Diaghilev," D Mag 53, no. 9 (September 1979), 48-55; "Au théâtre musical de Paris: Hommage à Diaghilev," SDLD 141 (10 February 1982), 15-16; BCS 256; A. Benois, Reminiscences of the Russian Ballet (London: Putnam, 1941); BOP 147-48, 150-69, 171-72; Paul Bourcier, "Diaghilev ou les occasions perdues," SDLD 143 (10 April 1982), 41; R. Buckle, Nijinsky (London: Weidenfeld, 1971); Marie-Françoise Christout, "Il y a cinquante ans mourut Serge de Diaghilev," SDLD 43 (10 April 1979), 37-41; CODB 157-58; Gilberte Cournand, "Diaghilev et les peintres," SDLD 10 (January 1972), 22-23; G. Détaille and G. Mulys, Les Ballets Russes de Monte-Carlo (Paris: Arc-en-ciel, 1954); Michel Fokine, Memoirs (London: Constable, 1961); GBAL 815; Arthur Gold and R. Fizdale, Misia (New York: Alfred A. Knopf, 1980); S. Grigoriev, The Diaghilev Ballet (London: Constable, 1953); A. Haskell, Ballets russes (London: Weidenfeld, 1968); HAZ 120-26; idem, Diaghilev (London: Gollancz, 1934); Serge Jouhet, "Magnifique et scandaleux Diaghilev," L'Avant-scène, Ballet-Danse, 3 (August-October, 1980), 12-15; Boris Kochno, Diaghilev and the Ballets russes, trans. Adrienne Foulke (New York and Evanston: Harper & Row, 1970); Bernard Laine, "Diaghilev Reconstruct-

ed," D Mag 53, no. 7 (July 1979), 80-83; "L'Hommage de l'Opéra à Serge de Diaghilev," L'Opéra de Paris IX (195?), 34-38; Tamara Karsavina, Theatre Street (London: Dance Books Ltd., 1981), 177, 249-60, 270-71, 277-78, 284-85, 292-94, 301, 310, 335-52; P. Lieven, The Birth of the Ballets russes (London: G. Allen, 1936); Serge Lifar, Serge de Diaghilev, sa vie, son oeuvre, sa légende (Monaco: Editions du Rocher, 1954); idem, Chez Diaghilev (Paris: Albin Michel, 1949); Nesta MacDonald, "Diaghilev Retrieved," D Mag 53, no. 3 (March 1979), 79-85; Olga Maynard, "In defense of Diaghilev," D Mag 54, no. 4 (April 1980), 79-85; idem, "Diaghilev and the Ballets russes," D Mag 45, no. 3 (March 1971), 50-56; John Percival, The World of Diaghilev (New York: Harmony Books, 1979); Francoise Reiss, Nijinsky ou la grâce: Sa vie, son ésthétique et sa psychologie (Plan de la Tour, Var: Editions d'aujourd'hui, 1980), 48-151; André Schaikevitch, "Diaghilev," SDLD 40 (January 1972), 16-20; TDB 565.

Diavolina was a pantomime ballet in a single act with music by César Pugni* a scenario and choreography by Arthur Saint-Léon,* and a set by Cambon and Thierry. It had its world premiere at the Imperial Theatre of the Opéra on 6 July 1863, and the striking dance productions in it by Saint-Léon assured its success despite its uninspired score overly dependent upon Italian songs found in the collection Passatempi musicali. The ballet was mounted on 21 dates between its premiere on 6 July 1863 and 30 December 1863. It was revived on 11 May 1864 for a second run of 24 presentations ending on 3 December 1866. Thus, it was billed at the Opéra on 45 occasions.

The ballet is set in the region around Caserte in about 1805, and it opens with two musicians called zambogari making as much noise as possible with their instruments on Diavolina's wedding day so that the bride's family will pay them to take their discordant music elsewhere. Marianna, Diavolina's cousin, cannot manage to get rid of them, but her assiduous suitor, Sergeant Bridoux, frightens them away. Don Peppino arrives with his buon augurio of bread and linen for the bride, and he is welcomed by a group of excited and chattering girls calling upon the bride and eager to see her wedding dress. Diavolina is worried because she has not seen her groom, the wealthy fisherman Gennariello, but she puts on her crown of orange blossoms for her guests. The girls help Marianna to finish sewing the bridal gown, and Diavolina waits nervously for her absent groom to bring her the customary bouquet. He appears finally; he is out of breath from running, but Diavolina decides to repay him for his tardiness by pretending to be asleep. When he attempts to kiss her, she awakens and describes to him how she has just dreamt of dancing with a young and handsome nobleman who squeezed her hand and kissed her tenderly. Gennariello is furious and reminds her that they have promised to be faithful to each other even in their dreams. She pretends not to understand him, and she tells him that she does not remember being in love with anyone. Gennariello is speechless and decides to return to work. He picks up his nets; Diavolina steps on a trailing end of the net that she picks up and throws over his head. They laugh and forgive each other.

The fishermen of Naples enter to congratulate the couple, and they are invited to dance the scarpetta with the girls of Caserte. Sergeant Bridoux falls to flirting with Marianna again, but he is interrupted by the arrival of Don Fortunata and his wife Francesca, wealthy bourgeois of the district. They are followed by the oaf Don Chichillo, who has rounded up all the amateur musicians of the countryside to entertain the wedding guests. He steps on everybody's toes and bumps into all the wives. Finally, the guests sit down to the table. Don Chichillo spills the wine, crawls under the table, and then stands up with it on his back after announcing to everybody that the bride and groom are holding hands.

The notary arrives to draw up the marriage contract, and Gennariello demands that his wife refrain from visiting the neighbors because he is jealous. Diavolina objects. He reserves the right to smoke, to drink, and to gamble, but the bride insists that her husband will have to stay at home. They both assert that they are to manage the house and the family. They fall into a heated debate, and Diavolina insists that she can spend money on expensive dresses and jewels if he can buy wine. She ends the discussion by running off to her room. Gennariello is licking his wounds, when he looks up to see Diavolina on the arm of Sergeant Bridoux, who is whispering sweet words of love into his companion's ear. He thinks that his sweetheart is trying to trick him, and he pretends to faint. Chichillo thinks he is dead and calls for help. Diavolina rushes up to him, and he opens his eyes and asks her to pray for him. Diavolina is overwhelmed and begs him to forgive her. She holds him in her arms, and he is so overjoyed that he stands up and kisses her. The lovers are reconciled; the dancing begins; the marriage contract is signed without disputes.

The male roles were filled by Dauty (Don Peppino), Lenfant (Fortunato), Louis Mérante* (Gennariello), Jean Coralli* (Don Chichillo), Francisque Berthier* (Sergeant Bridoux), Lefebvre* (the notary), and Cornet and Estienne (the zambogari). The female parts were created by Mlle Mourawieff (Diavolina), Mlle Louise Marquet* (Marianna), Mlle Aline (Francesca).

BIBLIOGRAPHY: AEM X, 1748; CB 343-47; Louis de Charolais, "Théâtre de l'Opéra: Diavolina," FM 27 (12 July 1863), 214; Chouquet 420; EDS VIII, 587-89; Ivor Guest, The Ballet of the Second Empire (Middletown, Conn.: Wesleyan University Press, 1974), 186-88, 259; Lajarte II, 234-35; Moniteur universel 193 (12 July 1863), 953.

Diaz de la Pena, Eugène-Emile (b. 27 February 1837, Paris; d. 12 September 1901, Coleville), composer, entered the Conservatoire in 1852 to study under Napoleon-Henri Reber* and Jacques Halévy.* He made his debut as a composer with Le Roi Candaule at the Théâtre-Lyrique on 9 June 1865. When the Opéra arranged a contest in 1867 for the best work entitled La Coupe du roi de Thulé,* his entry won and was performed at the theatre on 10 January 1873 after the new director, Halanzier, agreed to honor the original agreement made by the previous director, Perrin, before the war. The work that had pleased the judges was a failure with the public, but Diaz attempted one more opera, Benvenuto Cellini* of 1890. Ironically, the unfortunate fate of La Coupe du roi de Thulé was completed and sealed by the destruction of its manuscript in the fire of 1873 at the Opéra then located in the rue Le Peletier.*

BIBLIOGRAPHY: Chouquet 425; DBF XI, 253-54; Fétis Suppl. I, 268-69; Lajarte II, 245-46; LXIX VI, 745.

Dietsch, Pierre-Louis-Philippe (b. 17 March 1808, Dijon; d. 20 February 1865, Paris), composer, started his musical career as a choirboy in Dijon and took his first instruction from his choir-master, Travisini. His success induced his parents to send him to Paris in 1822 to study religious music under Alexandre Choron.* The Conservatoire accepted him as a student in 1830, and he enrolled in the classes of Antoine Reicha* and Chenié, but he left school prematurely to sing at the Théâtre-Italien and then at the Opéra. Religious music did not cease to interest him because he had been appointed chapelmaster at Saint-Eustache church in 1830, but this dual employment at the Opéra and Saint-Eustache did not prevent him from entering the competitions at the Institut or from completing his Le Vaisseau fantôme,* inspired by the same subject as Richard Wagner's* The Flying Dutchman. His work was given at the Opéra without success in 1842, and he never made a second attempt to do another composition for this theatre, but he did create a large corpus of religious music including 17 masses and a great number of hymns and motets. He became chapel-master at the Madeleine eventually and succeeded Girard as head of the orchestra at the Opéra in January 1860. Ironically, the author of Le Vaisseau fantôme directed the orchestra at the Opéra on the night that Wagner's Tannhäuser* had to endure its infamous Paris premiere on 13 May 1861.

BIBLIOGRAPHY: DBF XI, 320-21; Fétis III, 20; GE XIV, 516; Lajarte II, 171, 193.

Le Dieu et la Bayadère was an opera-ballet in two acts with music by Daniel Auber* and a libretto by Eugène Scribe.* Marie Taglioni* was the choreo-grapher. It had its premiere at the Opéra on 13 October 1830 and was mounted on 135 dates between 1830 and 1847 except 1839. It was revived on 22 January 1866. Thus, Auber's work was billed 145 times at the Opéra during its three runs at this theatre in 1830-38, 1840-47, and 1866.

The curtain rises in the opera-ballet with the people of Cachemire seeking protection and justice from Judge Olifour, who reveals his unsympathetic disposition by condemning the supplicants. He is moved to greater anger by the approach of the dancing Bayadères led by Zoloé, because he has forbidden them to enter the city

(I, 1-2). Zoloé defies Olifour with her dancing and derides him for his age; he orders her arrest, and an unknown stranger intervenes to protect her. Olifour decrees his execution for interfering but countermands his order at the last moment (I, 3). The stranger gives Zoloé a bracelet to show his gratitude for her pleas in his behalf (I, 4). Olifour's slaves bring precious gems to Zoloé as a sign of their master's love for her, but she gives these jewels to Ninka and the stranger. The bayadères join in a ballet to express their joy, and the grand vizier's head guardsman announces that a price has been put on the stranger's head (I, 6). Zoloé hides him at the risk of her own life (I, 7). Olifour enters to pay his court to Zoloé, but he is summoned by the grand vizier and sends Zoloé to his house in his sedan chair (I, 8).

Zoloé leaves the stranger in her hut to find food and drink, and he discloses in a monologue that he is a Brahma and cannot return to heaven until he finds "a heart taken with immortal love" for him (II, 1-2). Zoloé, Ninka, and Fatmé return with provisions. The stranger tests Zoloé by making her jealous to see whether or not she loves him (II, 3). She admits her love and begs to be his slave. The Brahma is about to reveal his identity because of Zoloé's completely dedicated love, when Olifour tries to enter her hovel. She pleads to die in the stranger's place (II, 4). The grand vizier's guards break down the door and threaten her life. She defies them, and the Brahma rescues her by taking her into paradise as his bride (II, 5).

The overture was but one of the enthusiastically received portions of Auber's music for Le Dieu et la Bayadère. Passages in both the first and second acts were applauded, especially "Quel vin! quel repas delectable" (I, 2), an aria by Olifour, and "Aux bords heureux du Gange" (II, 3), a nocturne sung by Ninka and the Brahma.

The Bayadère was danced by Mlle Marie Taglioni* assisted by Mlle Lise Noblet* as Fatmé. Adolphe Nourrit* sang "the unknown man" with Nicolas-Prosper Levasseur as Olifour.

One of the interesting features of this opera-ballet is its combining the functions of the singers and dancers in the manner of the eighteenth century by having the ballet coordinate its

movements with the emotions and concepts developed by the singers.
BIBLIOGRAPHY: CB 73-78; Chouquet 395; DDO I, 331; Lajarte II, 136-37; Charles Malherbe, Auber (Paris: Renouard, n.d.) 40; Moniteur universel 294 (21 October 1830), 1332; RBP 102-5; SS 96.

Dieulafoy, Joseph-Marie-Armand-Michel (b. 1762, Toulouse; d. 13 December 1823, Toulouse), librettist, held a post in the government of his native city before he left France to work on his family's plantations in Santo Domingo. He was fortunate enough to escape the massacres in the Indies, however, and he was able to return to France by way of Philadelphia. He started his theatrical career after reaching home by writing a series of comedies, vaudevilles, and comic operas that attest to his diligence, if not to his genius, as a librettist. He provided the words for Le Baiser et la quittance with Picard and Charles de Longchamps; this comic opera with a score by François Boïeldieu and Nicolò Isouard had its première at the Opéra-Comique on 18 June 1803 (see eighteenth-century volume for Boïeldieu and Isouard). He wrote the librettos for two of Gasparo Spontini's compositions billed at the same theatre: La Petite Maison (1804) and Milton (1804) (see eighteenth-century volume for Spontini). His collaborator on the poems for his two titles at the Opéra was Briffaut: Les Dieux Rivaux* was mounted in 1816 to celebrate the duke de Berry's marriage; Olympie* of 1819 was based upon Voltaire's tragedy of the same title. Dieulafoy also composed verse that was honored by the Académie des Jeux Floraux before his death.
BIBLIOGRAPHY: DBF XI, 332-33; GE XIV, 523-24; Lajarte II, 88, 94; LXIX VI, 825; Wks III, 250.

Les Dieux rivaux ou les fêtes de Cythère was an opera-ballet in a single act written for the program celebrating the marriage of the duke de Berry. It had its world premiere at the Royal Academy of Music on 21 June 1816. Its music was composed by Gasparo Spontini, Louis-Lue Persuis, Henri Berton, Rodolphe and Kreutzer (see eighteenth-century volume for Spontini, Persuis, Berton, and Kreutzer). Dieulafoy and Charles Brifaut wrote its libretto, and Gardel created its choreography.

The curtain rises on the work to disclose an untended and withered garden on Cythère, which the Cyclops have invaded. The invaders have occupied l'Amour's palace, where they are forging weapons for Mars. The conquered son of Vénus complains of the noise they are making and the havoc they are spreading throughout the region (sc. 1). La Renommée announces that Louis has restored peace to the earth; Mercure reveals that the gods are about to descend from Olympus to consult with the two most powerful rulers on earth. The angered Cyclops attack the forces of peace (sc. 2), but l'Amour and l'Hymen declare that they are determined to protect the throne upon which peace and happiness depend. They dispatch their followers to repel the Cyclops. The attack is successful, and the flowers begin to bloom again amidst the suddenly verdant grass and foliage. The royal insignia of France and Naples shine everywhere.

L'Amour, l'Hymen, and the chorus celebrate these welcome changes in song and herald the approach of the gods (sc. 3). Jupiter tells l'Amour to immortalize the day (sc. 4), and he assures France and Parthénope that their days of sorrow have passed. He asks the gods for a volunteer to guarantee the glory of France, and Minerve begs him to assign this task to her. The other gods make the same request of Jupiter. Apollon asserts that he can foster the arts in France; l'Amour argues that he can assure the entire country of happiness. Thémis warns that only she can make justice prevail on the banks of the Seine; Mars and Neptune boast that only they can support the glorious tradition of Turenne, Villars, Tourville, and Condé. Bacchus reminds his listeners that it was he who made Henri IV a great drinker, a memorable lover, and an undefeated warrior. Mars and l'Amour claim a share of credit for these latter two accomplishments of Henri IV. Jupiter calls a halt to the contention by ordering all the gods to share in maintaining the glory of France and the happiness of her inhabitants. Mars offers his sword, and Thémis contributes her scales, while Minerve relinquishes her shield and lance for the cause. Neptune presents his trident, Apollon surrenders his laurels, and l'Amour agrees to dedicate his blindfold to the future of the fortunate nation. L'Hymen sacrifices her torch. The king enters to accept these gifts, and the gods are overwhelmed by his resemblance to Louis XIV. A group of l'Amour's followers carries away the gods' offerings, and the new king and queen follow them, while the gods return to Olympus. A chorus announces the return of peace and the triumph of the arts under the new monarch.

It was never intended that Les Dieux rivaux should become a part of the repertory, and it was dropped after five presentations. Mme Rose Branchu and Mlle Gérard Grassari* filled the roles of France and Parthénope, respectively, and the parts of the goddesses were created by Mlle Paulin (Minerve, Thémis, and La Renommée) (see eighteenth-century volume for Branchu). The other actresses cast in the work included Mlle Allent (l'Amour) and Mme Cazot (l'Hymen). The male roles were assigned to Dérivis* (Jupiter), Lavigne (Mars), Bonnel (Neptune), Adolphe Nourrit* (Apollon), Eloi (Mercure), Laïs (Bacchus). The ballet was headed by Mlles Clotilde (Diane), Bigottini (Vénus), Delisle (Terpsicore) with the Graces danced by Mlles Aimée, Marinette, and Bertin.

BIBLIOGRAPHY: Charles Bouvet, Spontini (Paris: Editions Rieder, 1930), 93; Chouquet 387; DDO I, 331; EDS IX, 217-23; Albert Ghislanzoni, Gaspare Spontini: studio storico-critico (Rome: Edizioni dell'Ateneo, 1951), 112-13; Lajarte II, 88-89; Moniteur universel 175 (23 June 1816), 712.

Djelma was an opera in three acts with a score by Charles Lefebvre* and a libretto by Charles Lomon. It had its world premiere at the National Academy of Music on 25 May 1894 in a Lapissida production. Its sets were provided by Marcel Jambon* on this occasion, when Charles Bianchini provided its costumes. Joseph Hansen* established its choreography.

The opera opens in a room of Raïm's palace, where the first light of dawn is visible, and a choir is singing prayers to the Vishnou and Brahma. Kairam and Tchady are planning to leave Raïm and Nouraly in the desert to perish so that Kairam will be able to seize Raïm's power and wealth (I, 1-2). Djelma and Raïm enter to receive their guests' greetings and to announce a tiger hunt to protect the farmers of the region. All the courtiers volunteer to accompany Raïm (I, 3-4). Nouraly is promising Djelma that he and Kairam will protect Raïm when the seer Ourvaci warns Raïm that death awaits him on the hunt. Raïm refused to cancel the hunt despite the threatened danger and Djelma's protests. Djelma gives him a sachet and amulet before he leaves (I, 5-8).

Two years later, Djelma's slaves are urging her to stop waiting for her missing husband, but she continues to grieve. Nouraly proposes marriage to her, but she is shocked and refuses his offer. Ourvaci encourages her to discard her widow's raiment and to celebrate the imminent rites of abundance and happiness (II, 1-2). Kairam orders the palace prepared for the festival, and he reveals his plan to murder Nouraly so that he will have Djelma at his mercy (II, 3-4). Raïm staggers into the room. He is pale and dressed in tatters; he is still wondering why the bridle on his harness broke. He watches slaves scattering roses throughout the palace, and he overhears Kairam tell Tchady that Nouraly loves Djelma and plotted Raïm's death. When Kairam sees Raïm, the latter pretends to be a beggar, but Kairam orders him followed (II, 5-6). Djelma appears in festive costume, and the rites begin with the bayadères depicting the history of Lakmi in their dance (II, 7). Tchady reports to Kairam that the bedraggled intruder is Raïm, and Kairam seizes a rifle to shoot him while he is hiding in the foliage near the palace. Nouraly thinks that a tiger is lurking in the bushes, and he takes the weapon from Kairam. He takes aim and shoots at the moving branches. Nouraly calms the onlookers, but he knows that he has shot a man, and he sends Kairam and Tchady to investigate (II, 8).

It is dawn, and Kairam is still searching for the wounded intruder, but he cannot find him. He goes into the undergrowth, and Raïm emerges from the bushes with his knife in his hand. He vows to slay the other traitor, but he hides when Djelma and Nouraly approach (III, 1-2). Nouraly protests his lvoe to Djelma, but she rejects his most ardent declarations until she sees the amulet that Raïm has dropped. It is covered with blood, and Nouraly believes that he has murdered him. He is filled with grief and draws his knife to stab himself, but Raïm rushes from the bushes to save him. Djelma rejoices, and Raïm explains Kairam's treachery. He embraces Djelma, and Nouraly leaves for the desert to spend the remainder of his life praying for the reunited couple (III, 3).

It was beyond M. Lefebvre's ability to render this improbable libretto acceptable, but he tried, and he managed to create for it a few moving moments: Raïm's "Tu sais trop bein lire en mon âme" (a. 1), Djelma's "Jour fatal" (a. 2), Nouraly's hymn to Brahma (a. 3). The final ensemble also made a deep impression on spectators, but these passages were not enough to sustain the work, and it had to be withdrawn after its eighth performance on 29 December 1894, when a program of Djelma and Samson et Dalila* returned only 13,284 francs to the box office of the Opéra. The cast of Djelma on opening night was composed of Rose Caron* (Djelma), Meyrianne Héglon (Ourvaci), Albert Saléza* (Nouraly), Maurice Renaud* (Raïm), Auguste Dubulle* (Kairam), and Douaillier (Tschady). The ballet was led by Mlles Sandrini, Vangoethen, H. Régnier.

BIBLIOGRAPHY: AEM 8, 464-65; DDO I, 339-40; Arthur Pougin, "Première Représentation de Djelma à l'Opéra," Le Ménestrel 60 (27 May 1894), 163-64; Stoullig XX (1894), 26-31; SW 72; Thompson 988.

Docteur Magnus was an opera in only one act with music by Ernest Boulanger* and a libretto by Pierre-Etienne Cormon* and Michel Carré.* The libretto was poorly organized and failed to support whatever merit the score possessed. It had its premiere at the Opéra on 9 March 1864 and was dropped after its 11th performance on 11 July 1864.

The opera begins with Dr. Magnus reading the Bible to a group of listeners that includes his pupil Rosa and her fiance Fritz, and he manages to put everybody including himself to sleep (sc. 1). Gudule and Daniel find the group sleeping, and the latter greets his Cousin Rosa with a kiss. Rosa thinks Fritz has kissed her, and she slaps him. Fritz arouses the other sleepers with his screams. They greet Daniel after his long absence, and the doctor dismisses his audience to speak with his nephew (sc. 2). The doctor explains to Daniel that his example and lesson have banished drinking, flirting, inconstancy. In fact, no one sings or dances until the work in the fields is done. The doctor assures Daniel that the devil would be losing his time to come to the village (sc. 3).

Daniel resolves to return his friends to their former ways, and he decides to find out first whether the girls of the village have lost their coquettish ways (sc. 4). Rosa enters with a bouquet, and he admits to her that it was he who kissed her. She forgives him and makes a half-hearted attempt to escape, but he restrains her. He flatters her, and she is pleased. He gives her a mirror, and she is happy to adjust her coiffure and to appraise her appearance (sc. 5). Fritz appears, and she complains that he never charms her with his words, and she allows Daniel to kiss her again. Fritz is furious (sc. 6). The regional peddler stops to sell his trinkets to the girls of the village for the first time in many years, and the young men break into the doctor's cellar to sample the wine there. The boys and girls strike up a song celebrating pleasures long forgotten in the village (sc. 7). The doctor enters and demands to know why they are singing improper songs, and he insists upon knowing who has broken into his house. The young people leave in riotous haste, and the doctor looks with disbelief at the overturned tables and broken jugs (sc. 8). He accuses Daniel of being Satan himself and orders him to leave the village. The doctor sits down to read his bible and to nurse his righteous indignation, but Daniel keeps suggesting to him that he has not lost every memory of the joys of his youth. The doctor begins to recall the happier days of his earlier years; he and Daniel empty a glass and sing a duet in praise of wine (sc. 9). The girls return to ask the doctor's pardon for buying costume jewelry and ribbons, and he assures them that they have done no wrong. He forgives the young men for having broken into his cellar. The group celebrates, and Daniel rejoins them in a soldier's uniform. Rosa promises that she will wait for him until the end of the war, and he marches off with Fritz. The villagers arrange the chairs in their regular pattern, and they sit down in them to await Dr. Magnus' next Bible lesson (sc. 10-11).

The male roles were filled by Cazaux (Dr. Magnus), Victor Warot* (Daniel), Grisy (Fritz), and Portehaut (the peddler) with Mlle Levielly as Rosa and Mme Tarby as Gudule.

BIBLIOGRAPHY: *Chouquet 421; DDO I, 340; EDS III, 106-7; M. Escudier, "Théâtre Impérial de l'Opéra: Le Docteur Magnus," FM 28 (13 March 1864), 78-79; Lajarte II, 236; "Le Docteur Magnus," AM 4 (17 March 1864), 123; Wks III, 16532.*

Domenech, Consuelo (b. 5 October 1886, Montrichard; d. ?), vocalist, was a student of Mme Massart at the Conservatoire before she made her debut at the Opéra as Léonore in La Favorite* on 30 July 1890. After her debut, she sang no fewer than four major parts in the remaining five months of the year: Amnéris in Aïda,* Gerturde in Hamlet,* Uta in Siguard,* and Scozzone in Ascanio.* In 1891, she limited herself to doing Anne de Boleyn in Henry VIII* and Varédha in Le Mage*; she added only Ortrude of Lohengrin* to her repertory in 1892. Her last role at the Opéra was Fricka of La Walkyrie* in 1893. Her short career of four years at the Garnier Palace* made it possible for her to appear in only a single premiere, when she created the title-role of Thamara* on 28 December 1891.

BIBLIOGRAPHY: EFC 164; SW 27-30, 42, 89-90, 108-12, 134-36, 138, 202-4, 209, 224-26.

Dom Sébastien, roi de Portugal was an opera in five acts with a score by Domenico Gaetano Donizetti* and a libretto by Eugène Scribe.* It had its premiere on 13 November 1843 and enjoyed 30 performances before it was dropped on 2 April 1845. It might have remained in the repertory for a longer period of time if the burial scene in the third act had not cast a pall over the audience by recalling the recent death of the duke of Orléans on 13 July 1842.

The work opens with the Grand Inquisitor, Juan de Sylva, plotting to put Philippe II of Spain on the throne of Portugal during Dom Sébastien's coming voyage to Africa. The regent Dom Antonio, who is to replace the king, is unaware of this plot. A soldier-poet named Camoëns receives permission to travel with the king (I, 1-3). He calls attention to Zayda, who is about to be burned for returning to her Moslem faith after accepting baptism, and Sébastien commutes her sentence to exile in Africa. The Inquisitor swears vengeance for this usurpation of his authority. The king and his forces set sail; Dom Antonio and Juan de Sylva rejoice over his departure (I, 4).

Zayda returns to her father Ben Sélim. He asks his daughter why she refuses to wed Abayaldos and departs with his army to repulse the invading Christians (II, 1-4). The Arabs win a total victory but are deceived into believing that Dom Sébastien is dead. Zayda finds him unconscious but alive on the battlefield. Grateful, she revives him and declares her love to him (II, 5-7). Abayaldos and his men approach to slay all survivors, but Zayda saves Sébastien by agreeing to marry her African suitor. Liberated, Sébastien walks off into the distance (II, 8-9).

Abayaldos arrives in Lisbon to arrange a peace; he is accompanied by Zayda, whom he mistrusts (III, 1-2). Camoëns is back in Portugal, where a soldier warns him of the new king's hatred for veterans of the recent African campaign. Camoëns encounters Sébastien in the streets; the two friends rejoice and witness the sham funeral of Sébastien, a ruse planned by the usurper, Dom Antonio (III, 3-6). The three Inquisitors of the cortège describe the folly of the "dead" king, and Camoëns cannot restrain his indignation. Juan de Sylva orders his arrest, and Dom Sébastien countermands the directive while revealing his identity. Abayaldos swears that he buried Dom Sébastien in Africa; Dom Antonio and Juan de Sylva are quick to corroborate his assertion by insisting that the present claimant to the throne is and impostor. Abayaldos resolves to watch Zayda more carefully (III, 7).

Dom Sébastien stands before the tribunal of the Inquisition and argues that his regal status exempts him from answering questions. Zayda testifies that Dom Henrique died in battle and that Dom Sébastien was saved by her. She announces her love for Sébastien, moreover, and Abayaldos tears off his mask to denounce his wife as an adultress. The king and Zayda are condemned to death (IV, 1-3). Dom Luis guarantees to Juan de Sylva that the duke of Alba will be at the gates of Lisbon by nightfall to help him. Juan de Sylva offers to pardon Dom Sébastien and Zayda if she will convince him to sign a paper (V, 1-3). He explains to Zayda that he cannot affix his signature to the document because his enemies wish him to sign away his throne and rights to Philippe II. Ten o'clock strikes, the hour of Zayda's execution; Sébastien signs the paper to save her. suddenly, they hear Camoëns signing on the water (V, 1-4). The poet climbs to their cell and assures them that the people have risen to save their king. They try to escape from their prison on a rope ladder, but the soldiers cut it; Zayda,

Camoëns, and Sébastien fall to their death. The Spanish fleet appears on the horizon. Dom Antonio is left alone to rage at the prospect of seeing his plans thwarted; Juan de Sylva can exult at last with a total victory for Spain so close at hand (V, 5-6).

This romantic opera with its exotic sets and violent emotions boasted at least one effective musical passage in each act. Camoëns' Cavatine, "Soldats, j'ai cherché la victoire" (I, 3) stands out in the first act as does Dom Sébastien's cavatine in the second act: "Seul sur la terre" (II, 9). Camoëns and the unfortunate protagonist also dominated the third act with "O! ma patrie!" by Camoëns in scene three and the duet by the poet and the king in scene six: "C'est un soldat qui revient de la guerre." The barcarolle "Pêcheur de la rive" (V, 4) and the duet by Zayda and Sébastien in prison (V, 4) constitute the high points of the music in the closing scenes of the composition.

Mme Stoltz starred as Zayda and the men who sang included Dom Sébastien (G. Duprez), Camoëns (Barroilhet), Abayaldos (Massol), Juan de Sylva (Levasseur), Dom Antonio (Octave), Dom Henrique (F. Prévôt), Ben Sélim (Brémond).

BIBLIOGRAPHY: Guglielmo Barblan, L'opera di Donizetti nell'età romantica (Bergamo: Edizione del centenario, 1948), 214-22; Chouquet 405; DDO I, 342-43; Arnoldo Fraccaroli, Donizetti (Verona: Arnoldo Mondadori, 1945), 298-99, 309; Angelo Geddo, Donizetti; l'uomo, le musiche (Bergamo: Edizioni della Rotondo, 1956), 218-22; HUT 94-96; Lajarte II, 174; Richard Northcott, Donizetti: a Sketch of His Life and a Record of His Operas (privately printed, 1915), 10; Herbert Weinstock, Donizetti and the World of Opera in Italy, Paris, and Vienna in the First Half of the Nineteenth Century (New York: Pantheon Books, 1963), 206-10, 227-31, 365-66; Guido Zavadini, Donizetti: vita, musiche, epistolario (Bergamo: Instituto italiano d'arti grafiche, 1948), 648, 690-91, 703-6.

Don Carlos was the second work by Giuseppe Verdi* to have its world premiere in France. It was intended for Paris audiences and did not have to be translated from Italian. It was billed initially at the Opéra on 21 March 1867 with a libretto by Joseph Méry* and Camille du Locle.* Its choreography was created by Lucien Petipa,* and its sets were the work of Cambon and Thierry (a. 1, a. 3), Desplèchin and Lavastre (a. 2, a. 5) and Nolau, Rubé, and Chapéron (a. 4). The work was not overly popular because spectators found it too long or lacking in variety. It was based upon Schiller's drama, and Verdi was commissioned by the management of the Opéra to write it for the World's Fair in Paris, but it was never revived after its 43rd performance on 11 November 1867. It was given on 14 consecutive programs at the beginning of its history at the Opéra, and it returned more than 10,000 francs on six dates during this time, but these early hopes for success were soon shattered.

The lengthy opera starts in the forest of Fontainebleau during the winter with a party of hunters pursuing a stag. Elisabeth de Valois is concealed by the trees, and Carlos is rejoicing over being near his beloved Elisabeth. The latter appears with her page Thibault, but she fails to recognize the heir to the throne of Spain, and he pretends to be a member of the Spanish ambassador's staff. When the page leaves to procure transportation for Elisabeth, she takes advantage of the opportunity to question her Spanish companion about her fiance Carlos. He assures her that Carlos loves her, and he offers her a case containing his portrait. Thus, he reveals his true identity. She is touched by his declaration of love and admits her affection for him. They hear cannons announcing the establishment of peace between France and Spain (I, 1-4), and Thibault enters with the message that Henri II has given Elisabeth's hand in marriage to Philippe II of Spain. The lovers are crushed, and Elisabeth leaves for the court with the count de Lerme (I, 5-6).

Carlos is in the monastery of Saint-Just, where he is seeking solace near the tomb of Charles V, although a monk assures him that he will find peace only in death. The prince believes for a moment that the monk is Charles V returned to life, but he dismisses the idea immediately. Rodrigue comes to Carlos with the suggestion that he put himself at the head of the revolt about to occur in Flanders. He refuses to leave Spain, however, and he explains to his friend that he finds himself in love with his French stepmother. Rodrigue asserts that this love is reason enough for him to leave for

Flanders, and he agrees. His resolve is strengthened by the sight of the queen entering the convent on his father's arm (II, 3).

The second tableau of the second act presents Princess Eboli, Thibault, and the countess d'Aremberg on a grassy slope outside the monastery of Saint-Just, where they are awaiting Elisabeth. When the queen rejoins them, she is depressed and preoccupied. Rodrigue delivers a letter into her hands; he insists that she perform her duty as a mother by trying to cure her son of his morbid melancholy. Princess Eboli begins to think that Carlos' trouble may be caused by his unrequited love for her (II, 1-3 bis). Carlos informs Elisabeth that the Spanish climate does not agree with him; he announces his plans to leave for Flanders. Elisabeth remains impassive in the face of this declaration, but her defenses crumble when he reproaches her for her indifference. She reminds him of her duties as a wife and queen (II, 4). Philippe returns and ask Rodrigue why he has not seen him at court despite his long service to the Crown, and Rodrigue replies that he cannot support the royal policy toward Flanders. The king is angry at his answer, but he forgives his brashness and extends the freedom of the court to him amidst the approbation of the people (II, 5-6).

Preparations are in progress for a celebration in the queen's gardens at Valladolid, but Elisabeth is bored by the singing of the chorus and the prospect of dancing through the evening. She decides to retire and gives her mask and cloak to Princess Eboli, who decides to impersonate the queen because the king is passing the night in prayer before his coronation on the morrow. She decides to focus her attention on Carlos, to whom she sends a letter (III, 1-2). After the execution of Le Ballet de la Reine representing the queen as the only pearl worthy of the king of Spain, the third tableau of the act depicts Carlos reading a letter directing him to be at the palace fountain at midnight. Princess Eboli enters in the queen's garb, and he declares his love to her, and she unmasks in the belief that Carlos has recognized her. Carlos loses interest in her immediately, and she deduces that he loves the queen (III, 1-2 ter). Princess Eboli warns Rodrigue that she possesses the power of life and death over Carlos, and he is enraged by her threats. She dares him to kill her; she accuses Carlos of adultery (III, 3). Rodrigue asks Carlos for any important letters or papers that he may have (III, 4).

The fourth tableau of the third act represents the square before the cathedral of Valladolid filled with the people who come to honor their king. A chorus of monks leads in a procession of prisoners condemned to death by the Inquisition. The entire court enters to welcome Philippe II after his coronation. Carlos appears next at the head of a group of Flemish delegates in rags of mourning. Philippe dismisses the latter as rebels and heretics, and Carlos demands to rule Flanders if the king is not interested in its people. He draws his sword, and the king directs his men to disarm him, but Rodrigue takes his sword. The king orders the celebration to start, but the Flemings denounce the execution of the prisoners of the Inquisition, and a celestial voice invites the suffering souls on earth to find peace in God (III, 1-4).

The fourth act shifts to Philippe's study. He is aware that his wife does not love him, and he regrets that his subjects never seem to tire of conspiring against him. He obtains permission from the Grand Inquisitor to kill his son, but he refuses to deliver Rodrigue into the hands of the Inquisition (IV, 1-2). Elisabeth complains that a thief has stolen her jewel case, but she sees it on Philippe's desk. He opens it before her eyes to disclose Carlos' portrait. She explains that she has had the picture since her days in France, and that she treasures it like a mother. He accuses her of perjury and calls her an adultress. Princess Eboli enters to admit to Elisabeth that it was she who stole her jewel box because she loved Carlos. The queen allows her to choose between a convent and exile before dawn (IV, 3-5). The princess decides to save Carlos during the day left to her (IV, 6).

Carlos is in prison and overcome by despair. Rodrigue tells him that he has arranged for him to go free by forging papers that will prove that it was he, not Carlos, who stirred up the rebellion in Flanders. He urges Carlos to continue the struggle in the north, and he is killed by a bowman outside the cell. Philippe announces to Carlos that he is free to go, but the prince falls into a rage and berates his father as a murderer

(IV, 1-3 bis). The count de Lerne and Elisabeth announce that the people are in revolt to liberate Carlos, but Philippe orders the doors of the prison opened. He offers his life to the people, but the Grand Inquisitor frightens the populace into submissiveness. Elisabeth forgives Princess Eboli for her past misdeeds (IV, 4-5 bis).

Elisabeth is kneeling before the tomb of Charles V in the cloister of Saint-Just. When Carlos arrives, she reminds him that he must do his best in Flanders lest Rodrigue's death prove vain. He promises her to find victory or death, but the king enters with the Grand Inquisitor and hands him over to the Inquisition. A monk throws his cloak around Carlos and pulls him behind the gate to Charles V's tomb. The monk tells him that he will find peace only with God, and the chorus reveals him to be Charles V (V, 1-3).

The emphasis upon drama, intrigue, and incident in Don Carlos creates the impression that Verdi's genius or at least his manner had evolved from the Italian to the French style in the course of his contacts with the Paris stage and public over the previous decade. This view is misleading, however, because the French flavor of Don Carlos derives from its French libretto, not from any change in Verdi's techniques. The score, then, is not overly rich in ornate passages or in purely lyric moments, although it does contain certain dramatic peaks, for example, when Carlos supports the French deputies, "Sire, il est temps que je vive" (III, 3), or Philippe's solo beginning "Elle ne m'aime pas! non! son coeur est fermé!" (IV, 1).

The female parts were sung by Mme Marie Sass* (Elisabeth), Mme Gueymard-Lauters* (Princess Eboli), Mlle Dominique (the countess d'Aremberg). The male roles were filled by Jean-Baptiste Faure* (Rodrigue, marquis de Posa), Morère (Don Carlos), Louis Obin* (Philippe II), and David (the Grand Inquisitor). Mlle Levieilly was cast as Thibaut, the page of Elisabeth de Valois. Mlle Léontine Beaugrand* starred in Le Ballet de la Reine.

BIBLIOGRAPHY: Franco Abbiati, Giuseppe Verdi (Milano: Ricordi, 1959), III, 72-80, 87-88, 98-103, 108-15, 123-38, 149-74, 182-84; G. Bertrand, "Première Représentation de Don Carlos de Verdi à l'Opéra," Le Ménestrel 34 (17 March 1867), 121-23; Ferruccio Bonavia, Verdi (London: Dennis Dobson Ltd., 1947), 83-87; France-Yvonne Bril, Verdi

(Paris: Hachette, 1972), 65-70; Chouquet 422; DDO I, 344-45; Léon Escudier, "[La Première] de Don Carlos de Verdi," AM 7 (14 March 1867), 113-14, AM 7 (21 March 1867), 121-22; M. Escudier, "Première Représentation de Don Carlos," FM 31 (17 March 1867), 77-79; Carlo Gatti, Verdi, the Man and His Music (New York: G. P. Putnam's Sons, 1955), 196-212; idem, Verdi (Milano: Edizioni "Alpes," 1931) II, 119-62; Vincent Godefroy, The Dramatic Genius of Verdi (New York: St. Martin's Press, 1977), 135-71; Dena Humphreys, Verdi: Force of Destiny (New York: Henry Holt, 1948), 194-200; Dyneley Hussey, Verdi (London: J. M. Dent and Sons, 1973), 148-69; KCOB 617-29; Lajarte II, 241; LOA 171-72; George Martin, Verdi, His Music, Life and Times (New York: Dodd, Mead and Co., 1963), 414-27; MCDE 1074, 1089-90; MPPA 248-56; MSRL 242-44; OQE 409-15; PBSW 65-66, 215; Pierre Petit, Verdi, trans. Patrick Bowles (London: John Calder, 1962), 113-23; idem, "Don Carlos," Opera 21 (1962), 4-7; Andrew Porter, "Musical Events: the Shakespearen Truth," The New Yorker 26 February 1979, 96-99; idem, Porter, "Musical Events: Grand Opera," The New Yorker 23 January 1978, 86-95; Hippolyte Prévost, "Don Carlos et la critique," AM 7 (28 March 1867), 129-31 et seq.; Max de Schauensee, The Collector's Verdi and Puccini (Philadelphia: J. B. Lippincott, 1962), 70-73; SSBO 247-49; Francis Toye, Giuseppe Verdi; His Life and Works (New York: Alfred A. Knopf, 1946), 332-45; Joseph Wechsberg, Verdi (New York: G. P. Putnam's Sons, 1974), 126-30, 194-95; Franz Werfel and Paul Stefan, Verdi: the Man and His Letters, trans. Edward Downes (New York: L. B. Fischer, 1942, 247-48.

Don Giovanni by Wolfgang Amadeus Mozart is discussed in the twentieth-century volume after the entry, Don Juan. Also see Don Juan in the eighteenth-century volume.

Donizetti, Domenico Gaetano Maria (b. 29 November 1797, Bergamo; d. 8 April 1848, Bergamo), composer, was sent by his father to the newly opened music school in his native city, where it was planned to train boy vocalist to sing the parts formerly sung at masses and vespers by the now extinct castrati. Here, Gaetano studied singing under François Salari, piano under Antoine Gonzales, and composiiton under Simon Mayr, who became his lifelong friend as well as his musical mentor. His progress in Bergamo was so pronounced that the youth was sent next to the Liceo Filarmonico in Bologna to continue his work under Mattei. When he returned finally to Bergamo, he wrote three unpublished operas and Enrico di Borgogna (1818), which captured the fancy of the director of the San Luca Theatre in Venice. Since Donizetti was now serving as a soldier, and because his unit continued to be stationed at Venice, he gave his next three operas to the same theatre.

His reputation was now growing, and his subsequent 1821-30 titles were billed at theatres in Mantua, Roma, Naples, Palermo, and Genoa; more than two-thirds of these nearly 30 works were produced at the lyric theatres of Naples, because Barbaia had signed contracts with Donizetti for 1827-30 in his quest for a composer to replace Gioacchino Rossini.* These compositions had won over the hearts of all Italy, but it was Donizetti's next work that called the attention of all Europe to him, Anna Bolena mounted at Milan in 1830.

The composer had adhered almost constantly to the manner of Rossini until Anna Bolena, but he now found his own style, and the result at this point was a novel admixture of Rossini and an original manner resulting in a music filled with constant passion and sustained vehemence. This new work was considered his masterpiece even in the face of the uninhibited enthusiasm aroused by Lucrezia Borgia (1833), but it was his Lucia di Lammermoor* (1835) that became his most popular composition. Yet the world was not without its disappointments and shocks for Donizetti during the 1830s. He was refused the directorship of the Collegio di Musica at Naples, where he was already ranking professor at the time of the death of the previous director, Nicolas-Antoine Zingarelli, in 1837; his young bride Virginia, who was expecting the birth of their child fell victim to the cholera that was revishing Naples this same year (see eighteenth-century volume for Zingarelli). Finally, the censors of Naples provided the last straw by refusing to allow his Poliuto to be staged in their city. Donizetti packed his trunk and went to Paris.

The author of Lucia di Lammermoor stopped at Milan on his way to France because he wished to produce Gianni di Parigi (1839) at La Scala, but his first work in the French capital was La Fille du régiment given at the Opéra-Comique on 11 February 1840 with a libretto by Jules Saint-Georges* and Jean-François Bayard.* His Poliuto with a French poem by Eugène Scribe,* was now entitled Les Martyrs*; it was produced at the Opéra in 1840. Unfortunately, it was not much more successful at the Opéra than La Fille du régiment had been a few months previously at the Opéra-Comique. Donizetti's third work of 1840 was La Favorite* of 2 December, which met with a totally different reception. It would enjoy nearly 650 performances by 1896. A fourth work by Donizetti billed in Paris in the 1840s was his Lucrezia Borgia, although Victor Hugo* intervened to stop its presentation because his play had been the source of its libretto. It was taken to the Italian Opera of Paris, where it was offered to the public in Italian but under the title of La Rinegata.

Donizetti now left Paris on a trip that took him to Italy, Austria, and Germany. He enjoyed the fruits of success on his journey and was the recipient of fresh honors after the presentation of some newly written religious compositions in Germany. But he was back in Paris to produce Don Pasquale at the Théâtre-Italien on 3 January 1843 and Dom Sébastien, roi du Portugal* at the Opéra on 13 November 1843. His great success was yet to be billed at the Opéra, although it had already been performed at the Théâtre-Italien in 1837 and at the Théâtre-Lyrique in 1839. Lucie de Lammermoor* was given in its complete French version by Alphonse Royer* and Jean Vaëz* at the Le Peletier* opera house on 20 February 1846. Donizetti's only other composition to be heard at Paris was his Betly,* which was sung at the Opéra on 27 December 1853 in a French translation by Hippolyte Lucas.*

Donizetti was still in Paris, but his deteriorating health was a serious problem, and he was entertaining false hopes of being able to recover by moving to a sunnier clime. The French government refused to allow him to travel at first because it was feared that he could not survive a journey to Italy. He was transferred to a sanatorium in Ivry, but it was decided ultimately that he should be allowed to return home to Bergamo.

Like many artists, Donizetti had begun his career by imitating another master of his craft before finding his own style. Donizetti had started out under the influence of Rossini and had concluded by anticipating Giuseppe Verdi* in his ability to prepare his audiences for the sublime heights to which he takes them. Still, if he cannot be indicted for a lack of originality, it must be admitted with equal candor that he wrote too quickly in his haste to finish his scores, and his yielding to the temptation of hurrying detracted from the durable quality of his work that has not survived except for a relatively small number of his many composition. It is almost as though Donizetti succeeded despite himself, since it is difficult to know how a highly suspenseful and moving text like the last act of La Favorite could be the product of only a few hours of work. Also, it has been observed shrewdly that not all Donizetti's success came from his genius; he owed some of the applause he inspired to the artists who executed his work. For he was especially fortunate to be writing at a time when Duprez,* Grisi,* Lablache, Mario,* Pasta, Persiani, Rubini were in voice.

BIBLIOGRAPHY: *F. Alborghetti e M. Galli, Gaetano Donizetti e G. Simone Mayr (Bergamo: Goffuri e Gatti, 1875); William Ashbrook, Donizetti (London: Cassell, 1965); Guglielmo Barblan, L'opera di Donizetti nell'età romantica (Bergamo: La Banca mutua popolare di Bergamo, 1948); Bio. univ. XI, 207-15; EGC 111-14; Filippo Cicconetti, Vita di Gaetano Donizetti (Rome: Tipografia Tiberina, 1864); Arnaldo Fraccaroli, Donizetti (Milan: A. Mondadori, 1945); Giannandrea Gavazzeni, Gaetano Donizetti, vita e musiche (Milan: Fratelli Bocca, 1937); HUT 93-96; Lajarte II, 162, 164, 174, 180, 193, 215, 258-59; Charles Malherbe, Rapport sur l'exposition Donizetti à Bergame (Paris: Le Journal musical, 1897); MSRL 57-61; Giulano Donati-Pettèni, L'arte della musica in Bergamo (Bergamo: La Banca mutua popoiare di Bergamo, 1930; SSBO 153-56, 160-61, 164-65, 170-74, 177-79, 180-84, 186-90, 192, 194-200, 212-14, 236, 342; Herbert Weinstock, Donizetti and the World of Opera in Italy, Paris, and Vienna in the First Half of the Nineteenth Century (New York: Pantheon, 1963).*

Don Juan by Wolfgang Amadeus Mozart in the 1805 version by Chrétien Kalkbrenner is discussed in the eighteenth-century volume. For the original version by Mozart and Lorenzo Da Ponte, see the twentieth-century volume.

Don Juan was the title not only of Mozart's opera but also of the divertissement in this opera, when the latter section of the opera was given apart from its matrix work at the Opéra (see eighteenth-century volume for divertissement). The divertissement was provided with new choreography by Joseph Hansen,* when it was billed alone at the Garnier Palace* for the first time on 18 March 1899. The work did not prove to be very popular when it lacked the support of its parent composition, and it was mounted independently on only six occasions at the Opéra. The menuet was danced initially in these individual billings by Mlles Beauvais, Mante, and Soubrier with MM. Girodier, Javon, and Stilb, while Edouard Mangin conducted the orchestra.

Hansen's Don Juan is not to be confused with Mikhail Fokine's* ballet using the same title. This work used music by Christoph Willibald Gluck; its scenario was by Eric Allantini; it had its world premiere at the Alhambra Theatre in London on 25 June 1936 (see eighteenth-century volume for Gluck).
BIBLIOGRAPHY: BB 94-97; BOP 46; CODB 162-63; RLVB 162-65; SS 291; SW 269.

Don Pasquale by Domenico Donizetti* is discussed in the twentieth-century volume.

Don Quichotte was offered to the public as a heroic comedy in five acts with music by Jules Massenet* and a libretto by Henri Cain. Massenet's work had its world premiere at Monte Carlo on 19 February 1910 before being brought to Paris for its initial production in the French capital at the Théâtre Lyrique de la Gaîté on 29 December 1910 with Lucy Arbell* as Dulcinée opposite Vanni Marcoux* (Don Quichotte) and Lucien Fugère (Don Sanche). Only its fifth act was produced for its first billing at the Garnier Palace* on 10 December 1911, when Vanni Marcoux and André Gresse* filled the roles of the knight and his squire at a gala.

After Massenet's version of the Don Quixote story went on to enjoy 60 presentations at the Opéra-Comique between 1924 and 1950, it was brought back to the Opéra during the regime of M. Rolf Liebermann on 16 January 1974 (see twentieth-century volume for Liebermann). The work caused some unfavorable comment in this instance because it moved dangerously close to parody or caricature at certain moments, especially in its use of metal horses. Peter Ustinov was in charge of production, sets, and costumes, and Georges Prêtre provided the musical direction. The divertissements were created by Lélé de Triano (see eighteenth-century volume for divertissement). The sole female part of Dulcinée was sung by Viorica Cortez, and the male roles were filled by Nicolai Ghiaurov (Don Quichotte), Robert Dumé (Juan) (see twentieth-century volume for Cortez and Chiaurov). Peter Ustinov represented the mute head of the bandits; Pedro and Garcias were done in travesty by Renée Auphan and Anna Ringart. Willy Havrilo and Jean Deguara were cast as the two valets.

The opera begins in the public square of a Spanish town, where Dulcinée is being serenaded by a group of her admirers that includes Pedro, Garcias, Rodriquez, and Juan. The young men mock Don Quichotte and his squire, Don Sanche, when they enter astride their scrawny mounts and in rusting armor, but Don Quichotte ignores their jibes and instructs his servant to distribute alms to the cheering crowd. Twilight gathers, and Don Sanche takes leaves of his master to visit a nearby tavern while Don Quichotte begins to serenade his beloved Dulcinée. Juan interrupts him, and Don Quichotte challenges him to a duel, but Dulcinée prevents them from fighting. Fickle, she seems to favor Don Quichotte, but she smiles warmly upon Juan. The knight is troubled by her behavior, but she removes all doubt from his mind by promising him happiness beyond measure if he will recover the necklace stolen from her by the bandit chief, Ténébrun. She leaves on Juan's arm, but Don Quichotte is in raptures over the knowledge that it is he whom she really loves (a. 1).

It is dusk, and the earth is wet with mist. Don Quichotte is astride his mount and improvising love songs celebrating Dulcinée. Aggravated by his master's behavior, Don Sanche tries to convince Don Quichotte that Dulcinée is making a fool of him. He is delivering a tirade against women and their wiles when Don Quichotte notices a giant looming in the lifting mist. His squire assures him that the shadowy shape is a windmill, not a monster, but the valiant knight leaps upon his charger and rides to the attack. Don Sanche falls to his knees and prays for the return of his master's sanity. The curtain closes momentarily, and, when it parts again, Don Quichotte is seen caught in the sail of a windmill, while Don Sanche is attempting to retrieve him (a. 2).

It is dusk and Don Quichotte believes that he has tracked the bandits to their lair in the mountains, but Don Sanche has misgivings about only two men facing a band of 40 outlaws. When the brigands appear, there are 200 men in their force. Don Quichotte orders quaking Don Sanche to hide, and he alone approaches the foe while shouting his battle cry, "Dulcinée!" The bandit chief cannot believe that a single man would dare to oppose him with such calm and confidence, and he demands to know his identity. Chivalrous Don Quichotte replies that he is a knight errant, defender of the oppressed, champion of the wronged, friend of grieving widows and unloved orphans. Indeed, he is the Knight Supreme in search of his fair lady's necklace, the very necklace that the chief has stolen. Ténébrun is so impressed by Don Quichotte's dedication and courage that he returns the necklace, and his men ask for the knight's blessing. Don Quichotte calls to Don Sanche to witness the miracle that he has wrought in the name of chivalry (a. 3).

A gala is in progress at Dulcinée's home, where the hostess is expressing her lack of interest in her suitor's persistent proposals because she is awaiting new expressions of a nobler love from less stereotyped lovers. She asserts her independence to her company, seizes a guitar, and executes a solo dance for her applauding guests. Don Sanche announces Don Quichotte's arrival, and the knight tells his squire that he is about to wed Dulcinée. He is planning to take her to a lavish castle that Don Sanche is welcome to share with his master and his new mistress. Dulcinée greets her champion, who produces her necklace and claims her as his bride. She laughs at him again only to find herself touched by his sincere and noble love for her. She asks him to remain with her, and her guests mock and revile him. Indignant, Don Sanche refuses to allow his master to be humiliated, and he denounces the cruel stupidity of Juan and his companions (a. 4).

It is night, and the sky is filled with stars. Don Quichotte is resting against a tree, and Don Sanche is trying to make him more comfortable because he is dying. Don Quichotte expresses his gratitude to his servant; he bequeaths to him his Isle of Dreams and asks for his prayers. Don Quichotte looks toward Mars shining in the heavens and declares that he is leaving to rejoin Dulcinée. He dies in the arms of Don Sanche, who cannot restrain his tears (a. 5).

In his memoirs, Massenet was pleased to recall that his Don Quichotte enjoyed 80 consecutive performances at the Théâtre Lyrique de la Gaîté. The work was performed in the United States at the French Opera House in New Orleans as early as 1912 and at the Metropolitan Opera House of New York in 1914.

BIBLIOGRAPHY: *Charles Bouvet, Massenet (Paris: Henri Laurens, 1929), 111-12; René Brancour, Massenet (Paris: Félix Alcan, 1922), 118-19; José Bruyr, Massenet, musicien de la belle éopque (Lyon: eise, 1964), 109-12; René Dumesnil, La Musique contemporaine en France (Paris: Armand Colin, 1930) I, 66-70; Gabriel Fauré, Opinions musicales (Paris: Rieder, 1930), 81-82; Henry T. Finck, Massenet and His Operas (New York: John Lane Co., 1910), 220-25; James Harding, Massenet (London: J. M. Dent & Sons, 1970), 178-84; Demar Irvine, Massenet: A Chronicle of His Life and Times (Seattle: Demar Irvine, 1974), 324-32; KCOB 875-76; H. Ludwig, "Weiterhin unerloest: Peter Ustinov inszenierte Massenets Don Quichotte in Paris," Opern Welt 4 (April 1974), 44; Jules Massenet, My Recollections, trans. H. Villiers Barnett (Westport, Conn.: Greenwood Press, 1970), 172-77; Modern Drama and Opera: Reading Lists on the Works of Various Authors, ed. Frederick W. Faxon (Boston: The Boston Book Co., 1915), 187; OMEL 181-82; PBSW 215; Georges Servières, La Musique française moderne (Paris: Havard, 1897), 117-220; SSBO 350; SW 76; Thompson 465; WOC 63-64.*

Dorus-Gras, Julie Aimée Josephe (b. 7 September 1805, Valenciennes; d. 6 February 1896, Paris), vocalist, was the daughter of an ex-soldier who was the leader of the orchestra at the theatre in her native city. She received her first musical instruction from him, and her public appearances as a child impressed the citizenry of Valenciennes so favorably that she received a municipal scholarship enabling her to pursue her studies in Paris. Admitted to the Conservatoire in 1821, she was placed in the singing class directed by Blangini and Henri. Later, Bordogni and Paer helped her to improve her vocal style.

After Mlle Dorus had left the Conservatoire, she courted public interest by embarking upon a concert tour that took her to Brussels, where she scored a striking success in a concert given at the Théâtre-Royal. Count de Liederkerke became interested in her immediately and offered her a contract calling for operatic performances. The young artiste had never considered the possibility of appearing in dramatic works, but she accepted the invitation, because it was agreed that Cassel would coach her for six months to prepare her for this sort of work. She made her debut on schedule at the Théâtre de la Monnaie. It was now 1826, however, and Daniel Auber's* La Muette de Portici* was about to precipitate a revolution in Belgium for a few years later on account of its advocacy of independence and its glorification of freedom. Yet trouble was brewing in Belgium already, and the nascent star was alarmed at the unrest evident around her. She thought it prudent to return to France lest she be caught in the threatening storm.

Repatriated, Mlle Dorus accepted an invitation to appear at the Opéra, where she made her debut as the countess in Le Comte Ory* on 9 November 1830. Her performance was successful, and her attractive appearance along with her ability to execute complicated fiorature and to deliver high notes with ease encouraged the management to give her the opportunity to interpret Thérésine in Auber's Le Philtre.* because Mme Laure Cinthie-Damoreau* was unable to perform on account of illness. She then created the part of Alice at the premiere of Giacomo Meyerbeer's* Robert Le Diable* on 21 November 1831 and appeared as Mathilde in Guillaume Tell* during its 1832 revival. When Dr. Véron had become director of the Opéra in 1831, his first major project had been the production of Robert le Diable, and he had spared no expense in mounting this production which relied so heavily upon spectacle. It was Mlle Dorus' sensational performance in this work that had solidified her position with management and secured her reputation beyond all question. Meyerbeer himself compared her to an angel. Louis Hérold* begged to borrow her voice for the presentation of his Le Pré aux clercs at the Opéra-Comique, where she scored another triumph as Isabelle in this popular work during the last days of December 1832.

The star returned to do Oscar in Gustave III* at the Opéra on 27 February 1833, and she was so well received in the fifth act featuring the lavish ball that the spectators forgot that they had slept through the first four acts of Eugène Scribe's* complicated intrigue. She sang Elvire at the premiere of the French version of Don Juan* at the Opéra on 10 March 1834, and she created Eudoxie of La Juive* on 23 February 1835. Although the success of La Juive was uncertain at first, there was no question about the singer's next role as Marguerite de Valois in the initial staging of Les Huguenots* at the Opéra on 29 February 1836 with a cast led by Adolphe Nourrit* (Raoul) and Mlle Cornélie Falcon* as Valentine.

Mlle Dorus toured northern France and Belgium with a company of artistes during the summer of 1836, but she returned to the Opéra to appear in a revival of Guillaume Tell* with the new tenor sensation Gilbert Duprez.* She did Ginevra of Guido et Ginevra* by Jacques Halévy,* which had its premiere on 5 March 1838, and she sang Teresa for the first production of Hector Berlioz'* Benvenuto Cellini* at the Opéra on 3 September 1838. Her final creations for the Opéra were Ritta in La Xacarilla* on 1839, Pauline of Domenico Gaetano Donizetti's* Les Martyrs* of 1840, Isabelle in Chalres VI* in 1843, and Baptista of La Lazzerone* of 1844.

Mme Dorus-Gras had replaced Mme Cinthie-Damoreau as the leading soprano at the Opéra in 1835, and now, in 1845, she was growing tired of backstage intrigues and yielded to Mlles Rosine Stolz* and Maria Nau.* Her farewell program was composed of Robert le Diable and Les Rossignol,* but this occasion did not prove to be her final appearance before the public. She toured the principal cities of France in 1845-46, and, in 1847-49, she performed in Paris and London. She was still doing an occasional concert in the French capital as late as 1851.

Mlle Dorus had acquired the name Gras in 1833, when she had become the wife of the violinist Gras. Her husband was one of the leading instrumentalists in the Opéra orchestra.
BIBLIOGRAPHY: Chouquet 395-402, 404-5; DBF XI, 621-24; EFC 141-42; Escudier frères, Etudes biographiques sur les chanteurs contemporains (Paris: Just Tessier, 1840), 183-201; EZF 183; Fétis IV, 84-85; ICM 466; Lajarte 134-41, 147-50, 152-53, 156-58, 161-63, 172, 175, 178; PBSW 178; SW 64, 73, 106, 115, 129, 184.

Le Drapier was an opera in three acts with a score by Jacques Halévy* and a libretto by Eugène Scribe.* It did not prove to be a very popular work, and its first run lasted for only five performances between its premiere on 6 January and 20 January 1840. It was given once again on 10 February of the same year for a total of six billings.

The curtain rises to disclose the draper Bazu planning to marry his daughter Jeanne to Gautier despite the general concern about the course of the continuing civil war. Jeanne is unhappy over her father's choice of a husband for her. An unknown customer enters Bazu's shop to speak with him, and he orders Jeanne to close up the store. Urbain informs her that he has heard the news of her wedding and is going off to join the forces of the duke de Guise. He begs her to leave with him, but she refuses; he hears Gautier, Bazu, and the unidentified customer declare their loyalty to Henri de Valois and agree to allow Châtillon into Chartres. Friar Benoist knocks at Bazu's door (I, 1-5). He is accompanied by a crowd of citizens searching for a spy who has managed to enter the city. They seize Urbain, who protests that he has fled to Bazu's house to find security. He insists that he is not part of the conspiracy that includes Jeanne's father, and he is dragged away by the crowd (I, 6).

Friar Benoist accuses Bazu of being derelict in his duty as a municipal official, and he informs him that Urbain has been condemned to death. Bazu has been charged with the task of extracting the names of the enemy from him. Urbain promises Bazu to keep his lips sealed if he may wed Jeanne before his exeuction. Urbain backs up his demands with a threat to divulge Bazu's request for noble rank in return for helping the cause of Henri de Valois. Bazu agrees (II, 1-4). Jeanne and Urbain are about to be married when the latter's best man (II, 5-6) reminds Bazu that Urbain may still betray them (III, 1). Benoist enters to hear whether or not Urbain has disclosed the names of any guilty parties and to observe the large crowd gathered in the street to serenade the newlyweds. The unknown conspirator returns once more with a letter from Henri de Valois saying that a royalist army is in the nearby forest ready to attack at the sound of the cathedral bells (II, 2-5). Unaware that Urbain must be executed, Jeanne assures him of her enduring love. The clocks of the village strike noon, and Urbain tells her that he must die (III, 6-7). Gautier and Bazu enter to lead him to his death, and Gautier whispers to Bazu that he was so eager for Urbain to die that he ordered a carillon to accompany the regular striking of the hours. Benoist and Jeanne escort the condemned man to the block. Suddenly, the royalist forces overrun the city in response to the carillon. They rescue Urbain with the announcement of a general anmesty in the name of Henri III. The lovers rejoice (III, 8-10).

The rather complicated plot is redeemed in spots by the clever use of dramatic irony made possible by the disguises employed, but these clever turns in the intrigue, the romantic story and devices like the tolling bells, or the fine cast assembled for its production could not sustain Le Drapier for more than three weeks. The artists appearing in it included Mlle Maria Nau* as the heroine with the male parts filled by Giovanni Mario* (Urbain), Massol (Gautier), Nicolas Levasseur* (Bazu), and Adolphe Alizard* (Friar Benoist).

The most stirring portion of the music was the duet by Mlle Nau and Mario in the final act.

BIBLIOGRAPHY: Chouquet 402; DDO I, 367; Lajarte II, 162.

Dubois, François Clément Théodore (b. 24 August 1837, Rosnay; d. 11 June 1924, Paris), composer, studied at the Conservatoire in Paris, where he won the Prix de Rome in 1861. He produced his first work for the theatre in 1873, and he succeeded Camille Saint-Saëns* as organist at the Madeleine in 1877. He served as director of the

Conservatoire between 1896 and 1905, and he became an officer in the Legion of Honor in 1896.

Dubois wrote four operas for the theatre, and the first of them entitled La Guzla de l'emir was staged at the Athénée on 30 April 1873. Le Pain bis (1879) and Xavière (1895) were billed at the Opéra-Comique. His grand opera called Aben-Hamet was produced for the first time at the Théâtre du Châtelet on 16 December 1884. The only composition that Dubois had billed at the Garnier Palace* was La Farandole* of 14 December 1883, a ballet for which Louis Mérante* did the choreography.
BIBLIOGRAPHY: AEM III, 838-41; BBD 439; EDS IV, 1048-49; ELM I, 672; Grove II, 789-90; Hugues Imbert, Nouveaux profils de musiciens (Paris: Fischbacher, 1892), 45-112.

Dubulle, Auguste-Jean (b. 10 June 1858, Védrines-Saint-Loup, Cantal; d. ?), vocalist, won the prize for opera at the Conservatoire in 1879, when he was a student of Bussine and Louis Obin.* He made his debut as the Inquisitor of L'Africaine* on 14 November 1879 and sang the role of the king in Hamlet before the end of the year. He made such an immediate impression with his powerful bass voice that he was cast in a number of roles in quick succession over the next 17 years in addition to creating the following parts in the works indicated:

Role	Opera	Premiere
Mondor	Tabarin	12 January 1885
Aurilly	La Dame de Monsoreau	30 January 1888
Noircarmes	Patrie!	16 December 1886
High Priest	Thamara	28 December 1891
Giscon	Salammbô	16 May 1892
The King	Stratonice	9 December 1892
The King	Déidamie	15 September 1893
Kayran	Djelma	25 May 1894

Dubulle added five roles to his Garnier Palace* repertory in 1880: the king in Aïda,*

Balthazar in La Favorite,* Marcel in Les Huguenots,* Brogni in La Juive,* and Walther in Guillaume Tell.* his Wagnerian parts included Hounding in La Walkyrie* (1893) and Reinmar in Tannhäuser* (1895). Also, he did Dante and Guido in Françoise de Rimini* in 1882 and 1884, respectively, and Zacharie in Le Prophète* and Pedro in L'Africaine* during 1883. He filled the roles of Sparafucile in Rigoletto* (1889) and Frère Laurent of Roméo et Juliette* (1889) after being cast as Méphisto in Faust* (1884). He appeared at the Théâtre de la Monnaie in Brussels during 1886-87, but he was still at the Opéra in 1896 to do Hellé.*
BIBLIOGRAPHY: SW 68, 70, 72, 89, 99-100, 170-71, 177-78, 181-82, 193-94, 205, 209.

Duc, Valentin (b. 24 January 1858, Beziers; d. ?), vocalist, won first prizes in singing and opera at the Paris Conservatoire, where he was a student of Bussine and Louis Obin.* He made his debut at the Opéra as Arnold in Guillaume Tell* on 31 August 1885, and he remained at the Garnier Palace* until 1892. He was never really a favorite of Parisian audiences because he treveled widely and spent seasons in Lisbon, Madrid, Brussels, and La Haye as well as at the theatres of Marseilles, Bordeaux, and Anvers. He created only one part at the Opéra, Karloo in Patrie!* on 16 December 1886. His other roles at the Garnier included Eléazar in La Juive* (1885), Raoul in Les Huguenots* (1886) and Rodrigue in Le Cid* (1886) besides Jean in Le Prophète* (1889), Rhadamès in Aïda* (1890), Vasco in L'Africaine* (1890), and the protagonist of Sigurd* (1890).
BIBLIOGRAPHY: SW 25-30, 105-6, 115-18, 129-30, 170, 177-78, 202-3.

Dufranne, Eva, (b. 1856, Belgium; d. 1905, Paris), soprano, whose family name was spelled Dufrane at times, studied voice at the Conservatoire in Brussels, where she distinguished herself as a student. She left her native land to make her debut at the Opéra in Paris as Rachel in La Juive* on 16 August 1880. She was endowed with a robust constitution and a beautiful soprano voice that won her assignments in the longer and more arduous roles of the repertory. She remained at the Garnier Palace* for nearly a score of years, and her performances won her the support of the public until she withdrew from the Opéra to continue her career in the provincial theatres of France and in foreign countries.

At the Opéra, Mlle Dufranne appeared in the following roles during the years indicated:

Role	**Opera (Year)**
Valentine	Les Huguenots (1881)
Xaïma	Le Tribut de Zamora (1881)
Alice	Robert le Diable (1881)
Elvire	Don Juan (1881)
Agathe	Le Freischütz (1883)
Sélika	L'Africaine (1883)
Sapho	Sapho (1884)
Hermose	Le Tribut de Zamora (1885)
Anna	Don Juan (1887)
Dolorès	Patrie! (1887)
Aïda	Aïda (1887)
Catherine	Henry VIII (1888)
Elsa	Lohengrin (1892)
Ortrude	Lohengrin (1892)
Brunnhilde	Walkyrie (1893)
Fricka	Walkyrie (1894)
Hilda	Sigurd (1894)
Dara	La Montagne noire (1895)
Léonore	La Favorite (1896)
La Reine	Hamlet (1896)

Uta	Sigurd (1897)
Liba	La Cloche du Rhin (1898)

The soprano created only a single part during all her years at the Garnier Palace,* Francisquine in Tabarin* on 12 January 1885.
BIBLIOGRAPHY: EFC 156; "Necrologie . . . Eva Dufrane," Le Ménestrel 71 (1905) 200; PBSW 156; SW 25-29, 63, 73-75, 89-90, 100-102, 108-12, 115-17, 134-35, 151, 170-71, 184-85, 198-99, 202-3, 213-14, 225-26.

Dugazon, Gustave (b. 1782, Paris; d. 1826, Paris) studied harmony under Henri-Montan Berton at the Conservatoire, but he was obliged to interrupt his studies on several occasions, although he was able finally to return to study composition under François-Joseph Gossec (see eighteenth-century volume for Berton and Gossec). After winning second prize at the Institut in 1806, he gave piano lessons to support himself, and he started to publish the large corpus of airs, nocturnes, preludes, and tocattas he was to produce for the piano alone or in concert with other instruments. His first work for the theatre was Noémi, a ballet billed at the Porte Saint-Martin. He went on to do three unsuccessful compositions for the Feydeau Theatre between 1812 and 1818.

Yet despite these poor showings at these two less prestigious theatres, Dugazon had no hesitancy about submitting Les Fiancés de Caserte* to the Opéra. This ballet in a single act was accepted and executed in 1817, but it failed miserably. The pantomime ballet Alfred Le Grand* fared better in 1822, probably on account of its martial music, but it was Aline, reine de Golconde* of 1823, which earned the greatest applause for Dugazon. This ballet in two acts was his last contribution to the Opéra after a career in the theatre that must be described as mediocre despite the billing of his three titles at the Royal Academy of Music.
BIBLIOGRAPHY: DBF XI, 1488; Fétis III, 74; Lajarte II, 90, 102, 106, 115; LXIX VI, 1357.

Dukas, Paul (b. 1 October 1862, Paris; d. 17 May 1935, Paris) is discussed in the twentieth-century volume.

Du Locle, Camille (b. 16 July 1832, Orange; d. 9 October 1903, Capri), librettist and administrator, made his presence known on the musical scene in Paris by writing a series of three librettos for the lyric stage in the French capital. His first contribution to the Opéra itself was the poem he supplied for Jules-Laurent Duprato's* La Fiancée de Corinthe* that had its world premiere at the Imperial Academy of Music on 21 October 1867. Ultimately he was named adjunct director of the Opéra in 1870 after serving as secretary on the administrative staff of this theatre for several years.

In 1874, Du Locle became co-director of the Opéra-Comique with Count Adolphe Ribbing, DIT de Leuven. The latter had been director of the theatre since 1862, and the Comique had already entered a period of mediocrity when Du Locle assumed office there a dozen years later. This unsatisfactory situation did not improve very much under the new regime of Du Locle and de Leuven, however, although the closing of the Théâtre Lyrique had left the Comique with full rights to Mozart's Les Noces de Figaro (1872) and to Charles Gounod's* Roméo et Juliette* (1873) and Mireille (1874) (see eighteenth-century volume for Les Noces de Figaro). De Leuven left his directorship on 20 January 1874, and Du Locle resigned his post on 5 March 1876.

Yet Du Locle's interest in the operatic stage did not diminish with the passage of time, and he collaborated on a number of operas for which he helped to write the original French libretto or to translate into French the text of its libretto written in a foreign language:

Opera	**Collaborator**	**Date**
Aïda	Chalres Nuitter	22 March 1880
Sigurd	Alfred Blau	12 June 1885
Salammbô	none	16 May 1892
Othello	Arrigo Boïto	10 October 1894
Hellé	Chalres Nuitter	24 April 1896
Don Carlos	G. Méry	8 March 1966

Du Locle also translated La Forza del destino and Simon Boccanegra into French from the original Italian by Francesco Maria Piave, but these two compositions scored by Giuseppe Verdi* were produced at the Opéra in Italian in 1975 and 1978, respectively. Finally, it might also be noted here that Du Locle recommended Verdi over Gounod and Richard Wagner* in 1869 as the composer most capable of writing an opera suited to a program inaugurating a new opera house in Cairo. Aïda was the ultimate result of this recommendation.

BIBLIOGRAPHY: L'Avant-scène 19 (January-February 1979), 126; EDS IV, 1099; Jean Gourret, Histoire de l'Opéra-Comique (Paris: Les Publications Universitaires, 1978), 136-43; Lajarte II, 241-42; SW 27, 111, 165, 193, 202-3.

Dumanoir, Philippe-François, DIT Pinel (b. 1806, La Guadaloupe; d. November 1865, Pau), librettist, came to Paris to complete his education in 1825, but he began to write almost immediately for the theatre. He worked with collaborators on most of the works that he had produced, and his compositions were created with such alacrity and regularity that he and his co-workers were able to complete more than a hundred titles by the time that he had finished his last play in 1864, Les Drames du cabaret. His talents seemed more suited for creating works that satisfied the tastes and demands of the Gymnast, Palais-Royal, and Vaudeville theatres, but he had two librettos accepted by the Opéra. He provided the words for Griseldis* of 1848 set by Adolphe Adam* and for La Mule de Pedro* of 1863 with a score by Victor Massé.*

BIBLIOGRAPHY: Chouquet 409, 420; DBF XII, 100; GE XV, 33; Lajarte II, 187, 234; LXIX VI, 1371; Wks III 251-52.

Dumas, Alexandre **père** (b. 24 July 1802, Villers-Cotterets; d. 6 December 1870, Dieppe), writer, was the son of a general in the army of the French republic and the grandson of a negress. His single purpose in life was to earn large sums of money with his pen, and he set about doing this by composing an awesome array of historical novels and an almost endless series of historical dramas and plays dealing with the modern scene. He came to the attention of the public at large with the staging of his Henri III et sa cour (1829) at the

Comédie-Française, where his gift for developing melodramatic incidents and picturesque backgrounds won for him the plaudits of all Paris. His other hits for the legitimate stage included Antony (1831) and La Tour de Nesle (1832).

Although he was a prolific writer and seemed inevitably destined to contribute to the contemporary manner of grand opera as it was employed in Les Huguenots* of 1836 or Le Juif errant* of 1852, Dumas' only offering at the Opéra was the libretto he provided for the cantata Le Choeur des Girondins (1848) based upon his play entitled Le Chevalier de Maison-rouge.

BIBLIOGRAPHY: Fernande Bassan and Sylvie Chevalley, Alexandre Dumas père et la Comédie-Française (Paris: Lettres modernes, 1972); A. Bell, Alexandre Dumas, a Biography and Study (London: Cassell, 1950); J. Charpentier, Alexandre Dumas (Paris: Tallandier, 1947); H. Clouard, Alexandre Dumas (Paris: A. Michel, 1955); DBF XII, 109-13; R. Gaillard, Alexandre Dumas (Paris: Calmann-Lévy, 1953); Herbert Gorman, The Incredible Marquis, Alexandre Dumas (New York: Farrar & Rinehart, 1929); A. Mourois, Les Trois Dumas (Paris: Hachette, 1957); Hippolyte Parigot, Alexandre Dumas père (Paris: Hachette, 1902); Thieme I, 635-42; L. Thoorens, La Vie passionnée d'Alexandre Dumas (Verviers: Gérard et Cie., 1957).

Dumilâtre, Adèle (b. 30 June 1821, Paris; d. 4 May 1909, Paris), dancer, finished her studies at the ballet school of the Opéra and made her debut as a page with her sister in the premiere of La Chatte métamorphosée en femme on 18 October 1837. She was cast with her sister Sophie Dumilâtre* again as a Creole in La Volière* on 5 May 1838 and appeared in La Tarentule* and Filippo Taglioni's La Sylphide* before being assigned to more important parts that established her as a star and made her an idol of the public (see eighteenth-century volume for Taglioni). Her creations included:

Role	Opera	Premiere
Janetta	Le Diable amoureux	23 September 1840
Myrtha	Giselle	28 June 1841

Agnès	La Jolie Fille de Gand	22 June 1842
Lady Henriette	Lady Henriette	1 February 1844
Eucharis	Eucharis	7 August 1844

Adèle Dumilâtre's career also included successful tours of England and Italy before she retired from the stage in 1848 to live with her sister Sophie after the death of her husband. They dwelt in Pau. Adèle then moved to a château in Touraine with her two sons and daughter.

The ballerina was quite beautiful but had the reputation of being at times an overly disciplined dancer. Yet she was light, slight, and graceful, and Théophile Gautier* dubbed her the queen of the Wilis.

BIBLIOGRAPHY: CB 126, 129, 150, 169, 213-14, 323-24; CODB 167; DDD 93; EDS IV, 1117-18; Ivor Guest, The Ballet of the Second Empire (Middletown, Conn.: Wesleyan University Press, 1974), 37-38, 64, 69, 130, 255, 260, 263; idem, The Romantic Ballet in England (Middletown, Conn.: Wesleyan University Press, 1972), 68, 97, 100-101, 129; Lajarte II, 160, 163-64, 168, 171, 174-76.

Dumilâtre, Sophie (b. 1818, Paris; d. Pau?), dancer, was the elder of the two ballerinas who were daughters of the actor Marie-Michel Dumilâtre of the Comédie-Française. She appeared at the Opéra for the first time as an American Indian in the premiere of Les Mohicans* on 5 July 1837. Her next billing was with her younger sister as a page in the initial performance of Jean Coralli's* La Chatte métamorphosée en femme on 18 October 1837. Subsequently she created parts in the following works having their premieres on the dates indicated:

Opera	Premiere
La Volière	5 May 1838
La Tarentule	24 June 1839
La Péri	17 July 1843
Lady Henriette	1 February 1844
Eucharis	7 August 1844

Otello (Rossini) 2 September 1844

She also participated in the farewell program for Filippo Taglioni on 10 June 1844, when she danced the pas de deux from the second act of Dieu et la Bayadère* (see eighteenth-century volume for Taglioni).

Sophie Dumilâtre retired from the Paris stage about 1848 and went to Pau. Her tendency to withdraw from the spotlight encouraged the public to forget her or even to ignore her during her lifetime, especially because her younger sister was so pretty and prominent. Yet some critics have asserted that her style of dancing and techniques were more effective than those of her more popular sister Adèle.

BIBLIOGRAPHY: CB 126; CODB 167; EDS IV, 1117; Ivor Guest, The Ballet of the Second Empire (Middletown, Conn.: Wesleyan University Press, 1974), 38; Lajarte II, 157, 160, 173-74, 176-77.

Dupeyron, Ferdinand-Hector (b. 10 November 1861, Bordeaux; d. ?), vocalist, studied under the direction of Boulanger and Louis Obin* at the Conservatoire in Paris and made his stage debut at Nîmes as Eléazer in La Juive* during 1887. He filled subsequent engagements at Toulouse, Athens, and Brussels before making his first appearance on the stage of the Opéra as Matho in Salammbô* on 5 May 1892.

He never shared in the excitement of a premiere at the Garnier Palace'* and he remained with the company for only four years. His repertory at the National Academy of Music included Robert in Robert le Diable,* Shahabarim in Salammbô, and Eléazar in La Juive in 1892; Raoul in Les Huguenots,* the title-parts of Samson et Dalila* and Lohengrin,* Siegmund of La Walkyrie* in 1893; the male leads of Faust,* Sigurd,* and Othello* in 1894. The tenor's last role at the Opéra was Tannhaüser in 1895.

BIBLIOGRAPHY: Martin 138; SW 129-31, 134-35, 184-86, 193-94, 196-98, 205-7, 224-26.

Duponchel, Charles-Edmond (b. 1795, Paris; d. 1868, Paris), administrator and librettist, studied architecture and then went into designing jewelry and the goldsmith's trade. He founded one of the more prestigious Paris firms dealing in objects made of gold, and he accepted special commissions such as decorating the statue of Minerva by Simart. He was director of the Opéra between 1837 and 1843 and again between 1847 and 1849. He was also appointed co-director of the Vaudeville theatre with Dormeuil. These activities might have kept him from making a more extensive contribution to the repertory, because he shared in the composition of the libretto for La Tentation* for the Opéra with Hygin-Auguste Cavé* in 1832 before he became so involved in administrative and business matters in France and England.

BIBLIOGRAPHY: DBF XII, 426-27; GE XV, 85; Lajarte II, 143; LXIX VI, 1412; Wks 13769.

Dupont, Pierre Auguste, DIT Alexis (b. 1796, Paris; d. June 1874, Paris), vocalist, completed his studies at the Royal School of Music and became a substitute tenor at the Opéra in 1818. He was not satisfied with his status at the Royal Academy of Music under these conditions, and he transferred to the Opéra-Comique on 4 January 1821 to sing the male lead in Zémire et Azor.* He was still annoyed over his lack of progress, however, and he decided to go to Italy to improve his style.

After two years in Italy, Dupont returned to the Opéra to sing Pylade in Christoph Willibald Gluck's Iphigénie en Tauride on 24 May 1826 (see eighteenth-century volume for Gluck and Iphigénie en Tauride). His voice was quite charming, but it lacked the strength necessary for a completely effective performance in a large theatre. Yet his technique was flawless, and his delivery almost too precise, and he was assigned to a number of new parts at the Opéra during his 1826-40 stay there. He created Alphonse in La Muette de Portici* on 29 February 1829, Ruodi in Guillaume Tell* on 3 August 1829, and the count de Saint-Pol in François Ier à Chambord* on 15 March 1830. After doing a secondary role in Le Dieu et la Bayadère* on 13 October 1830, he was billed as Asmodée in La Tentation* on 20 June 1832 and as Warting in Gustave III* on 27 February 1833.

The last seven years of Dupont's association with the Opéra saw a decrease in the number of important parts he was asked to sing, although it was a time when Don Juan,* La Juive,* and other compositions with large casts were mounted at the

theatre. He was billed as Cossé in Les Huguenots* on 29 February 1836, but he was assigned a minor part in La Esméralda* on 14 November 1836, and he appeared as one of the students in Le Lac des feés* of 1 April 1839. He replaced Duprez in Benvenuto Cellini* after the fourth presentation of Hector Berlioz'* opera, but this substitution was scarcely balm to his easily injured vanity, and it was at this point in his career that he left the Opéra to concertize. He found that he was much more effective and successful in a smaller hall than in the larger theatre, and he was happier regulating his own affairs by himself.
BIBLIOGRAPHY: Chouquet 393-97, 399, 401; EZF 185-86; Fétis Suppl. I, 289; GE XV, 87; Lajarte II, 143; SW 105, 116, 152.

Duprato, Jules-Laurent (b. 26 March 1827, Nîmes; d. 20 May 1892, Paris), composer, came to Paris about 1844 to study composition under Fernand Le Borne* at the Conservatoire. His cantata entitled Damoclès won first prize at the Institut in the Prix de Rome competition of 1848. After his residence in Italy and Germany, he returned to France to give Les Trovatelles at the Opéra-Comique in 1854. His Paquerette was billed at the same theatre in 1856. A decade later, in 1866, he joined the faculty of the Conservatoire, where he was appointed to a professorship in harmony in 1871. The first and only dramatic work he had billed at the Opéra was La Fiancée de Corinthe* of 1867 that was not successful despite the enthusiasm that his earlier compositions had inspired. The only other piece that he did for presentation at the Opéra was the cantata of 15 August 1864 for which Henri Meilhac* and Ludovic Halévy had provided the words.
BIBLIOGRAPHY: Chouquet 423; Paul Clauzel, Jules Duprato, compositeur (Nîmes: F. Chastanier, 1895); Fétis III, 84; GE XV, 92; Lajarte II, 241, 255; LXIX VI, 1417.

Duprez, Alexandrine, née Duperron (b. Nantes; d. 27 February 1872, Brussels), French soprano, made her debut at the Odéon in 1827. She was billed on programs with her husband Gilbert earlier in life, but her voice lacked the quality to sustain a stage career, and she retired from the theatre to devote her attention to her daughter, Caroline.
BIBLIOGRAPHY: EZF 192.

Duprez, Caroline (b. 10 April 1832, Florence; d. 17 April 1875, Pau), soprano, sang with her father Gilbert on programs presented in Paris and London. She appeared at the Théâtre Italien in Paris during 1850, when she made her debut in the French capital in La Somnambula. She moved on to Brussels in 1851 to help produce the world premiere of her father's opera entitled Joanita.

In 1852, the young singer returned to the Opéra-Comique to create the role of Angela in Marco Spada* on 21 December 1852 and to execute the part of Cathérine in L'Etoile du nord in the same theatre. After a short stay at the opera house in Lyon (1856-58), she was billed into the Théâtre-Lyrique in Paris to fill the roles of the countess in Les Noces de Figaro and Marie in La Fille du régiment. Finally, on 3 August 1860, she was invited to the Garnier Palace* to sing Isabella in Robert de Diable.*

The soprano was called upon to sing subsequently at Bordeaux, London, and St. Petersburg, but she returned to France in 1866 to complete her career as the successor of Mme Caroline Carvalho* at the Théâtre-Lyrique.

BIBLIOGRAPHY: *Pierre Brunel and Stéphane Wolff, L'Opéra (Paris: Bordas, 1980), 178; EZF 192-93; Jean Gourret, Histoire de l'Opéra-Comique (Paris: Publications universitaires, 1978), 126.*

Duprez, Gilbert-Louis (b. 6 December 1806, Paris; d. 23 September 1896, Paris) was a dramatic tenor. He studied at the Conservatoire in Paris under Alexandre Choron* and made an unimpressive debut at the Odéon in 1825. He went to Italy in 1828 to continue his studies and to strengthen his voice, and, a decade after his Paris debut, he won acclaim finally in Naples with his rendering of Edgardo in Lucia di Lammermoor.*

Duprez decided that it was now the propitious moment to return to his native city, and he was correct in his conclusion. He scored a superb triumph at the Paris Opéra on 17 April 1837 with his presentation of Arnold in Guillaume Tell.* He sang the sustained high C in the last act from the chest instead of taking it in head voice, and this tour de force alone spelled the end of Adolphe Nourrit's* career at the Opéra.

After his successful debut at the Opéra, Duprez was engaged to remain with the company, and he embarked upon a series of performances that brought him money and glory for the next ten years. He created the parts of Guido in Guido et Ginevra* on 5 March 1838, the title-role in Benvenuto Cellini* on 10 September 1838, and Albert in Le Lac des fées* on 1 April 1839. When Domenico Gaetano Donizetti's* Les Martyrs* was at last ready for its premiere on 10 April 1840, he was cast as Polyeucte. The same year, on 2 December, he presented Fernand in the first mounting of La Favorite* in the rue Le Peletier.* Duprez was at the height of his popularity now, and he was acclaimed successively for his Gérard in La Reine de Chypre* on 22 December 1841, his dauphin in Charles VI* on 15 March 1843, and his Sébastien in Dom Sébastien, roi du Portugal* on 13 November 1843. His voice began to show signs occasionally now of weakening, but only his enemies and unrelenting critics found serious fault with him in the title-role of Othello* on 2 September 1844, as Edgard in Lucie de Lammermoor* on 20 February 1846, or as Gaston in Jérusalem* on 26 November 1847. Yet it was only a matter of time before his vulnerable voix sombrée had to yield. Finally, in 1849, Giacomo Meyerbeer* selected Gustave Roger* over him for the male lead in Le Prophète,* and Duprez had to take his last bow at age 43.

The tenor retired to a life of composing, wherein he found no success, and to a period of teaching declamation at the Conservatoire. Finally, he decided to devote himslef to the direction of his own singing school. He published an essay entitled L'Art du chant in 1845 before his retirement and a treatise called La Mélodie in 1873. His best-known student was doubtlessly Mme Caroline Carvalho,* who created Charles Gounod's* Marguerite and Juliette.

BIBLIOGRAPHY: AEM III, 973-75; DBF XII, 546-47; Ed. Duprez, "Gueymard," FM 19 (30 December 1855), 410-11; M. Escudier, "Reprise de Robert le Diable: Début de Mme Duprez-Vandenheuvel," FM 24 (12 August 1860), 328; MM. Escudier frères, Études biographiques sur les chanteurs contemporains (Paris: Just Tessier, 1840), 175-200; EZF 187-92; Fétis III, 84-85 and Suppl. I, 272-74; GIR 66-69; B. de Grimm, "Représentation au bénéfice de M. Duprez," FM 4 (2 May 1841), 151-52; HUT 112-16; Lajarte II, 133-34, 156-59, 162-65, 169, 172, 174, 180-81, 186-87; Lermina 502; PBSW 178; Alphonse

Royer, Histoire de l'Opéra (Paris: Bachelin-Deflorenne, 1875), 164-67; Thompson 479.

Durand-Ulbach, Emilie (b. 7 October 1857, Paris; d. ?), vocalist, studied under Mlle Poinsot and Mme Colonne and toured the provinces before appearing at the Théâtre de la Monnaie in Brussels during 1889. She was invited to the Opéra to fill the role of Madeleine in Rigoletto* on 11 July 1890. She sang Amnéris in Aïda* at the Garnier Palace* later this same year, but these two engagements to appear in Giuseppe Verdi's* two compositions constituted the mezzo-soprano's only two billings at the National Academy of Music.
BIBLIOGRAPHY: Martin 142; SW 27-29, 181-83.

Duvernay, Yolande Marie Louise, DITE Pauline (b. 1813, Paris; d. 2 September 1894, Nottingham), ballerina, danced for only five years at a time when Franziska Elssler* and Marie Taglioni* were striving for supremacy between themselves, and the conflict between the two stars was attracting the almost undivided attention of balletomanes. In fact, she made her Paris debut almost immediately after Taglioni danced La Sylphide* on 12 March 1832 and her London debut when the Elssler sisters had just opened there. Yet her ability attracted attention almost immediately and raised her to the rank of one of the foremost ballerinas of her time despite these circumstantial handicaps.

Mme Durvernay had ambitious plans for her daughter's future in the theatre, and she arranged for her to study ballet as a child at the school attached to the Opéra. Her teachers were Barrez and Auguste Vestris, and her achievements as a student encouraged her superiors to allow her to appear on stage with the corps de ballet at age 16 (see eighteenth-century volume for Vestris). She remained with this humble assignment for three years until Dr. Véron became interested in her and decided to give her the opportunity to become a première danseuse. He accepted a libretto entitled La Tentation* and charged the team of Jacques Halévy* and Casimir Gide* to set it.

Rehearsals for La Tentation lasted several months, and extreme care was taken with the production of this opera-ballet in five acts. It had its premiere on 20 June 1832, and the young girl turned in an excellent performance as Miranda in the Hell scene of the second act. The work was too long to win the unreserved approval of spectators, but Duvernay's accomplishments convinced the public that a new star had come to the Opéra. Word of her ability spread abroad, and she was invited to appear at the Drury Lane Theatre in London. She opened her engagement in England as princess Iseult in La Belle au bois dormant* on 13 February 1833 but was back in Paris the following April to meet her obligations at the Opéra. The new ballet of the 1833-34 winter season was La Révolte au sérail* in which Marie Taglioni danced Zulma, but la Duvernay stole the show for a moment with her satiric mime of a typical French general.

She was invited to return to London in the spring of 1834 to appear at the King's Theatre, and she scored triumphs with la Taglioni in Le Dieu et la Bayadère* and the famous La Sylphide.* When the elder ballerina left London in April, however, la Duvernay had the scene to herself in the subsequent productions of these two compositions. She hastened back to Paris as usual after the expiration of her contract in England, and she spent the entire year of 1835 at the Opéra. She was named to dance in the divertissement of La Juive,* which had its premiere on 23 February and the new ballet entitled Brézilia ou la Tribu des femmes,* which was mounted for the first time on 8 April 1835 (see eighteenth-century volume for divertissement). This latter composition in a single act was given on a benefit program for la Taglioni.

It was at this point in her life that Pauline Duvernay disappeared suddenly and without explanation. She had attempted suicide in May 1835, but she had recovered and was able to dance again before long. Her friends and associates were now wondering whether she had managed to kill herself this time, or whether she had perhaps been kidnapped. Ultimately, the conductor of the orchestra, M. Gide, received a note from her saying that she had retired to a convent but was now ready to dance again. On 21 September 1836, she appeared in La Fille du Danube,* the last premiere in which she was to participate at the Opéra.

She returned to England once again to perform at Drury Lane, and on this occasion she was to remain at the London theatre for nearly a year. She made her debut here in 1836 in La Fille du

Danube, now called The Maid of Cashmere, and she scored her biggest hit in Le Diable boiteux,* now billed as The Devil on Two Sticks. All London came to see her as Florinda and to witness her performance of the cachucha made famous by Fanny Elssler. She danced in a number of other pieces, including La Sylphide and Le Corsaire,* and her popularity continued to grow. Yet, when the theatre closed for the season on 19 August 1837, the ballerina retired permanently from the theatre. She was not yet 25 years old, and she gave no reason for her decision.

Pauline Duvernay became the wife of Stephen Lyne-Stephens on 14 October 1845, and she inherited his enormous wealth after his death in 1860. She was intensely religious and gave freely to charity and to religious projects.

BIBLIOGRAPHY: Charles de Boigne, Petits Mémoires de l'Opéra (Paris: Librairie nouvelle, 1857), 20-31; CB 78, 122, 213; Chouquet 396-98; CODB 171-72; DDD 95; EDB 129; EZF 193-95; GE XV, 150; Ivor Guest, The Romantic Ballet in England: Its Development, Its Fulfillment and Decline (Middletown, Conn.: Wesleyan University Press, 1972), 51, 62-64, 70-74, 78, 121, 128; idem, Romantic Ballet in Paris (Middletown, Conn.: Wesleyan University Press, 1966), 118-22, 140-43; Lajarte II, 147, 149-50; Parmenia Migel, The Ballerinas from the Court of Louis XV to Pavlova (New York: Macmillan, 1972), 225-30; Lillian Moore, Artists of the Dance (New York: Thomas Y. Crowell Co., 1938), 119-26; SST 209-13.

Duvernoy, Victor Alphonse (b. 30 August 1842, Paris; d. 7 March 1907, Paris), composer, enrolled at the Conservatoire in Paris to become a pupil of Barbereau, Bazin, and Antoine Marmontel. He won the Prix Chartier for his chamber music, and his cantata entitled La Tempéte earned him the Prix de Ville de Paris in 1880.

M. Duvernoy's initial contribution to the repertory of the National Academy of Music was his opera Hellé,* which had its world premiere at the Garnier Palace* on 24 April 1896. The composer never submitted a second opera to the jury at the Opéra, but he did contribute to the scores of three ballets choreographed by Joseph Hansen* between 1900 and 1902. He did all the music for Bacchus,* billed at the Garnier Palace for the first time on 26 November 1902, but he was only one of 28 compsoers whose work was used in the staging of Danses de jadis et de naguère* on 22 September 1900. Also, there were six other composers whose music was used in the production of Danses grecques* of 5 June 1901, to which he also contributed.

BIBLIOGRAPHY: BBD 450; ELM I, 680-81.

Duveyrier, Anne-Honoré-Joseph, DIT Mélesville (b. 13 December 1787, Paris; d. 7 November 1865, Marly), librettist, studied law and became a practicing lawyer at Montpellier in 1808. He pursued his career for two years but renounced law to write librettos for Paris theatres in 1815. He was encouraged to make this drastic decision by the fact that his L'Oncle rival had already been staged and accepted by the public at the Impératrice Theatre in 1811. He was extremely sincere about his new calling, moreover, and he managed to have at least two and sometimes four pieces billed at Paris theatres every year until his authorship came to number at least 150 compositions at the time of his death. He wrote for the Gymnase, Madame, Variétés, Vaudeville, and Porte Saint-Martin theatres in addition to furnishing scripts for the Palais-Royal and the Comédie-Française. He did 30 or 40 texts with Eugène Scribe* alone. Le Meunière (1821), Le Paradis de Mahomet (1822), La Petite Lampe merveilleuse (1822), Leicester (1823), Le Valet de chambre (1823), Le Concert à la Cour (1824), and Léocadie (1824) were only the first seven comic operas that they had performed at the Opéra-Comique during the first decade of the Restoration. Mélesville and Scribe also provided librettos for the Opéra. They were the authors of the words for Luigi Cherubini's Ali-Baba* of 1833, Daniel Auber's* Le Lac des fées* of 1839, and Giuseppe Verdi's* Les Vêpres siciliennes* of 1855 (see eighteenth-century volume for Cherubini). Mélesville had no collaborator while creating the poem for Jules Alary's* La Voix humaine* of 1861. Duveyrier, or Mélesville, had only these four works given at the Opéra.

BIBLIOGRAPHY: DBF XI, 1049; GE XV, 153; Lajarte II, 146, 159, 195, 218, 232; LXIX X, 1470-71 under Mélesville; Wks III, 254.

E

Eames, Emma (b. 13 August 1865, Shanghai; d. 13 June 1952, New York) was a world-famous soprano whose self-possession and calm on the stage were legendary. She was brought up in Bath, Maine, by her mother, who instructed her in the rudiments of singing before she went to Boston to continue her studies. Later, her talents and the range of her voice persuaded Mathilde Marchesi to accept her as a pupil. She made her debut in Paris at the Opéra as Juliette on 13 March 1889, and her performance as Charles Gounod's* heroine assured her continuance with the company. She also sang Marguerite in 1889, and she then created the role of Colombe at the world premiere of Camille Saint-Saëns'* Ascanio* on 21 March 1890 besides doing the title-part for the first presentation of Zaïre* on 28 May 1890.

The young soprano left the Opéra in 1891 to make her London debut at Convent Garden, and, this same year, she sailed for the United States to start her tenure of 18 years at the Metropolitan Opera House. She spent the remainder of her performing life in the United States except for two short excursions to England and to Spain. She resided in New York to teach and to write her memoirs after her retirement from the stage. Her last public appearance in France had been at the Opéra-Comique on 31 October 1904 to sing Tosca in Italian.

BIBLIOGRAPHY: American Annual 53 (1953), 203; EFC 158; Étude 70 (August 1952) 8; David Ewens, Living Musicians, 1st suppl. (New York: Wilson, 1957), 51; J. Haughton, "Opera Singers from the Golden

Age," Musical America 69 (February 1949), 166; ICM 487; KRJ 116; A.F.R. Lawrence, "Emma Eames," American Record Guide 29 (November 1962), 210-17; Martin 144; Musical America 72 (July 1952), 26; National Cyclopaedia of American Biography (New York: White, 1891-1968), Vol. 42, 680-81; Newsweek 39 (23 June 1952), 64; NY Times 14 June 1952, 15; G. Odell, "Famous Precedent," Musical America 73 (December 1953), 10; Henry Pleasants, Great Singers (New York: Simon and Schuster, 1966), 278-79; School and Society 72 (2 December 1950), 366; RC 253-56; SW 42, 88, 191, 227; WOC 250.

L'Eden was billed as a mystery in two parts, but this composition might be described more exactly as a cantata rather than as an operatic or choreographic work. Félicien David* created its score, and Joseph Méry* was the author of its poem. It was presented for the first time in Paris at the Théâtre de la Nation, and it had its premiere at the Opéra on 25 August 1848.

A preface in the piece is entitled Avant l'homme and offers 11 sestets describing the emergence of the first vegetable matter from the primeval ooze along with the appearance of the first of God's creatures on earth. L'Eden then depicts Adam in all his primitive innocence and joy. This first section of the poem proper also describes the arrival of Eve in the garden. A concluding duet is devoted to Adam's warning to Eve that they are forbidden to eat the fruit of the apple tree. The second portion of the piece begins with the temptation of Eve and Adam's subsequent disregard of his own warning. Lucifer expels them from the garden, and Adam realizes that he and Eve will have to earn their daily bread henceforth by the sweat of their brows.

L'Eden was not the type of work to enjoy extended popularity, and it was withdrawn after its fifth presentation on 13 September 1848. M. Placide Poultier* filled the role of Adam with M. Adolphe Alizard* as Lucifer, M. Portheault as the seducer, and Mlle Grimm as Eve.

BIBLIOGRAPHY: AEM III, 47-51; René Brancoeur, Félicien David: biographie critique (Paris: Laurens, 1914); DDO I, 376-77; Grove (1980) 5, 263-65; Lajarte II, 189; Thompson 491.

Elektra, by Richard Strauss,* is discussed in the twentieth-century volume.

Les Elfes was presented as a fantastic ballet in three acts and four tableaux with a libretto by Jules Saint-Georges,* a score by Count Nicolas Gabrielli,* and choreography by Joseph Mazilier.* It had its world premiere at the Imperial Theatre of the Opéra on 11 August 1856 with sets by Despléchin, Nolau, Thierry, and Martin. The future star Amalia Ferraris* made her debut at the Opéra in the first presentation of the work, and the theatre was crowded despite the unbearable heat that stifled Paris on this August evening. Even Napoleon III and his empress were in their box to share in the excitement of this almost unprecedented opening night.

The long and intricate ballet begins on a mountain top, where Prince Albert of Hungary is hunting with Count Frédéric de Hapsbourg (I, 1). A group of happy peasants offers flowers and fruit to the prince, but the count is interested only in the statue of a young dryad that he has discovered in an abandoned temple. The prince decides to take this piece of sculpture to his castle. The statue bears the name of Sylvia on its soclum (I, 2). The hunters continue on their way, but Frédéric decides to rest and falls asleep (I, 3). A band of elves emerges from a tree, and their queen becomes angry when she sees the sleeping intruder. The count awakens to find himself surrounded by a host of curious creatures, but Adda reassures him, and he takes her seriously when she observes that only a woman of stone could please him. He hastens to observe that he has never seen a woman more beautiful than the statue in the temple; he adds that he could indeed fall in love with her if she were alive. The queen reveals that she can effect this transformation. The sky grows dark, and a light shines on the temple, where the count sees a legend disclosing that the statue of Sylvia will live with the soul of an elf by day but return to stone at night. The count accepts these conditions, and the statue becomes animate. The storm dies, and the sun shines. The elves disappear with their dead companion, who has given her soul to the statue (I, 4).

The "statue" steps down from her soclum with great hesitation and views the scene with timidity. The count plays the shepherd's pipes and picks flowers for her, and she gains confidence until she is frightened by the returning hunters. She hides in the temple (I, 5). The prince orders his men to fetch the marble statue that has turned to stone again because night has fallen (I, 6).

The scene shifts to a salon in Prince Albert's palace, where preparations are under way for the wedding of the prince and Princess Bathilde, daughter of the Great Elector. The prince shows his art holdings to his guests, but he finds that his latest acquisition is missing from its base. No one can explain its disappearance, and the guests withdraw for the moment (II, 1). The "statue" emerges from her hiding place; she succumbs to the lure of Bathilde's beautiful and expensive presents. She puts the princess' diamonds and pearls in her hair; she is so charmed by her appearance that she fails to notice Count Frédéric watching her. The smitten count approaches her, but he realizes that her heart is not beating. He is overcome by the dreadful irony of the situation (II, 2), when the prince enters. The count presents Sylvia as his ward. Albert is charmed by the young girl, whom he seems to recognize, although he cannot understand her curious actions (II, 3). Bathilde appears with her retinue, but Albert continues to be so interested in the stranger that Frédéric grows jealous. The music affords a temporary distraction, especially when Sylvia rushes onto the dance floor to execute a series of original and bizarre steps. Frédéric tries to stop her, and she runs away (II, 4).

The second tableau of the second act shifts to Prince Albert's garden, where breathless Sylvia throws herself on a bench to rest. The count finds her and prevents her from falling when she tries to run away from him. He regrets that Sylvia lacks a heart and the power to reason or to love. The queen of the elves appears with three roses, and a rock in the waterfall offers a legend informing him that the three roses will endow the nymph with Reason, Grace, and Love if he will give the roses to her. One condition is attached to this situation. He will age ten years each time that he gives her a rose (II, bis). The queen disappears, and Frédéric gives Sylvia the rose of reason. She becomes shy and retiring (II, 2 bis);

she begins to compare the merits of Frédéric and Albert. She prefers the prince because he seems younger, but he is filled with terror upon feeling her cold hand and returns to Bathilde (II, 3 bis).

The festivities resume without interruption until Sylvia tries to dance. She is so clumsy that Frédéric gives her the rose of grace; her newly acquired skill and lightness reawaken the prince's interest in her. The music stops, and the count reveals his love to her, but she does not understand him. Hopeful, he gives her the rose of love, and she becomes vibrant. Happy Frédéric does not notice his white hair, stooped shoulders, and wizened skin until Sylvia runs to Albert. Jealous Frédéric draws his dagger, but he is without strength, and the prince disarms him easily. The Great Elector enters with his daughter to escort Albert to the wedding, and Frédéric explains to Sylvia that she has been rejected (II, 4 bis).

The theatre represents the Valley of Roses at dawn, where the queen of the elves and her subjects are burying the body of the elf who gave her soul to Sylvia (III, 1). Count Frédéric has come to the valley to greet Sylvia upon her return to life (III, 2), and he is followed by Prince Albert, who is still looking for Sylvia despite his marriage to Bathilde. The two men begin to argue, and they draw their swords. Sylvia throws herself between the rivals. Furious, the count lunges at Albert and seizes Sylvia. She announces her love for Albert, however, and the latter rescues her from Frédéric, who is placed under arrest and led away by the royal guard (III, 3). Albert and Sylvia embrace, but he finds himself obliged to return to his wife (III, 4-5).

The angry elves return to punish the creature responsible for their comrade's death, and they confiscate the roses of Reason and Grace. Undisciplined Sylvia leaps about until she collapses from exhaustion (III, 6), but she recovers long enough to confront Prince Albert mingling with his subjects. She tries to pull him away from his astonished bride, but he rejects her again, and she falls to the ground with a broken heart that she does not understand (III, 7). The sun sets, and Sylvia turns to stone slowly while trying instinctively to forgive Albert. Count Frédéric has escaped from prison, and he approaches with madness in his eyes. He finds

Sylvia already turned to stone, and he smashes the lifeless statue. A blue flame dances its way from the debris to the grave of the elves' dead companion. The grave opens, and the young elf emerges from the ground to rejoin her fellow elves and her queen (III, 8).

The ballet was a total triumph for Mme Ferraris in the part of Sylvia, and the press hailed her performance with unrestricted praise. Specifically, her elevation, grace, strength, and attack were described as perfect, excellent, or marvellous. Saint-Victor declared that her style recalled Marie Taglioni*; Saint-Georges sent her a laudium in verse complimenting her upon her ability to transform a statue into a butterfly. As for the spectators, it is said that the star was almost smothered by the deluge of bouquets thrown upon the stage. Yet there were some adverse comments. The score was uninspired; Domenico Segarelli* (Frédéric) tried too hard to call attention to himself by rolling his eyes like a madman; Lucien Petipa* (Albert) gave a dispirited performance when he danced his mazurka dressed in furs despite the heat; Victorine Legrain (Adda) was scarcely well cast as the queen of the elves. The other roles seem to have been filled competently by Lenfant (the Elector), Mlle Louise Marquet* (Mathilde), and Mlle Nathan (the young elf). Les Elfes remained in the repertory for nearly 40 performances, but the acclaim accorded to Mme Ferraris in her debut on its opening night is the most spectacular chapter in its history.

BIBLIOGRAPHY: CB 218-26; Chouquet 416; Ivor Guest, The Ballet of the Second Empire (Middletown, Conn.: Wesleyan University Press, 1974), 104-7, 258; J. de Heidwiller, "Théâtre Impérial de l'Opéra: Les Elfes," FM 20 (17 August 1856), 261-62; Lajarte II, 220; Moniteur universel 229, 230 (16, 17 August 1856), 913-14.

Elssler, Franziska, DIT Fanny (b. 23 June 1810, Vienna; d. 27 November 1884, Vienna), ballerina, was born into a family of professional musicians, and her father was able to support his wife and children in relative comfort as long as he was valet and copyist to Joseph Haydn (see eighteenth-century volume for Haydn). After the composer's death in 1808, her mother had to become a laundress to support her five offspring, while Thérèse and Fanny went to the ballet school at the Theater an der Wien to study under Jean Aumer and Filippo Taglioni in the hope of being able one day to add to the family income (see eighteenth-century volume for Aumer and Taglioni). Thérèse was nine, and Fanny was seven at this time, but they worked hard and progressed so rapidly that the younger sister made her first appearance on the stage before she was thirteen. The famous impresario Domenico Barbaia was now director of the San Carlo opera house in Naples as well as of the Kärntnertortheater in Vienna, and he was so impressed by the young girl's performance that he arranged for her to dance in Naples and Vienna. In Italy, she gave birth to Franz after becoming the mistress of Prince Leopold of Salerno.

Fanny returned to Vienna as soon as possible, where she resumed dancing at the Kärntnertotheater and became the mistress of Friedrich von Gentz, political adviser to Prince Metternich. Their liaison was disrupted when the Elssler sisters were offered a contract to appear in Berlin in 1830. Gentz died in 1832 after he had learned that Fanny had fallen in love with a Berlin dancer named Anton Stuhlmüller. When she discovered that she was about to have another child, she decided to avoid a scandal by going to England with her sister. The infant Theresa was born in London in 1833, and Fanny was able to resume her career because her new friend, Mrs. George Grote, was willing and able to care for her child. Then, in May 1833, Dr. Véron of the Opéra arrived in London to look for a ballerina to replace Marie Taglioni,* who was becoming temperamental and difficult to please. Dr. Véron favored the direct approach in contract negotiations, and he dazzled the Elssler sisters with extravagant gifts, a sumptuous banquet, and the offer of a three year contract. Thérèse and Fanny signed.

It was through Dr. Véron's initiative that the profitable Elssler-Taglioni rivalry was created, a rivalry that started with Fanny's paris debut as Alcine in the premiere of <u>La Tempête</u>* on 15 September 1834. The Austrian ballerina held the attention of Parisian audiences for two reasons. She was physically more attractive; she had now perfected her staccato style of dancing, which is described by the French as <u>taqueté</u> because it features sharp steps on pointes. Challenged, Taglioni rose to the occasion with her guaranteed-to-please La Sylphide* and La Révolte au sérail.* After Brézilia* was produced for their opponent's benefit on 8 April 1835, Fanny and Thérèse counterattacked with L'Ile des pirates* on 12 August 1835. If any theatregoers insisted on continuing the Elssler-Taglioni rivalry, they were now silenced forever in the spring of 1836, because Fanny was about to create her biggest box office sensation in Le Diable boiteux* of 1 June 1836 by introducing the cachucha into this ballet. This fiery Spanish dance and its sensuous vitality shocked audiences, but it raised receipts. The star's likeness in her Spanish costume appeared on souvenirs in cheap shops and in displays featuring the most expensive accessories of dress. It was about this time that Taglioni announced that she had "knee trouble" and retired temporarily to give birth to her child, but she returned to the theatre to dance in the premiere of La Fille du Danube* on 21 September 1836. The rivalry between the Elssler sisters and Taglioni then came to a halt, when Duponchel made manifest his reluctance to renew Taglioni's contract, and she left France for Russia. Fanny remained at the Opéra to execute the lead in La Gypsy* of 28 January 1839 and to join forces with her sister again for the premiere of La Tarentule* of 24 June 1839.

Yet even this success could not hold Fanny Elssler in Paris, when Henry Wikoff appeared on the scene with his Philadelphia accent. Attached to the American embassy, Wikoff knew Stephen Price, another American. The latter had explained to Wikoff that the only way he could avoid bankruptcy was to present Fanny Elssler in New York. Wikoff knew Fanny's latest flame, the marquis de La Valette, and he had promised Price to see what he could do through him. He kept his word and interviewed the ballerina, but now Stephen Price died suddenly. Interested in what promised to be a lucrative project, Wikoff took matters into his own hands and set sail for the United States on the famous Great Western on 15 April 1840 with Fanny and her retinue under his wing. The ballerina was greeted by New Yorkers with noise and excitement. Her month in the great city was punctuated by countless press notices, especially in the New York Morning Herald because Wikoff knew James Gordon Bennett. She made her New World debut at the Park Theatre on 14 May

1840, and she earned $10,000 for her 15 performances here before leaving for Baltimore, Philadelphia, Washington, New Orleans, and Havana. Finally, in the summer of 1842, she set sail for England.

The great Elssler began to show signs of temperament now, and she became hostile toward such close friends as Mrs. Grote and Wikoff. Her disposition was damaged further by the discovery that Caronne Grisi* had replaced her at the Opéra, and that the management of this theatre would have nothing to do with her. Annoyed, she sought and found greater triumphs in Berlin, Vienna, London again, Brussels, Budapest, Naples, and Milan. Her greatest glory was her engagement in St. Petersburg in 1848, where she had audiences at her feet with her execution of Giselle.* She went next to Vienna by way of Moscow and Hamburg. Here she bid farewell to the stage in the ballet Faust* on 21 June 1851.

Her retirement was saddened by her son's poor investments on the stock market and his subsequent suicide, but she was otherwise quite happy for the remainder of her life as the wife of Baron Victor Weber von Webenau, as the mother of her beloved Fanny, as a grandmother, and as the friend of her constant admirers.

BIBLIOGRAPHY: ACD 166-73; ACPM 326; Erik Aschengreen, "The Beautiful Danger; Facets of the Romantic Ballet," trans. Patricia N. McAndrew, Dance Perspectives 58 (Summer 1974), 2-6: BCS 299; Cyril W. Beaumont, Fanny Elssler (London: C. W. Beaumont, 1931); CB 72, 91, 113-28, 160-68, 262, 271-78, 360, 513; CODB 179; Joseph Cornell, "Fannyelssleriana," Dance Index 6 (1967), 205-11; DDD 96-98; EDB 132; Auguste Ehrhard, Une Vie de danseuse: Fanny Elssler (Paris: Plon-Nourrit, 1909); Fanny Elssler, The Letters and Journal of Fanny Elssler (New York: H. G. Daggers, 1845); Elssler's benefit performance at Opéra, "Spectacles, La Volière," Moniteur universel 127 (7 may 1858), 1150; EZF 195-96; Ivor Guest, The Romantic Ballet in England: Its Development, Fulfilment and Decline (Middletown, Conn.: Wesleyan University Press, 1972), 63-69; idem, Fanny Elssler (Middletown, Conn.: Wesleyan University Press, 1970); idem, Romantic Ballet in Paris (Middletown, Conn.: Wesleyan University Press, 1966), 132-39, 160-85; idem, "The Cachuca Reborn," The Dancing Times 685)October 1967), 18-21; idem, "Fanny

Elssler and Her Friends," Ballet 5 (June 1948), 33-36 and Ballet 6 (October, 1948), 38-43; Victoria Huckenpahler, "Fanny Elssler Comes to Wasington," D Mag 49, no. 7 (July 1975), 38-40; Lajarte Ii, 149, 151, 154, 158-60, 163-64; André Levinson, Ballet romantique (Paris: Editions du Trianon), 28-42; LTX 53-57; Parmenia Migel, The Ballerinas from the Court of Louis XV to Pavlova (New York: Macmillan, 1972), 145-67; idem, Artists of the Dance (New York: Thomas Y. Crowell Co., 1938), 91-109; idem, "Elssler and the Cachucha," The Dancing Times, new series 311 (August 1936), 495-97; Mark E. Perugini, A Pageant of the Dance and Ballet (London: Jarnolds, 1946), 180-82; Riki Raab, Fanny Elssler; eine Weltfaszination (Wien: Bergland Verlag, 1962); Kenneth Rapp, "The Legend of Fanny Elssler's Perouette by Moonlight," D Mag 49, no. 7 (July 1975), 41-42; RBP 131-85; SST 206-9; XXJ 33-36.

Emarot, Célestine, née Marguerite Adelaïde (b. 18 March 1824, Dijon; d. 7 October 1892, Paris), ballerina, was brought to Paris at age ten. She was enrolled at the dancing school attached to the Opéra in about 1836 through the influence of her mother's friends, and she showed herself to be a willing and energetic student. As time progressed, she failed to give promise of any brilliance or flair, but she did win a place in the corps de ballet. At age 17, she received an offer to appear at Her Majesty's Theatre in London. She became the mistress of the baron Charles de Chassiron about this time and gave birth to a dughter Emma toward the end of 1842. The child was to be known to the public as Emma Livry.*

Célestine had made her debut at the Opéra on 11 August 1845 in the premiere of Le Diable à quatre.* She danced the part of Yelva, but the audience remained indifferent to her dancing, which was decidedly ordinary despite her constant efforts to improve her art. She was returned to the corps de ballet for the premiere of Paquita* on 1 April 1846, and she proved woefully inadequate again in her second important role as the abbess in the 1850 revival of Robert le Diable.* Her second crushing blow in 1850 was her baron's marriage to Princess Caroline Murat, a cousin of Napoleon III. Yet she was never in financial need, despite her low earnings at the Opéra, and she was able to educate her talented daughter Emma in the best schools of the day with the help of Vicount Ferdinand de Montguyon, whose mistress she became shortly after her break with the baron Charles de Chassiron.

Célistine Emarot danced in the premieres of four other ballets at the Opéra: Stella* of 22 February 1850, Les Nations* of 6 August 1851, Vert-Vert* of 24 November 1851, and La Fonti* of 8 January 1855. She was also cast as Inès in Jovita* on 11 November 1853 and took part in the 1857 revival of Orfa.*

BIBLIOGRAPHY: CB 143-48, 177-83, 188, 190-208, 280-86, 337-43; Ivor Guest, The Ballet of the Second Empire (Middletown, Conn.: Wesleyan University Press, 1974), 123-25, 135-36, 151-54, 156-57, 160-61; Lajarte II, 140-41, 179, 181-82, 205-6, 209-12, 215, 217-18.

Empis, Adolphe-Dominique-Florent-Joseph Simonis DIT (b. 29 march 1795, Paris; d. 12 December 1868, Paris), playwright and librettist, was born into a wealthy family and received an excellent classical education. His family suffered a series of financial reverses when he was still a young man, however, and he was obliged to take a position with the government during the reign of Louis XVIII to support himself. His intelligence and diligence served him well, and he was promoted rapidly. At the same time he maintained his literary studies privately, and it was not long before he was collaborating on librettos for the lyric stage.

Empis' first work for the Opéra was done with Hippolyte Cournol, the libretto for Antoine Reicha's* Sapho* in 1822. Next he joined forces with Edouard Mennechet to provide the words for Vendôme en Espagne* set by Daniel-François-Esprit Auber* and Louis-Joseph-Ferdinand Hérold* in 1823. After additional collaborations with the dramatist Picard, Empis turned to writing comedies of character and manners without the help of a partner, and his talents were soon recognized. He was elected to the chair of Victor-Joseph Etienne Jouy at the French Academy in 1847, and the continuing success of his Vendôme en Espagne led to his appointment as secretary of the royal libraries (see eighteenth-century volume for Jouy). Finally, in 1856, he was chosen to succeed Arsène Houssaye as chief administrator of the

Comédie-Française, and he was appointed general inspector of libraries on 22 October 1859.

The playwright-administrator wrote a number of comedies in five acts that enjoyed a real measure of success between 1830 and 1846, but it was his Les Six Femmes de Henri VIII (1854) that inspired the most enthusiastic critical reviews, although this composition was not a theatrical piece.

BIBLIOGRAPHY: Chouquet 390-91; DBF XII, 1269; GE XV, 977-78; Lajarte II, 103, 106; LXIX VII, 468-69; Samuel Ustazade Silvestre de Sacy, Institut impérial de France. Académie française. Discours . . . prononcé aux funérailles de M. Empis (Paris: Firmin-Didot frères, 1868); SST 129-31; Thieme I, 685.

L'Enfant Prodigue, an oprea in five acts, had a score by Daniel Auber* and a libretto by Eugène Scribe.* It was presented for the first time on 6 December 1850 and went on to enjoy 40 performances by 26 July 1852, but it could not compete with more popular works by such composers as Domenico Donizetti* and Giuseppe Verdi.* It was never revived.

The curtain rises in L'Enfant prodigue with Ruben and his niece Jephtèle lamenting the continued absence of the former's son Azaël, when he returns with the two travelers, Aménophis and Nefté. He reassures Jephtèle of his love, and the guests present begin to speak of Memphis. Ruben predicts the downfall of this wicked metropolis, and he refuses to allow Azeël to take their farm produce there (I, 1-3). Jephtèle says he should make this trip before he settles down in marriage, and his father agrees reluctantly to his departure (I, 4-5). Azaël is overcome by the luxury and opulence of Memphis, and he and his companions gaze in awe upon the processions in honor of Apis and Isis to whom hymns are sung (II, 1-2). Nefté renounces the cult of the Nile, however, because the dancer Lia and her troop have been admitted to the rites honoring the river. Azaël is fascinated by her on the other hand, and he spends huge sums of money to buy gifts for her. In her turn, she is consumed by a desire to possess a veil that Jephtèle has given to Azaël, and she steals it from him. He begins to gamble and loses large sums of money with loaded dice; he quarrels with his companions, Nefté and Aménophis. He thanks

Lia for informing him that the dice were rigged (II, 3-4). Ruben comes to Memphis to find his son, but Azaël eludes him by deceit (II, 5-6).

Nefté and Azaël enter Isis' temple to recover Jephtéle's scarf, but they disturb Bocchoris and his comrades, who awaken from their drunken sleep. They save their lives by asserting that they have come to worship Isis (III, 1-2). Since the NIle is endangering the harvest by falling, the people have decided to offer up a sacrifice. They have chosen Jephtèle as the victim. Bocchoris offers to save her if she will give herself to him, but she refuses in anger (III, 3-5). Azaël is brought in for his trial by fire, and he discovers Jephtèle praying. He seizes an ax, and puts Bocchoris and the priests of Isis to route (III, 6). Lia helps Jephtèle escape, and the people take Azaël to the nIle (III, 7-9).

A period of time elapses between the third and fourth acts. Now Azaël is a servant of a camel driver who saved him from the river. Nefté and Aménophis stop at an oasis where the driver Nemrod is watering his animals. They recognize and quarrel with Azaël; they threaten to tell his father of the lowly state to which he has fallen (IV, 1-4). Azaël falls asleep, and Tobias' angel appears to him in a dream to tell him to return to his father (IV, 5). The scene returns to Azaël's home. Here, the harvesters are rejoicing over the completion of their tasks, but Ruben is bitter over his son's continued absence, while Jephtèle prays for his return (V, 1-3). Suddenly, Azaël appears and the two lovers are reconciled, although Jephtèle warns him of his father's wrath. But Ruben rejoices to see his son again, and his household shares his happiness (V, 4-6).

Although Auber's score was not enough by itself to keep L'Enfant prodigue in the repertory, it was quite colorful and matched the picturesque subject of the libretto. Among its most striking moments were the three romances by Jephtèle in act 1, scene 4 ("Allez, suives votre pensée"), by Ruben in act 2, scene 5 ("Il est un enfant d'Israël"), and by Azaël in act 4, scene 5 ("J'ai tout perdu, Seigneur"). The role of Ruben was especially noteworthy, and one of his most impressive and moving arias was his "Mon fils! . . . mon fils! . . . c'est toi!" (V, 6). The dances executed by Mlle Adèle Plunkett* as Lia were similarly well done and greeted with applause.

The major roles were done by Gustave Roger* as Azaël, Massol as Ruben, and Louis Obin* as Bocchoris opposite Mme Rosine Laborde as Nefté and Mlle Dameron as Jephtèle. Although the part of the camel driver was of lesser importance, Mlle Petit-Brière is remembered in this role because of her song "Ah! dans l'Arabie" (IV, 1).
BIBLIOGRAPHY: Chouquet 411; DDO I, 390; Lajarte II, 206-7; Charles Malherbe, Auber (Paris: Renouard, n.d.). 52-53; SSBO 220.

Engel, Pierre-Emile (b. 15 February 1847, Paris; d. 1927, Paris), vocalist, studied at the Ecole Duprez between 1861 and 1865 and made his theatrical debut at the Théâtre-parisien in Duprez' Jeanne d'Arc* in 1865. The following year, he was billed at the Fantaisies-Parisiennes. He traveled to New Orleans in 1868, but he returned to France before long to spend some time at the Gaîté before making his first appearance at the Opéra-Comique in La Dame Blanche on 6 September 1877. He journeyed abroad once more between 1879 and 1885 and was heard at the Théâtre de la Monnaie between 1885 and 1889.

His debut at the Opéra was sudden and unexpected. He was seated in the audience on 9 December 1889, when he was called upon to replace Emile Cossira in the role of Edgard during the first act of Lucie de Lammermoor.* He was billed next in the lead of Lohengrin* in 1891, and, in 1892, he was cast in four parts: Fernand of La Favorite,* the title-role of Faust,* a shepherd in Le Sicilien,* and Rhadamès in Aïda.* He created a single part during his short stay of three years at the Garnier Palace,* Nour-Eddin in Thamara* on 28 December 1891. He became singing professor at the Paris Conservatoire in 1906.
BIBLIOGRAPHY: DBF XII, 1289; Martin 147; SW 27-29, 85-90, 136-37, 209, 357.

Enlèvement au sérail is an opéra bouffe in three acts known as Die Entführung aus dem Serail in the original German and as The Abduction from the Seraglio in English. Gottlob Stephanie wrote its libretto based upon a play by Bretzner and Wolfgang Amadeus Mozart* composed its score. It had its world premiere at the National Theatre in Vienna on 12 July 1782, and it was performed in the original version for the first time in Paris at the Lycée des Arts on 26 September 1798. It was heard again in Paris on 11 May 1859 at the Théâtre Lyrique in a translation by Prosper Pascal, and a second French version by Kufferath and Solvay was performed at the Théâtre Royal de la Monnaie in Brussels on 15 February 1902. This latter text was used once more for its premiere at the Opéra in Paris on 1 December 1903. Mozart's work was also billed at the Opéra-Comique for the first time on 18 February 1937 in the Kufferath-Gidel version. At the Opéra, on 1 December 1903, the sets were designed by Marcel Jambon and Bailly.

The opera opens in the public square in front of the palace of the pacha Sélim, where Belmont is trying to find his fiancee Constance. He cannot obtain any information from the surly figpicker Osmin (I, 1-2), but he meets his former servant Pédrille, who has entered the pacha's service. Pédrille tells him to pretend to be an architect, and he will be readily accepted by the pacha, whose mania is constructing buildings (I, 3-4). The scheme works, and the men enter the palace gardens (I, 5-8).

Blondine gives orders to the annoyed pacha, who does her bidding and leaves the garden (II, 1). Constance despairs of seeing her sweetheart again, and she also defies Sélim (II, 2-4). Pédrille tells Blondine that Belmont has arrived, however, and he instructs her to be ready to escape after sundown. He specifies that they will leave through the window by using a ladder. Pédrille puts Osmin to sleep by giving him too much wine. Belmont and Constance are reunited, but jealous Belmont has to verify that his sweetheart loves him, not the pacha, while Pédrille is trying to make sure that Blondine loves him, not Osmin. The men have to apologize for their unjust suspicions, but all doubts are removed without delay (II, 5-7).

Belmont and Pédrille are in the midst of helping Constance and Blondine to escape from the palace when Osmin discovers them. He sounds the alarm, and Sélim's men capture the four fugitives (III, 1-2). Belmont and Constance are consoling each other, when Sélim enters to forgive the lovers because it would be madness to oppose love. Osmin flees the country in anger, but the lovers have words of praise and gratitude for their generous liberator (III, 3-4).

The libretto of L'Enlèvement au serail is almost childishly simple, and only the bottle scene between Belmont and Osmin has any real intrinsic interest as comedy, less comedy than is contained in the criticism made of the score by Emperor Joseph II: "There are too many notes in it." It is true, of course, that the work lacks the variety and grace found in the music of La Flûte enchantée* or Don Juan,* but there are moments in it that made it plausible to revive the work in other opera houses, for example, the quartet ending the second act. After it was finally brought to the stage of the Garnier palace* in 1903, it went on to enjoy 47 presentations by 28 June 1953, when it was produced in a new translation by Adolphe Boschot and J.-B. Prod'homme and with fresh choreography by Albert Aveline. The original 1903 cast at the Opéra included Jeanne Lindsay as Constance and Alice Verlet making her debut at the Garnier Palace as Blondine. The male roles were filled on this occasion by Agustraello Affre* (Belmont), André Gresse* (Osmin), Léon Laffitte* (Pédrille) and M. Douaillier (Sélim). Gabrielle Ritter-Ciampi, Solange Delmas, and Mado Robin are among the sopranos who have appeared as Constance at the Opéra.

BIBLIOGRAPHY: ABI, 139-44; AEM 9, 699-839; Alberta Albertini, Mozart: la vita, le opere (Milano: fratelli Bocca, 1946), 273-78, 283-86; Paul Bertrand, "Opéra: Un Enlèvement au sérail," Le Ménestrel 83, no. 45 (11 November 1921), 439; Louis Biancolli, The Mozart Handbook (Cleveland and New York: The World Publishing Co., 1954), 203-15; Eric Blom, Mozart (London: J. M. Dent & Sons, 1935), 282-86; Adolphe Boschot, Chez les musiciens (Paris: Plon, 1922), 13-21; Brigid Brophy, Mozart the Dramatist (New York: Harcourt Brace, 1964), 223-29; John N. Burk, Mozart and His Music (New York: Random House, 1959), 128-33, 218-20; Howard Chandler, Robbins Landon, Initiation à Mozart, tans. Yassu Gauclère (Paris: Gallimard, 1959), 357-405; Leopold Conrad, Mozarts Dramaturgie der Oper (Wunzburg: Konrad Triltsch, 1943), 226-47; COOM 167-96, 341; Henri de Curzon, "Mozart et l'Enlèvement au sérail," Le Ménestrel 83, no. 45 (11 November 1921), 437-39; DDO I, 391-92; E. J. Dent, Les Opéras de Mozart (Paris: Gallimard, 1958), 97-122; idem, Mozart's Operas (London: Oxford University Press, 1947), 67-87;

René Dumesnil, Mozart présent dans ses oeuvres lyriques (Bruxelles: La Renaissance du livre, 1965), 121-35; EDS VII, 899-915; Gabriel Fauré, Opinions musicals (Paris: Rieder, 1930), 88-89; Franz E. Gehring, Mozart (Freeport, N.Y.: Books for Libraries Press, 1972), 95-96, 121; Henri Ghéon, In Search of Mozart, trans. Alexander Dru (New York: Shead & Ward, 1934), 149-57; Aloys Greither, Die sieben grossen Opern Mozarts (Heidelberg: Lambert Schneider, 1977), 45-80; Charlotte Haldane, Mozart (Westport, Conn.: Greenwood Press, 1976), 24-25, 74-76; Jean-Victor Hocquard, Mozart (Paris: Du Seuil, 1970), 70-71; idem, La pensée de Mozart (Paris: Du Seuil, 1958), 549-52; Dyneley Hussey, Wolfgang Amade Mozart (Westport, Conn.: Greenwood Press, 1971), 144-48; Otto John, Life of Mozart, trans. Pauline D. Townsend (New York: Cooper Square Publishers, 1970) II, 194-95, 209, 216-48; Alec Hyatt King, Mozart (London: Clive Bingley, 1970) contains "books in English about Mozart," 52-67; Annette Kolb, Mozart (London: Victor Gollancz, 1939), 192-98; Ernst Lert, Mozart auf dem Theater (Berlin: Schuster & Loeffler, 1921), 311-25; Michael Levey, The Life and Death of Mozart (New York: Stein and Day, 1971), 141-53; Abram Loft, "The Comic Servant in Mozart's Operas," MQ 32 (1946), 376-89; Jean Massin and Brigitte Massin, Wolfgang Amadeus Mozart (Paris: Fayard, 1970), 893-908; MCDE II, 647-661; MSRL 143-44; G. N. Nissen, Biographie W. A. Mozarts (Hildesheim: Georg Olms, 1972), Anhang, 77-85; NMO 241-61; OEN II, 3-23; OQE 173-74; Bernhard Paumgartner, Mozart, trans. Paule Pascali (Paris: Gallimard, 1951), 273-86; Robert Pitrou, La Vie de Mozart (Paris: Renouard, 1935), 129, 150-54; Albert Protz, "Die Entfuhrung aus dem Serail" von W. A. Mozart (Berlin-Lichterfelde: R. Lienau, 1958); Arthur Schurig, Mozart, ed. J.-G. Prod'homme (Paris: éditions Corrêa, 1943), 194-97; Stoullig XIX (1903), 21-25; SW 79-80; Thompson 506, 2138; WOC 67.

Erlanger, Camille (b. 25 May 1863, paris; d. 24 April 1919, paris), composer, entered the Conservatoire in Paris at age 17, and he won a Grand Prix de Rome here in 1888 for his cantata entitled Velleda. He came to the attention of the general public a few years later, when his Saint-Julien l'Hospitalier was performed in concert at the

Opéra in Paris during 1895. Later, he composed a number of works for the Opéra-Comique including Le Juif polonais (1900), which enjoyed 53 performances in the rue Favart. His Aphrodite (1906) has been billed in this same theatre on 182 occasions. Erlanger's only contribution to the repertory at the Opéra was Le Fils de l'étoile* that had its world premiere at the Garnier Palace* on 17 April 1904.

BIBLIOGRAPHY: AEM III, 1501-4; BBD 483; EDS IV, 1552-54; ELM I, 699; Grove II, 965; NEO 216; PBSW 179.

Ernest II, Auguste-Charles-Jean-Léopold-Alexandre-Edouard, duke of Saxe-Cobourg-Gotha (b. 21 June 1818, Cobourg; d. 22 August 1893, Reinhardsbrunn), composer, studied music as a child and became interested especially in composition. His works for the stage were applauded generously in Germany, and two of them enjoyed enough success to tempt translators. His Casilda was produced in a French version at the royal theatre in Brussesl in 1855, and his Sainte-Claire* had its premiere in a French translation by Gustave Oppelt* at the Paris Opéra on 27 September 1855.

BIBLIOGRAPHY: Chouquet 415; EB IX, 751-52; Fétis III, 153; Lajarte II, 218-19; Anton Ohoron, Herzog Ernst II von Sachsen-Koburg-Gotha, ein Lebensbild (Leipzig: Renger, 1894).

Erostrate was an opera in two acts and three tableaux with a score by Ernest Reyer* and a libretto by Joseph Méry* and Emilien Pacini. It had its world premiere in Baden in a German translation on 21 August 1852, and it was billed initially in France at the Opéra on 16 October 1871. It returned only 1,817 francs, 16 centimes to the box office on the occasion of its second performance at the Paris theatre on 18 October 1871, and it was dropped from the repertory immediately.

The opera begins in the apartments of the courtesan Athénaïs, whose gardens feature a temple of Diana. A chorus of Diana's priestesses is singing the praises of the chaste goddess, and Athénaïs is assuring Rhodina that she has no intention of becoming involved in the complications that love fosters. Rhodina shows her a coffer of gold and ivory filled with jewels that Erostrate has sent to her as a sign of his love for her, but Athénaïs displays no interest in it or its donor (I, 1-2). Rhodina asks her why she perfers Scopas to Erostrate, and she replies that Scopas is a sculptor and can bestow glory and immortality upon the subjects of his art, and accomplishment that is beyond the powers of Erostrate (I, 3). Scopas tells Athénaïs that his work is finished. It is a Venus for which she has served as the model, and she is so flattered by the idea of becoming immortal in his art that she proposes marriage to him (I, 4). The populace is invited into Athénaïs' gardens to see the new statue, and the people pay homage to Scopas, his work, and his model. When everybody leaves, Athénaïs retires. Erostrate enters and sees her asleep. He is about to leave, when she admits in her sleep that she is in love. She awakens, and hopeful Erostrate declares his love to her, but she insults and maltreats him until he flees (I, 5-6).

Erostrate returns to Athénaïs' apartments to lament his unrequited love, and Rhodina tells him that he will not find her mistress at home because she is with Scopas. Erostrate regrets his lack of artistic ability and admits that he possesses only his love, his wealth, and his life. A peal of thunder is heard, and Rhodina wonders which of the gods is angry. They enter the temple of Diana (II, 1-2). Scopas and Athénaïs are filled with despair because angry Daina's thunderbolt has torn the arms from his statue. He asks Athénaïs not to abandon him, and she agrees to remain with him if he will take revenge for the ruined figure of Venus by destroying the statue of Diana. He refuses, and she calls him an ungrateful wretch and a coward; she assures him that no one will ever know the name of a sculptor from Milo who leaves only a broken statue to posterity. He admits defeat and decides to return to Milo; he can only hope that one day his damaged Venus will be retrieved and restored. She ridicules his vain hopes, and he leaves (II, 3-4). Athénaïs despairs of finding a lover worthy of her interest, and Erostrate volunteers to serve her, if she will have him. He catalogues the labors and miracles he will perform for her, and she agrees to favor him if he will avenge her. He shows her the temple of Daina already in flames, and she consents to leave Ephesus with him. Scopas warns them that the populace is looking for the arsonist to punish him, but Athénaïs and Erostrate remain calm and agree to die together (II, 5).

The four principal roles of Erostrate were filled by Mlle Hisson (Athénaïs), Mme Emmy Fursch-Madier* (Rhodina), Jacques Bouhy* (Erostrate), and Bosquin* (Scopas). Agar was called in from the Comédie-Française to do Chryseïs, a priestess of Apollo. Critics who attended one of the two performances of the work at the Opéra pointed to the merit of several passages in Reyer's score: "Sur nos luths d'lonie" (I, 2) by the chorus; "Oui, nous irons à Mytilène" (I, 4) by Athénaïs to Scopas; Erostrate's solo, "Le dieu Plutus, à ma naissance" (II, 1); and "La foudre a brisé ma statue" (II, 3) by Scopas.

BIBLIOGRAPHY: AEM XI, 352-53; Gustave Bertrand, "Première Représentation d'Erostrate à l'Opéra," Le Ménestrel 37 (22 October 1871), 370-71; Guy de Charnace, Musique et musiciens (Paris: P. Lethielleux, 1874) I, 109-21; Chouquet 424-25; Henri de Curzon, Ernest Reyer; sa vie et ses oeuvres, 1828-1909 (Paris: Perrin, 1924), 86-94; DDO I, 402; Adolphe Jullien, Ernest Reyer (Paris: Henri Laurens, n.d.), 20-25, 61-63; Lajarte II, 245; Ernest Reyer, Notes de musique (Paris: Charpentier, 1875), 371-80; Georges Servières, La Musique française moderne (Paris: Havard, 1897), 223-81.

Escalais, Leónce (b. 1859, Cuxac d'Aude; d. 30 August 1940, Cuxac d'Aude), vocalist, studied in Toulouse and Paris. He made his debut at the Opéra on 12 October 1883 in Arnold of Guillaume Tell.* Audiences were charmed by his brilliant tenor voice, and he was cast as Eléazar in La Juive* before the end of the year. In 1884, he did the title-role in Robert le Diable,* and the following year he was billed as Vasco in L'Africaine,* the protagonist of Sigurd,* and Raoul in Les Huguenots.* He created Lusignan in Zaïre* on 28 May 1890, and he did Zarastra in Le Mage* during 1891, but he had a dispute with the management of the theatre at about the same time, and he left Paris for Belgium, Italy, and the United States.

When Escalais returned to France, he began to teach, but he managed to make peace with the directorate of the Garnier Palace* in 1908. He sang parts from his regular repertory after this truce, and he added only Rhadamès to his Opéra repertory in 1908. The end of his career was accordingly more competent than spectacular despite the brilliance of his voice and its impressive range. He retired from the stage shortly before World War I to pay closer attention to a singing school he had founded. His farewell appearance at the Paris Opéra took place on 2 February 1910.

BIBLIOGRAPHY: DBF XII, 1408; A. Favia-Artsay, "Golden Book of Song," Hobbies 63 (June 1958), 26; KRJ 124-25; Martin 148; PBSW 179; Ronald Seeliger, "Tenor of High C," Opera News 33 no. 22 (29 March 1969), 16; SW 26, 28, 107, 118, 130, 138, 185, 203, 227.

L'Esclave was billed as an opera in four acts and five tableaux with a score by Edmond Membrée* and a libretto by Edouard Foussier* and François Got.* Louis Mérante created its choreography. It had its premiere on 17 July 1874 at the salle Ventadour* after the fiery destruction of the opera house in the rue Le Peletier* and before the completion of the Garnier Palace.* It enjoyed a dozen consecutive performances between the date of its first production and 10 August 1874, but it was dropped from the repertory after its 15th presentation on 28 August 1874.

The opera opens in a simple room in Paulus' home, where this pope of the Russian church is reciting the biblical account of Abraham and his son Isaac to his wife and daughter to illustrate the necessity of doing God's will. He assures Prascovia that he would sacrifice Paul, if the tsar demanded it, because their ruler is the representative of God on earth. In the course of his expatiation, he adds the tsar has been obliged to revive an old law that decrees that any woman having commerce with a slave becomes a slave herself. Paula counters that God's charity extends to all men, even slaves, but her father insists that a condemned slave cannot escape the law. After this socio-theological exposition, curfew sounds, and shots ring out. Wounded Kaledji supported by Moraskeff appears at the door (I, 1). Paulus offers them hospitality, but Kaledji confesses that he is condemned; Paulus shows them a hidden door leading to a hiding place, when troops approach (I, 2). Count Vasili demands that Paulus surrender the slave Kaledji to him, and Paulus is horrified to learn that he has harbored a fugitive slave. The count orders Paulus arrested but changes his mind and decides to take Paula captive when he notices her beauty. He offers not to harm Paula, if Paulus will deliver his slave, but Kaledji surrenders voluntarily. The count pardons Paulus and Kaledji, but no one understands his sudden clemency (I, 3-4).

The second act is set near the seashore with a chorus and ballet ushering in the month of roses. Kaladji recognizes Paula from a distance, but he remains apart to ponder his life of constant solitude and flight, which he refuses to ask Paula to share (II, 1-3). She complains of being unable to forget Kaledji, who draws close enough to overhear her declaring her undying love for him. Finally, they fall into each other's arms (II, 4). Count Vasili, Constantin, and a party of hunters interrupt their tender duet. Kaledji explains the scene to the skeptical count by assuring him that he was only thanking Paula for caring for him when he was wounded. The lovers are saved at least temporarily by the beaters announcing that a wild bull is headed in their direction. Kaledji grasps an ax and runs off to intercept the dangerous prey; the count asks Paula to explain her interest in a slave (II, 5-6); she is spared answering this difficult question by Kaledji giving the foot of the slain bull to Paula. Vasili usurps the honor of presenting her with this trophy (II, 7). Left along, Kaledji is nursing his hatred for the count, when his faithful companion Moraskeff announces that he has come to lead him to freedom. Kaledji explains that his love for Paula is holding him in Russia, and Moraskeff adds that there will be an uprising of the slaves who wish him for their leader. Kaledji sets the attack for the morrow (II, 8-9).

The scene shifts to a drunken orgy in Vasili's palace. The count presents Paula to his guests as his mistress, but Constantin suggests that they gamble for her. Vasili counters that they should duel to the death for her, and Kaledji enters to answer the challenge. Vasili denounces him as a slave and declares that no one will have Paula. He draws a knife. Paulus appears in his turn to place an anathema on Vasili's head and reads a summons ordering him to appear before the tsar to answer for his crimes. The count tries to extricate himself by asserting that he is marrying

Paula on the orders of the tsar. Paula refuses to become his wife, however, and the horrified bystanders, including her father, wish to know the justification for this open defiance of the tsar's will. Paula replies that she loves a slave, and her father's dismay deepens. Paulus reminds her that her love for a slave will make her a slave, but the count points out that she is not yet married to Kaledji, who vows to rescue her before the night is done (III, 1-4).

Paula is at home and hoping to see her love once again before her death (IV, 1). Prascovia tries to comfort her, but Paulus gives her a dagger to kill herself before dishonor overtakes her. She insists upon her love for Kaledji, and he raises the dagger over her, but he is interrupted by the sound of shouting and the pealing of bells (IV, 2-3). Kaledji tells Paula and her family to flee because his army is on the move, and his men will be able to rescue them within the hour. Paulus remains, but Prascovia and Paula leave (IV, 4).

The last tableau presents burned houses and dead soldiers. Paula is searchign for the body of Kaledji. She finds him, takes a knife from his belt, and kills herself (IV, 1 bis). Count Basili enters with Paulus to claim Paula's body (IV, 2 bis).

The female roles were filled by Mlle Mauduit (Paula) and Mme Grismar (Prascovia). The part of Kaledji was sung by M. Sylva with Lassalle as Count Vasili, Gailhard as Paulus, Bataille as Moraskeff, Grisy as Constantin, and Auguez as a Russian lord. The members of the ballet included Mlles Léontine Beaugrand,* Lapy, Montaubry, Pallier, Parent, Piron, Stoïchoff, and Valain. The musical passages that aroused the most enthusiasm included the chorus singing "C'est le mois des roses" (II, 1) and the duet by Paula and Kaledji (II, 4). The third act drew applause with Vasili's romance, "Pleure aujourd'hui, demain tu souriras." The duet between Paula and her mother at the start of the last act provided one of the most touching moments in the opera. These moments and the opera's sustained musicality suggest that it might have fared better at the Opéra if it had not been offered to the public in a temporary opera house.

BIBLIOGRAPHY: *DDO I, 406; Gaston Escudier, "L'Esclave, répétition générale," AM 13 (16 July*

1874), 229-30; M. B. Jouvin, "L'Esclave," AM 13 (23 July 1874), 240-41; Lajarte II, 246-47; Arthur Pougin, "Première Représentation de l'Eslcave d'Edmond Membrée à l'Opéra-Ventadour," Le Ménestrel 40 (19 July 1874) 259-60; Wks IV, 16927.

La Esméralda was an opera in four acts with music by Louise Bertin* and a libretto by Victor Hugo.* It was rehearsed under the title of Notre-Dame de Paris and had its premiere on 14 November 1836. The librettist's poetry was effective, and the composer's music was by no means dull, but these two basic elements of opera were not coordinated here. Later, in New Orleans, Eugène Prévost set Hugo's words with great success. The work was given in its entirety on six programs at the opera house in the rue Le Peletier,* but only the picturesque first act was produced after 16 December 1836. This initial portion of the composition was given a total of 19 billings in 1837 (5), 1838 (7), and 1839 (7). It was dropped after its 25th presentation on 23 October 1839.

The scene is set before Notre-Dame Cathedral on the night of the Feast of Fools with the beggars and tramps of Paris hailing Clopin Trouillefou as their king. Claude Frollo searches out Quasimodo in the crowd and calls upon him to help kidnap La Esméraida. When the priest and the hunchback seize the beautiful gypsy girl, she cries out (I, 1-2), and the archers of the watch under the command of Phoebus rescue her and arrest Quasimodo. Phoebus falls in love with La Esméralda, and he gives her his scarf, but she runs off after he attempts to embrace her (I, 3). The setting shifts to the place de Grève, where Quasimodo is in the pillory. The growd mocks him, and only the gypsy has enough compassion to give him a *drink of water (II, 1). A second change in* scenery brings the audience to the home of Aloïse, who is preparing a marriage feast for her daughter Fleur-de-Lys and Phoebus. The bride-to-be has doubts about the latter's constancy, and she asks him why is is not wearing the scarf she made for him. He protests, but she is unconvinced, and Phoebus must confess to himself that Fleur-de-Lys' suspicions are well founded (II, 2). The banquet begins, and some guests observe a beautiful gypsy girl dancing in the square below the windows. M. de Chevreuse points out that she is "Phoebus' gypsy"; jealous and spiteful, Fleur-de Lys invites her to the festivities. La Esméralda appears and declares her love for Phoebus; she pulls his scarf from her bodice. Indignant Aloïse and her outraged guests order the girl back into the street, but Phoebus declares he will defend her against all insults because he loves her (II, 3).

The third act opens with Phoebus and his companions drinking in a cabaret. Claude Frollo enters, and Phoebus declares in a loud voice that he will see La Esméralda in an hour. Curfew sounds, and only Phoebus and Calude Frollo tarry at the table (III, 1). When Phoebus rises to leave, Claude Frollo warns him that death, not his beloved gypsy, awaits him in the night (III, 2). The action now moves to a bedroom, where the priest and a band of men are hiding. Clopin assures Claude Frollo that La Esméralda and Phoebus will be visible, and the lovers enter immediately to declare their passion for each other. Jealous, Claude Frollo stabs Phoebus and escapes. The group of men appears to accuse La Esméralda of the murder (III, 3).

La Esméralda has been thrown into prison, where she is visited now by Claude Frollo in disguise. The priest declares his love to her and establishes his true identity, but she is revulsed and denounces him as an assassin. He tries to bribe her with promises of freedom, but she asserts that she prefers the scaffold to escape with him (IV, 1). The scene shifts next to Notre-Dame, where Clopin reports to Claude Frollo that Phoebus is still alive, and the priest reveals to Clopin that La Esméralda is to be brought to Notre-Dame. Quasimodo overhears their conversation (IV, 2-3). The gypsy is brought into the square before Notre-Dame in a tumbril, and Claude Frollo moves out at the head of the religious procession as if to hear her confession. He offers to rescue her again, but she refuses. Quasimodo dashes from the cathedral and carries her into the safety of the cathedral, but Claude Frollo denies her sanctuary. The archers intervene. Phoebus arrives in time to declare his love to her, but he dies immediately from his open wound, and La Esméralda falls across his lifeless body (IV, 4).

The title role of La Esméralda was sung by Mlle Cornélie Falcon* with the male parts assigned to Adolphe Nourrit* (Phoebus), Nicolas Levasseur* (Claude Frollo), and Massol (Quasimodo). One of the more popular passages in the score was the duet by La Esméralda and Claude Frollo, "Oh! je t'adore!" (IV, 1), sung in the prison scene.

BIBLIOGRAPHY: Chouquet 399-400; DDO I, 407; HAZ 136-37; Victor Hugo, Thöâtre complet, ed. J.-J. Thierry and Josette Mélèze (Paris: La Pléïade, 1964) II, 1900-902; Lajarte II, 155; Moniteur universel 329 (21 November 1836), 2134; PBSW 217; SSBO 210-11; 228, 258.

Espana is a ballet in a single act by Jane Catulle-Mendès with music by Emmanuel Chabrier* especially arranged by Albert Wolff. The choreography was elaborated by Mlle Rosita Mauri* and Léo Staats.* R. Pinchon created the costumes. It was performed for the first time at the National Academy of Music in Paris on 3 May 1911.

The ballet opens on a village square. It is very hot, and the carnaval performers are asleep in their wagons. Young Sylvaine and Sylvain enter chasing butterflies and eating the strawberries that they have picked in the adjacent woods. Magdeleine and Henry enter in their turn, and it is obvious from their actions that the former cannot arouse her companion's interest in her (sc. 1-3).

The performers emerge from their wagons, and the musicians form a parade which the strong man, the snake charmer, and the bird tamer join. It is the feast of St. Jean, and a crowd of dancing villagers appears with Marinette and Jean-Louis, whom the mayor agrees to join in matrimony. The scene ends with a divertissement (sc. 4-6) (see eighteenth-century volume for divertissement). After a dentist-magician pretends to pull his patient's tooth, a round is danced by the company, and St. Jean's fire is prepared to invoke the saint's blessing upon the impending marriage. The shepherds begin to dance after rustic incantations by the village sorceress. The friends of the engaged couple resume their dancing; Sylvain and Magdelaine try in vain to win admissions of love from Sylvaine and Henry (sc. 7-8).

A troupe of Spanish dancers arrives in the square. They are led by Pepito and Isabella, whose seductive dances disturb Sylvaine and Henry. The latter turns his back on Magdelaine to give all his attention to Isabella, while Sylvaine borrows a Spanish shawl and begins to imitate Isabella's lascivious dancing. Pepito becomes jealous immediately and drags Isabella away from Henry, whom Magdeleine tries to charm and to cajole. Sylvain in his turn challenges Pepito for Sylvaine's favor in similar fashion. The sorceress enters to present the young peasants with a red carnation to signify that the dance of love is about to begin. The entire company falls into an ardent dance signifying the power of love in the idyllic and voluptuous surroundings in which they live. When dancing resumes, the young lovers fall to flirting with each other once again (sc. 9).

The ballet boasted a large and distinguished cast, but it failed to evoke much response from spectators, and it had to be dropped from the repertory after its sixth presentation on 3 June 1911. The preponderantly female cast was headed by Mlles Carlotta Zambelli* (Sylvaine), Aïda Boni (Magdelaine), Johnsson (Jeune sorcière), Urban (Isabella), de Moreira (Marinette), and Lozeron and Jupin (Jeunes vagabondes). The principal male roles were filled by Albert Aveline* (Sylvain), Raymond (Henry), Cléret (José), Milhet (Jean-Louis), and Even (Juan).

Chabrier's rhapsody was played in public for the first time in concert at the Château d'Eau theatre on 6 November 1883.

BIBLIOGRAPHY: CB 345; Roger Delage, "Emmanuel Chabrier in Germany," MQ *49 (1963), 75-84; René Dumesnil,* La Musique contemporaine en France *(Paris: Armand Colin, 1930) I, 17-18 and II, 73-75; Rollo Myers,* Emmanuel Chabrier and His Circle *(London: J. M. Dent & Sons, 1969), 38-47; "Opéra . . .* Espana,*"* Le Ménestrel *77 (6 May 1911), 139; J.-G. Prod'homme, "Chabrier in His Letters,"* MQ *21 (1935); SW 273; Thompson 302-3, 511; Yvonne Tienot,* Chabrier par lui-meme et par ses intimes *(Paris: Henry Lemoine et Cie, 1965), 45-48.*

Etienne, Charles-Guillaume (b. 5 January 1777, Chamouilley, Haute-Marne; d. 13 March 1845, Paris), dramatist, journalist, and member of the French Academy, was raised by his uncle and his parish priest after the death of his parents. He completed his formal studies at age 14 and was sent to Lyon at age 16 to prepare himself for a business career under the direction of another uncle. Unfortunately he was caught up in the civil strife that erupted in Lyon during 1793, and he was involved in the disorders until he had an opportunity to return home.

Etienne married at age 18, and he settled in Bar-le-Duc to practice law and to fill his new post with the government of the Meuse department. These two sources of income failed to provide him with the sufficient money, however, and he decided to move to Paris, where he found more lucrative employment with a company dealing in military supplies. He also began to write short sketches and plays for the boulevard theatres. He made his debut as a playwright at the Théâtre Favart in 1799 with Le Rêve.

Etienne was now only 22 years old, but it was not long before he had his works billed at the Ambigu-Comique, the Louvois and Montansier theatres, and the Opéra-Comique. Yet the revenue derived from this activity was trifling at this time, and he followed the advice of a friend suggesting that he improve his lot by paying more attention to selling supplies to the army. Accordingly he left for Belgium, where circumstances conspired to present him with the opportunity to stage his latest play for the staff of general Davout. The general was so delighted with Une Heure de mariage that he rewarded the playwright with a position on his staff. This good fortune was compounded shortly thereafter, when Napoleon visited the area, and General Davout entertained him with a performance of Etienne's Une Journée au camp de Bruges. The emperor approved heartily of this unexpected theatrical performance presented in an improvised theatre, and he promoted the ingenious playwright to the position of private secretary to his minister, Maret. Subsequently Etienne moved on to Genoa, Naples, Vienna, Berlin, and Warsaw, where he acted as a sort of press agent and censor for the imperial armies. He remained loyal to Napoleon, whom he welcomed back to France upon the emperor's return to Marseilles from Elba.

These official duties demanded time, energy, and even a firm judgment at times, but the dramatist continued to write, and his position close to the emperor inevitably served to promote his works. His two great successes at this time were Brueys et palaprat at the Comédie-Française in 1807 and Les Deux Gendres at this same theatre in 1810. On 1 February 1814 he made his first contribution to the Opéra by supplying the libretto for L'Oriflamme,* a work designed to arouse patriotic resistance to the invading armies of hostile nations.

After Napoleon's departure for St. Helena and definitive exile, Etienne sided with His Majesty's opposition between 1815 and 1830, and he moved over to the progovernment faction after the Revolution of 1830. yet his political position and views were always respected, and his last three operas were staged without prejudice at the Royal Academy of Music on the following dates:

Title	Composer	Date
Le Rossignol	Louis-Sébastien Le Brun	23 April 1816
Zéloïde	Louis-Sebastien Le Brun	19 January 1818
Aladin	Nicolò Isouard	6 February 1822

BIBLIOGRAPHY: Bio. univ. XIII, 146-53; Lajarte II, 82-83, 87-88, 91, 100-101, 115; LXIX VII, 1052-53.

L'Etoile is a pantomimic ballet in two acts with a score by André Wormser,* a scenario by Adolph Aderer and Camille de Roddaz, and Choreography by Joseph Hansen.* It had its world premiere at the National Academy of Music on 31 May 1897 with scenery by Carpezat and costumes by Charles Bianchini.

The ballet is set in Paris on the right bank of the Seine during 1797. A hotel in the rue Prêtres-Saint-Germain-l'Auxerrois has tables set out on the sidewalk, and delivery boys are bringing packages to the draper's shop across the street because the draper's daughter is about to marry the son of the hotel owner. Séverin is munching on an apple while he sits on the steps of Bobèche's open-air theatre, and the residents of the quarter are filled with anticipation on account of the coming wedding celebration. Bobèche reminds Séverin that he has work to do. Séverin picks up a broom, and Bobèche practises a few dance steps. Bobèche leaves, and Séverin lays aside his broom. Zénaïde Bréju notices that Séverin is alone, and she calls to him. He fails to hear her; she kicks him and runs away, but he continues to ignore her until she emerges from her hiding place. He rushes at her suddenly, but she runs away. They stop their flirting long enough to discuss marriage. Séverin suggests that they could support themselves if he played his bagpipes and she danced (I, 1-2), but Mme Bréju interrupts their dreams of a happy life together (I, 3).

The guests begin to arrive for the wedding, and Mme Bréju observes to Mme Chamoiseau that it must be a glorious advantage to have a daughter who is a star at the Opéra. The wedding party forms and leaves for the city hall. The day progresses, and the crowd becomes denser in the square and near Pont-Neuf. Léocadie and Vestris arrive finally to attend the wedding party, but they find that the bride and groom have not yet returned. The two dancers from the Opéra decide to wait at the Hôtel de la Seine (I, 4-5). Bobèche returns and sees the crowd. He decides to profit by the occasion, and he mounts the boards to begin a dance with his troupe. Léocadie and Vestris join him in an impromptu divertissement that returns a shower of sous (I, 6) (see eighteenth-century volume for divertissement). The wedding party appears at this propitious moment, and a quadrille is organized, but Léocadie refuses to join in with the dancers. Zénaïde also remains in a corner because Séverin has to stand watch at Bobèche's theatre. Finally, impatient Zénaïde calls to Séverin. He seizes his bagpipes, and she dances the bourrée solo. Vestris notices her and asks her whether she can execute jetés battus. She has not trouble with the step, and he responds by dancing a gavotte. She follows his moves, and he is so impressed that he invites her to the Opéra. Zénaïde and her mother jump with joy, but furious Léocadie leaves (I, 4).

Mme Chamoiseau decides that she will also upbraid Vestris, and jealous Séverin warns the dancer to leave Zénaïde alone. Vestris is annoyed by these additional assaults, but a platoon of soldiers enters before he can say a word. The sergeant declares that all men 18 to 19 years of age must report for military service, and Vestris points to Séverin. The sergeant leads him away despite his protests (I, 9).

The scene shifts to the Opéra, where the candidates for a position with the corps de ballet are being examined in the presence of their families and close friends. Léocadie is on the jury, and she snubs Vestris when he enters. A letter is delivered to Mme Bréju; it is from Séverin. Mme Bréju cannot read, and she asks

Vestris to read it to her. When the dancer tells her that the missive is from her daughter's sweetheart, she loses her temper and throws the letter away. Léocadie retrieves it and pens an answer to it. She instructs Bobèche to deliver the answer to Séverin, who is in Paris (II, 1). The jury convenes; Zénaïde performs and is admitted to the corps de ballet with the rank of étoile. Séverin rushes in just as Vertris is congratulating Zénaïde by kissing her hand. He congratulates her in his turn, but he adds that he is no longer worthy of her because he is only a simple soldier. He leaves. Zénaïde discards her ballet belt and runs after him (II, 2-3). Mme Bréju is puzzled and exasperated; Vestris is upset. No one knows exactly what to do, but Zénaïde reappears to return her costume and slippers to Vestris. She explains that henceforth she will dance only with Séverin. Mme Bréju and Mme Chamoiseau are reconciled, and Zénaïde's friends applaud her decision. The ballet closes with the assembly joining Zénaïde and Séverin in the bourrée (II, 4).

The ballet was a signal success, and it enjoyed 78 performances before it was dropped from the repertory. Mlle Rosita Mauri* was cast in the part of Zénaïde at the initial performance of the work in 1897, when the other female roles were filled by Mlles Invernizzi (Mme Chamoiseau), Torri (Mme Bréju), Robin (Léocadie), and de Mérode (the bride). The male parts were created by Hansen (Vestris), Ladam (Séverin), de Soria (Bobèche), Ajas (the sergeant), and Régnier (the groom).

BIBLIOGRAPHY: KCOB 848-52; Arthur Pougin, "Première Représentation de <u>L'Étoile</u> . . . à l'Opéra," <u>Le Ménestrel</u> 63 (6 June 1897), 178-79; Stoullig XXIII (1897), 16-20, 41; SW 273.

L'Etoile de Messine was a pantomime ballet in two acts and six tableaux with music by Count Nicolas Gabrielli* and a libretto by Paul Foucher.* Borri created its choreography for Mme Amalia Ferraris,* and its sets were done by Despléchin, Thierry, Cambon, and Martin. It had its premiere at the Imperial Academy of Music on 20 November 1861, and its Italian-style score failed to inspire more than a moderate measure of interest in Paris. It was given on 34 dates in 1861-63, but it was withdrawn after its 14 January 1863 presentation, because Mme Ferraris left the Opéra after the benefit performance for her there on 21 March 1863, and no suitable replacement for her was found in time to save Count Gabrielli's composition from oblivion.

The ballet takes place during the time of the Spanish rule in Sicily, and the first tableau represents a casino in Messina, where a mascarade ball is in full swing. The marquis Don Flaminio is an old fool flirting with any lady half his age; Don Raphaël de Lemos is oblivious to everything around him except a picture in a locket at which he gazes steadily. A masked dancer approaches Don Raphaël with an invitation to dance with her, and she asks him the identity of the lady in the locket. He refuses to comply with her request, and she tears off her mask to reveal herself to be his fiancee, Countess Aldini. A masked gentleman notices her dismay and leads her away. At this moment, it is announced that the famous Gazella will dance for the guests. Don Raphaël notices the similarity between the ballerina and his portrait. He and the performer fall in love at first sight, but Don Flaminio reminds his friend of his duty to the countess. Gianni separates his sister from Don Raphaël by performing a pas de deux with her. The countess' escort unmasks. He is Don Raphaël's father, who disapporves his son's love for a dancer and informs him that his marriage contract with Countess Aldini is to be signed shortly.

The second tableau presents a hostelry where the traveling troupe is staying, and where Gianni reveals his hopes to marry. His sister Gazella enters, and all the performers except her retire. Don Raphaël finds her wondering whether or not he loves her, and he suggests that they elope. She refuses to abandon her brother, but she is convinced of his sincerity. A knock at the door puts Don Raphaël to flight, however, and Don Flaminio appears. He offers the dancer jewels and money, but she rejects them. Their noisy encounter arouses the performers. Don Flaminio explains that he wishes to hire the company to perform at the marriage celebration of Don Raphaël, son of the governor of Messina, and the niece of the viceroy of the Two Sicilies. The money offered to Gazella, he adds, was to pay for a sample of the dancing she would offer on this occasion. Jacopo cannot dispute this explanation, and he orders Gazella and Gianni to perform for him.

The third tableau depicts a beach with a hotel run by Rosetta, who is in love with the fisherman Momolo. The lovers and the villagers join in a dance to celebrate Momolo's return from a dangerous mission at sea, and Don Raphaël's marriage is announced with the traveling players sharing in these festivities because no local celebration is complete without "the star of Messina": Gazella. Gianni tells her that they will leave Sicily after being paid on the morrow because he will have enough money to take a wife. Also, he suspects her futile love for Don Raphaël. The latter signals to Gazella and suggests elopement again. She agrees. He has arranged for a boatman to take her to a distant island, where he will await her; she will recognize her guide because he will have a locket containing her portrait. Don Flaminio overhears these arrangements and buys the locket from Momolo as well as persuading the latter to part with his cloak and hat. He takes his place in Momolo's craft, but Gianni tears off Don Flaminio's disguise. The don receives a thrashing, but Gianni cannot support the conviction that Gazella was ready to abandon her friends for Don Flaminio's gold. He is about to punish her, but the villagers stop him. A total reconciliation is effected, and Gazella executes a lively tarantella.

The fourth tableau, designated as the first tableau of the second act, is designed to permit the presentation of a play in the palace of the viceroy. The guests are assembled for the wedding, but Don Raphaël has not yet returned from his island. Eager for revenge, Don Flaminio explains to the countess how she has been betrayed by her fiance. He shows her the portrait to prove his story, but their conversation is interrupted by the troupe presenting a "fantastic entertainment" in which Urgana, queen of the fairies, has fallen in love with Benvolio, a mere mortal. She sends beautiful Fiamma to tell him of the honor that has befallen him, but she has ordered her messenger to wear a veil lest Benvolio fall in love with her. Fiamma returns to the queen and takes off her veil; the countess recognizes the likeness of Don Raphaël's portrait in her features. No one notices her violent reaction, and the presentation continues. Benvolio will not come to Urgana, and the queen condemns Fiamma for treachery, but her subjects revolt because of her cruelty. They select Fiamma as their queen. She summons Benvolio and renounces her throne so that their love may not be jeopardized by her royal status. Don Raphaël enters when Gazella-Fiamma is describing her joy, and he kisses the countess' hand. Gazella realizes that she has deluded herself and heaps recriminations upon her former lover. The players disperse, and Gazella is overcome.

The next tableau returns to the players' hostelry. Don Flaminio enters with the countess and an order from the viceroy that the countess is to be hidden in the inn. Gianni enters with Gazella. Now aware of her love for Don Raphaël, Gianni cannot restrain his jealousy and declares himself to be in love with Gazella. She is horrified, but Gianni reveals that he is not her brother. The troupe found her as an infant. Raphaël appears, and Gianni's rage has no bounds. They fight, and the don is disarmed. The countess steps from behind the curtain and reminds Don Raphaël that his ring is on her finger. Gazella declares that she has no interest in Don Raphaël, and the duke de Lemos leads his son and the countess back to the palace.

The last tableau represents the port of Messina on the last day of the carnaval. It is also the appointed date of the marriage of the countess and Don Raphaël. Citizens are performing dances of the various regions of Italy. Raphaël is downcast, but the countess is filled with joy. The bride and groom enter the church, and Gazella is in tears. She refuses to dance until Don Flaminio aggravates her to the point where she feels obliged to prove that her lover is no longer in her thoughts. The people are held spellbound by her frenzied dancing until the tolling bell announces the end of the marriage ceremony. The dancer's heart breaks, and she falls dead into Gianni's arms. Don Raphaël approaches her, but Gianni throws his cloak over her, and the sound of a cannon signals the departure of the ship on which Gazella and her comrades were to sail.

Gazella was danced by Mme Amalia Ferraris* with the other female roles filled by Mme Louise Marquet* (Countess Aldini), Mme Aline (Jacinta), and Mme Morando (Rosetta). Louis Mérante* and Francisque Berthier* did Gianni and Jacopo, respectively, and the Spanish dons were represented by Jean Coralli* (Don Flaminio) and Alfred Chapuy* (Don Raphaël) with Lenfant as the latter's father, the duke de Lemos. The three principal parts in the divertissement entitled The Revolt of The Fairies were assigned to Mme Ferraris (Fiamma), Mlle Fanny Génat (Uragana), and Mérante (Benvolio) (see eighteenth-century volume for divertissement).

BIBLIOGRAPHY: AEM IV, 1213-14; CB 483; Chouquet 420; Léon Escudier, "L'Etoile de Messine," AM 1 (21 November 1861), 404; Ivor Guest, The Ballet of the Second Empire (Middletown, Conn.: Wesleyan University Press, 1974), 171-76, 180, 259; Lajarte II, 232; A. Lomon, "Théâtre Impérial de l'òpéra: L'Etoile de Messine," FM 25 (24 November 1861), 369-71; Moniteur universel 323 (24 November 1861), 1657-58.

L'Etoile de Seville was an opera in four acts that had its world premiere at the Royal Academy of Music on 17 December 1845. Hippolyte Lucas* wrote its libretto based upon Lope de Vega's play, and Michael Balfe* composed its score. Its choreography was created by Jean Coralli,* and the sets were provided by Philastre, Cambon, Diéterle, Despléchin, and Séchan.

The opera begins in the public square of Seville, which has been decorated to welcome the king. Don Bustos has forbidden his daughter to attend the celebration because he suspects that the monarch plans to seduce his daughter, and he is also opposed to welcoming a ruler who has won his crown by dethroning his father (I, 1-2). On the other hand, Don Sanche makes it quite clear that he honors the king for his rank and valor. He asks for Estrella's hand in marriage, and Don Bustos consents to this union, although he denies Don Sanche's request that the king preside at the wedding ceremony (I, 3). The king enters in triumph and greets Don Sanche as the support of his realm. A ballet is performed for his entertainment, and he asks Arias whether he has located the beauty from Seville whom he saw in Burgos. Aris informs him that she is known as the Star of Seville. He adds that her father suspects His Majesty's intentions and has ordered his daughter to remain hidden from public view. The angry king instructs his confidant to bribe his way to the girl so that he may visit her at midnight. The court leaves to attend a tournament, and the king declares his intention of fighting for Estrella. Don Bustos charges Don Sanche to represent his daughter, however, and the slave Zaïda gives him her mistress' scarf (I, 4).

The second act shifts to Estrella's bedroom, where her fiance tells her that her father has given his permission for them to marry on the morrow. She is overjoyed, but she tells him of her ominous dream wherein she sees her father mortally wounded. He dispels her fears (II, 1-2). The scene then moves to Don Bustos' garden, where Zaïda is telling her master that she saw a page bribe Diego to open the door to the garden at midnight. Don Bustos and the slave hide when they hear a signal. The king and Don Arias enter and reward Diego for his treachery, but Don Bustos stabs his disloyal servant when he approaches his hiding place (II, 1-2 bis). Don Bustos questions the intruders and recognizes the king's voice; he resolves to seize this opportunity to punish him. Don Arias tries to prevent the imminent duel by revealing the king's identity, but Don Bustos pretends to reject this warning as a lie invented to guarantee the intruders' escape. He insults the king by striking him with the flat of his sword, but Don Arias manages to lead the raging king from the garden (II, 3).

The third act opens with a ballet and a chorus inquiring into the reason for the king's obvious anger (III, 1). The king swears to have revenge for the insult that he has received (III, 2), and he confides to Don Sanche that he must remain silent about an affront that he has suffered. Don Sanche reminds him that he cannot tolerate dishonor for any reason, and he concurs. He writes a note in which he challenges Don Bustos to secret but mortal combat. Arias leaves to deliver the missive (III, 3). The setting changes to the banks of the Guadalquivir, where Don Bustos is fleeing from Seville lest he be murdered by royal henchmen. He gives a sealed letter to Don Gomez, who is to deliver it to the king only in an extreme emergency, and he is about to climb aboard Pedro's boat (III, 1 bis), when Arias delivers the king's note. Don Bustos accepts the challenge, but Don Sanche has taken the king's place. It is only after Don Busto has been wounded mortally that the duelists recognize each other (III, 2 bis). Arias flees, and Estrella finds her father.

She is crushed by grief and demands to know the identity of the murderer. Pedro informs her that he followed the assassins until they disappeared into the royal palace. She swears to avenge her father's death (III, 3-4 bis).

The final act transpires in a room of the royal palace overlooking a precipice. Don Sanche is torn by despair because he knows that he has slain the father of Estrella, and the king reproaches him for insisting upon fighting in his place. Estrella arrives at the palace to seek justice, and the king hides his champion (IV, 1). Estrella confronts the king and demands that he deliver the assassin. The king tries to calm her, but Don Sanche comes forward to admit his guilt. Estrella cannot believe that it is her fiance who has killed her father, and she arrives at the conclusion that he must have been ordered to murder him. She points an accusing finger at the king, but her sweetheart insists that he alone was responsible for the sorry deed. The king recalls an ancient law allowing members of an injured family to administer the punishment in cases involving honor, and he tells Estrella that Don Sanche is her prisoner. She falls speechless into a chair, and the king orders the lovers left alone with each other (IV, 2). Estrella tells Don Sanche that she is convinced of his innocence, but he begs her to take his life with the sword that killed her father. She suggests that they die together to find in death the happiness they cannot share in life (IV, 3). The king enters to prevent their fatal leap from the window because he has read Don Bustos' secret letter revealing that Estrella is the legitimate daughter of king Alphonse. The letter also forgives the king for dethroning his father, if he does not harm Estrella because she is a possible heir to the throne. The king admits his past wrongdoing and promises to mend his ways. He gives his blessing to the marriage of his half-sister and Don Sanche (IV, 4).

The opera was only moderately successful and had to be withdrawn from the repertory after 15 performances. Its score was not extraordinary, perhaps because it was written in only two months. Yet two passages in the music elicited applause: Zaïda's Moorish song at the beginning of the second act and a quartet in this same act. In general, however, critics felt that the performers deserved more praise than the work itself. Mme Rosine Stolz* made an especially good impression as Dona Estrella, and no one complained of Mlle Maria Nau's* portrayal of Zaïda. The male parts were filled by MM. Paul Baroilhet* (the king), Italo Gardoni* (Don Sanche), Brémont (Don Bustos), Menghis (Don Arias), F. Prévost (Gomez), Paulin (Pedro).

BIBLIOGRAPHY: AEM I, 1102-03; Chouquet 407; DDO 412; EDS I, 1311-12; Lajarte II, 179-80.

L'Etranger was billed as a "musical action" with a libretto and score by Vincent d'Indy,* when it was given its world premiere at the Théâtre Royal de la Monnaie on 7 January 1903 with Mme Claire Friche (Vita) and Henri Albers* (the stranger) in the leading roles. It was brought to the Garnier Palace* for its first presentation in Paris on 1 December 1903 in a production by M. Lapissida. Its scenery was created on this occasion by Marcel Jambon and Bailly, and Charles Bianchini designed its costumes.

The opera takes place near the ocean and opens with a group of fishermen returning home with nets and oars over their shoulders. Disaster threatens their settlement because no fish have been caught for a fortnight. One man is lucky, however, and the villagers begin to think that he is a sorcerer because he is a stranger and has been heard speaking to the sea. Vita admits that she speaks with the stranger because he has interesting tales to tell. She is in love with the customs officer, André, however, and she tells her companions that she and he are planning to wed in a few days. An old man complains that he has no money to feed his family, and the stranger enters to give him his catch. Vita witnesses this act of charity (I, 1), and she reveals to the stranger that she can no longer speak with the sea since his arrival in the village. She observes that she has the feeling of having seen him years previously, and he replies that her frank and innocent ways have persuaded him to settle in the village, although her companions dislike him and suspect him of sorcery. Yet he assures her that she will soon forget him because everybody is always happy to see him move on to another village. She assures him that her dream is to sail the seven seas with him, and he confesses that he loves her, although he insists that she should marry youthful André (I, 2).

André explains his tardy arrival to Vita. He has had to arrest a fisherman for smuggling. The prisoner begs André to release him because he has a family to feed, and the stranger supports his plea. André ignores their concern, and Vita is disappointed over his indifference to the fate of the wretched fisherman and his family (I, 3).

It is Sunday morning, and the weather threatens. The young girls are leaving church and discussing why Vita has asked the priest not to announce the bans of her imminent marriage. Vita explains to her angry mother that it was she who suspended the announcement of the bans. Her mother leaves her alone to consider her folly.

The stranger enters and explains that he is leaving the village. Vita insists that he reveal his identity to her, but he replies that he has no identity. He walks and sails forever; he dreams of love and happiness; his message to the world is charity. Vita begs him not to leave her, but he explains that youth no longer has a place in his life. He produces an enchanted emerald and explains that he has saved many vessels with its powers. He notes that this gem is useless to him now, and he admits that he creates hatred and suspicion wherever he goes. He must leave her, therefore, because he loves her. Vita begs him to remain with her, but he departs after giving her his emerald and proclaiming his love to her once more (II, 1-2).

Vita throws the emerald into the sea, and the fishermen enter complaining of the storm. They pray for Jean-Marie's safety because he has not yet returned to port after spending the night on the ocean. André cautions Vita against the rising tide, and he asks her why she canceled the announcement of their bans. She answers that she loves only the sea, and he leaves her. The storm increases in fury, and a ship appears driven before the wind. The stranger appears and orders the surfboat prepared. The crowd warns him that rescue efforts will prove vain, and only Vita enters the lifeboat with him. They embrace and strike out for the foundering vessel. A wave engulfs them, and a sudden calm prevails. An old sailor intones the <u>De Profundis</u>, and he is answered by the crowd of onlookers, who no longer see Vita and the stranger (II, 3).

L'Etranger is an unusually gloomy and excessively symbolic piece, but it enjoyed a reasonable success at the Opéra. It was billed at the Garnier Palace on 39 occasions, and it remained in the repertory from 1 December 1903 until 3 March 1952 with revivals in 1934, 1944, 1951. The important female roles were created at the Opéra by Lucienne Bréval* (Vita) and Mme Goulancourt (Vita's mother). The male members of the cast included Jean-François Delmas* (the stranger), Louis Dufranne (André), and Henri Stamler (the smuggler).

It has been suggested that L'Etranger is a symbolic representation of the life and works of César Franck,* d'Indy's teacher, and it will be recalled that d'Indy has written a biography of Franck published by Alcan.

BIBLIOGRAPHY: Michel D. Calvocoressi, Vincent d'Indy "L'Etranger": Le poème, analyse thématique de la partition (Paris: Editions du courrier musical, 1903); Joseph Canteloube, Vincent d'Indy (Paris: Henri Laurens, 1951), 85-88; André Coeuroy, La Musique française moderne (Paris: Delagrave, 1922), 77-82; Etienne Destranges, "L'Etranger" de M. Vincent d'Indy: Etude thématique et analytique (Paris: Fischbacher, 1895); René Dumesnil, La Musique contemporaine en France (Paris: Armand Colin, 1930) I, 23-27 and II, 95-103; Gabriel Fauré, Opinions musicales (Paris: Rieder, 1910), 55-60; Edward Burlingame Hill, Modern French Music (Westport, Conn.: Greenwood Press, 1970), 132-33, 387-88; Paul Landormy, La Musique française de Franck à Debussy (Paris: Gallimard, 1943), 84; MSRL 108; PBSW 217; Romain Rolland, Musicians of Today, trans. Mary Blaiklock (Freeport, N.Y.: Books for Libraries Press, 1969), 125-33; idem, "L'Etranger de Vincent d'Indy," RMI II (1904), 129-39; Gustave Samazeuilh, Musiciens de mon temps (Paris: Marcel Daubin, 1947), 67-75; idem "Le Théâtre lyrique de Vincent d'Indy," RM 18, no. 176 (August-September 1937), 129-39; SSBO 335; Stoullig XIX (1903), 21-25; R. A. Streatfeild, The Opera, ed. Edward J. Dent (Westport, Conn.: Greenwood Press, 1971), 256, 259-60; SW 81-82; Léon Vallas, Vincent d'Indy (Paris: Albin Michel, 1950) II, 308-26; idem, "La Mélodie de Vincent d'Indy," RM 21 (1946), 231-40.

Eucharis was billed as a pantomime ballet with choreography by Jean Coralli* and music by Ernest

Deldevez.* Its sets were created by Pierre Cicéri,* Séchan, Diéterle, Despléchins. It was danced for the first time at the Royal Academy of Music on 7 August 1844, but the shortcomings in its libretto by Léon Pillet* detracted too seriously from a well-done score, which did draw applause, and the work had to be dropped permanently from the repertory on 23 September 1844 after its sixth staging.

The ballet opens with disconsolate Calypso depressed over the departure of Ulysse from her island and swearing to slay any men appearing on her beaches. She has scarcely directed her nymphs to comply with this decision when a storm erupts, and two shipwrecked strangers swim ashore. The nymphs surround them, but the sorry plight of Télémaque and Mentor move Eucharis to compassion, and she grants the young man's request to spare his aged tutor. She includes the youth in her act of clemency because he reminds her of Ulysse (I, 1-2). Vénus is angry with Ulysse, and she decides to punish him by detaining his son Télémaque on Calypso's island; she directs L'Amour to make Calypso fall in love with him, and L'Amour transforms himslef into a sailor to execute his mother's order. The nymphs are preparing a festive celebration, when they are interrupted by the groans of a shipwrecked sailor. Eucharis is touched by his fate and Calypso yields to Télémaque's entreaty to spare him. The festivities resume, and L'Amour drops a love potion in Télémaque's wine. The latter starts to fall in love with Eucharis, and Calypso grows jealous of his sudden interest in her companion. Mentor tries to rescue his ward from this new danger by advising Calypso to hasten Télémaque's departure; she agrees and summons her dryads, hamadryads, and fauns to build a ship. The sailor realizes that his plans are being thwarted, and he asks Calypso for permission to teach her nymphs a new dance. She agrees; the nymphs begin to dance; the workers drop their tools to dance with them. L'Amour renews Calypso's interest in Télémaque, and she orders her retinue to burn the vessel. Mentor realizes that his plans have proven futile, and Télémaque is uncertain of what he should do, but the sailor smiles triumphantly (I, 3-4).

Eucharis has brought Télémaque to a grotto where Mentor shows him the names of Calypso and his father carved into the wall. The young man is determined not to delay on the island, but l'Amour prompts Eucharis to weaken his determination. Eucharis leads Mentor away to his quarters in the grotto, and l'Amour describes to Télémaque the advantages of remaining on the island because Eucharis loves him. Eucharis confirms the sailor's allegations, and Calypso enters crazed with love for Ulysse and believing that her lover is present. Télémaque and Eucharis try to help her, but her jealousy prompts her to attack Eucharis. She orders Eucharis' arrest and leaves with her frightened followers. Télémaque is about to help Eucharis, but angry Mentor casts a spell over him, and he falls asleep (II, 1).

In Télémaque's dream Pénélope's suitors are pressing her to choose a husband because Ulysse is still absent. She agrees to marry the man who can bend Ulysse's bow. Several pretenders for her hand try unsuccessfully to shoot an arrow, and their failure prompts them to declare the trial a fraud. Ulysse appears disguised as a begger and bends the bow with ease. Euryclée recognizes Ulysse by a scar on his leg, and Pénélope is overjoyed to be reunited with her husband. The thwarted suitors join forces to attack him, and Télémaque awakens with a start to behold a new suit of armor by his side. He seizes it and leaves to help his father. He is seeking a way to escape from the island when l'Amour enters to show him Eucharis in chains and exposed to the rapacity of vultures and sea monsters. He cannot understand this pitiful sight, but only Calypso can free the prisoner from her bonds. Télémaque pleads with the goddess to release her captive, and Calypso decides to have her vengeance by liberating Eucharis and bestowing immortality upon Télémaque. The latter finds himself once again unable to resist Eucharis' charms, and the sailor helps him to remove his armor, while the nymphs begin to dance. Mentor denounces Télémaque as a coward and swims out to an approaching ship so that he can sail back to Greece to help Ulysse. Inspired, Télémaque is moved to follow him. They arrive home in time to repulse Ulysse's attackers, and Mentor sets aside his human form to return to heaven as Minerva (II, 2).

The male parts in the ballet were danced by Petipa (Télémaque) and Elie (Mentor) with the four principal female roles filled by Mlles Leroux (Calypso), A. Dumilâtre (Eucharis), D. Marquet

(Vénus), Maria (L'Amour, the sailor). The three Graces were done by Mlles Wiétof, Pierson, J. Dabas. The fauns were represented by Mabille and Hoguet Vestris, and the choreographer cast himself as a satyr. The figures in the dream were created by Quériau (Ulysse), Lucien Petit (Eumée), Mlle Delacquit (Euriclée), Mlle Aline Dorsay (Pénélope).

BIBLIOGRAPHY: AEM III, 125-26; CB 113; Chouquet 405-6; Lajarte II, 176; Charles Malherbe, Notice sur Ernest Deldevez (Paris: Paul Dupont, 1899, 3-12; RBP 235-38.

Euryante is an opera in three acts with music by Carl Maria von Weber* that has had considerable success except in the French version by Castil-Blaze. The Paris public doomed it to failure right from the start by showing no interest in it, and it enjoyed only three performances after its premiere at the Opéra on 6 April 1831. Its fourth and last presentation took place on 25 April 1831, when it and Flore et Zéphire* combined managed to bring only 1,032 francs into the coffers of the company. Part of this failure must be attributed to Castil-Blaze, who tried to reduce Helmine von Chézy's libretto for Weber into a simple tale of innocence and virtue triumphant. He omitted Edelmar's cousin and her suicide with a poisonous ring, he ignored the episode of the snake at the start of the third act, and he made no effort to preserve the basic theme that Emma cannot find rest even in death until innocent tears have been shed upon the ring that caused her death. Also, the confused state of the last act in the 1931 edition of Castil-Blaze's translation suggests that he might not have finished or might not have understood his task from the beginning.

The opera opens in the year 1110 at Prémery, where Louis VII and the French leaders are celebrating peace with England. The king announces that a conspiracy against the crown has been discovered, and the Amaury is in prison, although his partners in this act of treason have not yet been identified. Adhémar and Lysiart seem relieved for an instant, but they are alarmed to learn that Amaury's daughter and Euryante are coming to Prémery. Louis congratulates Adhémar upon his fortunate love for Euryante, and the count sings a romance in her honor. Lysiart asserts to Adhémar that he can charm Euryante away from him, but Adhémar wagers his wealth and life upon her constancy. Lysiart and Adhémar deposit their rings with Louis to seal their bet (I, 1-2). Euryante announces her arrival with a cavatina, and Eglantine regrets her father's arrest while assuring Euryante that he will not name the other members of the conspiracy against a new crusade to the Holy Land. Euryante falls into the trap by expressing her gratitude because her beloved Adhémar is one of the plotters (I, 3-4). Alone, Eglantine reveals her unrequited love for Adhémar and rejoices to know that he is a member of her father's conspiracy because she can now take revenge upon her "odious rival" (I, 5). Her wrath is aggravated by Euryante being selected as queen of the coming tournament. Lysiart begins to court Euryante immediately, but she rejects him in anger (I, 6-7).

Eglantine suggests to Lysiart that they form a conspiracy to destroy Adhémar (II, 1-2). Euryante goes to bed, and Eglantine instructs Lysiart to steal Adhémar's ring from her. He enters her bedroom, where he is able to read a letter she has received from Adhémar, to steal her ring, and to observe the imprint of a violet upon her breast (II, 3-5). Euryante and Adhémar swear to be constant to each other the following morning, but Lysiart assures the king and his attendants that he has won the bet. Euryante is puzzled; Adhémar is furious. Lysiart produces the ring and confides to Adhémar that Euryante bears the imprint of a violet upon her body. Adhémar accuses Euryante of betraying him. She protests, but no one believes her, and Lysiart prepares to collect on the wager (II, 6-10).

Adhémar forgives Euryante but is determined to leave her (III, 1-2), and Lysiart gives orders to his four soldiers before meeting Euryante, now resigned to her fate (III, 1-5). Lysiart suffers pangs of conscience, however, and he regrets entering upon the plot (III, 6). The king has strayed from his hunting party, but he reappears with Euryante. He assures her that he has forgiven Amaury and Adhémar, because he has decided against the wisdom of mounting another crusade. She is grateful, but she reminds the king that Adhémar still believes that she has been unfaithful to him. He declares her innocent of all charges brought against her, and Lysiart continues to protest his love for her, but she rejects him in anger. Eglantine is next to repent her evil ways, and she announces that Lysiart has tried to have her killed. She adds that Adhémar rescued her. Lysiart is arrested as an imposter and liar; the king forgives Eglantine; Euryante and Adhémar are reconciled (III, 7-10).

The female roles were filled by Mme Damoueau (Euryante de Savoie), Mme Louise Debadie* (Eglantine), Mlle Jawureck (Berthe). Prévost was cast as Louis VII with Adolphe Nourrit* as Adhémar and Henri Dabadie* as Lysiart. The sets were created by Pierre Cicéri,* and Solomé was in charge of production.

BIBLIOGRAPHY: AEM 14, 286-323; Sir Julius Benedict, Weber (London: Sampsom Low, Marston and Co., 1899), 78-85, 109, 168; Karel Vladmir Burian, Carl Maria von Weber (Praha-Bratislava: 1970), 226-44; Henry Blaze de Bury, Musiciens contemporains (Paris: Michel Lévy frères, 1856), 62-64, 68; Chouquet 395; A. Coeuroy, Weber (Paris: Félix Alcan, 1925), 153-68; idem, "Le Problème d'Euryanthe," Le Correspondant, 25 October 1923; DDO I, 415; EDS IX, 1861-67; Carl Friedrich Glasenapp, Wagner-Encyklopädie (Hildesheim-New York: Georg Olms Verlag, 1977), 267-72; HBM 62-64; Martin Hürlimann, Carl Maria von Weber in seinen Schriften und in zeitgenössischen Dokumenten (Zürich: Conzett & Huber, 1973), 97-102, 194-96; JB 117-18; Adolphe Jullien, Weber à Paris en 1826 (Paris: A. Detaille, 1877), 15-16; Julius Kapp, Carl Maria von Weber (Berlin: Max Hesses Verlag, 1944), 190-93, 200-204, 212-14, 295-304; KCOB 157-60; Lajarte II, 137-38; MCDE 1152, 1157-58; Moniteur universel 98 (8 April 1831), 756; MPPA 170-71; J.-G. Prod'homme, "The Works of Weber in France, 1824-1926," MQ 14 (1928), 366-86; PBSW 48-51, 217; Ernest Reyer, Quarante ans de musique (Paris: Calmann-Lévy, n.d.), 215-29; William Saunders, Weber (New York: Da Capo Press, 1970), 137-43, 147-55, 205-9; Lucy Stebbins and Richard Stebbins, Enchanted Wanderer; the Life of Carl Maria von Weber (New York: G. P. Putnam's sons, 1940), 222-25, 234-35; Thompson 315, 2027, 2140; Baron Max Maria von Weber, Carl Maria von Weber, trans. J. Palgrave Simpson (New York: Haskell House, 1968) II, 243-56, 300-301, 331-41, 349-50; SSBO 145-47; Wks III, 9019.

F

Fabbri, Flora (b. ?, Florence; d. ?), ballerina, made her debut at the Fenice theatre in Venice and danced in Rome and Bologna before coming to Paris. Her decision to leave Italy was prompted by her marriage to the French choreographer Louis Bertin* in 1842, and she was accepted into the corps de ballet of the Opéra in 1845. She remained with the company until 1851, and she managed to establish herself as a leading ballerina at the Opéra in this era of Mlles Francesca Cerrito,* Caronne Grisi,* and Adeline Plunkett.*

In 1847, la Fabbri performed as one of the principal dancers in the premiere of Giuseppe Verdi's Jérusalem* on 26 November 1847, and, in June 1848, she appeared in the second act of La Sylphide.* She was then billed for the title-role of Paquita,* which had had its premiere on 1 April 1846. Finally, she was cast for the part of La Gloire, the central character of Les Nations,* a sort of scenic cantata that Théodore de Banville* and Adolphe Adam* concocted in five days to welcome the Lord Mayor of London to Paris on 6 August 1851.

After her departure from the Opéra, Flora Fabbi was seen on the stage of the Porte Saint-Martin Theatre, where she danced in Idalia, ou la fleur inconnue by her husband and Cazzoletti on 30 January 1855.

BIBLIOGRAPHY: Chouquet 411-12; CODB 187; Ivor Guest, The Ballet of the Second Empire (Middletown, Conn.: Wesleyan University Press, 1974), 39, 57, 255, 260, 265.

Fabert, Henri (b. 19 January 1897, Drôme; d. 22 February 1941, Marseilles), vocalist, studied law at Marseilles before he moved to Paris, where he decided to pursue a career in the theatre. He appeared with a few troupes including the Monte Carlo Company before he made his debut at the Opéra on 21 May 1909 in Mime of **Siegfried.*** He went on to specialize in Wagnerian roles at this point and sang Loge in L'Or du Rhin* in 1919, and David and Beckmesser of Les Maîtres Chanteurs* in 1912 and 1924, respectively. He did Chouisky of Boris Godounov* in 1922 and Robin of Le Fifre enchanté* in 1927 with the Opéra personnel at a gala in the Hôtel Claridge in Paris.

The striking feature of Fabert's career in retrospect is the number of roles he created at the Opéra between 1909 and 1934 despite the interruption of a half-dozen years in his singing caused by World War I. The following catalouge lists the 19 characters that he presented to the public for the first time on the dates indicated:

Role	**Opera**	**Premiere**
Mime	L'Or du Rhin	14 November 1909
Premier Juif	Salomé	3 May 1910
Pibrac-le-brancal	Le Miracle	30 December 1910
Gonzalve	L'Heure espagnole	5 December 1921
Bardolphe	Falstaff	3 April 1922
Une Voix	Le Renard	18 May 1922
Ragenhardt	La Fille de Roland	27 October 1922
Monostatos	La Flûte enchantée	22 December 1922
Le Clerc	Khovantchina	13 April 1923
Le Brahmane	Padmavâti	1 June 1923
Mégélius	Le Jardin du Paradis	29 October 1923
Don Sanche	L'Arlequin	22 December 1924
Silène	La Naissance de la lyre	30 June 1925

De Faninal	Le Chevalier à la rose	8 February 1927
Le Choryphée	Salamine	17 June 1929
Un Démon	La Tentation de Saint-Antoine	8 May 1930
Lope	L'Illustre Frégona	16 February 1931
Kuruchet-le-Gaucher	Perkain	25 January 1934
Squarciafico	Pa Princesse lointaine	22 March 1934

Fabert was billed in a single role at the Opéra-Comique. He created Fouché in Madame Sans-Gêne there on 10 June 1916. This occasion was a benefit performance given for soldiers made blind by the war.
BIBLIOGRAPHY: EDS IV, 1754-55; ICM 519; PBSW 179; SW 40, 60, 84, 95, 98, 114, 119, 124, 132, 140, 150, 154, 162, 167, 173, 176, 192, 195, 202, 207, 317; Thompson 519; WOC II, 111, 296.

Falcon, Cornélie (b. 28 January 1812, Paris; d. 26 February 1897, Paris), vocalist, displayed a precocious interest in music and was sent to the Conservatoire to study under Pellegrini and Bordogni. An industrious and capable student, she won her share of prizes and first appeared in public as a concert artist. She was invited to the Opéra by Adolphe Nourrit* to appear with him and Mlle Julie Dorus* in Robert le Diable* on 20 July 1832. She had a slight case of stage fright at curtain time, but she maintained her poise and managed to execute Alice's first aria without error. She performed the remainder of her role with ease and competence. Her voice was not perfect, but it was rich and moving, and her tragic air and dark bearing endowed her with the presence essential to her part. She was applauded warmly as the curtain fell, therefore, and her first appearance with the company made it obvious that an impressive career lay before her. Giacomo Meyerbeer* himself came to Paris to hear his new Alice, but, unfortunately, Cornélie fell ill after the fifth performance on 24 August, and he could not wait until she returned to the stage in his work on 17 September.

Mlle Falcon had made a great impression upon audiences with her dark eyes, her melancholy air and tragic appearance, and it was difficult for audiences to accept her in her next role, when she appeared as the countess Amélie in Auber's Gustave III* on 27 February 1833. She seemed an anomaly among the dancers at the Swedish court wearing fancy hoopskirts, powdered wigs, and dazzling jewels. Dancing and dancers were everywhere in this work, in which only men shared in the intrigue, and Mlle Falcon had the air of a frustrated vocalist waiting for all the commotion to stop so that she might begin without interruption from harlequins, dominoes, beggars, and clowns. In a word, Mlle Falcon came prepared to sing and found herself at a riotous mascarade. Luigi Cherubini asked her to do Morgiana in Ali Baba* on 22 July 1833, but his invitation was more flattering than substantial, because the part of Morgiana hardly constituted a real challenge to a young and ambitious singer (see eighteenth-century volume for Cherubini).

Mlle Falcon did not have another opportunity to make the most of her talents until the production of Don Juan* on 10 March 1834. She was cast as Donna Anna in Mozart's work and found herself in the company of Nourrit, Nicolas Levasseur,* Mlle Dorus, and Mme Damoreau. Her part and her situation in the plot matched her personality and ability in all respects, and she received louder approbation for her management of the Donna Anna role than she had won for her performance as Alice.

Yet the soprano's greatest moment arrived when she was chosen to do Rachel in La Juive* on 23 February 1835. M. Véron was about to leave the directorship of the Opéra, and he had spared no expense in providing the most magnificent costumes and breathtaking sets for Meyerbeer's work. Mlle Falcon's Semitic eyes, pensive grandeur, and passionate air made her a natural for her new part. Only her performance in Les Huguenots* would surpass her interpretation of Rachel.

When Les Huguenots was in rehearsal, Nourrit had suggested among other things that the "Blessing of the Daggers" scene be followed by a duet. The composer had hesitated but had agreed at last, and he had persuaded Emile Deschamps* to write words for him to set. After he had created the music for this new number, Meyerbeer handed the completed text to the orchestra for rehearsal with Nourrit and Mlle Falcon. The musicians and other personnel in attendance were so overwhelmed by the addition to the score that they arose in a spontaneous acknowledgement of Meyerbeer's genius. The public was equally impressed on opening night; critics and spectators were unanimous in their praise for la Falcon as Valentine. Marie Malibran* herself paid personal homage to her in the theatre after she had attended a subsequent production of Les Huguenots. The highlight of the opera, it was agreed, was the duet by Raoul and Valentine, the greatest moment that Meyerbeer created for the stage.

Yet time was running out for Cornélie Falcon. She joined Nourrit and Levasseur in the premiere of Stradella* on 3 March 1837, and the labors of the previous decade suddenly caught up with her shortly after Nourrit's retirement from the Opéra on 1 April 1837. Her voice left her during a performance of Louis Niedermeyer's* work, and the curtain was lowered. She rested for a while and then returned to the theatre to do Les Huguenots. She had changed to a contralto now, but she was able to sing, and a trip to Italy in 1838 seemed to restore her former power. She announced that her return to the stage of the Opéra would take place on 14 March 1840 and that, on this occasion, she would do La Juive, act 2, and Les Huguenots, act 4 with Duprez,* Massol, and Mme Dorus-Gras. On the night of her return, la Falcon was calm and well applauded at the moment of her entrance, but it became evident immediately that her voice was gone. She wept at her own pathetic fate but continued despite her inability to do much else besides make the audience regret the loss of her gifts. When she came to the painfully poignant words in Les Huguenots, "Nuit fatale, nuit d'alarmes, je n'ai plus d'avenir" ("Fatal night, night of alarms, I have no longer a future"), she could not support the dreadful irony of the line. She had no choice except to retire, but dramatic soprano roles like Rachel in La Juive and Valentine in Les Huguenots are still called by her name.

BIBLIOGRAPHY: *Charles Bouvet, Cornélie Falcon (Paris: F. Alcan, 1927); Chouquet 397-400; Ellen Clayton, Queens of Song (Freeport, N.Y.: Books for Libraries Press, reprint of 1865 edition), 32-39; DBF XIII, 505-6; DEO 143; EFC 70-73; EZF 197-200; Fétis III, 179; GE XVI, 1118-19; GIR 84-88; ICM 520; Lajarte II, 147-50, 152-53, 155-56; C. L. Osborne, "Too Much Too Soon," Opera News 31 (24 December 1966), 6-7; PBSW 55, 109, 143, 179; Alphonse Royer, Histoire de l'Opéra (Paris: Bachelin-Deflorenne, 1875), 160-62; N. Slonimsky, "Musical Oddities," Etude 74 (November 1956), 6; SST 311-18; Thurner 179-82.*

Falstaff by Giuseppe Verdi* is discussed in the twentieth-century volume.

Le Fanal is an opera in two acts with a score by Adolphe Adam* and a libretto by Jules-Henri Vernoy de Saint-Georges.* It had its world premiere at the Paris opera house on 24 December 1849. The work was seemingly designed to harmonize in places with the spirit of the Christmas season, but its spiritual appeal was not effective enough to sustain it, and it had to be dropped after 13 performances.

The opening scenes of Le Fanal present the coastal pilot Valentin and his brother Martial, the keeper of the lighthouse at Pornic in Brittany. Orphans since childhood, these two brothers have remained close friends, although Valentin admits to Martial that he has been keeping a secret from him (I, 1-3). Alone, Martial discloses that he too has a secret. He has not told Yvonne or Valentin of his love for Yvonne, niece of the tax collector Kergariou, because he is too poor to ask for her hand in marriage (I, 4). Yvonne now enters with a chorus of young girls on their way to decorate the chapel of Our Lady of Perpetual Help. She informs Martial that she has been watching for the ship that is bringing to Valentin the fortune that he has just inherited from his uncle. Valentin verifies that he has sighted the ship carrying his inheritance to Pornic. Martial is alarmed by Valentin's sudden acquisition of wealth because his riches have enhanced his status as a suitor for Yvonne's hand. He suggests that Yvonne choose between him and Valentin by offering to the preferred brother the rose that she is carrying. She gives the rose to Valentin to hide her love for Martial (I, 5-7). Falsely encouraged, Valentin asks greedy Kergariou to approve his marriage to Yvonne, but the tax collector refuses to take the pilot seriously until his wealth is safe in Pornic (I, 8-9). Valentin's ship approaches the harbor at last, but a storm arises. Valentin jumps into his skiff to guide the vessel to a safe anchorage, and he exhorts Martial to keep his beacon shining in the darkness. Yvonne and her companions pray to Our Lady of Perpetual Help, while a company of Breton sailors mobilizes for a rescue operation (I, 10-11).

The second and last act is set on the beach below the Pornic lighthouse, where Martial succumbs to the temptation to kill Valentin by extinguishing the beacon leading him to safety. His ensuing grief over having slain Valentin is increased by Yvonne's admission that it is he, Martial, and not Valentin whom she loves. Martial is reproaching himself for his treachery, when Valentin walks up the beach (II, 1-2) and assures Yvonne that he is now wealthy enough to become her husband. Embarrassed Yvonne leaves without relpying to her happy suitor (II, 3), and Valentin hurries off to secure Kergariou's permission to wed his ward now that his ship is safe in port (II, 4). Alone, Martial composes a letter designed to inform his brother that he, Martial, attempted to slay him so that he might marry Yvonne. He pays a peasant to deliver the missive as soon as the next ship leaves Pornic with him aboard (II, 5).

The villagers gather to celebrate the Yvonne-Valentin wedding that Kergariou has now approved. Yvonne seems strangely distracted in the midst of the festivities, and Valentin cannot understand why Martial has decided to leave Pornic. A group of sailors brings Martial back to the wedding, however, and Valentin insists upon knowing why his brother wishes to run away. Martial refuses to explain his actions (II, 6-7), but the peasant delivers his letter to Valentin at this crucial moment. The prospective groom is aghast to learn that his brother is in love with his bride, but Valentin's generosity knows no limits. He yields Yvonne to Martial as soon as he learns that she loves his brother. Also, he silences Yvonne's eternally greedy guardian by declaring that he plans to share his wealth with Martial. A happy chorus singing "Vive Valentin!" rings down the curtain (II, 8).

The roles of the orphan brothers were sung by M. Poultier (Martial) and M. Portheaut (Valentin) with M. Brémond in the part of Kergariou. Yvonne was sung by Mlle Dameron.

BIBLIOGRAPHY: Lajarte I, 205.

Fandango was a pantomine ballet in a single act with a score by Gaston Salvayre,* a scenario by Henri Meilhac* and Ludovic Halévy, and choreography by Louis Mérante.* It had its world premiere at the Garnier Palace* on 26 November 1877 with scenery by Daram and costumes by Eugène Lacoste.

The ballet is set in the public square of a village near the Pyrenees. The marquis' castle and a hotel dominate the square, where the villagers are awaiting the arrival of the baron de Flamberge, who is going to wed the marquis' daughter, Hélène. Albert is obviously unhappy about the prospect of this marriage because he and Hélène are in love (I, 1). The dancing master enters to rehearse the young girls scheduled to welcome the baron with a ballet (I, 2), but the lesson is interrupted by the music of a band of gypsies looking for lodging in the hotel (I, 3). Preparations for the reception resume, and Alvor emerges from the hotel with four or five gypsy girls. They belittle the dancing master's efforts, and they show him their version of a welcoming dance (I, 4-7).

The marquis, marquise, Hélène, and her governess come out of the hotel, and everybody takes his place. The baron enters with a bouquet for Hélène, who drops the flowers and begins to weep. The marquis assures the baron that nothing is amiss, and Albert rushes to Hélène. The baron demands an explanation, but no one volunteers to explain, and the matter is forgotten for the moment (I, 8-9). The review of the guards begins, and the marquis invites the baron to lead the maneuvers. All goes well until the gypsies decide to play, and their music interferes with the military band. Everybody begins to dance the fandango, and chaos results. The baron loses his temper, and the music stops. The marquis orders the arrest of the gypsies, but Carmencita falls at Hélène's feet and begs her to save her comrades. Hélène obtains their pardon on condition that they remain quiet until after the wedding, when they may dance the fandango in honor of the bride (I, 10).

The baron offers Hélène his portrait, and she begins to laugh. She explains that she can never love him, but her father enters with the notaries to sign the marriage contract, and her protests are silenced (I, 11-12). When Hélène is alone, Albert suggests that they elope. Carmencita offers to help them (I, 13). The wedding bells begin to ring, and the marriage procession begins to enter the church. Hélène and the baron are on a dais in the midst of the guests, and Carmencita enters disguised as one of a band of mountaineers. This latter group dances for the wedding party, and Carmencita passes the hat for contributions. When she arrives before the baron, she pretends to recognize him as her fugitive husband. She holds up the ring and portrait of the baron that Hélène has given her. He protests that he gave these two items to Hélène, but the bride denies ever having seen them before. The marquis is furious, and the outraged baron draws his sword. Albert responds by drawing his sword, and the baron finds it prudent to leave. The marquis consents to the marriage of his daughter and Albert, and Carmencita leads the guests in the fandango (I, 14).

The ballet enjoyed a limited success, and it was billed on 28 occasions before it was dropped from the repertory. The work was a disappointment especially to Léontine Beaugrand,* the current star of the Opéra who was given the lead in Fandango to compensate her for yielding the title-role in Léo Delibes'* Sylvia* to Rita Sangalli.* The other female roles in Fandango were created in Paris by Marie Sanlaville (Albert), Alice Biot (Hélène), and Mlle Aline (the governess). The male parts were danced by M. Vasquez (Alvar), M. Magri (the marquis de Luz), Cornet (the baron de Flamberge), F. Mérante (the dancing master). The orchestra was conducted by Jules Garcin.

BIBLIOGRAPHY: BOP 128-33; H. Moréno, "Le Fandango à l'Opéra," Le Ménestrel 44 (2 December 1877), 3; Stoullig III (1877), 45-47; SW 275.

Farandole is an old Provençal group dance performed by couples holding hands and moving through the streets of their town. It is danced in La Belle au bois dormant* and in Georges Bizet's* L'Arlésienne. Also, the word is used as a title to designate the ballet extracted from the latter opera and performed separately for the first time at the Garnier Palace* on 26 June 1909 on the occasion of a special performance. It was presented apart from its matrix work only on this single date. Mlles Mathilda Kschessinska and Aïda Boni starred on this program given for the benefit of the citizens of Marseilles. Other outstanding contributors to this program included Féodor Chaliapin,* Dimitri Smirnov, Lydia Lipkowska,* Marguerite Carré,* Paul Franz,* Félia Litvinne,* Anna Pavlova,* Mikhail Mordkin,* Lucien Muratore,* and Jeanne Hatto.*

BIBLIOGRAPHY: CODB 275; Stoullig VIII (1882), 55 and IX (1883), 22-26; SW 275.

La Farandole was a ballet in three acts with a score by Théodore Dubois* and a scenario by the team of Philippe Gille and Arnold Mortier. Louis Mérante* created its choreography. It has its world premiere at the Garnier Palace* on 14 December 1883.

The action of the ballet begins on a farm near Arles in the eighteenth century with a group of young girls working on the harvest. The farmer Rémy leaves for the city (I, 1) before Olivier can ask him for permission to marry his daughter Vivette. Valentin encourages him not to be so backward (I, 2), and Vivette emerges from her house. Olivier shows her the wedding ring that he has bought for her (I, 3), but she loses her temper, when she learns that Olivier has not yet spoken to her father. Vivette dresses Renaude in her father's hat, cloak, and cane, and the two girls demonstrate how Olivier should ask her father for her hand (I, 4).

An aged and unkempt man enters the courtyard. His name is Maurias. The girls consider him a sorcerer. They ask him to reveal their future. Reluctantly, he tells them that their future is dark because they are frivolous and quit work at the first sound of music to dance the _farandole_. He adds that they will have to dance in the arena of Arles for all eternity with the other spirits condemned to do the _farandole_ there forever. The girls grow angry with the old man because of his dismal prophecy, but Vivette and Olivier give him food and drink, and he promises them his life (I, 5). The inhabitants of the region begin the dance of the tambourines, and the girls execute the _farandole_ (I, 6), but the party is interrupted by

Rémy's return. Olivier rushes toward him to ask for Vivette's hand, but he pays no attention to his daughter's suitor. Maurias notices Olivier's desperation, and he seems to have an idea. He leads Olivier to the arena of Arles (I, 7-8).

The moonlight is shining upon Maurias and Olivier in the arena of Arles. Maurias tells Olivier that the souls of faithless lovers will appear at midnight, but he declares that Olivier must resist their wiles and refuse to dance the farandole with them if he would win Vivette's hand. Maurias leaves (II, 1), and the arena fills with the crowd of faithless souls. Olivier resists their wiles. The most beautiful and seductive phantom, Cigalia, uses all her charms in vain to tempt Olivier. Desperate, she assumes the appearance of Vivette herself. She demands the ring that he has bought for her, and the deluded youth gives it to her. The deceitful spirits laugh at him, and he learns that he has been tricked (II, 2-4).

The scene moves to a high rock in a clearing by the Rhône, where Maurias is sleeping. Olivier enters pale and haggard; he wishes to die by plunging from the rock, but he is stopped by Valentin and awakened Maurias. Vivette and her companions learn what has happened, and they tell Rémy of Olivier's fearsome experience, and he consents to the marriage of his daughter and Olivier. The inhabitants of the entire region gather to celebrate the coming wedding, and Olivier pins a bouquet to his financee's gown (III, 1-3). Suddenly, thunder rolls and lightning flashes. Cigalia appears and shows her ring; she claims Olivier as her husband. He follows her toward the forest (III, 4). Old Maurias appears on top of his rock with a tambourine. He plays the opening measures of the farandole. Cigalia forgets Olivier to rush to Maurias. When she arrives at the top of his rock, the old man seizes her and jumps into the Rhône with her in his arms. They drown. Vivette and Olivier kneel to pray for the man who gave his life to assure their happiness (III, 5).

The ballet enjoyed a reasonable measure of success, and it was billed on 30 occasions at the Opéra. Rosita Mauri* led the corps de ballet in the role of Vivette with Mlle Elisa Piron as Cigalia. The male dancers in the cast included

MM. Louis Mérante* (Olivier), Pluque (Rémy), and Cornet (Maurias).

The farandole is a native dance of Provence in which the dancers hold each other in a line by hand or by handerchiefs as they move through town to music in 6/8 time. It was also brought to the stage in Charles Gounod's* Mireille.

BIBLIOGRAPHY: Adolphe Jullien, Musiciens d'aujourd'hui (Paris: Librairie de l'Art, 1894) II, 316-20; H. Moréno, "Semaine théâtrale: La Farandole," Le Ménestrel 50 (9 December 1883), 11 and (16 December 1883), 18-19; SW 276; Thompson 527.

Farrar, Geraldine (b. 28 February 1882, Melrose, Mass.; d. 11 March 1967, Ridgefield, Conn.), vocalist, went to Europe with her family so that she might study in Paris. She began her training abroad with Trabadello in the French capital, and she completed her voice studies in Berlin with Lilli Lehman. She made her debut as a soprano at the Royal Opera House in the latter city on 15 October 1901.

Miss Farrar went on to sing in Monte Carlo, Stockholm, and Brussels. She appeared for the first time at the Garnier Palace* as Marguerite in Faust* on 18 May 1905, but she did only three other roles at the Opéra: the heroine of Roméo et Juliette* and Elisabeth of Tannhaüser* in 1907 and, in 1910, Mimi in La Vie de Boheme* with Enrico Caruso* as Rodolphe.

The soprano has made her first appearance with the Metropolitan Opera of New York in 1906. She enjoyed the rank of prima donna assoluta with this company with whom she remained until 1922. She became famous for her interpretations of Carmen and Cio-Cio-San, but she never returned to the Opéra after doing Mimi there in 1910 with her colleagues from the Metropolitan Opera. It is generally overlooked that Farrar also sang Ziriphine in Le Clown, Manon, and Tosca at the Opéra-Comique, when she was in Paris before World War I.

BIBLIOGRAPHY: AEM III, 1841-42; APD 299; Kevin Brownlow, Parade's Gone By (Berkeley: University of California Press, 1970), 366-70; I. Cook, "Visit with Farrar," Opera News (29 January 1966), 6; Gladys Davidson, Opera Biographies (London: Laurie, 1955), 96-98; DEO 146; EFC 177; Geraldine Farrar, The Autobiography of Geraldine Farrar:

Such Sweet Compassion (New York: The Greystone Press, 1938); idem, The Story of an American Singer by Herself (Boston: Houghton, Miflin Co., 1916); A. Favia-Artsay, "Grace Notes," Hobbies 61 (February 1957), 30; Renee B. Fisher, Musical Prodigies (New York: Association Press, 1973), 66-68; J. A. Haughton, "Opera Singers from the golden Age," Musical America 69 (February 1949), 277 ff.; "Historical Records," Hobbies 59 (September 1954), 24-25; ICM 529-30; KRJ 126-27; Kalton C. Lahue, Ladies in Distress (Cranbury, N.J.: A. S. Barnes, 1971), 88-97; Charles Matz and Mary Jane Matz, "First Ladies of the Puccini Premieres: Geraldine Farrar," ON 26, no. 26 (3 February 1962), 24-25; Newsweek 69 (20 March 1967), 78; New York Times 12 March 1967, 1; PBSW 179; Henry Pleasants, The Great Singers (New York: Simon and Schuster, 1966), 313-18; RC 264-71; Francis Robinson, "Geraldine Farrar, 1882-1967, a Memoir," ON 31 (15 April 1967), 14-15; SW 88, 191, 207, 223; Time 89 (24 March 1967), 64; Edward Chalres Wagenknecht, ed., Dramatic Impulse (New York: Dutton, 1946), 149-57; Mary Fitch Watkins, Behind the Scenes at the Opera (New York: Frederick A. Stokes Co., 1925), 301-13; S. T. Williamson, "Headliners," New York Times Magazine, 8 July 1951, 20; WOC 252.

Fauré, Gabriel Urbain (b. 12 May 1845, Parniers; d. 4 November 1924, Paris), composer, displayed such promising musical talent at age nine that Louis Niedermeyer* gave him a complete scholarship to attend his school in Paris. Here, Camille Saint-Saëns* took a special interest in him, and the young composer had his first music published as early as 1863. After graduation, Fauré held the post of organist in churches in Rennes and Paris, and he joined the faculty of the Ecole Niedermeyer in 1872.

When he reached the age of 50, Fauré found himslef the auther of an impressive number of songs and the recipient of an impressive array of honors. Still, he had not yet written a work that might convince the public at large of the true calibre of his genius and of his mastery over his art, although his Requiem had been played at the Madeleine. It was not until 26 August 1900 that Fauré had his first work produced on a stage in a genuinely theatrical manner.

On this summer evening in 1900, Fauré's lyric tragedy entitled Prométhée was produced in three acts at the Roman Theatre in Béziers. The importance and appeal of the composition were recognized slowly, but it was brought to Paris for production at the Ancien Hippodrome on 12 December 1907, and it was billed into the Garnier Palace* three days later, when the musicians of the National Guard assisted in its presentation. The work was revived at the Opéra on 17 May 1917.

The dramatic soprano Lucienne Bréval* was interested in Prométhée, and she suggested to Fauré in 1907 that he write a more traditional opera based upon the story of Penelope and her suitors. The project appealed to the composer. Although Fauré was now growing deaf, he had his Pénélope ready for its world premiere at the Monte Carlo opera house on 4 March 1913 with Mme Bréval in the lead and Lucien Muratore* as Ulysée. The work was staged for the first time in Paris on 10 May 1913 at the Théâtre des Champs-Elysées, but it was not given in its entirety at the National Academy of Music until 14 March 1943. Meanwhile, it had been performed at the Opéra-Comique, where it had started a run of 63 presentations on 20 January 1919 with Mme Lubin still in the title-role.

Fauré's last contribution to the repertory at the National Academy of Music would be made posthumously, when his music would be used for the score of the ballet Rayon de lune on 7 December 1928.

BIBLIOGRAPHY: AB I, 119-25; AEM III, 1867-80; BBD 502; "Bibliographie sommaire de quelques musiciens français depuis 1900," RM 210 (January 1952), 209; CBCM 835-40; DEC 194-96; EDS V, 75-80; ELM II, 29-34; F. Faure-Fremiet, Gabriel Fauré (Paris: Rieder, 1929); Grove III, 38-44; V. Jankelevitch, Gabriel Fauré, ses melodies, son esthétique (Paris: Plon, 1951); KT 167-81; Charles Koechlin, Gabriel Fauré (Paris: Plon, 1927); LD 1-28; C. Lombardi Giordano, Gabriel Fauré (Messina-Firenze: D'Anna, 1960); M. Long, Au piano avec Gabriel Fauré (Paris: Julliard, 1964); MCDE I, 343-51; MIT 150-55; MMFM 23-34; NEO 227; PBSW 179; Norman Suckling, Gabriel Fauré (New York: E. P. Dutton, 1946); Thompson 531-32; TWT 268-73; E. Vuillermoz, Gabriel Fauré (Paris: Flammarion, 1960).

Faure, Jean-Baptiste (b. 15 January 1830, Moulins; d. 9 November 1914, Paris), vocalist, helped support his mother by pumping the organ at Notre-Dame in Paris for 200 francs a year and a few free piano lessons. He was admitted to the Conservatoire in 1843, and his teacher Tariot was able to place him in the chorus of the Théâtre-Italien because he was a member of the staff there. Indefatigable, the boy sang in the choir of Saint-Nicolas-des-Champs and at the Madelaine. At the latter church, he was fortunate enough to attract the attention of Trévaux, who took a special interest in him and guided him into a career of singing with practical help wherever possible. Unfortunately, his voice changed at this time, and he lost his sources of income.

Young Faure ignored the injustices of fate and learned an instrument to support himself during his physiological crisis, and he found a position with the Odéon orchestra. After growing into his new voice, he returned to the chorus of the Théâtre-Italien and gained admission to the Conservatoire. A brilliant student, he won first prize for comic opera in 1851, and, on 20 October 1852, he sang Pygmalion in Galathée at the Opéra-Comique. He appeared in a few frivolities like Le Chien du jardinier, and he sang his roles with ease and competence until he aroused audiences' enthusiasm in Daniel Auber's* Manon Lescaut.* Fortune smiled upon him finally, when Bussine and Battaille retired to leave him the leading tenor of the troupe. He scored an immediate series of triumphs with the old as well as the new repertory, especially L'Etoile du nord, Quentin Durward, and Le Pardon de Ploërmel. Critics and spectators alike recognized the power and range of his voice as well as the skill of his delivery. An invitation to appear at the Opéra was inevitable.

M. Faure made his debut at the Opéra on 14 October 1861 as Julien in Pierre de Médicis by Prince Poinatowski,* and his next assignment was the creation of Pédro in La Mule de Pédro on 6 March 1863. This latter opera by Félix Massé* did not last beyond three performances, but the failure of the work was in no way attributable to the performers, and Faure was cast without prejudice as Nelusko in Giacomo Meyerbeer's* L'Africaine* on 28 April 1865. This role proved to be one of his favorite and most applauded parts. After creating the marquis de Posa in Giuseppe Verdi's Don Carlos* on 11 March 1867, Faure went on to appear as the protagonist in the premiere of Ambroise Thomas'* Hamlet* on 9 March 1868. He was cast as Méphistophélès in the initial production of Charles Gounod's Faust* at the Imperial Academy of Music on 3 March 1869. On 30 April 1870, he sang in the oratorio La Légende de Sainte Cécile on the benefit program for Mlle Christine Nilsson.* His last creation in the rue Le Peletier* before the fire of 29 October 1873 was Paddock in La Coupe du roi de Thulé* on 10 January 1873.

When the company transferred to the Garnier Palace* on 5 January 1875, Faure moved with his colleagues and created Charles VII in August Mermet's* Jeanne d'Arc* on 5 April 1876. This role was his only creation in the new opera house, but he was billed here in five revivals that were premiere performances of these works at the Garnier: Alphonse of La Favorite,* Méphisto of Faust,* Nevers of Les Huguenots,* and the protagonists of Guillaume Tell* and *Don Juan.*

Although this busy schedule does not suggest that Faure had much time to travel, he had gone to London almost every summer after 1860, and he had accepted invitations to sing in Berlin (1861), Brussels (1870-72), and Vienna (1878). He retired from the stage in 1878 but continued to perform at concerts.

The importance of Faure's career is evident by reason of his serving as a transitional figure between the last of the romantic composers and the first of the moderns. Also, his ability as a performer was remarkable from a purely professional point of view because he could act as well as he could sing. His ability to interpret and to communicate the nature of the drama unfolding on the stage while conveying the full impact of the music to the spectators resulted in moving and even perfect performances. His clear diction and vigorous delivery made for an exciting presentation especially in the case of works that he was interpreting for the first time, and on which he left an imprint despite the number of artists who were to do these roles after him. As for his own tastes, his preferences were for three parts: Don Juan, Hamlet, and Méphisto. When he sang his farewell performance at the Opéra on 13 May 1876, he chose Hamlet* for his opera, and the spectators paid the very generous sum of 21,229.50 francs to hear him.

BIBLIOGRAPHY: *Alfred Bablot d'Olbreuse, "Reprise de Don Juan," FM 33 (12 December 1869), 389-91; Gustave Bertrand, "Reprise d'Hamlet par Faure," Le Ménestrel 39 (8 December 1872), 11; A. de Bory, "Rentrée de Faure dans Guillaume Tell," FM 33 (8 August 1869), 246-47; Chouquet 420-25; Henri de Curzon, J.-B. Faure, 1830-1914 (Paris: Fischbacher, 1923; idem, Croquis d'artistes (Paris: Fischbacher, 1898), 53-67; DBF XIII, 751-52; DEO 147; M. Escudier, "Début de M. Faure dans Pierre de Médicis," FM 25 (20 October 1865), 330-31; Fétis, Suppl. I, 318-20; GE XVII, 55-56; ICM 532; Lajarte II, 234, 237-38, 241-47; L. E., "La Reconciliation: MM. Halanzier et Faure," AM 13 (29 October 1874), 351-52; Lermina 567; Martin 149; H. Moreno, "La Rentrée de Faure," Le Ménestrel 40 (1 November 1874), 379; idem, "La Solution de la question Faure," Le Ménestrel 40 (25 October 1874), 370; idem, "La Démission de Faure," Le Ménestrel 40 (18 October 1874), 363; idem "Les Adieux de Faure," Le Ménestrel 40 (10 May 1874), 179; SW 85, 89, 116, 125; XYZ 211-20.*

Faust with a score by Charles Gounod* and a libretto by Jules Barbier* and Michel Carré* was performed initially on 19 March 1859 at the Théâtre-Lyrique du Boulevard du Temple. Goethe's peom had been on the composer's mind for more than a score of years, and he had resolved to write a musical account of the story of Faust, Marguerite, and Méphistophélès as soon as he had seen Carré's version of the German poem in 1850. Barbier was eager to work on the project, and Carvalho agreed to put it on at his theatre. When another Faust was announced, however, Carvalho backed water and demanded a postponement, although his wife was to sing the female lead. Additional delays took place when Mme Carvalho demanded changes in the score to enhance her role and to enable her to display her virtuosity on the stage.

The work lasted for 57 performances during its first run at the Théâtre-Lyrique, a number of billings that was neither disheartening nor sensational. It was taken to the Théâtre Royal de la Monnaie in Brussels on 25 February 1861 and was back in Paris at the Théâtre-Lyrique du Châtelet on 18 December 1862 for 249 presentations in a revised form. The Théâtre-Lyrique de la Salle

Ventadour* mounted it only eight times beginning on 16 March 1868. In the meantime, it was heard in London (1863) and New York (1863). Finally, it had its premiere at the Opéra on 3 March 1869 with the "Nuit de Walpurgis" ballet included for the first time. The rest of its history at the Opéra is known, but it must be noted here that Gounod's work proved so popular that even management lost count of its performances after a while. First, Gounod was honored by the entire company on the occasion of what was supposed to be the 2,000th staging of Faust on 31 December 1934. This information is reported in the Journal de l'Opéra, and it would seem to be beyond dispute, but a later handwriting contradicts this assertion. As early as 27 August 1932, in fact, the Journal carries another notation indicating that statisticians had erred in tallying the billings of **Faust**. Recently, Stéphane Wolff pursued the matter and determined that the 31 December 1934 mounting of Faust was its 1,809th billing at the Opéra. He also points out that the true 500th performance of Gounod's work took place on 23 November 1887, although the artists celebrated this occasion on 4 November 1887. He dates the true 2,000th presentation of the work at the Opéra as 11 February 1944.

The intrigue of Faust begins with the antagonist's inability to drink his suicidal brew at dawn while listening to girls singing on their way to work in the fields, and he calls upon Méphistophélès in desperation. When the latter appears, he offers Faust gold, glory, and power only to learn that the supplicant hero seeks only youth. Méphistophélès offers him a contract of his soul in return for youth, and he persuades him to sign the document by showing him Marguerite at her spinning wheel. Faust drinks the elixir of youth, and his youth is restored (I, 1-2).

Wagner is drinking with a troop of soldiers in an inn, while a band of students flirts with a group of young girls, and a beggar enters to seek alms (II, 1). Only lovesick Siébel is reluctant to drink until a toast to Marguerite is proposed (II, 2). Valentin suggests a last toast before he departs on his journey with Siébel and leaves his sister Marguerite alone. Méphistophélès asks to sing with Wagner, but the latter is reluctant until he is convinced of the intruder's vocal gifts by his solo rendering of "Le Veau d'or" (II,

3). A quarrel ensues, however, and Valentin breaks his sword in midair (II, 4). Faust enters and demands that Méphistophélès keep his pact by awarding him Marguerite (II, 5). Marguerite enters and exits without paying attention to Faust. Méphistophélès laughs and leads Faust off in pursuit of his quarry.

Alone in Marguerite's garden, Siébel decides to declare his love to her but is dismayed to find that he kills every flower he touches. He puts his fingers in holy water to break this diabolical spell foretold by Méphistophélès in act 3, scene 4 (III, 1). Faust and his evil mentor watch Siébel picking a bouquet to leave at Marguerite's door (III, 2). Méphistophélès resolves to seek a more tempting gift to turn Marguerite's head, and Faust is left to sing the praises of his beloved's chaste beauty (III, 3-4). Reformed, he refuses to accept the jewels with which Méphistophélès returns and renounces his pursuit of Marguerite (III, 5). She returns to her spinning wheel and wonders about the identity of the stranger who accosts her. She finds the jewels and adorns herself with them (III, 6). Marthe surprises her admiring herself and her newly found gems, but Marguerite protests her ignorance of their origin (III, 7). Méphistophélès returns with Faust and tells Marthe that her husband is dead, a tragedy that he had also prophesied in act 2, scene 4. Faust asks Marguerite why she has removed her jewelry, and he flirts with her (III, 8). Siébel inquires about Marguerite's whereabouts, but Marthe induces him to leave (III, 9), and Faust bids an innocent farewell to Marguerite (III, 9-13).

Marguerite is at her spinning wheel again and wondering about her lover's intentions (IV, 1), when Siébel comes upon her weeping and learns of her love for the stranger. Marthe reveals that Velentin has returned to punish his sister (IV, 2-3). In the street, Siébel tells Valentin that Marguerite has gone to pray in the church, and Valentin reports that Wagner was killed in the first moments of battle. He, Valentin, becomes suspicious of his sister's actions and leaves for the church (IV, 1-2 bis). Faust and Méphistophélès return to find Marguerite, but they encounter Valentin and kill him in a duel (IV, 3-4). The dying man relates this episode to Marguerite, and he curses her with his last breath

(IV, 5). Marguerite returns to church, where Méphistophélès tells her that she is damned (IV, 3 ter).

After these variant scenes, the last act moves swiftly and in a single pattern of action. Méphistophélès has taken Faust to his kingdom in the Hartz mountains. It is Walpurgis night, and the mountain opens to disclose a golden palace, where the damned of the past are engaged in pagan revelry. Faust is about to join the festivities, when he utters Marguerite's name, and the palace disappears (V, 1-2). He makes his way to sleeping Marguerite and arouses her to declare his love to her. Suddenly, his hands drip with blood, and she repulses him, but they are redeemed at the last moment by the return of Christ and His redemption of the world (V, 3).

It has been suggested that Faust did not deserve the acclaim showered upon it, that it did not merit the popularity it continued to enjoy despite the critics because it relied too patently upon romantic diabolism and a pretty tale of young love. Whatever the merits of this observation, however, it is no less true that Gounod's work was popular almost immediately in the French provinces and abroad in Germany, Belgium, Italy, Sweden, and even England, where it acquired the second title of Daisy Faust. If it seems curious that this mystico-melodramatic romance between a cynical scholar and an innocent maid remains in the repertory despite its libretto, perhaps the secret of its longevity is lodged in the score that contains some of Gounod's best music: La Kermesse (II, 1), "Le Veau d'or" song (II, 3), the waltz and chorus during the first meeting of Marguerite and Faust (II, 5), Siébel's couplets in the flower scene (III, 1), Marguerite's "Il était un roi de Thule" and jewel song (III, 6), the soldiers' chorus (IV, 3), and the ballet of the damned beauties in the last act (V, 2).

The 1859 edition of Faust printed by Michel Lévy frères in Paris records that the cast at the Théâtre-Lyrique on 19 March 1859 was Faust: Joseph Barbot,* Méphisto: Balanqué, Valentin: Reynald, Wagner: Cibot, Marguerite: Caroline Carvalho,* Siébel: Mme Faivre, and Marthe: Mme Duclos.

BIBLIOGRAPHY: *L'Avant-scène 2 (March-April 1976), 1-97; Camille Bellaigue, Promenades lyriques (Paris: Nouvelle Librairie Nationale, 1924), 7-*

27; Henri Busser, "Souvenirs sur Faust," L'Opéra de Paris XII (1956), 10-15; Chouquet, 424: DDO I, 431-32; Norman Demuth, Introduction to the Music of Gounod (London: Dobson, 1950), 14-29; Jacques Dentan, "A propos de la nouvelle presentation de Faust," L'Opéra de Paris XI (1955), 16-19; Guy Ferchault, Faust: une légende et ses musiciens (Paris: Larousse, 1948), 74-95; James Harding, Gounod (New York: Stein and Day, 1973), 97-99, 105-14, 153-54; Coit Roscoe Hoechst, Faust in Music (Gettysburg, Pa.: Gettysburg Compiler Print, 1916); JB 237-38; KCOB 782-90; Lajarte II, 243-44; Paul Landormy "Faust" de Gounod: étude et analyse (Paris: Mellottée, 1944); idem, "Faust" de Gounod (Paris: Mellottée, 1922); MPPA 281-92; MSRL 91-93; OQE 104-8; PBSW 61-62, 109-10, 163, 217-18; Max de Rieux, "La Nouvelle Mise en scène de Faust," L'Opéra de Paris XII (1956), 7-9; Albert Soubies and Henri de Curzon, Documents inédits sur le "Faust" de Gounod (Paris: Fischbacher, 1912); SSBO 234; SW 84-89.

La Favorite is an opera in four acts with a score by Gaetano Donizetti* and a libretto by Alphonse Royer* and Jean-Nicolas-Gustave Vaë.* The choreography was created by Mabille. The work was extremely successful and did not disappear from repertory until 1918. It had its world premiere at the Royal Academy of Music in Paris on 2 December 1840 and went on to enjoy 692 performances at the Opéra. Léon Carvalho* staged it in 1875 with new choreography by Joseph Hansen.*

The work starts with Fernand's explanation to his superior that he must renounce his vows and leave the monastery of Saint-Jacques de Compostelle to search for a beautiful pilgrim with whom he has fallen in love. Balthazar releases him with a warning about the treacherous ways of the world (I, 1-2). He becomes a regular visitor to Léonore's pleasant island, but she refuses to reveal her identity to him and explains ultimately that he must leave her island forever. Fernand learns that she has dismissed him because she is attracted to a king. Fernand resolves to improve his status in the world (I, 3-8).

Alphonse XI reminds Don Gaspard that he is planning to honor young Fernand, who saved his life and turned the tide of battle in the recent struggle against the Moors. The king complains simultaneously of the plotting courtiers trying to create trouble between the Vatican and him because of his love for Léonore. Inès tells the royal mistress of Fernand's exploits, and she complains to Alphonse that she is living in a shadow by staying at Seville without being queen. The king promises to divorce his wife, but Léonore is more frightened than reassured by this prospect (II, 1-4). Léonore's position is weakened further when Don Gaspard shows the king an anonymous love letter written to her. Balthazar declares to Alphonse that the pope has condemned his liaison with Léonore and that he must dismiss her under penalty of anathema. The members of his household flee in fright (II, 5-6).

Fernand arrives at court, and the king asks him to name his own reward for his services. The hero answers that he seeks the hand of Léonore. The king agrees and sets their wedding for an hour hence. Léonore is troubled to think that Fernand will come to know of his dishonor, and she resolves to tell him of her relationship with Alphonse (III, 1-5). The king confers upon Fernand the titles of count of Zamora and marquis of Montréal, and the wedding takes place despite the indignation of the outraged nobles, who refuse to acknowledge the groom's newly acquired status. Fernand challenges them to combat on the field of honor (III, 6-10). Balthazar recognizes Fernand at last, and Fernand asks him what dishonorable thing he has done. When Balthazar informs him that Léonore was Alphonse's mistress, he renounces his titles, his wealth, and his sword. Upbraiding the king for deceiving him, he leaves Léonore and the court (III, 11-12).

Fernand has returned to Saint-Jacques de Compostelle, where he ponders his recent experiences. He and Balthazar enter the chapel, where Léonore dressed as a novice asks Fernand for forgiveness. He refuses to listen to her in his bitterness, but she explains how Inès was to inform him of her dishonorable status. He pardons her at last and suggests that they go away to live together. Weakened by her trails, she can no longer stand. She urges him to keep his vows and dies on the floor of the chapel (IV, 1-7).

Every act of La Favorite offered at least one musical passage to which the spectators responded with emotion or admiration. In the first act, it was the cavatine by Fernand, "Un ange, une femme inconnue." The second act contained an aria by the king, "Léonor! biens, j'abandonne," and a duet by Léonore and the king, "Dans ce palais, règnent pour te séduire," in the second and third scenes, respectively. The third act was especially noteworthy with a trio by Léonore, the king, and Fernand (III, 3); an aria by Léonore, "O mon Fernand" (III, 4); the chorus of the Spanish lords (III, 9); the finale of the act by Fernand, "Sire, je vous dois tout" (III, 12). Fernand's cavatine, "ange si pur" (IV, 3) and a duet by Léonore and Fernand stood out in the last act.

The original cast included Mmes Rosine Stoltz* as Léonore and Elian as Inès opposite Gilbert Duprez* (Fernand), Nicolas Levasseur* (Balthazar), and Pierre Wartel* (Don Gaspard). Paul Barroilhet* made his debut at the Opéra as King Alphonse in the premiere of La Favorite on 2 December 1842. The corps de ballet was led by Mlles Lise Noblet,* Dupont, and Blangy. François-Antoine Habeneck* conducted the orchestra.

BIBLIOGRAPHY: *Guglielmo Barblan, L'Opera di Donizetti nell'età romantica (Bergamo: Edizione del centenario, 1948), 175-81; Chouquet, 403; DDO I, 434-35; Arnoldo Fraccaroli, Donizetti (Verona: Arnoldo Mondadori, 1945), 247-51; Angelo Geddo, Donizetti, l'uomo-le musiche (Bergamo: Edizioni della Rotanda, 1956), 187-93; KCOB 468-78; Lajarte II, 164-65; MSRL 60; Richard Northcott, Donizetti: a Sketch of His Life and a Record of His Operas (privately printed, 1915), 11-12; OQE 81; PBSW 218; SSBO 190; SW 89-90; Herbert Weinstock, Donizetti and the World of Opera in Italy, Paris, and Vienna in the First Half of the Ninteenth Century (New York: Pantheon Books, 1963); Guido Zavadini, Donizetti: vita, musiche, epistolario (Bergamo: Istituto italiano d'arti grafiche, 1948), 526-28.*

Fedora was an opera in three acts with a score by Umberto Giordano* and a libretto by A. Colautti based upon the play by Victorien Sardou. It had its world premiere at the Teatro Lirico in Milan on 17 November 1898 with Gemma Bellincioni in the title role and Enrico Caruso* as her sweetheart and husband Loris. It was booked into the Théâtre Italien in Paris in 1905, but only its second act was produced at the Opéra on 20 October 1910, when it was part of a gala program organized to raise money for the Sardou monument.

The opera begins in the living room of Count Vladimir Andrejevich, where the servants are discussing their master's dissolute way of life. Princess Fedora is inquiring after the whereabouts of the count, who is her fiance, when he is brought in covered with blood and severely wounded. His servants carry him to his bedroom. The police arrive and question the members of the household about events preceding the attack upon the victim. Suspicion falls upon Loris Ipanov, and upset Fedora reaches the unfounded conclusion that Ipanov is the guilty party. The count dies (a. 1).

The scene shifts to Paris, where Fedora is greeting her friends at a reception. She has traced Ipanov to the French capital, and she has managed to convince him that she is interested in him so that he will confess that it was he who murdered Count Andrejevich. Loris now declares his love to the princess, and she protests that she is planning to return to St. Petersburg. He explains that he cannot go back to Russia because he is wanted in the Andrejevich murder case. He adds that he was responsible for the count's death, but, he insists, he is morally innocent of any criminal act. Fedora rejoices and writes a letter to inform the Russian authorities of Loris' imminent return to Russia. She then arranges to have her accomplices kidnap the fugitive and take him to St. Petersburg.

Loris returns to Fedora's apartment to show her proof of his innocence, a letter establishing that the count was hving a secret love affair with his wife, Wanda. He adds that he apprehended the couple in the act of adultery and had to shoot the count to defend his own life. His story and tears move Fedora to admit her love for him, and she cancels her plans to have him repatriated for prosecution (a. 2).

The setting moves to the Swiss Alps, where Fedora and Louis are living in connubial bliss. The count leaves the villa to collect the mail, and a former confederate of Fedora enters to inform her that her letter to Russia was intercepted with the result that Loris' brother has been executed and his mother has died of grief. Loris enters with the mail, and he opens a letter informing him of what has happened to his brother and mother. He begs Fedora to help him find the woman who has destroyed his family. Fedora is crushed by remorse over her letter and tries to appease her husband by reminding him that Wanda must have suffered for his misdeeds. Unmoved, Loris insists upon revenge. Fedora begins to understand the force of his anger, and she swallows poison out of the fear that he may discover the entire truth and murder her. Her actions bring him to the realization that it was she who wrote the fatal letter, but he forgives her as she dies in his arms (a. 3).

At the Opéra, Lina Cavalierei* filled the role of Princess Fedora, while Fernando de Lucia sang Count Loris Ipanov. The composer himself was at the desk.

BIBLIOGRAPHY: AEM 5, 148-50; EDS V, 1313-18; KCOB 706-10; PBSW 218; SSBO 317-18; SW 90-91; Thompson 667, 2144.

Ferrari, Gabrielle (b. 14 September 1851, Paris; d. 4 July 1921, Paris), composer, studied at the Milan Conservatory and then went to Paris to take private lessons with Charles Gounod.* She became known for her piano pieces, but she was not afraid to attempt the composition of operas. Her operas included Le Dernier Amour (1895) Sous le masque (1898), and Le Tartare (1906). Her most successful work for the lyric stage was Le Cobzar.* This lyric drama in three acts had its world premiere at the Monte Carlo opera house in 1909, but it was brought to the Garnier Palace* for its Paris premiere on 30 March 1912.

BIBLIOGRAPHY: BBD 510.

Ferraris, Amalia (1830, Voghera; 8 February 1904, Florence), ballerina, studied ballet with Carlo Blasis* and made her debut at La Scala in Milan in 1844. She danced in the light and airy style popular at the time, and it was not long before she had won a host of admirers in her native land. Word of her triumphs spread abroad, and she was offered engagements in London and Vienna.

Ferraris made her debut at the Opéra in Jules Saint-Georges' Les Elfes* on 11 August 1856. Joseph Mazilier* did the choreography for this work in three acts which was billed as a pantomime ballet. The supporting cast including Lucien Petipa* and Domenico Segarelli* were criticized for various reasons, but Ferraris scored a personal triumph that brought unanimous applause from an audience over which Napoleon III and his empress presided. The press extolled her for her elevation, her pointes, and the strength of her movements. Spectators showered her with flowers after her representation of Sylvie, and Saint-Georges paid tribute to her in verse.

Alphonse Royer* was director of the Opéra at this time, and he proved to be a shrewd man of affairs as well as a skilled administrator by charging Mazilier to compose a ballet in which the talents of Carolina Rosati* and la Ferraris might be exploited for the benefit of the box office. The choreographer agreed, and Marco Spado* was ready for its premiere on 1 April 1857. Mme Ferraris danced la Marchesa, and Mlle Rosati appeared as Angela. This obvious contest between the two ballerinas was greeted with enthusiasm by the public, and Ferraris was praised for her elevation, while Rosati was acclaimed for her ability to mime. Royer was satisfied, and Ferraris' contract was renewed for a year at a salary of 40,000 francs.

The large amount of money paid for Ferraris' services meant that she had to dance almost constantly at the theatre, and special measures were taken to furnish her with a vehicle until new compositions could be completed for her. She was billed as the heroine of Orfa,* revived on 15 July 1857, and she performed in the divertissement of Le Cheval de bronze* on 21 September 1857, although her contract excused her from appearing in divertissements (see eighteenth-century volume for divertissement). Finally, Sacountala* was ready for its premiere on 14 July 1858, and Ferraris danced the lead. Once again she received rave notices in the press for the ethereal quality of her performance. Some critics suggested that she had found a way to suspend the force of gravity and could float across the stage at will. Lightness, grace, and brilliance were the words favored by journalists engaged in describing her style.

Carolina Rosati now left the Opéra for Russia in 1859, and la Ferraris found herself the most valuable ballerina in the corps de ballet and the highest paid member of this group. She consented to do Diane in the divertissement entitled Les Amours de Diane in Pierre de Médicis,* written especially for her by Lucien Petipa. Its premiere was scheduled for 9 March 1860, and she was acclaimed once again for the strength and precision of her pointes and her ethereal grace. Then, after the disaster of Tannhaüser,* she was assigned to the first new ballet at the Opéra since 1858, Graziosa,* in which she danced the heroine and inspired members of the Jockey Club to throw flowers at her obviously enchanted feet.

On 20 November 1861, she appeared in the ballet that had been promised to her in return for her willingness to dance in divertissements. The long awaited work was L'Etoile de Messine* by Borri, a reworked version of the choreographer's La Giuocoliera in which Ferraris had already danced at Bologna five years previously. No expenses were spared for sets, costumes, or cast. Ferraris filled the part of Gazella, the star of an itinerant troupe of players. The work was so carefully rehearsed that the extras as well as the principals won praise for their skill, while Ferraris opposite Louis Mérante* scored still another victory on the stage. She was applauded not only for her virtues but also for her capability to convey the comic moments of her role. Cries of "Bis!" greeted her tarantella, and she held the audience enthralled in her closing death scene. The only complaints of the evening were lodged against Nicolas Gabielli's* score.

It was suggested next that Ferraris might do the heroine's role in Zara, but she was not enthusiastic about this project and fell to arguing with the new director, Emile Perrin, over certain changes that he wished to make in this work. The argument continued until Ferraris aggravated the situation by demanding a salary of 60,000 francs in a new contract to be issued to her after 4 June 1863. Perrin refused to meet her demands, and she asked for an early release from her contract. She was given a benefit performance on 21 March 1863, and the emperor and empress presented her with a farewell gift of precious earrings. She received a deafening ovation and was showered with flowers before the night was done.

Ferraris filled engagements in London and Brussels before returning to Italy for a final tour of her native land. She retired from the theatre in 1868, but came back to Paris to teach for a time.

Amalia Ferraris' greatest importance derived from the perfection to which she brought her technique, a feat by which she contributed more than any other dancer to the victory of Italian virtuousity in the ballet at Paris during the second half of the nineteenth century.

BIBLIOGRAPHY: ACD 185; CB 136, 160, 218-32, 361-69, 384; CODB 193; DDD 100-101; M. Escudier, "Représentation d'adieu de Mme Ferraris au Théâtre Impérial de l'Opéra," FM 27 (29 March 1863), 94-95; EZF 201-2; Ivor Guest, The Ballet of the Second Empire (Middletown, Conn.: Wesleyan University Press, 1974), 1-3, 103-11, 118-20, 179-83; Lajarte II, 211-12, 220, 222-25, 231-32; Parmenia Migel, The Ballerinas from the Court of Louis XIV to Pavlova (New York: Macmillan, 1972), 209, 230-32, 238, 247, 253, 256.

Fervaal was described by its author as a musical action. It is composed of a prologue and three acts, and its score and libretto are by Vincent d'Indy.* It had its world premiere in Brussels at the Théâtre de la Monnaie on 12 March 1897, and its Paris premiere took place at the Opéra-Comique on 10 May 1898. It was not produced at the National Academy of Music until 31 December 1912, when it was provided with costumes by Pinchon and sets by Simas (a. 1), Rochette and Landrin (a. 2, 3).

The opera opens on the northern shore of the Mediterranean with Fervaal and old Arfagard struggling against a group of bandits. Fervaal is knocked unconscious, and the highwaymen are about to assault Arfagard, when the enchantress Guilhen enters with her retinue to interrupt the robbery. She arouses Arfagard's anger by approaching Fervaal, who stirs for an instant. Guilhen notices his golden collar and noble dress; she decides to restore the injured man to health. Guilhen's servants make a litter for him; old Arfagard follows the litter (prol.).

Fervaal is resting in Guilhen's gardens when Arfagard enters with his armor. He tells Fervaal that his wound has healed and that he must leave for his native land, Cravann, the only Celtic region still untouched by invaders. He reminds Fervaal that he is the last descendant of his gods, but he will be worthy of this honorable rank only as long as love does not trouble his soul. Fervaal dons his armor, and Arfagard discloses that the nation will elect a new leader at the next full moon (I, 1). Fervaal puts on the jeweled sword given to him by Guilhen, who appears to ask him why Arfagard wishes two strong horses and why he is wearing his sword. He explains his unusual background and describes his carefree youth in the Land of the Clouds, and he reveals why he had to hide in the sacred forest of Cravann. He asks her who she is, and she replies that she too led a carefree life until she met him. He declares his love for her and urges her to flee with him to the mountains. Arfagard reminds him that he must leave alone, because he is bound by an oath. He abandons Guilhen, and she falls victim to her grief (I, 2). She faints but recovers to call upon the sons of the winds and fire to smite Fervaal's land. A band of Saracens enters her gardens intent upon plunder because Guilhen left them to starve. Guilhen begs them to listen to her, and she tells them of a wondrous country in the north filled with grain, bread, and gold. She proclaims a holy war in the name of Allah, and they march toward the north (I, 3).

The second act opens before an altar in the forests of the north, where Fervaal is thinking of Guilhen. A shepherd announces a meeting of the chiefs at dawn. The night mists form strange shapes over the stone altar, and Arfagard calls upon the goddess Kaito to reveal coming events. Kaito answers that she will never appear again, and Arfagard instructs Fervaal to don his armor (II, 1). The chiefs assemble, and Arfagard reveals to them that an overwhelming force is preparing to attack them. Each chief proposes himself for the post of leader. Arfagard reminds them that the oracle has proclaimed that only a man untouched by love may lead their nation. Fervaal enters (II, 2); he is elected to head the army of the free Celtic nations. The council is about to congratulate Fervaal, when a messenger announces that a foreign horde is scaling the heights to Cravann. Fervaal assigns each chief to a sector of the line of battle; he tells Arfagard that he will perish in this fight because he has fallen in love with Guilhen and is not eligible to lead his compatriots. Arfagard is aghast (II, 3).

Fervaal is wandering across the battlefield and lamenting his survival, while his peers have been punished by death. He begs Arfagard to sacrifice him to Esus to expiate his impure leadership. Arfagard forgives him and prepares to offer him as a sacrifice. Suddenly, Guilhen's voice is heard calling to Fervaal, who kills

Arfagard in a fit of passion (III, 1). The lovers embrace and rejoice over their reunion. Guilhen complains that she is cold, and Fervaal assures her that they will return to her country in the south. She insists that it is too late for her to think of going home because she will be dead within hours. The clouds cover the moon, and she dies. The thunder rolls (III, 2), and Fervaal begs Thrann not to disturb the dead. He has visions of the roses in the south and lifts Guilhen in his arms. He climbs the mountain with her until he passes into the clouds and leaves the stage empty. A ray of light from the morning sun strikes the top of the mountain, and the curtain falls (III, 3).

This work composed under the impact of the "vague wagnérienne" was not supported by Parisian audiences, and it had to be dropped after its tenth presentation on 27 October 1913. The two female roles were filled at its Garnier Palace* premiere by Lucienne Bréval* (Guilhen) and Lyse Charny (Kaito). The two principal male parts were sung at this time by Lucien Muratore* (Fervaal) and Jean-François Delmas* (Arfagard). Vincent d'Indy conducted his own work at the Opéra on 10 June 1913.

Fervaal was the composer's first sustained effort for the lyric theatre, and it boasted a polished and flawless score. Its great fault from the point of view of the public was its reliance upon Wagnerian techniques: the use of a symphony in an opera, the employment of leitmotivs to indicate characters or incidents, the choice of the Celtic mythos for its story, and its emphasis upon ritual. Yet even this dependence upon Wagnerian technique might have been overlooked, if the score had exhibited more feeling.

BIBLIOGRAPHY: Camille Bellaigue, Impressions musicales et littéraires (Paris: Ch. Delagrave, n.d.), 240-45; Louis Borgex, Vincent d'Indy (Paris: Durand, 1913), 25-28; Adolphe Boschot, Chex les musiciens (Paris: Plon, 1922), 196-202; Pierre de Bréville and H. Gauthier-Villars, "Fervaal": étude thématique et analytique (Paris: A. Durand, 1897); Joseph Canteloube, Vincent d'Indy (Paris: Henri Laurens, 1951), 41-42, 46-48, 80-85; Martin Cooper, French Music from the Death of Berlioz to the Death of Fauré (London, New York, Toronto: Oxford University Press, 1951), 113-14; DDO II, 1219; Norman Demuth,

Vincent d'Indy (London: Rockcliff, 1951), 48; Etienne Destranges, "Fervaal" de Vincent d'Indy: Etude thématique et analytique (Paris: A. Durand, 1896); G. Jean-Aubry, "Villiers de L'Isle Adam and music," M&L 38 (1957), 404; Maurice Kufferath, "Fervaal . . . de V. d'Indy," RMI 4 (1897), 313-27; Paul Landormy, La Musique française de Franck à Debussy (Paris: Gallimard, 1943), 82-84; Daniel Gregory Mason, Contemporary Composers (New York: Macmillan Co., 1918), 189-92; Léon Morris, "Opéra . . . Fervaal . . . répétition générale à ce théâtre le 31 décembre 1912," Le Ménestrel 79 (4 January 1913), 2-4; MSRL 107-8; Gustave Samazeuilh, "Le Théâtre lyrique de Vincent d'Indy," RM 18, no. 176 (August-September 1937), 129-39; SSBO 119-21; Stoullig XXXVII (1912), 30-35 and XXXIX (1913), 1-3, 12; SW 91; Léon Vallas, Vincent d'Indy (Paris: Albin Michel, 1950) II, 283-308; idem, "La Mélodie de Vincent d'Indy," RM 21 (1946), 231-40.

Festin is a ballet in the form of a suite of dances first performed by the Ballets russes* at the Châtelet Theatre on 19 June 1909. Serge Diaghilev's* company brought the work to the Opéra for its initial presentation in this theatre on 19 June 1909. It did not become a part of the repertory at the Opéra, but it was danced there by the Russian troupe on five occasions: 19 June 1909 and 4, 7, 9, 15 June 1910.

Le Festin is a ballet that was created at the last moment because Diaghilev lacked a third work to complete his offerings during the first season of the Ballets russes in the French capital. He assembled a collection of dances and music already in the repertories of the Maryinsky and Grand theatres in Russia, and he tied his "anthology" together by having Michel Fokine* compose a finale for it by setting a Ukrainian folk dance to music from Piotr Ilyitch Tchaikovsky's* Symphony No. 2. His scenery was borrowed from the opening scene of Fëdor Glinka's Russlan et Ludmilla (1842), which he was also producing at the time, and he commissioned a group of Russian painters to supply him with sketches for costumes.

The pieces that were coordinated to furnish Le Festin with a score and dances included the march from Nikolay Rimsky-Korsakov's* Le Coq d'or,* the lezzinka from Glinka's Russlan et Ludmilla, a pas de deux from Tchaikovsky's La

Belle au bois dormant,* the czardas from the divertissement of Alexander Glazounov's* Raymonda, the gopak from Modest Mussorgsky's* The Fair at Sorochinsk, the mazurka from Glinka's La Vie pour le tzar, and the trepak in the final divertissement of Tchaikovsky's Casse-noisette* (see eighteenth-century volume for divertissement). Thus, Le Festin was a veritable smorgasbord of Russian tidbits.

The dancers called upon to execute Le Festin were headed by such stars as Vera Fokina,* Tamara Karsavina,* Vera Karalli, Bronislava Nijinska,* Alexandra Baldina, Ludmila Schollar, and Yelena Smirnova. The male dancers who appeared alongside these eminent danseuses at the Châtelet numbered Michel Fokine, Vaslav Nijinsky,* Mikail Mordkin,* Nicholas Kremnev, Adolphe Bohm, Laurent Novikov, and Alexis Koslov.

BIBLIOGRAPHY: AEM 13, 858-68; Alexandre Benois, Reminiscences of the Russian Ballet, trans. Mary Britnieva (London: Putnam, 1947), 353-54; BK 30; Richard Buckle, Nijinsky (New York: Simon and Schuster, 1971), 91-92; Boris Kochno, Diaghilev and the Ballets russes, trans. Adrienne Foulke (New York & Evanston: Harper & Row, 1970), 30-31; "Opéra . . . Saison russe," Le Ménestrel 76 (11 June 1910), 186-87; SW 277.

La Fête chez Thérèse was a ballet in two acts with a score by Reynaldo Hahn* and an argument by Catulle Mendès. It was choreographed by Mme Stichel, its sets were designed by Rochette, and Pinchon created its costumes. It had its world premiere at the National Academy of Music on 13 February 1910.

The ballet begins in the workshop of Palmyre, where apprentices and working girls are listening to Mimi Pinson recount her amorous adventures. The famous dancer Carlotta Grisi* enters in the midst of all the noise to try on her dancing costumes, and Mimi asks her to execute the Giselle* waltz. The boss Palmyre enters with the duchess Thérèse to try on the latter's dresses, and the poet Théodore is immediately attracted to the duchess, although he is regarded as Mimi's sweetheart. Inevitably, Mimi is crushed and reduced to tears (a. 2).

The second act shifts to a beautiful park, where the duchess is giving a festive ball. The park is filled with masquerade characters dressed in costumes of every sort and color. Gilles and Arlequin begin to act out a pantomime, and Théodore finds himself shoulder to shoulder with the duchess. The masked poet arranges a rendezvous with Thérèse, who is curious to know his identity, but Mimi is aware of what he is doing. She begs her hostess to ignore her sweetheart's efforts to arouse her interest in him, and the generous duchess complies with Mimi's request. She arranges matters so that Mimi and her adored poet are blissfully reunited.

Hahn's touching and illustrative score assured the success of the ballet that reached 35 performances by 1921 despite an intervening war. It was revived on 9 December 1921 for its 36th presentation, and it was not withdrawn from the stage until after its 45th billing at the Opéra on 3 August 1924. The important female roles were filled for the first time by Mlles Carlotta Zambelli* (Mimi), Aïda Boni (Duchess Thérèse), Marthe Urban (Carlotta Grisi), Sirède (Palmyre), and Anna Johnsson (Arlequine). The male parts were created by P. Raymond (Théodore), Albert Aveline* (Gilles), and Gustave Ricaux (Arlequin).

BIBLIOGRAPHY: BOP 152, 158; René Dumesnil, La Musique contemporaine en France (Paris: Armand Colin, 1930) I, 164 and II, 137-38; EDS VI, 98-99; Bernard Gavoty, Raynaldo Hahn (Paris: Buchet-Chastel, 1976), 221; P. de Lapommeraye, "Opéra: La Fête Chez Thérèse," Le Ménestrel 83, no. 50 (16 December 1921), 498-99; LOB 61-62; PGB 120-23; Gustave Samazeuilh, Musiciens de mon temps (Paris: Marcel Daubin, 1947), 212-14; "Semaine théâtrale . . . "La Fête chez Thérèse," Le Ménestrel 76 (19 February and 19 March 1910), 59-60, 95; Stoullig XXXVI (1910), 2-9, 34; SW 278-79; VBO 45-47.

La Fête hongroise is a makeshift divertissement in a single act that was created for performance at the salle Louvois in 1821, while the company of the Opéra was waiting to get back into their theatre in the rue Le Peletier (see eighteenth-century volume for divertissement). At this time, the schedule of performances became rather confused, and programs were given on only five dates: 25 May; 1, 8, 15 June; and 16 August 1821. La Fête hongroise was produced on only one of these five dates, 15 June 1821, and it was never returned to the stage of the Royal Academy of Music after its world premiere there, when its companion piece was Le Devin du village (see eighteenth-century volume for Le Devin du village). The score of La Fête hongroise was composed by Adalbert Gyrowetz,* and Jean Aumer established its choreography (see eighteenth-century volume for Aumer).

As a divertissement and a hastily composed piece designed to fill a passing need, La Fête hongroise had no structured narrative or significant theme, and Aumer never bothered to publish a libretto in connection with its creation. Certain newspaper reviews make it possible to say little more than that it presents an opening crowd scene where a Hungarian count stages an entertainment for his household staff that includes a cossack, a hussar, and a group of peasants. The master supplies casks of wine, and the singing and dancing begin in earnest. At this point in the production, a city slicker finds himself attracted to one of the pretty peasant girls, and he begins to court her with more zeal than judgment. The peasants resent his actions and undertake to teach him to behave by tossing him in a blanket. The remainder of the divertissement is devoted to dancing featuring pas de deux and pas de trois.

The costumes were gay and colorful in this Hungary-oriented work, and it aroused enthusiasm despite its abrupt withdrawal from the repertory. The cast included Jean Aumer (the count), M. Regaine (the petit-maître), M. Godefroi (an intendant), M. Brocard (the hussar), Mlle Gaillet (the countess).

BIBLIOGRAPHY: Richard Banks, "Structure of the Romantic ballet, La Fête hongroise," undated typescript in archives of the Opéra; reviews in Le Miroir, 16 June 1821 and Courrier des Spectacles, 17 June 1821 and 18 June 1821; Lajarte II, 100.

Fête russe was a ballet using for its score a medley assembled by Paul Vidal* and employing choreography by Joseph Hansen.* The six musical pieces forming its score included Fëdor Glinka's music for the entr'acte, divertissement and finale of La Vie pour le tzar,* Piotr Ilyitch Tchaikovsky's * Polacca, and Anton Rubinstein's* Danse circassienne (see eighteenth-century for divertissement).

Fête russe had its world premiere at the Garnier Palace* on 21 October 1893, and it enjoyed

11 performances at the Opéra before it was dropped from the repertory. Its cast was headed by Rosita Mauri,* and the other female roles in the ballet were filled by Mlles Désiré, Hirsch, Lobstein, Sallé, and Subra. MM. Vasquez, de Soria, and Ajas appeared in the male parts. M. Vidal provided the musical direction for his own score.
BIBLIOGRAPHY: SW 279.

Février, Henri (b. 2 October 1875, Paris; d. 6 July 1957, paris), composer, studied at the Paris Conservatory with Gabriel Fauré,* Xavier Leroux,* and Jules Massenet,* and he composed a number of operas an operettas that found their way to the stages of the Opéra and the Opéra-Comique:

Opera	Theatre	Premiere
Le Roi aveugle	Opéra-Comique	8 May 1906
Monna Vanna*	Opéra-Comique	10 January 1909
Gismonde	Opéra-Comique	15 October 1919
L'lle désenchantée	Opéra	19 November 1925
La Femme nue	Opéra-Comique	23 March 1929

BIBLIOGRAPHY: AEM IV, 148-49; BBD 514; EDS V, 265-66; ELM II, 54; NEO 234.

La Fiancée de Corinthe was an opera in a single act with a libretto by Camille Du Locle* and a score by Jules Duprato.* It had its world premiere at the Imperial Theatre of the Opéra in Paris on 21 October 1867.

The opera opens in Polus' home near the sea, where Chloris has been waiting for a year in the hope that Lysis will return to Corinth. Her sister Daphné has died by drowning since Lysis' departure, but Chloris is certain that Lysis will be back before long to marry her sister, because he does not know that she is dead. Her father Polus would like to move to the mountains so that he can forget the sea, but he reports to his daughter that Lysis has already returned to Corinth, and she instists upon remaining where she is. She voices the secret hope that she may look enough like her sister to capture Lysis' heart despite his inevitable grief over Daphné's death.

Lysis is heard singing in the distance, and Chloris persuades her father to swear that he will not tell Lysis of Daphné's death (sc. 1-2).

Chloris enters her house. Lysis greets Porus and inquires about Daphné. The father offers an evasive reply, and the youth recalls that his fiancee was carrying a lamp and a basket of fruit when he met her for the first time. Chloris returns from the house with a lamp and a basket of fruit, and Lysis mistakes her for Daphné. They express their mutual joy over being reunited, and even Polus believes he is looking at Daphné. Lysis declares his love to her; he tells her how he used to see her at night during his long voyage. Suddenly Chloris sees Daphné's shade wandering in the background. Polus cannot continue the deception, and he reveals that Daphné is dead. Chloris expresses the ambiguous hope that Lysis will love her enough on the morrow to marry her. She and her father retire (sc. 4), but Lysis remains outdoors to sleep. Daphné calls out to him and begs him to ignore her dissembling sister. Lysis recognizes Daphné, and they swear their undying love to each other. Lysis asserts that he will follow Daphné into death if they are ever obliged to separate from each other. They consecrate their promises with a libation and repeat the marriage vows of ancient Corinth. Dawn begins to break, however, and Daphné must return to the company of the unburied dead. She kisses him farewell, and he falls asleep (sc. 5).

Lysis awakens and believes that his reunion with Daphné was a dream. Chloris admits to him that she has deceived him, but she assures him that she loves him. She asks him to become her husband. Lysis sees marriage to Chloris as a way of returning to Daphné, and he accepts her proposal. Distant voices call to him. He begs Chloris to forgive him and dies (sc. 6).

Audiences objected to the libretto of La Fiancée de Corinthe on account of the too human conduct of Daphné's wine-drinking shade and to the casual way in which Lysis dies without breaching the rules of etiquette, although the score seems to have compensated for these infractions of vraisemblance. At least witnesses have reported that Chloris' "Tu ne reverras plus ta belle et jeune amante" and the trio "O delice! ô nuit d'ivresse" moved the spectators who attended one of the 14 performances that the work enjoyed. The small cast included David (Polus), Mlle Rosine Bloch* (Lysis), and Mlle Mauduit (Daphné and Chloris).

BIBLIOGRAPHY: *Gustave Bertrand, "Semaine théâtrale: premières représentations . . . la* *Fiancée de Corinthe* *à l'Opéra,"* *Le Ménestrel* *34 (27 October 1867), 378-79; Chouquet 423; DDO I, 451-52; EDS IV, 1156-57; Lajarte II, 241-42; M. Stern, "Théâtre Impérial de l'Opéra:* *La Fiancée de Corinthe*,*"* *FM* *31 (27 October 1867), 334-35, 338.*

Les Fiancés de Caserte is a ballet in a single act and 17 scenes with a scenario and choreography by the team of Pierre Gardel and Louis-Jacques Milon (see eighteenth-century volume for Gardel and Milon). The ballet was billed originally for 14 July 1817 under the title of L'Echange des roses, but its world premiere was postponed until 17 September 1817, when it was given its ultimate title of Les Fiancés de Caserte, ou les Mariages de Caserte. It was presented with a score by Gustave Dugazon.*

The libretto notes that the ballet was inspired by a story appearing in the Journal Général of 12 May 1776 describing the marriage customs established in the Italian city of Caserte near Naples by Ferdinand IV, king of the Two Sicilies. These procedures surrounding marriages demanded that the groom be at least 20 years old while the bride had to be 16. If the parents consented to the marriage, the couple exchanged bouquets in church before the baptismal fonts on Pentecost Sunday. A date for the wedding was set, if the young man accepted the girl's white roses and if she accepted his red roses. The couple carried their bouquets wherever they went on the Sunday of their betrothal.

The ballet opens in a Caserte neighborhood in front of Margarita's silk shop. Her daughters, Rosina and Vittorina, are overjoyed to read a bulletin announcing that the exchange of roses is to take place on schedule. Vittorina and Paolino lay plans to win Margarita's consent to their marriage, but Antoni has to reassure Rosina of his determination to marry her because she is aware of her mother's designs upon him. Margarita appears and orders her daughters back into the shop. She starts to flirt with Antoni, but she is interrupted by the civil officer making his rounds to distribute the roses for the impending ceremony (sc. 1-3). When Margarita leaves with the officer, her daughters emerge from the shop to run into the arms of their sweethearts. Unfortunately, Margarita returns immediately. She starts to scold Paolino, but he interrupts her to ask for permission to wed Vittorina. Margarita dismisses him immediately and also decides to give Rosina's hand in marriage to Geronimo (sc. 4-5).

Margarita suggests to Geronimo that Rosina would be an ideal wife for him, and he plays the mandolin and dances in an effort to dispel Rosina's obvious indifference toward him. Finally even a dull witted suitor like Geronimo can see that Rosina is interested only in Antoni, however, and he turns his attention from her to her mother while advising Margarita that Rosina prefers to wed Antoni (sc. 6-7). Margarita clings to her original plans nevertheless, and she prevents disconsolate Vittorina and Paolino from registering with the civil officer while she makes an effort to place Antoni and herself on this official's marriage rolls. The wedding clerk misunderstands her intentions, however, and he records Geronimo as her intended groom (sc. 8-10).

Vittorina and Paolino persuade Geronimo to help them win Margarita's approval of their marriage, while Antoni can only pretend to yield to Margarita's insistant advances. Rosina is inevitably crushed by her sweetheart's unexpected response to Margarita's displays of affection, but Antoni is quick to assure her that he is only dissembling and is truly faithful and constant to her alone (sc. 11-15).

The governor arrives for the ceremony of the roses, and Vittorina and Paolino beg him and his wife to allow them to exchange their roses in the church and to set a date for their wedding. The sympathetic governor grants their wish. The ceremony begins. Margarita is surprised to see Vittorina and Rosina exchange their white roses for the red roses offered to them by Paolino and Antoni, but she is speechless when Geronimo approaches her with his bouquet. Geronimo advises her to accept his bouquet lest she appear ridiculous. She acquiesces, and the entire affair is settled (sc. 16-17).

The ballet was a pronounced failure and was dropped from the repertory after its second performance on 22 September 1817, when only 2,515 francs were left at the box office. It had been paired with La Caravane du Caire for its first presentation five days previously and with Les Bayadères for its final produciton at the Royal Acedemy of Music (see eighteenth-century volume for La Caravane du Caire and Les Bayadères). The major female roles were filled by Mlles Marie Delisle (Margarita), Emilie Bigottini (Rosina), and Courtin (Vittorina) opposite MM. Albert (Antoni), Louis Mérante* (Geronimo), and Antoine Coulon* (Paolino). Louis Milon was cast as the governor in this ballet that he helped to create (see eighteenth-century volume for Delisle, Bigottini, Albert, and Milon).

BIBLIOGRAPHY: BP 82, 306-7; CB 7; Lajarte II, 90-91.

Fidelio was a comic opera in three acts with a score by Ludwig Van Beethoven* and a libretto by Josef Sonnleithner and Georges Friedrich Treitschke. It had its world premiere on 20 November 1805 in this form at the Theatre an der Wien in Vienna under the title of Léonor ou l'Amour conjugal. After a booking in Prague, it was returned to Vienna on 20 March 1806 as Fidelio in two acts, and it was under this title that it had its Paris premiere at the Odéon in a French version by François-Joseph Blaze* during 1825. A German troupe produced it next in Paris at the Favart Theatre in 1831 in its original version in German, and, in 1852, it was offered in Italian at the Théâtre Italien. M. G. Antheunis did a second version in French for presentation at the Théâtre-Lyrique in 1862, and the team of Jules Barbier* and Michel Carré* completed a third text in French for the Opéra-Comique on 30 December 1898. It was not until 15 February 1926 that it was brought to the stage of the Opéra, when the Royal Opera of the Hague presented it. After two revivals by the Vienna Opera Company at Paris in 1928 and 1936, it was given in French by the artists of the Garnier Palace* at the Champs-Elysées Theatre in a French version by Maurice Kufferath with sets and lighting effects by Klausz in 1937.

The opera opens in the courtyard of a state prison near Seville, where Jacquino is reproaching Marcelline for ignoring him in favor of Fidélio (I, 1). Florestan's wife Léonore enters in her male disguise as Fidélio. She has been on an excursion to purchase supplies for the jail, and she has saved so much money that the warden Rocco decides that "he" may marry his daughter Marcelline as soon as the governor leaves for Seville. Léonore-Fidélio asks Rocco to allow "him" to help him in the prison cellars. Rocco agrees to allow his future son-in-law to assist him, although it is against the governor's orders. He is under orders especially to keep one prisoner hidden from all eyes, the captive who is being starved to death. Léonore-Fidélio takes a lively interest in this unfortunate creature because she believes that he may be her missing husband (I, 2-5). Pizarro receives an anonymous letter saying that a government inspector is about to examine his prison, and he decides to expedite his starving prisoner's death because he is being held unlawfully. He posts a lookout on the Seville road and tells Rocco to dig Florestan's grave in an old cistern below the jail (I, 6-7). Marceline and Rocco explain to Jacquino that he cannot marry Marceline, and Fidélio persuades Rocco to allow the prisoners into the yard for a breath of fresh air (I, 8-10). A chorus of prisoners sings the praises of freedom, and Rocco returns from the governor's office with the news that Fidélio is now his assistant. He adds that their first task will be to bury the prisoner whom Pizarro plans to kill. Pizarro orders the prisoners back into their cells and tells Rocco to begin his assigned task without delay (I, 11-14).

The setting of the first tableau of the second act depicts a dungeon with Florestan stretched out on a stone bench and a heap of stones beside a cistern. The prisoner sees a ray of light, when the door of his cell opens, and he has a premonitory vision of his wife Léonor. Rocco and his helper start to dig. The prisoner lifts his face to drink from his pitcher, and Léonore recognizes him as her husband. She faints but recovers to offer him bread and wine. Finally, the grave is dug, and Rocco gives the signal for Pizarro to appear (II, 1-2). The governor enters and dismisses Fidélio, who hides behind a pillar to watch him; he is planning to kill her and Rocco to hide his crime. He draws a dagger and defies Florestan; Léonore throws herself between her husband and his assassin. Rocco tries to protect Fidélio, who reveals her identity. Pizarro tries to slay her and Florestan. Suddenly the sentry on the Seville road sounds his trumpet. The king's minister is approaching. Jacquino appears at the head of the stairs with a squad of soldiers to lead the prisoners from their cells. Léonore and Florestan are saved (II, 3-4).

The second tableau of the act presents the esplanade of the prison, where a lively crowd is gathered to witness the liberation of the prisoners and the reunion of families. Don Fernando announces that the king has sent him to restore justice (II, 5). Rocco pushes through the crowd to describe the wrongs done to Léonore and Florestan, while he establishes their identities. Fernando gives to Léonore the opportunity to cast off her husband's chains, and he orders Pizarro led away to receive his just desserts (II, 6).

The opera was quite popular at the Garnier Palace,* where it enjoyed its 84th performance on 20 May 1960 after revivals in 1936, 1940, and 1955. This last production was offered by the Stuttgart Opera Company under the direction of Wieland Wagner, who was responsible for its sets and costumes at this time. More recently, _Fidélio_ has been billed at the Opéra on 16 dates between 1962 and 1968. Beethoven's work is recognized as one of the most typical of rescue operas (see eighteenth-century volume for rescue opera).

BIBLIOGRAPHY: _L'Avant-scène_ 10 (May-June 1977), 1-129; Camille Bellaigue, _Impressions musicales et littéraires_ (Paris: Delagrave, n.d.), 177-89; Henry Blaze de Bury, _Musiciens contemporains_ (Paris: Michel Levy frères, 1856), 73-85; Jean Chantovoine, "Théâtre national de l'Opéra . . . _Fidélio_, de Beethoven," _Le Ménestrel_ 99, no. 4 (22 January 1937), 27-28; idem, "Représentations de l'Opéra de Vienne (à l'Opéra de Paris)," _Le Ménestrel_ 90, no. 21 (25 May 1928), 231-32; idem, "Représentations de l'Opéra de La Haye: _Fidélio_ . . .," _Le Ménestrel_ 88, no. 9 (26 February 1926), 94-95; Guy de Charnacé, _Musique et musiciens_ (Paris: P. Lethielleux, 1874), 59-72; Edward Joseph Dent, _Opera_ (Westport, Conn.: Greenwood Press, 1978), 59-61; EDS II, 140-46; Louis C. Elson, _Famous Composers and Their Works_ (Boston: J. B. Miller Co., 1900), 149; HBM 73-85; Dyneley Hussey, "Beethoven as a Composer of Opera," _M&L_ 8 (1927), 243-52; Edgar Istel, "Beethoven's _Léonor_ and _Fidélio_," _MQ_ 7 (1921), 226-51; JB 110-12; KCOB 145-52; Maurice Kufferath, _"Fidélio" de L. van Beethoven_ (Paris: Fischbacher, 1913); René

Leibowitz, "Fidélio ou l'amour de l'opéra," Les Temps modernes 10 (1955), 1505-17; Jean Massin and Brigitte Massin, Ludwig van Beethoven (Paris: Fayard, 1967), 643-50; MCDE I, 84-86; MSRL 10-12; OCM 258-68; ON 27, no. 12 (26 January 1963), insert; OQE 19-22; PBSW 47-48, 219; Ernest Reyer, Notes de musique (Paris: Charpentier, 1875), 277-91; SSBO 119-21; SW 92-94; Thompson 541, 2145; WOC 74.

Le Fifre enchanté is an opéra-comique in a single act with a score by Jacques Offenbach* and a libretto by Charles Nuitter* and Tréfeu. It had its world premiere at Ems in 1867, and it was produced for the first time in Paris on 30 September 1868 at the Théâtre des Bouffes-Parisiens. This work by Offenbach was never performed before the public at the Opéra, but it was rehearsed there in preparation for a private presentation given by the performers from the Opéra at the Hotel Claridge in Paris during a gala celebration honoring King Fouad of Egypt on 24 October 1927.

The action of Offenbach's work evolves in the living room of M. and Mme Robin, where Caroline is dusting the furniture and awaiting the arrival in town of her sweetheart, a fifer with the First Grenadiers. M. Popelinet arrives to see Mme Robin, to whom he has been writing fervent love letters. Recently Mme Robin answered one of these letters because she was angry with her husband, and lawyer Popelinet has had his hopes aroused. He confesses his love for Mme Robin to Caroline and bribes her to remain silent, but she ushers him out of the house.

Charlotte and Robin enter from the bedroom, where they have been arguing. They sit down on opposite sides of the room to pout and to frown. Robin is dressed in his best clothes, but Charlotte does not believe that he is going to a business conference with the director of his firm. He insists that he is telling the truth, and he bribes Caroline to corroborate his story that he is needed urgently at the office. Charlotte remains skeptical, and Robin storms out of the house. Charlotte now bribes Caroline to tell her the truth, and Caroline admits that Robin bribed her to say that his presence at his office was necessary. Charlotte tells Caroline that she has had enough deception in her marriage. She plans to get a divorce, and she explains that she is going to see a lawyer, M. Popelinet. She leaves the house.

Caroline hears the Grenadiers' fife and drum corps in the street. She rushes to the window, where she waves to Rigobert. He enters the house, and they embrace with enthusiasm, but a knock on the door announces Charlotte's return. Caroline hides Rigobert in the closet. Charlotte explains her premature return by saying that Popelinet was not in his office. She adds that he will come to her home as soon as he is free.

A knock on the door announces lawyer Popelinet's visit, and Charlotte orders Caroline to leave her alone with her adviser. Popelinet offers flowers and flattering love poetry to Charlotte, who protests against his advances. She insists that she seeks only legal advice.

A waitress from a nearby restaurant knocks at the door. She has a sumptuous dinner ordered by Popelinet for his tête-à-tête with Charlotte, who rebukes the lawyer once again for his impertinence. The unexpected sound of a key in the front door announces that Robin has returned home, and Charlotte hides the telltale supper. Popelinet conceals himself in a second closet. Charlotte and Caroline then turn off the lights and rush upstairs to their rooms.

Robin enters with a coachman whom he thanks for rescuing him in the rue Corbeau, where his dinner with Isabelle was interrupted by a colonel from the Grenadiers. The two men in the closets hear every word. Popelinet lives in the rue Corbeau; the colonel is from Rigobert's regiment. Suddenly, Popelinet and Rigobert see each other peering through the transoms of their respective closets. The coachman leaves.

Charlotte and Caroline return downstaris, when Robin calls. They all smell the hidden supper, especially the truffles, and Robin wishes to know how these delicacies have come into the house. He asks for something to eat because he is hungry, but he is interrupted by a noise in the closet. He opens the door and finds a grenadier. Caroline and Charlotte look surprised. Robin demands to know why the interloper is in the house, and Rigobert explains that he is a devil, a fact that he sets out to prove with his flute. First, he tells Robin how he was taken unawares by a colonel in Isabelle's apartment. Second, he produces the hidden supper for hungry Robin. When Robin calls for a drink, the waitress reappears with flaming punch.

Charlotte challenges her husband to explain his presence in Isabelle's apartment and asks for a divorce. He replies that he would give her a divorce on the spot, if there were a lawyer on hand. Rigobert calls upon his magic flute for the fourth time, and Popelinet appears. Rigobert extracts Charlotte's impetuous letter from Popelinet's pocket and returns it to Charlotte. He asks Caroline to marry him, and she agrees. M. and Mme Robin forgive each other and plan a second honeymoon, while Popelinet marches out the front door as the curtain falls.

The principal female roles in Le Fifre enchanté were filled by Mmes Ketty Lapeyrette* (Mme Robin) and Ritter-Ciampi (Caroline), while Marcelle Denya sang Rigobert in travesty. André Baugé (Popelinet) and Henri Fabert* (Robin) were cast in the two other important male parts.

BIBLIOGRAPHY: AEM 9, 1892-1901; EDS VII, 1293-98; Richard Northcutt, Jacques Offenbach: a Sketch of His Life and a Record of His Operas (London: The Press Printers, 1917), 44; David Rissin, Offenbach ou le rire en musique (Paris: Fayard, 1980); SW 94.

La Fille de marbre was a pantomic ballet in two acts and three tableaux with a score by Cesare Pugni.* Its book and choreography were the work of Charles Saint-Léon.* The sets were designed by Cambon and Thierry. It had its world premiere at the Royal Academy of Music in Paris on 20 October 1847.

The ballet begins in the place of the Genius of Fire to which Satan and the sculptor Manassès have come to obtain a soul for the beautiful marble statue that the artist has just completed. He is willing to sell his own soul to Satan to obtain this favor, and Belphégor, chief of the salamanders, agrees to animate the statue. He performs the rite of animation and names the figure Fatma, but he cautions that she will return to stone if she yields to love. Manassès is overjoyed, although Satan puts his mark on Fatma, and the artist himself assumes a hellish appearance. Belphégor tells Manassès that the Moorish prince Alyatar is already in love with Fatma, and he warns him that this love may prove fatal. The cavern of the salamanders closes, and the two earthlings are wafted back to Seville on Satan's breath (I, tabl. 1).

In Seville, Alyatar awakens suddenly from a deep sleep. He believes that Fatma is a product of his dreams, but Satan assures him that she is alive and close at hand. It is a feast day, and Manassès alarms a group of dancers when he appears in his infernal costume, but he dispels their fright by presenting Fatma as a gypsy dancer. A constable stops her performance because gypsies are not allowed in the city. A sign announcing this ordinance changes its text mysteriously, however, and the dancer is allowed to continue. The corregidor enters to inform her that she is breaking the law, but he finds that he is helpless and unable to enforce his own orders. The celebration reaches its height, and Alyatar is attracted to the square. He is surprised to see the girl of his dreams. He rushes up to her, and alarmed Manassès tries in vain to lead the girl away. The absorbed dancers do not notice a procession of penitents crossing the Guadalquivir river until their leader orders the corregidor to arrest the gypsies. Manassès and Fatma escape in a boat, and the nobles among the dancers pursue them. Alyatar leaps from a bridge to swim after Fatma, when he cannot find an empty boat (I, tabl. 2).

The scene shifts to Grenada, where the Spanish king is celebrating his victory over the Moors. Fatma enters with the nobles led by Sandoval, who are still trying to dance with her, and the king is so struck by her beauty that he gives her a necklace. Manassès is not disturbed by the attention paid to his companion by the king and the nobles because the Moorish prince is not on the scene. Yet Alyatar is present, and he manages to declare his passion to the beautiful gypsy. She is moved to tears by his words, but she warns him not to speak of love to her again. He reveals that his compatriots are waiting for him to give the signal to arise in revolt against the Spaniards. Bugles blow, and he runs off with Satan at his heels to join his troops. The Moors are victorious and regain possession of the Alhambra. Alyatar is proclaimed king of Grenada, and he asks Fatma to share his throne. She yields to the urgings of her heart and accepts his offer. She is about to ascend the throne when the sky darkens and thunder rolls. The new queen turns to stone, and Alyatar smashes his crown. Manassès is struck dead by a lightning bolt, and Satan claims his soul (II, tabl. 1).

It has been suggested that this ballet based upon a variation of the Pygmalion story is a first version of the librettist's Les Elfes.* Also, it is noteworthy that the vocal portion of the original text of La Fille de marbre was suppressed at rehearsals because it was decided that the composition was to be produced in pantomime. The score was competent but not outstanding, although it did furnish Sain-Léon (Manassès) and his wife Francesca Cerrito* (Fatma) the opportunity to demonstrate that they were exceptional performers. The other male roles were created by Elie (Cadavel), H. Desplaces (Alyatar), Quériau (Belphégor), Francisque Berthier* (the Corregidor), Toussaint (Don Sandoval), Adici (the constable), and L'Enfant (the penitent, the king). The ballet was billed on only a score of dates at the opera house in the rue Le Peletier,* but it had served the purpose for which it had been produced so hastily, that is, to present Fanny Cerrito and her husband to the public. It was not long before the two dancers were invited to perform for Louis Philippe at Saint-Cloud, where the ballerina received jewelry and her husband was rewarded with cash.

BIBLIOGRAPHY: CB 319-24; Chouquet 408; CODB 195; Ivor Guest, The Ballet of the Second Empire (Middletown, Conn.: Wesleyan University Press, 1974), 29-33, 258; Lajarte II, 186; PBR 117; SS 119.

La Fille de Mme Angot is an opéra-comique in three acts with a score by Charles Lecocq and a libretto by Clairville, Konig, an Giraudin. It had its world premiere in Brussels on 4 December 1872, and it was produced for the first time in Paris at the Théâtre des Folies Dramatiques on 21 February 1873. As an opéra-comique, it was not traditionally suited for adoption into the repertory at the Opéra, where its second act was performed only once on 28 Arpil 1912. The occasion of this presentation was a gala organized by Aviation Française.

The daughter of Mme Angot is Clairette, who has been adopted by the merchants of the marketplace, where the action begins with the plan to marry the young girl to the barber Pomponnet. This matrimonial project runs into difficulty because Clairette has fallen in love with Ange Pitou, a poet dedicated to defending the Royalist cause in his writings, although the Revolution of 1789 has already begun, and France is now ruled by the Directorate.

Ange Pitou's latest piece of poetry is a satirical song about Mlle Lange, an actress who is also the mistress of Barras, head of the Directorate. Mlle Lange leads an unexpectedly complicated life, however, because she has a secret lover named Larivaudière, and, as might be expected, Larivaudière is not eager to have Pitou's song sung all over France. Thus, he pays the poet not to publish his composition dealing with the life and loves of Mlle Lange.

Yet Larivaudière's bribe does not succeed in suppressing the song, since Clairette does not wish to marry Pomponnet; she is in love with Pitou. She decides to sing Pitou's song because Pitou is arrested whenever he sings it, and, if she is arrested, her unwanted marriage will be postponed because she will be in jail. Thus, she sings the song and is thrown into prison (a. 1).

The setting changes to Mlle Lange's drawing room, where the curious mistress of Barras uses her lover's influence to bring Clairette to her home. While Pomponnet is dressing Mlle Lange's hair, he suggests that it is Ange Pitou's fault that innocent Clairette has been arrested because it was Pitou who wrote the song. The barber leaves to get a copy of the song to support his argument. When Clairette and Mlle Lange find themselves alone together, they discover that they are old friends and went to school together. When Larivaudière arrives, he becomes jealous of Pitou, but Lange assures him that they must have Pitou on their side, because they are aligned with Barras, who is in fact hatching a Royalist plot. Pomponnet now returns, but he is arrested because he has a copy of Pitou's song (a. 2).

A meeting of the Royalists takes place in a hall later the same day, and the Hussars arrive on the scene to arrest the subversive agitators. Resourceful, the Royalists assert that they are having a dance. They invite the Hussars to join them. The Hussars are deceived by this ruse, and they share in the festivities. In the meantime, Clairette discovers that Lange is in love with

Pitou, and she decides to expose them. Finally, however, she concludes that Lange and Pitou deserve each other, and she agrees to marry Pomponnet (a. 3).

Mme Amélie Legallois* (Mlle Lange) and Edmée Favart (Clairette) filled the female roles at the sole performance of La Fille de Mme Angot at the Opéra, and the male parts were assigned to MM. Sardet (Ange Pitou), Dinh Gilly* (Pomponnet), and Alberti (Larivaudière).

BIBLIOGRAPHY: Gabriel Couret, "La Fille de Madame Angot," L'Opéra de Paris 24 (n.d.), 60-61; Maurice Decerf, "La Fille de Madame Angot à la salle Favart," L'Opéra de Paris 8 (n.d.), 44-47; H. Moréno, "Première Représentation de la Fille de Mme Angot," Le Ménestrel 39 (23 February 1873); PBSW 219; SW 94; Thompson 544; WOC 74-75.

La Fille de Roland was billed as a musical tragedy in four acts with a score by Henri Rabaud* and a libretto by Paul Ferrier. It had its world premiere at the Opéra-Comique in Paris on 16 March 1904, and it was then performed in Brussels at the Théâtre Royal de la Monnaie on 7 October 1921. It was not produced at the Garnier Palace* until 27 October 1922, when it was furnished with sets by Paquereau.

The opera begins in the vast hall of Montblois castle within sight of the mountains of Saxony, where Radbert and Théobalt are awaiting the return of Count Amaury from Roncevaux. Amaury has gone to Roncevaux to expiate an unspecified crime that he has committed in the past. His son Gérald has captured Ragenhardt and freed his Frankish captive Berthe; Amaury pardons Ragenhardt after his return to Montblois on condition that he become a Christian. Ragenhardt warns Amaury and his men that the younger Saxons are about to rise against him to avenge their fathers' deaths (I, 1-3). Count Amaury offers protection to Berthe, who reveals that she is the daughter of Aude and Roland. Amaury is terrified when he learns her identity, but Gérald expresses his admiration for the hero of Roncevaux (I, 4). Amaury has visions of the Christian defeat at Roncevaux and recalls the Franksih soldiers denouncing him as a traitor (I, 5).

Gérald regrets Berthe's imminent departure and admits his love for her to his father, but Amaury reminds him that his lower rank forbids him to think of marrying her. He makes Gérald swear not to follow her to Aix-la-Chapelle (II, 1-2). Radbert announces the approach of the imperial escort for Berthe, and Amaury cannot restrain himself from remarking upon the incongruity of the duke de Nayme entrusting himself to Ganelon's hospitality. Also, Amaury wonders whether he will be recognized (II, 3). The duke acknowledges Gérald's prowess in protecting Berthe and suggests a toast and some poetry. All present except Ragenhardt drink to the health of Charlemagne; Ragenhardt proposes a toast to Ganelon. The duke and his men object that Ganelon betrayed Roland (II, 4), and the duke adds that his greatest regret is that he saved Ganelon's life at Verdun by slaying King Morglan. Ragenhardt reveals that he is Morglan's son, but he fails to recognize Amaury as Ganelon. The duke de Nayme asks Count Amaury to permit his son to come with him because Charlemagne wishes to honor Berthe's rescuer. Gérald has sworn not to follow her, but she declares her love for him to Amaury, and he cannot avoid granting her request (II, 5-8).

The setting shifts to the imperial palace at Aix-la-Chapelle, where Charlemagne is explaining to Berthe that more than 30 barons have perished in trying to wrest Roland's sword Durandal from the Sarracen champion. He insists that he will permit no more bloodshed over the precious relic. Berthe suggests that Gérald may be able to retrieve it (III, 1-2). Noéthold presents himself for battle once more, and Charlemagne declares that there will be no fighting for Durandal except the duel between Noéthold and himself. The court protests (III, 3), and Gérald rings the ball as a signal of his challenge. Charlemagne gives Gérald his sword Joyeuse, and the warriors leave for the arena, where Gérald wins the day (III, 4-5). Gérald returns the swords to Charlemagne, who gives Berthe's hand in marriage to the victor (III, 6). Amaury feels that his son's success will protect him now, but Charlemagne encounters him by chance and recognizes him. Amaury reveals that Gérald is his son, and Charlemagne does not know what to do in the name of justice (III, 7-8).

The court has assembled to celebrate the marriage of Gérald and Berthe at which the duke de Nayme is officiating. When the duke asks whether any man opposes the marriage, Ragenhardt voices his opposition and asserts that he will give his reasons to the emperor (IV, 1). Gérald suggests to his father that Ragenhardt is insane, but Amaury confesses to his son that he is Ganelon. Gérald laments his father's situation and is crushed by the suffering that he must have endured. Amaury flees before the court returns, and Gérald faces his peers alone. Charlemagne asks his advisers for a judgment, and the barons declare that Gérald has redeemed the honor of his name. Berthe testifies that she wishes to be Gérald's wife, but he responds the he no longer dares to become her husband. He and his father must go into exile to restore their honor. Charlemagne commends this noble decision, and Berthe bids farewell to Gérald, who leaves with Durandal and his father at his side (IV, 2-3).

The tortured exposition of the first act along with the improbable basis of the intrigue hurt the opera, and it was dropped from the repertory after a dozen performances. It was revived for its 12th billing on 11 January 1926. The title-role was filled for the first time at the Opéra by Germaine Lubin, and the male parts were created there by Paul Franz* (Gérald), Edouard Rouard (Amaury), Jean-François Delmas* (Charlemagne), Henri Fabert* (Ragenhardt), and André Gresse* (duke de Nayme).

BIBLIOGRAPHY: *Paul Bertrand, "Opéra: La Fille de Roland," Le Ménestrel 84, no. 44 (3 November 1922), 435-36; André Coeuroy, La Musique française moderne (Paris: Delagrave, 1922), 115-20; René Dumesnil, La Musique Contemporaine en France (Paris: Armand Colin, 1930) II, 117-20; Gabriel Fauré, Opinions musicales (Paris: Rieder, 1930), 103-7; Henri Rebois, Les Grands Prix de Rome de musique (Paris: Firmin-Didot, 1932), 73-74; SW 95.*

La Fille du Danube was a pantomime-ballet in two acts and four tableaux with a score by Adolphe Adam* and a libretto by Filippo Taglioni, who also created the choreography (see eighteenth-century volume for Taglioni). Pierre Cicéri* designed the scenery for the first, third, and fourth tableaux, while the second tableau was a result of a collaboration by Diéterle, Feuchère, and Séchan. It had its world premiere at the Royal Academy of Music in Paris on 21 September 1836. A sequel to *La Sylphide*,* *La Fille du Danube* was billed on 30 programs between the time of its first presentation and 11 September 1840. It was mounted at the Theatre Royal in Drury Lane under the title of The Daughter of the Danube on 21 November 1837, and it was taken to St. Petersburg by its choreographer and his daughter in 1837.

The ballet is set in the Doneschingen valley nestled among the Férenbach mountains and leading down to the Danube at Neyding. Here, at the junction of the Brig and the Danube, rare aquatic flowers and plants grow in abundance and have brought the name of Vallée des Fleurs to the region. This fragrant and colorful country is under the dominion of the baron de Willibald, whose father and older brother have been slain in an assult upon Prague in 1420. The brother had buried three wives before his own death, and each of his brides had died in sudden and seemingly diabolical circumstances that deter the surviving brother from seeking a wife among the nobility. Thus, he prefers a bride of humble provenance, and he decides to look for her in the Vallée des Fleurs. He hears of a young girl found among the flowers one morning by Irmengarde. She is called Fleur-des-Champs because no one knows her true identity. It is to her that the baron de Willibald proposes marriage through his squire Rudolph. Inevitabley, the young couple fall in love, and one day the undines emerge from the Danube to lull them to sleep, while the nymph of the river puts rings on their fingers. They awaken and throw themselves into each other's arms. Irmengarde comes upon them, however, and she dismisses Rudolph in anger. The baron does not dismiss his suit for Fleur-des-Champs' hand, however, and he invites all the girls of the valley to visit him so that he may select a bride. He resorts to this ploy because he cannot single out Fleur-des-Champs as his choice at this time (I, tabl. 1).

The baron welcomes his guests to his lavish reception at his château de Neyding, where the knights and ladies of the court have gathered in sumptuous elegance. The young girls enter dressed in white and wearing flowers; they dance among themselves. The ladies of the court grow indignant over their presence, and the baron angers the nobles with the proposal of marriage that he extends to Fleur-des-Champs. He is dismayed in his turn, when Rudolph steps forward to claim Fleur-des-Champs as his bride. Alarmed by this disturbing development, the young girl runs to the balcony overlooking the Danube. She rejects the baron and throws her bouquet to Rudolph before leaping into the river (I, tabl. 2).

Rudolph has become mad, and he wanders about the court and along the river in search of his sweetheart. One day, the nymph and undines of the Danube seem to confront him with Fleur-des-Champs, but it is only a vision. Whoever wishes Fleur-des-Champs must take her from her father's arms. The baron hits upon a scheme to restore his squire to health. He will have one of the village maidens dress as Fleur-des-Champs. The ruse is executed, but the girl's veil falls from her face, and Rudolph realizes that he has been deceived. Despairing, he throws himself into the river (II, tabl. 3).

The Danube overflows its banks, and thunder rolls across the skies. The river has received into his arms the husband of his daughter. Rudolph is carried down to the sacred grotto of the Danube, where his reason and life are restored. Yet one trial remains. He must pick Fleur-des-Champs from among all the veiled nymphs without being deceived a second time. He withstands all their tricks and wiles by fighting off the imposters with his sweetheart's bouquet. Finally he detects Fleurs-des-Champs, and he persuades the nymph of the river to allow him and her to return to the world, where no one can separate them from each other by any means (II, tabl. 4). A final note in the libretto adds that the heartbroken baron presented the happy couple with a generous dowry before entering an Italian monastery, where he died in 1430.

The three female roles were filled by Mlles Marie Taglioni* (Fleur-des-Champs), Florentine (Irmengarde), and Pauline Leroux (a young girl). The male parts were created by MM. Montjoie (the baron), Joseph Mazilier* (Rudolph), Ragaine (the Danube), and Quériau (an officer of the baron). The ballet was praised for its settings and choreography, but at least one critic felt that the performers failed to endow the action with sufficient animation.

BIBLIOGRAPHY: ACD 186; Camille Bellaigue, Notes brèves (Paris: C. Delagrave, 1914), 167-86; CB 99-103; Chouquet 399; CODB 195; Jacques François F. E. Halévy, Souvenirs et portraits (Paris: Michel Levy frères, 1861), 300-301; Lajarte II,

154; J. M., "Reprise de La Fille du Danube," FM 1 (23 October 1838), 1; Moniteur univresel 277 (5 October 1836), 1940; PBR 100; Arthur Pougin, Adolphe Adam, sa vie, sa carrière, ses mémoires artistiques (Geneva: Minkoff reprint, 1973), 120-22; RBP 154-57; SS 101-2.

La Fille du Far-West, known in Italian as La Fanciulla del West, is an opera in three acts with a score by Giacomo Puccini* and a libretto by Guelfo Civinini and Carlo Zangarini. It is derived from David Belasco's play entitled The Girl of the Golden West, which Puccini saw one evening on Broadway. The work had its world premiere at the Metropolitan Opera in New York on 12 December 1910. It was performed in Rome and London during 1911, and it had its first presentation at the Monte Carlo opera house on 2 April 1912. Finally, the company of the Monte Carlo Opera gave the second act of Puccini's composition at the Garnier Palace* on 16 May 1912. The French version of the opera by Maurice Vaucaire is entitled La Fille du Far-West, a title that ignores the significance and pertinency of the phrase "Golden West" in the original English title.

The action of the opera unfolds during the Gold Rush of 1849 in California, and the curtain rises to disclose the interior of the Polka saloon, where a $5,000 reward has been posted by Wells Fargo for the arrest of the outlaw Ramerrez. A group of miners starts a game of cards, and other customers call for drinks or food. Jack Wallace sings a song about his mother; homesick Larkens begins to weep, and the miners take up a collection to purchase his ticket to England. A fight starts, when Sonora catches Sid cheating at cards. The players wish to hang him, but sheriff Jack Rance interferes. The Wells Fargo agent Ashby discloses that Ramerrez is thought to be in the region. He adds that he and Minnie are going to be married, and Sonora laughs at him. A fight starts again, but Minnie stops this brawl before it becomes serious. The miners offer her gifts, and she gives them a Bible lesson. The mail arrives, and Ashby receives information from an informer: Ramerrez will be at nearby Palmes.

Dick Johnson enters and orders whisky. Rance begins to annoy him, but he and Minnie continue to discuss the days when they knew each other in

Monterey. Jealous Rance interrupts them again. He tries to arouse the miners against Johnson, but Minnie vouches for him. Minnie and he begin to waltz, and Rance sulks, but the situation changes immediately when a crowd enters with Castro. The crowd is led by Ashby, who is calling for the prisoner to be hanged. Castro tries to save himself by promising to reveal Ramerrez' hideout. Rance leads a posse after the fugitive, and Nick leaves Minnie to guard the gold dust with Johnson. Alone, they fall to talking, and Minnie invites him to see her simple home (a. 1).

The second act is set in Minnie's cabin an hour later. The Indian Wowle is crouched near the fireplace with her child on her back. Her man Billy enters, and they sup together. Minnie welcomes Johnson with a kiss. The lovers hear three shots, and they ignore them, but Minnie decides that Johnson must spend the night in her cabin on account of the heavy snowfall. A voice calls out in the night. It is Nick and the men from Polka come to protect her because Ramerrez has been identified. He is the stranger calling himself Johnson. Minnie assures them that she is safe. She confronts Johnson-Ramerrez, and he pleads that he has known only an outlaw's life since childhood. He leaves the cabin an shots ring out. Minnie runs to him and finds him wounded. She hides him on the rafters of her cabin. Rance enters looking for Ramerrez, but he seizes Minnie to kiss her. She threatens him with a bottle, and he moves away. A drop of blood falls on his hand. It is followed by other drops of blood. He orders Johnson to descend from his hiding place; Rance grants him a few moments of grace, and he faints. Minnie invites Rance to gamble at cards. If he wins, she will belong to him; if he loses, Ramerrez will be hers. He agrees, and she wins by pulling a full house from her stocking. He leaves in disgust. She bursts out laughing and kisses Johnson's head, which is still on the table (a. 2).

Ashby, Nick, and Rance are in a clearing in the mountains, where they are still cursing and hunting Ramerrez. Their trackers inform them that they have surrounded their prey, but Ramerrez escapes again. He runs into Sonora's men eventually, however, and his captors emerge from the forest with their pale and disheveled prisoner. Rance assures him that his punishment will be swift and certain, and the men accuse him of a string of crimes that he denies. He begs his captors not to tell Minnie how he died at the end of a rope; he asks them to say that he is free and determined to reform his ways. Rance refuses his request. He walks to the tree where he is to be hanged when Minnie rides in with Nick. Rance calls for Ramerrez' execution, but his henchmen ignore him, and Minnie defies him. He warns her not to interfere, but she aims her gun at him and tells the crowd that the prisoner has already started to mend his ways. Sonora agrees that they owe Minnie at least one kind act, and she declares that she alone has taught them love and the meaning of redemption. Sonora cuts the rope away from Johnson's neck, and he and Minnie bid farewell to California and its gold (a. 3).

La Fille du Far-West did not enjoy a long run at the Opéra, where it has been performed in its entirety on only three occasions. Its second act has been performed in this theatre on another three dates. When it was given at the Garnier Palace for the first time, the cast featured Carmen Melis* as Minnie, Enrico Caruso* as Dick Johnson, and Titta Ruffo* as Jack Rance. The second act was given in the French version by Vaucaire on 4 May 1916 with Claire Friche as Minnie, John Sullivan as Dick Johnson, and Louis Lestelly as Jack Rance.

BIBLIOGRAPHY: Giuseppe Adami, Puccini (Milan: Fratelli Treves, 1938), 54-57; Dominique Amy, Giacomo Puccini (Paris: Seghers, 1970), 70-76; Mosco Carner, Puccini: a Critical Biography (Old Woking, Surrey: Duckworth, 1974), 401-14; Claudio Casini, Giacomo Puccini (Turin: Utet, 1978), 346-58; Norbert Christen, Giacomo Puccini (Hamburg: Karl Dieter Wagner, 1978), 292-96; Arnaldo Fraccaroli, La Vita di Giacomo Puccini (Milan: G. Ricordi, 1925), 135-53; Guido M. Gatti, "The Work of Giacomo Puccini," MQ 14 (1928), 216-54; André Gauthier, Puccini (Paris: Du Seuil, 1961), 114-28; GM 149-59; A. Goléa, "A l'Opéra-Comique: La Fille du Far-West," Journal Musical Français 182-83 (July-August 1969), 17-18; Edward Greenfield, Puccini: Keeper of the Seal (Tiptree, Essex: The Anchor Press, 1958), 54-56, 58-59, 225-29; Cecil Hopkinson, A Bibliography of the Works of Giacomo Puccini, 1858-1924 (New York: Broude Brothers, 1968), 30-34; KCOB 1182-87; Gaston Knosp, G. Puccini (Brussels: Schott frères, 1937), 125-48;

LOA 192-94; Giorgio Magri, Puccini e rue rime (Milan: Giorgio Borletti, 1974), 344-46, 356; George R. Marek, Puccini: a Biography (New York: Simon and Schuster, 1951), 260-73, 344-47; Wolfgang Marggraf, Giacomo Puccini (Leipzig: Philipp Reclam, 1977), 131-40; Guido Marotti, Giacomo Puccini (Florence: Valecchi, 1949), 141-46; MCDE 735-36; MOC 149-59; Modern Drama and Opera: Reading Lists on the Works of Various Authors, ed. Frederick W. Faxon (Boston: The Boston Book Co., 1915), 215-17; MSRL 175; "Opéra représentation italienne . . . La Fille du Far-West," Le Ménestrel 78 (25 May 1912), 163-64; OQE 273-77; PBSW 217; Leonardo Pinzauti, Giacomo Puccini (Turin: Eri, 1975), 107-25, 192-94; idem, Puccini: una vita (Florence: Vallecchi, 1974), 107-26; Giacomo Puccini, Letters, ed. Giuseppe Adami, trans. Ena Makin (New York: AMS Press, 1971), 172-73, 177, 180; Claudio Sartori, Puccini (Milan: Nuova Academia Editrice, 1958), 279-91, 369-70; Vincent Seligman, Puccini Among Friends (London: Macmillan 7 Co., 1938), 131-216; Enzo Siciliano, Puccini (Milan: Rizzoli, 1976), 249-77; Richard Specht, Giacomo Puccini: the Man, His Life, His Work (Westport, Conn.: Greenwood Press, 1970), 192-205; SSBO 351-52, 356-57; R. A. Streatfeild, The Opera (Westport, Conn.: Greenwood Press, 1971), 303-4; SW 95-96; Thompson 526, 2141-43; Richard Valente, The Verismo of Giacomo Puccini (Ann Arbor, Mi.: Braun-Blumfield, 1971), 189-207; William Weaver, Puccini, the Man and His Music (New York: E. P. Dutton, 1977), 69-89, 137-39.

La Fille mal gardée was a pantomime-ballet that Jean Bercher Dauberval had composed for the Grand Théâtre at Bordeaux in 1786 and that Jean Aumer returned to the larger stage of the Royal Academy of Music with considerable changes on 17 November 1828 (see eighteenth-century volume for Dauberval and Aumer). The music was the work of Aumer. The ballet was performed on a score of dates during the 1828-29 season, and it was withdrawn temporarily after its 36th presentation on 4 January 1833. It was then returned to the stage on 30 December 1836 as a companion piece for Guillaume Tell.* This program returned only 1,098 francs 40 centimes to the box office, but the ballet was kept alive and given on another 16 dates between 1837 and 1840 before it was dropped from the repertory after its 53rd billing on 9 September 1840. Subsequently, it was danced on another 26 dates.

The ballet is set in a hamlet near Paris, where Lise is looking for Colas. She cannot find him and ties a ribbon to a tree before going back into her house. Colas notices the ribbon and throws a kiss through the window to Lise, but her mother sees him and starts to throw kitchen utensils at him. He runs away, and Simone scolds her daughter; Colas sneaks into the stable. Simone gives Lise a churn and cream to make butter, and Colas starts to flirt with her while helping with the churning. He is frightened away by the noise of the young village girls coming to take Lise to work with them, but Simone chases everybody away. Thomas and his son Alain arrive, and Simone accepts Thomas' suggestion that Lise and Alain marry. Lise leaves for the fields with her mother, Thomas, and Alain, despite her disapproval of their plans for her future.

The scene shifts to a field filled with harvesters. Colas rejoins Lise and her company for lunch. When the dancing starts, he picks Lise for his partner. Thomas and Alain become resentful and leave. The dancing continues until a storm interrupts the harvesters' activities.

The second act opens with Simone and her daughter at home. Simone is tired from working and sits down by her spinning wheel after closing the door for the night. She drops off to sleep, and Colas appears at the barred transom. Simone awakens and frightens him away. Lise dances to distract her mother, and the harvesters arrive with sheaves of wheat. They ask for their wages and a drink. Simone takes them to the cellar after barring the door behind the workers. Lise looks for her spindle to resume spinning, and Colas emerges from the sheaves. She is angry because her lover has been so bold, but she forgives him quickly and begins to weep over her predicament. Her sympathetic lover rushes to hold her up when she appears on the point of fainting. Suddenly Simone comes upstairs while Colas is holding Lise, and he rushes into Simone's bedroom in a panic. Lise pretends to be asleep. Simone accepts the situation, although she is suspicious and orders Lise upstairs. Thomas, Alain, and the notary arrive to conclude the marriage between Alain and Lise; the contract is signed. Simone produces her daughter's dowry. Simone suggests to Alain that he go upstairs to get his bride, and Colas refuses him admission to the bedroom. He asks Simone for Lise's hand, and the notary and guests support his request. Simone yields to their entreaties. Thomas and his son depart in haste and anger, but the remainder of the company lingers to share in the wedding celebration.

The principal female roles were filled by Mmes Lise Noblet,* Marie Taglioni,* and Pauline Montessu* with Albert and Paul in the male parts (see eighteenth-century volume for Albert). Although this ballet is now nearly 200 years old, it is still danced by the Soviet Ballet, and Anna Pavlova* appeared in it in London with her company under its English title of Useless Precautions. In Paris, it was given its 79th presentation under its French title at a gala benefit on 23 February 1922. Lise, now called Licette, was danced by Mlle A. Balachova with Smolzoff as Colin, Moysennko as Simone, Alexandroff as Thomas now known as Michot, and Strouknoff as Alain renamed Nicaise. Simone was frequently filled by a man, and Enrico Cecchetti was often cast in this role.

BIBLIOGRAPHY: ACD 186-87; AEM VI, 250-59; L'Avant-scène, Ballet-Danse 5 (February-April 1981), 115-58; Clive Barns, "La Fille mal gardée," Dance and Dancers 11, no. 3 (March 1960), 6-10; CB 2-5; Chouquet 394; CODB 195-96; EDS I, 1139-41; GBAL, 228-35; GBGB 160-69; GMSM 142-61, 189, HAZ 145-46; André-Philippe Hersin, "A l'Opéra, La Fille mal gardée," SDLD 136 (Summer 1981), 8-11; idem, "A Roven . . . La Fille mal gardée," SDLD 113 (10 April 1979), 11-12; Lajarte II, 132-33; Bruce Merrill, "A French Fille: Back at the Opéra," D Mag 55, no. 8 (August 1981), 47; Moniteur universel 324 (19 November 1828) 1726; PBR 76; Grace Robert, The Borzoi Book of Ballets (New York: Alfred A. Knopf, 1946), 130-34; SS 76-138; SW 279-80.

La Filleule des fées was billed as a grand fairy ballet in three acts, seven tableaux, and a prologue. The libretto was the work of Jules Vernoy de Saint-Georges* and Jules Perrot*; its score was composed by Adolphe Adam* and Clemenceau de Saint-Julien.* It had its world premiere at the Opéra on 8 October 1849 with sets by Cambon, Despléchin, and Thierry.

The curtain rises in the prologue to disclose a large room in a farmhouse with a hill and the village church visible through an open door. Servants are decorating the room with flowers and preparing for the reception after a baptism. Guillaume and his infant daughter Ysaure are seen emerging from the church followed by the nurse Berthe and the godparents. The group arrives at the farm, and Guillaume invites his guests to supper (prol., 1); he receives presents of fruit and flowers from the young girls of the region. He blesses his child, and the godfather, M. Jobin, is moved to tears. They are beginning to dine, when an old woman knocks at the door and asks for hospitality. He invites her to be seated, and a second old woman makes the same request, and then a third. Guillaume repeats his invitation, but he notices suddenly that he has 13 people at his table, and he dismisses the last guest. She objects and slaps M. Jobin before storming from the room (prol., 2). The guests continue with the celebration until night falls, and it is time for them to leave. The two aged guests in black remain (prol., 3-4), however, and the nurse rocks Ysaure to sleep. Thunder sounds in the distance, and Berthe falls asleep. The two old women arise and conjure up a crowd of other old women. This company turns without warning into a group of dazzingly dressed fairies among whom are Blanche and Rose, Ysaure's two godmothers. The fairies endow the child with the gifts of charm and beauty; they present her with a shining belt to protect her from all harm (prol., 5). The third old woman returns through the fireplace and casts a pall over the gathering. She is the Black Fairy, and she waves her wand of serpents over the infant with a promise to offer her gifts when she is 15 years old. The Black Fairy drives Rose and Blanche away and a storm erupts. The nurse awakens and takes Ysaure into her arms (prol., 6).

The first act begins at Ysaure's house with the château of Hugues de Provence visible on the hill in the distance. It is spring, and Ysaure is 15 years old. She is celebrating the season with her companions, and her foster brother has fallen in love with her. She assures him of her friendship but insists that she does not love him. He is desolate and about to jump into a well when a tiny old woman stops him. She promises to help him if he will kiss her. He overcomes his reluctance and is about to embrace her, when she turns into the Black Fairy (I, tabl. 1, sc. 1-4). An exhausted hunter enters. Two old women ask him for alms and tell his fortune. He will fall in love with the girl in the adjacent house. They touch the house with their crutches, and it becomes transparent; the hunter sees Ysaure in her room and falls in love with her. He rushes forward to speak with her, but the Black Fairy restores the original walls to the house. The hunter summons his followers to break down its door, and they hasten to comply with his order, but the Black Fairy transports the house to a platform on a hill. The two old women promise that he will see Ysaure again (I, tabl. 1, sc. 5). Ysaure descends the hill to rejoin the celebration with her godfather Jobin. Alain is confident of winning her hand with the help of the Black Fairy, but he is no less upset when the hunter proves to be Hugues de Provence. The count crowns Ysaure Queen of the Spring, and the company dances until nightfall. At the close of the celebration, Alain grasps Ysaure by the arm to separate her from the count, and the good fairies transport the prince to her room (I, tabl. 1, sc. 6).

Berthe and Alain are in Ysaure's room, where the girl is obviously angry at Alain for being so possessive. She refuses his flowers at first, but she feels sorry for him before long. Encouraged, he leaves to pick a fresh bouquet for her (I, tabl. 2, sc. 1-2). The count reveals his presence to Ysaure and proposes to her. She accepts his offer of marriage (I, tabl. 2, sc. 3). Alone, Ysaure wishes for a beautiful wedding gown, and a sumptuous dress and veil appear before her eyes. She wishes for new furniture, and her request is granted. The rooms of her home grow larger and are decorated with magnificent tapestries and expensive draperies (I, tabl. 2, sc. 4). The Black Fairy intrudes to inscribe upon the walls of her suddenly palatial residence, "You have made her so beautiful that no man can see her without losing his reason." Thunder rolls and the Black Fairy disappears. The prince returns with his retinue just as Alain appears with his fresh bouquet. The youth looks at the girl, and he is so struck by her beauty that he becomes mad. He assaults Hugues, but the count manages to escape, and Ysaure flees in terror. She leaps from a windown, but a band of genii catches her (I, tabl. 2, sc. 5-8).

The second act shifts to a wooded park furnished with statues and a fountain playing in the moonlight. The good fairies animate the statues while awaiting Ysaure, who enters on a swan (II, 1-2). Blanche and Rose warn her not to meet with Hugues lest he become mad like Alain, whom they produce as a reminder. The spectacle of her foster brother chasing his own shadow grieves her so deeply that her godmothers try to distract her by giving her almost all the powers of a fairy. She dances over the water with her companions; she conjures up Hugues (II, 3-5). Alain returns, and he becomes jealous upon seeing the preference shown to his rival. He seizes Ysaure's wand and touches Hugues with it. The prince is awakened from his protective trance. Ysaure tries to run away to protect him, but Alain touches her, and she turns into marble. Hugues tries to approach motionless Ysaure, and he is about to be driven mad when one of the good fairies revives Ysaure and spirits her away. Furious, Alain rushes after her with Hugues in tow (II, 6).

The first tableau of the third act unfolds in a cave lined with aquatic flowers and foliage. It is the home of the Springs, who are dining when Ysaure and her godmothers arrive. Ysaure is looking at her reflection in the waters here (III, 1) when Alain appears with Hugues. The madman tries to make Hugues look at Ysaure, but the good fairies strike the prince blind. Ysaure and Hugues despair over his predicament, and she retrieves her want to restore his sight, but the Black Fairy breaks her talisman. Ysaure and her godmothers beg the hostile fairy not to be so cruel and she relents. Hugues may have his sight if he will recognize Ysaure among the water-nymphs in the cave. The prince passes the test by falling at the feet of his beloved (III, 2). The mist disappears from the cave to reveal the fairies' paradise filled with jewels and gold. All the fairies of the earth arrive to celebrate the marriage of Ysaure and the prince. Alain's reason is restored, and the sight of the two happy lovers makes him regret his folly (III, 3).

La Filleule des fées has the distinction of being the last ballet in which Caronne Grisi* appeared at the Opéra. Also, it was a long work, and it was one of the most ambitious balletic productions ever attempted at the Paris opera house in the rue Le Peletier.* It enjoyed only 19 performances between its premiere and 21 December 1849, however, and it must be admitted that this was scarcely an impressive showing for a composition that Théophile Gautier* described as "a double perfection" on account of Perrot's choreography and Grisi's dancing. Also, as the forgoing synopsis of the libretto indicates, the presentation of this work entailed much ingenuity. The walls of Ysaure's cottage had to disappear and reappear, it had to be transported to the platform on the hill, and it had to be transformed into a palace before the spectators' eyes. The last two tableaux with their moonlight, sunrise, and watery effects constituted breathless spectacles and difficult staging problems by themselves. The leading roles of the ballet were created by Lucien Petipa* (prince Hugues de Provence), Jules Perrot (Alain), Francisque Berthier* (Jobin), Lenfant (Guillaume), Caronne Grisi (Ysaure, Célestine Emarot* (Blanche), Marie Taglioni* (Rose), Marquet (Black Fairy), and Aline (Berthe). Lastly, it should be noted that Grisi's last appearance at the Opéra was in the 21 December 1849 presentation of La Filleule des fees.

BIBLIOGRAPHY: CB 280-86; Ivor Guest, The Ballet of the Second Empire (Middletown, Conn.: Wesleyan University Press, 1974), 47-50; Lajarte II, 204.

Le Fils de l'etoile was a musical drama in five acts with a score by Camille Erlanger, a libretto by Catulle Mendès, and choreography by Joseph Hansen.* It had its world premiere at the Opéra on 17 April 1904 in a production by Lapissida for which Amable created and sets and Charles Bianchini designed the costumes.

The opera opens with a group of priestesses meandering through the ruins of the Israelites' temple in the city of Liberty. They are jubilant because Astarté, Bélial, Baalzébub, and Moloch have triumphed, and they predict that the jews will never restore their city. Beltis warns them that the prophet Akiba has announced that a warrior will appear in the east and that his army will be the light of heaven and earth. The priestesses reply that he will never overcome the cities of Magdala and Endor. Séphora asserts that the son of the star may have already been born to serve the God of Abraham, whom she adores. The priestesses try to seize her, but Akiba comes to the rescue of his daughter. They pray for help, and the surviving Jews rush in from the desert to ask Akiba when the Messiah will come to protect them from the legions of Rome. He can only repeat the prophecy that a star will rise. They curse him, and he prays for the coming of the Messiah. A lily grows from a rock; Séphora becomes radiant. A star appears in the firmament, and a young man shines in their midst. He is Bar-Kokeba, who tells the frightened people that he has come to rebuild the temple and to deliver his people. He will marry Séphora, and he will overturn the throne of the wicked. The priestesses return to assert their power, but the Jews place their faith in Bar-Kokéba (a. 1).

The Israelites are rebuilding the city of Liberty, Bethar. Akiba is encouraging the workers, and Séphora is awaiting the return of her husband. A messenger announces Bar-Kokéba's crushing victory over the pagans. Séphora is beginning to worry that he may have succumbed to temptation among the pagans, but he returns with his captives, among whom is Lilith. The people urge him to march against the Roman forces dispatched by the emperor, but he prefers to rest, and his followers are perplexed over this decision. He gives Lilith to Séphora as a servant, and Séphora is dismayed to see her beauty. When Lilith tries to follow Bar-Kokéba to his quarters, Séphora blocks her way, but the captive asserts that she must follow her master. Frantic, Séphora throws herself at Bar-Kokéba's feet, but he cannot withstand Lilith's charms and obeys her order to pick up her ring. Lilith's companions from Magdala mock Séphora, and Akiba warns that Lilith has come to destroy Israel. Bar-Kakéba's conscience bothers him, but he remains with his captive, while Séphora departs with her husband's sword to prove her love for him by killing Caesar (a. 2).

The third act shifts to Endor, where the pagan priestesses are warning the sorceress Beltis that the Israelites are threatening Rome. Lilith informs her allies that Séphora is on her way to Endor. Baltis disguises herself as an old woman and awaits Séphora on the steps of the temple. The Israelite sees her when she arrives in Endor, and she asks her the location of the Roman camp.

Beltis volunteers to guide her there, but she lulls her to sleep on the way. She hypnotizes Séphora and her companion so that they will awaken in the belief that they have already done what they came to do (a. 3).

Julius Séverus has been sent by Hadrien to crush the Hebrew revolt, and Séphora dreams that she is in his tent, where the general's staff is drinking, singing, and watching a divertissement (see eighteenth-century volume for divertissement). She sees herself having a private interview with Séverus. He cannot resist her charms, and she plies him with wine until he is drunk. She pulls her sword from her dress and decapitates him; her servant puts his head in a sack, and they start back to the city of Liberty. Séphora awakens and believes that her dream is a reality. She picks up a sack conveniently provided by Beltis and sets out on the journey home (a. 4).

The daughters of Magdala are in Bar-Kokéba's palace, where the leader of the Hebrews has been passing days and nights in a drunken stupor with Lilith. A chorus of Lilith's companions are singing the praises of love, and a group of dancers is portraying the mystery and power of death. Akiba urges the Hebrew servants to abandon the dissolute palace, and the soldiers of Israel are marching in an attitude of defeat. Bar-Kokéba is filled with remorse but is too weak to protest or to move. Séphora enters brandishing her sword and announcing that she has served God by slaying the emperor. Lilith and the dancers call her a fool, and she responds by emptying her sack. It contains only a stone. The Roman trumpets are heard at the walls, and Bar-Kokéba recovers his strength. He dismisses Lilith; she and her followers are chased from the city. He apologizes to Séphora, and they are reconciled. He calls for his sword and rushes into the fray, while Lilith returns defiantly to pray for a Roman victory that will destroy Hierosolyma and disperse the Kingdom of Israel. Her prayer is answered, and the surviving Israelites can only mourn the destruction of their city and the death of their lost king (a. 5).

The opera was only moderately successful and was withdrawn after its 26th presentation on 30 January 1905. At its premiere, it was furnished with an excellent cast that included Lucienne

Bréval* (Séphora), Mayrianne Héglon (Lilith), and Marcelle Demougeot* (Beltis). The male parts were created by Albert Alvarez* (Bar-Kokéba), Charles Delmar (Akiba), and Joseph Hansen (Julius Séverus). Mlle Carlotta Zambelli* starred in the ballet.

BIBLIOGRAPHY: AEM 3, 1501-4; EDS IV, 1552-54; H. Moréno, "Première Représentation du Fils de l'étoile à l'Opéra," Le Ménestrel 70 (24 April 1904), 129-31; Stoullig XXX (1904), 4-8, 12; SW 96.

Fiocre, Eugénie (b. 2 July 1845, Paris; d. 1908, ?), ballerina, entered the ballet school attached to the Opéra in 1858 and made her stage debut in the rue Le Peletier* on 19 February 1864 as a minor character in La Maschera.* She had little or no opportunity to distinguish herself as Pier Angelo, the first of the travesty roles she was to fill at the Opéra between 1864 and 1873, but she caused a sensation in her second part here. As Cupid in Néméa* on 11 July 1864, she was acclaimed for her beauty alone, and Théophile Gautier* went so far as to say that she was beauty itself, sexless and as pure as Parian marble. Yet he was not the only critic to give voice to ecstatic expressions of joy upon beholding the charms of this attractive girl of 19 capable of dazzling an entire audience. Fiocre was besieged by a phalanx of protesting suitors of whom the most serious were the Spanish banker Salamanca and the French baron and banker Soubeyran. La Fiocre perferred her compatriot.

The dancer's interests now seemed to turn more in the direction of wealthy and titled admirers, although she continued at the Opéra without difficulty because her lack of imposing talent did not become too obvious in the roles selected for her. She was cast as Fenella in the 17 February 1865 revival of La Muette de Portici,* and she managed to satisfy the public with her portrayal of Daniel Auber's* heroine as a happy lass unable to understand events transpiring around her. Gautier was still more impressed with "her sculptural beauty . . . her fine body" than her pointes and entrechats. When Perrin* was casting his new ballet Le Roi d'Yvetot,* he thought it wise to have her on the stage and adhered to the policy of assigning a travesty part to her. He gave her the role of the colonel.

Predictably enough, Gautier approved her performance in the premiere of his work on 28 December 1865; he noted that "her slender figure and proud bearing" endowed her with the presence of an Amazon queen. She was given another costume that would display her form to good advantage in the last revival of Le Dieu et la Bayadère* beginning on 22 January 1866, but Nestor Roqueplan had some complimentary things to say about her dancing on this occasion, and he was especially pleased with her pointe work and pirouettes. Yet despite these kind observations Eugénie Fiocre was selected to dance still another minor part, the shepherd Aristée in the divertissement written by Louis Mérante* for Le Juif errant* in the summer of 1866 (see eighteenth-century volume for divertissement).

These assignments given to Eugénie Fiocre may not have afforded her the opportunity to win spectacular triumphs with her dancing, but they kept her before the public eye and in the mind of the administration. Thus, when La Source* was being cast, she won the role of Nourreda in Léo Delibes'* ballet, which had its first presentation on 12 November 1866. Unfortunately, her lovely face and form notwithstanding, her ability as a dancer could not and did not measure up to the performance expected of her. Gautier flew into poetic ecstacy over "her charming body" again, but other critics were not as impressed. One journalist observed sarcastically that Fiocre had now almost learned to dance, and one of his colleagues remarked that her pas was "a kind of Oriental cancan." It was hinted strongly that her costume was too brief and certainly not within the bounds of propriety. But a young painter named Dégas was attracted to her strongly enough to choose her as his first operatic subject.

The reactions in the press to her dancing in La Source had no effect upon Eugénie Fiocre's career after 1866. She remained at the Opéra, and she was given roles in which her performance was neither a disaster nor a sensation. She appeared in the divertissement written by Petipa* for Ambroise Thomas'* Hamlet* on 9 March 1868; she was cast in another travesty role as a hunter on this occasion. She did the courtesan Phryné in the ballet added to the last act of Faust* on 3 March 1869, and her part called upon her to divest herself of her veils in an attempt to seduce

Charles Gounod's* protagonist. Lastly, she shared in the success of Coppélia* on 25 March 1870 as Frantz and took part in Gretna Green* on 5 March 1873. In 1875, at age 30, she retired to the country, where she could indulge in her favorite sport of hunting, but she was seen from time to time at the Opéra in the company of admiring friends.

BIBLIOGRAPHY: CB 294, 351, 354-59, 483-89; CODB 198; EDB 143; Ivor Guest, The Ballet of the Second Empire (Middletown, Conn.: Wesleyan University Press, 1974), 198-202, 205-8, 210-11, 217-19, 226-27; Lajarte II, 235-37, 244-47; SW 108, 258, 326; XYZ 315.

Fioretti, Angelina (b. 1846, Italy; d. July 1879, Milan), ballerina, studied under the direction of Carlo Blasis* and joined the corps de ballet at La Scala, where Marie Taglioni* noticed her and arranged for her to come to Paris.

She made her debut at the Opéra on 28 December 1863 in the divertissement of Gioacchino Rossini's* Moïse* (see eighteenth-century volume for divertissement). She created a good impression with her early appearances at the Garnier Palace*, and she was cast next as Gloriette in Le Marche des Innocents* on 7 February 1864. Her third role was in the divertissement of Auguste Mermet's* Roland à Roncevaux* on 3 October 1864. She replaced Muravieva, in the female lead of Néméa* on 26 May 1865 and danced Thérèse in Théodore Labaree's* Le Roi d'Yvetot* on 28 December 1865. After appearing in the divertissement of Don Juan* on 2 April 1866, she supplanted Adèle Grantzow* as Naïla in Léo Delibes'* La Source.*

The second half of Mlle Fioretti's stay at the Opéra began with her filling the role of Gulnare in Le Corsaire* on 21 October 1867. Her next assignment was to do the polka with Eugénie Fiocre* in La Fête du printemps, the divertissement written by Lucien Petipa* for Ambroise Thomas'* Hamlet* (1868). Lastly, she represented Hélène in the divertissement of Faust* on 3 March 1869. She married the baritone Napoleone Verger on 18 July 1870 and retired from the stage.

Mlle Fioretti's career lasted for only seven years (1863-70), and she spent all this time at the Opéra. She was not a great dancer, but her competency was beyond question. It was her animated manner on the stage that was most responsible for her success.

BIBLIOGRAPHY: EDS V, 365; Ivor Guest, The Ballet of the Second Empire (Middletown, Conn.: Wesleyan University press, 1974), 7, 14, 64, 204-5, 208, 210, 214, 221, 223, 225-28, 230, 255, 259, 261; Lajarte II, 125-26, 219-20, 239-40, 243-44.

Fledermaus by Johann Strauss, Jr., is discussed in the twentieth-century volume under its French title, Chauve-Souris.

Les Fleurs is the ballet from the third entree of Les Indes galantes by Jean-Philippe Rameau (see eighteenth-century volume for Les Indes galantes and Rameau). It was given as a separate unit for the first time at a celebration in the Bureau of Public Education in Paris on 11 June 1878, and Mme Laure Fonta* provided fresh choreography for it on this occasion, while M. Théodore Lajarte* restored its score. There were parts for 13 flowers in the ballet, and Mme Fonta danced the rose, while Mlles Fatou (daisy), Bernay (carnation), and Roumier (lily-of-the-valley) filled some of the other roles. M. Basquez executed both winds, Zéphir and Borée. It was not produced separately for the second time by the Opéra until the corps de ballet mounted it in London at Covent Garden on 28 September 1954 with its music revised by Henri Busser, its choreography renewed by Harald Lander, and its sets and costumes redesigned by Fost. Mlle Micheline Bardin danced the rose on this occasion with Liane Daydé as the butterfly, Roger Ritz as the Persian, Michel Renault and Jean-Paul Andréani as the winds. Mlles Paulette Dynalix, Denise Bourgeoise, Claude Bessy, Jacqueline Rayet, and Rigel were among the dancers representing the flowers (see twentieth-century volume for Busser, Lander, Bardin, Daydé, Renault, Andréani, Dynalix, Bourgeois, and Rayet).

The revival of Les Indes galantes in its entirety on 18 June 1952 in a lavish super-production by Maurice Lehman precluded any subsequent revival of Les Fleurs as a separate unit at the Paris opera house, especially because this entree was redesigned with new éclat on this occasion. It was staged to the accompaniment of floral perfume being sprayed over the spectators so that their noses as well as their eyes and ears might be tickled; as a part of Les Indes galantes, it has been performed on nearly 250 occasions at the Opéra since 18 June 1952. This elegance and these statistics suggest how many spectators may have seen this eighteenth-century work after World War II.

BILBIOGRAPHY: BOP 156, 201; CODB 270; OMEL 152-56; SS 64-65; SW 120-21.

Flore et Zéphire is a ballet-divertissement in a single act for which Charles-Louis Didelot wrote the book and the choreography (see eighteenth-century volume for Didelot). Cesare Bossi created its original score, and Liparotti provided it with machinery and scenery for its initial run. It had its world premiere at King's Theatre in London on 7 July 1896 with Mme Rose Colinette and its choreographer in the title-roles. It had its first performance in Paris at the Royal Academy of Music on 12 December 1815 with fresh music by Venua. Its sets were created in Paris by Pierre Cicéri, while Marches provided its costumes.

The curtain rises to reveal Cléonice asleep in a grassy grove and Zéphire descending from the skies with Cupid in his arms. Zéphire begs Cupid to make Erigone fall in love with him when she arrives to tend to her roses in the grove. He sees sleeping Cléonice at this moment, however, and he is enthralled by her charms. He awakens her and begs Cupid to wait for Erigone.

Zéphire now flutters about Cléonice until the breeze from his wings awakens her. He declares his love to her, but she dismisses him with a smile, although she agrees to dance with him. She notices his silhouette on the wall of an adjacent temple, and she traces its outline with a pin. At this moment, Cupid announces Erigone's arrival in the grove, and Zéphire flees in panic. Cléonice is puzzled and amused by the god's disappearance, and she rushes off to thank Apollo for granting her the ability to paint.

Erigone waters her roses and notices Cléonice's portrait of Zéphire. She seems charmed by the drawing. Her rose bush opens suddenly, and Cupid emerges from it. He encircles Erigone with his fire, and she feels herself being consumed by the flames of love. She turns around to see Zéphire, who asserts his love for her. She reminds him that he is a winged and alien creature. Cupid rushes in to punish Zéphire for his inconstancy by removing his wings and attaching them to Erigone's shoulders. Wounded Zéphire tries to recover his wings, but Erigone flies off into the sky.

Zéphire is distraught over the loss of his wings and the disappearance of Erigone, and he threatens Cupid with the destruction of the world's flowers. Cupid responds with a compromise. He will guarantee Zéphire's happiness if Zéphire will vow to control his fickle heart and will record his oath on the temple wall. Zéphire agrees to remain faithful to Erigone if she becomes a goddess and will share the empire of flowers with him under the name of Flore.

Cupid and Zéphire hide behind a fountain when they see Erigone returning to earth. She approaches the fountain, and Zéphire grasps the tips of her wings. Cupid points to Zéphire's oath written on the temple wall, and Chloris becomes Flore by accepting Zéphire's love and returning his wings.

Didelot had had almost 20 years to polish and to perfect his ballet between its London and Paris productions, and it was such a success in the latter city that Louis XVIII invited Didelot to the royal box to congratulate him. The public was enthusiastic about the work because Didelot had elaborated for it a system of wires whereby the newly designed apparatus made it possible for Zéphire to fly through the air with Flore in his arms. The ballet remained in repertory until 8 March 1826, when it enjoyed its 169th performance at the Opéra.

Geneviève Gosselin created the role of Flore in Paris, where the part of Zéphire was filled initially by François Decombe Albert (see eighteenth-century volume for Gosselin and Albert). The other roles were danced by Mme Constance Gosselin (Vénus), Mlle Marie Delisle (Erigone), and M. Beaupré (Pan) (see eighteenth-century volume for Gosselin, Delisle, and Flore et Zéphire).

BIBLIOGRAPHY: BOP 76-77; CB 22-27; DDD 234; Lajarte II, 86; PBR 77.

Florestan ou le conseil de dix was an opera in three acts with a score by Manuel-Vincent Garcia* and a libretto by Etienne Delrieu.* The work had been given at the Opéra-Comique on 12 June 1819 under the title of Marini with music by Dourlens, but it was not well received and was withdrawn. It was then taken to the Royal Academy of Music for its premiere here with its new score on 26 June 1822, but it had to be dropped from the repertory after its fifth presentation on 17 July 1822.

The opera is set in Venice during the sixteenth century, and it opens with a group of singing and dancing sailors and gondoliers gathered near the palace of Octavie, a wealthy and influential noblewoman. The chorus is singing the praises of Florestan, a French knight who has conquered Soliman. Orseo disperses the celebrants, however, and he hides with his guards (I, 1-3). Octavie welcomes Florestan back to Venice; Octavie and Florestan renew their pledge of constant love (I, 4-6). Now an admired officer in the Venetian navy, Florestan declines to lead a public triumph because he wishes to obey the Council of Ten. Octavie warns him to beware of Pezari, who is jealous of his success (I, 7-8). An ensuing victory celebration is interrupted by Orseo, who arrests Florestan (I, 9-10), and the sailors and soldiers present rush off to rescue their hero from a jealous tribunal (I, 11).

Noradin the Moor regrets serving the murderous council, but he blames Florestan for his predicament because the Frenchman made him a slave instead of allowing him to die (II, 1). Pezari rejoices to have Florestan in his power (II, 2). He charges him with insubordination for attacking Soliman despite an order to retreat, and he accuses him of subversion as well. The council condemns Florestan to death, although the president, Marcello, is absent. The latter enters angrily to challenge the hero's arrest and the council's verdict. He calls upon Florestan to testify, and the accused indicates that he refused to retreat at the moment of victory. Pezari's lies and insults provoke Florestan, and the trial degenerates into a quarrel (II, 3-5). All the judges except Marcello condemn Florestan for the second time, and Orseo announces that Octavie is approaching with a crowd of angry citizens. The council agrees to ignore her defense of Florestan and adjourns (II, 6-7), but Marcello assures her of help in the senate (II, 8). Pezari promises Octavie that he will free Florestan if she will marry him. Outraged by her scornful refusal of his proposal, he offers Noradin his liberty, if he will murder Florestan in his cell. Noradin is happy to slay the man who killed his father, and he accepts the proposition (II, 9-12).

Florestan is in chains, but he falls asleep. Noradin enters his cell to slay him, but the Moor hesitates, and Florestan awakens. Noradin loses his thirst for vengeance on account of Florestan's courage; he decides to help him to escape through a secret outlet to the canal. Florestan learns from Noradin that Pezari has kidnapped Octavie (III, 1-3), and the setting changes to her cell. Marcello frees her and assures her that Florestan is alive and has appeared before the senate, where he has won his case. The people rejoice to see their hero free again, and preparations are completed in Saint Mark's square for his triumph (III, 4-8). Florestan acknowledges Noradin's help, and he and Octavie announce their marriage and their willingness to occupy the royal thrones of Venice (III, 9-8).

Prosper Dérivis* appeared as Florestan with the other male roles being filled by Henri Dabadie* (Marcello), Bonel (Pezari), Adolphe Nourrit* (Noradin), and Prévot (Orseo). Mme Rose Branchu was cast as Octavie (see eighteenth-century volume for Branchu). The music of Florestan left no lasting impression upon spectators or posterity.

BIBLIOGRAPHY: Anna, contesse de Brémont, The World of Music (London: W. W. Gibbings, 1892), 37-42; Chouquet 390; DDO I, 472; EDS V, 918-22; Lajarte II, 101-2; Louise Héritte de La Tour, Une Famille de grands musiciens (Paris: Stock, 1922), 511; John Mewburn Levien, The Garcia Family (London: Novello and Co., 1932), 9-18; M. Sterling Mackinlay. Garcia the Centenarian (New York: D. Appleton and Co., 1908), 3-12; Wks II, 4241, 4873.

Flotow, Friedrich, Freiherr von (b. 27 April 1812, Teutendorf; d. 24 January 1883, Darmstadt), composer, was destined for a career as a diplomat, but his father allowed him to study music in Paris under Antoine Reicha* after the youth had made a trip to France in 1827. The apprentice composer left the French capital to escape from the disorders of 1830, but he returned after the revolution to present several works at private performances and to mount Le Naufrage de la Méduse (1839) at the Renaissance Theatre. La Duchesse de Guise (1840) was given at the Ventadour.

L'Esclave du Camoëns was a disappointment at the Opéra-Comique in 1843.

It was at this time that Flotow made his initial contribution to the Opéra by collaborating with Frédéric Burgmuller* and Ernest Deldevez* on the score of Lady Henriette* of 1844, a ballet in three acts that Jules Saint-Georges* converted later into the opera Martha set by Flotow for performance in Vienna in 1847. L'Ame en peine* of 1846 was his other title billed at the Opéra.

Flotow did nothing in Paris between 1856 and 1863, because he was serving as intendant of the court theatre at Schwerin during this interval, and, from 1869, he lived in Austria. The French government did not fail to recognize his presence on the contemporary scene, however, and he was named a corresponding member of the Institut in 1864. He did a number of instrumental compositions including duos and trios for piano, violin, and cello, but his works for the stage did not survive, except Martha, on account of their similarity of style and monotony of manner. Yet he does have a certain historical importance by reason of having introduced the French operetta into Germany during the romantic period in this country.

BIBLIOGRAPHY: Benno Bardi-Poswiansky, Flotow als Opernkomponist (Königsberg: Diss., 1924); Edward J. Dent, "A Best-Seller in Opera [F.'s Martha]," M&L 22 (1941), 139-154; EGC 129-31; Fétis III, 276-77; Rosa Flotow, Friedrich von Flotow's Leben von seiner Witwe (Leipzig; B & H, 1892); Lajarte II, 174, 183; PBSW 5, 180; Wks, 6246, 6285, 8679, 8958, 10474, 11627, 12827.

Fokina, Vera Petrovna (b. 3 August 1886, Russia; d. 29 July 1958, New York), ballerina, née Antonova, studied at the St. Petersburg Imperial Ballet Academy and joined the Maryinsky Theatre in 1904. She married Michel Fokine* in 1905 and joined the Ballets russes* with him for the 1909 excursion of Serge Diaghilev's* company to Paris, where she interpreted roles created by her husband.

Vera Fokina danced in the initial performances of four works at the start of her career at the Opéra: Le Festin* on 19 June 1909, Schéhérazade* on 4 June 1910, and Les Orientales and L'Oiseau de feu* on 25 June 1910. She created five roles between 1910-21:

Role	Ballet	Premiere
Chiarina	Carnaval*	4 June 1910
La Sulamite	La Légende de Joseph*	14 May 1914
Ta-Hor	Cléopâtre*	2 June 1914
La Marquise	Le Rêve de la marquise	11 May 1921
Chloé	Daphnis et Chloé	20 June 1921

Three of these works had their world premieres elsewhere, and the date listed is the day of their first billing at the Opéra. The compositions having their first presentations at the Garnier Palace* were Carnaval and La Légende de Joseph.
BIBLIOGRAPHY: ACD 188; CB 571-75, 581-84, 598-602; CODB 200-201; Charles Spencer, Léon Bakst (London: Academy Editions, 1973), 69; SW 250, 255, 265-66, 277, 294, 304-5, 318.

Fokine, Mikhail Mikhailovich (b. 25 April 1880, St. Petersburg; d. 22 August 1942, New York), choreographer, called Michel Fokine in Western Europe and America, studied at the Imperial Ballet Academy from which he was graduated in 1898 to become a member of the Maryinski Theatre. He was raised to the rank of first soloist here in 1904 and choreographed his first ballets almost immediately.

Fokine's reputation as a dancer and choreographer was quite impressive by 1909, and Serge Diaghilev* invited him to join his newly formed Ballets russes* preparing for their first season in Paris. Fokine accepted the impresario's offer, because the idea of being official choreographer for the company attracted him by providing him with the opportunity to put into practice his new ideas about ballet composition. The Ballets russes paid their first visit to the Garnier Palace* on 19 June 1909, and they presented two works that Fokine had already choreographed: Les Sylphides* and Le Festin.* His Danses russes* was presented a week later on 26 June 1909 in a gala featuring Anna Pavlova* and Mikhail Mordkin.*

The Ballets russes returned to the Garnier during the following decade to present a number of works that Fokine had choreographed for their initial presentations at the Opéra, although they might have already had their world premieres elsewhere. In 1910, the Ballets russes arranged for their first extended stay at the Opéra, and they added six new compositions to the two works they had already mounted as a corporate entity in 1909: *Schéhérazade** (4 June), *Carnaval** (4 June), *Danses polovtsiennes** (7 June), *Cléopâtre** (11 June), *Les Orientales* (25 June), and *L'Oiseau de feu** (25 June). The company returned to the Opéra in 1911 with only a single work choreographed by Fokine, *Le Spectre de la rose** (24 December), and they did not return to the Garnier until 1914, when they mounted five Fokine compositions: *La Légende de Joseph** (14 May), *Les Papillons** (14 May), *Le Coq d'or** (24 May), *Pétrouchka** (21 May), and *Midas* (2 June). Ignoring the international scene, the Ballets russes posted programs at the Garnier in 1915, but their only new pieces were choreographed by Massine. After the war Serge Diaghilev's company resumed appearances at the Opéra in 1919, but it was not until 25 January 1920 that Fokine had another composition billed at the Opéra: *Thamar*. The other six new works which the visiting troupe had brought to the opera house for the first time in 1920 had choreography by Massine. In 1921, however, Fokine's *Le Rêve de la marquise* was staged without benefit of Diaghilev's company. He, his wife Vera Fokine, and Solange Schwarz mounted it independently on 11 May 1921 (see twentieth-century volume for *Thamar, Le Rêve de la marquise*, and Schwarz). Fokine and Fokina also appeared with the corps de ballet of the Garnier to perform *Daphnis et Chloé* for the first time at the present opera house on 20 June 1921. His *Le Martyre de St. Sébastien* had its Garnier premiere on 17 June 1922 (see twentieth-century volume for *Daphnis et Chloé* and *Le Martyre de St. Sébastien*). These arrangements were obviously unsatisfactory for Fokine, however, and he sailed for New York in 1923.

The ensuing years saw the choreographer travel to South America and Australia, and he returned to Europe from time to time, although he resisted Soviet efforts to persuade him to return to his native land. His *Diane de Poitiers* and *Sémiramis* were produced at the Garnier on 30 April 1934 and 11 May 1934, respectively. The Bolchoï Ballet of Moscow mounted his *Valse* for the first time at the Opéra on 9 June 1958 (see twentieth-century volume for Diane de Poitiers, Sémiramis, and Valse).

Fokine has come to assume the importance of Noverre or Petipa in the history of ballet not only on account of his 60 or 70 ballets given wherever ballet is known, but also because his ideas on the nature and function of a ballet have influenced so many contemporary dancers and choreographers. He has expounded his ideas in his "five points" program published in the London Times for 6 July 1914. Briefly, his doctrine holds that new movements must be created for new topics and times, while the dancing and mime must be relevant to the drama evolving upon the stage. The entire body must be used in order to obtain a full and satisfactory interpretation of the subject matter, and the dancers as a group have the same esthetic responsibility and function as the individual performer. Finally, dancing is to be allied to all the arts, not only to music and painting, because the choreographer and his creation must cultivate and foster complete liberty of expression.

BIBLIOGRAPHY: ACD 188-91; ACPM 367-70; BCS 330; Nicholas Beriosoff, "Remembering Fokine," Ballet 12 (August 1952), 16-23; CB 553-613; Marie-Françoise Christout, "Fokine," SDLD (February 1973), 15-20; CODB 201-2; Gladys Davidson, Ballet Biographies (London: Werner Laurie, 1952), 78-84; EDB 144; Michel Fokine, Fokine: Memoirs of a Ballet Master, trans. Vitale Fokine (Boston: Little, Brown, 1961); Stephen Greco, "Michel Fokine's Work and World View: Centenary Exhibit at Lincoln Center," D Mag 55, no 5 (May 1981), SC 42-SC 43; HAZ 148-52; IBB 73-86; Joan Lawson, A History of Ballet and Its Makers (New York: Putnam, 1964), 96-112; Pierre Michaut, Le Ballet Contemporain, 1929-1950 (Paris: Plon, 1950), 143-71; Walter Sorell, The Dance through the Ages (New York: Grosset and Dunlap, 1967), 164-65; Charles Spencer, Léon Bakst (London: Academy Editions, 1973), 50, 56-57,67, 73, 77, 87, 90, 95, 98, 102-3, 105, 113, 117, 127-28, 134, 136, 140, 142, 150; SW 65-66, 250, 255, 264-65, 268, 294, 298, 304-6, 311, 318, 323-24, 326, 331, 335, 373.

Fonta, Laure (b. 1845; d. Paris, ?), ballerina, née Laure Poinet, suffered from a nervous ailment as a child, and her doctors advised her to study dancing to help eliminate this condition. She entered the ballet school affiliated with the Imperial Academy of Music, therefore, and became a pupil of Lucien Petipa.* She completed her studies and joined the corps de ballet at the Opéra, where she was scheduled to make her debut as Daphné in Zara. This work was dropped on account of the tragic death by fire of Emma Livry,* however, and it was not until the revival of La Muette de Portici* on 19 January 1863 that Fonta made her debut in the rue Le Peletier* as a sujet in the divertissement of Daniel Auber's work (see eighteenth-century volume for divertissement).

The young dancer earned the confidence of management with her initial performance at the Opéra, and she was cast as Myrtha, queen of the Wilis, for Martha Muravieva's* revival of Giselle* on 8 May 1863, and, on 28 December 1863, she was assigned to a part in Giacchino Rossini's Moïse.* A series of important roles followed. First she was given a major part in the divertissement of Roland à Roncevaux* which had its premiere on 3 October 1864, and next she was selected for the role of Rosette in the premiere of Le Roi d'Yvetot* on 28 December 1865. She returned to dancing Myrtha in 1866-67, and, after doing Fenella in La Muette de Portici, she was selected to appear as Erigone in the revival of Félicien David's* Herculanum* on 29 June 1868. Her last roles at the Opéra included Cléopâtre in the divertissement of Faust* (1869), the abbess Hélène in Robert le Diable* (1870), Aurore in Coppélia* (1870).

When the Franco-Prussian War began, Mlle Fonta kept active at the Opéra as a teacher and as a member of the jury responsible for accepting young dancers into the corps de ballet. After 1881, she severed connections with the Opéra and devoted herself entirely to teaching and research.

BIBLIOGRAPHY: EDS V, 498-99; Ivor Guest, The Ballet of the Second Empire (Middletown, Conn.: Wesleyan University Press, 1974), 12-14, 150, 158, 178-79, 183, 208, 210, 223, 226-27, 241, 249, 255, 259, 261; Lajarte II, 125-26, 129-30, 140-41, 168, 239-40, 243-44.

La Fonti was a ballet in two acts and six tableaux with a score by Théodore Labarre,* a libretto by Eugène Deligny,* and choreography by Joseph Mazilier.* The public was pleased with its music and scenario at its premiere before the Imperial Family on 8 January 1855, and the ballet went on to enjoy 24 performances before it was dropped from the repertory. Martin, Cambon, and Thierry designed its scenery, and the costumes were created by Lormier, who did nearly all the costuming for the Imperial Academy of Music and the Imperial Theatre of the Opéra until 1855, when Albert became active in this aspect of production. The combined efforts of its creators and the artistes prompted Théophile Gauthier* to describe La Fonti as the outstanding ballet since Giselle.*

The ballet opens in 1750 in the dressing room of Amalia Fonti, premiere danseuse at the Pergola Theatre, who is trying to prepare for her performance while avoiding the advances of her hairdresser and dispelling the fears of the balletmaster Babinella that she may not be ready to dance on schedule. Her dressmaker is following her about the room arranging the costume she is wearing to portray Flore, when she suggests to Babinella that her performance will suffer this evening because she has not received top billing. Babinella promises to print her name in larger letters on the next batch of posters, and they begin to argue over a sequence of steps she is to execute in Flore et Zéphyre. When Count Angelo de Monteleone appears in her doorway, she dismisses her partner Carlino and Babinella, and the count presents her with an expensive piece of jewelry. She refuses it with the explanation that she could accept a gift of this value only from her fiance, but he replies that he has not planned on this eventuality. She is obviously hurt by his attitude, when the baron San-Pietro and a group of gentlemen enter her dressing room followed by a secretive old man with a scowl on his face. The old man manages to hide in her room, and the baron begs her to favor one of their number with a mark of preference so that the others may leave. She replies that she prefers whoever will marry her. The baron San-Pietro and his friends laugh at her answer, but her partner Carlino offers to marry her. She is not impressed by his proposal, and the count de Monteleone asks her to become his wife. The old man emerges from his hiding place to forbid his son to wed a dancer. The obedient count acquiesces and leaves. La Fonti flies into a rage but dries her tears and answers the three taps calling her to the stage (sc. 1).

The orchestra plays the overture, and the chair on the stage reserved for Count Angelo de Monteleone is vacant. The ballet opens with Flore announcing that she is going to make fickle Zéphyre fall in love with her. She enlists Eros' aid and is successful; Monteleone takes his place among the spectators at this moment, and Carlino and la Fonti become so flustered that they forget their parts. Babinella manages to restore the course of action on the stage. Zéphyre abandons Flore, but Eros revives his love for her. Flore ignores him in her turn, and Zéphyre summons his breezes to lay waste to Flore's garden. The couple decide to restore calm by marrying each other, and the ballet ends. Count de Monteleone sends a note to la Fonti, but his alert father notices it (sc. 2).

The marquis de Monteleone bribes la Fonti's maid to give him the missive in which his son suggests to the dancer that they elope to France. The dancer defies the marquis' order that she leave Florence, and he has her arrested. Count de Monteleone waits in vain for her in his coach (sc. 3) because she has been thrown into the prison governed by the baron San-Pietro. The baron tries to win her favor by plying her with food and wine in her cell, but Carlino finds a way into the jail so that she may escape in his clothing. They execute this plan by getting San-Pietro drunk on wine and dizzy from dancing. San-Pietro realizes finally that he has been tricked, when he notices that his prisoner has grown a beard. He calls his guards, but agile Carlino eludes them and escapes through an open door (sc. 4).

Count Angelo de Monteleone and Princess Carolina Tornasari are discussing their wedding plans when la Fonti enters disguised as a dancing master charged with creating a quadrille for the wedding celebration to be held in the evening. Carolina is afraid of "him" because of his constant interest in her. Finally "he" declares his love for Carolina, but, when la Fonti is alone with her, "he" warns her that the man she is about to marry is in love with a dancer named Amalia Fonti. "He" displays the letters that her beloved count has written to la Fonti; "he" assures Carolina that he will be a more faithful lover than her prospective groom. "He" threatens to kill himself, if she signs the marriage contract. Convinced, Carolina agrees to reject the contract, and Monteleone is about to attack the dancing master, when he recognizes "him" as la Fonti. He declares his love to her, but she reminds him that the difference in their social rank is too great to allow them to marry. She apologizes for having subjected him to ridicule and leaves (sc. 5).

The closing tableau shifts to the Corso in Rome during Carnaval. A woman enters in disarray and with madness in her eyes. The crowd makes way for her, because they recognize her as Amalia Fonti, the danseuse whom they applauded so generously only two months before. Accompanied by her maid and Carlino, she believes that she is still on stage and begins to dance. This effort drains her strength, and she falls lifeless to the pavement (sc. 6).

The ballet was written for Carolina Rosati* at the suggestion of Nestor Roqueplan, director of the Opéra, and she was inevitably cast as Amalia Fonti. The other female roles were filled by Forli (Princess Carolina Tornasari), Aline (Carolina's mother, also designated as Princess Tornasari), Emarot (Amalia Fonti's maid), Léontine Rousseau (Carolina Tornasari's maid), Mercier (the dressmaker). The male parts were created by Lucien Petipa* (count de Monteleone), Lenfant (marquis de Monteleone), Louis Mérante* (Carolino), Francisque Berthier* (Babinella), Dauty (baron de San-Pietro), and Vandris (haridresser).

BIBLIOGRAPHY: AEM VIII, 9-10; Chouquet 414-15; EDS VII, 339-40; L. Escudier, "Théâtre Impérial de l'Opéra: La Fonti," FM 19 (14 January 1855), 9-10; Ivor Guest, The Ballet of the Second Empire (Middletown, Conn.: Wesleyan University Press, 1974), 87-91, 258; Amédée Labarre, Variétés littéraires et musicales (Paris: Calmann-Lévy, 1878), 119-25; Lajarte II, 217-18.

La Forêt was a musical legend in two acts with a score by Augustin Savart,* a libretto by Laurent Tailhade, and choregoraphy by Mme Stichel. It had its world premiere at the National Academy of Music on 13 February 1910 with sets by Rochette and costumes by Pinchon. It was not very popular at the Opéra, and it was dropped from the repertory after its seventh performance on 6 April 1910.

The opera opens in a forest clearing at dawn. The woodcutter Pierre promises his superiors that he will keep his word. He will have the forest cut down within a day. Afterward he mutters to himself that he will flee to the city with his handful of ill-begottn gold (I, 1). Jeanne interrupts his soliloquy to remind him that the village festival is about to begin, and their comrades wish to celebrate their marriage. Pierre explains that he must remain in the woods to clear the way for the new road to the Fairies' Pool. She assures him that they will have a better living if he works their farm, but he insists upon remaining in the forest. She accuses him of loving the woods more than her, or of having a gypsy girl in his camp, but he reveals that he is under the spell of a sylvan lady who wears a crown of lavender. Frightened, Jeanne insists that he return to the village so that the priest may exorcise him. He refuses and hears the subtle song of Nemorosa. He pushes Jeanne away. She begs him to be back in the village by evening (I, 2).

The second act shifts to a second clearing near the Fairies' Pool. A profusion of flowers is seen everywhere, and Pierre is about to begin his work. He raises his axe, but an invisible choir urges him to desist. He recognizes the voices, but he believes that madness is overtaking him, and he attacks the trees. The hamadryads look at him in terror, and the nymphs of the oak, yew, birch, and beech trees enumerate their virtues and charms to him in an effort to stave off his attack. The woodcutter refuses to be persuaded or intimadted, and he reminds the trees that their day of glory has passed (II, 1-3). Nemorosa tries to convince him to lay down his axe and to live with her in the depths of her grove. He refuses because he is pledged to Jeanne, but Nemorosa warns him that he will never destroy the forest. He may know its peacefulness, but he has not yet discovered its traps and its pitfalls. She calls upon the spirits of the trees, flowers, birds, moths, lakes, and springs to unite against an aggressor, and the sprites appear in a parade led by fireflies and elves. Angry, Pierre rushes to the attack, but the sprites bind him in their belts, veils, and scarves, while the trees invade the clearing and begin to grow before Pierre's astonished eyes. The Spirits of the Waters emerge from the swamp to encircle the woodcutter, who takes a step forward only to fall into the water.

He drowns (II, 4-5). Jeanne enters in search of Pierre, and she hears a voice advising her to return to the village. Fear overcomes her, and she warns the forest that wheat fields and meadows will replace it, but the trees look down at her with an appeased air (II, 6).

The three leading roles in La Forêt were created by Louise Grandjean (Nemorosa), Ketty Lapeyrette* (Jeanne), and Jean-François Delmas* (Pierre).

BIBLIOGRAPHY: "La Forêt," Le Ménestrel 76 (19 February 1910), 58-59; Stoullig XXXVI (1910), 2-9; SW 99.

Foucher, Paul-Henri (b. 21 April 1810, Paris; d. 1875, Paris) received an excellent education and held several posts in the government before resigning to devote all his time to writing. He favored the theatre and made his debut at the Odéon with Amy Robsart (1829), a drama in five acts that he had composed in collaboration with his brother-in-law, Victor Hugo.* After the unsuccessful premiere of this work, he went on to do compositions for the Porte Saint-Martin, Ambigu-Comique, the Opéra-Comique, and the Gaîté theatres before becoming Paris correspondent for L'Indépendance belge in 1848 and joining the editorial staff of La France in 1865. He was responsible alone or with a literary partner for nearly 60 titles posted at Parisian theatres during the 1831-50 surge of romanticism in the theatre. His librettos for the Opéra were not always impressive successes, but he did have four titles posted here that revealed a lively imagination and a feeling for the picturesque situations dear to the audiences of his time: Le Vaisseau fantôme* of 1842, Richard en Palestine* of 1844, Paquita* of 1846, and L'Etoile de Messine* of 1861.

BIBLIOBRAPHY: GE XVII, 874; Lajarte II, 171, 177, 181-2, 232; LXIX VIII, 651-12; Wks, III, 256.

Fournier, Emile-Eugène-Alix (b. 11 October 1864, Paris; d. 12 September 1897, Joinville-le-Pont), composer, studied under the direction of Léo Delibes* and François Dubois* at the Conservatoire in his native city. He won the second Grand Prix de Rome in 1891, but his only contribution to the repertory of the Opéra was his Stratonice* in one

act that had its world premiere at the Garnier Palace* on 9 December 1982.
BIBLIOGRAPHY: BBD 540.

Foussier, Edouard (b. 23 July 1824, Paris; d. 15 March 1882, Paris), librettist, studied law and became interested in writing after publishing his impressions of a trip he had taken to Italy. He turned almost immediately to the theatre and had a comedy entitled Héraclite et Démocrite (1850) billed at the Comédie-Française, where most of his plays were produced. After three more dramatic compositions entitled Les Jeux innocents (Gymnase, 1850), Une Journée d'Agrippa d'Aubigné (Comédie-Française, 1853), Le Temps perdu (Gymnase, 1855), his Le Chercheur d'esprit (1865) was mounted at the Opéra-Comique, but it was not until five plays and 20 years later that his first and only contribution to the repertory of the Opéra was offered to the public. He and François Got* collaborated on the libretto of this opera in five acts entitled L'Esclave* and given its premiere on 17 July 1874.
BIBLIOGRAPHY: GE XVII, 933; Lajarte II, 246-47; LXIX VIII, 686; Wks 9860, 11850, 14794, 14842, 15396, 15594, 16927, 17038, 17572, 18344, 18415, 18542, 18769, 21760, 21812.

Franck, César (b. 10 December 1822, Liége, Belgium; d. 8 November 1890, Paris), composer, attended the Paris Conservatoire, where he won prizes for piano, fugue, and organ between 1837 and 1842. After graduation, he returned to Belgium for two years, but he then gave up his residence in his native land to come back to Paris, where he spent the first years of his adult life earning a living by playing the organ in various churches in the French capital. He managed to survive the siege of Paris during the Franco-Prussian War, and recognition of his talents was at last forthcoming. He was appointed professor of the organ at the Conservatoire in 1872, and, in 1878, he was selected to play his own music at the inauguration of the organ at the Trocadéro. Finally, in 1895, he was named Chevalier of the Légion d'Honneur.

Although Franck's reputation grew with the passage of time, his works for the theatre are mostly forgotten today in favor of his orchestral, choral, and chamber compositions. His pieces for the stage include Le Valet de Ferme, Hulda, and Ghisèle, but none of these compositions was ever staged at the Opéra, although the jury at this theatre had heard and rejected Le Valet de Ferme in 1851. Yet his music was played at the Garnier Palace* posthumously, when, on 25 May 1918, his Rebecca was produced there with a scenario by Paul Collin. Later, on 1 March 1950, his music was also used to score Serge Lifar's ballet, Passion (see twentieth-century volume for Rebecca, Lifar, and Passion).

BIBLIOGRAPHY: AEM IV, 637-53; BBD 543-44; CBCM 630-41; Norman Demuth, César Franck (New York: Philosophical Library, 1949); EDS V, 660-62; EGC 131-35; ELM II, 161-65; Vincent d'Indy, César Franck (New York: Dodd, Mead, 1931); MCDE I, 352-64; PBSW 62; Thompson 620-24; Léon Vallas, César Franck (London: Harrap, 1951).

François Ier à Chambord is an opera originally in two acts and later reduced to a single act in a futile effort to lengthen its first and only run at the Opéra. It had its world premiere at the Paris opera house on 15 March 1830. The composer responsible for its score is not indicated in its libretto, but its music was created by Prosper de Ginestet.* Alexandre-Pierre Moline de Saint-Yon* and Fougeroux collaborated on its words, while Auguste Vestris provided the choreography for the divertissements in the first and second acts (see eighteenth-century volume for Vestris and divertissement). Pierre-Luc-Charles Cicéri* painted the canvas set depicting the Chambord Château that would also be used in the staging of Les Huguenots* until 13 October 1873, when the opera house in the rue Le Peletier* burned to the ground.

The opera is set in the Chambord château in 1516, and the curtain rises on the first act to disclose a richly decorated room provided with a writing table. A chorus composed of lords and ladies from the retinue of Marguerite de Valois is weaving garlands in preparation for the ceremony honoring François Ier for his victory at Marignan. The seneschal exhorts his companions to be especially careful with the decorations because he wishes François Ier to be so delighted with them that he will agree to his marriage with Carina, a beautiful lady-in-waiting of Marguerite de Valois. Unfortunately, Carina is in love with Léonard de

Vinci (I, 1-2). Marguerite reveals that it was the king, not Nemours, who saved Carina on the battlefield in Italy, although the Italian girl is still unaware of the true identity of her rescuer. Marguerite vows to guarantee Carina's future happiness (I, 3), and Carina swears that her beloved Léonard's paintings and newly designed lyre will find acceptance at court despite Michelangelo's jealous opposition (I, 4). François Ier enters in simple dress to disguise his presence at court; he reveals his love for Carina, who still believes that he is Nemours. She asks him to intercede with the king on Léonard's behalf, and he guarantees to honor her request (I, 5-6) just as the seneschal enters and realizes that the king is his rival for Carina's hand, although the king believes that the seneschal wishes to marry his sister, Marguerite de Valois. François Ier orders the seneschal to bring Léonard to him, and he swears that his love for Carina will never fade (I, 7-8). The king's courtiers welcome him back to court, but he is annoyed by the noise of the celebration, while Carina is amazed to learn that her "Nemours" is really François Ier. The king arranges to meet Carina later in the gardens of the castle, and he leaves the celebration to greet his subjects at the castle gates (I, 9-10).

The second act is set in the castle gardens with signs of an elaborate celebration everywhere. The seneschal is explaining to Léonard that he must agree to paint the portrait of a court beauty whom he once loved, but whose charms have now captured the king's fancy (II, 1). Carina and Léonard swear eternal love to each other, but he notices the royal ring on her finger (II, 2-3). The seneschal encounters the loving couple in the garden, moreover, and he accuses Carina of infidelity while assuring Léonard that he will also find Carina to be fickle and unfaithful (II, 4). The king enters and declares that Léonard's genius is beyond question, and that he will remain at the French court. Marguerite and Carina are overjoyed by this announcement. Léonard is perplexed when he concludes that the king and the seneschal are in love with Carina, and he is further frustrated by Marguerite's announcement that Carina and the seneschal will be wed before midnight. The king suggests to his sister that she refrain from choosing a husband for Carina, and Carina interprets Léonard's growing dismay as a sign of his love for her. The king gives the signal for the festivities to begin (I, 5).

Marguerite directs Léonard to lead the chorus with his newly designed lyre (II, 6), and the king meets with Carina in the garden according to plan. He declares his love to her, but she rejects him in favor of Léonard. She shows him his ring while pleading for him to understand her predicament. The confused king decides finally that only the marriage of Carina and Léonard can resolve the complicated situation for which he, his sister Marguerite, the seneschal, Léonard, and Carina are responsible (II, 7-9).

The opera was overloaded with exposition and complications, and it had to be withdrawn from the stage after its sixth representation. The parts of the three suitors for the hand of the beautiful Italian orphan were sung by M. Adolphe Nourrit* (Léonard de Vinci), M. Henri Dabadie* (the seneschal), and M. Nicolas Levasseur* (François Ier). Mme Dammoreau sang the soprano part of Carina, while Mme Gosselin interpreted the ancillary role of Marguerite de Valois. Alexandre Dupont was cast as the count St.-Pol.

BIBLIOGRAPHY: Lajarte II, 135; Moniteur universel 77 (18 March 1830), 506.

Françoise de Rimini was an opera in four acts, a prologue, and an epilogue with a score by Ambroise Thomas* and a libretto by Jules Barbier* and Michel Carré.* The choreography was created by Louis Mérante.* The costumes were designed by Eugène Lacoste, and the sets were the work of the younger Lavastre (tabl. 1, 2), the elder Lavastre and Carpezat (tabl. 3), Daran (tabl. 4), Rubé and Chapéron (tabl. 5). The composition had its world premiere at the Opéra in Paris on 14 April 1882.

The prologue of the opera opens before the gates of hell with Dante wondering where he is until Virgil volunteers to guide him through the underworld (prol., tabl. 1).

The two poets enter the first circle of hell, where they encounter the shades of Paolo and Francesca. Dante asks them what bond holds them together, and they explain that they are united in a criminal love that started one day when they were reading the same book. The lovers regretfully move on before they can finish their tale, but Virgil promises to retell the story that started one day when the two lovers were reading in the same book.

The first act presents Paolo and Francesca seated next to each other and reading a book that tells the story of Queen Guinèvre and Lancelot and how they kissed one day. Francesca turns to Paolo and kisses him in like fashion while declaring her love to him. He hastens to assure her of his love for her (I, 1). Francesca's father Guido enters to tell her that the Guelfs have triumphed over Florence and are on their way to destroy Rimini. Paolo promises Guido that he will fight until the end; Francesca asks her father for permission for her and Paolo to wed. Guido consents and urges them to flee. They refuse, and Guido reveals that the Guelfs are being led by Paolo's exiled brother, Malatesta (a. 1, tabl. 1).

The second tableau depicts the fearsome citizens of Rimini awaiting the assault of Malatesta's 10,000 men. The soldiers have laid down their arms, and only Ascanio and Paolo seem willing to resist the attack. Malatesta enters the city unopposed, but Paolo defies him. Malatesta insists to his brother that he is trying to unify Italy with his victories, and Guido offers himself as a hostage for his compatriots, but Malatesta frees him. He declares a day of festival and celebration before disappearing with Francesca as his hostage (a. 1, tabl. 2).

Francesca refuses to marry Malatesta, although her father reminds her that she can save the citizens of Rimini by becoming his bride. Guido also points out to her that Paolo is dead (II, 1). Ascanio reports to Francesca that he saw Paolo die upon the battlefield (II, 2). Malatesta escorts Francesca to the chapel for their wedding (II, 3). Ascanio remains behind for a moment to mourn Paolo before leaving for the wedding (II, 4). Paolo enters wan and weary; he calls to astonished Ascanio and asks him about the wedding in the adjacent chapel. Ascanio is speechless, and Paolo climbs the steps to the chapel to see Francesca and Malatesta at the altar. He tears open his wound in a suicidal rage and falls to the floor (II, 5). Francesca and Malatesta emerge from the chapel. Paolo is carried away. Guido promises Francesca to go to the emperor for aid (II, 7). Francesca is overcome by grief despite her joy at knowing that Paolo is alive (II, 8).

Malatesta is enraged by his brother's survival (III, 1), but he hides his anger lest he displease Francesca (III, 2). A chorus sings the delights of love at a celebration in honor of Francesca, and a ballet featuring a pas de deux is in progress when the sounds of revolt are heard outside the palace. Guido enters with his assault group that includes Ascanio and Paolo (III, 3). Guido exhibits an imperial decree. Malatesta must submit to interrogation on the morrow (III, 4).

Francesca is alone in her apartment with the book that she and paolo read together, but she refuses to open it because he has left Rimini. She retires to her bedroom (IV, 1-2). Paolo returns suddenly to say farewell to his beloved, however, and he picks up their book impulsively. She returns from her bedroom because she cannot sleep, and he hides behind a tapestry. She notices that the book is open, and she realizes that he is in the room. She cries out for him to leave, but he refuses to abandon her until he has said farewell. She warns him that he will destroy them both and protests her love to him. They are recalling the fatal day that they read their book when Ascanio opens the door and falls dead without uttering a word. Malatesta is about to lunge at them with his sword when a curtain of clouds crosses the theatre (a. 4, tabl. 1).

Dante beseeches Béatrix to come to the aid of Paolo and Francesca, and she appears in a radiant vision, while the stage setting is transformed into a representation of the upper regions of light. Virgil and Dante bow before this apparition, and Francesca, Béatrix, Paolo, Dante, Virgil, and the choir of angels unite to sing the glory of God (epilogue).

<u>Francoise de Rimini</u> was neither an outright failure nor an outstanding success with its 41 presentations at the Opéra between the time of its premiere there and its last performance at the Garnier Palace* on 12 December 1884. The composition was Thomas' last opera, however, and it reveals traces of the composer's extreme care with his score. The prologue has a moving salute to Virgil stressing the violins, and "Italie! Italie!" opening the second tableau of the first act is a stirring anthem. The music of the wedding in the second act and of the <u>divertissement</u> of the third act are likewise worthy of separate mention (see eighteenth-century volume

for divertissement). Some critics considered the duet by Paolo and Francesca in the fourth act the most powerful passage in the entire score. Mme Caroline Salla made her debut at the Opéra as Francesca in the premiere of the work, and the other two female roles were filled on this occasion by Hélène Richard* (Ascanio) and Andréa Barbot* (Virgil). The male parts were created by Henri Sellier* (Paolo), Jean Lassalle* (Malatesta), Pierre Gailhard* (Guido), and Alfred-Auguste Giraudet* (Dante). Mlle Rosita Mauri* starred in the ballet alongside Louis Mérante.*

BIBLIOGRAPHY: DDO I, 484-86; Adolphe Jullien, Musiciens d'aujourd'hui (Paris: Librairie de l'Art, 1894) I, 57-66; Lermina 644-45; H. Moréno, "Françoise de Rimini: première représentation et notes de repétitions," Le Ménestrel 48 (16 April 1882), 153-57 (23 April 1882), 162-65 (30 April 1882), 171-73 (7 May 1882), 178-80 (14 May 1882), 186-88; Grace Robert, The Borzoi Book of Ballets (New York: Alfred A. Knopf, 1946), 138-40; SSBO 247, 284; Stoullig VIII (1882), 14-22 and X (1884), 15; SW 99-100.

François Villon was an opera in a single act with a score by Edmond Membrée* and a libretto by François Got* of the Comédie-Française. It had its premiere at the Imperial Academy of Music on 20 April 1857 and managed to survive for 18 presentations before it was dropped from the repertory on 14 October 1857. Its principal weakness lay in its libretto, which depended too heavily upon a false view of Villon's character.

The opera opens in Tours in 1473 on the feast day of Saint Louis. Captain Stewart of the Scottish guards enters Gauthier's inn looking for the gypsy Aika (I, 1-2). The Enfants Sans-Souci return from their performance of a farce by Villon, and Gossoyn regrets that the poet is to be hanged on the morrow. The Enfants Sans-Souci sing a burlesque De Profundis for their doomed comrade and order supper, but Gauthier refuses to serve them until they pay their bill. A fight breaks out, and Villon walks through the door (I, 3). His comrades explain that the cause of the trouble is Gauthier's negative attitude towards them, and Villon asserts that he will make the innkeeper say "yes" to them in spite of himself. Villon asks him a series of questions to which he answers negatively. Villon then asks him if guests must pay their bills in his inn, and he forgets himself and answers affirmatively. He is downcast because he has lost his wager and must feed his guests, but Villon pulls out a fat purse. He offers to pay the players' bill if Gauthier will acknowledge that he is their servant by bowing to them. Gauthier agrees (I, 4).

Gossoyn asks Villon why he is free, and the poet explains that the king has given him a pardon and the purse for his feast day, and he adds that his confinement was brightened by a beautiful singer who threw him a coral bracelet. They invite the gypsies to dine with them, and Aïka appears among them (I, 5-6). Villon tries to return her bracelet, but she refuses to accept it. The grateful poet scatters his gold around the room and invites his friends to share it. Aïka prepares to leave, and Villon is ready to depart with her, when Gauthier tells her that Stewart has been looking for her (I, 7). Stewart declares his love to her, but she reminds him that she is a gypsy without rights or a home. She asserts that he would be nothing but another master to her, but he ignores her words and tries to drag her away with him (I, 8). Villon intercedes. He picks up a stool when Stewart reaches for his knife, and Aïka reminds them that she is not in love with either one of them. Stewart leaves in disgust, but Villon is saddened by the gypsy's words until she admits that she loves him. The lovers sing a duet confirming their mutual love, but Villon refuses to allow her to leave Tours with him because he has nothing to offer her (I, 9-10). Aïka departs for Spain, and Villon decides to return to Paris. The gypsy's farewell song is heard through an open window in the inn, and Villon answers her with a glass in his hand and a toast on his lips (I, 11).

The male leads were sung by Louis Henri Obin* (Villon), Boulo (Stewart), Sapin (Gossoyn), and Guignot (Gauthier) with Mlle Delisle filling the part of Aïka. The score of the opera was noteworthy in several places, especially the music for Villon's "Mais où sont les neiges d'antan" and the drinking song in the inn, "Rions, buvons, chantons, compères!"

BIBLIOGRAPHY: Chouquet 417; DDO I, 484; EDS V, 1506-7; L. Escudier, "Chronique: François Villon," FM 21 (26 April 1857), 137; Lajarte II,

223; Moniteur universel 116 (26 April 1857), 457-58; Wks IV, 17572.

Franz, Paul (b. 30 November 1876, Paris; d. April 1950, Paris), vocalist, originally named Franz Gauthier, was invited to sing at the Opéra after he had won a singing contest in 1907. He made his debut as a tenor in the title-role of Lohengrin* on 1 February 1909, the same year that he sang the male leads in Samson et Dalila,* Sigurd,* Roméo et Juliette,* Faust,* and Tannhaüser in a display of virtuosity and versatility that had to impress even the most demanding spectators. In his second year at the Opéra, he was cast as Faust in La Damnation de Faust,* Siegmound in La Walkyrie,* and Rhadamès in Aïda.* His success with the public justified his continuing to appear in major roles, and he did Walther in Les Maîtres Chanteurs de Nuremberg* and Rodrigue in Le Cid* in 1911, and, in 1912, he appeared as Jean in Le Prophète.* His last parts before the invasion of 1914 included Tristan in 1913 and Toloïk in Le Vieil Aigle* of 1914.

Franz was billed in only two works during the war, as Kerloo in Patrie!* in 1916 and as Guillaume in Messidor* in 1917, but he returned to the stage of the Garnier Palace* for a second sequence of appearances almost as soon as peace was restored: the lead in Othello,* Prinzivalle in Monna Vanna,* and Mâtho in Salammbô* in 1919. Then, after an interval of six years during which time he added no new parts to his Garnier repertory except for the roles he created, the tenor was billed as Raoul in Les Huguenots* and Siegfried in Le Crépuscule des dieux* in 1925. It was not until 1933 that he sang Eléazar in La Juive.*

Franz' long tenure at the Opéra provided him with the opportunity to create 15 parts at the theatre between 1914 adn 1930. In this interval, he brought the following characters to the stage of the Garnier for the first time:

Role	Opera	Premiere
Parsifal	Parsifal	4 January 1914
Comte de Dunois	Jeanne d'Arc (Roze)	24 November 1917
Pâris	Hélène	20 June 1919

Auférus	Légende de St. Christophe	6 June 1920
Antar	Antar	14 March 1921
Enée	Les Troyens	10 June 1921
Jean	Hérodiade	22 December 1921
Gérald	La Fille de Roland	27 October 1922
Rata-Sen	Padmavâti	1 June 1923
Prince Assur	Le Jardin du Paradis	29 October 1923
Le chevalier Roland	Esclarmonde	24 December 1923
Mardochée	Esther	28 April 1925
Solnik	L'Ile désenchantée	19 November 1925
Xerxès	Salamine	17 June 1929
Satan	La Tentation de St. Antoine	8 May 1930

A glance at Franz' repertory reveals that he was an excellent and durable Wagnerian tenor as well as a versatile and dramatic performer. In fact, his constant appearance in heroic roles created by Richard Wagner* won for him the reputation of being the most competent interpreter of this composer in France.
BIBLIOGRAPHY: EDS V, 684; ICM 626; KRJ 141-42; PBSW 180; RC 292-4; SW 28, 37, 62, 66, 69, 80-81, 95, 110, 113, 118-19, 124, 126, 130, 133, 139, 148, 151, 165, 167, 169-71, 178, 191-93, 203, 307, 218, 223, 225.

Fredegonde was presented to the public as a lyric drama in five acts. The libretto was written by Louis Sallet. Ernest Guiraud* began the score that was finished by his friend Camille Saint-Saëns* after the former's death on 6 May 1892. Joseph Hansen* was in charge of the choreography. Charles Bianchini designed the costumes, and the sets were created by Chapéron and his son (a. 1),

Carpezat (a. 2), Marcel Jambon and Bailly (a. 3), Amable (a. 4, 5). It had its world premiere at the Opéra on 18 December 1895 in a production by Lapissida.

The drama begins in the place of Thermas in Paris, where a crowd is milling about in a multiplicity of costumes, and a chorus is singing the praises of Brunhilda, who has been acclaimed queen of all Gaul and mistress of Paris. The people call upon the poet Fortunatus to honor her in his verse (I, 1). He recites a poetic welcome to her, and she is pleasant to the poet, but her first act is to swear to make Hilpérik and Frédégonde suffer for having murdered her sister. She calls upon the members of her court to help her, but she declares that a celebration is in order first (I, 3). Suddenly, a guard announces that the Neustrians have stormed the walls of Paris, and she is informed that Frédégonde convinced Sigoald to betray the city. Victorious Frédégonde, Hilpérik, and Mérowig appear before Brunhilda (I, 3). Hilpérik assures her that he will treat her as befits her station, but she asks him why he had to insult her by appearing at her court with Frédégonde. The latter insults Brunhilda, and Hilpérik announces that he has decided to replace her as a ruler of Gaul. Brunhilda is plunged into despair. Her kindgom has been stolen, her sister has been murdered, and her brother-in-law has cast his lot in with a prostitute. Hilpérik orders Brunhilda taken to a convent in Rouen by his son, Mérowig. The victors fall to dividing the spoils (I, 4). Brunhilda thanks Mérowig for making her captivity endurable, and a messenger tells him that his father is impatient for him to take his prisoner to Rouen. Mérowig prepares to leave in the evening (II, 1-3) and assures Brunhilda that he is performing this task with great reluctance. She reminds him that Frédégonde will not hesitate to have her killed when she is hidden in a convent, and she warns him not to be too kind to her lest harm befall him too. She realizes suddenly that she may have hurt Mérowig because Frédégonde is his mother, but he assures her that she is his stepmother. He adds that she would slay him in a moment if she believed that his death would profit her natural sons. He confesses his love to her, and she responds by admitting that she has fallen in love with him (II, 4).

Contingents of Austrasians and Neustrians under Mérowig's command are awaiting the coming struggle against Hilpérik near Rouen. They pass the time with games and by watching the girls of the region dance. Fortunatus announces that he is entering the monastery in Rouen. Brunhilda and Mérowig arrive at the camp to await the biship of Rouen, who is going to marry them (III, 1-3). At first the biship tries to persuade them to cancel the wedding, but they insist, and he accedes to their wishes. They are wed and are being congratulated by their followers, when the alarm is sounded. Landéric's Neustrian army is approaching. Wine is poured for the wedding feast, however, because the battle will not take place until dawn (III, 4).

The setting returns to the palace of Thermes, where Frédégonde assures Hilpérik that everybody is condemning his son for his disobedience and treason. Hilpérik vows to punish his son, who has fled to sanctuary in the monastery of Saint-Martin after his defeat. Frédégonde wishes to see her stepson punished immediately and severely. She accuses Chilpérik of deceiving her and ignoring her sons. She makes him swear that he will seize Mérowig and isolate him in a cloister for the rest of his life (IV, 1).

Fortunatus, Mérowig, and Brunhilda remain under the protection of Saint-Martin's monastery (V, 1), and the bishop tells Fortunatus that Chilpérik wishes to speak with him to establish peace. When Frédégonde warns the biship to be her friend, he replies that he fears only God, and she becomes angry immediately. She asks whether Mérowig is in the cloister, and he replies that he is in sanctuary. He leaves, and she vows to have Mérowig and Brunhilda in her power. The king arrives (IV, 4); he and Frédégonde confront Brunhilda and Mérowig standing inside the area of sanctuary. The king requests his son to repent his revolt by placing himself in his hands and confessing his wrongdoing. Mérowig is hesitant; Brunhilda suspects a trap. Mérowig crosses the line finally to fall at his father's feet. The king asks his bishops and doctors whether he should execute his son or confine him to a monastery for the remainder of his life. Frédégonde threatens the jury, and Mérowig is sentenced to pass the reminder of his days in a cloister. The outraged biship places anathema upon the heads of the king, the queen, and the jury. Brunhilda and Mérowig demand a pardon; Frédégonde and Hilpérik ignore their plea. Mérowig stabs himself because Frédégonde has been able to steal his father, his love, and his liberty. Brunhilda is overcome by grief, but Frédégonde is filled with joy (V, 5).

The pulbic was not impressed by Frédégonde, probably because the militant tone of the first three acts that Guiraud scored were not in the vein of his style. Saint-Saëns did better with the last two acts, however, but the end result of these two men composing this work was to create an uneven tone for it. Also, the division of the opposing forces in the drama into Neustrian and Austriasian camps left puzzled spectators unable to decide to which faction they should direct their sympathy and loyalty. The work was dropped from the repertory after its ninth presentation on 14 February 1896. Lucienne Bréval* sang the role of Brunhilda at the dress rehearsal on 14 December 1895, but this part was filled by Marie Lafargue at the premiere four days later with Mlle Meryianne Héglon as Frédégonde. The male parts were created by Albert Alvarez* (Mérowig), Maurice Renaud* (Hilpérik), Albert Vaguet* (Fortunatus), and René Fournets (the bishop).

BIBLIOGRAPHY: *Jean Bonnerot, C. Saint-Saëns, 1835-1921; sa vie et son oeuvre (Paris: A. Durandet et fils, 1922), 151, 159-60; DDO I, 487; Edward Burlingame Hill, Modern French Music (Boston and New York: Houghton Mifflin Co., 1924), 276; Arthur Hervey, Master of French Music (Boston: Milford House, 1973), 107-72; idem, Saint-Saëns (Westport, Conn.: Greenwood Press, 1970), 69; Hugues Imbert, Médaillons contemporains (Paris: Fischbacher, 1903), 285-94; Watson Lyle, Camille Saint-Saëns, His Life and Art (Westport, Conn.: Greenwood Press, 1970), 38, 63-64; Otto Neitzel, Camille Saint-Saëns (Berlin: Harmonie, 1899), 64-65; Georges Servières, La Musique française moderne (Paris: G. Havard fils, 1897), 377-81; Stoullig XXI (1895), 19-24; SW 100.*

Le Freischutz is an opera in three acts with a score by Carl-Maria von Weber* and a libretto by Johann-Friedrichkind that was first translated into French by Sauvage and Castil-Blaze* for presentation at the Théâtre-Lyrique de l'Odéon on 7 December 1824 under the title of Robin des bois.

Seven years later, in 1831, it was staged in its original German form at the Opéra-Comique by a German groupe. The Opéra-Comique used the translation by Sauvage and Blaze when they decided to give Weber's work in French on 15 January 1835. Finally, Emilien Pacini made a second and more faithful translation, and Hector Berlioz* was called upon to furnish music for the portions of the text that were spoken in German and that had to be given in recitative form in France, where the law prohibited the use of spoken word on the stage of the Opéra. Ultimately, on 7 June 1841, the Pacini-Berlioz translation had its premiere at the Le Peletier* opera house. This text became the official version used by the Opéra. The work proved to be extremely popular, and it was given on 104 dates at the Le Peletier opera house. It had its premiere at the Garnier Palace* on 3 July 1876, and it has been billed on 130 dates at this theatre. The composition has not been revived since its 234th presentation at the Opéra on 9 June 1927. In later years, Louis Mérante* (1876) and Joseph Hansen* (1905) have done the choreography for the ballet entitled L'Invitation à la Valse that is included in the French version of Weber's work.

The opera opens with Kilian winning a shooting contest by shattering the target. Defeated Max is disappointed, and Kilian teases him until Max loses his temper and lunges at Kilian with his knife (I, 1). The huntmaster Kouno reproaches Max for allowing a peasant to outshoot him. Gaspard assures Max that the devil is involved in this affair and suggests that he go to the old forest. Here, on Friday, he should trace a mystical circle with a bloody knife while repeating the name of the Black Hunter three times. Kouno orders Gaspard to leave because he does not wish a man of his questionable reputation in his presence; he urges Max to win the royal shooting match the following day if he wishes to wed his daughter Agathe and to inherit the position of Prince Ottokar's huntmaster (I, 2). The hunters dance and then leave Max alone to lament his impossible love for Agathe. He surrenders to despair (I, 3-4), and Gaspard returns to share a glass of wine with him. He pours a potion into Max's glass, urges him to drink, and suggests that he shoot at a hawk soaring high in the night sky. Max is skeptical, but he fires, and a giant eagle falls at his feet. Gaspard puts some feathers in Max's hat and confides to him that the bullet he shot was enchanted. Max asks for a supply of these magic bullets, and Gaspard tells him to be at the Wolf's Glen at midnight. Max is hesitant, but he agrees finally lest he lose Agathe. The Black Hunter directs a threatening glance in his direction (I, 5), and Gaspard rejoices over his triumph (I, 6).

Annette and Agathe are in a hunting lodge discussing love and youth, while they await Max. Annette retires (II, 1), and Agathe prays that Max will win the shooting contest and her hand (II, 2). Max arrives with the sad announcement that he has been beaten in the recent shooting meet, but he shows Agathe and Annette the feathers of the bird that he has just killed. He asserts that he has strong hopes for success on the morrow because he is shooting well. He has also knocked down a 16-point buck that he has left at the Wolf's Glen. The woman are horrified by the mention of this place, where the Black Hunter is often seen. He reassures them and leaves (II, 3) to return to Wolf's Glen. Here, Gaspard is forming a circle of stones to serve as a frame for a death's head. Midnight sounds, and Gaspard calls upon Samiel. He asks for an extension of time to pay his debt, but Samiel rejects his plea. He or Max must be at the gates of hell tomorrow to pay for the benefits he has received (II, 4). Max enters, and the ghost of his mother warns him to flee. Gaspard casts the bullets, six for Max and his targets and the seventh for Samiel. A storm breaks out, trees fall, the rocks of the ravine spilt. Samiel appears for his bullet, and Max faints (II, 5).

The last act opens in Agathe's bedroom, where she is dressed in her wedding gown and praying. She weeps and tells Annette that she fears for Max on this stormy night, but Annette assures her that her fears are groundless (III, 1-2). Agathe's attendants present her with her flowers. Annette opens the box holding the bridal crown, and she is terrified to see the crown of death. She hides the dreaded object, but Agathe persists in her fears and wonders whether the flowers are for the altar or for her tomb. Desperate, Annette seizes the roses from a vase and makes a crown of them (III, 3).

The setting changes to the country, where Ottokar is presiding over the hunt. Koumo, Max,

Gaspard, and Annette but not Agathe are on the scene. The prince calls a halt to the banquet, singing, and dancing so that the shooting may begin. Ottokar orders Max to shoot a white dove flying overhead. He takes aim, but Agathe enters crying prophetically that she is the white dove. The bird flies into a tree, where Gaspard is watching the contest. Max fires; Agathe and Gaspard fall to the ground. Agathe recovers her senses, but Gaspard dies, and Samiel claims his soul. The prince asks Max to explain these mysterious events, and he confesses that his bullets were the work of the devil. Ottokar is aghast and refuses to permit him to wed his daughter. The hermit reprimands the prince for being too severe, and the guests at the contest urge clemency for Max because he has always been a man of honor. The prince agrees that Agathe and Max may marry after a year, and the couple's faith in the future is restored (III, 4).

The male roles of Le Freischutz were filled at its premiere on 7 June 1841 at the Le Peletier theatre by Marié (Max), Bouché (Gaspard), Massol (Kilian), E. Prévost (Koumo), Pierre Wartel* (Ottokar), Goyan (Samiel), Adolphe Alizard* (the hermit). Agathe and Annette were sung by Mme Rosine Stoltz* and Mme Maria Nau,* respectively. The ballet at the first presentation of Weber's opera at the Garnier was danced by Mlles Laure Fonta,* Parent, Fatou. Max has been performed at the Opéra by such stars as Chapuis, Edmond Vergnet,* Laurent, François Dubois,* and Verdière with Pierre Gailhard,* Jean-François Delmas,* Paul Plançon,* and André Gresse* cast as Gaspard. The score of Le Freischütz made an especially deep impression upon audiences from the start, especially the overture. The moving moments in the first act included Max's "Ah! trop longtemps de mes souffrances" (I, 4) and Gaspard's ominous "Non, tu ne m'échepperas pas" (I, 6). The opening duet by Annette and Agathe, "Ca, tiens bien" (II, 1), Annette's dramatic "Sans le revoir encor" (II, 2), and the scene in which the bullets are cast (II, 5) provided the suspense of the second act. The hunting chorus (III, 4) and the finale sustain the earlier pace.

BIBLIOGRAPHY: *Karlovich Arnold, Der Freischütz. 1. Max. 2. Agathe. 3. Aennchen. 4. Kaspar. Opern-Charaktere in Bezug auf deren musikalisch-deklamatorische, wie dramatische-mimische*

Darstellung (Leizip: F. Voigt's Buckhandlung, 1869); Alfred Louis Bacharach, Lives of Great Composers (London: Gollanex, 1935), 623-40; Hector Berlioz, Voyage musical en Allemagne et en Italie: études sur Bethoven, Gluck et Weber (Paris: J. Labitte, 1844); Gustave Bertrand, "Opéra: reprise de Freyschütz," Le Ménestrel 37 (29 May 1870), 202-3; Ange Henri Blaze de Bury, Musciens du passé, du présent et de l'avenir (Paris: Calman Lévy, 1880), 151-95; Chouquet 403; André Coeuroy, "Une Nouvelle Adaptation française du Freischütz," RM 7, no. 8 (1 June 1926), 249-59; idem, Weber (Paris: F. Alcan, 1925), 144-53; Thilo Cornelissen, "Der Freischütz" von C.M.V. Weber (Berlin-Lichterfelde: 1959); DDO I, 488-89; Nathan Haskell Dole, A Score of Famous Composers (New York: T. Y. Crowell & Co., 1891), 258-82; Heinrich Ludwig Egmont Dorn, "Die grosse Arie der Agathe," in "Aus meinem leben," (Berlin: B. Behr, 1870-86) VI, 94-106; "Freyschütz à l'Opéra," in Guy de Charnacé, Musique et musiciens (Paris: Lethielleux, 1874), 73-86; R. Gorer, "Weber and the Romantic Movement," M&L 17 (1936), 13-24; Friedrich Gotz, "Der Freischütz in 1977," Opéra 27 (1977), 142-47; Felix Hasselberg, Der Freischütz: Friedrich Kinds Opernidichtung und ihre Quellen (Berlin: Dom Verlag, 1921; Gunter Hausswald, Carl Maria von Weber, eine Gedenkschrift (Dresden: VVV Dresdner Verlag, 1951), 155-83; Martin Hurlimann, Carl Maria von Weber in seinen Schriften und in zeitgenossichen Dokumenten (Zurich: Manesse-Verlag, 1973); JB 113-17; Adolphe Jullien, Weber à Paris en 1826 (Paris: A. Detaille, 1877); Julius Kapp, Carl Maria von Weber (Berlin: M. Hesse, 1944), 267-74; KCOB 152-57; Friedrich Kind, Der Freischütz (Berlin: Dom Verlag, 1921; Wolfgang Kron, Die angeblichen Frischütz-Kritiken E.T.A. Hoffmanns; eine Untersuchung (Munich: Mittueber, 1957); P. Lacome, "Le Freyschütz et le public," AM 10 (23 June 1870), 236-37; Lajarte II, 166-67; Gilson MacCormack, "Weber in Paris," M&L 9 (1928), 240-48; Gottfried Mayerhofer, "Abermals vom Freischützen" der Münchener "Freischütz" von 1812 (Regensburg: G. Bosse, 1959); MCDE II, 1151-53, 1155-59; Paul Alfred Merbach, "Parodien und Nachwirkungen von Webers Freischütz," ZfMw 11 (1919-20), 642-55; Hans Joachim Moser, Carl Maria von Weber, Leben und Werk (Leipzig: Breitkopf & Hartel, 1955), 68-93; MPPA 176-94; MSRL 268-69; Edmond Neukomm, Histoire du "Freischütz" . . .

tirée de la biographie de Charles Marie de Weber écrite par son fils le baron Max-Marie de Weber (Paris: A. Fauré, 1867); OQE 503-5; PBSW 220-21; J.-G. Prod'homme, "The Works of Weber in France, 1824-1926," MQ 14 (1928), 366-86; Henry Prunières, "Le Freischütz à l'Opéra," RM 8, no. 2 (1 December 1926), 156-58; Ralph, "Théâtre impérial de l'Opéra: reprise du Freyschütz, Coppélia," AM 10 (2 June 1870), 209-10; William Saunders, Weber, with a New Bibliography Compiled by Frederick Freedman (New York: Da Capo Press, 1970), 124-32, 135-40, 153-55, 198-204, 295-348; SSBO 137, 141-44, 147, 152; SW 100-102; Edward M. Terry, A Richard Wagner Dictionary (Westport, Conn.: Greenwood Press, 1971), 40; Johann Georg Theodor, Die Quelle des "Freischütz" (Dresden: R.v. Zahn, 1875); Thompson 628, 2027, 2149-50; John Hamilton Warrack, Carl Maria von Weber, 2d ed. (Cambridge: Cambridge University Press, 1976), 210-39, 319-25; Max Maria Weber, Carl Maria von Weber; the Life of an Artist trans. J. Palgrave Simpson (New York: Greenwood Press, 1969) II, 192-94, 211-13, 218-28, 256-60, 263-65, 423-26.

La Fronde was an opera in five acts with music by Louis Niedermeyer* and a libretto by Jules Lacroix* and Auguste Maquet.* Lucian Petipa* created the choreography, and the sets were done by Cambon and Thierry (a. 1), Despléchin (a. 2, 3), Nolau and Rubé (a. 4), and Martin (a. 5). The work was produced for the first time at the Imperial Academy of Music on 1 May 1853, but it did not prove very successful despite an impressive score and a gallery of convincing characters marred only by the distortion of the duke de Montfort's personality. La Fronde was dropped from the repertory after its eighth performance on 27 May 1853, and it is a temptation to attribute its sudden demise to political influence, because the composition treated an insurgent faction with sympathy and made martyrs of prisoners of the state.

As its title indicates, La Fronde begins at the start of the regency of Anne of Austria, and it opens in the garden of Renard's cabaret near the Tuileries, where Croisilles, Valence, and several members of the bourgeois party are awaiting Jarzé, captain of the royal guards. He enters followed by Marthe, who is looking for Richard de Sauveterre. She has a letter for

Richard and leaves when she cannot find him (I, 1-2). Duchess Hélène de Themines appears on the balcony, and she is also looking for Richard. He appears, and she overhears him confess his love for Loïse. Hélène confronts him, and he reminds her that she caused him to lose his captaincy in the queen's guards and to suffer exile from Paris. Hélène protests her love to him, and he rejects her, but she vows to destroy him and the woman he loves (I, 3-4). The nobles sit down to dine, and they assure Hélène that they have convened to honor the queen; the duchess agrees to preside at the banquet because she is the queen's staunch friend. She then reminds her cousin Jarzé that he should be thinking about his marriage to Loïse, and Richard starts to tremble, a reaction noticed by the jealous duchess. Crafty Hélène suggests a toast to Loïse, and Richard can scarcely control his feelings. When the marquis de Jarzé recites a poem belittling the absent duke de Beaufort, Richard accuses the recitant of calumny. They draw swords, and the duke de Beaufort enters with a group of subversive frondeurs. He defies and silences the nobles with his own poem, and they leave quietly. Beaufort discloses that the royal party is withdrawing to Saint-Germain to starve Paris into sumbission and that civil war is about to begin. Beaufort's plan is to kidnap young Louis XIV and Mazarin, the queen's prime minister. They will place the king in the Louvre and Mazarin in the Bastille. Richard agrees to deliver the letter that will open Saint-Germain to the kidnappers. Hélène sees the letter change hands from a distance, and Jarzé leads his troops into the café. Beaufort and his men repulse the attack to the sound of violins and to the cheers of the populace (I, 5-7).

The second act moves to Saint-Germain, where Hélène extracts from Loïse an admission that she plans to wed Richard. She assures Loïse that this marriage will be a disaster for her because Richard does not love her. She adds that the name of Richard's true love is written in a letter that he is bringing to Saint-Germain in the hilt of his sword (II, 1-3). Richard obtains a truce of four hours to celebrate the feast of Saint-Germain in Paris (II, 4), and festivities begin in the park of Saint-Germain with singing and dancing. Richard makes contact with his accomplices; a lantern at nine o'clock will be the signal to start the kidnapping. Curfew sounds (III, 1), and Loïse accuses Richard of inconstancey. She points to the hilt of his sword, but he denies the letter he carries there is from another woman. Yet he cannot withstand her pleas and reproaches, and he reads her the letter while Hélène is listening. The lovers are reconciled and plan to marry secretly in the chapel at eight o'clock. Hélène knows everything about the conspiracy and the lovers' projected wedding (III, 3).

The fourth act opens in the chapel of Saint-Germain during a storm. Loïse and Richard are awaiting the monk who is to marry them (IV, 1-3). When the monk arrives and asks for their witnesses, Beaufort marches in with his men in chains, wounded, and under guard to say their final prayers. Beaufort accuses Richard of denouncing the conspiracy and taking a bride while his friends suffer for his treachery. Richard protests in vain, but the duke accuses him specifically by showing the letter to the queen. This reference to the letter persuades Richard that Loïse has betrayed them. Recriminations pour forth once more, and it is Loïse's turn to protest her innocence in vain (IV, 4).

The last act transpires in prison, where Richard wonders why he has been separated from his friends and given the freedom of an open parapet. Hélène enters to offer him escape to freedom. She assures him that Beaufort has fled and that no harm can come to his friends, but he will not accept her offer (V, 1-2). Loïse tells Richard that it was Hélène who denounced the conspirators to the queen. She tries to poison herself, but Hélène prevents her suicide to prolong her suffering. Suddenly, Hélène repents her treachery and confesses her madness in betraying Richard. She asks Loïse to help her to save Richard, but the jailer announces that it is time for them to leave. Richard decides to escape at the last moment, but he changes his mind when he hears the prayers of the prisoners on their way to the block. Determined to rejoin his friends in death, he hurls himself from the parapet to the yard below (V, 3).

The female roles were filled by Mmes Fortunata Tedesco* (Hélène de Themines), E. Lagrua (Loïse de Champvilliers), and Maria Nau* (Marthe). Louis Henri Obin* and Gustave Roger* sang the duke de Beaufort and Richard de Sauveterre, respectively, with Lucien and Koenig as the marquis de Croisilles and the count de Valence. F. Prévot did Renard the innkeeper and Marie was cast as the marquis de Jarzé. The individual dancers included Louis Mérante* and Louis Taglioni in the pas de deux and Mlles Regina and Forli with Bauchet and Minard in the pas de quatre. The high spot in the score of the opera was the romance sung by Richard de Sauveterre in the fourth act, but applause was also evoked by the opening chorus of the work in Renard's cabaret and the finale of the fourth act.

BIBLIOGRAPHY: AEM IX, 1507-9; Chouquet 413; DDO I, 490-91; Marie Escudier, "Académie Impériale de Musique: La Fronde," FM 17 (8 May 1853), 149-50; Lajarte II, 213; L. A. Niedermeyer, Vie d'un compositeur moderne, 1802-1861 (Paris: Fischbacher, 1893) 91-124; Wks IV, 17597.

Fuoco, Sofia (b. 16 January 1830, Milan; d. 4 June 1916, Carate Lario), ballerina, née Maria Brambilla, began to study ballet under the direction of Carlo Blasis,* when she was age seven. Incredibly, she made her debut at La Scala in 1839, and she was promoted to the rank of ballerina in 1843. At the Milan opera house, she had the distinction of being the first Giselle to dance on the stage of this theatre. Also, she appeared there in Jules Perrot's* Pas de quatre with Marie Taglioni,* Carolina Rosati,* and Carolina Vente.

The ballerina made her debut at the Opéra in Paris on 10 July 1846 in the world premiere of Betty.* Joseph Mazilier's* work drew some criticism from the press, but critics were enthusiastic about the new star from Milan, and the newspapers used words like ease, vigor, and precision to evaluate her performance. The poet Theophile Gautier* proclaimed his amazement at her "astounding pointes." She remained at the Opéra until 1850, but she did not create any other roles except Betty. She appeared in Nisida* in 1848, and she danced in the divertissements of Jérusalem* (1847) and Jeanne la folle* (1849) (see eighteenth-century volume for divertissement).

After leaving France, she went on tour to London, Madrid, and Barcelona before returning to Italy. She withdrew from the stage in 1858 to love a life of comfort and ease in her villa on Lake Como.

BIBLIOGRAPHY: ACPM 389; CB 160, 190, 195-96, 262; Chouquet 408; CODB 210; Ivor Guest, The Ballet of the Second Empire (Middletown, Conn.: Wesleyan University Press, 1974), 2, 39, 41, 256, 260; Lajarte II, 183-84.

Fursch-Madier, Emmy (b. 1847, Bayonne, France; d. 20 September 1894, Warrenville, N.J.) was a dramatic soprano trained at the Conservatoire. She made her debut in Paris, but she traveled almost continuously and never, stayed in the French capital for any extended periods of time. She gave performances in Brussels as well as in Paris after 1870, and she traveled to New Orleans to sing there in 1874. She appeared at Convent Garden during 1879-81 and then returned to the United States to sing at the Metropolitan Opera House and the Academy of Music in New York City. It was at the Metrolopitan that she bid farewell to the stage as Ortrud in Lohengrin* in February 1894.

After her debut at the Ventadour* opera house on 4 December 1874 as Marguerite in Faust,* Mlle Fursch-Madier remained in Paris long enough to sing Valentine in Les Huguenots* in 1875, and Elvire in Don Juan* and Berthe in Le Prophète* in 1876. It would be impossible to tell from her Paris repertory, therefore, that her favorite roles included Dona Anna, Lucrezia Borgia, Leonora, and Aïda, which she sang at Giuseppe Verdi's* request.

BIBLIOGRAPHY: EFC 151; ICM 637; SW 27, 75, 117, 178.

G

Gabrielli, Count Nicolas (b. 21 February 1814, Naples; d. 14 June 1891, Paris), composer, took music lessons from Busti and Domenico Gaetano Donizetti,* but his natural gift for composing led him into a prolific career of writing before he had time to acquire an extensive and formal education in harmony, counterpoint, and the other aspects of composition that a musician is supposed to learn in school or with a master. He began his career by contributing a dozen texts almost exclusively to the Nuovo Theatre in Naples between 1835 and 1847. Then, almost as if it entailed no effort, he provided the music for more than 60 ballets at the San Carlo and Fondo theatres. He moved on to Paris next, where he furnished Théophile Gautier* with the score for Gemma,* which was danced initially at the Opéra on 31 May 1854. He set the libretto of Les Elfes* by Jules Saint-Georges* and Joseph Mazilier* for the production of this ballet at the Imperial Academy of Music in 1856. He gave Don Gregorio to the Opéra-Comique in 1859 and made his last contribution to the repertory of the Opéra in 1861 with L'Etoile de Messine.*

BIBLIOGRAPHY: Lajarte II, 216, 220, 232.

Gade, Niels Wilhelm (b. 22 February 1817, Copenhagen; d. 21 December 1890, Copenhagen), composer, started his career as a musician by becoming a violinist with the royal orchestra of Denmark. Also, his talents earned him enough prize money during his younger years to enable him to travel in Italy and Germany, where he became conductor

for several orchestras. He did not limit his activities to conducting, however, and it was not long before he won the reputation of being an important composer on the musical scene in Europe with his eight symphonies, multiple pieces for the piano, and numerous vocal works characterized by a genuine melodic charm. He was director of music for a brief period at the Royal Theatre in Copenhagen, and he composed the scores for at least three ballets between 1840 and 1854. Yet he had only one of these last works performed at the Opéra in Paris, when Napoli was presented on the stage of the Garnier Palace* by the troupe of the Copenhagen Opera on 14 June 1937 (see twentieth-century volume for Napoli).
BIBLIOGRAPHY: AEM IV, 1223-28; BBD 565-66; EDS V, 811-12; ELM II, 196; Grove III, 537-38; SW 300.

Gailhard, André (b. 29 June 1885, Paris; d. 3 July 1966, Ermont, Val d'Oise), composer, was the son of the singer Pierre Gailhard.* His father enrolled him in the Paris Conservatoire, where he won the Grand Prix de Rome in 1908 after studying with Xavier Leroux,* Jules Massenet,* and Paul Vidal.* He became interested in theatrical music at the start of his career, and his Amaryllis was produced at Toulouse in 1906.

Gailhard's lyric tragedy entitled La Fille du soleil was produced initially at the ancient arena in Béziers during the summer of 1909, and it was brought to the Garnier Palace* for its first presentation there on 3 April 1910. His only other composition staged at the Opéra was Le Sortilège,* which had its world premiere at the National Academy of Music on 29 January 1913.
BIBLIOGRAPHY: BBD 567; ELM II, 198-99; Grove III, 545-46.

Gailhard, Pierre or Pedro (b. 1 August 1848, Toulouse; d. 12 October 1918, Paris), vocalist, studied at the Conservatoire in Paris and made his theatrical debut as a bass at the Opéra-Comique in 1867 before appearing at the Opéra for the first time on 3 November 1871 as Méphistophélès in Faust.*

He remained at the Imperial Academy of Music to sing the Inquisitor in L'Africaine,* Saint-Bris in Les Huguenots,* and Léporello in Don Juan* during 1872. In 1873, he did Gaspard in Le Freischütz,* and he was cast as the king in

Hamlet* at the first presentation of Ambroise Thomas'* opera at the Garnier Palace* on 31 March 1875. He also did the first portrayals at the Garnier of Charles Gounod's* Méphistophélès on 6 September 1875 and of Pythéas in Sapho* on 2 April 1884.

While he was performing at the new opera house, he created three roles: Richard in Auguste Mermet's* Jeanne d'Arc* on 5 April 1876, Simon in La Reine Berthe* on 27 December 1878, and Guido of Françoise de Rimini* on 14 April 1882.

M. Gailhard became involved in the administration of the Opéra when he was named its codirector with Ritt in 1885. Their partnership lasted until 1892, when Bertrand replaced them and then shared the position with Gailhard during 1893-98. M. Gailhard served his third term alone between 1899 and 1906. He was codirector with P. B. Gheusi in 1907 and then withdrew within a few months to go into permanent retirement.

BIBLIOGRAPHY: DEO 168; GE XVIII, 351; ICM 641; KRJ 147-48; Lajarte II, 244, 247; Martin 161; PBSW 181; Hugo Riemann, Musik Lexikon, ed. Alfred Einstein (Berlin: Max Hesses Verlag, 1929), I, 561; SW 85, 90, 109, 125, 179, 199; XYZ 221-24.

Gall, Yvonne (b. 6 March 1885, Paris; d. 1972, Paris), vocalist, studied at the Conservatoire in Paris and made her debut at the Opéra as a soprano in the part of Mathilde in Guillaume Tell* on 29 January 1908. She had studied under Auguste-Jean Dubulle at the Conservatoire since 1904, and she distinguished herself immediately by her performances as Marguerite in Faust,* Aricie in Hippolyte et Aricie, and Gilda in Rigoletto* before the end of her first year at the Garnier Palace.* In 1909, she was billed as la Naïade in the revival of Christoph Willibald Gluck's Armide and filled the part of Juliette in Charles Gounod's* Roméo et Juliette* (see eighteenth-century volume for Hippolyle et Aricie, Gluck, and Armide). She did only Elsa in Lohengrin* in 1910, Eva in Les Maîtres Chanteurs de Nuremberg* in 1911, and Fausta in Jules Massenet's* Roma* in 1912. The war years saw her remain surprisingly active despite the curtailment of theatrical activities at the Opéra. She sang the title-role in Thaïs* (1914), Ascanio in La Duchesse d'Estampes (1915), Desdémone in Othello* (1916), the title-role again in Briséis* (1916), and Hélène in Messidor* (1917).

Mme Gall agreed to appear at the Chicago Opera between 1918 and 1920, and she returned to Paris in 1921 to join the company of the Opéra-Comique in the world premiere of Les Noces corinthiennes on 10 May 1922, when she sang Daphné. She accepted other invitations to perform in the more prestigious theatres of England, Italy, Belgium, Germany. Yet she also returned to the stage where she had made her debut. In 1924, she did Salomé and Marguerite in Hérodiade and Faust (see twentieth-century volume for Hérodiade). Six years later, she returned to appear at the Opéra as Valentine in Les Huguenots* (1930) and the princess in Marouf (1931) (see twentieth-century volume for Marouf). She was billed as Phoebé in Castor et Pollux by Jean-Philippe Rameau and in a Chopin-Schubert Soirée romantique in 1935 (see eighteenth-century volume for Castor et Pollux and Rameau).

The approximately twenty years of Mme Gall's affiliation with the opera saw her do a dozen new parts at the Opéra. When Woglinde of L'Or du Rhin* was sung initially at the Garnier Palace* on 14 November 1909, it was Yvonne Gall who filled the part. She also created Iole in Déjanire* on 22 November 1911, Kundry in Parsifal on 4 January 1914, Francesca in Scemo* on 6 May 1914 after appearing as one of the nymphs in the initial presentation of Henri Cain's Icare on 19 December 1911. She represented Tatiana in Eugène Oneguine, which had its Garnier premiere on 9 December 1915, Francesca in Les Amants de Rimini on 2 March 1916, and she was the soloist for Florent Schmitt's Chant de Guerre on 18 May 1916. Her last four creations for the Paris Opera were La Fée in Le Jardin du paradis on 29 October 1923, the title-roles in Miarka on 16 January 1925 and Esther on 28 April 1928, and La Vérité in Guercoeur on 21 April 1931 (see twentieth-century volume for Eugène Oneguine, Les Amants de Rimini, Le Jardin du paradis, Miarka, Esther, and Guercoeur).

It would be superfluous to observe that Mme Gall possessed a rich and varied repertory and that her reputation was international in scope. She was an excellent musician who unserstood and practised her craft with skill and warmth. After she had left the stage, her knowledge and brilliant voice won her a professorship at the

Conservatoire. Unfortunately, these many accomplishments have overshadowed Mlle Gall's second "career" at the Opéra-Comique, where her offerings have included Tosca, Louise, Manon, Marguerite, Dona Anna.
BIBLIOGRAPHY: EFC 179-80; ICM 643; KRJ 148; Opera 23 (1972), 1036: obituary; PBSW 81; SW 33, 71, 81, 83, 105, 118, 124, 135, 139, 149, 169, 189, 199, 362, 375; WOC 254.

Gallenbert, Wenceslas-Robert, count de (b. 28 December 1783, Vienna; d. 13 March 1859, Rome), composer, perferred music to all his other studies, and he was still a youth when he undertook the composition of songs, overtures, and operettas. He went to Italy, made the acquaintance of the impressario Barbaia, wrote ballets for his theatres, and persuaded him to return to Austria with him to establish an Italian theatre in Vienna. The new company installed themselves in the theatre of the Porte-de-Carinthie, but the venture did not survive, although the count had spent a fortune to finance and to support it. Faced with financial chaos and bankruptcy, Gallenberg fled to Italy, where he settled down to compose a large number of ballets. Some of these works proved quite popular, and two of them were taken to Paris for performance at the Opéra: Alfred le Grand* of 1822, on which Gustave Dugazon* collaborated, and Brézilia* of 1835, which did not live up to its promises of success.
BIBLIOGRAPHY: Lajarte II, 102-3, 116, 151.

Gallon, Jean (b. 25 June 1878, Paris; d. 23 June 1959, Paris), composer, and his brother Noël both studied piano and theory at the Conservatoire in their native city. Jean became chorus director at the Opéra in Paris between 1909 and 1914, and he taught harmony at the Paris Conservatoire between 1919 and 1949, while his brother Noël taught counterpoint and fugue at the same institution. The two brothers collaborated on the ballet Hansli le bossu,* which had its world premiere at the Garnier Palace* on 20 June 1914.
BIBLIOGRAPHY: AEM IV, 1327-28; BBD 570; ELM II, 208; SW 285.

Gallon, Noël (b. 11 September 1891, Paris; d. 26 December 1966, Paris). See Gallon, Jean.

Garcia, Manuel-Vincent (b. 22 January 1775, Seville; d. 2 June 1832, Paris) entered the choir of the Seville cathedral at age six. Since there was no theatre in his native city, the boy heard only church music until the director of the theatre at Cadiz invited him to come to his city to perform in a tonadilla. He went on to Madrid from Cadiz and thence south again to Malaga, where he wrote his first opera, Preso, imitated from a French comic opera, but he hurried back to the Spanish capital because of an outbreak of yellow fever along the coast. In Madrid, he started to create a series of scores and librettos for the theatre, and he looked once more to French comic operas for his models. Confident of his ability, the composer-singer journeyed to Paris to appear in Griselda at the Opéra-Bouffe in 1808, although he was still ignorant of the Italian language. He then moved over to the Théâtre-Italien to sing his own El Poeta calculista at a benefit performance, and his reputation as a musician was known throughout the French capital by morning.

After a trip to Italy, where he was hailed as one of the great artistes of the day, Garcia returned to Paris to join the Théâtre-Italien as its first tenor. Success followed success for him, and the help he had received in Italy from the singer Anzani, along with his native talents and exhuberance, made him the toast of the French capital. Eventually annoyed by internal jealously at the theatre, he left for England in 1817. He had just completed his Le Prince d'occasion at this time, but it was not a success abroad. His real triumph in England was his appearance in Le Barbier de Séville.

Finally admitting to himself that Paris was his home as an artiste, Garcia sailed for the continent and remanied with the Théâtre-Italien between 1819 and 1824. These years were the time of his greatest accomplishments as a performer and composer. He had his La Mort du Tasse* staged at the Opéra in 1821 and his Florestan* mounted in the same theatre the following year. His La Meuniere (1821) was billed at the Gymnase, and his Les Deux Contrats de mariage (1824) was performed at the Opéra-Comique. Then, in 1824, he left Paris for London once again, and later he crossed the ocean to perform in New York and Mexico with his specially recruited troupe. His tour was a triumph, although he was attacked by bandits and robbed of all his possessions including 1,000 ounces of gold. When Garcia returned to Paris finally, he discovered that these trials, travels, and labors had altered his voice, and he retired to teach and to compose. He has left 17 Spanish, 14 Italian, and 17 French operas.

Garcia was a personality who captured people's imaginations with his personal ways and professional performance, and he was not above exploiting his talents by indulging in Italian virtuosity upon the stage. In a word, he was "box office" to perfection. His talents as a composer were by no means as sensational, but he must be credited with fecundity. Yet if ideas came easily to him, he never took the time or made the effort to develop or to discipline his works. Indeed, he did not even take the time to give titles to some of his still unedited works.

BIBLIOGRAPHY: *Enciclopedia universal ilustrada europeo-americana* *(Barcelona: Hijos de Jespasa, n.d.) XXV, 764; Fétis III, 403-5; Lajarte II, 97, 101, 116; LXIX VIII, 1012-13; Wks 3814, 4241, 4931, 5045, 5498, 5750.*

Garden, Mary (b. 20 February 1874, Aberdeen, Scotland; d. 3 January 1967, Aberdeen), vocalist, lived in the United States as a young girl before going to France to study with Trabadello and Lucien Feugère. She and Sybil Sanderson* met one day, and the famous singer presented her to Albert Carré. M. Carré was director of the Opéra-Comique and was rehearsing Gustave Charpentier's Louise* starring Mlle Rioton. He had Mary Garden learn the star's part of Louise, and, on the evening of 13 April 1900, when Mlle Rioton could not go on for the third act, Mary Garden made her stage debut as Charpentier's midinette. She had worked hard to learn her role, and she enjoyed a resounding success as the unknown actress who had saved the day. She was given a new contract that quadrupled her salary.

The new star went on to do Rouget de Lisle's financée in Lucien Lambert's La Marseillaise, and the leads in Gabriel Pierné's La Fille de Tabarin and La Traviata (see twentieth-century volume for La Traviata). Her second hit in Paris was in Jules Massenet's* Manon,* but it was not until 1902 that the second really important event of her theatrical career occurred. Late in the season, M. Carré came to his troupe with a new text by an unknown composer named Claude Debussy.* The work was Pelléas et Mélisande,* and Mary Garden was chosen to create the part of Melisande in its world premiere at the Opéra-Comique on 30 April 1902. She remained at the Opéra-Comique until 1906, and she appeared in Chérubin by Massenet (1905) and Aphrodite by Camille Erlanger* (1906) during this time.

The meteoric soprano returned to the United States during the ensuing decade to appear at the Metropolitan Opera House (1907) and at the Chicago Opera, where she would remain for a score of years as its leading light and inspiration. But she was also billed at the Paris Opéra before her definitive return to Illionis and the mid-West of America. She sang Thaïs in her debut at the Garnier Palace* on 11 May 1908 in Massenet's now world-famous composition. She appeared in the same theatre in 1908 as Charles Gounod's* Marguerite and Juliette and as Ambroise Thomas'* Ophélie. The following year she was cast as the heroine of Henri Février's* lyric drama, Monna Vanna.* Yet she created only a single role at the Garnier theatre, Salomé in Richard Strauss'* musical drama by the same name that was given its premiere in its French version at the Opéra on 3 May 1910 with Lucien Muratore* as Hérode.

Mary Garden made one last trip to Paris in 1930 before embarking upon her lengthy lecture tours in America and England. Then, on this occasion, she decided to remain at the Opéra-Comique for four years. She said farewell to her Paris public after her last performance as Katiuska in Risurrezione (1934). Finally, in 1939, she returned to Scotland to spend the remainder of her days in her native Aberdeen. In her lengthy career as a performer and lecturer, perhaps her greatest service had been to introduce to the American public the celebrated roles of Erlanger, Fevrier, Charpentier, Massenet, Debussy. Her forte was not the traditional repertory.

BIBLIOGRAPHY: APD 331; Britannica Book of the Year, 1968 (London: Encyclopedia Brittanica, 1968), 590; Gladys Davidson, Opera Biographies (London: Laurie, 1955), 111-16; EFC 180; David Ewen, Living Musicians, 1st suppl. (New York: Wilson, 1957), 61; Mary Garden and Louis Biancolli, Mary Garden's Story (New York: Simon and Schuster, 1951); "Garden in Paris." Newsweek 27 (20 May 1946), 92; GIR 144-48; ICM 648; KRJ

150; P. L. Miller, "Two Great Ladies: Mary Garden and Geraldine Farrar," American Record Guide 34 (February 1968), 464-66; Newsweek 69 (16 January 1967), 72; New York Times, 5 January 1967, 1; PBSW 109, 181; Henry Pleasants, Great Singers (New York: Simon and Schuster, 1966), 308-13; SW 88, 109, 151, 191, 195, 208; Time 89 (13 January 1967), 68; André Tubeuf "Quelques Violetta inoubliades . . . Mary Garden," Opéra de Paris 7 (March 1983), 10; Edward Charles Wagenknecht, Seven Daughters of the Theatre (Norman: University of Oklahoma Press, 1964), 159-79; WOC 254.

Gardoni, Italo (b. 12 March 1821, Parma; d. 26 March 1882, Paris), vocalist, studied voice under the tutelage of A. De Cesari and made his earliest stage appearances in Turin, Berlin, and Milan. In Italy, he distinguished himself especially as Cassio in Giacchino Rossini's* Otello.*

Gardoni appeared at the Opéra in 1844-46, when he created three roles: Bothwell in Louis Niedermeyer's* Marie Stuart,* Jonathas in Auguste Mermet's* David,* and Léopold in Friedrich Flotow's* Ame en peine,*

After his 1844-46 engagement at the Opéra, Gardoni accepted a contract with the Théâtre-Italien now occupying the Salle Ventadour,* where he made his first appearances in Domenico Gaetano Donizetti's* Elisire d'Amore and La Sonnambula. He moved on to London in the summer of 1847 to perform with Jenny Lind, but he returned subsequently to the Italian troupe in Paris, where he remained until the end of his career in 1874. Yet he did accept other billings in Vienna and St. Petersburg (1848-50, 1872), Madrid (1950), Amsterdam, and especially London, where his pleasant voice assured him a permanent welcome as the best of the second-rate tenors.

BIBLIOGRAPHY: DDOI, 43, 299; EDS V, 944-45; Lajarte II, 178, 182-83; Thompson 649.

Garnier, Charles (b. 1825, Paris; d. 1898, Paris), French architect, won the Grand Prix de Rome in architecture for 1848, and he toured Turkey with Théophile Gautier* and Greece with Edmund About before returning to his native city in 1854. Garnier showed no evidence of unusual ambition until 1861, when he decided to enter the heated contest to design the winning plans for a new opera house in Paris. The competition was sponsored by the imperial government of Napoleon III, and 170 other contestants also submitted blueprints for the new theatre destined to replace the previous facility in the rue Le Peletier.*

Garnier's plan was selected by the judges, and, when the new building was completed, it was designated as a national monument. Also, it has come to be known as the Garnier Palace,* and posterity considers Garnier's structure as the outstanding example of nineteenth-century theatrical architecture. Garnier never achieved a second success in his chosen art, although he built a replica of his Paris opera house in Monte Carlo.

BIBLIOGRAPHY: Jean Gourret, Histoire de l'Opéra de Paris (Paris: Publications universitaires, 1977), 71, 74-75; PBSW 18, 181; Petite Encyclopédie illustrée de l'Opéra de Paris (Paris: Théâtre national de l'Opéra, 1974), 11-37.

Garnier Palace, or Opéra and Palais Garnier in French, are terms designating the new opera house that was built after a decree of 29 December 1860 had made official the construction of a more effective and attractive theatre to replace the Le Peletier,* which the Imperial Academy of Music was using at this time and which would be destroyed by fire in 1873. Architects were invited to submit plans for the new structure, and 171 contestants presented their designs. Charles Garnier's entry won.

The surveyors laid out the new location of the Opéra in July 1861, and ground was broken immediately, but the construction schedule was delayed when springs were encountered during excavation. Eight steam pumps were installed and operated without interruption between 6 November 1861 and 21 May 1862. Later, this subterranean water would be available and used for heating, cooling, and fighting fires when nine reservoirs and two tanks would be available to feed the 14 furnaces and almost endless air ducts. The basements and subbasements were kept dry, moreover, because the foundation was built of alternating layers of concrete, cement, and asphalt; barrel vault construction was used in the footing of the structure. The cornerstone of the Garnier Palace was laid by Count Waleski on 21 July 1862.

Work proceeded at a surprising pace despite interruptions by the Franco-Prussian War, the

Commune Uprising of 1871, and a fire. The workers were ready to concentrate upon finishing the roof in 1868; Garnier announced in September 1873 that the new opera house would be finished by January 1876. The marble and stone necessary for the completion of the work had already arrived in Paris from Italy, Sicily, Africa, Spain, Belgium, Scotland, Sweden, and Finland. Also, Garnier was able to overcome a series of special engineering problems that had to be solved before he could open his theatre; for example, the disposal of the enormous quantity of water that would fall on the roof of the Opéra during heavy storms.

The theatre was ready to open its doors to the public on 5 January 1875. Its final dimensions were especially impressive more than a century ago. It was 564 feet long, 331 feet wide, and 79 feet high from the floor of its fifth cellar to the top of Aimé Maillet's Apollo on the roof. The government of France had spent 35,400,000 francs for this incredible structure boasting a stage large enough to hold the entire Comédie-Française. This stage measured 85 feet wide, 170 feet deep, 197 feet high. The theatre boasted 2,156 seats, and the concierges had to worry about 7,593 keys and 1,606 doors to close whenever the Garnier was to remain closed. Nearly a hundred artists, especially sculptors, contributed the decorations that included the lavish use of figures, although it must be said that not all segments of the art work met with universal approbation. Jean-Baptiste Carpeaux's* group representing The Dance evoked numerous attacks in the press right from the beginning, and a bottle of ink was hurled at it one dark night.

The Opéra had its "try out" on 1 December 1874, when a select audience was invited to hear Ernest Deldevez* direct the orchestra in the overtures to La Muette de Portici* and Der Freischutz,* and the chorus singing the blessing-of-the-daggers scene in Les Huguenots* and the soldiers' chorus in Faust.* The theatre made a good impression upon the "experts" present at the "pre-first night" program, and it was decided to open the Garnier Palace to the public on 5 January 1875. The distinguished guests included the president of the Republic, the duchess of Magenta, the lord mayor of London, Alphonso XII and the queen mother Isabella of Spain, and the former king of Hanover. There were 2,400 other spectators. Mme Gabrielle Krauss* appeared in the first two acts of La Juive,* and Pierre Gailhard* starred in the blessing-of-the-daggers scene in Les Huguenots* because Jean-Baptist Fauré* refused to perform after a quarrel with management. The orchestra contributed the overtures of La Muette de Portici* and Guillaume Tell* to the program. The evening closed with Eugénie Fiocre* presenting the corps de ballet in the second tableau of the second act of La Source.* Management was quite happy with the tidy sum of 36,282 francs left at the box office, and Garnier's labors of 14 years had come to a close in a burst of glory.

As time progressed, it became evident that certain changes had to be made in the theatre to take full advantage of its basic structure and to profit by the technological advances of the period. Gas was used for illumination at first, and a clumsy series of batteries supplied the electricity to operate bells used to give signals to the performers. These batteries were also called upon for the creation of moonlight effects. In 1881, the seating area was provided with electric lighting, and, in 1887, electricity was installed to illuminate the stage. Another invention came to the Opéra on 19 April 1881, when the director Vaucorbeil invited a few select guests to listen to Les Huguenots over the telephone in the second basement of the theatre. The following month, this crude network was extended to include four microphones installed in the prompter's box and hooked up to the storehouse for scenery and costumes in the rue Richer. Jacques Rouché took advantage of the lull caused by the war of 1914-1918 to eliminate the foremost loges that interferred with the view of the stage from certain seats. A radio broadcast was arranged for September 1932, when Faust* was performed. The theatre was closed in 1936, when management decided to refurbish it completely; an electric organ and a cyclorama were installed at this time, and the latter was unveiled on 21 January 1937. The interior of the theatre was redecorated again between 28 July and 15 September 1955; Marc Chagall's new ceiling was presented to the press and public on 21 and 23 September 1964. Redecorating work was done once again during the interval of 27 May 1969 and 18 November 1970, when the opera house was closed twice. 220 electricity was installed in September 1970 without anyone suggesting that this improvement might be celebrated by singing "Terre, eclaire-toi", which had been sung for the Electrical Exposition of 1881.

Unfortunately, the Garnier Palace also suffered misfurtunes before it was able to celebrate its 100th birthday on 5 January 1975. The first mishap was the fire in the warehouse in the rue Richer on 6 January 1894, and this misfortune was followed by the death of a spectator in the fall of a counterweight of the main chandelier on 18 May 1896. A zeppelin raid interrupted the performance of Guillaume Tell* on 11 January 1917, and German planes caused another disruption on 17 February 1918. A second fire closed the theatre from 25 to 31 December 1950. One of the more serious strikes suspended all activity at the theatre between 17 October and 7 November 1953, and labor disputes became so frequent and bitter that the theatre remained closed for nearly nine months between 16 November 1970 and 21 May 1971. Inflation and labor unrest resulted ultimately in the abolition of the Opéra-Comique and the appointment of Rudolf Liebermann in 1973 to try to satisfy the public, the workers, the performers, and management itself.

BIBLIOGRAPHY: *François Agostini, "L'Electricité règne sur l'Opéra," Opera 20 (1961), 54-57; Gérard Bauer, René Bourdon, Roland Bierge, "Chagall à l'Opéra," Opéra 23 (1964), 2-19; H. M. Delaage, "Hommage à Charles Garnier," Opéra 20 (1961), 51-53; Pierre Flinois and Jean-Loup Roubert, "Promenades avec Charles Garnier: 1, En montant l'escalier," Opéra de Paris (6 February 1983), 3236; idem, "Promenades avec Charles Garnier: 2, En descendant dans les caves," Opéra de Paris 7 (March 1983), 37-40; idem, "Promenades avec C. Garnier: 4, Au-dessus de Paris," Opéra de Paris 9 (18 March 1983), 36-40; Charles Garnier, Le Nouvel Opéra de Paris (Paris: Ducher, 1878), 2 vols; M. Garnier-Lançon, "Quinze Theatres pour l'Opéra de Paris," Musica 123 (31 June 1964), 24-31; Jacques Hillairet, Dictionnaire historique des rues de Paris (Paris: Les Editions de minuit, 1963) II, 197-98; Albert Laprade, "Charles Garnier et son palais," L'Opéra de Paris 25 (1967), 5-10; André Lejeune et Stéphane Wolff, Les Quinze Salles de l'Opéra de Paris (Paris: Librairie théâtrale, 1955), 31-38; Oliver Merlin, L'Opéra de Paris (Paris: Hâtier, C. 1976); Maurice Moulène, "L'Opéra connu et inconnu," L'Opéra de Paris 8*

(195?), 18-23; "L'Opéra connu et inconnu," L'Opéra de Paris 7 (n.d.), 21-25; Monika Steinhauser, Die Architektur der Pariser Oper (Munich: Prestel-Verlag, 1969); Charles Louis Etienne Truinet, DIT Charles Nuitter, Le Nouvel Opéra (Paris: Hachette, 1875); H. Weinstock, "Great Opera Houses: Paris," ON 25 (17 December 1960), 22-27. X.Y.Z., pseud. of T. Faucon, Le Nouvel Opéra (Paris: Michel Lévy frères, 1875).

Gastinel, Léon Gustave (b. 13 August 1823, Villers; d. 1906, Fresnes-les-Rungis), composer, studied at the Conservatoire in Paris, where he won the Grand Prix de Rome in 1846. He composed a number of masses and oratorios as well as chamber music, but he was also attracted to the theatre. His contribution to the repertory of the Opéra was slight, however, because he favored light operas. His ballet entitled Le Rêve* had its world premiere at the Garnier Palace* on 9 June 1890, and his music was used in the anthology piece called Danses de jadis et de naguère,* which had its world premiere at the National Academy of Music on 22 September 1900.
BIBLIOGRAPHY: AEM IV, 1437, BBD 578; ELM II, 233.

Gaubert, Philippe (b. 4 July 1879, Cahors; d. 8 July 1941, paris), composer, began his studies for the flute under the guidance of Claude Taffanel* at the Paris Conservatoire. He won the 1905 Prix de Rome for his skill with this instrument, and it was not long before he was recognized as one of the more accomplished flautists in the French capital, where he was invited constantly to execute the solo parts for flute with the leading orchestras of the region.

M. Gaubert's ability as a conductor led to his appointment to the post of conductor at the Garnier Palace,* where he remained at the desk from 19 September 1929 until 30 June 1941. He presided at the world premieres of a number of ballets and operas during this period, which saw the first performances at the Opéra of such significant works as Les Troyens, Le chevalier à la rose, and Le Vaisseau fantôme (see twentieth-century volume for Les Troyens, Le Chevalier à la rose, and Le Vaisseau fantôme).

The compositions by Gaubert himself that were billed at the National Academy of Music include the opera Naïla of 6 April 1927 and the following four ballets:

Ballet	Premiere
Philotis	18 February 1914
Fresques	9 May 1923
Alexandre le Grand	21 June 1937
Le Chevalier et la demoiselle	2 July 1941

BIBLIOGRAPHY: AEM IV, 1463-5; APD 332-33; BBD 579; ELM II, 235; Grove III, 577; HAZ 157; NEO 258; PBSW 181.

Gautier, Théophile (b. 31 August 1811, Tarbes; d. 22 October 1872, Neuilly), writer, left his native city for Paris as a very young child. After completing his studies in the capital, he decided to embark upon a career of painting, but he relinquished this ambition in favor of literature. He took part in the battle over Hernani in 1830, the year of the publication of his first volume of verse, and he was soon accepted as one of the foremost figures on the literary scene in France. His writings appeared in many newspapers of the day as well as in the volumes of fiction, verse, and travel literature that he published. His special field of activity for the newspapers was art and drama criticism. He moved about freely in theatrical circles in Paris during the Second Empire and married Ernesta Grisi, by whom he had two daughters. The fall of Napoleon III in 1870 destroyed his favored position, however, and he spent the last days of his life regretting his previous successes and prosperity. It was during the 1841-58 period of his career that he was especially active at the Opéra, and he provided no fewer than five ballets for the company during this interval: Giselle* of 1841, La Péri* of 1843, Pâquerette* of 1851, Gemma of 1854, and Sacountala* of 1858.

BIBLIOGRAPHY: Bernard Delvaille, Théophile Gautier (Paris, 1968); Lajarte II, 168, 173, 194, 207, 216, 225; Charles de Spoelberch de Lovenjoul, Histoire des oeuvres de Théophile de Gautier, Slatkine reprints (Geneva, 1968); PBSW 52, 112,

142; Jean Tild, Théophile Gautier et ses amis (Paris, 1951); H. Van der Tuin, L'Evolution psychologique, esthétique et littéraire de Théophile Gautier (Amsterdam, 1933).

Gemma was a ballet in two acts and five tableaux with music by Count Nicolas Gabrielli,* words by Théophile Gautier,* and choreography by Mlle Francesca Cerrito.* It had its premiere at the Opéra on 31 May 1854, but its music was ineffectual, and it had to be dropped from the repertory after its seventh billing on 8 September 1854.

Gemma is set near seventeenth-century Naples, where the heroine is deciding which costume to wear to a ball being held to celebrate her leaving the convent, and her guardian is doing everything within his means to make her attractive on this occasion because he wishes to marry her to the prince de Tarente despite her love for the painter, Massimo. The situation is complicated further by the marquis de Santa-Croce, who hopes to become wealthy by subjecting Gemma to his "magnetic forces" and then marrying her under his spell (I, 1). The ball begins with Gemma wearing the "mesmerized" rose prepared for her by Santa-Croce, but jealous Massimo makes her discard the powerful flower, and she returns to her natural personality and disposition. Santa-Croce is furious to see that Gemma has rejected him for Massimo once again. The alchemist renews his spell and leads docile Gemma to his henchman, who kidnaps her (I, 2).

The third tableau at the start of the second act presents Gemma plunged into somnambulism in Santa-Croce's castle. She has signed a marriage contract with him. Massimo tries to rescue her, but the contract and Gemma's apparent coldness toward him convince him that she is in love with her captor. Santa-Croce allows her to return to her normal self to determine whether or not she can withstand him in her right mind, and she takes advantage of her restored acumen to steal his dagger. Unable to use the weapon, she climbs through a window and down a tree to faithful Giacomo, who rides away with her (II, 1). Massimo's sister Angiola tries to comfort her brother, and she is aided in her task by Gemma, who has come to the painter's studio. Massimo does not recognize his sweetheart until she poses for him within a frame. Gemma has to return to her picture frame to pose as her own portrait when Santa-Croce enters in search of her. The ruse works, and she is able to flee to San-Severino's castle with Angiola, Giacomo, and Massimo (II, 2).

In the last tableau, the fugitives stop on their way to the castle of San-Severino long enough to share in the celebration of the Marietta-Beppo wedding in the mountains. Santa-Croce catches up with them. He hypnotizes Gemma and tries to lead her away once more, but Massimo kills him in the ensuing swordplay. San-Severino is at the wedding feast, and he agrees at last that his ward and Massimo may wed because the painter has saved Gemma's life (II, 3).

Although Gemma was given only seven times at the Opéra, some musicologists have been misled by the praise that its libretto inspired in the press and have entertained the notion that the work was a success. The scenes that prompted especially favorable comment were the mirror scene opening the ballet and presenting animated reflections of Gemma's bridal attendants, Santa-Croce's attempts to seduce Gemma in the second act after he has restored her to normalcy, and the Abruzzaire executed in the last scene by the two lovers. The ballet must also have profited initially by being the first work of its kind to be based upon the newly discovered phenomenon of hypnotism. The cast was likewise quite impressive with Mlle Cerrito as Gemma opposite Lucien Petipa* as Massimo.

BIBLIOGRAPHY: CB, 377-82; Edwin Binney, Les Ballets de Théophile Gautier (Paris: Nizet, 1965), 185-209; Chouquet, 414; Lajarte, II, 216; PBR 121; Spoelberch de Lovenjoul, Histoire des oeuvres de Théophile Gautier (Paris: Didier, 1887) II, 171; SS 121-22.

Gilbert, Etienne (b. 5 December 1859, Jonquières, Gard; d. ?), vocalist, studied at the Conservatoire in Paris under the direction of Crosti and Louis Henri Obin.* He made his theatrical debut at Rouen in 1887 before going to the Opéra-Comique in 1889. He was invited to make his debut at the Opéra on 6 November 1893 as Vasco da Gama in L'Africaine.* He went on to fill the role of Lohengrin in 1893, but his remaining assignments as a tenor at the Garnier Palace* included only two other parts, Tybalt of Roméo et Juliette* in 1894 and Tannhaüser in 1898.

BIBLIOGRAPHY: Martin 171; SW 25-26, 134-35, 205-7.

Gide, Casimir (b. 4 July 1804, Paris; d. 18 February 1868, Paris), composer, was the son of a wealthy bookstore owner whose principal wish was that his son would carry on his business. Casimir had only a cursory knowledge of music, therefore, but his interest in this art grew to be his principal concern after his admission to the Conservatoire in 1817. No longer a casual student, he made a serious effort to learn composition, and he wrote scores for vaudevilles and dramas to test his knowledge and talent. Finally, he set Duport's Les Trois Marie, which was billed at the Nouveautés in 1828. The Opéra-Comique accepted his Le Roi de Sicile in 1831.

Not satisfied with the scope of these two compositions, which had failed to evoke much enthusiasm, Gide turned next to doing a grand ballet in five acts entitled La Tentation.* Jacques Halévy* was his collaborator on the music for this work performed at the Opéra in 1832. His second piece for this theatre was L'Ile des pirates,* which he and Carlini set using selections from Giaochino Rossini* and Ludwig van Beethoven.* After L'Ile des pirates of 1835, Gide scored Le Diable boiteux* of 1836 alone, and he had no collaborator for La Volière* of 1838. His fifth contribution to the repertory of the Opéra was his music for La Tarentule* of 1839 with a libretto by Eugène Scribe.* It was not until 1847 that his last title for the Opéra was posted at the Le Peletier* theatre, Ozai* with choreography by Jean Coralli.* Gide was to do L'Angélus (1854) for the Opéra-Comique, but shortly afterwards the composer decided to do what his father had planned for him since birth, and he turned to the business of selling books without apparent regrets.

BIBLIOGRAPHY: GE XVIII, 922-23; LXIX VIII, 1249.

Gilly, Dinh (b. 1877, Algiers; d. 19 May 1940, London), vocalist, was born into an army family and had the opportunity to study voice in Toulouse, Rome, and the Paris Conservatoire. He made his theatrical debut as a baritone in Sylvio of Paillasse* at the Garnier Palace* premiere of Ruggiero Leoncavallo's* work on 14 December 1902. A strong baritone, Gilly went on to visit the more prestigious opera houses of South America, Spain,

Germany, England, and New York, but he enjoyed a brilliant success at the Opéra in Paris during the first five years of his career.

The year after his debut, Gilly was cast at the Garnier as Valentin in Faust* and Marcutio in Roméo et Juliette.* The following year, he was billed as Amonasro in Aïda,* Spendius in Salammbô,* and de Luna in Le Trouvère.* His assignments in 1905 included the high priest of Odin in Sigurd,* the king in Le Cid,* and Kilian in Le Freischütz.* When Christoph Willibald Gluck's Armide was revived, he did Ubalde in 1905 and Hidraot in 1907 (see eighteenth-century volume for Gluck and Armide). Simultaneously, he appeared as Wolfram of Tannhäuser* in 1906 and Khirvan of Thamara* in 1907. His final billings at the Garnier theatre were scheduled in 1908: the king in Tannhäuser and de Nevers in Les Huguenots.*

Gilly, sometimes booked as Dinh-Gilly, sang his farewell performance at Covent Garden in 1924. He performed on the British radio from time to time during his retirement in London, where he also taught at this time. He had had only a brief career at the Opéra-Comique after his debut there as Scarpia in La Tosca on 10 July 1922.

BIBLIOGRAPHY: ICM 666; KRJ 159; PBSW 18; SW 30, 41, 62, 89, 101, 118, 168, 191, 209, 217; WOC II, 293.

Ginestet, Prosper de (b. 1796, Aix; d. 1860; Paris), composer, gave up music to join the royal guard under Louis XVIII, and he became a regimental officer a short time later, but he resigned his commission after the Revolution of 1830 because of his oath of loyalty to the Bourbons. His sympathies were with the Royalists, and he left public life to join the staff of their publication, L'Avenir, where he published articles on the musical theatre and theatrical music. His renewed interest in music led him to write compositions for piano, violin, and cello, and he went on to offer texts to the troupes of the Opéra and Opéra-Comique. He did the scores for L'Orphelin et le brigadier (1827) and Le Mort fiancé (1833) performed at the latter theatre. François Ier à Chambord* of 1830 was his only composition given at the Opéra.

BIBLIOGRAPHY: Fétis IV, 6; Lajarte II, 135; LXIX VIII, 1261; Wks 11531.

Girrdano, Umberto (b. 27 August 1867, Foggia; d. 12 November 1948, Milan), composer, began his musical studies in his native city and continued them at the Conservatory in Naples. Here, he composed his first opera. It was entitled Marina and attracted the attention of the publisher Sonzogno, who convinced the musician to do a second opera called Mala Vita (1892). Encouraged by the eventual success of this composition, Giordano went on to create a failure, Regina Diaz (1894), and the well-known Andrea Chénier (1896). He added Fédora* (1898) and Siberia (1904) as well as Madame Sans-Gêne (1915) to his growing authorship, which continued to attract spectators by its genuine theatricality.

Only the second act of Fédora was produced at the Opéra in Paris on 20 October 1910, but his Siberia* was billed there in its entirety on seven dates in 1911-12 before it was withdrawn from the repertory. Madame Sans-Gêne was produced on nine occasions at the Opéra-Comique, where it had its Paris premiere on 10 June 1916 as part of a program organized for the benefit of soldiers blinded in the early years of World War I. Madame Sans-Gêne had had its world premiere at the Metropolitan in New York on 25 February 1915, and it was produced for the first time in Europe at Turin on 28 February 1915.

BIBLIOGRAPHY: AEM V, 148-50; BBD 603-4; CBCM 874-78; EDS V, 1313-18; ELM II, 268; Grove III, 648; PBSW 71, 182.

Giorza, Paolo (b. 1838, Milan; d. 4 May 1914, Seattle, Wash.), composer, took his first music lessons from his father and made a specialty of writing ballets because of the popularity of this type of composition in Italy. His sole dramatic work was a failure, Corrado, console di Milano (1860), but the many successes among his 40 choreographic creations more than compensated for this single disaster at Milan. His only title billed at the Opéra was La Maschera ou les nuits de Venise* of 1864, and he had no scores played at the other lyric theatres in Paris.

BIBLIOGRAPHY: Chouquet 421; Fétis Suppl. I, 383-84; Lajarte II, 235.

Giovanna d'Arco by Giuseppe Verdi* is discussed in the entry for Jeanne d'Arc in the twentieth-century volume.

Giraudet, Alfred-Auguste (b. 28 March 1845, Etampes; d. ?), vocalist, made his theatrical debut as Méphisto in Faust* at Boulogne-sur-mer in 1866 and appeared initially in Paris at the Théâtre Lyrique in the same role the following year. After engagements at Bordeaux in 1871-72 and in Italy during 1873-74, he returned to France to sing at the Théâtre-Italien in 1874 and at the Opéra-Comique in 1875.

In 1880, Giraudet was invited to perform at the Opéra, where he remained until 1883. The color of his baritone voice won him several engagements elsewhere before his retirement from the stage. He was admitted to the facutly of the Conservatoire in 1888.

Giraudet's repertory at the Opéra had included:

Role	**Opera (date)**
Marcel	Les Huguenots (1880)
Brogni	La Juive (1880)
Ramphis	Aïda (1880)
Don Pédro	L'Africaine (1880)
Zaccharie	Le Prophète (1881)
Claudius	Hamlet (1881)
Bertram	Robert le Diable (1881)
Walther	Guillaume Tell (1881)
Balthazar	La Favorite (1882)

He had created two parts during his tenure at the Garnier Palace: Ramire II in Le Tribut de Zamora* on 1 April 1881 and Dante in Françoise de Rimini* on 14 April 1882.

BIBLIOGRAPHY: *Martin 172; "Nécrologie . . . Alfred-August Giraudet," Le Ménestrel 77 (14 October 1911), 328; SW 25-30, 89-90, 99, 105-10, 115-18, 129-31, 177-78, 184-86, 213-14.*

Giselle is a fantasy ballet in two acts with music by Adolphe Adam,* a libretto by Théophile Gautier* and Jules-Henri de Saint-Georges,* and choreography by Jean Coralli* and Jules Perrot.* It found a place in the international balletic repertory almost immediately after its premiere on 28 June 1841 and was staged at the Opéra on 400 dates by 18 October 1961. It is still danced at the Opéra and was executed initially on the stage of the present Paris opera house on 18 June 1910 by the Ballets russes* of Serge Diaghilev.* Nicolas Sergueev created a third choreography for its 1924 revival at the Opéra.

The ballet Giselle ou les Wilis is based upon a German tradition described by Heinrich Heine, who explains that the Wilis are brides who have died before their wedding day. At midnight, they rise from their tombs in their bridal gowns to dance in troupes along the highways in an effort to satisfy an urge for dancing that they could not fulfill during their abbreviated lifetimes. They are beautiful but perfidious because whoever stops to dance with them has to continue dancing until he drops dead.

The first act of the ballet is set in a valley in Germany, where Hilarion is spying on the hut of Loys, whom he distrusts because the latter is his rival for the hand of Giselle (I, 1-2). Duke Albert of Silesia, known as Loys and dressed as a peasant, emerges from his humble dwelling to visit Giselle. He knocks at her door, and she rushes out to embrace him and to assure herself that her nightmare about him loving another woman is false. Outraged Hilarion cannot support this tender scene and tells Giselle that he has seen her and her lover all the while. Giselle flaunts her indifference toward him (I, 3-4). Although it is time to go into the vineyards for the harvest, she persuades her coworkers to forget the grapes so that they may dance. She has to rest after her dancing because she is now too tired to work (I, 5-6). The prince and his daughter Bathilde enter Giselle's house to escape the heat of the day, and Bathilde gives Giselle a golden chain. She explains that she is in love like Giselle and wishes to meet her fiance. Giselle leaves to find Loys, and she comes upon Hilarion leaving her hut with a sword. Hilarion knows his rival at last. He is an aristocrat disguising himself as a peasant. Loys rejoins Giselle (I, 7-10), and the peasants celebrate the completion of the harvest. Giselle is named queen of the festival; she grasps Loys and begins to dance. Hilarion accuses Loys of being a disguised nobleman and a suborner; he produces the sword to substantiate his accusations. Albert rushes at Hilarion in anger. Giselle is overwhelmed, but Loys-Albert still tries to deny his noble rank. She is about to believe him, when the prince's hunting party and the prince recognize Loys as Duke Albert. The prince asks him for an explanation for his strange conduct and costume, and Giselle runs home in tears over being tricked. She attempts suicide but fails. Irrational, she dances until she drops dead from exhaustion (I, 11-12).

The blue moonlight hits the cross on Giselle's tomb, and Hilarion fears that the treacherous Wilis will appear. Myrtha, queen of the Wilis, emerges from the shadows to conjure up her companions of every nationality (II, 1-4). Giselle is among them. They disperse at the sound of approaching villagers and then seduce the younger peasants into dancing (II, 5-6). Albert appears; he is worn and haggard. He tries to move toward Giselle, but she continues to elude him. He attempts to embrace her and finds himself before the cross on her tomb. He looks around and beholds Hilarion obliged to dance with an endless series of Wilis until he is so overcome with fatigue that he falls into the lake and drowns. The Wilis turn to Albert for their next victim, but Giselle intervenes (II, 7-11). She urges her lover to flee and places him under the protection of the cross on her tomb. The queen of the Wilis touches Giselle with her wand and forces her to dance until Albert is charmed away from the cross by her seductive manner. They begin to dance together, and Albert is about to collapse when the sun rises. Gradually, the Wilis disappear, but Albert tries to detain Giselle. The duke's daughter and followers arrive to save him; Giselle disappears after exhorting Albert to save his love for his daughter Bathilde, because she, Giselle, is irrevocably of another world (II, 12-3).

The original cast at the Royal Academy of Music in 1841 included Mlle Caronne Grisi* (Giselle), Mlle Adèle Dumilâtre* (queen of the Wilis), and Mlle Forster (Princess Bathilde) opposite Lucien Petipa* (Albert) and Mabille

(Hilarion). Subsequently, Serge Lifar became associated with the role of Albert, while Mlles Spessivtzeva, Darsonval, and Chauviré stood out in the title-role during the first half of the twentieth century (see twentieth-century volume for Lifar, Spessivtzeva, Darsonval, and Chauviré).

BIBLIOGRAPHY: ACPM 404; L'Avant-scène, Ballet-Danse 1 (January-March 1980), 1-151; Cyril W. Beaumont, The Ballet called "Giselle" (New York: Dance Horizons, 1969); Edwin Binney, Les Ballets de Théophile Gautier (Paris: Nizet, 1965), 60-104, 335-50; BK 48; CB 129-37; Chouquet 403-4; CODB 509-10; Simone Dupuis, "Comment elles abordent Giselle," SDLD 140 (10 January 1982), 44-45; Jacques Feuilly, "Giselle," SDLD 101 (10 February 1978), 16; GMSM 32-55, 191; HAZ 158-62; A.-P. Hersin, "Alternance a l'Opera, SDLD 101 (10 February 1978), 6-8; idem, "Reprises a l'Opera," SDLD 113 (10 April 1979), 6-8; John Mueller, "Films: Alonso's Giselle," D Mag 52 no. 12 (December 1978), 38; PBR 104; Joanna Richadson, Theophile Gautier, His Life and Times (New York: Coward-McCann, 1959), 47-51, 190; Frank W. D. Ries, "In Search of Giselle," D Mag 53, no. 8 (August 1979), 59-74; RNI 54; SS 105-8; SW 282-83; Violette Verdy, "Giselle" or the Wilis, Adapted from Theophile Gautier (New York: McGraw-Hill, 1977); idem, "Gieselle," A Rôle for lifetime (New York: Marcel Dekker, 1977).

Glazunov, Alexander Konstantinovich (b. 10 August 1865, St. Petersburg; d. 21 March 1936, Paris), composer, began to study music at age nine, and he wrote his first symphony at age sixteen. His career began so early and in such a spectacular manner that his teacher Balakirev persuaded Nikolay Rimsky-Korsakov* to accept him as a student. It was not long before he became known to Parisians, who heard his music for the first time at the Paris Exhibition of 1889. His international reputation was formally acknowledged in 1907, when he received honorary degrees from Oxford and Cambridge.

Glazunov composed in various traditions or manners, and he was equally capable of writing in a lyric, heroic, religious, or nationalistic style. Yet his work never entered the repertory at the Opéra, where his music was heard only when guest ballet companies employed it. The Ballets russes* drew upon his work for three compositions

that they executed at the Garnier Palace* before World War I: Le Festin* on 19 June 1909, Cléopâtre* on 11 June 1910, and Les Orientales on 25 June 1910. More recently, George Balanchine,* who admired Glazunov, used his work for two ballets that he presented on programs at the Opéra: Pas de dix, which he produced initially in Paris on 17 October 1956, and his Raymonda Variations, which he mounted for the first time at the Garnier Palace on 29 June 1965.
BIBLIOGRAPHY: AEM V, 214-17; BBD 607-8; CBCM 855-59; CAR 431-35, 501-2; DEC 235-38; EDS V, 1366-68; ELM II, 272-77; Grove III, 660-62; PBSW 68; Thompson 670-71; TWT 308-11.

Gosselin, Louis F. (b. 28 February 1800, Paris; d. 1860, Paris), dancer, studied ballet with his older sister and took more advanced lessons privately with Antoine Coulon.* He passed the entrance examination for the Royal Academy of Music and was assigned a part in a pas de deux from Les Pages du duc de Vendôme* on 5 September 1821.

Young Gosselin made a favorable impression on spectators and management alike with his impressive stage presence and noble demeanor. His ability was verified by his interpretation of the count's role in Le Carnaval de Venise* in 1822. After dancing the part of the duke in Clari* and Almaviva in Le Page inconstant,* he was billed for the premieres of Alfred le Grand* on 18 September 1822 and Aline, reine de Golconde* on 1 October 1823. He was now clearly and firmly established at the Royal Academy of Music, and he was assigned to roles in the initial presentation of Cendrillon* on 3 March 1823 and Ipsiboë* on 31 March 1824.

Gosselin spent 1839-52 at the King's Theatre in London, but he was tempted back to Paris with an offer of the equivalent of an advanced professorship at the Opéra, which was now the Imperial Academy of Music. He remained in this post until his death, and he could boast of having had Francesca Cerrito,* Carolina Rosati,* and Marie Taglioni* among his pupils.
BIBLIOGRAPHY: CB 104, 241, 247, 254, 297, 375; CODB 229; DDD 110; EDS 1505-6; Ivor Guest, The Ballet of the Second Empire (Middletown, Conn.: Wesleyan University Press, 1974), 7, 74, 177, 254; idem, The Romantic Ballet in England (Middletown,

Conn.: Wesleyan University Press, 1972), 34, 65, 96-97, 103, 115.

Got, François-Jules-Edmond (b. 1 October 1822, Lingnerolles; d. 1901, Paris), librettist, studied at the collège Charlemagne and was employed by the government after graduation. He left this position in 1841 to enter the Conservatoire to study drama, and he won second prize in comedy the following year. After completing military service, he joined the troupe of the Comédie-Française, and his talent for acting earned him the reputation of being one of the most effective performers in the company. He was not long in reaching stardom, and he came to excel in such classic roles as Figaro and Crispin while creating such contemporary parts as Giboyer in Les Effrontés and Guérin in Maître Guérin. A man of ideas, he organized a road company to represent the Comédie-Française in the provinces, but his other projects were sometimes bold and drastic enough to dismay the members of the administration and to bring him into conflict with them.

These activities did not prevent Got from finding time to compose two librettos for the Opéra. His first text for this theatre was the poem he did alone for François Villon* of 1857. Edouard Foussier* helped him provide the words for L'Esclave* mounted in 1874.

BIBLIOGRAPHY: Chouquet 417; GE XIX, 31; Edmond Got, Journal de Edmond Got, sociétaire de la Comédie-française (1822-1901), ed. Méderic Got and Henri Lavedan (Paris: Plon, 1910); idem, La Comédie-française à Londres (1871-79), ed. George d'Heylli (Paris: P. Ollendorff, 1880); Lajarte II, 223, 246; LXIX VIII, 1381.

Gottschalk, Louis Moreau (b. 8 May 1829, New Orleans; d. 18 December 1869, Rio de Janeiro), pianist, went to Paris to study piano with Hallé and Stamaty. It was not long before he became the toast of Paris, and even Frédéric Chopin* had words of praise for his piano playing. Gottschalk returned to the United States in 1853 to make a successful and lucrative tour of his own country, where he was applauded with frenzied enthusiasm whenever he appeared in concert. It was on one of his spectacular tours that the pianist contracted yellow fever in Brazil, where he died and left behind him a large corpus of works derived from Creole and Afro-Hispanic sources.

Gottschalk's music was used for the score of Tarantella, a ballet by George Balanchine that was danced at the Garnier Palace* for the first time on 28 June 1965, nearly a century after the pianist-composer's death. The ballet was presented by the New York City Ballet on this date with an arrangement of Gottschalk's music by Hershy Kay.

BIBLIOGRAPHY: BBD 630; GBAL 632.

Gounod, Charles-François (b. 17 June 1818, Paris; d. 17 October 1893, Saint-Cloud). composer, studied at the lycée Saint-Louis, where he excelled in Latin, and he entered the Conservatoire in 1836 to study under Henry Berton, Jean Lesueur, and Jacques Halévy* despite his widowed mother's misgivings about his choice of a career in music (see eighteenth-century volume for Berton and Lesueur). After two unsuccessful attempts to win the Prix de Rome contest in 1837-38, Gounod carried off first prize with his 1839 cantata entitled Fernand.

Gounod arrived in Rome on 27 January 1840. His director at the Villa Medici was the painter Ingres, whom he came to know quite well and for whom he did sketches in his spare time. Other acquaintances to exert an influence upon the young musician included Fanny Hensel, Felix Mendelssohn's* sister who increased his knowledge of German music, and père Lacordaire, the Dominican friar and disciple of Lamennais who felt that Gounod and his gifted compatriots would provide valuable support for his new religious movement. There was one unhappy note in Gounod's life at Rome: the extremely hostile condemnation that his Palestrina-inspired composition evoked in the Paris evaluation of this work written by Gasparo Spontini and expressing the official opinion of the Conservatoire (see eighteenth-century volume for Spontini).

The composer's stay in Rome was extended until June 1842, when he left Italy to travel to Vienna by way of Florence, Venice, Trieste, and Grätz. He was welcomed to Austria by Count Stockhammer, who arranged for his Requiem to be played by the Vienna Philharmonic and for his choral mass to be sung at Karlskirche on Easter 1843. Moving on to Berlin, he saw Fanny Hensel again, and she gave him a letter of introduction to her brother in Leipzig. After a pleasant visit with Mendelssohn in this latter city, Gounod returned to Paris and his waiting mother. He obtained the post of organist at the Missions Etrangères church, where his desire to play Palestrina and Bach brought him into conflict with his superiors and the parishioners. These differences were resolved shortly, but Gounod's increasing religious fervor prompted him to leave his post to enter the Carmelite seminary of Saint-Sulpice. His enthusiasm for a life of sacrifice and prayer seemed to wane with the approach of the 1848 revolution, and he left the religious community to try his fortune in the theatre.

The composer's first task now was to find a libretto, and this problem was solved by Emile Augier's* willingness to provide a text, if Pauline Viardot* were to star in the production. Although Gounod's life was upset drastically at this crucial moment by the death of his brother, he was able to complete by September 1850 the score for the poem that Augier had given him in April 1850. The work was entitled Sapho,* and it had its unsuccessful premiere on 16 April 1851. Gounod's marriage to Anna Zimmerman at this time caused a repture in his relationship with Pauline Viardot, but he did not appear troubled and began to do the incidental music for François Ponsard's Ulysse which was given its first presentation at the Comédie-Française on 18 June 1852. Then, in April 1853, the public heard the musician's Ave Maria for the first time in a concert by Jules Pasdeloup. This piece had been literally saved from oblivion by Pierre Zimmerman, the musician's father-in-law, who suggested that Gounod might do something with this "Meditation on the first prelude of Bach." When his wife's father died in 1853, he left his beautiful Saint-Cloud mansion to Anna and Charles.

Gounod had given Sapho and Ulysse to a publisher without any serious thought of payment in return, but he was now entertaining the possibility of being paid for his labors. Perhaps it crossed his mind, moreover, that the public had to be given a product for which it was waiting before it would pay to see and to hear it. Thus, he was tempted when Nestor Roqueplan offered him the libretto entitled La Nonne sanglante* based upon the thrilling tale of horror by Matthew Lewis entitled The Monk. It was known that Giuseppe Verdi,* Hector Berlioz* Giacomo Meyerbeer,* Jacques Halévy,* and Félicien David* had rejected this text, but its author was Eugène Scribe,* and it possessed all the features of Gothic romanticism. Gounod accepted the offer by Roqueplan, but his gamble was without profit to all concerned. The premiere of La Nonne sanglante on 18 October 1854 was a failure. Gounod suggested to Scribe that they try again, but the peevish librettist refused to entertain the suggestion.

Three failures in succession did nothing to encourage the composer, but he returned to his desk to work on an opera he would never finish, Ivan le terrible, and to apply for election to the Academy of Fine Arts, but these activities were interrupted by a nervous breakdown. When he recovered, Jules Barbier* suggested to him that they collaborate on an operatic version of Goethe's Faust, and the director of the Théâtre-Lyrique agreed that such a work should be done, but he demanded that a Molière comedy be given first. Gounod's resultant Le Médecin malgré lui of 1858 was his first successful composition. Léon Carvalho* kept his promise, and Faust* was mounted next on the stage of the Théâtre-Lyrique on 19 March 1859. Gounod also started work this same year on Philémon et Baucis,* which was based on La Fontaine but with the added theme of youth restored and love refreshed. It had its premiere on 18 February 1860 at the Théâtre-Lyrique.

Faust and Philémon et Baucis had brought a quiet revolution to the French operatic stage because the natural quality of the vocal passages sounded the death knoll of romantic bombast and declamation. Yet this new style puzzled audiences at first, and neither composition was a complete success immediately except for spectators like Berlioz and Meyerbeer. The third work in the 1859-60 triad of compositions by Gounod was his light-hearted La Colombe, also based on La Fontaine but given in Baden-Baden because of the composer's promise to create a work for the theatre there if its director would waive his claims and permit Philémon et Baucis to be billed first at Carvalho's Théâtre-Lyrique.

The empress Eugénie now suggested that she and Gounod might pool their talents to compose a ballet in the fall of 1860, but he preferred to finish his La Reine de Saba* for the Opéra. The rehearsals were stormy because the singers, dancers, stagehands, and even the leader of the orchestra grumbled over the difficulty of their assignments. The situation became so difficult that Gounod had to appeal to the government to restore order. The work was given its premiere finally on 29 February 1862 with some financial success despite its uneven quality.

The failure of La Reine de Saba along with the death of his teacher, Halévy and the loss of his mother depressed Gounod to such a degree that he decided to journey to Italy with his son Jean and his wife Anna. In Rome, he visited Saint Peter's to hear Palestrina's music again, and he made a sentimental visit to the Villa Medici. He continued on to Naples and then returned to Paris by way of Florence and Switzerland. Back at his desk, he toyed with the idea of doing a Cid, but he decided finally to accept Carré's suggestion that he do an opera based on Mistral's Mirèio. Arrangements were made, and an enthusiastic Gounod left for Provence. He had a long and pleasant stay with the poet and then rented a room in the Ville-Verte hotel to pass a happy five or six weeks communing with nature and creating his score. He returned to Paris with his music almost complete. Unfortunately, he was now persuaded to go to London ostensibly to promote Faust but in truth to line the pockets of his editors and the entrepreneurs. Upset by the discovery of the real reason for his sudden excursion across the Channel, Counod suffered a second breakdown and had to be placed under the care of Dr. Blanche in Passy. It was not until 19 March 1864 that Mireille was performed, and the lack of enthusiasm that greeted it made Carvalho insist that Gounod revise it by endowing it with a happy ending, by keeping the heroine alive, and by reducing the five acts to three acts. The formula worked.

Gounod's next score was Les Deux Reines, which would not be performed until 1872 because of governmental opposition to it during the Second Empire. He also started on Fiesque, but he set this work aside to try to do a score for an adaptation in four acts of William Shakespeare's Romeo and Juliet that Barbier and Carré had brought to him. He was especially interested in the subject because of his admiration for Berlioz' symphony. He finished most of the music for this new libretto during his stay in Provence in the spring of 1865. The immense effort of writing almost an entire opera in a month sent Gounod back to Dr. Blanche in salubrious Passy, but Carvalho had the manuscript of Roméo et Juliette* in hand by August 1866. Still, Carvalho had his usual adamant suggestions about inserting a "show-stopper" in the text for his wife, already cast as Juliette. Rehearsals dragged on because of such problems as incorrect costumes. Yet the work was ready for its premiere on 27 April 1867, and Gounod was able to enjoy his first immediate success.

The Academy of Fine Arts elected Gounod to its membership, and the Legion of Honor chose him as an officer. It seemed that Gounod was now becoming a great personage in the musical theatre, especially since Faust had become a part of the Opéra repertory. The composer himself was growing grandiloquent and pontifical. But all these matters were overshadowed by the outbreak of the Franco-Prussian War. Gounod took his family to Liverpool. He performed his Gallia in England and set a number of English songs, but the most important event of his stay in Great Britain was his making the acquaintance of Georgina Weldon. He took such an obvious interest in her that Mme Gounod had no choice but to return to France without her husband. Even an invitation to become head of the Conservatoire could not persuade Gounod to return to the Continent. Ultimately he did go back to France, but he also persuaded Mrs. Weldon to follow him because he wished her to star in Gallia about to be performed in Paris. They recrossed the Channel, and Gounod tried to go to work on his new composition, Polyeucte.* Yet his constant struggle with his wife, the relentless attacks upon "the Englishman Gounod" by the French press, and a distracting lawsuit undermined his health again. Then, in the spring of 1874, Dr. Blanche arrived at the home of the Weldon family to bring Gounod back to France.

After three years of war and Mrs. Weldon, Gounod tried to resume his work. Encouraged by a revival of his Jeanne d'Arc at the Gaité, he accepted Carvalho's suggestion to set a libretto entitled Cinq-Mars for the Opéra-Comique. Once again there were the usual problems at rehearsal that Gounod always seemed to encounter, but the work, based on Alfred de Vigny's novel, was declared a success the evening of its premiere on

5 April 1877. Then, after ten years of intermittent labor, *Polyeucte* opened at the Opéra on 7 October 1878. The tragedy was too far in the ideal realm of Corneille, and it failed, but Gounod composed one last piece to redeem this failure, *Le Tribut de Zamora*,* which was everything that lofty *Polyeucte* was not. It offered picturesque settings, a murderess, a slave auction, an orphaned heroine, and the irreproachable conclusion of love triumphant. It had its premiere at the Opéra on 1 April 1881 and was an instant success. Mrs. Weldon was among the spectators.

Gounod was now 63, and he would write no more music for the theatre. He assumed the role of patriarch in his new and elegant mansion in the place Malherbes and kept himself occupied not only with the composition of religious music but also with the promotion of his pet projects. He was generous with his time, and he never refused to see reporters, who never grew tired of describing his flowing beard, clerical garb, and Mosaic wisdom. His last work was a *Requiem* for his grandson Maurice that he finished only two days before his own death.

BIBLIOGRAPHY: L'Avant-scène 41 (May-June 1982), 3-103, 118-39; Camille Bellaigue, Gounod (Paris: Alcan, 1919); Marie Anne de Bovet, Charles Gounod, His Life and Works (London: S. Low, Marston, Searle & Rivington, 1891); H. Busser, Charles Gounod (Lyon: E. I. S. E., 1953); Chouquet 411, 414, 420, 424; J. J. Debillemont, Chalres Gounod (Paris: Nouvelle Revue de Paris, 1864); Henri Delaborde, Notice sur la vie et les oeuvres de Charles Gounod (Paris: Institut de France, 1894); Théodore Dubois, Institut de France. Académie des beaux-arts. Notice sur Charles Gounod . . . lue dans la séance du 24 novembre 1894 (Paris: Firmin-Didot, 1894); EGC 160-63; Fétis IV, 70-72; Charles François Gounod, Autobiographical Reminiscences, trans. W. Hely Hutchinson (New York: Da Capo Press, 1970); James Harding, Gounod (New York: Stein and Day, 1973); P.-L. Hillemacher, Charles Gounod, Biographie Critique (Paris: H. Laurens, 1906); Hugues Imbert, Charles Gounod: les mémoires d'un artiste et l'autobiographie (Paris: Fischbacher, 1897); JB 236-41; Lajarte II, 208, 217, 233, 243, 256; P. Landormy, Gounod (Paris: Gallimard, 1942); MPPA 281-315; MSRL 88-93; PBSW 61-62, 182; Michel Poupet, "Gounod et

Bizet," L'Avant-scène 41 (May-June 1982), 106-17; J. G. Prod'homme and A. Dandelot, Gounod 2 vols. (Paris: Delagrave, 1911); Henry Tolhurst, Gounod (London: Bell & Sons, 1904).

Grahn, Lucina Alexia, DITE Lucile (b. 30 June 1821, Copenhagen; d. 1907, Munich), ballerina, studied ballet along with her first lessons in spelling, and August Bournonville* was so impressed by her talent that he took a personal interest in her future. He accompanied his pupil to Paris, where the adolescent girl was so amazed by the Opéra that she determined to perform there as soon as circumstances would permit.

When Mlle Grahn returned to her native Denmark, she danced at age 16 in her teacher's Valdemar, and, in 1836, she did the title-role in La Sylphide,* now newly arranged for her by Bournonville. She was applauded generously for this latter performance, and the royal family rewarded her with a piece of jewelry and an invitation to the palace for afternoon chocolate.

Yet these accomplishments were really secondary for Lucile Grahn, because it was the Paris opera house that was still occupying her mind. While her compatriots were still hailing her as their Danish Taglioni, she applied for a fellowship to study ballet in the French capital. Bournonville tried to interfere, but she refused to be outmaneuvered and appealed to the royal family. She left for Paris in the spring of 1837.

In France, she studied under the direction of Hippolyte Barrez,* now director of the ballet school, and her progress was so evident that it was decided that she should make her debut in La Juive* in October. Unfortunately, her leave from the Copenhagen ballet expired, and she had to return to Denmark. She was bitter, and Bournonville was spiteful; their quarrel spread through government circles as each sought redress for offenses real or imagined. The king brought the dispute to a swift conclusion by giving the ballerina permission to fill an engagement in Hamburg. Once outside her country, Lucile felt free to follow her own wishes, and she journeyed to Paris after leaving Germany. Her angered government revoked her membership in the national ballet and her pension, but the dancer exhibited no regret and never set foot on Danish soil again.

Lucile Grahn made her debut at the Opéra in Le Carnaval de Venise* on 1 August 1838. She inspired some enthusiasm, but this work was mounted only once, and it was not until the following year that she scored her first real triumph by substituting for Franziska Elssler* in La Sylphide on 10 January 1839. Then, in preparation for her part in a benefit for Cornélie Falcon* scheduled for 14 March 1840, Mlle Grahn suffered a severe injury to her knee. She was disabled for a period of weeks, and her total recovery required several months. She never danced at the Opéra again, although she did appear in Russia in 1843 and in Italy in 1844. It was in England that she enjoyed prolonged success, however, especially as one of the performers in the famous Pas de quatre.

She married the English tenor Friederich Young in 1856, but she returned to her profession as a teacher after he became an invalid as a result of injuries sustained in a fall at the theatre. She passed this later part of her life in Munich, and she survived her husband by more than a score of years. She had no heirs and willed her entire fortune to this city that named a street after her.

BIBLIOGRAPHY: ACPM 424; CODB 231; Margaret Crosland, Ballet Carnaval (New York: Arco, 1955), 29; EDB 160-61; LXIX VIII, 1428; Parmenia Migel, The Ballerinas from the Court of Louis XIV to Pavlova (New York: Macmillan, 1972), 168-76; Mark Edward Perugini, A Pageant of the Dance and Ballet (London: Jarrolds, 1946), 208-12; Walter Terry, Star Performance (New York: Doubleday, 1954), 83-86.

Grantzow, Adèle Camille (b. 1 January 1845, Brunswick; d. 7 June 1877, Berlin), ballerina, received her first dancing instructions from her father, the balletmaster in her native city. She made her first public appearance at the Brunswick Opera House and then moved on to Hanover with the rank of première danseuse. Ambitious, she went next to Paris, where she lived with her teacher, the famous Mme Dominique. Charles Saint-Léon* had known her from her Hanover days, and he interrupted her sojourn in the French capital by persuading her to become première danseuse at the Bolshoi Theatre. She made her debut in Moscow on 27 November 1865.

Saint-Léon grew enthusiastic about Grantzow's work, and he sent word of her progress and success to Paris. The director of the Opéra, Emile Perrin, became interested immediately, and a contract for the dancer's return to France was drawn up to the satisfaction of both parties. Mlle Grantzow was to make her services available to the Opéra from April to September 1866. She arrived in Paris for her debut in Giselle* on 11 May 1866. Reactions to her performance were favorable, although a critic here and there like Nestor Roqueplan proved hard to please and found flaws in her technique. She was credited with scoring an overall success, however, and the general consensus was that she deserved the applause that had greeted her miming and pas.

The Opéra was now planning to produce Léo Delibes'* La Source* as its next balletic attraction, and Adèle Grantzow had already been selected to do Naïla. Fate intervened when she hurt her foot, and a second delay was caused by a decision to add a third act to the work. It was then realized that Grantzow's contract ran only to September, and she had to return to Russia to meet her obligations there after the expiration of her contractural engagement in Paris. Mlle Guglielmina Salvioni* was named to replace her, and La Source was given without her on 12 November 1866.

La Grantzow returned to Paris on 10 May 1867 after an incredibly successful series of appearances in St. Petersburg and Moscow. Her first vehicle at the Opéra was La Source, and critics acknowledged that she had revived a dying ballet by appearing in it in the nick of time. But her most extravagant albeit brief victory in the French capital was as the lead in the first act of Giselle* on 4 June 1867 before Tsar Alexander II, who was visiting the Universal Exposition in Paris. The imperial box was filled with rulers and dignitaries of nearly every description from a far away as Japan. The public was so curious and enthusiastic that 30,000 francs were left at the box office. Giselle was repeated with Le Trouvère* on 10 June for the king of Prussia and on 5 July for the sultan of Turkey.

It was at this point that Perrin realized that he had failed to arrange for a new ballet to be given at the Opéra during the Exposition, and he decided to revive Joseph Mazilier's* Le Corsaire* of 1856. A budget of more than 70,000 francs financed the new production, and Grantzow was cast as Médora. Unfortunately she had to disobey her physician's order not to dance on her injured foot on the evening of the premiere, 21 October 1867, but she managed to remain on stage throughout the performance, although her foot became so swollen that she had to slit open her slipper. She repeated her role on 25, 28, 30 October and 4, 8 November before fever set in, and she was obliged to rest with her foot off the ground. After her foot had healed, she returned to the stage to dance Médora again on 20, 22, 28 November before leaving for Russia. When she came back to Paris in the spring of 1867, she resumed her role in Le Corsaire on 17, 27, 29 April and 7, 15 May.

The ballet seemed to be in the doldrums in Paris during 1867-68 for a number of reasons. It was enjoying fewer and fewer billings at the Opéra. Lucien Petipa* had retired and had not been replaced. Well aware of this situation, Perrin charged Saint-Léon with choreographing a work to fill the gap. He was to collaborate with Charles Nuitter* and Delibes. Adèle Grantzow was to be given the lead. She reported to the theatre for rehearsals eventually on 30 July 1868. The new composition was entitled Coppélia.* Inevitably, problems arose and delays occurred. Saint-Léon had to go to Russia, and he fell ill there. Adèle became sick in her turn and had to withdraw from the part. An unknown Italian named Giuseppina Bozzachi* replaced her.

When la Grantzow recovered her health, she traveled to St. Petersburg to dance in Saint-Léon's new composition, Le Lys. It was obvious that she had lost some of her efficiency and strength, but Perrin entertained Saint-Léon's suggestion that she might do well in a revival of Pâquerette* or in a new composition by Jules Duprato* based upon Don Quixote. These projects did not materialize, because Grantzow was stricken suddenly with typhus when she was still in St. Petersburg. She hovered between life and death for nearly a month, but she recovered to enjoy good health and to make plans to marry an officer in the Prussian cavalry. She noticed a rash on her leg one day, however, and she sought medical treatment for it. The physician was careless with procedures, and blood poisoning resulted. An amputation was ordered, but Adèle was not strong enough to survive the operation and died in the Augusta Hospital in Berlin.

BIBLIOGRAPHY: ACD 217; CB 136, 218, 247, 249, 351, 354, 359, 410-16, 488; CODB 233; DDD 111-12; EDB 165; M. Escudier, "Théâtre Impérial de l'Opéra: Début de Mlle Grantzow," FM 31 (20 May 1866), 150-51; Ivor Guest, The Ballet of the Second Empire (Middletown, Conn.: Wesleyan University Press, 1974), 211-18, 220-23, 227-33; Lajarte II, 219-20; Parmenia Migel, The Ballerinas from the Court of Louis XIV to Pavlova (New York: Macmillan, 1972), 228-29, 255, 262, 264.

Grassari, Mlle Gérard DITE (b. 1793, Tongres, Belgium), vocalist, was brought to Paris by her divorced mother around 1814 and enrolled in the Conservatoire to complete her musical studies. She left the Conservatoire in 1816 and made her debut at the Opéra on 13 February 1816 under her stage name of Grassari. Her first role was Antigone in Oedipe à Colone (see eighteenth-century volume for Oedipe à Colone).

Mlle Grassari had a striking soprano voice, and she was assigned immediately to act as a stand-in for performers unable to meet their schedules. After she had appeared in Les Dieux rivaux* (1816), Nathalie* (1816), and Les Croisés (1819), however, it became evident that her talents deserved more serious consideration, and she was promoted to the rank of leading soprano. In this position, she created ten roles at the Royal Academy of Music between 1819 and 1825.

Role	Opera	Premiere
Aspasie	Aspasie et Périclès	17 July 1820
Stratonice	Stratonice	30 March 1821
Almasie	Aladin	6 February 1822
Virginie	Virginie	11 June 1823
Lasthénie	Lasthénie	8 September 1823
The queen	Vendôme en Espagne	5 December 1823
Zénaïre	Ipsiboé	31 March 1824

The princess	La Belle au bois dormant (Carafa)	2 March 1825
Phédore	Pharamond	10 June 1825
Elzire	Don Sanche	17 October 1825

Mlle Grassari remained at the Opéra until 1828, but she was not assigned to any new roles after Mlle Laure Cinthe-Damoreau's* debut at the Royal Academy of Music on 4 February 1826. Mlle Grassari left the Opéra finally in 1828, and she dropped from sight without saying anything about her plans to her colleagues.
BIBILIGRAPHY: Chouquet 387-88, 390-92; EFC 140; Fétis Suppl. I, 416; George Jellinek, "Napoleon and the Prima Donna," ON 39 (8 February 1975), 14-15; Lajarte II, 89, 98, 100-101, 104-7, 109-10.

Graziosa was a pantomime-ballet in a single act with music by Théodore Labarre,* a libretto by Darley, and choreography by Lucien Petipa. Its set was created by Cambon and Thierry. It had its world premiere at the Imperial Theatre of the Opéra on 25 March 1861, and it was given on 20 dates during its first year at the Opéra. It went on to enjoy another 22 performances in 1862-63, and it was revived on 15 December 1871 for another 7 productions in 1871-72, but it had to be dropped from the repertory after its staging on 13 March 1872. Ultimately its score was lost in the conflagration that destroyed the opera house in the rue le Peletier* in 1873.

The ballet is set in a small city near Naples, where local girls are dancing the tarentella. One of the dancers distinguishes herself by her elevation. She is Graziosa, who is awaiting her fiance Pietro. The latter appears almost immediately at the head of his mule train. He greets his sweetheart at the moment when a group of nobles enters, and one of their number is speaking tenderly to a lady of the group wearing the customary street mask. Don Rodrigo bars the passage of Don Manuel and his companion; he demands that she unmask. A duel ensues; Pietro leaves to summon the police; Graziosa leads the masked lady from the square. The mysterious woman returns to ask the duelists to put up their swords. She unmasks. The men are surprised to see that she is Graziosa. Don Rodrigo apologizes to Don Manuel, who walks off with the resourceful dancer on his arm.

Pietro returns with the mayor and the municipal guards, but the square is empty. Afraid, he runs away, but the soldiers catch him and throw him into a convenient room until he can be transferred to prison for giving false information to the authorities. The soldiers sit down to a glass of wine at the café, and Graziosa returns to hear Pietro calling her. She notices that Moscatello and his men are absorbed in the their game of cards. She dances in front of the guards to lure them away, but alert Moscatello orders them back to the table. He chases Graziosa in his turn, and it is not long before all the police are standing around the dancer in a circle. She pours them a drink, and Pietro grasps the opportunity to escape. Graziosa laughs at her admirers and disappears.

The mayor enters with his clerk and surprises a bewildered Moscatello, who orders one of his men to fetch the prisoner. The police discover that he has escaped, however, and they explain that a charming dancer distracted them from their work. The exasperated mayor orders them to recapture the fugitives or face a firing squad. The square now fills with people eager to see the bullfight ordered by the governor, Don Manuel, and dancing in the streets follows the corrida. The mayor is wondering whether his mysterious dancer is among the celebrants, when Graziosa appears in her wedding dress. She and Pietro are about to be married, but the presence of the mayor makes her uneasy. She is about to slip away through the crowd when he asks her to dance. She dances clumsily to avoid suspicion, and he leaves. Pietro appears, and she forgets herself and dances with her usual lightness and skill. The mayor observes her and orders her arrest. She begs for clemency, but the mayor remains deaf to her pleas. She turns to Don Manuel, who remembers the favor she did for him, and he intervenes in her behalf. The populace celebrates the governor's kindness and the loving couple's future happiness.

Mme Amalia Ferraris* scored a triumph in the title-role of this ballet that was supposed to serve as a companion piece for Richard Wagner's* Tannhäuser.* The work appealed to audiences because it was gay, lively, and amusing, and it had a dash of Spanish and Italian theatre. The male parts were filled by Alfred Chapuy* (Pietro), Jean Coralli* (Don Manuel), Estienne (Don Rodrigo), Dauty (the mayor), and Francisque Berthier* (Moscatello).

BIBLIOGRAPHY: *AEM VIII, 9-10; Aidmo Aldini, "Théâtre Imperial de l'Opéra:* _Graziosa_*,"* _FM_ *25 (31 March 1861) 97-98; CB 365-69; Chouquet 419; EDS VIII, 44-45; Léon Escudier, "*_Graziosa_*,"* _AM_ *1 (28 March 1861), 132; Ivor Guest,* _The Ballet of the Second Empire_ *(Middletown, Conn.: Wesleyan University Press, 1974), 166-68, 259; Lajarte II, 231;* _Moniteur universel_ *90 (31 March 1861), 457; Wks IV, 17786.*

Gresse, André (b. 23 March 1868, Lyons; d. 1937, Paris), vocalist, studied at the Conservatoire in Paris and made his theatrical debut in _Don Juan_* at the Opéra-Comique in 1896. He then stepped into his father's shoes as one of the leading baritones at the Opéra, where he made his first appearance as Saint-Bris in _Les Huguenots_* on 7 January 1901. His association with the Opéra lasted for 25 years, and he performed in nearly 60 roles at the Garnier Palace* during this time.

In his first year at the Garnier opera house, Gresse sang Méphisto in _Faust_,* the kings in _Aïda_* and in _Lohengrin_,* the Landgrave in _Tannhaüser_,* Gessler in _Guillaume Tell_,* Capulet in _Roméo et Juliette_,* and Oberthal in _Le Prophète_.* He was almost as active and versatile in the second year of his tenure at the Opéra, when he represented the Brahmine in _L'Africaine_,* Wotan in _Siegfried_,* the bishop in _Orsola_,* Ramphis in _Aïda_,* and Leporello in _Don Juan_.* After filling these 12 parts in two years, Gresse did only the high priest of _Sigurd_* in 1903 and Hagen in this same work along with Don Diègue of _Le Cid_* in 1905.

The decade before World War I saw him posted as Gaspard in _Le Freischütz_* in 1906, and then as Sparafucile in _Rigoletto_,* Pluton in _Hippolyte et Aricie_, the ghost in _Hamlet_,* and Frère Laurent in _Roméo et Juliette_* in 1908 (see eighteenth-century volume for _Hippolyte et Aricie_). In 1909, he sang Hagen in _Le Crépuscule des dieux_,* Marco in _Monna Vanna_,* the aged Hebrew in _Samson et Dalila_,* and Hounding in _La Walkyrie_.* The last roles that he added to his Garnier repertory before the outbreak of hostilities included Méphisto in _La Damnation de Faust_* in 1910 and Sancho in _Don Quichotte_* in 1911.

Gresse interpreted nine additional characters during the war: the king in Hamlet* and the duke of Alba in Patrie!* during 1915; Alphonse in La Favorite,* Oreste in Niccolò Piccinni's Iphigénie en Tauride, and Strakoklès in Briséis* in 1916; Hephristos in Prométhée, the legate in Henry VIII,* and L. Cornelius in Roma* in 1917; and Jupiter in Castor et Pollux in 1918 (see eighteenth-century volume for Piccinni, Iphigénie en Tauride, and Castor et Pollux).

After 11 November 1918, the baritone was cast as Ermite in La Légende de Saint Christophe in 1920, and, in 1922, as Varlaam in Boris Godounov.* The following year, he was billed as Fernand in Le Trouvère,* and he did Phanuel in Hérodiade as well as the emperor Phorcas in Esclarmonde in 1924 (see twentieth-century volume for La Légende de Saint Christophe, Hérodiade, and Esclarmonde). His father had created the role of Pogner in Les Maîtres Chanteurs de Nuremberg* on 10 November 1897 at the Garnier, but André did not appear in this part at the same theatre until 1926. It was his last role at the Opéra.

The younger Gresse created a dozen parts in works that had either their world, Paris, or Garnier premieres during his 25 years at the theatre:

Role	Opera	Premiere
Osmin	L'Enlèvenment au sérail	1 December 1903
Roi Marke	Tristan et Isolde	11 December 1904
Le Révérend	Bacchus	2 May 1909
Fasolt	L'Or du Rhin	14 November 1909
L'Evêque	Le Miracle	30 December 1910
Titurel	Parsifal	4 January 1914
Arrigo di Leca	Scémo	6 May 1914
Barbacala	Mlle de Nantes	9 December 1915
A male voice	Une Fête chez la Pouplinière	25 May 1916
Le Grand Père	Le Retour	6 June 1919

Hérode	Salomé (Mariotte)	2 July 1919
Térence	Néron	27 January 1921
Duc de Nayme	La Fille de Roland	27 October 1922

M. Gresse also found time to sing at the Opéra-Comique and to make a limited number of guest appearances at other theatres. When he retired from the stage, he accepted a professorship at the Conservatoire in Paris. At the Opéra-Comique, where he was especially active after his debut as the Commandeur in Don Juan on 17 November 1896, he created only one part: "Le President du Tribunal" of Le Juif Polonais on 11 April 1900. Yet he was billed for 14 other roles at the theatre including Fernando in Fidélio, Gaveston in La Dame Blanche, the count in Manon, Ramon in Mireille, and Colline in La vie de Bohème.
BIBLIOGRAPHY: ICM 701; KRJ 170; SW 26, 28, 44, 51-52, 56, 63, 67, 69, 74, 76, 79, 81, 86, 95, 102, 106, 109-10, 112, 114-16, 123, 134, 136, 140, 150-51, 162, 164, 169-71, 178, 181-82, 189, 194, 197, 199, 202-3, 207, 215, 217, 225, 278, 295, 374-75; WOC II, 100-101, 301-2.

Gresse, Léon (b. 22 July 1845, Charolles; d. ?), vocalist, made his theatrical debut at Le Havre and then filled an engagement at Toulouse before coming to the Opéra for the first time to do one of the gravediggers in Hamlet* on 20 October 1875. When his initial contract at the Garnier Palace* expired, he moved over to the Théâtre-Lyrique and thence to Brussels and London before returning to the Opéra for a second engagement on 6 May 1885. At the Garnier, he sang nearly every major part in the current repertory:

Role	**Opera (date)**
Saint-Bris	Les Huguenots (1875)
Gessler	Guillaume Tell (1876)
Marcel	Les Huguenots (1885)
Walther	Guillaume Tell (1885)
Balthazar	La Favorite (1885)

Brogni	La Juive (1885)
Sparafucile	Rigoletto (1886)
Bertram	Robert le Diable (1886)
Don Pédro	L'Africaine (1886)
Don Diègue	Le Cid (1886)
Ramfis	Aïda (1887)
Zaccharie	Le Prophète (1887)
Claudius	Hamlet (1888)
The old Hebrew	Samson (1893)
Frère Laurent	Roméo (1894)

Also, he created another five roles: Hagen in Sigurd* on 12 June 1885; Hounding in La Walkyrie* on 12 May 1893; Ludovic in Othello* on 10 October 1894; Père Saval of La Montagne noire* on 8 February 1895; and Pogner in Les Maîtres Chanteurs de Nuremberg* on 10 November 1897.

BIBLIOGRAPHY: Martin 178; SW 25-28, 89, 105-6, 108-9, 115-17, 129-30, 139, 151, 165, 177-78, 181-82, 184-85, 189-91, 196-97, 202-3, 224-25.

Gretna-Green was a pantomimic ballet in a single act with music by Ernest Guiraud,* a libretto by Charles Nuitter,* and choreography by Louis Mérante.* It had its world premiere at the Théâtre National de l'Opéra on 5 March 1873, but it did not arouse much enthusiasm among spectators, and it was dropped rom the repertory after its tenth performance.

The ballet is set in Gretna-Green, a Scottish village where eloping couples seeking hasty marriages may wed without parental consent. The curtain rises on the ballet to disclose a blacksmith's shop and Tom's Union Hotel. Tom and his servant Mary emerge from the hotel to purchase flowers, fish, and vegetables, and Mary hears young Williams returning from the hunt. She teases him about his interest in Pretty, daughter of the blacksmith Toby. Williams tarries to speak with Pretty and to offer her a dead lark for her kitchen, but she is unable to support the sight of the poor creature, although she is quick to accept some pheasant feathers. Her father appears at this moment and Williams leaves, while Pretty pretends to be weaving a garland of flowers.

Williams returns to give Toby a pheasant, and the blacksmith's helper Bob informs his boss that a couple wishes him to marry them. The young pair approach; the groom Jackson explains that he is rich, but Jenny's parents have forbidden her to marry him. Toby agrees to officiate at their wedding, of course, and he calls upon Bob and Williams to serve as witnesses. Toby prepares for the ceremony by standing behind his anvil with his hammer in his hand. According to the custom of Gretna-Green, Jenny must initiate the rite by announcing her desire to become Jackson's wife. She complies with this requirement, and the groom kisses her. Tony smites the anvil and declares them married.

This marriage prompts Pretty and Williams to entertain thoughts of becoming man and wife, and he kisses her as a sign of his affection at the moment of her father's return to his shop. Frightened, Williams asks Toby for his daughter's hand, but the blacksmith reminds him that he is too poor to think of taking a wife. Toby orders Pretty into the house. Williams leaves only to return for his gun. Toby is so angry to see him that he has to drink a large glass of beer to calm his nerves.

A stage arrives at the Union Hotel, and a footman approaches Toby in the hope of finding the blacksmith. Toby reveals his identity, and the servant explains that he wishes him to perform a marriage. Angelica and Sir Edward descend from the coach, and Toby walks toward them. Angelica is outraged that Toby should dare to speak to her without being presented to her. Sir Edward complies with her demand for a formal introduction, and Toby then explains that the bride must be the first to request the marriage. Angelica is indignant that she should be asked to initiate the marriage, and Sir Edward tries in vain to pacify her. Toby refuses to violate the rules governing marriages in Greta-Green, however, and Angelica grows more stubborn by the minute. Suddenly, a hunting horn is heard, and Sir Edward's servant reveals to his master that his father is approaching. Mary and Tom come to the couple's rescue and hide them.

Williams rides in with the duke, who accepts a bouquet from Pretty. One of the duke's servants recognizes Sir Edward's footman, but the two domestics do not reveal that they know each other. The duke enters the inn, and the dancing begins. Beer is opened by the barrel. Sir Edward and Angelica decide to cancel their wedding, and they agree to leave the village. Sir Edward's coachman has gotten drunk, but Pretty and Williams come to the rescue of Angelica and Sir Edward by hiding them. Toby consumes more than his share of beer and decides to return home. He comes upon a company of his daughter's friends, however, and he tries to kiss one of them. They agree that he can kiss whomever he catches in a game of blindman's buff. He grabs old Mary by mistake, and she slaps him. He returns to the party for another drink and falls asleep.

Sir Edward and Williams come back to the inn in each other's clothes. Pretty appears in Angelica's dress, and the latter enters in a peasant's costume. Toby awakens. He is groggy, and he does not realize that Pretty and Williams are dressed as Angelica and Sir Edward. He calls for witnesses when his daughter and her sweetheart express their readiness to marry each other. Pretty assumes Angelica's haughty airs to assure the deception. She expresses her desire to wed the groom, who kisses her without delay, and Toby strikes the hymenal anvil before he is aware of what he is doing. The duke is furious because he believes that his son has married Angelica, but Toby insists that such marriages are a local custom. The blacksmith insists that nothing can be done to annul the union of the couple whom he has joined in matrimony, and he begins to laugh until he recognizes Williams. When he understands at last that the bride is his own daughter, he flies into a rage. The unsympathetic bystanders remind him that such marriages are a local custom. The ballet closes with the national music and dances of Scotland.

The score of <u>Gretna-Green</u> was destroyed in the fire of 1873 at the Le Peletier* opera house, but it does not seem to have aroused great enthusiasm among spectators. As for the cast, the most interesting feature of this aspect of the ballet was the decision to cast Mlle Eugénie

Fiocre* in the part of Williams, because the tendency to assign this ballerina to travesty roles between 1863 and 1873 marked the total triumph of the female dancer over her male counterparts. Curiously enough, a commentary on the apogee of the danseuse at this time is found in the fact that Degas never thought it necessary to depict a male dancer in his works inspired by the theatre. The other female performers to share in the premiere of Gretna-Green were Mlles Beaugrand (Pretty), Bourgoing (Angelica), Pallier (Jenny), and Mme Aline (Mary). The male parts were created by Francisque Berthier* (Toby), Rémond (Sir Edwards), Pluque (the duke), and Cornet (Tom), Gonforino (Bob). F. Mérante, Ponçot, Monfallet, and Guillemot danced the servants. A second travesty role was executed by Mlle Sanlaville (Jackson). The sets for the work were provided by Rubé and Chaperon.

BIBLIOGRAPHY: CB 483; Guy de Charnacé, Musique et musiciens (Paris: Lethielleux, 1874) I, 251-55; M. Léon Escudier, "Théâtre National de l'Opéra: Gretna-Green, première représentation," AM 12 (8 May 1873), 148; Ivor Guest, "Gretna-Green," Ballet 12 (January 1952), 29-31; Adolphe Jullien, Musiciens d'aujourd'hui, 2me série (Paris: Librairie de l'art, 1894), 290-95; Lajarte II, 246; M.L.E., "Théâtre national de l'Opéra, Gretna-Green, première représentation," AM 12 (8 May 1893), 148; H. Moréno, "Première Représentation de Gretna-Green à l'Opéra," Le Ménestrel 39 (11 May 1873), 188.

Grieg, Edvard (b. 15 June 1843, Bergen; d. 4 September 1907, Bergen), composer, received his first piano instruction from his mother before he left his native city to study under Moscheles, Reinecke, and Wenzel at Leipzig. He went to Copenhagen in 1863 and returned to Norway finally in 1866 to found a Norwegian Academy of Music.

Grieg now joined forces with Ibsen and Björnson to enrich and to spread the culture of his homeland, and he displayed an active interest in the stage by doing the music for Björnstjerne Björnson's Jorsalfar and Henrik Ibsen's Peer Gynt.

Although the composer was never prompted to write an opera, his music was heard at the Opéra on three occasions. He was one of five musicians whose works Serge Diaghilev* selected for the score of his Les Orientales mounted at the Opéra

on 25 June 1910. Queen Marie of Rumania took extracts from his work for Le Lys de la vie that Loïe Fuller presented at the Garnier Palace* on 1 July 1920. Grieg's Lumières was one of seven pieces by six musicians that Loïe Fuller chose in making up the score for her Fluorescences of 9 February 1938 (see twentieth-century volume for Le Lys de la vie and Fluorescences). Couriously enough, therefore, Grieg contributed only to works having scores derived from the music of four or more compsoers.
BIBLIOGRAPHY: AEM V, 896-908; BBD 646-47; EDS V, 1742-3; ELM II, 355-58; Thompson 704-11.

Griseldis ou les cinq sens was a pantomime-ballet in three acts and five tableaux with music by Adolphe Adam,* a scenario by Philippe Dumanoir,* and choreography by Joseph Mazilier.* It had its premiere only a few days before the revolution of February 1848, and the ensuing violence within Paris diminished whatever success this composition might have had in more normal times. It enjoyed its first presentation on 16 February 1848, and the theatre had to close between 22 and 29 February. Subsequently, Griseldis had to be dropped from the repertory after its 14th production on 28 April 1848.

The ballet opens in the royal residence in Prague, where Elfrid is paying no attention to dancers trying to entertain him. He is about to go hunting, when the ambassador from Moldavia enters to propose the marriage of Elfrid and the daughter of his king. Elfrid shows no emotion and promises to do his father's bidding. The marriage proposal is accepted, therefore, and Elfrid and his squire Jacobus prepare to travel to Moldavia for the wedding (I, 1-3). Griseldis enters alone and replaces the crown that Elfrid has just received with a crown of flowers and her picture; she vows that her humble birth will not keep her beloved prince from her. She hides at the sound of approaching footsteps, but it is Elfrid. He finds the picture and the crown on the cushion, and he recognizes the girl of his dreams. He feels his heart beating, and he realizes for the first time the meaning of sensitivity (I, 4-6). He refuses to travel to Moldavia, and his father is angry to learn that he has fallen in love with a peasant when his son shows him the portrait of Griseldis. His father's anger turns to tears, however, and Elfrid decides that he must be obedient. He leaves Bohemia (I, 7).

The tableau devoted to the sense of hearing begins at dawn in front of a village inn, where Elfrid and Jacobus are staying. Peasants on their way to the fields obey Jacobus' suggestion to dance in the street to honor their illustrious guest. Griseldis appears with her goats. The villagers do not know her, but they invite her to dance, to sing, and to play her mandolin. After the dance she hides in the ruins of a gothic chapel until Elfrid appears. He looks at her picture and is wondering where she is, when he hears her playing and singing. He is moved for the second time in his life, and he rushes to the ruins because he senses a bond between the portrait he sees and the music he hears (II, 1-5). Jacobus persuades him to depart from the village (II, 6-7).

The opening of the second act and the third tableau devoted to the sense of touch coincide and are set in Belgrade. Governor Hassan welcomes Elfrid after dismissing the dancers of his harem. Elfrid elects to spend the night in the gardens of the palace; he falls asleep, and Griseldis kisses his forehead because she discovers that he is carrying her picture. Awakened, Elfrid takes her in his arms, caresses her, and tries to find out whether or not she is Griseldis, but she eludes him (II, 1-3, bis). Elfrid tells Jocobus what has happened, and his squire thinks that he is mad. Griseldis appears again only to escape once more because Elfrid is surrounded by the dancers of the harem (II, 4-6, bis).

The fourth tableau illustrating the senses of smell and taste is included in the third act and transpires in a forest, where Griseldis appears with a hunting party. She picks a bouquet of flowers and rides off before Elfrid and Jacobus arrive. The latter are about to dine, when they are interrupted by a festival of gardeners laden with flowers. Each of the dancers invites him to enjoy the perfume of her bouquet but Griseldis enters and throws her bouquet at his feet. He prefers her modest gift, and the dancers leave. Elfrid tries to identify the woman who continues to appear before him (III, 1-5). She is off to one side at this very moment and hypnotizes him. She pours a goblet of wine, drinks a sip, and gives the remainder to Elfrid. When he opens his eyes, he swallows the wine with special pleasure because it has come from his mysterious love (III, 6-7).

The fifth tableau presents Elfrid about to meet his future queen but consumed with regret because the stranger of his dreams is still beyond his reach. He hears her singing, however, and she appears once again. She is dressed as a goatherd now, and she identifies herself as the lady of the portrait, the bouquet, the kiss, and the wine. She reproaches him for marrying a stranger because it was she who awakened his senses and showed him the delights of life. He protests that he wishes to marry her, and he puts his ring on her finger, but she runs away. Jacobus prevents his master from following her, but Elfrid is resolved not to marry the princess. He is about to tell his veiled fiancee that he cannot become her husband, when he recognizes her as Griseldis as soon as she begins to sing (III, 1-5, bis).

Lucien Petipa* was cast in the part of Elfrid with Mazilier as his father and Francisque Berthier* as his squire. Mlle Caronne Grisi* scored another triumph in the title-role. Lenfant and Monnet were selected to represent the ambassador and Hassan, governor of Belgrade.

BIBLIOGRAPHY: AEM I, 76-77; Chouquet 409; EDS I, 112-14; Ivor Guest, The Ballet of the Second Empire (Middletown, Conn.: Wesleyan University Press, 1974), 33-37, 102; Lajarte II, 187; Arthur Pougin, Adolphe Adam: sa vie, sa carrière, ses mémoires artistiques (Geneva: Minkoff reprint, 1973), 192-93, 274; Wks III, 9758.

Griselidis was billed originally as a "lyric story" in three acts and a prologue with a score by Jules Massenet* and a libretto by Armand Silvestre and Eugène Morand. It had its world premiere at the Opéra-Comique on 20 November 1901 with Mme Lucienne Bréval* in the title-role and MM. Fugère and Dufranne in the parts of the devil and the marquis de Saluces. It was heard for the first time at the Garnier Palace* on 29 November 1922 in a production by Pierre Chéreau. The dance of the spirits in the second act was directed by Raymond Legueult and Maurice Brianchon.

The prologue is set in a forest in Provence, where Alain is filled with joy because he is about to meet beautiful Grisélidis. Alaine assures Gondebaud that Grisélidis is indeed so beautiful that the marquis would marry her without hesitation (prol., sc. 1-2). The marquis reveals that he has already seen her, and, when Grisélidis arrives on the scene, he proposes marriage to her. She accepts his offer (prol., sc. 3).

The first act opens in Grisélidis' apartments in the Château de Saluces, where the furnishings include an oratory, a triptych, and a statue depicting St. Agnes holding a lamb and crushing the devil under her heel. Grisélidis' lady-in-waiting Bertrade is singing a spinning song when Gondebaud enters to reveal that the marquis is about to depart for the Holy Land (I, 1-2). The marquis describes his reluctance to leave his wife and son behind him, and the prior warns him that a husband is looking for trouble when he leaves a beautiful wife unguarded. The marquis belittles this warning, but the prior warns him again that he is underestimating the devil. Suddenly, the sculptured devil in the oratory becomes animate (I, 3) and explains to the marquis that he and his wife spend their nights promoting adultery on earth. He offers to lay a wager that the marquis' beautiful wife will not remain faithful to her husband. The marquis accepts, and he pledges his wedding ring as a guarantee that he will honor the terms of this infernal bet (I, 4). Alone, the marquis ponders the sacrifices he will make by leaving home, and he bids his wife farewell in a tender love scene in which the couple renew their vows of fidelity (I, 5-6).

The second act is set on the terrace of the marquis' château by the edge of the sea. Here, the devil is describing how happy his life has been since he has been away from his wife, when she appears. Fiamina accuses him of philandering, but he assures her that he has been busy promoting adultery in Provence. When Fiamina learns that her husband's latest target is a marchioness, she volunteers to help him (II, 1-2). Grisélidis and her son Loys pray for the safe return of the marquis, and the devil and his wife enter disguised as a merchant and a slave from the East. The devil announces that the marquis bought Fiamina from him and ordered him to deliver her to his château in Provence. Here, she is to be châtelaine until the marquis returns from the Holy Land to marry her. The devil produces the marquis' ring to verify his story, and gulled Grisélidis falls victim to his lies. She surrenders her husband to the Oriental slave, and the devil plans his next step. He will arrange for Grisélidis to succumb to the poet Alain (II, 3-5). He summons up his spirit servants to help him execute his plan (II, 6). Alain and Grisélidis meet; they recognize each other. Their mutual unhappiness draws them together, and they recall their love for each other. Loys' presence returns Grisélidis to her senses, but the devil maintains control of her by kidnapping her son (II, 7-8).

Grisélidis is praying for the return of her son when she notices that the image of St. Agnes has disappeared. The devil presents himself to her again. He is dressed as an Oriental, and he tells the desperate mother that her son has been kidnapped by pirates whose handsome leader has fallen in love with her. He will return Loys, if she will kiss him. Reluctant Grisélidis agrees to meet the pirate's demands, but she arms herself with a dagger dipped in holy water. She leaves to rescue her son just before the return of her husband (III, 1-3). The devil informs the marquis that his wife has not remained faithful to him, and he gives the outraged crusader a knife with which to slay her (III, 4). The marquis discards this weapon, and Grisélidis comes back to the château. She asks the marquis whether she is still his wife, and he asks her whethere she has remained faithful during his absence. Eventually they swear their fidelity to each other, and they fall into each other's arms when they realize that they have been victims of the devil. The devil returns to destroy their happiness by reminding them that their son is still missing, and the furious marquis swears to rescue his son. Grisélidis prays for his success, and the cross in the oratory bursts into flame. St. Agnes reappears with Loys, and the family is reunited. The exhausted devil entertains thoughts of retirement (III, 5-8).

This drama of good and evil did not appeal to spectators, and Grisélidis was withdrawn from the repertory after its eighth performance on 11 March 1923. Yet it was returned to the stage of the Opéra-Comique on 30 October 1942, and it went on to enjoy 73 presentations at this theatre. When it was revived at the Comique, Mme Ellen Dosia sang the female lead opposite José Beckmans (the devil) and Louis Musy (the marquis). The leading roles had been filled for the first time at the

Garnier Palace by Marthe Davelli (Grisélidis), Jeanne Laval (Fiamina), Jean Aquistapace (the devil), and Robert Cousinou* (the marquis). Mme Davelli was making her debut at the Opéra on this occasion, when the Dance of the Spirits was executed by Mlle Branca, Mlle Alice Bourgat, and the corps de ballet.

Grisélidis was produced at the Manhattan Opera House on 19 January 1910.

BIBLIOGRAPHY: *Charles Bouvet, Massenet (Paris: Henri Laurens, 1929), 92-94; René Brancour, Massenet (Paris: Félix Alcan, 1922), 105-8; José Bruyr, Massenet, musicien de la belle époque (Lyon: eise, 1964), 97-98; Henry T. Finck, Massenet and His Operas (New York: John Lane Co., 1910), 120-27; James Harding, Massenet (London: J. M. Dent & Sons, 1970), 143-47; Demar Irvine, Massenet: a Chronicle of His Life and times (Seattle: Demar Irvine, 1974), 268-82; Albertine Morin-Labrecque, Jules Massenet et ses opéras (Montréal: éditions de l'étoile, 1914), 18-21; Arthur Pougin, Massenet (Paris: Fischbacher, 1914), 118-20; Louis Schneider, Massenet: l'homme, le musicien (Paris: L. Castaret, 1908), 234-44; SSBO 330; SW 104; Thompson 713.*

Grisi, Caronne Adèle Josephine Marie, DITE Carlotta (b. 28 June 1819, Visinada; d. 22 May 1899, Geneva), ballerina, started her formal study of ballet at age seven, and her progress was so evident that she was admitted to the children's corps de ballet at La Scala three years later. Her parents allowed her to go on a tour of Italy at age 14, when she met Jules Perrot* in Naples. A skilled dancer and choreographer, he became her teacher and then her lover. The couple toured London, Vienna, Munich, and Milan so that Carlotta might gain experience and perfect her art. In Paris, they performed in Le Zingaro at the Renaissance Theatre in early 1840. They were billed here as man and wife, and, the following year, Carlotta obtained a contract with the Opéra, where it was agreed that her husband was to be her choreographer during her engagement.

The story of la Grisi's stay at the Opéra is curious, because she appeared on the stage for only three or four months before becoming one of the best-known ballerinas in Europe. In February 1841, she executed a pas de deux with Lucien Petipa* in Domenico Gaetano Donizetti's* La

Favorite,* and she appeared next in the ballets of several operas. Then, on 28 June 1841, she created the title-role in Giselle,* one of the two greatest ballets of the century. Jean Coralli* had done the choreography for this work in two acts, and Jules Perrot's name did not even appear on the program. In fact, Carlotta was billed as Mlle Grisi without any reference to her coach, mentor, and husband.

After the astounding success of Giselle, an attempt was made immediately to provide Mlle Grisi with a second hit, and management accepted La Jolie Fille de Gand* for her. The choreography had been created by Albert Decombe, known in the theatre simply as Albert (see eighteenth-century volume for Decombe). Cast as Béatrix in this ballet of three acts, Carlotta enjoyed a maximum effort on the part of management now willing to invest twice the amount of money spent on Giselle. It was successful to a degree, nearly 70 billings by 1848, but it failed to overwhelm audiences as Giselle had done.

The search for another profitable scenario for la Grisi continued throughout the months of 1842 that she spent as a soloist in England with faithful Perrot and Théophile Gautier.* The poet was now suffering from unrequited love for the ballerina, and, just before Christmas, it was revealed that he had completed a "ballet fantastique" for his beloved star. It was entitled La Péri,* and Frédéric Burgmuller* had done the score for it. It had its premiere on 17 July 1843 and offered the same theme as La Sylphide*: man in search of the ideal of his dreams. Grisi danced in the title-role, and her performance was hailed as her finest accomplishment. The Opéra renewed her contract for three years and quadrupled her salary. Two outstanding works with choreography by Joseph Mazilier* were selected for her new term: Le Diable à quatre* of 1845 scored by Adolphe Adam,* in which she danced Mazourka; Paquita* of 1846 with music by Ernest Deldevez,* an in which she filled the title-role with such effectiveness that critics described her performance as brilliant and inimitable.

La Grisi was now approaching the end of her Paris career, although she had two other major parts at the Opéra between 1847 and the time of her departure from France. She created the heroine of Griséldis,* which had its premiere on

16 February 1848, although the first run of this ingenious ballet in three acts was cut short by the revolution that removed Louis-Philippe from power. Then, on 8 October 1849, she appeared in the central role in La Filleule des fées,* for which Perrot had done the choreography.

The ballerina left France for a stay of three years in Russia after these successes, and Perrot accompanied her as her partner and her ballet-master as well as her husband. After a cautious start on account of her status as a visitor, la Grisi was soon the dominant and most popular figure on the dancing scene in St. Petersburg. She appeared on more than a hundred programs, and it was apparent to all that she was still in full possession of her physical strength and artistic ability. She could have returned to Paris or have accepted a London engagement after her sojourn in Russia, but she went instead to Poland in 1854.

It was at this point in her life that she interrupted her career to have her child by Prince Radziwill. After the birth of her daughter, she accepted the advice of Théophile Gautier* and retired of her own accord before her years could diminish her capacity to perform. She was 34 when she put away the boxed slippers that she had been the first to wear upon the stage.

BIBLIOGRAPHY: ACPM 432; Susan Au, "Prints of a Parisian Péri," Dance Perspectives 61 (Spring 1975), 30-45; BCS 391; Cyril W. Beaumont, The Ballet Called "Giselle" (New York: Dance Horizons, 1969), 22-23, 70-74; Charles de Boigne, Petits Mémoires de l'Opéra (Paris: Librairie Nouvelle, 1857), 248-52, 340-41; CB, 129-43, 149-59, 177-90, 233-35, 241-47, 250-54, 280-86, 360; CODB 237; Margaret Crosland, Ballet Carnaval (New York: Arco, 1955), 31; DDD 113; EZF 207-9; EDB 167; Ivor Guest, The Ballet of the Second Empire (Middletown, Conn.: Wesleyan University Press, 1974), 33-37, 39, 46-50; idem, Fanny Elssler (Middletown, Conn.: Wesleyan University Press, 1970), 211-12; idem, The Romantic Ballet in Paris (London: Sir Isaac Pitman and Sons Ltd., 1966), 186-225; Lajarte II, 168, 171, 173, 179, 181-82, 187; André Levinson, Ballet Romantique (Paris: Editions du Trianon, 1929), 43-48; Serge Lifar, Les Trois Grâces du xxe siècle (Paris: Corrêa, 1957), 58-65; idem, Carlotta Grisi, trans. Doris Langley Moore (London: Lehmann, 1947); Parmenia Migel, The Ballerinas from the Court of Louis XIV to Pavlova (New York: Macmillan, 1972), 139-40, 194-209; Doris Langley Moore, "Carlotta Grisi," Ballet 2 (December 1946), 57-62; Lillian Moore, Artists of the Dance (New York: Thomas Y. Crowell Co., 1938), 127-35; idem, "The Origin of Adagio in Ballet: Grisi's Leap in La Péri," The Dancing Times, new series 307 (April 1936), 16-17; Mark E. Perugini, A Pageant of the Dance and Ballet (London: Jarrolds, 1946), 202-5; Henry Pleasants, Great Singers (New York: Simon and Schuster, 1966), 178-80; RBP 186-225; Walter Sorell, The Dance Through the Ages (New York: Grosset and Dunlap, 1967), 139-41; Susan Reimer Sticklor, "Angel with a Past," Dance Perspectives 61 (Spring 1975), 18-29; Walter Terry, Star Performance (New York: Doubleday, 1954), 75-79; XXJ 36-43.

Le Guerillero was billed as an opera in two acts with a score by Ambroise Thomas* and a libretto by Théodore Anne.* It had its world premiere at the Royal Academy of Music on 22 June 1842 with sets by Séchan, Despléchin, and Diéterle.

The action of the opera transpires in Portugal, near Oporto during 1640 when this country broke with Spain to place Duke Juan de Bragance on the throne with the title of Don Juan IV. The curtain rises to disclose a cluster of ruins near a forest. Ferdinand's soldiers enter with a discouraged air because their casualties have been so high. They complain of Don Juan's continuing absence from the battlefield, but Pédro defends the king, although the men assert that he has forgotten them for a woman (I, 1). Thérésa and Francisco are led in as prisoners, and Ferdinand reminds the outraged girl that she is now in his power. She berates him as a tyrant, and Francisco warns him that Thérésa's brother is Pédro, a man who does not ignore insults and threats, but Ferdinand orders his men to jail the prisoners (I, 2). Pédro informs Ferdinand that he is losing the confidence of his followers, and the leader of the group swears to make Thérésa his wife. Pédro does not appear upset, and Ferdinand goes on to reveal that his announcement of Don Juan's imminent arrival was a ruse to control his men. He falls asleep because it is late (I, 3-4), and a stranger enters the camp. He declares himself to be an ally, but Pédro challenges him, although Ferdinand agrees to meet privately with the intruder (I, 5). A chorus of soldiers threatens to mutiny on account of Ferdinand's orders to imprison Thérésa and Francisco; they ask Pédro to become their leader, but he urges his supporters to remain loyal to Ferdinand (I, 6). The men ignore his plea and rush at Ferdinand, who regains the upper hand by announcing that the stranger is the king. The insurgents forget their differences and swear to follow Don Juan into battle (I, 7).

The scene shifts to the great hall of a Moorish castle. Francisco has not forgotten that Ferdinand has tried to betray the cause of Don Juan, and Thérésa is hoping to find her brother, Pédro. She reminds her sweetheart that she cannot marry him until she has obtained vengeance for the wrongs done to her family (II, 1-2). Vicenzio announces that Ferdinand is advancing toward the castle with the king, who declares that Portugal has been liberated (II, 3). Thérésa approaches the king to ask for justice, and she is overwhelmed with surprise to see that he is not Don Juan. She persists in her request, however, and she accuses Ferdinand of having threatened her life and her honor. The king decides to give her satisfaction by forcing Ferdinand to marry her. Ferdinand rejoices over this unexpected decision, and Francisco protests. The king exits with Thérésa and Ferdinand (II, 4-5), and the chapel bell rings offstage. Francisco ponders royal justice and despairs (II, 6). The king returns, and Francisco accuses him of perpetuating an injustice. Shots ring out, and the king assures Francisco that he can wed the widow of a soldier, and he presents Thérésa to him. He then reveals himself to be Pédro disguised as Don Juan. He has resorted to this deception to take vengeance for Ferdinand's despicable plan to deceive the people by presenting his lieutenant, Pédro, as Don Juan, a ruse that would have succeeded on account of his resemblance to the king.

The work was reasonably successful. It enjoyed a run of 41 performances between the date of its premiere, 22 June 1842, and 30 July 1845. The score had two passages that evoked applause. The first of these moments was the disguised king's aria closing the first act, "De nos jours glorieux" (I, 7), and the other admired interval was the chorus, "Pour nous, plus de souffrance" (II, 2). The part of Thérésa was sung initially by Mme Nathan-Treilhet, and the male roles were created by Massol (the unknown king), Bouche (Ferdinand), F. Prevost (Pédro), Octave (the young peasant, Francisco), Molinier (Vicenzio). The officers in the insurgent army were represented by MM. Molinier, Koenig, and Hens.

BIBLIOGRAPHY: Camille Bellaigue, Musical Studies and Silhouettes (New York: Dodd, Mead and Co., 1900), 309-14; Alfred Bruneau, Musiques de Russie et musiciens de France (Paris: Bibliothèque-Charpentier, 1903), 208-15; Chouquet 404; DDOI, 529; Escudier, "Le Guerillero," FM 5 (26 June 1842), 232; Arthur Hervey, Masters of French Music (Boston: Milford House, 1973), 1-35; Lajarte II, 170.

Guerra, Antonio (b. 1806, Naples; d. 1846, Vienna), choreographer, studied ballet at the school attached to the San Carlo Opera in his native city and moved to Vienna, where he made his debut as a choreographer on 16 August 1827 at the Hoftheater with Der erste Schiffer set to music by Adalbert Gyrowetz.* He returned to Italy to perform at La Scala and the San Carlo opera house before traveling to Paris in 1837.

At the Garnier Palace*, he composed the ballet Les Mohicans* with music by Adolphe-Charles Adam* in which Mlle Nathalie Fitz-James distinguished herself on 5 July 1837, but he left Paris before long to travel to London and then to return to Italy and to Austria. He was influenced strongly by the French Romantic ballet, but he contributed relatively little to the French stage, despite his interest in it and his sojourn at the Opéra. He was a skilled and graceful dancer, and he is remembered as a partner of Franziska Elssler* as well as the choreographer of Les Mohicans.

BIBLIOGRAPHY: ACPM, 433; CODB 239; DDD 114; EDS VI, 21-22.

Gueymard, Louis (b. 17 August 1822, Chappanay; d. July 1880, Paris), vocalist, completed his studies at the Conservatoire in 1848 and was engaged as a tenor by the Opéra almost immediately. He remained at the theatre for a score of years, and his voice never lost its strength during this time. He participated in cantatas on 28 October 1852, 12 January 1856, 17 March 1856, and he was a member of the group that presented the victory song Magenta on 6 June 1859. As far as the regular repertory was concerned, he appeared in a number of the revivals of the standard compositions that continued to appeal to audiences, although they were already familiar with their scores and librettos. In this type of work, he sang Arnold in Guillaume Tell* in 1856, Raoul in Les Huguenots* in 1861, and Robert in Robert le Diable* in 1867.

Most of Gueymard's energy was devoted to creating new characters in operas having their premieres between 1848 and 1864. The following list indicates these characters and the 13 works in which they appeared:

Role	**Opera**	**Premiere**
Philippe d'Autriche	Jeanne la Folle	6 November 1848
Jonas	Le Prophète	16 April 1849
Phaon	Sapho	16 April 1851
Rodolphe	Louise Miller	2 February 1853
Rodolphe	Le Maître Chanteur	17 October 1853
Rodolphe	La Nonne sanglante	18 October 1854
Henri	Les Vêpres siciliennes	13 June 1855
Manrique	Le Trouvère	12 January 1857
René	La Magicienne	17 March 1858
Tébald	Roméo et Juliette	7 September 1859
Pierre de Médicis	Pierre de Médicis	9 March 1860
Adoniram	La Reine de Saba	28 February 1862
Roland	Roland à Roncevaux	3 October 1864

M. Louis Gueymard was married to Mme Pauline Gueymard* née Lauters in 1858, but their marriage ended in divorce a decade later.

BIBLIOGRAPHY: Chouquet 410-11, 413-16, 417-18, 420-21; EZF 209; Fétis Suppl I, 430; GE XIX, 540;

ICM 718; Lajarte II, 153, 189-90, 208, 213-15, 217-18, 221-22, 226-28, 233, 239; Lermina 731.

Gueymard, Pauline, née Lauters (b. 1 December 1834, Brussels), vocalist, studied painting until friends of her family noticed the quality of her singing voice and persuaded her to enroll at the Brussels Conservatoire. After distinguishing herself as a student in Belgium, she went to Paris to pursue a career in the musical theatre. She had married a painter named Deligne, and she made her debut at the Théâtre-Lyrique as Mme Deligne-Lauters in the autumn of 1855. Her charm, beauty, and striking mezzo-soprano voice inspired enthusiastic applause for her performances in a series of works that included Gevaert's Le Billet de Marguerite (1854) and Les Lavandières de Santarem (1855). Her success won her a contract at the Opéra, where she met and married the singer Louis Gueymard* in 1858. The marriage ended in a divorce in 1868, but this development had no effect upon her career, and she continued to perform at the Opéra until 1876. After her retirement, she appeared for an interval at the Théâtre-Italien to sing Amnéris in Aïda.*

Her career of a dozen years at the Opéra included two cantatas, Victoire! (1858) and Paix, Charité, Grandeur (1866), and roles that she created almost annually until fire destroyed the opera house in the rue Le Peletier* on 29 October 1873. The eleven works in which these parts are found and the dates of their premieres at the Opéra are:

Role	**Opera**	**Premiere**
Léonore	Le Touvère	1 April 1857
Blanche	Le Magicienne	17 March 1858
Lélia	Herculanum	4 March 1859
Juliette	Roméo et Juliette (Bellini)	7 September 1859
Laura Salviati	Pierre de Médicis	9 March 1860
Balkis	La Reine de Saba	28 February 1862

Gilda	La Mule de Pédro	6 March 1863
Alde	Roland à Roncevaux	3 October 1864
Eboli	Don Carlos	11 March 1867
Gertrude	Hamlet	9 March 1868
Myrrha	La Coupe du roi de Thulé	10 January 1873

Mme Gueymard's repertory also included the title-role of Christoph Willibald Gluck's Alceste, Léonore of La Favorite,* and Fidès of Le Prophète (see eighteenth-century volume for Gluck and Alceste).

BIBLIOGRAPHY: *Chouquet 416-18, 420-23, 425; Ed. Duprez, "Gueymard," FM 19 (30 December 1855) 410-11; EFC 146-47; EZF 209-11; Fétis Suppl. I, 429-30; GE XIX, 540; Lajarte II, 108, 216; SW 32, 90, 108, 178, 216-17; Thurner 253-60; Wks 14953, 18492; XYZ 249-54.*

Guido et Ginevra was an opera in five acts with a score by Jacques Halévy* and a libretto by Eugène Scribe.* Joseph Mazilier* was its choreographer. It had its first presentation at the Opéra on 5 March 1838 and was given on 32 occasions during the year of its premiere. It lost its appeal quickly and was billed at the Opéra on only a dozen dates between 1839 and 1841 and dropped after its performance on 15 October 1841.

Subtitled La Peste de Florence, this somber work opens with the villagers of Arc celebrating their feast day by drinking to the welfare of Florence and the health of Cosme de Médicis but with the less peaceful condottieri and their leader Forte-Braccio picking their pockets and planning a kidnapping. The singer Ricciarda joins the festivities while paying little attention to her escort Manfredi, duke of Mantua, because of her interest in Guido, a young farmer of Arc. She invites the youth to join Manfredi's household because he is a sculptor, but he refuses on account of his desire to locate a certain beautiful woman of the region (I, 1-3). After an intermezzo of dancing, Ginevra appears in the dress of a villager, but she will not divulge her identity to Guido. The condottieri kidnap her, because they have seen her magnificent carriage and richly dressed retinue. They make off with her and stab Guido, but his comrades and her escorts capture Forte-Braccio. Lorenzo forces Ginevra to leave the fair, but he does not wish it known that she is a Medici, and he is afraid that Manfredi, duke of Mantua, will recognize her (I, 4-7).

Ricciarda and Guido meet in the Medici palace, where Ginevra laments her approaching marriage to the duke of Ferrara. Ricciarda is furious, and Guido is desperate to learn of Ginevra's wedding; Manfredi notices Guido's jealousy and directs his assassin, Braccia-Forte to slay him (II, 1-4). Ricciarda discovers this plot and bribes the murderer to kill Ginevra instead of Guido. Cosme de Médicis leaves the nuptial celebration to verify the outbreak of a plague in Florence; Forte-Braccia gives Ginevra a scarf as a wedding present; it poisons her, and her sudden death is attributed to the plague (II, 5-7).

The third act opens with Ginevra's burial in the cathedral of Florence. The sacristan Téobaldo orders Forte-Braccia from the church and persuades grieving Guido to leave the crypt (III, 1-3). Ginevra recovers her senses in her tomb but cannot escape before lapsing back into unconsciousness (III, 4). Forte-Braccio and his men return to the cathedral to steal her diamond necklace; they find her standing before them and throw themselves at her feet. She runs from the church (III, 5). Ginevra interrupts an orgy in Manfredi's palace, and the duke shoots her with an arquebus. Ricciarda is filled with apprehension and tries in vain to flee from Manfredi (IV, 1). Forte-Braccio and his band have stolen expensive items from the empty palaces of Florence and are crossing the main square of the city with their booty, when wounded Ginevra tries to enter her father's home (IV, 2-3). She comes upon startled Guido, who recovers and swears to protect her from Manfredi (IV, 4).

The last act begin in a village of the Apennines, where Guido and Ginevra encounter the latter's father on the highway. Ginevra cannot reveal her identity to Cosme de Médicis because he has sworn to kill Guido before her eyes whenever and wherever he finds him. Cosme is puzzled by her appearance and voice, but he does not recognize her until she throws herself into his arms.

Overjoyed to find his daughter, Cosme recants and approves her marriage to Guido (V, 1-3).

The cast of Guido et Ginevra was an asset to its production with Gilbert Duprez,* Nicolas Levasseur,* and Massol in the parts of Guido, Cosme de Médicis, and Forte-Braccio, respectively. Mme Julie Dorus-Gras* sang Ginevra with Mme Rosine Stoltz* as Ricciarda.

The noteworthy musical passages in Halévy's opera included Guido's romance, "Pendant la fête, une inconnue" (I, 4); the duet by Ricciarda and Forte-Braccio, "Où vas-tu?" (II, 5); Cosme de Médicis' prayer, "Sa main fermera ma paupière" (III, 1); the duet by Ginevra and Guido, "Ombre chérie (IV, 4); and the trio by Cosme de Médicis, Guido, and Ginevra, "Ma fille, à mon amour ravie" (V, 2). It might also be recalled in reference to the score of Guido et Ginevra that the valve trombone and the melophone were introduced into the orchestra for the presentation of this composition. The music of the opera was doubtlessly effective enough to support a run longer than the work enjoyed, but the libretto was marred too seriously by such unacceptable scenes as the resurection of the heroine to be shot again for no compelling reason and the chorus of bandits singing "Vive la peste!" On the other hand, of course, it must be remembered that Guido et Ginevra was written at the height of the vogue for romantic grand opera, which thrived on acts of passion and violence.

BIBLIOGRAPHY: Chouquet, 400; DDO I, 531; Lajarte II, 156-57; Moniteur universel 65 (6 March 1838), 482 and 68 (9 March 1838), 530.

Guillaume Tell is an opera in four acts with a score by Giacchino Rossini* and a libretto by Hippolyte Bis* and Victor Jouy (see eighteenth-century volume for Jouy). It had its world premiere at the opera house in the rue Le Peletier* on 3 August 1829 and became quite popular despite the charge of mediocrity that some critics leveled at the librettists' adaptation of Friedrich Schiller's play to the operatic stage. It was billed at the Park Theatre in New York as early as 16 June 1845 and at the Drury Lane Theatre in London on 28 November 1884, and it was mounted at the Opéra for the 528th time on 2 September 1870, when it was decided to close the theatre on account of the German attack on the

French capital. In all, the artists at the Opéra have offered it to the public on more than 900 dates with revivals in 1916, 1920, 1929, and 1932 in the twentieth century alone.

The action of Guillaume Tell opens in Burgeln in the canton of Uri on the shore of Lake Lucerne, where the protagonist is lamenting the loss of liberty in Switzerland (I, 1). His compatriot Arnold reveals his love for Mathilde, the Hapsburg princess, despite his part in an active conspiracy to restore Swiss independence (I, 2-4). Guillaume asks him why he is so distraught and reminds him of his obligation to liberate his country (I, 5). Melchtal enters at this instant to bless the marriage of Guillaume and Hedwige, but Guillaume runs after Arnold to discover what is troubling his coconspirator (I, 6-7). Leuthold appears covered with the blood of one of the governor's soldiers who has tried to kidnap his daughter, and Guillaume returns after failing to catch up with fleeing Arnold. Leuthold asks him for protection against the soldiers. Guillaume bids farewell to his family; he and Leuthold escape across the lake in a violent storm (I, 8-10). Rodolph marches in at the head of the governor's archers and vows to punish the fugitives, who are now safely beyond his reach. He orders the countryside pillaged, and Arnold's father, Melchtal, is taken prisoner (I, 11).

The scene shifts to the heights of Rutli, where a royal hunting party obeys the governor's order to return to the valley. Alone in the dark forest, Mathilde reveals her love for Arnold before he appears to sing with her the duet in which the two lovers declare their mutual and eternal passion for each other (II, 1-3). The approach of Guillaume and Walter Furst frightens Mathilde away, and Guillaume accuses Arnold of deserting to the enemy because of his feelings for Mathilde. Arnold refuses to reject the Hapsburg cause until he learns that his father Melchtal has been executed by the governor. After renewing his pledge to defend Swiss liberty against Austrian tyranny, Arnold welcomes the soldiers of Unterwald with Guillaume and Walter Fürst. The inhabitants of Schwitz and Uri arrive to lend their strength to the common cause (II, 4-6).

The third act begins in Altdorf at the castle of Governor Gesler, who is demanding public recognition and supervising preparations for the royal festival celebrating the formal installation of Hapsburg rule. The soldiers force the Swiss women to dance with them, and Gesler requires a show of total obeisance. Guillaume and his son Jemmy infiltrate the crowd, and the father defies the governor. He is recognized as Leuthold's rescuer, and his concern for Jemmy betrays the latter as his son. Gesler picks an apple from a tree and orders Guillaume to shoot it from his son's head, if he wishes to avoid death for his son and himself. He agrees, and he steals an extra arrow from his quiver when his arms are returned. He shoots the apple from Jemmy's head, but Gesler notices the second arrow concealed in his tunic. Guillaume angers Gesler by asserting that this second arrow was planned for him, and the governor orders both prisoners executed (III, 1-2). Mathilde countermands this cruel directive and forces Gesler to remand Jemmy into her custody. The governor's senseless behavior arouses the people, but the governor controls them by threatening to stab Guillaume (III, 3).

The fourth act returns to Melchtal's dwelling, which Arnold hesitates to enter because he despairs of having revenge for his father's death on account of Guillaume's capture (IV, 1). A crowd of angry Swiss appear and ask for arms, which Arnold is able to supply. He urges his compatriots to follow him to Altdorf to stay Gesler and to free Guillaume (IV, 2). Hedwige joins them (IV, 3), and Jemmy announces that Mathilde will help the Swiss against Gesler (IV, 4). Leuther reveals that he has seen Guillaume at large (IV, 5), and the tyrannical governor approaches shore with a group of soldiers in his boat. Guillaume emerges from the forest to find his house set on fire by his son to signal the revolt against oppression. Guillaume slays Gesler with a single arrow. Arnold announces the fall of Altdorf, and the curtain falls with the message that victory and liberty have been returned to Switzerland despite the invading tyrants (IV, 6-9).

This libretto may have been deficient in certain respects, but lack of variety was not one of its faults. It provided the composer with opportunities to write music in the martial, sentimental, rustic, patriotic, or festival styles. The choice of Switzerland as a setting was a stroke of genius in itself because it made possible the presentation of Italian cavatinas or Germanic choruses as well as allowing descriptive passages based upon the natural scenery provided by the stormy lakes, peaceful valleys, and wooded countryside against which the action unfolds. And the human drama presented by the librettists is singularly rich in opportunities for a gifted composer like Rossini. The married relationship existing between Hedwige and Guillaume fostered such passages as the wife's fearful "Tu me glaces d'effroi" (I, 3); the love affair between Arnold and Mathilde made possible the latter's "Sombres forêts," sung by moonlight before the Arnold-Mathilde duet, "Oui, vous l'arrachez à mon âme." At the other pole, there is Jemmy's terrified "Pâle et tremblant, se soutenant à peine" after he sees Leuthold covered with his victim's blood in the first act. Also, there are the production scenes at the end of the first and at the start of the third acts. Nor can the famous "apple scene" be forgotten, where the father expresses his anguish at the possibility that his skill with the bow may fail him at this crucial moment.

The three female roles in the oprea were created by Laure Cinthie-Damoreau* (Mathilde), Dabadie* (Jemmy), and Mori (Edwige) with the major male parts filled at its premiere by Adolphe Nourrit* (Arnold), Dabadie* (Guillaume), Nicolas Levasseur* (Walter), and Prévost (Gessler). Other stars to make an exceptional impression in Rossini's 37th and last opera have included Mlles Maria Nau,* Bosman, and Josephine de Reszké* as Mathilde and Gilbert Duprez* as Arnold in the nineteenth century. Jean Noté* and Marcel Journet* as Guillaume as well as Jeanne Laval as Jemmy have been applauded more recently for their performances, but it must be remembered that the continuing popularity of Guillaume Tell has resulted in literally dozens of stars appearing in it over the past 150 years.

BIBLIOGRAPHY: AB I, 46-52; Fedele d'Amico, L'Opera teatrale di Gioacchino Rossini (Rome: Elia, 1974), 261-80; AWL 91-96; Alexis Azevedo, G. Rossini, sa vie et ses oeuvres (Paris: Heugel, 1864), 273-93; Riccardo Bacchelli, Rossini (Turin: Unione tipografico-n-Editrice torinese, 1945), 278-87; Camille Bellaigue, Promenades lyriques (Paris: Nouvelle Librairie Nationale, 1924), 79-96; W. Armine Bevan, Rossini (London: George Bell, 1904), 48-53; Charles de boigne, Petits

Mémoires de l'Opéra (Paris: Librairie Nouvelle, 1857), 261-62, 302-4; Alfredo Bonaccorsi, *Gioacchino Rossini* (Florence: Leo S. Olschki, 1967) includes Guido Pannain "Rossini nel *Guglielmo Tell*," 131-39, also printed in *RMI* 31 (1924), 473-506; Jean-Louis Caussou, *Gioacchino Rossini* (Paris: Seghers, 1967), 53-55, 127-32; Umberto Gozzano, *Rossini: il romanzo dell opera* (Turin: G. B. Paravia, 1953), 171-77; James Harding, *Rossini* (London: Faber and Faber, 1871), 62-67; Franz Heinemann, "Schillers *Wilhelm Tell* in der Musikgeschichte des 19. Jahrhunderts," *Zeitschrift für Bücherfreunde* 11, no. 2 (1907), 321-38; HUT 80-84; JB 103-8; KCOB 434-37; Adolph Kohut, *Rossini* (Leipzig: Philipp Reclam, n.d.), 70-77; Lajarte II, 133-5; Arturo Lancellott; *Gioacchino Rossini* (Rome: Fratelli Palombi, 1942), 91-115; Marcello, "La prima rappresentazione del *Guglielmo Tell* a Parigi," *RMI* 16 (1909), 664-70; *Moniteur universel* 216 (4 August 1829), 1376 and 217 (5 August 1829), 1382; A. Moutoz, *Rossini et son "Guillaume Tell"* (Paris: A. Pilon, 1872); OQE 304-5; Guido Pannain, "Rossini nel *Guglielmo Tell*," *RMI* 31 (1924), 473-506; PBSW 55, 222; Jacques Gabriel Prod'homme, "Rossini and His Works in France," *MQ* 17 (1931), 110-37; Giuseppe Radiciotti, *Gioacchino Rossini: vita documentata, opere ed influenza su l'arte* (Tivol: Artigrafiche Majella di Aldo Chicca, 1928) II, 98-165; Luigi Rognoni, *Gioacchino Rossini* (Turin: Edizioni Radiotelevisione italiana, 1968), 131-32, 191-92, 217-35; Gino Roncaglio, *Rossini l'Olimpico* (Milano: Fratelli Bocca, 1953), 465-97; SSBO 105, 157, 159-61; SW, 105-6; Francis Toye, *Rossini: a Study in Tragi-Comedy* (New York: Norton, 1963) 136-51, 169-71; Herbert Weinstock, *Rossini: a Biography* (London: Oxford University Press, 1968), 160-69; Roberto Zanetti, *Gioacchino Rossini* (Milan: G. Ricord;, 1971), 62-65.

Guiraud, Ernest (b. 23 June 1837, New Orleans; d. 6 May 1892, Paris), composer, was given his musical training by his father, who had won the Prix de Rome competition in Paris before leaving France for the New World. When he was 12, his father took him back to Paris to give him an idea of his patrimony and to obtain a collection of librettos to use in his son's exercises in dramatic composition. *Le Roi David* was among these books, and the young man is said to have set Auguste Mermet's* poem and to have had his score performed by the French opera company in New Orleans at age 15. This feat made it evident that Guiraud was ready to study in Paris.

When he arrived in the French capital, he was fortunate enough to be able to call upon his father's friends, especially M. Croizilles, violinist at the Opéra-Comique. The older musician watched over his ward like a father and saw to it that he was enrolled at the Conservatoire to study piano with Marmontel. He distinguished himself with honors in 1855 and won second prize in the contest of 1857; he carried off top honors in 1858. At the Conservatoire, his program included courses in harmony with Barbareau and in composition with Jacques Halévy.* He won the Prix de Rome on his first attempt at the Institut in 1859, when he captured the vote of every judge. He sent back a composition from Rome to Paris every 12 months during his three years residence in Italy: a solemn mass, an opera buffa in one act called Gli Avventuri, a comic opera entitled Sylvia.*

He was back in Paris only a few months when his Slyvia was produced at the Opéra-Comique on 11 May 1864. Then, on 5 march 1869, his En Prison was performed at the Théâtre-Lyrique. His third work, Le Kobold, was mounted at the Opéra-Comique on 2 July 1870.

The Franco-Prussian War saw Guiraud enlist in an infantry battalion, although his status as a Prix de Rome winner exempted him from military service. After the end of hostilities, he returned to his desk and created a suite for orchestra given at the Concerts populaires on 28 January 1872. This nontheatrical composition strengthened his reputation with the public, and he returned to the boards with an oprea entitled Madame Turlupin mounted at the Athénée on 23 November 1872. The Opéra then accepted his ballet Gretna Green* on 5 May 1873. This collaboration with Louis Mérante* was followed by his most effective work for the Opéra-Comique, Piccolino of 11 April 1876. Carvalho* called upon him to complete Jacques Offenbach's* score for Les Contes d'Hoffmann* also given at the Opéra-Comique on 10 February 1881 with a stellar cast that included the tenor Taskin and Mlle Isac. His one and only lyric composition for the Opéra was Frédégonde* of

18 December 1895, and Camille Saint-Saëns* had to complete this postumous work. Finally, his music was included in two ballets by Joseph Hansen* danced at the Opéra, Danses de jadis et de naguère* of 1900 and Danses grecques* of 1901.
BIBLIOGRAPHY: Mina Curtiss, Bizet and His World (New York: Knopf, 1958), 96-97, 100-102, 416-17, 426; Winton Dean, Georges Bizet (London: Dent, 1965), 33-35, 77-79, 124-29, 209-11, 219-21, 274; Fétis Suppl. I 436-38; GE XIX, 599; Arthur Hoérée, "Les Entretiens Debussy-Guiraud," L'Avant-scène 11 (September-October 1977), 140-45; Lajarte II, 246; PBSW 62, 72-73, 124; SW 263-64.

Guiraud, Pierre-Marie-Thérèse-Alexandre (b. 25 December 1788, Limoux; d. 24 February 1847, Paris), librettist, received his education from a private tutor for 15 years and then studied law at Toulouse. His father's premature death compelled him to give up his plans for a career before the bar because he had to turn his attention to the management of the cloth factory that he had inherited. After he had obtained help to operate this family establishment, he turned to literary pursuits and published his Ode sur les Grecs in 1820. The poet went on to do volumes of verse and a handful of tragedies, but his contribution to the Opéra was minimal. He collaborated with Jacques Ancelot* and Alexandre Soumet* on the libretto for Pharamond,* for which François Boïeldieu, Pierre Berton, and Rodolphe Kreutzer did the music (see eighteenth-century volume for Boïeldieu, Berton, and Kreutzer). This opera of 10 June 1825 dealing with the mythical first king of France was performed on the occasion of the coronation of Charles X.
BIBLIOGRAPHY: Bio. univ. XVIII, 219-21; GE XIX, 598-99; Lajarte II, 110; LXIX VIII, 1636; Wks 3631, 4732, 5398, 6049.

Gungsbourg, Raoul (b. 25 December 1859, Bucharest; d. 31 May 1955, Monte Carlo), administrator and composer, served as director of several opera companies in Russia before becoming director of the Monte Carlo Opera. While he was at this latter theatre, he had the distinction of becoming the first director to present the complete version of Hector Berlioz'* La Damnation de Faust* on a legitmate stage. Also, he wrote a few operas that he produced for the first time in the Monte Carlo opera house. Le Vieil Aigle* was among these works. It was brought to the Opéra for its Paris premiere on 26 June 1909 with Feodor Chaliapin* in the leading role. It was given five billings at the Opéra, and it is the only work by Gungsbourg that has been billed into the Garnier Palace.*

It was as the manager of the Monte Carlo opera house that M. Gungsbourg made his greatest contribution to operatic history because so many well-known works were created on this stage when it was under his egis. These works that he created included Jules Massenet's* Jongleur de Notre-Dame (1902), Camille Saint-Saëns'* Hélène (1904), Gabriel Fauré's* Pénélope* (1913), Maurice Ravel's L'Enfant et les sortilèges (1925), and at least another dozen compositions that became famous wherever there was an opera house (see twentieth-century volume for Ravel and L'Enfant et les sortilèges).

BIBLIOGRAPHY: AEM V, 1125 a; BBD 662-63; Grove III, 852.

Gustave III was offered as an historical opera in five acts with a score by Daniel Auber,* a libretto by Eugène Scribe,* and choreography by Filippo Taglioni (see eighteenth-century volume for Taglioni). It had its premiere on 27 February 1833 and was given in whole or in part on 156 dates by the end of 1850. It was produced in its entirety on 117 occasions during this interval with 63 stagings taking place in the first two years of its history at the Opéra. The work is subtitled Le Bal masqué because of the lavish ball in the last act, and it was this spectacular conclusion of the opera that was given separately at first and most frequently: 20 times between 1835 and 1850, including the special benefit for Gilbert Duprez* on 14 December 1849. The second act was seen as a selection on 15 dates, but the fourth act was done by itself on only four dates in 1839. Thus, selections from Gustave III were included on 39 programs. It will also be recalled that Somma translated Scribe's work into Italian for Giuseppe Verdi* to set in Un Ballo in maschera. Edouard Duprez then turned Somma's Italian text into French for Le Bal masqué given at the Théetre-Lyrique on 17 November 1869.

The action of Auber's most energetic work occurs in the palace of Gustave III in Stockholm on 15-16 march 1792 with De Horn, Warting, and their accomplices plotting to assassinate the Swedish king. Gustave III exhorts his artists to work and orders a ball, to which the countess Ancharstroem has been invited (I, 1-2). He is suspicious when the latter's husband asks to speak to him, but he is relieved to find that this gentleman of the court wishes to inform him of a plot against his life, not of his interest in his wife. He busies himself with the campaign against Russia and his coming opera Gustave Wasa instead of bothering with the conspiracy. He is given a decree to sign that will banish the soothsayer Arvedson, and he decides suddenly to visit this popular fortune-teller (I, 3).

The scene shifts to Arvedson's apartment, where the soothsayer promises Gustave III, disguised as Christian, that the king will reward him for his service, and the Swedish monarch gives him a purse of gold. The countess Anckarstroem enters, and the king hides behind a curtain to hear her ask for a potion to cure her of a troublesome love. Arvedson directs her to a place of punishment and torment, where she will find a greenbriar bush to serve as a base for her elixir (II, 1-2). She reads Gustave's palm and foretells his death. The first man to shake his hand will slay him. The king ridicules the prophecy (II, 3) and grasps Anckarstroem's hand in a gesture of defiance. All present recoil in terror when the king reveals his identity, and the conspirators try to slay him in the street after he leaves Arvedson's quarters. The cheers of his subjects thwart their plan (II, 4).

Amélie Ancharstroem has come to the field of tortures, where Gustave declares his love for her. Her husband comes upon them and warns the king of assassins waiting to murder him; he does not recognize his veiled wife. Amélie threatens to reveal her identity to her husband if the king refuses to flee (III, 1-3). After his departure, Amélie and her husband are accosted by the conspirators, and Amélie's presence is revealed to the consternation of her husband and the surprise of the assassins (III, 4-5). Anckarstroem prepares to execute his wife as an adultress, and he joins the conspiracy led by De Horn and Warting (IV, 1-2). The countess picks his name by lot to slay the king, and she guesses the meaning of events transpiring among the company (IV, 3). Oscar announces that the masked ball is scheduled for the coming night, and the conspirators decide to strike (IV, 4).

Amélie and her husband Anckarstroem are supposed to leave for Finland. The scene changes to the ballroom, where a variegated crowd of dancers occupies the scene. Anckarstroem hears that the king has been informed of the plot and will not attend the ball, but Oscar reveals that he is present dressed as a black domino with a ribbon cross upon his chest. A woman dressed as a white domino removes the cross from the king's costume; Gustave recognizes her as Amélie and tells her that he has made her husband governor of Finland so that she will not be at the court in Stockholm (V, 1-4). But Anckarstroem shoots Gustave, and the assassins are arrested without the murderer knowing of the royal decision to send him and his wife away from the capital (V, 5).

The introduction of an adulterous love into Gustave III was one of the reasons for its limited popularity despite an otherwise striking libretto, because it was quite widely known in Europe that the regicide upon which the opera is based was a purely political affair. On the other side of the ledger, the work was known throughout the musical world because of the hero's galop and the dancing airs of the last act. Yet it was probably the third act with its gibbet and macabre atmosphere that was designed specifically to hold the attention of romantic theatre-goers of the day.

The original cast included Adolphe Nourrit* in the title-role and Nicolas Levasseur* as Anckarstroem opposite Mlle Cornélie Falcon* in the part of Amélie.

BIBLIOGRAPHY: Chouquet, 397; DDO I, 537; B. Jouvin, D.F.E. Auber (Paris: Heugel, 1864), 59-62; Lajarte II, 145-46; Charles Malherbe, Auber (Paris: Renouard, n.d.), 44; Moniteur universel 59 (28 February 1833), 557 and 61 (2 March 1833), 580; PBSW 2220.

Guy-Stéphan, Marie (b. 1818, ?; d. 21 August 1873, Paris), ballerina, returned to Paris from Madrid at the time that Joseph Mazilier* was creating a new ballet for Olimpia Priora,* and the choreographer received word from management that he was to revise his composition so that it would provide a second major role to be assigned her. When Aelia et Mysis* had its premiere on 21 September 1853, therefore, Priora and Guy-Stéphan had leads in it. Fortunately, critics were agreed that each dancer had excelled in her role, and the evening was a success not only for the performers but also for queen Maria Cristina of Spain, the duchess of Alba, and the latter's sister, Empress Eugénie.

After the enthusiastic welcome given to the new star at the Opéra, it might be supposed that management would feel no reluctance about assigning roles to her even without orders from high places, but Nestor Roqueplan had other ideas after a quarrel with her. He failed to renew her contract. The dispute became public and bitter, and Guy-Stéphan asserted that the Opéra was not honoring its contract with her. The government intervened in the plaintiff's favor before the court could reach a decision, and Marie returned to the theatre in triumph. She was given a part to do in the divertissement of La Muette de Portici* presented on 13 December 1854 in the presence of the emperor and empress (see eighteenth-century volume for divertissement). La Guy-Stéphan caused a flurry of excitement and gossip by lifting her skirts to eye level in front of Napoleon's box in the course of her dancing.

A new work entitled Les Gaîtés champêtres had been readied for Guy-Stéphan in the spring of 1854, but the dancer had fallen into a second disagreement with management. This dispute with Crosnier, appointed director of the Opéra on 11 November 1854, did not end as happily as the first argument with Roqueplan, however, and it was Guy-Stéphan who had to beat a retreat on this occasion. She left the Opéra permanently before the end of the summer of 1855.

BIBLIOGRAPHY: DDD 115; Ivor Guest, The Ballet of the Second Empire (Middletown, Conn.: Wesleyan University Press, 1974), 70, 72-73, 83-84, 102, 198, 256, 258; Lajarte II, 213-14.

Gwendoline is an opera in three acts with a score by Emmanuel Chabrier* and a libretto by Catulle Mendès. It had its world premiere at the Théâtre Royal de la Monnaie in Brussels on 10 April 1886 and was produced subsequently at Carlsruhe (1889) and Munich (1890) before it had its French premiere in Lyon at the Grand theatre on 19 April 1893. It was brought to the Garnier Palace* for its first presentation in Paris on 27 December 1893 in a production by Lapissida. Amable and

Gardy designed its sets on this occasion, and Charles Bianchini created its costumes.

The action of Gwendoline takes place on the coast of Great Britain before the advent of the Romans. The curtain rises to disclose the Saxon maidens greeting the dawn, and a mixed chorus urging the villagers to begin their work in the fields and at sea. Gwendoline's father, Armel, leaves with his nets and harpoon, and his daughter warns him against the warlike Danes, who appear suddenly on a raiding party (I, 1-2). Harald proclaims his victory over the Saxons and demands that Armel surrender his gold. The old man refuses to be intimidated, and the Danes threaten to destroy him, his village, and his fields. Harald is about to slay his captive, but Gwendoline intervenes; Harald is speechless, when he beholds Gwendoline's beauty (I, 3). The warrior reveals that he is a stranger to feminine ways and charm, and she weaves a crown of flowers for him. He dashes it to the ground in anger, but he obeys her orders to pick it up and to return her spinning wheel. She sings a spinning song for him, and he cannot resist the charm of her manner or the beauty of her voice. He asks Armel for Gwendoline's hand, but the old man asserts that his daughter is mistress of her fate. Gwendoline refuses to commit herself to Harald, and Armel plans to slay him and his men in the evening when they have laid aside their armor and are drunk from wedding wine (I, 4).

The Saxon girls depress old Armel with their nuptial songs for his daughter, but Aella assures him that they are ready to ambush the Danes when the moment arrives (II, 1). Gwendoline and Harald enter in nuptial garb, and the wedding ceremony begins. The Danes offer the bride presents of gold and precious cloth, and the Saxon girls extend gifts of fruit and flowers to Harald. Old Armel pronounces Gwendoline and Harald man and wife, and the couple declare their mutual love, but he gives his daughter a knife to stab her husband on their wedding couch. She exhibits alarm, but her consternation is forgotten quickly in the midst of the festivities (II, 2). Suddenly, Gwendoline warns Harald to flee and assures him of her love again in an effort to protect him against her father's plan. He ignores her warnings. The sound of overturning tables and fighting interrupts Harald's vows of love to his young bride, and his men run in to warn him of the incumbent danger. He rushes off to the fray, but he remembers that he has no weapons. Gwendoline gives him her knife (II, 3).

The Danes are attacked mercilessly on their retreat to their ships, and Harald enters wounded and with his knife shattered. Armel wounds him mortally, but the Danish leader defies him (III, 1). Gwendoline seizes Harald's knife and stabs herself. A light pierces the darkness of the night to shine upon the heights where the dying lovers defy their fate. The Danish ships sink in flames at their feet in a Wagnerian conclusion (III, 2).

The libretto of Gwendoline reflects the fact that its author was an accomplished poet, but the score is somewhat uneven with the more impressive passages compensating for the lapses. The first act is the best of the three acts, although the choruses are uniformly well done. The composition was billed at the Opéra on 38 dates and enjoyed revivals in 1911, 1926, 1941. Mme Lucy Berthet created the title-role with a cast that included Maunce Renaud* (Harald), Albert Vaguet* (Armel), and Mme Douaillier (Aella).

BIBLIOGRAPHY: Martin Cooper, French Music from the Death of Berlioz to the Death of Fauré (London, New York, Toronto: Oxford University Press, 1951), 40-42; DDO I, 538-39; Roger Delage, "Emmanuel Chabrier in Germany," MQ 49 (1963), 75-84; René Dumesnil, La Musique contemporaine en France (Paris: Armand Colin, 1930) I, 17-18 and II, 73-75; Edward Burlingame Hill, Modern French Music (Boston and New York: Houghton Mifflin Co., 1924), 65-67, 72-76; Hugues Imbert, Médaillons contemporains (Paris: Fischbacher, 1903), 90-91; Rollo Myers, Emmanuel Chabrier and his circle (London: J. M. Dent & Sons, 1969), 52-68, 118-19, 158; MSRL 40-41; "Opéra . . . reprise de Gwendoline," Le Ménestrel 77 (6 May 1911), 138-39; Christopher Palmer, Impressionism in Music (London: Hutchinson University Library, 1973), 105-8; PBSW 64, 222; J.-G. Prod'homme, "Chabrier in His Letters," MQ 21 (1935); Gustave Samazeuil, Musiciens de mon temps (Paris: Marcel Daubin, 1947), 43-49; SSBO 292-93, 295; Stoullig XIX (1893), 41-50 and XX (1894), 5-6 and XXXVII (1911), 3-9 and XXXVIII (1912), 28; SW 107-8; Thompson 724, 2155; Yvonne Tienot, Chabrier par lui-même et par ses intimes (Paris: Henry Lemoine et cie, 1965), 52-59, 74-78, 120-21; Mario Versepuy, "Chabrier et ses origines auvergnates," Le Ménestrel 99, no. 11 (12 March 1937), 89-91.

La Gypsy is a ballet in three acts and five scenes with a libretto by Jules-Henri Vernoy de Saint-Georges* and Joseph Mazilier.* Its score was composed by François Benoist,* Ambroise Thomas,* and Count Aurelio Marliana.* Joseph Mazilier* was responsible for the choreography of this work, which had its world premiere at the Royal Academy of Music on 28 January 1839 with sets by Philastre and Cambon. Paul Lormier created its costumes.

The ballet opens on the grounds of Lord Campbell's estate located outside Edinburgh. Here in the country, the Campbell clan is enjoying a reunion and celebrating the accession of Charles II to the throne of England. Lord Campbell leads a hunting party off on a foray, and his foppish nephew, Narcisse de Crakentorp, remains behind to watch over Sara, Lord Campbell's only child. A fugitive Roundhead named Stenio enters. He is bent upon escaping from Scotland, but he delays to enter a nearby tavern just as Trousse-Diable and his band of gypsies enter. When Stenio emerges from the tavern, he encounters a platoon of soldiers, but he is protected from possible arrest by the gypsies, who dress him as one of their band. He drops a parchment roll certifying his army commission, but he retrieves it in time to preserve his anonymity, despite the soldiers' curiosity.

After the soldiers' departure, the noise of the hunting party is heard in the distance, and a wild beast is seen crossing the bridge in the valley. The savage animal appears headed towards Sarah, Narcisse, and nurse Meg. Narcisse runs away in fright, but Stenio seizes his gun and runs up an adjacent path as if to save endangered Sarah. The Roundhead fires his gun as soon as he disappears. Lord Campbell hears the report of the weapon and rushes in to see Stenio carrying his daughter to safety. She is suffering from a lacerated arm, however, and Meg tells her father how Stenio saved his daughter from the savage beast. A physician assures him that Sarah will recover, and the relieved Lord Campbell invites his guests to a banquet.

The dinner is proceeding without incident until Stenio refuses to toast the king's health and pours his wine on the ground. the royalists draw their swords, but Lord Campbell reminds his irritated guests that Stenio has just saved Sarah's life. Angry Trousse-Diable insults his guest and is arrested for his trouble, but Stenio is allowed to leave. The banquet continues, and a man is seen suddenly on the castle wall. He enters the castle through Sarah's bedroom window. After a brief interval, Meg leans out the window to warn the diners that Sarah has disappeared, and Tousse-Diable is seen dashing down a mountain path with the child in his arms (I, 1).

The second act opens a dozen years later in Edinburgh, where a full moon is glistening on a large tent set up in a street by the gypsies. Sarah is now eighteen and quite beautiful. She is asleep in the tent, but Trousse-Diable and his gypsies are preparing to rob unwary citizens. Narcisse comes out from the tavern, and they accost him. Mab, queen of the gypsies, forces the thieves to return their loot. Unfortunately, Trousse-Diable has run away with the miniature that he wrested from Narcisse, and this precious object is not restored to its owner.

Sarah is awakened by the commotion outside the tent, and she comes into the street. Stenio enters to declare his love to her, and jealous Mab threatens her for daring to encourage him. Sarah admits her love for Stenio; she demands that Stenio choose between her and Mab. He responds by declaring that he loves her, and Mab is obliged to consent to the marriage of Sarah and Stenio. Trousse-Diable enters wearing Narcisse's miniature, and Mab orders him to surrender it to her. The scene ends with a set of dances led by Sarah (II, 1).

The setting moves to the square before the town hall of Edinburgh where a fair is in progress. Crowds swarm around the exhibitions, and gypsies gather to execute communal dances.

When the dancing concludes, Narcisse tries to kiss Sarah, and she slaps him. Mab recognizes Narcisse as the victim of the robbery, and she hits upon a plan for revenge. She gives Narcisse's miniature to Sarah. In timely fashion, Narcisse now returns to notice his miniature hanging from Sarah's neck. He accuses her of larceny, and she asserts that she received the stolen object from Queen Mab. Sarah is arrested by the sherrif's deputies when she cannot find Mab to corroborate her allegations (II, 2).

The scene moves to the home of Lord Campbell, now sheriff of Edinburgh. He is a troubled man because the gypsy's dancing reminds him of his lost daughter. He is mulling over this situation when his assistant informs him that he must serve as judge in a trial involving a gypsy girl accused of robbery. He hears the case and declares Sarah guilty despite her protests of innocence. She tries to kill herself, and he intervenes only to notice her scarred arm. He asks her to tell him the story of her scar, and she explains how she was attacked by a wild beast when she was a child. He recognizes he as his missing daughter, but forgotten Stenio is led away by Trousse-Diable (II, 3).

Lord Campbell celebrates the return of his daughter by giving a ball. Sarah enters in a beautiful gown, but she snubs Narcisse and then decides to inspect her gypsy clothes in the adjoining study. Trousse-Diable and Stenio enter the room through a window just as Lord Campbell arrives in the ballroom with his guests. Meg attempts to return Sarah's gypsy garments to storage, but Sarah prevents her from entering the study lest she discover Stenio. At this moment, Mab enters wearing a veil. She tells Lord Campbell that his daughter is hiding a man in his castle, and he initiates a search that uncovers Stenio. Sarah tries to save the situation by presenting Stenio as her husband, and angry Mab flounces out of the room. Stenio establishes his noble standing by producing his army commission, and a complete reconciliation follows. Mab appears unexpectedly at a window with another gypsy, however, and her companion fires a revolver at Stenio. He falls to the floor, and Sarah goes into shock. Suddenly she believes that she is a gypsy once again, and she stabs Mab before fainting in her father's arms. The deputies arrest defiant Mab and her gypsy accomplice (III, 1).

The ballet was well received by the public, and it was performed on 29 dates in 1839. During the first year of its billings at the Opéra, it was often paired with and act of another work such as <u>Le Philtre</u>,* <u>Le Serment</u>,* or <u>Le Siège de Corinthe</u>.* Only its first two acts were presented on the program of 20 January 1840, but it was revived without cuts on 7 February 1840, when it was presented as a companion piece for La Xacarilla.* It was staged at the Royal Academy of Music on a total of five dates in 1840 and 1841 before it was dropped after its presentation on 23 April 1841. Subsequently it was returned to the stage of the Royal Academy of Music on 23 January 1843 for another run of eight billings before being removed from the repertory after its performance of 8 January 1844.

Sarah Campbell as a young girl was danced by Mlle Guérino in the first act, and the role of Sarah as a young lady in the second act was filled by Franziska Ellsler,* while Montjoie and Joseph Mazilier were cast, respectively, as Lord Campbell and Stenio. MM. Elie and Simon did the minor male parts of Narcisse and Trousse-Diable. The press was especially enthusiastic about Mlle Ellsler's performance, and it has been suggested that La Gypsy was the first ballet to call attention to the true extent of her talents.

BIBLIOGRAPHY: CB 194-204; CODB 241; DDD 337; Lajarte II, 158-59; Moniteur universel 32 (11 February 1839), 212; RBP 173-77; SS 103.

Gyrowetz, Adalbert (b. 19 February 1765, Budweis; d. 22 March 1850, Vienna), composer, left home to follow courses in philosophy and jurisprudence at the University of Prague but continued to study music in his spare time. Illness forced him to return to his home in Bohemia within a short time, however, and his extracurricular interest became his principal occupation. Count Fünfkirchen became interested in his work and invited him to become his chapelmaster. A few pieces he wrote while in the count's retinue won him local fame and the financial means to travel to Italy to study counterpoint for two years at Naples under Sala. He then journeyed to London via Milan and Paris, and he remained in England for three years, where he wrote an opera, Semiramide, as well as several cantatas. When the weather in Great Britain proved too severe for him, he went to Vienna.

His travels and experiences along with his ability as a linguist won him diplomatic posts that took him abroad temporarily, but it was not long before he decided to devote all his time to music. He became music director of the Imperial Opera at Vienna in 1804, and he retained this position as long as this theatre was under government control. He wrote his last composition for the theatre in Prague in 1828 at age 64.

Gyrowetz was extremely prolific, and his publications include at least 30 works for the musical theatre and more than two dozen symphonies as well as serenades, quartets, quintets, nocturnes, sonatas, and more than 20 collections of dances and 15 volumes of songs and romances. He was as successful in concerts as well as on the boards, although he lacked one essential quality: originality of style. Despite his having composed more works quantitatively than Haydn or Mozart, he had only three titles posted at the Paris Opéra: Les Pages du duc de Vendôme* of 1820, La Fête hongroise* of 1821, and Nathalie* of 1832, which he scored with Michel Carafa.* These three titles amounted to four acts in all, hardly an impressive contribution from so prolific a composer.

BIBLIOGRAPHY: AEM V, 1146-58; Allgemeine deutsche Biographie (Leipzig: Duncker & Humbolt, 1879) X, 247-49; Fétis IV, 167-69; GE XIX, 669; Lajarte II, 96, 100, 116, 145; LXIX VIII, 1663.

H

Habeneck, François-Antoine (b. 1 June 1781, Mézières; d. 8 February 1849, Paris), administrator, was the eldest of three brothers taught to play the violin by their father. Precocious, he played concertos in public at age ten before going to Brest, where he composed concertos by instinct rather than by calling upon any formal education in music. He did not get to Paris until after he was 20 years old, but he was admitted to the Conservatoire to study under Denis Baillot, and his ability secured his reputation as a musician almost immediately (see eighteenth-century volume for Baillot). The empress Josephine was so impressed by his playing that she awarded him an income of 1,200 francs, and he was placed as a violinist in the orchestra of the Opéra-Comique and then of the Opéra. When Rodolphe Kreutzer became leader of the latter orchestra, he chose Habeneck to be his first violin (see eighteenth-century volume for Kreutzer).

Habeneck's special talent was not composing but rather organizing and directing concerts, and his gift in this direction was recognized early. He was placed in charge of the Conservatoire concerts until their suppression in 1815, and he was later reassigned to this same responsibility, when the concerts were renewed in 1828. He was also director of the Opéra between 1821 and 1824 and became first violin in its orchestra after the 1830 revolution as well as its director until 1846.

His compositions include concert pieces for violin and piano, a polonaise for violin and orchestra, and violin solos. His only contributions to the repertory of the Opéra were the few passages he wrote for the conclusion of Aladin* of 1822 after the death of Ange-Marie Benincori* and his arrangement of Jean Dauberval's Le Page inconstant of 1823 (see eighteenth-century volume for Dauberval).

BIBLIOGRAPHY: N. Demuth, "Habeneck and La Société des Conserts," Music Survey I, 133-36; Fétis IV, 172; GE XIX, 681-82; GIR 163-69; HBM 188-90; Lajarte II, 100-101, 107-8; LXIX IX, 4; PBSW 183; Schrade, Beethoven in France (New Haven: Yale University Press, 1942) 3, 26, 116.

Hahn, Reynaldo (b. 9 August 1875, Caracas, Venzuela; d. 28 January 1947, Paris), composer, came to France at age three and was admitted to the Paris Conservatoire, when he was eleven. He studied under the direction of Dubois, Lavignac, and Jules Massenet*; he published his first music at age 14.

Hahn showed an early interest in the theatre, and his Ile de rêve was produced at the Opéra-Comique as early as 23 March 1898. This comic opera was followed by La Carmélite at the Opéra-Comique on 16 December 1902, and his Nausicaa was produced at Monte Carlo in 1919 before it had its premiere at the Opéra-Comique on 18 June 1923. His other works for the stage included La Colombe de Bouddha (1921) and Mozart (1925).

The composer had three works produced at the Opéra during his lifetime. He contributed the ballet entitled La Fête chez Thérèse* to the repertory of the Garnier Palace* on 13 February 1910, and he scored Fête triumphale for the victory celebration of 14 July 1919 at the Garnier Palace. His most important composition, Le Marchand de Venise, was staged at the Opéra on 21 March 1935 (see twentieth-century volume for Fête triumphale and Le Marchand de Venise).

Hahn conducted operatic programs in Paris, Cannes, and Salzburg, and he served as director at the Opéra in Paris during 1945-46.

BIBLIOGRAPHY: AEM V, 1319-20; BBD 673-74; Louis Beydts, "Mon souvenir de Reynaldo Hahn," L'Opéra de Paris 6 (1953), 47-49; EDS VI, 98-99; ELM II, 398-99; Grove IV, 15-16; René de Laromeguière, "Le

Souvenir de Reynaldo Hahn," *L'Opéra de Paris* *4 (1951), 33-35; NEO 289; PBSW 63-64, 70, 112, 183.*

Helévy, Jacques-François-Fromental-Elie (b. 27 May 1799, Paris; 17 March 1862, Nice), composer, entered the Conservatoire in 1809 to study under Cazot but also became a student of Lambert for the piano, of Berton for harmony, and of Luigi Cherubini for counterpoint (see eighteenth-century volume for Cherubini). He won the Prix de Rome competition in 1819 for his cantata on the prescribed subject of Herminie. After the completion of his residence in Rome, he returned to Paris in 1822 to embark upon a career as a composer of music for the theatre. He had two librettos at his disposal, a grand opera entitled Pygmalion and a comic opera called Les Deux Pavillons, but he wasted two years trying to get them accepted. He managed to have L'Artisan performed at the Feydeau Theatre in 1827, but it did not impress the public. Le Roi et le batelier, produced in 1828, was a special effort to honor Charles X, but it added nothing to his reputation, although Clari at the Théâtre-Italien gave evidence of genuine talent the following year.

Halévy made his first offering to the Opéra with the grand ballet Manor Lescaut* in three acts of 1830. After a disappointment with his unproduced Yella and an almost colorless La Langue musicale (1831), he returned to the Opéra in 1832 with another work in the grand style, La Tentation,* which mingled nearly equal portions of lyric drama and ballet. Then, in 1835, Halévy did La Juive,* a grand opera that has withstood the passage of time and intervening changes in taste. Typical of its genre, it extended lavish offerings to eye and ear alike despite the tendency of its author to become heavy or repetitious at times. In only six months, he gave the public another smash hit with L'Eclair (1835) at the Opéra-Comique. Unlike La Juive, it was both bright and elegant to such an extent that it seemed designed to capture spectators who might have been unimpressed with the less sparkling La Juive at the Opéra.

Curiously enough, a period of 30 months' silence followed these two hits offered in such rapid succession by Halévy, but the composer was back in 1838 with Guido et Ginevra* at the Opéra and Les Treize (1839) at the Opéra-Comique. Le Drapier* was billed at the Opéra in 1840. These three works were done with care, especially Guido et Ginevra, but none of them matched the success of La Juive. Halévy remedied this lack of a brilliant piece between 1835 and 1840 with La Reine de Chypre* of 1841 at the Opéra, a work that would enjoy more than 150 presentations by 1878. Halévy had by no means come to the end of his resources, and he had another seven titles billed at the Opéra-Comique as well as another four compositions accepted at the Opéra: Charles VI* of 1843, Le Lazzarone* of 1844, Le Juif errant* of 1852, and La Magicienne* of 1858.

Halévy's production for the theatre amounted to more than 35 works, and his significance as a leading figure in the romantic school of grand opera is undisputed. He used all the tricks of his day, but he used them well: the big ensembles, the exotic and colorful settings, the almost epic ballets, the emotional conflicts and dilemmas. His music endured after these trappings of the earlier nineteenth-century style of theatre became obsolete, however, and even his more learned or melodramatic creations have bequeathed excerpts to concert orchestras. His importance as a contributor to the theatre tends to make posterity forget the services he rendered to music as a teacher at the Conservatoire, although his students included Charles Gounod,* François Bazin,* Victor Massé,* Ernest Deldevez,* and other figures who became important upon the musical scene in Paris. His many honors including his membership in the Academy of Fine Arts attest to the respect in which his colleagues held him as artist and teacher. The last century has seen La Reine de Chypre reach its 152nd presentation at the Garnier Palace* on 20 July 1878, while La Juive enjoyed its 562nd billing at the Opéra on 9 April 1934, when Marjorie Lawrence sang Rachel (see twentieth-century volume for Lawrence).

BIBLIOGRAPHY: Charles-Ernest Beulé, Institut impérial de France: Notice sur la vie et les ouvrages de M. F. Halévy (Paris: F. Didot, 1862); EGC 171-73; Fétis IV, 205-7; GE XIX, 754-55; Léon Halévy, F. Halévy, sa vie et ses oeuvres, récits et impressions personarelles, simples souvenirs (Paris: P. Dupont, 1862); HUT 137-39; J. W. Klein, "Jacques Fromental Halévy, 1799-1862," MR 23 (February 1962), 13-19; Lajarte II, 136, 143,

149, 156, 162, 169, 172, 175, 194, 211, 224, 260; LXIX IX, 29-30; Edouard Monnais, F. Halévy, souvenirs d'un ami, pour joindre à ceux d'un frère (Paris: N. Chaix, 1863); MPPA 215-45; PBSW 55, 183; Arthur Pougin, F. Halévy, écrivain (Paris: A. Caludin, 1865); Wks 3184, 3203, 3897, 4656, 4788, 5655, 7539, 8192, 8657, 8721, 9154, 9798, 9808, 10434, 10520, 10670, 11557, 12536, 12764, 13222, 13379, 13505, 13657, 13839; Riemann 316-17; SW 129, 180.

Hamlet was billed as an opera in five acts with music by Ambroise Thomas,* a libretto by Michel Carré* and Jules Barbier,* and choreography by Lucien Petipa.* Its sets were by Rubé and Chaperon (a. 1, 5), Cambon (a. 2), and Despléchin (a. 3, 4). It had its premiere at the Imperial Academy of Music on 9 March 1868, and it enjoyed an extraordinary success from every point of view. Financially, it surpassed the operas being presented at the same time, and the receipts it returned to the box office did not fall below 10,000 francs for the first 22 presentations after its premiere. It earned the record sum of 14,147 francs on 28 April 1868; it was given on 21 of the 24 programs mounted at the opera between 9 March and 26 April 1868; it was performed on 57 dates this same year. Subsequently, it remained in repertory for a total of 99 billings at the opera house in the rue Le Peletier,* and it was billed for its 100th showing on the evening of 28 November 1873, but the theatre burned to the ground that morning, and it enjoyed its 100th performance at the salle Ventadour* on 23 March 1894. It had its premiere and 110th presentation at the Garnier Palace* on 31 March 1875, and it went on to reach its 384th and last showing at this theatre on 28 September 1938.

This operatic version of Shakespeare's tragedy opens with Claudius placing the crown of Denmark upon Gertrude's head, and the courtiers hailing her as their queen. She appears worried about Hamlet's continued absence (I, 1), however, and he enters brooding over his mother's marriage to Claudius only two months after the death of his father, the previous king of Denmark and the prior husband of Gertrude (I, 2). Ophélie reproaches the prince for his sudden moodiness and complains about his plans to leave Elsinore (I, 3). Laërte entrusts Ophélie to Hamlet because the king is sending him to Norway. Laërte and his sister leave for the royal wedding banquet, and Hamlet goes off alone just before his friends, Marcellus and Horatio, arrive to tell him that the ghost of his father has been seen on the ramparts (I, 5). The scene shifts to the ramparts, where Hamlet and his friends are awaiting the spectre. Midnight strikes, and the ghost enters to tell his son to take vengeance on Claudius for seducing his mother and poisoning his father (I, 1-3 bis).

Ophélie laments Hamlet's sudden indifference toward her (II, 1-3), and she asks the queen for permission to leave the court, but Gertrude begs her to remain to help her to cure Hamlet's increasingly strange conduct (II, 4). The fearsome queen expresses her alarm to the king, who warns her to be silent (II, 5). Hamlet speaks harshly to his frightened mother, who leaves hurriedly with the king, but he remains to explain to his troupe of players that he wishes them to stage Le Meurtre de Gonzague at the castle, where the courtiers assemble to witness the pantomime presenting an old king and a queen with Gertrude's features engaging in murder and adultery. The king goes to bed and falls asleep; the queen hands a cup of poison to her lover, who poisons her husband. Hamlet describes the action and interrupts his commentary long enough to accuse his stepfather of growing unreasonably pale. The king dismisses the actors in a panic, and Hamlet is certain of his guilt. He feigns madness and accuses Claudius of murder. Marcellus and Horatio try to restrain him, and Caludius rushes off in terror with the horrified queen.

Hamlet is pondering the problems of existence in his mother's apartments when the king enters. Hamlet is about to stab him, but the king kneels to pray and to ask his brother for forgiveness. Hamlet decides that the king should die on the throne instead of on a prayer bench. Claudius calls out to Polonius that he has seen the ghost of the late king, and Hamlet realizes that his father's murderer has an accomplice, Polonius (III, 1-3). Gertrude enters with Ophélie to tell Hamlet that the altar is prepared for his wedding to his betrothed, but he replies that he is unwilling to think of marriage. He suggest that Ophélie enter a nunnery, and she leaves in tears (III, 4). Hamlet accuses his mother of adultery and murder. She pleads for mercy and understanding, and he replies to her with hatred and scorn. The spectre warns Hamlet to limit his vengeance to Claudius and to leave his mother to heaven (III, 5).

The fourth act begins with a salute to spring by a group of Danish peasants. Ophélie joins them and sings of her love for Hamlet and his love for her. She explains that the story of their quarrel is a lie; her song is interspersed with laughter and tears. She moves through the rushes and drowns in the stream (IV, 1-3).

The gravediggers are singing and drinking at the start of the last act, and Hamlet asks the identity of the deceased, but the workers have forgotten his name. Hamlet pauses long enough in his flight from the king's assassins to regret Ophélie's madness, and Laërte comes upon him. He wishes to know the reason for his sister's misfortune, and they fall into a duel that is interrupted by a funeral procession. Hamlet inquires about the deceased for the second time, and Laërte puts up his sword when he realizes that Hamlet is unaware of Ophélie's death (V, 1-3). Hamlet sees the king and queen, and he hides behind the tomb until he recognizes dead Ophélie. He is about to kill himself, but the spectre intervenes and orders Hamlet to slay the king. Hamlet obeys. The queen feels death overtaking her. The courtiers, soldiers, and chorus greet melancholy Hamlet with shouts of "Long live the king!" (V, 4).

Mme Christine Nilsson created the role of Ophélie in Paris, and she was followed in the part over the next 70 years by such famous sopranos as Mme Caroline Carvalho,* Lillian Nordica,* Nellie Melba,* Mary Garden,* Jeanne Campredon, Gabrielle Ritter-Ciampi, and Solange Delmar (see twentieth-century volume for Ritter-Ciampi). Hamlet was sung initially by Jean-Baptiste Faure* and subsequently by Jean Lassalle,* Maurice Renaud,* Tita Ruffo,* Jean Noté,* Endrèze, José Beckmans, and Martial Singher (see twentieth-century volume for Endréze and Singher). The remainder of the men in the original cast included Jules Belval* (the king), Collin (Laërte), David (the ghost), Grisy (Marcellus), Castelmary (Horatio), Ponsard (Polonius), Gaspard and Mermand (the gravediggers) with Mme Pauline Gueymard-Lauters* as the queen.

The noteworthy passages in the score included the opening coronation march and chorus (I, 1) as well as the first duet between Ophélie and Hamlet, "Ah! doute de la lumière" (I, 3). Gertrude's anxious description of her son's apparent madness, "Dans son regard plus sombre" (II, 4), stands out in the second act as does the comedians' chorus, "Princes sans appanages" (II, 7). The third act provides two climactic moments: the trio with Hamlet's famous line to Ophélia ("Get thee to a nunnery!") translated as "Allez dans un cloître" (III, 4); the duet between Hamlet and his mother in act 3, scene 5. The touching "Un doux serment nous lie" by Ophélie to the chorus in the celebration of Spring (IV, 2) and Hamlet's "Comme une pâle fleur" (V, 2) are among the most moving passages in the last half of the tragedy.

BIBLIOGRAPHY: AEM XIII, 351-55; Camille Bellaigue, Musical Studies and Silhouettes, trans. Ellen Orr (New York: Dodd, Mead and Co., 1900), 312-14; idem, "Première Représentation d'Hamlet," Le Ménestrel 35 (15 March 1868), 122-23; Gustave Bertrand "Une Nouvelle Ophélie, Mlle Fidès Devries," Le Ménestrel 39 (8 December 1872), 11; Chouquet 423; DDO I, 541-44; Oscar Comettant, "Ce qu'on voit dans l'opéra d'Hamlet," AM 11 (7 March 1872), 76-78; Henri de Curzon, Ambroise Thomas (Paris: Heugel, 1921) 12-16; M. Escudier, "Hamlet, première représentation," FM 32 (15 March 1868) 77-79; Arthur Hervey, Masters of French Music (Plainview, N.Y.: Books for Libraries Press, 1976) 27-31; Lajarte II, 242; Lermina 747-48; H. Moréno, "Reprise d'Hamlet à l'Opéra; le baryton Bouhy et Mlle Daram," Le Ménestrel 44 (18 August 1878), 297-98; OQE 360; PBSW 61, 143, 222; SSBO 252; Stoullig XXXIV (1908), 33-34, 35-43, I (1875), 6-12, 22-23, 29, 57, XXII (1896), 22-24; SW 108-10; Albert Vizentini, "Première Représentation d'Hamlet," AM 8 (12 March 1868), 113-16; idem, "Ambroise Thomas, Hamlet," Le Ménestrel 37 (23 January 1870), 57-58; Mabel Wagnalls, Stars of the Opera (New York: Funk & Wagnalls Co., 1899), 145-65.

Hamlet is the title given to the touching Fête du printemps scene that constitutes the divertissement at the opening of the fourth act of Ambroise Thomas'* Hamlet,* whenever this segment of the opera is produced alone (see eighteenth-century volume for divertissement). It was given separately for the first time on 30 April 1870 at the theatre in the rue Le Peletier,* only two years

after the world premiere of its parent composition was billed at this same opera house on 9 March 1868. Mlles Eugenie Fiocre,* Lamy, Montaubry, Parent, and Stoikoff made up its cast on this occasion. The divertissement enjoyed its second representation apart from its matrix work on 24 October 1893 at the Garnier Palace,* but it was not brought back to the stage of this theatre again until its production there on 9 April 1918 with Mlles Jeanne Dumas, G. Franck, and Antonine Meunier. This work has enjoyed only five billings at the Opéra despite the praise that critics and spectators have always showered upon it.
BIBLIOGRAPHY: SW 285.

Hansen, Joseph (b. 1842, Belgium; d. 1907, Asnieres), choreographer, was an indefatigable worker who seems never to have received credit for his work. He was director of the Moscow Bolshoi Theatre from 1879 until 1884, when his most striking accomplishment was a revival of Swan Lake (1880); he became balletmaster at the Alhambra Theatre in London for the 1884-87 interval. In the meantime, he had produced Coppélia* for the first time in Brussels in 1871 and in Moscow in 1882.

In 1887, Hansen became balletmaster at the Opéra in Paris, and he remained at the theatre in this capacity until 1896, when Ladam replaced him. Hansen's activity as a choreographer for the Opéra did not diminish at this time, however, because his remaining years by no means constituted a period of inactivity for him. He did ballets and divertissements for 24 longer works between 1888 and 1907, although these pieces were never separated from their matrix works to distinguish themselves with separate performances (see eighteenth-century volume for divertissement). The titles of the compositions for which he wrote more than casual choreography are La Dame de Monsoreau* (1888), Charles Gounod's* Roméo et Juliette* (1888), Ascanio* (1890), Le Mage (1891), Thamara* (1891), Salammbô* (1892), Samson et Dalila* (1892), Déïdamie* (1893), Othello* (1894), Djelma* (1894), Frédégonde* (1895), Hellé* (1896), Messidor* (1897), La Burgonde* (1898), La Prise de Troie (1899), Lancelot* (1900), Astarté (1901), Le Roi de Paris* (1901), Les Barbares* (1901), La Statue* (1903), Le Fils de l'étoile* (1904), Daria* (1905), Ariane* (1906), and La Catalane*

(1907). Only in 1889 and 1902 did Hansen not create the choreography for some sort of lyric drama. Also, in 1901 he choreographed as many as three compositions.

As for ballets, it is surprising but true that Hansen had the time to choreograph no fewer than 14 of these compositions in the same period of time; that is, between 1889 and his death. Thus, he contributed to 38 works added to the Paris repertory during the last 20 years of his life. These ballets and the dates of their premieres were:

Ballet	**Premiere**
La Tempête	26 June 1889
Le Rêve	9 June 1890
La Vie pour le Tzar	19 May 1892
La Maladetta	24 February 1893
Fête russe	21 October 1893
L'Etoile	31 May 1897
Don Juan (divertissement)	18 March 1899
Danes de jadis et de naguère	11 November 1900
Bacchus	26 November 1902
Automobile Club Ballet	17 December 1903
La Nuit de Walpurgis	3 June 1905
La Ronde des saisons	22 December 1905
Le Ballet des nations	24 December 1907
Thaïs (divertissement)	1 July 1910

The divertissement from Thaïs was in reality the Ballet de la Tentation in the second act that had been produced for the first time at the premiere of Thaïs on 16 May 1894.

BIBLIOGRAPHY: ACPM 440-41; CODB 245; DDD 115; SW 38-39, 42-43, 46, 53-54, 56, 68, 70, 72, 96, 100,

111, 133, 138, 148, 165, 176-77, 187, 189-90, 193-94, 196-97, 204, 209, 240-41, 244, 263, 269, 273, 279, 296, 302, 317, 320, 331, 338.

Hansli le bossu was a ballet in two acts and three tableaux with an argument by Henri Caïn an Edouard Adenis. Its music was composed by Noël and Jean Gallon,* and its choreography was created by Yvan Clustine. Bailly designed its scenery, and Pinchon did its costumes. It had its world premiere at the National Academy of Music on 20 June 1914.

The ballet is set in a village near the Alsace-Lorraine border that boasts of a hunch-backed violinist of great talent. The poor and deformed youth loves Suzel, the wealthiest and prettiest girl of the region. Hansli has kept his love hidden, however, because Suzel is the daughter of the burgomaster Hauser, who is intent upon marrying his Suzel to handsome Fritz.

A crowd is in the village to celebrate the Feast of the Hops, and a contest is in progress to select the Queen of the Feast. Suzel wins the title not only on account of her beauty, but also because Hansli has written an exceptionally striking waltz for her dance performance. Hansli is so jubilant over the success of his music that he declares his love to Suzel, who is hardly overjoyed to hear this declaration. Hauser is angered by Hansli's presumption, moreover, and he orders him to leave the celebration. Hansli weeps bitterly, especially because he cannot support the idea of cruel and sarcastic Fritz marrying gentle Suzel (tabl. 1).

Night has fallen, and the square is deserted. The wind rustles through the trees, and the gnomes arrive to enjoy their nightly amusements. They dance, climb trees, do somersaults, peek in windows, listen at doors. Suddenly, they hear a sigh. It is Hansli come to say a last farewell to Suzel on his violin. the gnomes hide in corners and in trees, and they listen to the musician's playing. They cannot resist his art, and they surround him with tapping feet. After he has finished playing, Hansli gives his violin to the delighted gnomes, who set about to make model violins for themselves. Hansli tries to hang himself, but the grateful gnomes refuse to let him die. When they learn the reason for the musician's desire to kill himself, they summon their three doctors who excise the hump on Hansli's back. The operation is a success. The violinist cannot contain his joy, and the gnomes begin to play with the hump as if it were a balloon. Fritz enters. He is drunk and tries to strangle his rival. The gnomes seize him, however, and they affix Hansli's hump to his back (tabl. 2).

It is morning, and the village has assembled for the wedding of Suzel and Fritz. Hansli enters, and the villagers notice that he has become gay an lively. Fritz appears, and the guests observe that he is quite depressed. The villagers now begin to wonder why the groom is wearing so large a cloak, and why he continues to keep his back against the wall. When Fritz moves forward to sign the wedding contract, however, Hansli pulls away his cloak. Everybody is aghast upon seeing that he is a hunchback, and he disappears in humiliation. Yet Hauser refuses to accept Hansli as his son-in-law even if he is not deformed because he is still poor. Desperate, the violinist calls upon his tiny friends. The sky darkens, and they appear. They give Hansli a pot of gold and dress Suzel like a small madonna. Finally, Hauser gives his permission for the happy couple to wed (tabl. 3).

The ballet would most probably have enjoyed more than seven performances because it was a lively and ingenious composition, but the war cut its first run short. It was not billed at the Opéra again after 27 July 1914. The Garnier, it will be recalled, was closed after the performance of Les Huguenots* on 29 July 1914, and the theatre remained dark until 9 December 1915, when a relief program was organized to help Belgium.

The female roles in Hansli le bossu were created by Carlotta Zambelli* (Suzel), Aïda Boni (Catherine), and Jeanne Barbier (Marguerite). The male parts were filled by Yvan Aveline (Hansli), Bourel (Fritz), Girodier (old man Hauser), Charles Javon (the notary). Henri Rabaud* conducted the orchestra.

BIBLIOGRAPHY: Stoullig XL (1914-15), 23-25; SW 285.

Hatto, Jeanne (b. 30 January 1879, Lyons; d. ?), vocalist, was the stage name of Marguerite Jeanne Frère. She showed an early interest in music and was enrolled at the Conservatoire in Paris. She distinguished herself as a student and made her debut as a soprano at the Garnier Palace* in Brunehilde of Sigurd* on 22 December 1899.

Mlle Hatto was only 20 years old at the time of her first performance at the Opéra, and she enjoyed a comparatively long and active association with the company. She was billed in nearly a score of roles during her more than 20 years of performing at the Paris opera house. In 1900, she was cast in the title-role of Salammbô,* and, the following year, she sang Elisabeth in Tannhaüser* and Eva in Les Maîtres Chanteurs.* She added Nedda of Paillasse* to her personal repertory in 1902 and Margyane of La Statue* in 1903. She returned to Richard Wagner* with Sieglinde of La Walkyrie* in 1904, and she was billed as Annette for Le Freischütz* in 1905. After doing the title-role of Thamara* and Marguerite of Faust* in 1907, she appeared in Diane of Hippolyte et Aricie and Elsa of Lohengrin* in 1908 (see eighteenth-century volume for Hippolyte et Aricie). She was assigned next to the female lead of Monna Vanna* in 1909 and Stephana of Sibéria* in 1912. Her last parts before World War I were Guilhen in Fervaal* and Alix in Le Miracle* during 1913.

After the end of hostilities, Mlle Hatto sang Marguerite of La Damnation de Faust* in 1919, Nicéa of La Légende de Saint Crhistophe in 1920, and Télaïre of Castor et Pollux in 1921 (see eighteenth-century volume for Castor et Pollux and twentieth-century volume for La Légende de Saint Christophe).

Mlle Hatto's creations were neither as numerous nor as significant as the forgoing assignments that she filled in some of the landmark operas of the nineteenth century. She portrayed the following six characters for the first time at the Opéra over a score of years:

Role	Opera	Premiere
Iole	Astarté	15 February 1901
Floria	Les Barbares	30 October 1901
Iana	Le Cobzar	30 March 1912
Hermione	Mademoiselle de Nantes	16 December 1915

Genièvre	Le Roi Artus	30 March 1916
Une Esclave	Néron	27 January 1921

Mlle Hatto made her debut at the Opéra-Comique on 13 October 1910, but her association with this theatre was limited to her performances as Tosca and her creation in Le Voile du Bonheur of Si-Tchun on 26 April 1911.
BIBLIOGRAPHY: EFC 173; ICM 759; SW 43, 46, 63, 91, 101, 115, 135, 140, 150-51, 168, 186, 193, 201, 204, 207, 226, 295, 374; WOC 180, 256.

Hébert-Massy, Marie (b. 1814?; d. May 1875, Toulouse), vocalist, known first as Massy and née Giacomasci, married her colleague Hébert at the Opéra-Comique after she had joined this company as a soprano in 1832. She scored a series of striking successes at the Opéra-Comique but left this theatre after a few years to tour Europe. When she returned to Paris from this profitable trip, she was invited to appear at the Opéra as the heroine of Lucie de Lammermoor* in 1847. She did not remain at the Royal Academy of Music, however, but transferred to the Porte Saint-Martin Theatre, where Adolphe Adam* wrote work specifically for her so that she might exploit her ability to act as well as to sing. Finally, in 1850, she returned to the Opéra for a second brief interval to do Berthe in Le Prophète* and a few other roles. She was not offered a serious contract and returned to Toulouse to join the faculty of the Conservatoire of this city.
BIBLIOGRAPHY: Fétis Suppl. I, 454-55; SW 137, 178.

Heilbronn, Marie (b. 1849, Lyon; d. 1886, Nice), vocalist, made her theatrical debut at age eight in a performance of La Fille bien gardée* at the theatre in Bruges. She was admitted to the Conservatoire in Brussels, where she studied under Cornelis and obtained prizes in singing and piano. She moved to Paris subsequently to continue her studies with Duprez,* and she was given a contract by Adolphe de Leuven* to sing at the Opéra-Comique. She remained here during 1868 and moved on to Ems in 1869, but she was soon back in Paris with a contract to appear at the Variétés. Her next engagement was at the Théâtre-Italien, where

she proved to be a sensation as Violetta in 1877. She returned to the Opéra-Comique, but she left this company to perform at the Opéra, where she made her debut as Marguerite in Faust* during 1879. Unfortunately, she had differences with management at the Garnier Palace* and handed her resignation to M. Vaucorbeil on 1 March 1880. She went to the Opéra-Comique in 1884 for her third engagement there, and she was able to win new laurels for her interpretation of the role of the heroine in Charles Gounod's* Roméo et Juliette.* At the Opéra, she had sung only Zerline of Don Juan* and Ophélie of Hamlet* after her premiere at the Garnier theatre in the role of Gounod's Marguerite.
BIBLIOGRAPHY: EFC 155; Lermina 754; SW 73-75, 86-88, 108-10.

Heilbronner, Rose (b. 1884, Paris), vocalist, studied under Mme Martini and Rosa Bauer in Paris before making her stage debut at the Opéra-Comique in 1907. She remained at this theatre until 1912, and it was during this interval that she made her only appearance at the Opéra in a gala on 20 October 1910, when she sang the countess Olga in Fédora.* The special occasion which prompted her sole performance at the Garnier Palace* was a benefit to raise money for a monument to Victorien Sardou.* Mme Heilbronner continued to sing in French theatres during and after World War I, but she never returned to the Opéra.
BIBLIOGRAPHY: EFC 185; KRJ 184; SW 90-91; WOC 257.

Hellé was an opera in four acts with a score by Alphonse Duvernoy* and a libretto by Camille Du Locle* and Charles Nuitter.* Joseph Hansen* established its choreography, and Bianchini designed its costumes. Its sets were created by Amable (a. 1), Jambon and Bailly (a. 2), Carpezat (a. 3), Rubé and Moisson (a. 4). It had its world premiere at the Garnier Palace* on 24 April 1896.

The curtain rises on the opera to present an ancient and half-ruined temple on a hill by the sea, where priestesses led by Hellé are offering gifts to the ancient gods in an attempt to rejuvenate the temple. A ship anchors in the harbor (I, 1-2), and the priestesses give food and drink to its crew (I, 3). The landing party is Christian, and their leader asks Hellé about the priestesses' religion, but she urges him to leave her and her companions as soon as possible. Gauthier replies by inviting Hellé to sail away with him, but she insists that she must remain in Thessaly to perpetuate the memory of her ancient gods (I, 4). Gauthier feels that he is falling in love with Hellé (I, 5), and he decides to force her to leave with him (I, 6). Hellé enters to bid farewell to him. She refuses to depart with him, and he orders his crew to carry her to his ship. He sails away with her despite the prayers of her priestesses (I, 7).

The scene shifts to the square in front of Santa-Maria Novella in Florence. Here, Gauthier's palace dominates the other structures. Gauthier's soldiers are drinking opposite the palace, and the citizens are preparing to celebrate the feast of the patron saint of the city, Saint-Jean. The soldiers sing the praises of their leader and warn the bourgeois merchants not to murmur against his rule. Gauthier appears on his loggia with Hellé to urge his pople to enjoy their celebration, but the crowd is restless because they suspect that Hellé is a sorceress. A ballet representing the story of Hérode, Salomé, and John the Baptist is danced in the square.

After this divertissement, Gauthier proposes marriage to Hellé, but she remains silent, and he threatens her with violence (II, 1-2) (see eighteenth-century volume for divertissement). Hellé calls upon the goddess Diana to come to her aid (II, 3). The soldiers now insist upon dancing with a group of girls offering flowers to the Madonna. Roger loses his temper when the people try to protect the frightened girls, and Jean de Brienne upbraids Roger and his soldiers. The popular opposition to Gauthier's rule becomes quite apparent, and Gauthier is attracted by the commotion. He recognizes Jean, his son finally returned from France. Hellé notices how deeply Gauthier loves his son, and she decides that it is through Jean that she will strike at him. When Jean sees Hellé on the loggia, he is overcome by her beauty (II, 5-7).

The action moves to a villa outside Florence. It is evening, and Hellé's attendants are dressing her in splendid raiment to welcome Gauthier (III, 1-2). Gauthier arrives, but Roger enters immediately to tell him that he must return to Florence because a revolt seems imminent. He is reluctant to leave because he is certain that Hellé is no longer angry. Roger suggests that she may seem more pleasant because she loves another man (III, 3-4). Roger and Gauthier leave, and Jean enters to declare his love to Hellé and to implore her to elope with him. She feels herself falling in love with him and pleads with him to leave (III, 5-7), but it is too late. Gauthier returns to discover his son at Hellé's feet. Gauthier is crushed. Florence is seen burning in the distance (III, 8). Roger returns to announce that the people have put Gauthier's palace to the torch. Gauthier disowns his son, and Hellé begs Diana to forgive her for her weakness (III, 9).

The citizens flee from Florence in panic and blame Hellé and Gauthier for their misfortunes. They have condemned Hellé to the stake, but Jean has rescued her. She admits her love to him (IV, 1-2), and a chorus warns her that Hecate has sworn to avenge Diana's betrayal at her hands. She urges Jean to release her, and Hecate appears before her. She dies, and he stabs himself in despair (IV, 3). Gauthier runs toward them in his grief, and an invisible chorus declares that sacrilege leads to only one conclusion (IV, 4).

The opera was criticized immediately for presenting a Greek enclave of the twelfth century clinging to the religious beliefs of ancient Greece, and there were other comments to the effect that the score was too mediocre to inspire much excitement, although it was admitted that the music of the first and third acts had its moments. Yet Hellé had a run of 24 performances at the Garnier Palace,* where it remained in the repertory for five years from 24 April 1896 until 19 September 1900, when it was dropped. One accident marred its history at the Paris theatre. On 20 May 1896, one of the counterweights of the main chandelier crashed into the amphitheatre boxes killing one woman and injuring two men.

The principal roles of Hellé were created by Rose Caron* (Hellé) and Laure Beuvais* (Myrrha), while the male members of the cast included Albert Alvarez* (Jean), Charles Delmas (Gauthier), and René Fournets (Roger). The divertissement featured Carlotta Zambelli* as Salomé.

BIBLIOGRAPHY: *DDO I, 549; Arthur Pougin, "Première Représentation d'Hellé à l'Opéra," Le Ménestrel 62 (26 April 1896), 131-32; Stoullig*

XXII (1896) 1, 13-17, 20-22; SW 111.

Henry VIII is an opera in four acts and six tableaux with a score by Camille Saint-Saëns* and a libretto by Léonce Détroyat and Armand Sylvestre. Its choreography was provided by Louis Mérante* for its world premiere at the Garnier on 5 March 1885, but Joseph Hansen* and Léo Staats* furnished fresh choreography for its revivals in 1889 and 1909, respectively. Its scenery was created by Lavastre aîné an Carpezat (a. 1), Jean Baptiste Lavastre (a. 2 and a. 4, tabl. 2), and Rubé and Chaperon (a. 3, tabl. 2 and a. 4, tabl. 1). Eugène Lacoste created its costumes.

The opera is set in the palace of Hnery VIII in London, where two large windows open on a public square. Norfolk and the Spanish ambassador are speaking with each other, and the latter reveals his love for beautiful Anne de Boleyn, but Norfolk cautions him about a rumor reporting that the king loves this same woman. He adds that Henry is ruthless and allows nothing to interfere with his desires, and the validity of Norwalk's warning is confirmed by the news that the king's former favorite, Buckingham, has been condemned to death (I, 1-2). Henry enters, and Norfolk presents Don Gomez to him. The king invites the ambassador to attend the imminent presentation of a new lady-in-waiting to the queen, and the surprised ambassador leaves with Norfolk (I, 3). Surrey confirms that the pope has refused Henry's request for an annulment of his marriage to Catherine d'Aragon (I, 4), and Henry reveals to Catherine that she is about to have a new lady-in-waiting. She thanks the king and asks for Buckingham's pardon, but he refuses her request. She is alarmed, when Henry suggests that their marriage should be annulled because it breaks the law forbidding a man to marry his brother's widow. She cites the pope's approval of their union, but he suggests that the pope is not infallible. Catherine realizes that she has a rival (I, 5), and her new lady-in-waiting enters: Anne de Boleyn. The Spanish ambassador and Anne recognize each other, and Henry notices their reactions to each others presence. He presents Anne to Catherine and bestows upon her the title of marquise de Pembroke at the moment when the courtiers are looking through the windows at Pembroke being led to the scaffold. When Anne realizes what is transpiring, she is filled with fearsome premonitions (I, 6).

The scene moves to Richmond's gardens, where Don Gomez is pondering recent developments. Henry has left London with Anne to escape the plague, but he has left Catherine there. He concludes that Anne is as treacherous as the king, but she enters to reassure him of her undiminished love (II, 1-2). The king invites him to a party he plans for Anne. Henry declares his love to Anne, but she refuses to listen to his fervent assertions until he promises to make her his queen. Henry swears to Anne that he will honor his word (II, 3-4), and Anne yields to her lust for power (II, 5). Catherine warns her that her folly will lead to her ruin, but she defies the queen (II, 6). Henry returns to the gardens, and Catherine protests to him; he warns her that their marriage is about to end. The papal legate reports that Rome will not dissolve Henry's marriage, but the king declares that the party for Anne is about to begin, and he leaves with her on his arm (II, 7).

Henry refuses to speak with the papal legate (III, 1-2), and Anne tells him that she cannot be his queen, because marriage with her might mean his ruin. He suggests that her reluctance to marry him might be caused by her love for another man, but she denies his charge. The insistant legate appears before Henry to warn him of the consequences of his disobedience to Rome, but Henry remains firm (III, 3-6). Alone, the terrified legate asks God to pity the innocent people of England (III, 7).

The action shifts to Parliament, where the queen argues for the sanctity of her marriage. She is supported by Don Gomez, but the archbishop of Canterbury declares her marriage null and void. The papal delegate describes this verdict as unacceptable. Henry appeals to his subjects, and they agree to follow him into the new Church of England. He declares Anne de Boleyn his wife, and the legate excommunicates him (III, tabl. 2, sc. 1).

The last act opens in Anne's apartments, where the courtiers have gathered for a party. They remark that the king seems morose despite his wedding. Don Gomez enters, and his presence terrifies Anne. He assures her that he no longer loves her, and he adds that he has destroyed all her letters except one that is in Catherine's possession (IV, tabl. 1, sc. 1-3). The king enters and is furious to find Don Gomez with his queen, but he is mollified when he learns that the ambassador has a message from Catherine, who wishes him to know that she will love him until death takes her. Calm, Henry orders Don Gomez to follow him to Kimbold (IV, tabl. 1, sc. 4-5).

The last tableau transpires in Catherine's retreat at Kimbold. The local people are celebrating Henry's birthday, and Catherine is seated by her fireplace. She is aware that she is about to die, and she distributes gifts among her ladies-in-waiting, but she sets aside the letter proving that Anne has loved Don Gomez since her days at the French Court (IV, tabl. 2, sc. 1-2). Anne begs Catherine for an interview so that she may obtain her forgiveness, but it becomes apparent before long that she is looking for the fatal letter. Catherine waves the missive in Anne's face just as Henry enters with Don Gomez. The king tries to deceive Catherine into thinking that he is truly contrite for having caused her such unbearable suffering, but she refuses to be misled by this gambit. He tries to anger her by taking Anne into his arms, but she remains firm and throws the letter into the flames of her fireplace. She beseeches Don Gomez to follow her example and to forgive Anne. She dies. Outraged, Henri swears that he will put Anne's head upon the block, if he learns that she loves another man (IV, tabl. 2, sc. 3-4).

Saint-Saëns' opera created a storm of controversy in its time, because some spectators objected to its symphonic use of the orchestra in the style of Wagner,* while others praised the skill with which the composer had blended the score with the libretto. Yet it was generally agreed that the characters were too pale for the highly dramatic situations in which they became involved. Catherine was viewed as an unhappy woman worthy of inspiring some sympathy, but Anne was seen as a cheap flirt who set a price on her charms, while Don Gomez lacked the depth of character required of a convincing hero. As for Henry VIII, he was too thoroughly vicious to escape being labeled as an uncomplicated villain ready for any evil deed. It was the combination of the situations and the score that seemed to save the day; for example, the love scenes between Anne and Henry at the end of the first act and at the beginning of the second act, Catherine's efforts to redeem Anne in the second act, the pompous march in the Parliament tableau (III, tabl. 2), and the quartet by Catherine, Anne, Henry, and Gomez in the concluding tableau.

Henry VIII reached its 50th performance at the Garnier Palace* on 29 May 1891, and it remained in the repertory at the Opéra until 9 May 1919, when it enjoyed its 87th presentation. The role of Catherine d'Aragon has been filled by some of the greatest sopranos to sing at the Garnier: Gabrielle Krauss,* Rose Caron,* Lucienne Bréval,* Félia Litvinne,* and Marcelle Demougeot.* The title-role has been filled by Jean Lassalle,* Berardi, Jean-François Delmas,* and Maurice Renaud.*

The original cast also included MM. Etienne Dereims* (Don Gomez), and Auguste Boudouresque* (papal legate), Lorrain (Norfolk), and Gaspard (archbishop of Canterbury) with Mme Alphonsine Richard as Anne.

BIBLIOGRAPHY: *Jean Bonnerot, C. Saint-Saëns, 1835-1921; sa vie et son oeuvre (Paris: A. Durandet et fils, 1922), 102, 104-5, 107, 110-12, 133; DDO I, 550-51; René Dumesnil, La Musique contemporaine en France (Paris: Armand Colin, 1930) I, 12-15 and II, 64-66; Gabriel Fauré, Opinions musicales (Paris: Rieder, 1930), 127-28; Edmond Hippeau, "Henry VIII" et l'opéra français (Paris: La Renaissance musicale, 1883); James Harding, Saint-Saëns and His Circle (London: Chapman & Hall, 1965), 162-64, 171, 205-6; Modern Drama and Opera: Reading Lists on the Works of Various authors, ed. Frederick W. Faxon (Boston: The Boston Book Co., 1915), 201-2; Arthur Hervey, Saint-Saëns (Westport, Conn.: Greenwood Press, 1970), 58-62; Edmond Gabriel Hippeau, Henry VIII et l'opéra français (Paris: La Renaissance musicale, 1883); Adolphe Jullien, Musiciens d'aujourd'hui (Paris: Librairie de l'Art, 1894) I, 290-99; Watson Lyle, Camille Saint-Saëns, His Life and Art (Westport, Conn.: Greenwood Press, 1970), 31-32, 55-56, 73, 158-65; MCDE 822, 826; H. Moréno, "Henry VIII, opéra en 4 actes de M. Camille Saint-Saëns," Le Ménestrel 49 (11 March 1883), 113-16; Otto Neitzel, Camille Saint-Saëns (Berlin: Harmonie, 1899), 36-41; D. C. Parker, "Camille Saint-Saëns: a Critical estimate," MQ 5 (1919), 561-77; PBSW 222; J. G. Prod'homme, "Camille Saint-Saëns," MQ 8 (1922), 469-86;*

Georges Servières, La musique française moderne (Paris: Havard, 1897), 285-404; SSBO 285, 292; Stoullig VIII (1882), 25, and IX (1883), 3-13, 20-22, and XIX (1903), 7-10, and XXXV (1909), 20-22; R. A. Streatfeild, The Opera, ed. Edward J. Dent (Westport, Conn.: Greenwood Press, 1971), 235-36; SW 111-14.

Herculanum was an opera in four acts with music by Félicien David* and a libretto by Joseph Méry* and Hadot. Joseph Mazilier and Emma Livry* did its choreography, and its sets were created by Cambon and Thierry (a. 1, a. 4) and Despléchin (a. 2, a. 3). It had its premiere at the Imperial theatre of the Opera on 4 March 1859, and it proved impressive enough in musical circles to win the prize of 20,000 francs posted by the Institut in 1867. Its third act came to be given separately as early as 1 June 1859, and it was performed in whole or in part on 44 occasions during its first 12 months at the Opéra. It was returned to the stage for another 15 billings in 1861-62, and it was not dropepd from the repertory until after its eighth presentation in 1868 on 6 November. It had been given in its entirety or partly on 82 dates.

The first act of the opera opens in Olympia's palace in Herculanum during 79 a.d. with a chorus singing the beauty, power, and glory of this queen of the eastern empire, whom Rome has chosen to undermine Christianity in the Euphrates valley. Her brother Nicanor assures her that she will be successful, and he invites her friends and allies to share in a feast with her. Two noble Romans named Lilia and Hélios, who have defected to Chrisianity, are brought before her; they explain that they wish only to be left alone to pray and to adore God until their deaths. Nicanor wishes to kill them, but Olympia insists that their souls must be converted to the cult of pagan pleasure because death means nothing to Christians (I, 1-2). She dismisses Lilia but is attracted to Hélios, whom she urges to renounce Christ to rule with her. He is tempted but refuses her offer to become her king, and she gives a secret order to Locusta (I, 3-4). She then sings a bacchanalian air and directs Hélios to drink with her. He agrees to toast the virtues of his faith, and he empties his goblet, but the drugged wine makes him forget his religion for the pleasures of the world and the charms of his hostess (I, 5). Magnus enters to berate Olympia for her debauched life, and he reads her a passage from Apocalypse foretelling her destruction. He threatens her with Vesuvius, the scourge of sinners, and Olympia urges her guests to forget this harmless lunatic, although the chorus urges them to heed his fearsome words (I, 6).

The second act presents the Christians assembled before a cross and remembering the martyrs in their prayers. Nicanor orders them to disperse and directs his soldiers to bring Lilia to him (II, 1-2). He declares his love to her and invites her to leave for the East with him; she protests that she is about to marry Hélios. He asserts that he is a Christian; she is not deceived. Nicanor insists that she will not be able to escape from him, and, when he seizes her, he is struck dead by an unseen force. Lilia faints, and Satan appears (II, 3). He reminds Lilia that she is not without her faults because she still succumbs to jealousy. He invites her to look into Olympia's palace, where Hélios is stretched out at the queen's feet, and she is crushed. Satan picks up Nicanor's mantle and leaves (III, 4).

Hélios and Olympia are in the latter's gardens, where she is assuring Hélios that he is not dreaming. He realizes that he has deserted Lilia, however, and Olympia threatens to kill her if he does not become her king (III, 1). After a celebration in honor of Bacchus, Lilia enters to remind Hélios of his promises to her. He warns her that she is courting death by defying Olympia, but she refuses to curry favor with him, the queen, or the court. Her open declaration of her belief in Christ provokes the chorus to call for her death, and Olympia orders her arrest (III, 2). "Nicanor" enters, and Lilia warns that he is Satan. "Nicanor" urges Olympia to allow Lilia to live so that she may suffer to see Hélios as her king. Sarcastic Olympia tells Hélios to go out into the desert with his beloved to live on air and hope; "Nicanor" urges him in similar fashion to shun the radiant throne and the pleasures of the world being thrust upon him. Hélios debates with himself. Finally he proclaims his love for Olympia and declares himself doomed. Satan rejoices over his victory, and Lilia regrets that Hélios has sold his soul (III, 3).

The curtain rises on the fourth act to disclose that Vesuvius has already begun to erupt. The molten lava has ruined the houses in the neighborhood of Olympia's palace, and the people are beginning to climb to the top of her home to escape the holocaust. Satan incites a band of slaves who have regained their freedom during the panic, and they rejoice in the knowledge that the empire is disintegrating (IV, 1-2). Hélios finds Lilia, but she rejects him as a blasphemer. He begs her to pardon him before God punishes him; she forgives him and suggests that they await death together. Magnus announces that heaven has decided to speak at last (IV, 4). Olympia greets Satan as her brother, but he informs her that Nicanor is dead. He adds that he is Satan and had come to carry her off to hell. He points to the rising lava. Olympia defies death, Lilia and Hélios welcome it, and Herculanum disappears (IV, 5).

The male parts in Herculanum were created by Gustave Roger* (Hélios), Louis Obin* (Nicanor and Satan as Nicanor), Antoine Coulon* (Satan), Marie (Magnus). The female roles were filled by Mme Adélaide Borghi-Mamo* (Olympia) and Mme Pauline Gueymard-Lauters* (Lilia). The score included several unusually impressive passages, for example, the orgy at the end of the first act (I, 6), Lilia's "Credo" in the third act (III, 2), and the duet by Lilia and Hélios in act 4, scene 4.

BIBLIOGRAPHY: AEM III, 47-51; G. Jean-Aubry, "Villiers de l'Isle Adam and music," M&L 19 (38), 391-92; Alexis Jacob Azevedo, F. David (Paris: Heugel 1863), 79-80; René Brancour, Félicien David (Paris: Henri Laurens, n.d.), 78-85; Chouquet 417-18; DDO I, 552-54; EDS IV, 231-32; M. Escudier, "Théâtre Impérial de l'Opéra: reprise d'Herculanum," FM 32 (5 July 1868), 205; idem, "Reprise d'Herculanum," FM 25 (12 May 1861), 145; "Herculanum: première représentation," Le Ménestrel 26 (6 March 1859), 105-6; (13 March 1859), 113-15; (27 March 1859), 131; Lajarte II, 225-226; Moniteur universel 65 (6 March 1859) 261-62; PBSW 222; Albert Vizentini, "Première Représentation (reprise) d'Herculanum," AM 8 (2 July 1868), 241-42.

Hérold, Louis-Joseph-Ferdinand (b. 28 January 1791, Paris; d. 19 January 1833, Thernes), composer, did not have a musical career planned for him, although his father was a musician, but he graviated toward the piano after the death of his father in 1802 and entered the Conservatoire to study this instrument under Adolphe Adam.* He distinguished himself by winning first prize in the piano competition of 1810, and it was agreed that he should study with Charles Catel and Etienne Méhul (see eighteenth-century volume for Catel and Méhul). Hérold learned rapidly, and he won the Prix de Rome in 1812 with his version of the contest cantata entitled *Mlle de la Vallière*.

The young musician left for Italy in November 1812 and passed three profitable and happy years in Rome and then in Naples, where he wrote *La Gioventù di Enrico Quinto*. François Boïeldieu had become interested in Hérold and decided to help him on his return to Paris by inviting him to collaborate on *Charles de France* (see eighteenth-century volume for Boïeldieu). This work was mounted at the Opéra-Comique on 18 June 1816, and it provided an auspicious start for the composer's career in addition to persuading the management of the Opéra-Comique to give him the libretto of *Les Rosières* to set for performance by the end of the year. He finished *La Clochette* next, and it was scheduled for staging in 1817. This last of his first three compositions at the Opéra-Comique established his status as a reliable and talented composer.

A lull followed in Hérold's work for the theatre, however, and he created a few pieces for the piano until it was suggested over a year later that he set *Le Premier venu* for the Opéra-Comique. He accepted the commission against his better judgment, because the libretto was ordinary, and its story had already been used for a play still running at the Louvois Theatre. Hérold did not wish to antagonize the director of the Opéra-Comique, and he did the score for a late 1818 opening in the hope that something better would appear. He waited patiently again, but nothing was forthcoming. Eager to get on with a project for the theatre, he decided to resurrect and to revise *Les Troqueurs* (1753), which had been the delight of the previous century. Yet even this gambit failed in 1819, because the work had so little in common with Restoration tastes and interests. He seemed justified in believing that he was the victim of some cruel plot when his next piece, *L'Amour platonique*, was withdrawn before it had a chance to succeed or to fail. Then, in 1820, Planard gave him L'Auteur mort et vivant. It failed. Hérold refused to pick up his pen for the theatre during the next three years.

In 1823, the management of the Opéra-Comique sent Hérold to Italy to recruit singers, and he returned to Paris from this trip stimulated by the new surroundings through which he had passed. His Le Muletier with a libretto by P. de Kock was his first success at the Opéra-Comique. It was presented on 12 May 1823. Then, on 8 September 1823, he did his first score for the Opéra, Lasthénie,* which was followed by the almost political Vendôme en Espagne* at the same theatre on 5 December 1823. After a few mediocre titles at the Opéra-Comique, he had his most successful work to date also given here, Marie (1826), but his appointment as chorusmaster at the Opéra prevented him from exploiting the streak of good fortune that he seemed about to enjoy.

He did not give up the struggle to produce a hit at the Opéra, however, but his contributions to the repertory here lacked the spark necessary to the production of an inspired and superior piece of work. These compositions included four ballets: Astolphe et Joconde* of 1827, which had some musical moments; La Somnambule* of 1827, the most successful of these later creations; La Fille mal gardée* of 1829, a revision of Dauberval's 1786 ballet; and La Belle au bois dormant* of 1829, which was considered a success, although it was withdrawn after fewer than 50 billings.

When Hérold returned to the Opéra-Comique, he did his best work for the stage. L'Illusion (1829) had all the melancholy music needed to support its emotional and romantic appeal. Zampa (1831) assured its author a place among the immortals of comic opera. Its overture was given on the program inaugurating the third salle Favart in 1898. Le Pré aux clercs (1832) was selected for the first bill at the second salle Favart in 1840, and it was revived again at the time of the Exposition Universelle of 1855. It had its 100th performance on 10 October 1871 on the program designed to remedy the financial difficulties of the Opéra-Comique after its troubles during the Commune. It reached its 1,229th presentation by 1880.

Hérold had a busy career in the course of contributing so many compositions to the two principal musical theatres of France during the Restoration, but it was certain individual works rather than his entire production that won him audiences and kept his name alive. His trip to Italy influenced him profoundly, and the Italian quality of his music became more evident as time progressed. Yet his style is energetic, and his desire for accent and rhythm fills his work with syncopation and melodies beginning on the first beat of the measure. His lasting compositions were all produced initially at the Opéra-Comique, since his coloratura style was more indigenous to this stage at this time. Also, since his successes were gained in his later years, and because he died at such an early age, it is to be regretted that he did not have the good fortune to find better librettos sooner.

La Fille mal gardée was revived for a single performance at the Garnier theatre on 23 February 1922, its 79th presentation, and Le Roman d'Estelle of 9 March 1916 used music by Hérold in its score.

BIBLIOGRAPHY: Hector Berlioz, Les Musiciens et la musique (Paris: Calmann-Lévy, n.d.), 131-41; Raoul Duhamel, "Ferdinand Hérold," RM 14 (1933), 278-90; EGC 187-88; Fétis IV, 308-11; GE XIX, 1198-9; HBM 165-68; Benoît Jean Baptiste Jouvin, Hérold, sa vie et ses oeuvres (Paris: Au Ménestrel, 1868); Lajarte II, 105-6, 125, 128, 132-33; LXIX IX, 210; Gérald Mannoni, "Hérold et la danse," SDLD 137 (October 1981), 42-43; MPPA 195-214; PBSW 55, 63, 143, 184; Arthur Pougin, Hérold, biographie critique (Paris: H. Laurens, 1906); Wks 3198, 3207, 3223, 3291, 3501, 2576, 3786, 3990, 4472, 4660, 4662, 4721, 4861, 4947, 5063, 5483, 5658, 5674, 5806, 5946, 5987, 10670, 11121, 11204, 12496, 14098.

L'Heureux Retour was billed as ballet in a single act with music arranged by Henri Berton, Louis Persuis, and Rodolphe Kreutzer and choreography created by Louis-Jacques Milon, except for the last divertissement by Pierre Gardel (see eighteenth-century volume for Berton, Persuis, Kreutzer, Milon, divertissement and Gardel). It had its premire on 25 July 1815 and was given at the Opéra on a dozen dates during the year of its first presentation. In 1816, it was included on the free program of 24 August and then dropped from the repertory. As its dates might indicate, the prime purpose of the work was to welcome the Bourbons back to Paris.

L'Heureux Retour is set in a Paris square, where the National Guard is being mobilized to serve as an escort for the returning king. Caroline Deschamps fears that her sweetheart Edouard might be killed in the service of this outfit, but her mother assures her of his safety (sc. 1-2). A deputation of women from the markets of Paris enter singing "Rendez-nous notre père de Gand," and their dancing attracts a crowd of curious onlookers. The king passes through the square. A wounded member of the old guard forgets Napoleon in his joy and shouts, "Long live the king!" A restauranteur provides free wine to toast His Majesty. Caroline asks the old guardsman about her sweetheart, and he recognizes his picture; he reports that Edouard is dead. Caroline is led away in tears (sc. 3). A parade forms, but it is dispersed by the old guard in retreat; an English colonel enters with Edouard, who explains that he owes his life to the colonel (sc. 4-5). Caroline is filled with happiness and thanks the Englishman. The colonel insists upon marrying Caroline and Edouard, and he gives the bride a ring of great value (sc. 6-8).

The setting changes to the Tuileries, where there are dancing and singing to celebrate the restoration of the monarchy. Edouard and Caroline sing "Charmante Gabrielle" and execute a pas de deux. The curtain falls amidst cries of "long live the king!"

Mme Courtin filled the part of Caroline with Louis Mérante* and Mlle Saulnier as her parents. Elie did her sweetheart Edouard, and Louis Montjoie executed the part of the colonel (see eighteenth-century volume for Montjoie).

BIBLIOGRAPHY: AEM VII, 1781-83; Chouquet 386; DDOI, 560; Lajarte II, 85-86; Wks I, 1324.

Hillemacher, Paul Joseph Wilhelm (b. 29 November 1852, Paris; d. 13 August 1933, Versailles) and **Hillemacher, Joseph Edouard** (b. 10 June 1860, Paris; d. 2 June 1909, Paris), composers, were brothers who entrolled in the Conservatoire in their native city, where they distinguished themselves by winning a number of prizes including the Prix de Rome. They decided to collaborate, and they signed the fruits of their labors as P. L. Hillemacher. Their impressive production

included a quantity of songs and compositions for orchestra, but their titles also include two operas that were billed at the National Academy of Music: Orsola* of 21 May 1902 and Le Drac of 29 June 1942, which had had its world premiere at Karlsruhe on 14 November 1896 under the title of Der Flutgeist (see twentieth-century volume for Le Drac). Their contributions to the repertory at the Opéra-Comique included Circé of 17 April 1907 and Fra Angelico of 10 June 1924. This latter composition was in fact a work by Paul alone. Lucien had been dead since 1909.
BIBLIOGRAPHY: AEM VI, 397-99; BBD 749; ELM II, 470; Grove IV, 280; PBSW 87.

Holmes, Augusta (b. 16 December 1847, Paris; d. 28 January 1903, Paris), composer, baptized Mary Anne Holmes by her Irish parents, began life as a prodigy composing her own works and playing the piano at an unreasonably young age. Eventually, she became a pupil of César Franck* and launched her own career as a composer by winning a municipal music competition organized by the city of Paris. Her success with this work entitled Lutèce encouraged her to enter the same contest the following year, when she earned honorable mention with Les Argonautes. She kept herself in the public eye with subsequent successes, and, on 8 February 1895, she saw her La Montagne noire* billed at the Garnier Palace* with her own libretto. Also, she was one of the 28 composers whose music was played in the production of Danses de jadis et de naguère* on 22 September 1900.
BIBLIOGRAPHY: AEM VI, 648-50; BBD 766; ELM II, 482; Grove IV, 328-29.

Hugo, Victor-Marie (b. 26 February 1802, Besançon; d. 22 May 1885, Paris), writer, visited Italy and Spain as a boy because his father's military career took him to these countries during Napoleon's supremacy in Europe. He returned to Paris to finish his education after the political situation in Madrid became ominous for the French, and he began his literary career with occasional verse and a book of poetry in 1822.

Victor Hugo turned to the theatre in 1829 after the success of Alexandre Dumas père* at the Comédie-Française; his Hernani became the rallying point of the romantic school of writers only months later in 1830. His political differences with Napoleon III forced him into exile with the establishment of the Second Empire, but he returned in triumph to Paris after the creation of the Third Republic in 1870.

His literary production included historical novels and plays, and lyric and epic poetry, but he made only a single contribution to the Opéra, the libretto of La Esméralda* of 1836 which Louise Bertin* set. He might well have written other texts for the company, if they and their theatre had not been so firmly under the control of Napoleon III.

BIBLIOGRAPHY: P. Audiat, Ainsi vécut Victor Hugo (Paris: Hachette, 1947); J.-B. Barrère, Hugo, l'homme et l'oeuvre (Paris: Boivin, 1952); P. Berret, Victor Hugo (Paris: Garnier, 1927); P. and V. Glachant, Essai sur le théâtre de Victor Hugo (Paris: Hachette, 1902-3); Lajarte I, 155; Denis Mahaffey, A Concise Bibliography of French Literature (London and New York: Bowker, 1975), 167; Thieme I, 970-97.

Les Huguenots is a grand opera in five acts with music by Giacomo Meyerbeer,* a libretto by Eugène Scribe* and Emile Deschamps, and choreography by Filippo Taglioni* (see eighteenth-century volume for Taglioni). Deschamps' greatest effort was expended on the fourth act, for which Adolphe Nourrit* suggested the conclusion. It had its world premiere at the Royal Academy of Music on 29 February 1836; it enjoyed its 500th billing at the Opéra on 4 April 1876, and it was retained in the repertory until its 1,120th performance at the Garnier Palace* on 22 November 1936, more than a century since the first time it had been offered to the public. Louis Mérante* furnished new choreography for Meyerbeer's composiiton, when the famous impresario Léon Carvalho* revived it at the present opera house in Paris on 26 April 1875 with his wife as Queen Marguerite. Lapissida mounted his version of the work with choreogrpahy by Joseph Hansen* in 1897. An interesting incident in the history of Meyerbeer's masterpiece took place at the performance of 19 April 1881, when the director of the Opéra, M. Vaucorbeil, arranged for Les Huguenots to be heard in the subcellar of the theatre over the telephone. This was the first time that a live performance of a theatrical composition had been transmitted.

The action of Les Huguenots unfolds in France during the sixteenth century at the time of the religious wars. Specifically, the time is August 1572, and the king has just made an effort to reconcile the Protestant and Catholic factions by inducing the Catholic count de Nevers to invite the Huguenot Raoul de Nangis to a banquet at his château in Touraine. On this festive occasion celebrating the count de Nevers' coming marriage to Valentine de Saint-bris, daughter of the count de Saint-Bris, Raoul rises to toast love and to admit his own sudden love for an unknown lady whom he has encountered recently near the château of Amboise (I, 1-2). Raoul's manservant Marcel enters at this juncture and upbraids his master for sharing in the unbecoming self-indulgence tolerated by Catholics; he points to the evils of wine and song and terminates his tirade with a Protestant hymn attacking nuns, monks, and the pope (I, 3). A veiled woman enters the castle, and the count de Nevers leaves the festive gathering to speak with her. The guests spy upon her through a tapestry, and Raoul recognizes her as the lady of Amboise (I, 4-5). He believes that the veiled stranger must be the mistress of the count de Nevers, but she is in fact Valentine de Saint-Bris, whom the queen has sent to the count de Nevers to persuade him to release her from her promise to marry him. De Nevers returns to the banquet to announce with some asperity that his plans to marry Valentine de Saint-Bris have been canceled. A second development occurs when Urbain delivers a mysterious letter to Raoul. It asks him to keep a secret rendez-vous. De Retz and Cossé recognize the handwriting of the letter. It has been penned by Marguerite de Valois, sister of the kings of France. Raoul's prestige rises to new heights among the guests, and he is led away blindfolded to meet his unknown correspondent as a chorus in his honor closes the act (I, 6-7).

If the first act is carried by the male members of the cast, the second act presents the women involved in the intrigue, and the setting moves to the stately gardens of Chenonceaux. Here Queen Marguerite sings the praises of bountiful and beautiful Touraine, and Valentine assures her that the count de Nevers has agreed not to marry her. Valentine expresses her fears that she may not be able to marry Raoul because he is a Huguenot (II, 1-2). Marguerite and her attendants bathe in the Cher. Raoul is led in blindfolded. The queen and he are attracted to each other, but Marguerite refuses to betray Valentine or to jeopardize the royal effort to establish peace in the kingdom (II, 3-5). Raoul learns finally that he is speaking to the queen, and he promises unhesitatingly to marry the Catholic daughter of the count de Saint-Bris to help the cause of peace (II, 6). The nobility arrives at Chenonceaux to witness the wedding of Valentine and Raoul. Charles XI sends word that Saint-Bris and de Nevers are to go immediately to Paris, but they do not leave until they and Raoul have pledged their eternal friendship for each other. Also, they make arrangements to attend the imminent wedding, which never takes place. Raoul refuses suddenly to accept Valentine as his bride because he still believes that she is the mistress of the count de Nevers. He offers no explanation for his decision, which almost precipitates a quarrel in addition to leaving Queen Marguerite and rejected Valentine stupefied (II, 7-8).

The third act featuring the choruses and orchestra moves to the Pré aux Clercs area in Paris, and the set represents two taverns facing each other with a chapel in the center background. The Catholics and Protestants are hurling hostile remarks at each other from their respective taverns after Valentine's wedding cortege has entered the chapel. The wedding party reappears finally led by the groom, de Nevers, and the bride's father, Saint-Bris. Valentine remains inside the chapel to pray. Marcel enters to inform Saint-Bris that Raoul wishes to meet him on the field of honor. Saint-Bris accepts the challenge and initiates a plot to ambush Raoul on the way to the duel (III, 1). Curfew tolls, and Valentine leaves the chapel. She encounters Marcel in the darkness and warns him that his master is about to walk into a trap. She cautions that he should be escorted to the field of honor by a company of armed friends (III, 2-3). Marcel urges Raoul to postpone the encounter, but he refuses. Marcel, Raoul, and their two companions are attacked during their preparations for the combat, but Huguenots rush into aid them. Men and women pair out of the neighboring taverns to join the scuffle (III, 4). Queen Marguerite stops the riot, and Marcel asserts that Saint-Bris inspired the disorder. He points to a women on the steps of the chapel who will corroborate his allegations. Saint-Bris tears away her veil and discovers his daughter, Valentine. Marguerite explains to Raoul that Valentine has always loved him, even on the day that she came to de Nevers' château to escape an unwelcome marriage. Raoul's joy is short lived because de Nevers arrives to claim his bride and to leave Raoul sulking on the banks of the Seine (III, 5-6).

The fourth act of Les Huguenots is generally considered the most effective segment of the opera. It transpires in the count de Nevers' residence and opens with a touching aria often omitted from production in the interests of brevity. Valentine's sad complaint that her love for Raoul is a dream to be forgotten. Her lament is interrupted by Raoul's unannounced appearance before her to beg her pardon for his cruel rejection of her hand. Suddenly the couple hear the sounds of the count de Nevers returning home with his fellow conspirators, and Valentine is obliged to hide Raoul. The leaders of the Catholic faction unite in a plot to slay every Huguenot in Paris, and they swear to undertake this deed most foul as soon as midnight strikes. They plan to wear white scarves to identify themselves in the darkness. De Nevers breaks his sword and refuses to participate in this heartless slaughter. He is placed in custody (IV, 1-3). Saint-Bris assigns the conspirators to their posts, and three monks bless the weapons to be used (IV, 4-5). Raoul leaves his hiding place, but anxious Valentine detains him. The bells of Saint-Germain-l'Auverrois begin to peal at midnight, and the Saint-Barthélemy massacre begins before Raoul can spread the alarm (IV, 6).

The last act is often cut or even entirely omitted in some productions of Meyerbeer's opera, but it remains an integral portion of the composition and is certainly not a superfluous appendage. It is divided into two tableaux and opens with a ball celebrating the imminent marriage of Marguerite de Valois and Henri de Navarre. These festivities are taking place at the hôtel de Nesles when Raoul enters. He is bleeding severely from his wounds, but he is able to announce that the massacre of the Protestants has begun and that Coligny is dead (V, 1-2). The setting then shifts to a cloister where Raoul comes upon wounded Marcel. They are discussing the course of action they should take when Valentine enters wearing the white scarf of the Catholic faction. She offers to save them if they will renounce their religion at the Louvre. She adds that she is free now because de Nevers is dead. Raoul an Marcel refuse to abjure their Protestantism, and Valentine accepts their decision. Total reconciliation occurs when Marcel marries Valentine and Raoul before the altar and in the eyes of God. The Catholics break down the doors of the chapel and drag Valentine, Raoul, and Marcel outside to their deaths. Saint-Bris realizes that his soldiers have slain his daughter, and the curtain falls with Queen Marguerite trying to stop the bloodshed (V, 3-5).

This large-scale spectacle was filled with dramatic moments that offered almost countless possibilities to the composer, and Meyerbeer took full advantage of them to move his romantic spectators. The first act offered the orgy chorus, "A table, amis, à table" (I, 2) and Raoul's romance, "Plus blanche que la blanche hermine" (I, 2). The second act opened with Marguerite's memorable "O beau pays de la Touraine" (II, 1) and moved directly to the bathers' chorus, "Jeunes beautés, sous ce feuillage" (II, 3). Then, in the fourth act, Meyerbeer scaled new heights in the scene of the blessing of the daggers (IV, 3) and the immortal duet of Valentine and Raoul starting with the former's "Où vas-tu?" (IV, 6). Lastly, there was the touching trio in the wedding scene of the final act beginning with Marcel's question to the lovers, "Savez-vous qu'en joignant vos mains dans les ténèbres..." (V, 4).

The artistes who shared in the 160,000 franc production authorized by Duponchel included Mlle Cornélie Falcon* as Valentine and Mme Julie Dorus-Gras* as Marguerite opposite Adolphe Nourrit* (Raoul), Levasseur (Marcel), Dérivis* (Nevers), and Serda (Saint-Bris). The 13 runs enjoyed by Les Huguenots allowed nearly every singer of note in the company between 1836 and 1936 to perform in it. More than 50 stars have sung the role of Valentine, for example, and the last interpreters of Raoul have included John Sullivan, who made his debut in this part on 28 July 1914, Georges Thill, and Raoul Jobin (see twentieth-century volume for Thill and Jobin). It may be of interest to note that Albert Huberty was cast as Marcel at the

Opera between 1920 and 1936, although other artistes also appeared in this part from time to time during this post World War I period.

BIBLIOGRAPHY: Neil Cole Arvin, Eugène Scribe and the French Theatre, 1815-60 (Cambridge: Harvard University Press, 1924), 207-8, 212; Henri Blaze de Bury, Meyerbeer et son temps (Paris: Levy Frères, 1865), 114-32; Chouquet 399; Henri de Curzon, Meyerbeer (Paris: Renouard, n.d.), 45-56; DDO I, 564-65; Christhard Frese, Dramaturgie der grossen Opern Giacomo Meyerbeers (Berlin-Lichterfelde: Robert Lienau, 1970), 90-152; Edgar Istel, "Act IV of Les Huguenots," MQ 22 (1936), 87-90; JB 147-52; KCOB 725-40; Lajarte II, 152-53; Moniteur universel 67 (7 March 1836), 417-18; Giacomo Meyerbeer, Briefwechsel und Tagebücher (Berlin: Walter de Gryter, 1970) III, 509, 679-80; NMO 178-217; OQE 153-54; PBSW 55-56, 223; SSBO 179-80; SW 115-18.

I

L'Ile des pirates is a pantomime-ballet in four acts with a libretto by Adolphe Nourrit* and Louis Henry and choreography by Henry. Oreste Carlini* wrote the music for the first act and the pas de deux in the third act, while Casimir Gide* provided the remainder of the score for the last three acts except for two passages by Giocchino Rossini* and a sonata by Ludwig van Beethoven.* The sets for the first two acts were created by Léon Feuchères, Charles Séchan, and Jules Diéterle, while Cambon and Philastre provided the scenery for the last two acts. The ballet had its world premiere at the Royal Academy of Music on 12 August 1835, when it was presented with Rossini's <u>Moïse</u>* on a program that returned the unremarkable sum of 4,917 francs, 60 centimes, to the box office.

The action of the ballet begins in the Roman states of Italy a short distance from the seashore, and the setting represents the formal garden of a villa where an orchestra is playing, and a nearby beach and the sea are visible through tall trees. The hurried goings and comings of the master gardener and his apprentices indicate that an event of importance is about to take place at the Montalbano villa (I, 1). Isabella, the widow of the marquis of Montalbano, and her two daughters approve the floral arrangements, but Mathilde's preoccupied and melancholy air indicate that the marchioness' younger daughter is unhappy over the imminent marriage arranged for her by her mother (I, 2). The Montalbano family enters the villa, and a naval officer appears. He is obviously surprised by the lavish preparations being made for what is obviously to be a wedding, and he writes a hasty note to one of the marchioness' daughters who return to the garden before long. When Mathilde sees Ottavio, she faints because she has been misled into believing that he has been killed in a duel. Only the false report of her sweetheart's death induced her to agree to marry Moncaldi, a foreign dignitary. Unfortunately, the two lovers are forced to separate without being able to formulate a plan to forestall the Mathilde-Moncaldi marriage (I, 3-6). Moncaldi enters with his future mother-in-law to distribute presents among the villagers who execute a series of dances to honor the coming marriage (I, 7). A group of pilgrims approach Moncaldi to ask for alms, and one of the mendicants whispers into his ear. The dancing comes to a halt, and the marchioness affixes her daughter's bridal veil to her forehead. The distraught girl announces abruptly that she has no intention of marrying Moncaldi, who reacts by throwing his handkerchief into the air. A shot rings out in the direction of the orchestra. Armed men fill the garden. They are in disguise, but it is apparent that they are being led by Archipel, a local brigand. the intruders seize and run off with the young women, and Ottavio is wounded seriously when he attempts to rescue Mathilde (I, 8-10).

The scene shifts to the deck of a pirate ship anchored off one of the islands on the Barbary Coast. It is dawn and the crew is asleep except for the watch. Rosalie persuades her sister Mathilde not to leap into the sea, and the two girls begin to weep in desperation (II, 1). Mathilde is reassured when a Dutch sailor manages to give her a note explaining that Ottavio has recovered from his wounds and is on his way to rescue her. Encouraged Mathilde recovers her wits and decides to use her wiles to circumvent Akbar's persistent advances (II, 2). Akbar, known previously as Moncaldi, inspects his ship and pays off his pirate crew for their loyalty, but he discovers that the Dutchman in his crew has betrayed him. He orders him flogged, and his wife begs Mathilde to intervene on his behalf before he is scourged to death. Mathilde agrees to help the poor man, but Akbar is unmoved by her plea. The Dutchman's son, a cabin boy on the pirate ship, is outraged by Akbar's cruelty, and he tries to stab the leader of the buccaneers. Akbar is amused and touched by the boy's courage, and he releases his father while rewarding the son with a draught of wine and a vermeil goblet (II, 3).

The pirates sit down to eat and to be entertained by a Creole drummer and a negro flautist, but a quarrel erupts on the afterdeck, and one of the pirates slays his assailant. Akbar shoots the survivor forthwith in the name of pirate justice, and order is restored promptly. the merrymaking resumes and is reaching new heights when a stranger clambers aboard ship. He is Ottavio in disguise, and Mathilde recognizes him (I, 4-7). Ottavio deceives the pirates, however, and he is received into their infamous brotherhood. A general celebration before the mast marks his acceptance as a member of the crew (II, 8).

The third act is set in the women's compound on the pirates' island where Ottavio is selecting the two female companions allotted to him by pirate law. Inevitably he selects Mathilde and Rosalie. Thwarted Akbar has to accept Ottavio's choice because it is ratified by the brotherhood of pirates. A ceremonial parade of women living in the enclave terminates the act (I, 1-3).

Akbar has summoned Ottavio to his tent to try to purchase Mathilde and Rosalie from him. Ottavio refuses to sell his wards, and the pirate leader challenges him to a duel to decide the ownership of the sisters (IV, 1). The noise of the rivals' clashing sabers attracts the other pirates when the fighting moves into the open (IV, 2-3). Mathilde begs Akbar to lay down his sword, but she only irritates him, and he tries to strike her. The pirates now interfere to remind their chief that the two women belong to Ottavio by law. Angry Akbar threatens to ignite an adjourning powder magazine (IV, 4-6). The pirates have to set aside their internal differences at this moment, however, because the sound of hostile cannon is heard. The reconciled buccaneers rush off to intercept the common enemy (IV, 7).

The setting now moves to the beach, where the enemy fleet is maneuvering offshore. The Dutch sailor threatened by Akbar has spiked the guns on the pirate ship. The outlaws' vessel is sunk by the enemy, and Ottavio joins the landing party from the invading fleet. He takes Akbar prisoner, but the pirate leader is able to free himself long enough to stab himself. He dies at the feet of Mathilde, who has rushed to her hero's side (IV, 8-11).

L'Ile des pirates was not an exceptionally popular work, but its exotic subject and spectacular sets kept it alive at the Opéra until 6 July 1838, when it was dropped from the repertory after its 24th performance at the Royal Academy of Music. M. Henry was quite disappointed in the lack of enthusiasm shown to his work, and it was not long before he returned to his home in Naples, where he accepted an invitation to join the company of the San Carlo opera house. The cast of the ballet was distinguished despite its lack of impact upon Parisian audiences: Joseph Mazilier* (Ottavio), Franziska Elssler* (Mathilde), Amélie Legallois* (the marchioness Isabelle), Louis Montjoi (Akbar), and Térèse Elssler (Rosalie) (see eighteenth-century volume for Montjoie). Pauline Montessu* filled the role of the Creole in the second act. The libretto reports the names of 110 extras appearing as peasants and disguised pirates in the first act, while 72 sailors and cabin boys from various regions of Europe, Asia, and Africa were used in the second act. The Elssler sisters executed a pas de deux in the third act.

BIBLIOGRAPHY: BOP 308; Lajarte II, 151; PBR 99.

Illica, Luigi (b. 9 May 1857, Castell' Arquato; d. 16 December 1919, Colombarone), Italian librettist, ran away from home and school to go to sea at an early age, and he found himself involved in naval combat against the Turks before he reached age 20. He gave up his romantic maritime career to settle in Milan in 1879, and in 1881 he moved to Bologna. Here he started a republican literary journal with the help of Carducci, but he returned to Milan in 1882 to publish his first volume of verse and to collaborate on the creation of a play. The success of this latter work induced him to continue to write for the theatre.

The poet-playwright-journalist's first libretto was done in partnership with Francesco Pozza for Smareglia. The relative success of this work entitled II Vassallo di Szigeth induced him to continue as a librettist, and eventually he collaborated on three well-known operas for which Giacomo Puccini* created the scores: La Vie de Bohème, La Tosca, and Madame Butterfly (see twentieth-century volume for La Vie de Bohème, La

Tosca, and Madame Butterfly). These three compositions have been produced at the Opéra in Paris with the usual success that they have come to enjoy elsewhere. Later, Illica wrote for Giordano (Andrea Chenier, 1896) and Mascagni (Iris, 1898; Isabeau, 1911), but these titles have not yet been billed at the Garnier Palace.*

BIBLIOGRAPHY: PBSW 184; SW 137-38, 210-11, 222-23.

d'Indy, Vincent (b. 27 March 1851, Paris; d. 1 December 1931, Paris), compsoer, was raised by his paternal grandmother, who gave him his first music lessons and then placed him under the tutelage of the pianist Marmontel at the proper time. When the youth was sixteen, he came upon Hector Berlioz'* writings on instrumentation, and he was so excited by this composer's revelations that he decided to become a professional musician. The Franco-Prussian War interrupted his progress, but, as soon as peace was restored, he set out to learn all that he could about the music and musicians of the day. He became friendly with Pasdeloup, who agreed to play his first compositions; he studied at the Conservatoire; he played piano, horn, and drums in the pit of the Théâtre-Italien. Next he traveled to Germany, where he met Franz Liszt, and where he became familiar with Richard Wagner's* music.

It was during this period in d'Indy's life that he wrote his first piece for the theatre, Attendez-moi sous l'orme, with a text based upon the eighteenth-century play by Regnard with the same title. It was a curious choice of subject, but its librettist was a friend of d'Indy, and the work was produced at the Opéra-Comique on 11 February 1882.

After this first contribution to the theatre, the composer was more inclined to incorporate his personal tastes and prejudices into his writings, and it is almost possible to follow the evolution of his thought and beliefs by tracing the attitudes developed in his works. His Le Chant de la cloche composed between 1879 and 1883, was a faithful echo of Wagner and Parsifal; it was suggested by a poem by Friedrich Schiller with the same name (see twentieth-century volume for Le Chant de la cloche and Parsifal). Next came Fervaal,* done between 1882 and 1895 and revealing his renunciation of Germanism through a resolve to return to his own national roots in the manner endorsed by Maurice Barrès. It was also the time of his Symphonie cévanole, L'Etranger,* and creative summers in the colorful Cévannes. Later he would reflect his religious convictions in La Légende de St. Christophe (see twentieth-century volume for La Légende de St. Christophe).

The following catalogue indicates the dates of the world premieres of d'Indy's works at the Théâtre de la Monnaie in Brussels and of their premieres at the Opéra. All three of d'Indy's operas had their world premieres in Brussels, while his two ballets were danced for the first time in Paris. Istar was presented initially at the Châtelet Theatre in the French capital, whereas La Légende de St. Christophe had its world premiere at the Opéra (see twentieth-century volume for Istar).

Opera	Brussels	Opéra
L'Etranger	7 January 1903	1 December 1903
Fervaal	12 March 1897	31 December 1912
Le Chant de la cloche	21 November 1912	13 January 1916
La Légende de St. Christophe		9 June 1920
Istar		10 July 1924

BIBLIOGRAPHY: AEM VI, 1199-1210; BBD 796-97; DEC 289-92; Norman Demuth, Vincent d'Indy (London: Rockcliffe, 1951); EDS VI, 545-47; ELM II, 550-57; Grove IV, 467-76; MMFM 34-40; NEO 185; PBSW 184-85; Gustave Samazeuilh, "Le Centenaise de Vincent d'Indy," L'Opéra de Paris 3 (n.d.), 32-34; Thompson 865-68; TWT 390-94.

Ipsiboé was the last of 33 operas for which Rodolphe Kreutzer wrote the music (see eighteenth-century volume for Kreutzer). The libretto for this opera in four acts was done by Alexandre Moline de Saint-Yon,* and its dances were created by Pierre Gardel (see eighteenth-century volume for Gardel). Pierre Cicéri* provided the sets for its world premiere at the Royal Academy of Music on 31 March 1824, but it was not very successful.

Its action was based on a popular contemporary novel by the viscount d'Arlincourt dealing with the struggle between the Bozons and Bérengers in twelfth-century Provence. The opera was harmed more than helped by the overabundance of night scenes it contained, and it had to be dropped from the repertory after its 13th performance on 28 July 1824.

The curtain rises in the first act to disclose a pleasant countryside with a lighthouse on the heights and the château of the duke de Solamire below it. The latter swears to his men that they will return Provence to the Fernands after banishing the usurper Zénaïre. They also vow to destroy Ipsiboé, a sorceress living in the lighthouse (I, 1-2). A group of villagers advances upon Ipsiboé's dwelling covered with magic symbols (I, 3) despite Alamède's plea that they spare her because she has raised him from the cradle. They agree if he and his friend Izorin will persuade the witch to leave the country (I, 3). Alamède discloses that Ipsiboé has promised to tell him the secret of his birth this very evening among the tombs of the Fernands at Aix. He adds that he has fallen in love with Raimond's daughter, Zénaïre, and it is for this reason that he has dressed himself as a troubadour. He wishes to sing of the queen's beauty wherever he goes after leaving Ipsiboé (I, 4). Zénaïre enters with the duke de Solamire, and she demands to see Ipsiboé. The villagers dance for her entertainment (I, 5), and she recognizes Alamède as the man who saved her life and with whom she has fallen in love. She requests him to recite a poem in honor of constancy, but she hides her feelings so well that Alamède does not notice her love for him. He sings his poem, and Zénaïre realizes that he is complaining of her indifference. She asks him to join her court (I, 6). A storm arises, and the hieroglyphics on Ipsiboé's lighthouse gleam as if aflame, but Zénaïre is not intimidated (I, 7). Ipsiboé herself appears against a curtain of fire, and she predicts that death will visit Zénaïre (I, 8).

The setting shifts to the neglected burial grounds of the ancient kings of Provence, where Ipsiboé swears to restore the Fernands to the throne in the person of Alamède (II, 1). The duke assures her that they will succeed because he has won the confidence of Zénaïre (II, 2). The duke overhears Alamède rejoicing that he has aroused the queen's interest, and he reproaches him for neglecting his family honor. Alamède debates between love and duty; he decides to follow the honorable path by ignoring his love for Zénaïre (II, 1-4). Ipsiboé tells him that it is time for him to save his country, and he accepts this task without understanding exactly what he is supposed to do. She calls her army from hiding (II, 5), however, and her officers receive Alamède as a knight. Ipsiboé presents him with his badge of leadership (II, 6). Ipsiboé opens the secret tunnel leading from the graveyard to Zénaïre's throne room, where a group of warriors is seen advancing toward the queen with daggers in their hands. They take her away. Alamède is about to rush to her assistance, but the witch leads him into the vault (II, 7).

Ipsiboé and Alamède arrive in the gardens of Zénaïre's palace. He does not understand the significance of the revolt against the queen, but Ipsiboé warns him that he must dismiss Zénaïre from his mind. The duke informs his accomplice that the queen is planning a counteroffensive; Ipsiboé promises Alamède that a wise man in the nearby hermitage will tell him his family name at six o'clock. She leaves after ordering her ward to meet her in the gardens after sunset, and Alamède cannot conceal his impatience, because he has failed once again to discover the secret of his birth (III, 1-3). Zénaïre appears with her court; she calls to Alamède, and he cannot resist her. He lingers to watch the ballet, and, after the performance, the queen announces that a celebration will be held in the palace. Alamède sings of his sorrow over his humble birth; Zénaïre wishes that he were a knight worthy of her hand. Suddenly, Ipsiboé's horn sounds a summons for the youth, but he ignores it (III, 5), and dawn finds him still in the gardens with Zénaïre. Izorin announces that the palace guard has defected, and Ipsiboé's horn sounds again, but Alamède resolves to protect the queen (III, 6-7). The duke enters with his soldiers, who pay homage to Alamède, and the duke himself addresses the poet as "noble count Edgart." Alamède decides to fight for the glory of his name, and Ipsiboé reminds him that Zénaïre is his chief foe. When his supporters put the royal palace to the torch and call for the queen's death, however, he swears to protect her (III, 8-9).

The last act depicts a lovely landscape with Ipsiboé's lighthouse in the background. The duke reveals that the queen has been deposed, although she has escaped. Alamède enters supporting Zénaïre. The duke's soldiers advance to seize the tired couple, but Alamède draws his sword. He displays the badge of his authority and ordres the attackers to lay down their arms. They respect his command (IV, 1-2).

The two female roles were filled initially by Mme Rose Branchu (Ipsiboé) and Mlle Gerard Grassari* (Zénaïre), and the male parts were created by Prosper Dérivis (the duke de Solamire), Adolphe Nourrit* (Alamède), and Henri Dabadie* (Izorin) (see eighteenth-century volume for Branchu and Dérivis).

BIBLIOGRAPHY: DDO I, 585; Lajarte II, 108; Moniteur universel 93 (2 April 1824), 370.

Isaac, Adèle (b. 1854, Calais; d. 1915, Paris), French soprano, studied under the direction of Gilbert Duprez* and made her theatrical debut at a charity performance in Paris during the Franco-Prussian War.

After the cessation of hostilities, Mme Isaac was billed as Marie in La Fille du régiment at the Opéra-Comique on 1 July 1873, and she returned to this same theatre to create Stella, Olympia, and Antonia at the premiere of Les Contes d'Hoffmann* at the Comique on 10 February 1881.

The soprano made her first appearance at the Garnier Palace* as Marguerite in Mefistofele* and Gilda in Rigoletto* at a gala on 5 April 1883. This same year, she was cast as Ophélie in Hamlet,* Marguerite in Faust,* and the countess in Le Comte Ory.* Now firmly established, she remained at the Opéra during 1884 to sing the parts of Zerline in Don Juan,* the queen in Les Huguenots,* and Isabelle in Robert le Diable,* and to execute the title-role of Françoise de Rimini.* Her 1885 roles at the Garnier included Mathilde in Guillaume Tell* and Xaina in Le Tribut de Zamora.*

Mme Isaac retired from the stage after her marriage in 1888.

BIBLIOGRAPHY: EDS VI, 617-18; EFC 157; Lermina 810; Martin 194; PBSW 185; SW 73-75, 84-88, 99-100, 105-6, 115-18, 184-85, 412.

Isnardon, Jacques (b. 1860, Algiers; d. 1930, Marseilles), French singer, made his debut as a tenor in Montpellier in 1884, but he had shifted to bass roles by the time that he sang his first role at the Opéra-Comique in Paris on 23 February 1885. Also, he was hired as a bass, when he was given a contract to perform at the Théâtre Royal de la Monnaie in Brussels during 1886.

After appearances in Italy and Monte Carlo, M. Isnardon received an invitation to sing Méphistophélès in Faust* at the Garnier Palace* on 15 August 1892, but he left the Opéra to create the part of Landrinier in Xavière at the Opéra-Comique on 26 November 1895. He was cast as Colline in La Vie de Bohème and as Don Juan in Beaucoup de bruit pour rien on 13 June 1898 and 24 March 1899, when these two works by Giacomo Puccini* and Puget, respectively were performed for the first time at this theatre. He was also billed as Bazile in Le Barbier de Séville,* and Sulpice in La Fille du régiment, and as Lothario in Mignon* by Ambroise Thomas* at the Comique.

M. Isnardon served on the faculty of the Conservatoire in Paris for a time after his retirement from the stage, but it was not long before he left the French capital to settle in Marseilles and to found a music school there.

BIBLIOGRAPHY: PBSW 185; SW 480; WOC 177, 181, 226, 304.

J

Jambon, Marcel (b. 1838, Barbezieux; d. 1908, Paris), French artist, learned the art of painting scenery under the direction of Rubé. He became his master's partner before long, and, after Rubé's death in 1899, he opened his own studio. His son-in-law, Marcel Bailly, became his partner. He produced so many sets for the Opéra that he was finally commissioned to organize the storehouse where the Opéra stored its sets in the boulevard Berthier. So much material was involved in this project that Jambon managed to have a railway installed between the warehouse and the Garnier Palace* to facilitate the shuttling of sets.

Some of the sets created by Jambon alone or with Bailly were used in the following works:

Composer	Work
Saint-Saëns	Ascanio (1890), tabl. 3, 6
Wagner	La Walkyrie (1893), a. 2
Massenet	Thaïs (1894), tabl. 1, 5, 6, 7
Verdi	Othello (1894), a. 1
Lomon	Djelma (1894)
Holmes	La Montagne noire (1895)
Brumeau	Messidor (1897), a. 4
Vidal	La Burgonde (1898), a. 1, 2, 3

Méhul	Joseph (1899)
Chabrier	Briséis (1899)
Saint-Saëns	Les Barbares (1901)
Leoncavallo	Paillasse (1902)
Mozart	L'Enlèvement au serail (1903)
D'Indy	L'Etranger (1903)
Marty	Daria (1905)
Massenet	Ariane (1906), a. 1, 2, 5
Wagner	Le Crépuscule des dieux (1908), a. 2
Gounod	Faust (1908), a. 3
Saint-Saëns	Henry VIII (1909)

BIBLIOGRAPHY: PBSW 185; SW passim.

Javotte was a ballet in one act and three tableaux with a score by Camille Saint-Saëns* and a scenario by J.-L. Croze. It had its world premiere at the Grand theatre in Lyon on 3 December 1896. It was brought to Paris on 23 October 1899 to fill a billing at the Opéra-Comique. Here, it enjoyed 31 presentations with choreography by Mme Mariquita, ballet master in the rue Favart between 1898 and 1920. It was staged next at the Opéra for the first time on 5 February 1909 in choreography by Léo Staats.*

The ballet opens in a village square, where a holiday is being celebrated by dancing couples. Jean refuses to dance because he is waiting for his sweetheart, Javotte. When they appear upon the scene, the latter's parents report to the local constable that their daughter is missing, but Javotte is seen running toward Jean at this very moment. Vespers call a halt to the dancing, and Jean and Javotte are left alone in the village square with a few drinkers. She begins to weep because she has left her house against her parents' wishes. Remorseful, she bids Jean goodnight and returns to her father and mother, who forgive her because she admits her disobedience (tabl. 1).

The setting shifts to a room in Javotte's house, where she is performing tasks assigned to her as punishment. Her parents leave for the festival after locking Javotte in the house, where the girl continues to work dutifully but despondently. She hears a rap on a window. It is Jean. The reunited lovers engage in a wild waltz. They knock everything over and then decide to go to the village square. They leave an instant before Javotte's parents return to find their home in complete disorder. The constable enters to announce that he has apprehended Javotte and Jean, but his prisoners are two different people. The annoyed parents attack the constable because they believe that he is trying to play a joke on them (tabl. 2).

Night has fallen, but the square is illuminated for the selection of the Queen of the Ball. There are three finalists for the title, but they are so evenly matched that the crowd calls for Javotte to enter the contest. She agrees and wins first prize. Her parents appear at this very moment, and Jean and Javotte try in vain to hide. Jean confesses his guilt, and he begs for Javotte's hand in marriage. Her mother convinces her father that Jean is a good match for their daughter, and it is agreed that the young couple may wed. The bride and groom dance a pas de deux, and the curtain falls after an animated and happy ensemble (tabl. 3).

Saint-Saëns work proved quite popular over the years at the Opéra, where it was accepted into the repertory on 5 September 1909 and revived in 1919 and 1935 for a total of 44 presentations. Albert Aveline* did new choreography for its revival and its 33rd presentation on 14 October 1935. The principal roles in the ballet were created by Carlotta Zambelli* (Javotte), Olga Soutzo (the mother), Léo Staats (Jean), and Girodier (the father).

BIBLIOGRAPHY: *Jean Bonnerot,* <u>C. Saint-Saëns, 1835-1921; sa vie et son oeuvre</u> *(Paris: A. Durandet fils, 1922), 163-65, 170; BOP 148-50; CB 533-36; René Dumesnil,* <u>La Musique contemporaine en France</u> *(Paris: Armand Colin, 1930) I, 12-15 and II, 64-66; Gabriel Fauré,* <u>Opinions musicales</u> *(Paris: Rieder, 1930), 131-32; James Harding,* <u>Saint-Saëns and His Circle</u> *(London: Chapman &*

Hall, 1965), 202, 204; Arthur Hervey, Saint-Saëns (Westport: Conn.: Greenwood Press, 1970), 77; Watson Lyle, Camille Saint-Saëns, His Life and Art (Westport, Conn.: Greenwood Press, 1970), 170; Otto Neitzel, Camille Saint-Saëns (Berlin: Harmonie, 1899), 61-64; PBSW 155; SS 157; Stoullig XXXV (1909), 6-9; SW 289-90; VBO 44-45; WOC 207.

Jeanne d'Arc was billed as an opera in four acts and six tableaux with words and music by Auguste Mermet.* It had its world premiere at the National Academy of Music on 5 April 1876.

The opera opens in the village square of Domrémy with a chorus of young girls singing beneath an ancient oak. Their song deals with the legend surrounding the tree (I, 1), and Jacques d'Arc reproaches them for their inappropriate behavior in time of war. Gaston de Metz informs his soldiers and the inhabitants of Arc that the English have conquered France and are about to take Orleans. He curses Queen Isabeau for having betrayed the country, and he laments the suffering that the population has endured. The distant sky is red with flames, and the people pray for protection against the pitiless invader. Jeanne calls upon her compatriots to have faith in God; she announces that the English leader Salisbury is dead. She predicts that a virgin on a white horse will rescue France (I, 2-3). Richard enters on his way to Vaucouleurs; he discloses that Orleans is about to be surrendered to the English. Jeanne disputes his words, and he is thunderstuck to learn that she knows the details of Salisbury's death (I, 4). Jeanne informs Gaston that she must go to Vaucouleurs because it is time for her to rescue France. She reveals that Saint Catherine, Saint Marguerite, and the archangel Michael have ordered her to save the dauphin, but Gaston reminds her that she lacks the strength to lift a sword. She is firm in her intentions, however, and he agrees to lead her to the prince (I, 5). The act closes with Jeanne absorbed in prayer, while a celestial choir reminds her to abide by the will of God (I, 6).

Richard is lamenting the dauphin's indifference to the fate of France when he appears with his mistress Agnès at the castle of Chinon (II, 1). He sings a love song to her; he describes his lack of concern about Orleans (II, 1). Richard informs the prince that he has brought Jeanne to speak with him, but he answers that she is a creature of Satan. He refuses to see her, but the astrologer Maître Jean recalls that Merlin has predicted that a virgin will come from a forest of oak to save France. The dauphin replies that a celebration for Agnès is the order of the day, and he drinks a toast to his mistress. Minstrels entertain the court (II, 3-5). Le Bar-de-Duc approaches to announce that the English are attacking; he falls dead, and Gaston suggests that they listen to the maid from Arc. The dauphin decides to test Jeanne, and he puts Lore on the throne (II, 6). Jeanne enters and berates Lore for attempting to deceive her. She turns to her sovereign and reminds him that his future is in the hands of God. She convinces him to follow her, although Richard and Gaucourt are certain that she is Satan's emissary (II, 7).

The third act shifts to the French camp near Blois, where Richard urges Agnès to destroy Jeanne before Jeanne can betray Charles. He swears to Agnès that Jeanne is an imposter and the mistress of Gaston de Metz. Maître Jean reads in the stars that Jeanne will lead Charles to the altar at Rheims, where he will receive the crown of France; he notes that the death of sacrilegious Isabeau is also predicted in the heavens (III, 1). Jeanne wonders why the dauphin has failed to appear, and she falls asleep. Gaston comes upon her and declares his love for her so loudly that he awakens her (II, 2-3). Agnès overhears him and denounces Jeanne as a dissembler. Jeanne explains to her accuser that she has been deceived by Isabeau. Convinced, Agnès becomes Jeanne's ally (III, 4-5).

The second tableau of the third act depicts the camp at sunrise with the army complaining of being held at Blois instead of being ordered to Orleans. They begin to drink and to sing; they dance with the gypsies and idlers of the region (III, 6-7). Jeanne reprimands them and restores order. She dismisses Richard as the instigator of the orgy, and he threatens her (III, 8). She leaves with the army for Orleans (III, 8).

The last act is set beneath the walls of Orleans held by the English archers. Gaston has been taken prisoner by the enemy, and he shouts a warning for Jeanne to be careful (IV, 1-2). The maid is able to deliver Orleans, however, although she finds Gaston dead. An invisible choir of angels urges her to move to Reims for the coronation of Charles (IV, 3), and the scene shifts to the cathedral of this city. The dauphin vows to protect France, and he is anointed Charles VII. Jeanne bids him farewell and asks royal permission to return to her mother in Arc. The king asks her to stay with him until the English are expelled from France. She agrees to his request before looking up to behold a vision of a flaming pyre in the public square of Rouen (IV, 4).

Mermet's Jeanne d'Arc was a disappointment at the box office, and it had to be dropped after its 15th performance at the Opéra on 5 April 1876. The sets were impressive, especially those for the scene on the banks of the Loire (III, 8) and for the coronation scene in the cathedral at Reims (IV, 4), but the uninspired score was too ordinary to be overlooked by audiences. However, certain passages in the music were approved by critics and paying spectators alike, especially the chorus sung by the invisible angels (I, 6); Gaston's ecstatic "Elle est pure, elle est chaste et belle" (II, 2), sung to sleeping Jeanne; and the "Veni Creator" in the coronation scene (IV, 4). The female roles were created by Mmes Krauss (Jeanne d'Arc), Daram (Agnès Sorel), and Saune (le page). The men singing the male parts included Faure (Charles VII), Salomon (Gaston de Metz), Gailhard (Richard), Gaspard (Ambroise de Loré), Caron (Maître Jean), Menu (Jacques d'Arc), and Sapin (the sorcerer). Gally made his debut as Bar-de-Duc at the premiere. The ballet was led by Mlles Laure Fonta,* Amélie Columbier, Louise Marquet, Marie Sanlaville, and Montaubry.

The sets were created by Cheret (tabl. 1), Jean-Baptiste Lavastre and Despléchins (tabl. 2), Rubé and Chaperon (tabl. 3, 4), Cambon and Carpezet (tabl. 5, 6). Frémiet and Eugene Lacoste designed the costumes.

BIBLIOGRAPHY: DDO I, 604-5; Adolphe Jullien, Musiciens d'aujourd'hui (Paris: Librarie de l'art, 1892), 179-87; Lajarte II, 247; H. Moréno, "Première Représentation de la Jeanne d'Arc de Mermet," Le Ménestrel 42 (9 April 1876), 147; Stoullig II (1876), 8-19, 24, 48, 55-56; SW 125; M. de Thémines, "Jeanne d'Arc au théâtre," AM 12 (21 August 1873), 265-67.

Jeanne d'Arc by Giuseppe Verdi* is discussed in twentieth-century volume.

Jeanne la folle was an opera in five acts with a score by Antonin-Louis Clapisson* and a libretto by Eugène Scribe.* It had its premiere on 6 November 1848, but it had to be dropped after its eighth presentation on 11 December 1848, perhaps because its score was too labored or because its subject matter was too depressing and sombre.

The curtain rises with Aben-Hassan hiding in the mountains near Grenada with a band of Moors. He is preparing a counterattack against the Christians. Don Philippe is traveling through the forest with the Moorish girl Aïxa, and he comes upon the castle occupied by Don Fabrique, who is a relative of and in love with Jeanne, wife of Philippe (I, 1-4). Don Fabrique arrives at his castle and expresses surprise to see Jeanne's husband Philippe, but the latter explains that Jeanne is awaiting his return to Grenada so that he may be with her at the Alhambra during her cornation (I, 5). Aben-Hassan announces to Don Fabrique and Philippe that his daughter is missing and that he will kill the kidnappers. He accuses Philippe, who swears on his honor that he has not seen her. At this very moment, her voice is heard within the castle walls. Aben-Hassan attacks only to find that his forces are outnumbered (I, 6). The scene changes to the Alhambra, where king Fernand confides to Don Fabrique that his daughter loves her husband to the point of madness. He adds that he saw signs of this weakness during Philippe's recent absence, and he suggest that any indication of infidelity on his part might prove fatal. Fernand agrees to watch over her (II, 1-3). Jeanne is crowned in the Alhambra, and Aben-Hassan emerges from the crowd to petition her for justice because his daughter has been stolen from him by a nobleman whose name he does not know. Philippe enters, and Aben-Hassan indicts him in a loud and angry voice. Jeanne begins to act strangely. Don Fabrique protests that he was the kidnapper, and Jeanne decides to correct the alleged wrong by having him marry Aïxa (II, 4-5).

Aben-Hassan explains to Aïxa that she has run away with a man of great power, and that she and he are to be married if she becomes a Christian. She agrees to the arrangement, but her father reminds her that he and his men are about to massacre the Christians (III, 1-2). Philippe sends word to Aïxa to leave his home because Jeanne will be there. He promises to see her at the Alhambra. Aben-Hassan intercepts the note. Philippe plans to ask Jeanne for a marital separation, but she forestalls this possibility by suggesting that he become her king of Castille. He replies that he will wed her because of his love for her, and he determines to bid farewell to Aïxa (III, 3-6). The Moors revolt; Don Fabrique advises Jeanne and Ferdinand to escape (III, 7). Aïxa warns Philippe to avoid the raging Moors coming to regroup their forces in the Alhambra. They put the palace to the torch but are forced to flee before the victorious Christians. Aïxa faints and is found by Jeanne. The misinformed queen tells her that she may marry Don Fabrique if she becomes a Christian, but Aïxa replies that he holds no interest for her (IV, 1-5). Jeanne can find no logical answer to this confusion until Aïxa tells her that the man with whom she is involved is in another part of the basement. Aïxa volunteers to get him, and she returns with Philippe. Jeanne loses her sanity and stabs Philippe while believing that she is rescuing him (IV, 6-8).

Jeanne's father and attendants are with her when she awakens believing that her madness was a dream. She gives orders for her coronation and her wedding to Philippe, who enters dying. She insists upon knowing the identity of his assailant (V, 1-5). Don Fabrique blames Aïxa for the attack upon Philippe because he found her and a dagger near the wounded man. Aben-Hassan praises his daughter for doing away with a Christian, but she denies the deed. Jeanne insists that the guilty party be exposed, and Aïxa promises to tell her privately. The queen loses her sanity again upon hearing herself named, but she recognizes her dagger. She decides to find a saint or relic able to awaken Philippe from his "sleep" and sets out on her mad trip (V, 6).

The music of the opera did not create a favorable impression, although there were some passages that were applauded: the duet between Don Fabrique and Ferdinand (II, 3); the chorus singing "La cloche sonne" (V, 1). The female roles were filled by Mlle Masson as Jeanne and Mlle Grimm as Aïxa. The male parts were done by Brémond (Ferdinand d'Aragon), Louis Gueymard*

(Philippe d'Autriche), Portehaut (Don Fabrique), and Euzet (Aben-Hassan).
BIBLIOGRAPHY: Chouquet, 410; DDO I, 605; Lajarte II, 189-90.

Jérome, Henri (b. 5 April 1860, Monplaisir, Rhône; d. ?), vocalist, studied at the conservatories of Lyon and Paris. He was a student of M. Crosti in the capital and distinguished himself by winning prizes in singing and opéra-comique in 1888. He made his debut at the Opéra as Faust on 15 October 1888 and remained at the Garnier Palace* until 1891. He moved next to Bordeaux, where he sang the regular repertory, but he returned to Paris to sing at the Opéra-Comique on 15 November, when he appeared in Les Pêcheurs de perles.

When he was at the Garnier, Jérome created Norestan in Zaïre on 28 May 1890, and he was billed in the following roles:

Role	**Opera, Year**
Léopold	La Juive, 1889
The duke	Rigoletto, 1889
Laërte	Hamlet, 1889
Raimbaut	Robert le Diable, 1890.

BIBLIOGRAPHY: Martin 196; SW 108-10, 129-31, 181-86, 227.

Jérusalem was an opera in four acts with a score by Giuseppe Verdi,* a libretto by Alphonse Royer* and Gustave Vaëz,* and choreography by Joseph Mazilier.* Originally entitled l Lombardi alla prima crociata with words by Solera, the work had had its world premiere at La Scala on 11 February 1843. It has also been given at Her Majesty's Theatre in London on 3 March 1846 before its French derivative was produced for the first time at the Royal Academy of Music in Paris on 26 November 1847 with scenery by Séchan, Diéterle, and Despléchin for the whole production except the sets that Cambon and Thierry created for the second tableaux of the second and third acts. Jérusalem was the first work by Verdi that was produceed in French in Paris, and it enjoyed only a moderate measure of success. None of its 12 stagings in 1843 returned under 6,000 francs to the box office, but the receipts it earned in 1844 began to drop as early as 1 January, and spectators left only 3,455 francs, 70 centimes, at the box office for its 18th presentation on 23 January. It was dropped from the repertory after its 31st performance on 14 February 1849, when receipts fell to 2,273 francs, 12 centimes.

The opera opens in the palace of the count de Toulouse on a night in 1095 a.d. Hélène and Gaston are debating over whether or not Gaston can forgive Hélène's father for killing his father in a senseless war involving both their houses. At daybreak, Gaston assures Hélène that he can forget everything for her love, and he leaves (I, 1). Hélène and Isaure pray for the success of Gaston's interview with Hélène's father, and a chorus celebrates the coming day, when peace is to be restored so that both armies may embark upon the imminent crusade (I, 2-3). The count de Toulouse welcomes Gaston and suggests that they become one family in accordance with the pope's wish. He offers him Hélène's hand in marriage; Roger is consumed by jealousy, while Hélène and Gaston make no effort to conceal their joy (I, 4). The papal legate announces that the pope had named the count de Toulouse to lead the French crusaders, and it is decided that the expedition will leave on the morrow. The company retires to the chapel to pray after Gaston dons the white mantle of the crusaders as a special honor from his future father-in-law (I, 5). Roger remains outside the chapel to tell his hired assassin to kill the man clothed in white. The murderer performs his deed and rushes out of the chapel with the royal guards in hot pursuit. Roger rejoices. Shortly therafter, Hélène and Gaston leave the chapel, and stupefied Roger learns that it is his brother, the count de Toulouse, who has been stabbed. The count is alive but wounded seriously. When the soldiers return with his assailant, the count's friends press him to reveal the identity of the man who paid him to commit this heinous crime. The prisoner points to Gaston. The onlookers denounce him, but Roger can scarcely support the weight of his guilt. The papal legate saves Gaston from violence by observing that God will find and punish the criminal without human help, and he places an anathema on Gaston's head despite the accused's objections (I, 6-8).

The scene shifts to the mountains near Ramla and Jerusalem, where Roger has spent three years atoning for his crime. He is saying his prayers, when Gaston's squire Raymond enters in a state of complete exhaustion. Roger gives him water and leaves to help his comrades (II, 1-2). Hélène enters to consult with the pious hermit living in these mountains because he may have news of Gaston, who left France in disgrace to come to Palestine. She finds Raymond, who tells her that Gaston is a prisoner of the Arabs in Ramla. She is resolved to visit this city despite Raymond's warnings (II, 3). A group of lost pilgrims wanders into the area praying for their safe return to France, when the crusaders' trumpets sound (II, 4). The count de Toulouse and the papal legate enter with their army, and the holy man appears. Roger is not recognized, and he does not reveal his identity. He is accepted into the Christian army, which continues on its way to Ramla (II, 5-6).

The second tableau of the second act depicts the apartments of the emir of Ramla, where Gaston is awaiting the emir. Hélène is also brought before the emir after her capture in Ramla despite her disguise. The two Christians recognize each other but remain silent in the presence of their captor. Suspicious, the emir leaves them alone (II, 7-9). They fall into each other' arms, but Gaston urges her to forget him because of the disgrace he suffers. She refuses to abandon him. Suddenly, an alarm is sounded, and the lovers try to escape, but Arab soldiers intercept them (II, 7-10).

Hélène is now a captive in the harem, where a chorus and ballet prepare the entrance of the emir. An officer warns that the Christians have begun their assault, and the emir orders Hélène's head to be thrown at their leader if he gains entry into the city. Hélène prays for deliverance, and Gaston fights his way to her. He assures her that they must pursue their fate with the Christians (III, 1-4). The count de Toulouse breaks into the harem, finds the lovers together, and realizes that Hélène has entered Ramla to rescue Gaston. Angered, he orders Gaston's death. Hélène accuses her father and his knights of doing the devil's work; she declares that God will visit His justice upon their heads. The count accuses her of sacrilege and arrests her (III, 5).

The second tableau of the third acts offers a scaffold draped in black. Gaston is escorted to the place of his execution, but he stops long enough to assert his innocence before God and man. He is stripped of all his honors, rank, and standing on this occasion, when his helmet is smashed and his sword is broken. He will die on the morrow (III, 6).

Roger stands before Jerusalem with the Christian army ready for the assault. The papal delegate recognizes him as the holy man of the wilderness and suggests that he console the condemned criminal in the nearby tent. The legate orders the guards to obey the holy man's orders, and Roger directs them to leave when he recognizes Gaston. He returns Gaston's sword to him and tells him that he is free to depart, and the condemned man rejoices that he may die with honor in the attack upon Jerusalem (IV, 1-4).

Isaure announces that the Holy City is in Christian hands. The victorious warriors return to the count's tent to report to their leader. The count asks Gaston to reveal his identity because he was the first to hoist the Christian standard over the city. Gaston raises his vizor, and he is recognized. Hélène asks the papal delegate whether he must die (IV, 5). Roger enters wounded mortally; he discloses his identity to his brother and confesses his guilt to exonerate Gaston (IV, 6).

The score of Jérusalem embraced all Verdi's original music for I Lombardi, and the composer added several passages; for example, the degradation scene (III, 6) and the chorus "Enfin voici le jour propice" (I, 3), but the high points in the music remained the sextet in the first act and the final trio sung by Hélène, Roger, and Gaston in the French work (IV, 4). Mazilier's divertissement (III, 1) was also an addition (see eighteenth-century volume for divertissement). The male parts were created by Gilbert Duprez* (Gaston), Adolphe Alizard* (Roger), Portehaut (the count de Toulouse), Brémond (papal legate), Joseph Barbot* (Raymond), F. Prévost (a soldier), Molinier (a herald), Guimot (the emir), and Koenig (emir's officer). The female roles were filled by Mme Julian Van Gelder (Hélène) and Mme Muller (Isaure).

BIBLIOGRAPHY: Franco Abbiati, Giuseppe Verdi (Milan: Ricordi, 1959) I, 727-37, 761; A. Basevi,

Studio sulle opere di Giuseppe Verdi (Florence: Tofani, 1859), 19-38, 123-32; Ferruccio Bonavia, Verdi (London: Denis Dobson Ltd., 1947), 30-31; Julian Budden, The Operas of Verdi (London: Cassell, 1973) I, 113-35, 339-59; H.C., "Jérusalem," FM 10 (28 November 1847), 389-91 and FM 10 (5 December 1847), 397-98; Chouquet 409; DDO I, 607-8; Carlo Gatti, Verdi (Milan: Edizioni Alpes, 1931), 299-304; "Gerusalemme: opera in quattro atti," Quaderni dell'Istituto di Studi Verdiani 2 (14 November 1974), 1-109; Carlo Gatti, Verdi, the Man and His Music (New York: G.P. Putnam's Sons, 1955), 63-65, 104-8; Luigi Gianoli, Verdi (Brescia: La Scuola, 1961), 105-6; paul Hume, Verdi, the Man and His Music (New York: E. P. Dutton and Metropolitan Opera Guild, 1977), 122-24; Dena Humphreys, Verdi: Force of Destiny (New York: Henry Holt, 1948), 82-88, 110; Dyneley Hussey, Verdi (London: J. M. Dent & Sons, 1973), 60; Lajarte II, 186-87; George Martin, Verdi, His Music, Life and Times (New York: Dodd, Mead and Co., 1963), 210-11, 549; SSBO 198-99, 206, 248; Thompson 1039, 2174-75; Francis Toye, Giuseppe Verdi; His Life and Works (New York: Alfred A. Knopf, 1946), 207-12; Guiseppe Verdi, Gerusalemme (n.p.: Istituto di studi verdiani, 1963); Franz Werfel and Paul Stefan, Verdi: the Man and His Letters, trans. Edward Downes (New York: L.B. Fischer, 1942), 46-47, 134, 150.

Jeux by Vaslav Nijinsky* is discussed in twentieth-century volume.

Les Jeux floraux was an opera in three acts with a score by Pamphile-Léopold Aimon* and a libretto by Jean-Nicolas Bouilly* that had its premire at the Montansier opera house on 16 November 1818. Although the work by Aimon dealt with a subject inspired by the Middle Ages, it failed to please romantic audiences, and it had to be dropped from the repertory after its seventh presentation on 8 January 1819.

The setting is Toulouse at the start of the fourteenth century, where the daughter of count Raymond of Toulouse named Clémence-Isaure has just finished her poem for the *jeux floraux*. She shows her maid Berthe the jeweled case containing three flowers that she will award to the winner of the games. She and Berthe recall how her wedding was canceled after her intended husband unhorsed her father in a tournament for a few years previously. Isaure observes that the rules of the coming games will permit her former suitor to return to Toulouse. Lautrec enters the garden at this very moment, and the runited lovers are ecstatic to see each other again, but she warns him of her father's resentment if he should win her hand. Lautrec fears that Montfort and Béranger may surpass him in poetry, however (I, 1-2), and the latter poets debate their literary projects and tastes. Isaure announces that she will wed the winner of the games, but her father construes this maneuver as a ruse to enable her to marry Lautrec by crowning his work (I, 3-5). Literature is forgotten, however, when it is announced that Alphonse of Aragon has begun an invasion. Raymond restores Lautrec to his rank and title so that he may help to repulse the invaders, but he appears to have some mental reservations about this pardon that he has extended to Lautrec. The act ends in a divertissement of song and dance celebrating Flore and spring (I, 6-7) (see eighteenth-century volume for divertissement).

Raymond asserts to Montfort that he hopes that he will win the contest and Isaure's hand, and Béranger demonstrates his ability to write verse despite his age (II, 1-2). Alphonse's defeat is announced, and Raymond declares that two poets will be nominated to give thanks to the valiant soldiers of Toulouse for having defeated Alphonse. His elation over a victory is turned to alarm by the news that the tide of battle has now turned in favor of the Spanish army. Raymond decides to send Lautrec into the fray in the hope that he may be killed (II, 3-4). Despairing Isaure and Lautrec bid each other farewell (II, 5-7).

Isaure is still bewailing her predicament when Raymond announces gleefully that Montfort has won the prize for poetry. His daughter protests that she loves Lautrec, and her obstinacy infuriates her father. The judges of the literary contest announce that Béranger has defeated Montfort. Raymond orders the competition repeated so that the people may select the winner. The poets obey Raymond's command, but the people of Toulouse return a divided verdict (III, 1-4). A herald announces that Lautrec has defeated Alphonse, and the victorious hero requests permission to enter the poetry contest. He wins the prize, and Raymond acknowledges his debt to him by accepting him as his future son-in-law (III, 5-7).

Raymond was sung by Nicolas Levasseur* with Mme Rose Branchu as his daughter, Clémence-Isaure (see eighteenth-century volume for Branchu). Adolphe Nourrit* filled the part of Lautrec, while François Lays and Prosper Dérivis* were cast in the roles of the two poets (see eighteenth-century volume for Lays).

BIBLIOGRAPHY: Chouquet 388; DDO I, 612; Lajarte II, 93-94; Moniteur universel 322 (18 November 1818), 1852.

La Jolie Fille de Gand was a pantomime-ballet in three acts and nine tableaux with a libretto by Jules-Henri Vernoy de Saint-Georges,* a score by Adolphe Adam,* and choreography by Albert Decombe (see eighteenth-century volume for Decombe). It had its world premier at the Royal Academy of Music in Paris on 22 June 1842 with sets by Pierre Cicéri,* Philastre, and Cambon.

The ballet begins at Gand in the shop of the goldsmith Césarius, where the dancing master Zéphiros is giving a lesson to Agnès and Béatrix, daughters of Césarius. Julia joins her two cousins to demonstrate certain steps, but the lesson is interrupted by Bénédict, who is engaged to marry Béatrix. The latter accepts his flowers with indifference, however, and Julia mocks him while giving a letter from an unknown suitor to Béatrix (I, 1-3), but Césarius informs Bénédict and his daughter that their marriage contract has been signed. Only the prospective groom seems happy with the news that the wedding is scheduled for the morrow (I, 4). The marquis de San Lucar and his friend Bustamente enter the shop, and Julia identifies the marquis as her cousin's unknown suitor. Béatrix has already fallen in love with the marquis, and he loses no time in declaring his love to her. He purchases a gem for each of the three girls (I, 5). Césarius presents Bénédict to San Lucar as his future son-in-law; Julia urges the marquis not to lose hope. Césarius, his family, the marquis, and his entourage leave for the municipal fair (I, 6-7).

The second tableau represents the main square in Gand filled with merchants, entertainers, and onlookers of every description. An archery contest begins. Bustamente's arrow goes wild and pierces Zéphiros' wig. The marquis wins the prize of a crown of flowers, which he gives to Béatrix. Agnès tries to persuade Béatrix to reject Bénédict for the marquis, who notices Béatrix giving the key to her room to Julia. Dancing begins, but the fair is disrupted by a storm. San Lucar manages to profit by the ensuing confusion. He steals the key to Béatrix' room from Julia, who rushes off with Bénédict (I, tabl. 2).

The setting moves to Béatrix' bedroom, where Césarius is scolding his daughter for her coolness toward her fiance. The young girl is moved by her faithful suitor's tears and constancey, but she cannot stop thinking of the marquis. After her father has left, San Lucar himself opens her door. She begs him to leave before he is discovered, but Julia appears next in the doorway, and the marquis is delighted to see her because he considers her an ally in his suit for Béatrix' hand. He declares his love to the frightened girl; Julia supports him. Béatrix ignores them. Thwarted, the marquis pulls his dagger and threatens suicide. The two girls disarm him, and there is a knock on the door. Julia hides the marquis behind the bed curtains, and Béatrix opens the door (I, tabl. 3, 1-4). Agnès has come to tell her that her wedding is scheduled for 6:00 a.m. Agnès suggests that it is time for Béatrix to retire, and she leaves with Julia, while San Lucar withdraws through the window. Tired Béatrix casts a last look at her crown of roses and falls asleep (I, tabl. 3, 5).

The stage is now decorated as a sumptuous boudoir in San Lucar's palace in Venice. He has kidnapped Béatrix, and she is his mistress. Zéphiros has become director at La Fenice Theatre, and he enters to invite her and San Lucar to a ball he is giving because he believes them to be married (II, tabl. 1, 1-3). Julia is now a dancer for Zéphiros, and she reveals to her cousin that the handsome count Leonardo has replaced Bustamente as her protector. The latter appears next with Diana, première danseuse at La Fenice, and the social gathering degenerates into a quarrel. San Lucar manages to restores order in his house at last, and Bustamente invites Béatrix' visitors to his ball. The marquis orders his valets to bring in costumes, and his guests select their garments for the coming masquerade (II, tabl. 1, 4-5).

The ball is in progress on the stage of La Fenice, which has been transformed into a ballroom. The dancing is interrupted long enough to present a divertissement starring Diana (see eighteenth-century volume for divertissement). San Lucar applauds the dancer with such enthusiasm that jealous Béatrix persuades Zéphiros to place her in the ballet. She performs with complete perfection (II, tabl. 2, 1-5), and she is chosen to be queen of the ball. Suddenly an angry domino tears the crown from her head. It is her father. Weeping, she asks his forgiveness, and he is about to take her back to Gand when San Lucar interferes with a vow to marry her. The old man refuses to have the debaucher of his daughter as a son-in-law, and he curses Béatrix for dishonoring her family. Béatrix cannot withstand this blow, and she falls into the marquis' arms (II, tabl. 2, 6).

The last act opens in the gardens of San Lucar's castle during a full moon. An orgy is coming to an end. Young nobles are stretched out near tables covered with dishes and empty bottles; courtisans dressed as nymphs and bacchants complete the scene. Some guests are dancing, and others are gambling, while San Lucar devotes his energy and wit to distracting depressed Béatrix (IV, tabl. 1, 1-2). The gambling fever seizes the marquis, and he loses his fortune to Bustamente despite Béatrix' pleas that he leave the gaming table. Béatrix departs, and he continues to wager until he loses even his mistress' jewelry. Bustamente goads him into betting Béatrix herself against Bustamente's winnings. He agrees and loses. Bustamente disguises himself as San Lucar. Béatrix returns to the room. She is unaware of what has happened, and Bustamente leads her away to his gondola, while the marquis' guests witness the deceit with smiles (IV, tabl. 1, 3-4).

The setting shifts to San Lucar's apartment, to which Bustamente has led Béatrix. She takes her companion's hand in the semidarkness and begs him to discard his mask. When he refuses, she tears it from his face and faints (III, tabl. 2, 1). The marquis arrives in time to protect his mistress, but Béatrix cannot forgive him for wagering her like a chattel. San Lucar attacks Bustamente and kills him. Béatrix flees (II, tabl. 2, 1-2).

The third tableau returns to Gand, where Agnès and Bénédict are about to wed. The villagers gather to watch Zéphiros' dancers from the fair. Béatrix enters enhausted but with enough strength to scold Julia for becoming a carnaval performer with Zéphiros, who has lost his position at La Fenice (III, tabl. 3, 1-4). Bénédict does not recognize despairing Béatrix, who cannot forget her past innocence. She is especially troubled because she cannot support the thought of her sister marching to the altar with her former fiance. Finally, she learns that her father is dead. She hurls herself from the nearby cliff (III, tabl. 3, 5-6)

The scene changes suddenly to Béatrix' bedroom. The young girl opens her eyes and realizes that her misadventures are dreams. She falls to her knees in gratitude, and her clock strikes 6:00 a.m. There is a knock at her window. It is the marquis come to take her with him. The door opens at the same time, and she sees her father with Agnès and Bénédict ready to escort her to church. The angry marquis disappears, when she throws herself into her father's arms, and decides to lead a virtuous life with Bénédict (III, tabl. 4, 1-3).

La Jolie Fille de Gand was popular from the start. It enjoyed 23 presentations in the year of its premiere; it was billed on 56 dates before it was dropped from the repertory on 12 May 1845. Caronne Grisi* as Béatrix was a huge success as usual, and she was supported by Adèle Dumilâtre* as Agnès. Mlle L. Fitzjames danced Diana, the première danseuse at La Fenice. The male roles were created by Albert Decombe (San Lucar), Montjoie (Césarius), Hippolyte Barrez* (Zéphiros), Elie (Bustamente), Lucien Petipa* (Bénédict), and Jean Coralli* (Léonardo) (see eighteenth-century volume for Decombe). The first pas de trois was executed by Barrez, Frémolle, and Sophie Dumilâtre*; the second pas de trois was danced by Mabille, Mlle Maria, and Mlle Adèle Dumilâtre. Mme Grisi and Petipa starred in the pas de deux. Yet it was Grisi's miming that proved to be the most surprising feature of this work.

BIBLIOGRAPHY: CB 149-59; Chouquet 404; CODB 284; Escudier, "La Jolie Fille de Gand," FM 5 (26 June 1842), 229-32; Lajarte II, 171; RBP 108; PBP 216-20; SS 111.

Joncières, Victorin de (b. 12 April 1839, Paris; d. 26 october 1903, Paris), composer, studied painting as a youth, but he turned to music when he found himself obliged to compose an operetta for one of his friends. He entered the Conservatoire in Paris, but he left this institution after a quarrel there with one of his professors. Now obliged to act independently, he composed a number of orchestral pieces. He made his debut in the theatre on 8 February 1867 at the Théâtre-Lyrique with Sardanaple, but this work was rejected by the audience despite the presence of Christine Nilsson* in the cast. His second opera, Le Dernier Jour de Pompei (1868), was scarcely more successful at the same theatre.

Joncières was now completely without hope of having a theatre accept his works because he had disappointed the management of the Théâtre-Lyrique. Also, the Opéra was not interested in examining his manuscripts, and he was unwilling to offer anything to the Opéra-Comique. Finally, a path opened for him when the Théâtre-Lirique de la Gaîté reopened under the direction of Vizentini, and his Dimitri (1876) was chosen for the inauguration program. This work was such an improvement over his previous productions that the Opéra accepted his La Reine Berthe* on 27 December 1878, and the Opéra-Comique produced his Chevalier Jean on 11 March 1885. These two pieces did little to help his reputation at either theatre, although the Opéra did agree to bill his lyric drama Lancelot* on 7 February 1900. But this work endured for only eight presentations, and Joncières' efforts for the theatre terminated with the last performance of Lancelot on 24 April 1900.
BIBLIOGRAPHY: AEM VII, 158; BBD 833-34; EDS VII, 790; ELM II, 632; Grove IV, 655-56; PBSW 185.

Joseph was billed originally as a lyric drama in three acts with a score by Etienne-Nicolas Méhul and a libretto by Alexandre Duval (see eighteenth-century volume for Méhul). It had its world premiere at the Opéra-Comique in the Feydeau Theatre on 17 February 1807 with Jean Elleviou in the title-role (see eighteenth-century for Elleviou). It was revived at the Favart Theatre (1851) and the Théâtre Lyrique (1862) before it was given for the first time at the Garnier Palace* on 26 May 1899, the same year that it was returned to the stage of the Opéra-Comique.

Ultimately, it was revived for its 123rd presentation at the Opéra-Comique on 24 November 1910, and it was given its 21st and last performance at the Garnier Palace on 20 October 1946. Thus, it remained in the repertory for 140 years, and, during this time, it was billed on 150 occasions at the two most important national lyric theatres in France. When it was brought to the Garnier Palace for its premiere in this theatre on 26 May 1899, its scenery was supplied by Marcel Jambon* and Marcel Bailly, and Charles Bianchini created its costumes. Its recitatives had to be set to music at this time, and Louis Bourgault-Ducoudray* supplied this service.

The opera begins in Joseph's palace in Memphis, where Joseph is ruling as governor under the name of Cléophas. He is thinking of his aged father growing old without him, and he recalls how his brothers attacked him and sold him to some Arabs because he disapproved of their crimes. At this time, however, his brothers have sent to Egypt to request food because Palestine has been stricken by a famine. They submit their request to Cléophas, who recognizes them. Joseph bids Siméon to return home to tell their father that Cléophas has invited the Israelites to find sanctuary in Egypt. The crowd outside the palace hails their governor because of his compassion for the common people (a. 1).

A choir beseeches the God of Israel to make the land green with the coming harvest, and Benjamin recalls how he was called upon in his boyhood to replace Joseph in Jacob's affections. Joseph greets his father, who is now blind, and he overhears him asking God to return him to his own land to die. He recognizes his son Joseph, and his heart is filled with joy, although Benjamin assures him that the man he believes to be his son is really Cléophas. Joseph invites Benjamin and Jacob to ride in Cléophas' chariot during the triumph organized to recognize Cléophas' generosity toward the Israelites (a. 2).

A chorus of children calls upon the Israelites to praise God, who has brought them so many blessings, and the sons of Jacob add their voices to this song of thanksgiving. Jacob praises God for giving him Benjamin to guide his steps, and he urges Benjamin to abandon his treacherous brothers. Jacob's other sons ask their father to forgive them, and Siméon assures

Jacob that he alone is guilty. Joseph reveals his identity to his father, and he pardons his brothers for the suffering that they have brought to him. He reminds his father that God's mercy is boundless, and Jacob is persuaded to forgive his sons (a. 3).

Joseph was the most popular of Méhul's 30 or more compositions for the theatre, and, as already noted, its serious simplicity impressed spectators for many years. The three leading roles in this oratorio-like work were created in 1807 by Jean-Baptiste Gavaudan (Benjamin), Jean Elleviou (Joseph), and Solié (Jacob), and, in 1899, these parts were executed initially at the Garnier by Aïno Ackté* (Benjamin) in travesty and MM. Albert Vaguet* (Joseph), and Jean-François Delmas* (Jacob) (see eighteenth-century volume for Gavaudan and Elleviou). The revival of 1946 at the Opéra saw Méhul's work provided with dances by Serge Peretti, and Mme St.-Arnaud was cast in travesty as Benjamin with MM. Ramboud* (Joseph), Endrèze (Jacob), and Fronval (Siméon) cast in the other leading roles (see twentieth-century volume for Peretti and Endréze).

BIBLIOGRAPHY: Adolphe Boschot, Chez les musiciens (Paris: Plon, 1922), 61-62; DDO I, 617-19; MSRL 130; PBSW 225; Arthur Pougin, "Joseph de Méhul," Le Ménestrel 65 (4 June 1899), 178-80; P. Scudo, Critique et littérature musicales (Paris: Victor Lecou, 1852) II, 347-52; Stoullig XXV (1899), 9-11; R. A. Streatfeild, The Opera, ed. Edward J. Dent (Westport, Conn.: Greenwood Press, 1971), 75-76; SW 127-28; Thompson 2168; WOC 98-99.

Journet, Marcel (b. 25 July 1867, Grasse; d. 9 September 1933, Vittel), bass, studied at the Conservatoire in Paris with Louis Henri Obin* and Seghettini, but he made his theatrical debut in Montpellier. He moved on to Brussels after a year in the Midi, but he was back in the French capital before long to make his first appearance at the Opéra on 2 October 1908 as the king in Lohengrin.* Subsequently he enjoyed great success at various European theatres, especially at La Scala, but his career over the next score of years was associated principally with the Opéra.

The year after his debut at the Garnier Palace,* he did Méphisto in Faust,* Hounding in La Walkyrie,* the king in Hamlet,* Frère Laurent in Roméo et Juliette,* the legate in Henry VIII,*

Marcel in Les Huguenots,* and the Landgrave in Tannhäuser.* It was obvious that the public was far from tiring of his rich bass voice because he was nearly as active at the theatre in 1910 as he had been in 1909. In 1910, he added five parts to his Garnier repretory: Sparafucile in Rigoletto,* Ramphis in Aïda,* Hagen in Sigurd,* Walther in Guillaume Tell,* and Wotan in La Walkyrie.* During the three years before the war, he sang Pogner of Les Maîtres Chanteurs de Nuremberg* in 1911, Zaccharie of Le Prophète* in 1912, and Méphisto of La Damnation de Faust* in 1913.

The war years witnessed an inevitable lessening of Journet's activity at the Opéra. He portrayed the old Hebrew of Samson et Dalila,* Athanaël of Thaïs,* and Gurnemanz of Parsifal,* in 1914, but he did nothing in the 1915-18 interval. In 1919, however, he demonstrated that his voice was still colorful and robust by representing the high priest in Thaïs, de Rysoor in Patrie!* and Don Diègue in Le Cid.* His 1920 season offered to the public for the first time Guido in Monna Vanna* and Tonio in Paillasse* followed in 1921 by Benvenuto Cellini in Ascanio.* After doing Wotan of L'Or du Rhin* in 1922, he undertook nothing that was new for him right away, probably because he was busy preparing for the world premiere of Boïto's Nerone at La Scala on 1 May 1924. In 1926, however, he sang the count in Manon* at paris, and, in 1928, he was billed at the Opéra as Wotan in Siegried* and as Hagen in Le Crépuscule des dieux.* Finally, he sang the role of the hero of Guillaume Tell* in 1929.

While M. Journet was building up his repertory at the Garnier Palace* to 29 parts, he removed all doubts about his dramatic ability and vocal versality by creating eight roles in composition that had their world or local premieres at the Garnier between 1909 and 1930:

Role	Opera	Premiere
Fafner	L'Or du Rhin	14 November 1909
L. Cornélius	Roma	24 April 1912
Klingsor	Parsifal	4 January 1914
Phanuel	Hérodiade	22 December 1921

Dosiféi	Khovantchina	13 April 1923
Don Jacintho	Tour de Feu	12 January 1928
Sultan	Marouf	21 June 1928
Antoine	Tentation de St. Antoine	8 May 1930

M. Journet was nearly 63 years old at the time that he walked onto the stage of the Opéra to sing the lead in the world premiere of Brunel's La Tentation de Saint Antoine (see eighteenth-century volume for La Tentation de Saint Antoine). M. Journet was not only one of the most celebrated bass singers of his day, but he was also the most durable.

BIBLIOGRAPHY: APD 403-4; EDS VI, 811-12; A. Favia-Artsay, "Marcel Journet," Hobbies 72 (May 1967), 36; ICM 914; KRJ 211; RC 414-19; PBSW 185; Harold Simpson, Singers to Remember (McMinnville, Oreg.: Oakwood Press, 1974), 71-73; W. Violi, "Madelon and Journet," Hobbies 57 (January 1953), 33; SW 42, 62, 66, 70, 86, 106-7, 109, 112-13, 118, 132, 136, 139, 141, 144, 151, 162, 168, 170-71, 178, 184, 189, 191, 202-3, 207, 209, 211, 225-26.

Jovita ou les boucaniers was a pantomime-ballet in three tableaux with a score of Théodore Labarre.* Joseph Mazilier* wrote its libretto and choreographed it. Its sets were created by Despléchin, Thierry, and Cambon. Victor Sacré was the chief machinist who engineered the sensational blast and its spectacular effects in the outlaws' grotto at the end of the second tableau. The ballet had its world premiere at the Imperial Academy of Music on 11 November 1853. It enjoyed 23 performances during its first run lasting until 8 December 1854. It was revived for another dozen billings at the Opéra between 16 May 1856 and 17 August 1859.

The opera is set in Mexico at the start of the seventeenth century. It is dawn, and Don José Cavallines' slaves are preparing floral pieces for his daughter Jovita on her feast day. She thanks her father and the slaves for their gifts, but she is distracted by the appearance of the young officer Don Altamirano, who posts a reward for whoever will rid Mexico of the outlaw Zubillaga. Altamirano protests his love to Jovita, but she rebukes him for ignoring her feast day. She leaves him to speak with her neighbors; she promises to dance only with Don Alvar.

An old man in rags and on a crutch asks for hospitality, and Don Altamirano decides to ignore Jovita because of her real or feigned indifference toward him. This ploy is successful, and the lovers are reconciled. Don José Cavallines reproaches Altamirano for not speaking to him about marrying his daughter, but the young officer replies that he has been awaiting his promotion to a captaincy before asking him for Jovita's hand. He adds that his promotion is imminent, because he expects to capture Zubillaga, dead or alive. The old man warns him that pursuing the outlaw will be a dangerous business, but he offers to serve as Altamirano's guide. The old man goes off to tell his wife that he is leaving at nightfall with an expedition formed to track down Zubillaga. Altamirano gives his ring to Jovita and explains that they will be married with her father's permission as soon as he returns from his mission. The musicians arrive; the masters and slaves execute European and native dances, respectively. The old man returns after the dancing and reveals to Altamirano that he is the real Zubillaga. Altamirano orders his men to seize him, but he blows his horn, and his armed followers appear on every side. He allows Don Cavallines to remain free because he offered him hospitality, but he announces that he is holding Altamirano for ransom. The bandit makes prisoners of the guests and slaves on the plantation, but Jovita manages to hide, and the band of brigands rides away without her. She sees a dagger on the floor and picks it up; she interprets its presence in her home as a sign that she must free Altamirano or kill Zubillaga because her father cannot pay her sweetheart's ransom (tabl. 1).

The second tableau depicts Zubillaga's hideout tucked away in a remote and almost inaccessible corner of the Cordilleras mountains. The bandit has sold the slaves but retained his European captives for ransom. One of his sentries hears a noise. It is Jovita disguised as a gypsy and entering the camp. Altamirano realizes immediately what is transpiring, and he asserts that he has never seen the intruding woman. Zubillaga asks Jovita why she has come into his camp, and she replies that she admires him and wishes to thank him for the trouble that he has caused for the Spaniards, the oppressors of her people. She volunteers to dance for them before she leaves, but the bandit declares that she cannot leave the camp because she might be tempted to divulge its location. She assures him that she is most happy to become a member of their band, and the outlaws accept her as their peer. As a final test, Zubillaga leaves her alone with Altamirano. He spies on the couple, but Jovita sees through this ruse and continues to act like a stranger with her sweetheart. The bandit is convinced at last and asks Jovita to be his wife. He throws his arms around her; Jovita struggles; Altamirano notices his ring on her finger. He rushes at the bandit with a stool as a club, but the soldiers knock him out. Unfortunately, he has revealed Jovita's true identity in the scuffle, but she manages once again to convince Zubillaga that she is a gypsy, not the Creole daughter of Don Cavallines. Zubillaga primes a rifle to shoot Altamirano, but he is persuaded that it would be foolish to lose the handsome ransom Altamirano will bring. He allows him to live.

The camp has become quiet, and Jovita takes advantage of the lull to dance for the outlaws in the hope that she can stir up trouble. They start to fight over her, and Zubillaga declares that she is his wife, but his men are unimpressed by his vehemence. The chief sees that the situation is becoming dangerous, and he suggests a compromise. They will draw lots for the gypsy. He writes his own name on each of the pieces of paper to outwit his illiterate men. He explains this gambit to Jovita, who manages to cut his powerhorn from its cords. She pours his powder from the entrance to the grotto over to the powder barrel. She severs Altamirano's bonds, warns the other prisoners, and throws a lamp into the powder train. They find shelter behind the rocks, but the outlaws are killed to a man in the ensuing explosion (tabl. 2).

A reception is given to honor the beautiful Jovita, who makes her entrance in a car drawn by white horses. She is greeted by the viceroy of Mexico and his staff for having rid the country of its worst plague. Don Altamirano receives his promotion, and the lovers are free to wed (tabl. 3).

The ballet boasted a number of interesting moments: the tremendous explosion, a comic dance by Mme Dominique and Francisque Berthier, and melodies by the harpist Théodore Labarre.* Yet it was Carolina Rosati* who stole the show. She made her debut at the Opéra in the part of Jovita, and she inspired generous praise in the press for her miming ability, her ballet talents, the lightness and vivacity with which she executed her part. Yet the most indisputable tribute paid to her was probably Nestor Roqueplan's decision to increase her salary by 1,500 francs a month after the premiere of Paquita. The other female roles were not as significant, but the male parts were important enough to have merited the services of Lenfant (José Cavallines), Louis Mérante* (Don Altamirano), and Lucien Petipa* (Zubillaga).

BIBLIOGRAPHY: CB 204-8; Chouquet 413; CODB 286; Marie Escudier, "Jovita, ballet de M. Mazillier," FM 17 (13 November 1853), 367-68; Ivor Guest, The Ballet of the Second Empire (Middletown, Conn.: Wesleyan University Press, 1974), 75-78, 166; Lajarte II, 215.

Les Joyaux de la Madone, originally entitled I Gioielli della Madonna, was billed as "scenes of popular Neapolitan life" in three acts with a score by Ermanno Wolf-Ferrari* and a libretto by C. Zangarini and E. Golisciani. The work had its world premiere in Berlin at the Kurfürstenoper on 2 December 1911 in a German version by Liebstockl. It was produced in Chicago, New York, and London in 1912, but it was not brought to the Garnier Palace until 12 September 1913. The French version of René Lara was produced by Paul Stuart and was provided with fresh choreography by Yvan Clustine. Carmelo Preite made his debut as conductor of the orchestra at the Opéra on this occasion. Its sets were created in Paris by Ronsin, Marc-Henri Laverdot (a. 1), Mouveau (a. 2), and Rochette (a. 3); its costumes were designed by Pinchon.

The opera begins in front of Carméla's house in Naples. Her neighbors are the blacksmith Gennaro and the public secretary Biaso. It is the hour of vespers on the feast of the Madonna, and the houses are decorated with flowers. The crowd is composed of every segment of the local population: mothers sewing or combing their children's hair; merchants selling rosaries, candles, and sherbert; beggars asking for alms; fishermen passing with nets on their shoulders; girls and boys with mandolins or guitars. A blind man is playing a flute in a corner, and a riotous game of morra is in progress near the center of the square. Boats dock with a troupe of children dressed as angels. They swarm over the balloon vendor, and he loses his wares. The square grows quiet finally, and the blacksmith Gennaro appears with his candalabra. He places candles in it and offers his work to the Madonna with a prayer that he be cured of his unrequited love. Maliella enters pursued by her stepmother Carméla, who begs her to be reasonable and not to run around in disarray. Gennaro approves of Carméla's words, but she accuses him of being jealous and stares at him in defiance. The embarrassed blacksmith is too upset to answer, and Biaso breaks the tension by donning a paper hat. The outlaw Camorristes disembark and begin to flirt with Maliella. She sings and dances for them to annoy Gennaro. She runs away with Biaso. Carméla explains to Gennaro that unruly Maliella is not her child. She is an orphan whom she swore to raise if the Madonna would cure Gennaro of a childhood illness. She assures her son that they will be rid of the girl when she marries. Gennaro shudders at the thought of losing her. The Camorristes Rocco and Ciccilio return with Biaso more dead than alive. They order him into his house, and they cheer, when Raphael declares his love to Maliella. Annoyed, she stabs Raphael with a hatpin, but he asserts that his wound is a sign of her love. He offers to steal the Madonna's jewels for her to prove his love, and she is charmed by his boldness. He throws a flower to her as the statue of the Madonna passes with the returning crowd (a. 1).

The second act shifts to the orchard near Carméla's home. Here, Maliella defies Gennaro by threatening to pack her clothes and to leave Carméla's house forever. She returns to her room to pack, and he declares his love to her when she is ready to depart. She boasts of Raphael's offer to steal the Madonna's jewels for her, and he orders her back into her room. He gathers up a stack of keys and files; he leaves just before Raphael and his Camorristes appear to serenade her. She promises to elope with him on the morrow. He leaves and Gennaro returns to give the precious gems to Maliella. She is terrified, but

Gennaro asserts that the Virgin has forgiven him. She adorns herself with the jewels and can think only of Raphael. In fact, she is quite unaware that it is Gennaro who takes her into his arms to seduce her (a. 2).

The action moves to the hideout of the Camorristes in a suburb of Naples. Stella pulls the cloth from the table, and the women climb upon it to dance. The bandits toast Raphael and his new love, but Grazia and Stella begin to flirt with him. He ignores their advances, and they mock him. An orgy begins, and the superstitious outlaws cover their picture of the Madonna. Suddenly, Maliella enters to reveal that Gennaro is following her. She faints and Raphael calls for Gennaro's capture. Maliella recovers consciousness and confesses to Raphael that she has succumbed to Gennaro's advances. Raphael denounces her; she pleads in vain for forgiveness. He pushes her away; she falls to the ground to reveal the Madonna's jewels. Ciccilio returns with Gennaro as his prisoner, and Maliella denounces him while throwing the gems to the floor. The company is horrified to learn that the jewelry has been stolen from the Madonna, and they flee. Alone, Gennaro places the jewels on the altar beneath the picture of the Madonna. He prays for forgiveness and stabs himslef. Dying, he kisses Maliella's shawl just as the first rays of sunlight penetrate the Camorristes' hideout (a. 3).

Wolf-Ferrari's work was only moderately successful in Paris, where it enjoyed 17 performances before it was dropped from the repertory on 1 July 1914. Andrée Vally made her debut at the Opéra in the leading role of Maliella at the premiere of Les Joyaux de la Madone, when the other principal female roles were filled by Lyse Charny (Carméla), Jeanne Campredon (Stella), Antoinette Laute-Brun* (Concetta), and Georgette Couat (Grazia). The male parts were created by MM. Léon Campagnola* (Gennaro), Vanni Marcoux* (Raphael), François Dubois* (Biaso), and Gonguet (Cicillio).

BIBLIOGRAPHY: KCOB 1235-59; MSRL 273; PBSW 225; Stoullig XXXIX (1913), 16-20, 22; SSBO 358; SW 128; Thompson 667, 2152-53.

Le Jugement de Paris, heard at the Opéra for the first time on 27 October 1905, was neither an opera nor a ballet. It was the symphony with which Edmond Malherbe won a current contest organized by the Opéra for this sort of musical composition. M. Malherbe based his work upon a painting by paul Baudry called Le Jugement de Paris that hung in the foyer of the Garnier Palace.* The canvas presented Paris, Mercury, Venus, Cupid, Pallas, and Juno, and the composer developed a theme representing each of these mythological figures. Some critics dismissed Le Jugement de Paris as an overly long lesson in counterpoint that relied too heavily upon the percussion section of the orchestra. The symphony was played on four dates at the Garnier Palace before it was dropped from programs.

BIBLIOGRAPHY: Henri Rebois, Les Grands Prix de Rome de musique (Paris: Firmin-Didot, 1932), 83-87.

Le Juif errant was a grand opera in five acts with music by Jacques Fromenthal Halévy,* a libretto by Eugène Scribe,* and Jules-Henri Vernoy de Saint-Georges,* and choreography by Arthur Saint-Léon.* It had its world premiere at the Opéra on 23 April 1852 after the theatre was closed for a week for rehearsals. It ran on 17 straight programs until 31 May, when it began to alternate with other works. Its receipts ran as high as 11,040 francs, 61 centimes, during this interval. In all, it was given 41 times in 1852, but its popularity began to diminish after the novelty of the spectacle and the music wore off, and receipts for the day now dropped as low as 2,975 francs, 65 centimes, during the slower summer months. Receipts increased in the fall, but Halévy's work was mounted on only seven dates in 1853. It was evident by this time that the public was not overly enthusiastic about it. Le Juif errant was accordingly dropped from the repertory on 28 October 1853 after 31 presentations.

The curtain rises on the city of Anvers at the start of Halévy's work, and Théodora and her brother Léon are attending a twelfth-century fair. When Théodora is asked about a certain picture, she explains that it is a portrait of the Wandering Jew from whom she is descended. She adds that her forbear was condemned by the Lord to walk the face of the earth without rest (I, 1-2). Curfew rings, and Ashvérus appears wandering in the darkness and followed by a band of brigands

(I, 3-5). Ludgers tells his men that they are in trouble because it was the countess of Flanders whom they have murdered for her jewelry and whose daughter they have kidnapped. They are about to slay the child when Ashvérus intervenes. The bandits attack him but break their weapons upon his immortal body. They recognize him as the Wandering Jew and flee in terror (I, 6-7). Théodora offers Ashvérus drink and lodging, but he cannot accept. His actions convince her that he is her father. He gives her the countess' child to guard and departs (I, 8-9).

The second act shifts to Bulgaria 12 years later. Irène believes that Théodora and Léon are her siblings. Théodora has brought Irène to Bulgaria because her father Boudoin was emperor of the Orient before his death, and she wished to return Irène to him. Léon has fallen in love with Irène. Ludgers and his band ask for lodging on their way to Byzance to attend the coronation of Nicéphore, who has been named emperor because Irène is believed to be dead (II, 1-2). Ludgers has turned to slaving and kidnaps Irène to sell her to Nicéphore (II, 3), and Léon admits his love for her to his sister, but she adds that she can never be his wife. When Léon discovers that Irène has been kidnapped, however, he and Théodora leave for Thessalonica to find her. Ludgers displays her to Nicéphore, but Ashvérus declares to the people that Irène is their empress. Nicéphore agrees to accept this assertion as the truth if the Jew will pass a trial by fire. He is tied to the stake, the fire is lighted, and the flames are extinguished by a mysterious force. Irène is acclaimed empress by the people (II, 4-8).

Irène mounts the throne in Constantinople; Léon despairs of his love for her (III, 1-2). The empress orders Théodora and Léon to remain with her to watch the shepherd Aristée charm a swarm of bees and to help her greet petitioners. Nicéphore enters first to propose that Irène marry him to maintain peace in the empire, and she is about to abdicate, but Nicéphore gives her the crown that she places on her head (III, 3-5). She and Léon declare their mutual love, and the empress swears to reject Nicéphore (IV, 1-2). Nicéphore and Ludgers have overheard them, however, and they vow to slay the lovers (IV, 3). The Wandering Jew prays for an end to his suffering, and Ludgers' bandits lay in wait for Léon (IV, 4). Invulnerable Ashvérus tries to come to Léon's aid, but the latter rejects his help, and Ludgers stabs him before throwing him into the sea (IV, 5-6).

Léon reappears on the beach to greet his father, who has prayed for his rescue. Ashvérus tells his son and daughter, Théodora and Léon, to return to Constantinople with Irène because Nicéphore is dead. The Wandering Jew's prayers for death are answered (V, 1-2) because it is finally the Day of Judgment, but he is reawakened by the angel and ordered to continue on his way across the earth (V, 3-4).

The score of Halévy's Le Juif errant did not match his music for La Juive,* but a few passages in it did move the spectators to applaud. The first act included Théodora's "Marche! marche! marche!" (I, 2) and her duet with her father, "Un pauvre voyageur" (I, 9). The bandits' quartet in scene 3, beginning "Moi, j'ai parcouru l'Asie" and the duet, "A moi, ta soeur et ton ami, in scene 5, were outstanding in the second act. Yet the rest of the composition contained little that was exceptional except perhaps for "Je t'attendais, mon frère," the duet by Irène and Léon in act 4, scene 2. The one certain sensation in the work was not in the music, but in the ballet, when Mlle Marie Taglioni* executed "the step of the bees" in the third act. It might be added here that the part of trumpets in the Last Judgment scene of the final act was played by saxophones.

The artists appearing in the premiere performance of Le Juif Errant included Gustave Roger* as Léon, Massol as Ashvérus, and Louis-Henri Obin* as Nicéphore. Mme Fortunata Tedesco and Mlle Emmy La Grua appeared in the parts of Théodora and Irène, respectively.

BIBLIOGRAPHY: Chouquet, 412; DDO I, 625-26; Lajarte II, 211; SSBO 221, 224.

La Juive is an opera in five acts with music by Jacques Fromenthal Halévy,* a libretto by Eugène Scribe,* and choreography by Filippo Taglioni (see eighteenth-century volume for Taglioni). It had its world premiere at the Opéra on 23 February 1835 in a production promoted by Duponchel that cost 150,000 francs, and the sets and costumes alone were enough to impress the public. The work enjoyed its 100th performance as early as 5 June 1840, and it was billed on more than 350 dates by the time that the opera house in the rue Peletier* was destroyed by fire on 28 October 1874. Its first two acts were included on the program celebrating the inauguration of the present Opéra on 5 January 1875, and, three days later on 8 January 1875, it was given in its entirety on the first bill available to the paying public at the new opera house. On this last occasion, the impresario Léon Carvalho* was in charge of production, and Louis Mérante* provided fresh choreography for Halévy's work. Although La Juive was not billed at the Opéra between 1893 and 1933, it has been given in this theatre on nearly 200 dates. In all, the Opéra has offered it to the public on 562 occasions. The Théâtre-Lyrique also presented La Juive in 1910.

The curtain rises on the first act of La Juive with Léopold ordering his workers to continue with their tasks on his house, although it is a feast day in Constance and despite the murmurings of the people. Albert recognizes Léopold disguised to keep his presence unknown to Sigismond, who is coming to open the ecclesiastical council designed to eradicate the Hussite schism (I, 1). Ruggiero announces the gift of free wine to the people on this feast day, and he denounces Eléazar for working. Eléazar and his daughter are arrested and led away for burning (I, 2-3). Cardinal Brogni emerges from the cathedral and recognizes Eléazar as the Jew whom he banished from Rome for usury. He pardons Eléazar (I, 4). Léopold serenades Rachel, who believes that the singer is Samuel; she invites him to celebrate Passover with her father and her in the evening. The wine begins to flow in the public fountains, and the drinkers celebrate in song and dance. The crowd pushes Rachel and Eléazar to the church, where Ruggiero denounces them a second time for profaning a holy place, and the people carry them off to cast them into the lake (I, 5-6). Léopold sees his beloved Rachel being mauled by the mob, and he drives the aggressors away with his sword. A group of soldiers led by Albert recaptures Rachel and seizes Léopold dressed as Samuel, but Léopold orders Albert's soldiers to desist, and Rachel is surprised to see Christians obey her Jewish Samuel (I, 7). Eléazar enters bleeding and pursued by Christians, and Léopold orders the crowd to break off their chase. Rachel is amazed at his power once again, but he resolves that she will never know his name or the source of his power as prince of the Empire. The act closes with the pageantry of Sigismond's entrance with the members of the council (I, 8).

Léopold is observing Passover in Eléazar's house, and he is obliged to discard the unleavened bread, an act noticed by Rachel. The emperor's niece Eudoxie enters to reveal that she is the wife of Léopold and wishes to purchase from Eléazar a special necklace encrusted with jewels; she intends to give it to her husband as a memento for having conquered the Hussites (II, 1-2). Léopold asks Rachel to meet him later, and he leaves after the night prayer (II, 3-4). He returns to admit to Rachel that he is a Crhistian, however, and he suggests that they run away and try to live happily by themselves (II, 5-6). Eléazar appears suddenly and asks where they are going; Rachel persuades her father to allow them to marry despite the injunction against mixed marriages. Léopold rushes into the street without explaining why he cannot become her husband (II, 7).

Eudoxie and Léopold give a dinner and ballet for the emperor, the kings of the earth, and the princes of the church. Eléazar and Rachel enter the banquet hall to deliver the necklace to Eudoxie. They are astonished to behold Léopold-Samuel there, and the latter is overwhelmed, while Rachel and her father are speechless upon learning that Eudoxie is the wife of Samuel-Léopold. Rachel tears the necklace from Eudoxie's hands and denounces her former suitor by describing him as the lover of a Jewess. When she adds that she is this Jewess, Cardinal Brogni places her, Eléazar, and Léopold under anathema. The damned trio are led off to prison (III, 1-2).

Eudoxie persuades Rachel to testify for Léopold (IV, 1-2). Cardinal Brogni tries to save Rachel, but he cannot persuade Eléazar to renounce his faith. Eléazar reminds him that the Jews came to his aid during the sack of Rome by the king of Naples when his daughter was saved from the flames. He reveals that he knows the whereabouts of his daughter, but he refuses to divulge this information (IV, 3-4). Eléazar decides momentarily to save Rachel but then proves to be unwilling to let her be lost to Israel (IV, 5).

Eléazar and Rachel are led in to be boiled alive, and Léopold has been sentenced to banishment. Rachel admits that she has testified in behalf of Léopold (V, 1-3). Eléazar and his daughter are brought before the boiling cauldron, and Cardinal Brogni asks Eléazar whether his daughter is alive. He assures the cardinal that she lives. She is before him and is about to die. But it is too late for the cardinal to intervene. The Jew and his "daughter" die (V, 4).

La Juive marks the summit of Halévy's musical genius, and the score is filled with passages that have been played at social and military concerts. Perhaps the most impressive piece of music in the entire opera is Cardinal Brogni's aria, "Si la rigueur et la vengeance" (I, 4), which is followed almost immediately by two other memorable moments in the work: Léopold's serenade, "Loin de son ami" (I, 5), and the drinking chorus by the populace, "Du vin! du vin! du vin!" (I, 5). The second act is the richest portion of the composition musically. It opens with the celebrated Easter scene and includes the trio by Eudoxie, Eléazar, and Léopold, "Tu possèdes, dit-on, un joyau magnifique" (II, 2), as well as Eléazar's "Dieu, que ma voix tremblante" (II, 1), Rachel's "Il va venir" (II, 5), and the duet, "Lorsqu'à toi je me suis donnée" (II, 6). The fourth act features the suspenseful duet between Brogni and Eléazar, "Ta fille en ce moment est devant le concile" (IV, 4), words laden with dramatic irony that becomes fully apparent only at the conclusion of the opera. A second passage in this act that moved spectators was Eléazar's "Rachel! quand du Seigneur la grâce tutélaire" (IV, 5).

The role of Rachel based upon Sir Walter Scott's Rebecca was filled initially by Mlle Cornélie Falcon,* and the part of Eléazar inspired by Shakespeare's Shylock was created by Adolphe Nourrit.* Mme Julie Dorus-Gras* did Eudoxie with Marcel Lafont as Léopold and Nicolas Levasseur* as the cardinal. Gilbert Duprez* made a deep impression upon the public during the 1847 revival of La Juive; Mme Marie-Gabrielle Krauss* made her debut as Rachel on 5 January 1875. Albert Aveline* created new choreography for the work in 1933.

BIBLIOGRAPHY: *Neil Cole Arvin, Eugène Scribe and the French Theatre, 1815-1860 (Cambridge: Harvard University Press, 1924), 202-7; Chouquet 398; DDO I, 626-27; HUT 92-93; KCOB 749-55; Lajarte II, 149-50; Moniteur universel 59 (28 February 1835),*

438; NMO 320-40; OQE 109-10; PBSW 55, 109-10, 225; SSBO 176, 178, 221; SST 299-318; SW 129-31.

Les Jumeaux de Bergame was a pantomime-ballet in a single act with a score by Théodore de Lajarte,* a scenario based upon Florian by Charles Nuitter* and Louis Mérante,* and choreography by Louis Mérante.* It had its world premiere at the casino de Paramé during the summer of 1885, and it was brought to the stage of the Garnier Palace* on 26 January 1886. Unfortunately, it failed to win support at the Opéra, and it had to be dropped from the repertory here after its fourth presentation.

In Les Jumeaux de Bergame, the curtain rises to disclose a public square lined with busy shops of every sort. Lélio keeps walking up and down in front of Pantalon's place of business because he hopes to catch a glimpse of his beloved Isabelle. He is disappointed and about to leave when he meets Pantalon's servant, Nérine, who refuses to deliver a note to Isabelle. At this same moment, Pantalon appears with his daughter and his lackey, Arlequin. Lélio follows them in the hope of finding an opportunity to speak with Isabelle. Coraline sets up her floral displays, and Arlequin begins to throw kisses at her because he is captivated by her charm and beauty. Pantalon rebukes him. Lélio buys an expensive bouquet from Coraline, and he gives Arlequin an écu to deliver it to Isabelle. Pantalon discovers Lélio's card in the flowers and chases Arlequin away with threats.

Arlequin begins to curse Pantalon because he has dismissed him from his service for having delivered Lélio's bouquet to Isabelle. He decides to return to his beloved Coraline to find solace, but Pantalon's servant Nérine stops him because she is in love with him despite his love for Coraline. Arlequin lacks malice, and he begins to dance with Nérine in an effort to distract her. She thinks that he is now in love with her, but he assures her that he can think only of Coraline. She is furious and rushes off to her master's home.

Arlequin is alone again, and he now turns to Coraline. He is speaking with her as the lottery cart comes down the street. She purchases a ticket. The cart is filled with actors from the Théâtre Italien, and one of them is a second

Arlequin, that is, the brother of the first Arlequin. The younger brother, Arlequin II, goes in search of Arlequin I, Coraline's sweetheart, and he knocks on Pantalon's door. Pantalon opens the door and mistakes Arlequin II for his former servant. He kicks him downstairs. Puzzled but not discouraged, Arlequin II now knocks at Coraline's door. She gives him her portrait and the lottery ticket. Arlequin is perplexed by the mixed reception he is receiving in Bergamo, especially when Nérine seizes his lottery ticket and runs off with it.

Night falls, and Arlequin I returns to call upon Coraline. She emerges from her house to speak with him, but she is puzzled when he professes to know nothing of her portrait and lottery ticket. Finally, she loses her temper and goes back into her house. Arlequin II comes past Coraline's house now and recognizes it. He serenades the young lady who gave him a lottery ticket, but his song is soon interrupted by Arlequin I. The two Arlequins begin to fight, but the neighbors separate them. Coraline and Nérine cannot believe their eyes when they see the two Arlequins, who resemble each other so closely. Arlequin I identifies himslef to Coraline; he recognizes his brother and suggests to Nérine that she marry him. Nérine agrees; she returns the portrait and lottery ticket to Coraline. The two Arlequins announce their weddings, and Coraline wins the lottery. Small Pulcinellas bring her the sacks of money. She gives Pantalon two sacks of écus, and consents to the marriage of Isabelle and Lélio. She divides the remaining money between Nérine and herself.

The male parts in this unsuccessful ballet were danced by Louis Mérante (Pantalon) and Vasquez fils (Lélio). The female roles were filled by Julia Subra (Coraline), Marie Sanlaville (Arlequin I), Marie Biot (Arlequin II), Invernizzi (Isabelle), Gina Ottolini (Nérine).

BIBLIOGRAPHY: Stoullig XII (1886), 2-4; SW 291; Thompson 970.

K

Karsavina, Tamara Platonovna (b. 9 March 1885, St. Petersburg; d. 26 May 1978, Beaconsfield, Buckinghamshire, U.K.), Russian ballerina, was the only daughter of the dancer Platon Karsavin, but it was her mother who guided her into a career as a ballerina by arranging for her to take preparatory lessons with Varvara Nikitina and to enter the School of the Imperial Ballet in 1894. Here she studied under the direction of Pavel Gerdt and distinguished herself as an alert, gifted, and graceful dancer.

After graduation from ballet school in her native city, she continued to study under the direction of her father. Also in 1902, she made her stage debut in a minor role in Javotte* at the Maryinski Theatre. She was likewise assigned to her first important part in 1902, when she was cast as Flore in Le Réveile de Flore.

It now appeared that the young danseuse was beyond all doubt destined for a brilliant stage career; then she fell ill in May 1904. Her malady was diagnosed as malaria, and it was suggested that she interrupt her dancing to go to Italy for a cure. She responded well to the regimen prescribed for her in the more moderate climate in southern Europe, and she decided to profit from her leave of absence by taking lessons from the prestigious teacher Caterina Beretta under whom Vera Trefilova and Anna Pavlova* had already studied. When she returned to Russia in the fall, she had regained her strength and was ready to resume her career. She added The Trial of Damis and Graziella to her repertory. She went on her first Russian tour in 1906, and she filled leading roles in such classical ballets as Le Lac des cygnes and Paquita.* More importantly perhaps, she began to enlarge her circle of acquaintances at this time and came to know such important personalities as Léon Bakst,* Olga Preobrajenskaya, and Mikhail Fokine.* Yet Karsavina did not feel that she could lay claim to stardom until her trip to Prague and her filling the leads at the Maryinski Theatre in Swan Lake and Corsair in 1909.

It was also in 1909 that Serge Diaghilev* offered the ballerina a contract to appear with his troupe at the Châtelet Theatre in Paris. She was quick to accept the opportunity to visit this city where she "expected the streets to be like ballroom floors and to be peopled exclusively with smart ladies walking along with a frou-frou of silk petticoats." Thus, Karsavina come to open the first season of the Ballets russes* in Paris on 19 May 1909 by dancing in Le Pavillon d'Armide with Vaslav Nijinsky* and his sister Bronislava Nijinska.* She was also billed at the Garnier Palace* on the followign dates when Diaghilev moved to the Opéra:

Character or Assignment	Work	Date
Pas de deux	Le Festin	19 June 1909
Chopin Valse op. 64	Les Sylphides	19 June 1909
Zobéide	Schéhérazade	4 June 1910
Esclave favorite	Cléopâtre	11 June 1910
Giselle	Giselle	18 June 1910
Oiseau de feu	L'Oiseau de feu	25 June 1910
La Jeune Fille	Spectre de la rose	19 December 1911
-	Coq d'or	24 May 1914
La Ballerine	Petrouchka	24 May 1914
Cléopâtre	Cléopâtre	2 June 1914

La Ballerine	<u>Pétrouchka</u>	24 December 1914
Colombine	<u>Carnaval</u>	27 December 1919
Mariuccia	<u>Les Femmes de bonne humeur</u>	27 December 1919
Miller's wife	<u>Le Tricorne</u>	23 January 1920

These roels at the Opéra and other parts executed in the theatres of Europe made Karsavina as well as Nijinsky one of Diaghilev's most successful stars, and her interpretations of Fokine's ballets inspired applause whenever and wherever she appeared. In her turn, she remained faithful to her compatriot's company and returned to his organization until his death in 1929, when she appeared in <u>Pétrouchka</u>* during the impresario's last London season. Her marriage in 1915 induced her to reside in London, however, and her stage activities were limited largely to this city after World War I. She threw her lot in with Marie Rambert's company after Diaghilev's death.

Tamara Karsavina was named prima ballerina in 1910.

BIBLIOGRAPHY: Alexandre Benois, <u>Memoirs</u>, trans. Moura Budberg, intro Tamara Karsavina, 2 vols. (London: Chatto and Windus, 1960); CODB 289-90; DDD 124-25; HAZ 192-94; Tamara Karsavina, <u>Theatre Street: The Reminiscences of Tamara Karsavina</u> (London: Dance Books Ltd., 1981); idem, <u>Classical Ballet: The Flow of Movement</u> (New York: Dance Horizons, c. 1962) 1-94; LTX 154-215.

Keys and Doors might seem to have no place in a work devoted to opera and ballet, but these two things do provide a certain interest, and, in their picturesque fashion, they furnish an idea of the complexity of managing an opera house and representing its productions. Also, the keys to the Garnier Palace* offered a touch of dour humor on the evening of the German occupation of 1940, when Serge Lifar remembered in panic that he had forgotten to lock the theatre (see twentieth-century volume for Lifar).

The doors encountered in the Opéra may not be dismissed simply as doors because there are double as well as single doors in this structure. Too, there are closet and cupboard doors, and all of them require keys at least in theory. Then there are three separate areas in the opera house, and each of them has different needs. When M. Charles Nuitter* drew up his catalogue of keys and doors in 1875, the year of the inauguration of the theatre, he arrived at the following statistics:

Administration area doors

Single Doors, 675

Double Doors, 196

Cupboard doors, 813

Total administration doors, 1,684

Audience area doors

Single doors, 452

Double doors, 249

Cupboard doors, 47

Total audience doors, 748

Stage area doors

Single doors, 34

Double doors, 1

Cupboard doors, 65

Total stage doors, 100

Yet no fewer than 7,593 keys were made and distributed to open and to close the locks on these 2,532 doors.
BIBLIOGRAPHY: *Petite Encyclopédie illustrée de l'Opéra de Paris* *(Paris: Opéra, 1978), 140.*

La Korrigane was billed as a fantastic ballet in two acts with a score by Charles-Marie Widor* and a scenario by François Coppée. Louis Mérante* created its choreography, and its sets were designed by Lavastre, Rubé, and Chaperon. Eugène Lacoste was responsible for its costumes. It had its world premiere at the Garnier Palace* on 1 December 1880.

The ballet begins in the public square of a Breton village in the seventeenth century. It is the Feast of the Pilgrimage, and the square is filled with drinkers, gossips, peddlers, beggars, and children. The tavernkeeper Loïc greets the hunchback Pascou, and the crowd disperses.

Yvonnette appears. She is downcast because she must continue to work as a tavernmaid. Pascou makes advances to her, and she flees. The begger boy Janik threatens Pascou, but vespers sound, and Yvonnette gives Janik his supper. Handsome Lilez enters with a cheerful greeting for everybody but Pascou. A peddler sells a rosary to Lilez with the reminder that the beads will protect him against Korriganes. Lilez pockets the rosary, and Pascou derides him for being superstitious.

Yvonnette brings a drink of cider to Lilez, who gives her some money to help her ease the strain of her poverty, but she hands the coins to Janik. An old woman passing by slips and falls. Yvonnette helps her, and she promises to help Yvonnette because she knows that the girl loves Lilez. The old woman reveals herself to be the queen of the Korriganes, and she conjures up a company of dwarfs, who bring lovely clothes and precious jewels to the tavernmaid. There is a condition attached to these gifts, however, because Yvonnette must become a Korrigane if Lilez does not prove his love for her before the first stroke of the Angelus. The dazzled girl accepts this condition. Pascou has witnessed this agreement.

The crowd emerges from the church, and Lilez is stunned by Yvonnette's charm and appearance. They dance, and Pascou steals his rosary. Lilez proposes marriage to Yvonnette to prove his love to her, and the jealous hunchback pushes the hands of the clock ahead so that the Angelus will ring. The Korriganes appear and seize Yvonnette, who protests. The queen refuses to listen to explanations, and Yvonnette is carried away despite Lilez' efforts to protect her (a. 1).

The scene shifts to a deserted heath, where eerie music is playing, and the Korriganes are dancing. The beggar boy Janik and the hunchback Pascou enter with some drunken companions. Pascou is fearless because he has a rosary, and he accepts wine from Janik. He becomes drowsy and falls asleep; Janik steals his rosary and runs away. The dwarfs seize the unprotected hunchback, and Yvonnette explains to the queen that it is he who turned back the hands of the clock to sound the Angelus prematurely. The queen touches the culprit with her wand, and two jackass ears sprout from his head. The dwarfs force him to dance until he falls into a hole.

Lilez enters in search of Yvonnette, and the Korriganes surround him. The queen tells him that he can have his sweetheart if he can find her. Each Korrigane throws her arms around his neck, but he rejects them all. Finally, he repulses Yvonnette herself when the queen reinforces her spell over her. But Yvonnette has an idea. She will dance the same steps that caught Lilez' eye when they met for the first time. She begins the dance, and the Korriganes try to imitate her to confuse Lilez, but they fail. Lilez rushes to his beloved, but the Korriganes try to stop him. Janik arrives in the nick of time with the rosary, and the Korriganes flee, especially because dawn is breaking. Lilez thanks the beggar and embraces his happy Yvonnette (a. 2).

The score and the music of La Korrigane were hailed as a great success by the critics who were especially impressed by the contrast between the earthy Breton peasants of act 1 and the ethereal Korriganes of act 2. In fact, the critics' judgment proved correct, and the work was exceedingly well received. It enjoyed its 100th billing at the Opéra on 18 May 1896, and it was revived subsequently in 1916 and 1933. Eventually, it was performed on 160 dates between 1880 and 1935. The leading roles at the world premiere were filled by Rosita Mauri* (Yvonnette), Marie Sanlaville (queen of the Korriganes), and Isabel Ottolini (Janik) alongside Louis Mérante* (Lilez), M. Ajas (the hunchback Pascou) and Cornet (Loïc). Mauri scored a complete triumph in La Korrigane, especially with the number that she danced in sabots. Unfortunately, it was not long before she hurt her foot in one of these tricky exhibitions.

BIBLIOGRAPHY: AEM 14, 584-85; René Baron, "La Korrigane," RM 16, no. 147 (June 1934), 126-27; BOP 134-35, 150; CB 501-7; CODB 302; EDS IX, 1936; H. Moréno, "Semaine théâtrale: La Korrigane," Le Ménestrel 47 (5 December 1880), 3-4; Stoullig XLI (1916), 12-14; SW 292; VOP 58, 68, 71, 81-83.

Kousnetzoff, Maria (b. 1880, Odessa, Russia; d. 26 April 1966, Paris), vocalist, began her theatrical career as a ballet dancer in St. Petersburg, where she decided to become a singer about 1905. She came to Paris in 1906 or 1907, and she made her debut at the Opéra as Elsa in Lohengrin* on 1 February 1908. She sang Marguerite in Faust* and the female leads in Roméo et Juliette* and Thaïs* this same year. The following three years saw her do three roles at the Garnier: the title-parts of Gwendoline* in 1911, of Salomé* in 1912, and Aïda* in 1913.

Mme Kousnetzoff returned to Russia during World War I, but she had to emigrate to Sweden in 1917 because of the Revolution. She returned to Paris finally in 1920, but the Opéra no longer interested her. She turned to making movies to improve her financial situation, and she founded the Opéra Russe in the French capital in 1927. This venture demanded all her energy until 1939.

Mme Kousnetzoff had sung at the Opéra-Comique when she had first arrived in Paris, but she never returned to this theatre in later years. Her roles here had included Manon, in which she had made her debut on 19 April 1910, Tosca, Cio-Cio-San, and Violetta.

BIBLIOGRAPHY: A. Favia-Artsay, "Maria N. Kouznetsova," Hobbies 73 (July 1968), 36ff.; EFC 181; KRJ 227; PBSW 186; SW 29, 88, 108, 135, 191, 196, 208; WOC 259.

Krauss, Marie Gabrielle (b. 24 March 1842, Vienna; d. 6 January 1906, Paris), soprano, studied at the Conservatorium in Vienna and was one of Mme Marchesi's favorite pupils. She was invited to join the Imperial Opera in her native city, and she made her theatrical debut there as a soprano on 20 July 1860 as Mathilde in Guillaume Tell.* She was greeted with so much enthusiasm in the large number of roles that she sang during her first months at the Vienna opera house that M. Bagier asked her to perform at the Théâtre-Italien, of which he was director. She agreed and made her Paris debut in Il Trovatore on 6 April 1866, but it was not until 1867 that the public became aware of the power of her genius and the scope of her artistry. She did Norma, Polito, Otello, and the other principal works of the Italian repertory, and the public was vociferous in its approbation of her performances until the political events of 1870 interfered with Franco-

Austrian relations and Mme Krauss' career in Paris.

The soprano returned to the Théâtre-Italien in 1873, and she was billed at the Opéra on 5 January 1875, when she made her debut at the Garnier palace* by singing Rachel in the first two acts of La Juive* at the inauguration at this new opera house. She went on to sing Valentine and Dona Anna in the first presentations of Les Huguenots* and Don Juan* at the Garnier on 26 April 1875 and 29 November 1875, respectively. The next year, she was cast as Alice in Robert le Diable* on 6 December and, in 1877, as Agathe in Le Freischütz* and Sélika in L'Africaine.* She did not do Marguerite in Faust* until 1882, but she was billed in the title-role of Sapho* for the first production of this work by Charles Gounod* at the Garnier on 2 April 1884.

She created eight roles on the following dates during her association with the Opéra:

Role	Opera	Premiere
Jeanne d'Arc	Jeanne d'Arc (Mermet)	5 April 1876
Pauline	Polyeucte	7 October 1878
Aïda	Aïda	22 March 1880
La Vierge	La Vierge	22 May 1880
Hermosa	Le Tribut de Zamora	1 April 1881
Cathérine d'Aragon	Henry VIII	5 March 1883
Gilda	Rigoletto	27 February 1885
Dolorès	Patrie!	16 December 1886

Mme Krauss was praised for her clear delivery and her ability to convey the drama as well as the pathos in the roles in which she was cast. Her versatility was linguistic and theatrical, because she never hesitated or made errors, whether she was singing in German, Italian, or French. Her stage presence was commanding, and, as if this quality were not enough to assure her stardom, she was as beautiful and as gracious as she was talented and intelligent. It is a pertinent commentary upon her personality that she was as popular in Naples, Milan, Paris, and St. Petersburg as she was in Vienna.

BIBLIOGRAPHY: Anon., "Mlle Krauss," FM 33 (28 November 1869), 374-75; Guy de Charnacé, "Les Etoiles du chant; Gabrielle Krauss," Le Ménestrel 36, (21 November 1869), 404-5; Henri de Curzon, Croquis d'artistes (Paris: Fischbacher, 1898), 71-82; DEO 247; EFC 153; Fétis, Suppl. II, 47-49; GE XXI, 641-42; ICM 954; Lermina 846; Martin 199; PBSW 186; SW 25, 27, 74, 88, 102, 111-12, 116, 125, 129, 170, 175, 182, 185, 198, 213, 378; Thurner 295-304; XYZ 243-48.

L

Labarre, Théodore (b. 5 March 1805, Paris; d. 9 March 1870, Paris), composer, took his first music lessons on the harp from Cousineau between ages 7 and 9, and he continued with this instrument until 1820 under the direction of Bochsa and Naderman. Convinced that their son might have a bright future in music, his parents entered him in the Conservatoire to study harmony under Dourlen, counterpoint under Eler, and composition under François Boïeldieu (see eighteenth-century volume for Boïeldieu). Although he was only 18, he entered the Prix de Rome competition in 1823, but he placed second and went to England instead of to Italy in 1824.

Now a professional musician, Labarre gave concerts in London, Brighton, and Bath in addition to performing in Ireland and Scotland. He made England his temporary home, and he returned to the Continent only between seasons to make personal appearances wherever possible in Switzerland, Italy, and France. After a few years, however, he decided to write for the theatre in Paris, and he moved to the French capital, where he did his first lyric drama entitled Les Deux Familles (1831) for the Ventadour. This work was not a success, but he was not discouraged and gave La Révolte au sérail to the Opéra in 1833. This second composition was greated with enthusiasm by the public, but Labarre must have felt inclined to return to making personal appearances because he recrossed the Channel. His plans did not work out to his satisfaction, however, and he spent most of his time giving lessons during this stay in

England, when he married the singer Mlle Lambert in 1837.

Labarre returned to Paris once more in 1847 to succeed Girard at the Opéra-Comique, when the latter administrator moved up to the directorship of the Opéra. Labarre seemed to be content in his new position, and he produced Le Ménétrier at the Opéra-Comique in 1849. Then, suddenly, he went back to England because of the political atmosphere in Paris or for some other personal reason. In any event, he was in London during the coup d'état of Napoleon III in 1851, and he returned to Paris because he must have felt that the winds of fortune were blowing in his direction again. Apparently he was correct because he joined the emperor's private group of musicians without delay, and he was able to take advantage of his political position by having his Jovita* of 1853 staged at the Opéra. His ballet La Fonti* was billed at the same theatre in 1855. Labarre had written only ballets for the Opéra until this time, but his opéra-bouffe called Pantagruel* was performed here on Christmas eve of 1855. He reverted to ballet, however, with his last two compositions at the Opéra, Graziosa* of 1861 and Le Roi d'Yvetot* of 1865.

Labarre's two most popular works proved to be Jovita and Graziosa, but his most important addition to the literature of music is doubtlessly the hundred or so pieces for the harp that he left after his death. These compositions included duets for harp and piano; trios for harp, horn, and bassoon; and duets for harp and oboe, violin, or horn.

BIBLIOGRAPHY: AEM VIII, 10; CB 204-8, 365-69; Fétis V, 147-48; Lajarte II, 147, 195, 215, 217, 219, 231, 239; LXIX X, 4; Wks 6562, 8376, 11232, 12877, 12879.

Le Lac des aulnes is a fairy ballet in two acts and five tableaux with an argument and a score by Henri Maréchal.* It was given its world premiere at the Garnier Palace on 25 November 1907 with sets by Marcel Jambon* and Marcel Bailly, costumes by Charles Bétout, and colored projections in light at the start of the second act by Eugène Frey. Vanara created its choreography.

The action of the ballet takes place in Bohemia during the Middle Ages, and the first act is set at the home of a magician who is working in his laboratory. He waves his wand to capture three butterflies that he places with his other captive creatures in an adjacent room. Elfen detaches himself from the tapestry and makes himself invisible with his sprig of alder, and he watches the magician capture three winged genii. After Elfen discovers the magician's procedures, he thwarts his operations. The angry magician sees that Elfen has disappeared from the tapestry, but he cannot find him to punish him.

The magician's attractive daughter, Lulla, enters to reproach her father for working too late at night, and she discovers that he has put winged creatures in a prison. Elfen makes the same discovery and decides to become visible only to Lulla. He dances with the young girl, and, when the magician hears them kiss, he sends his daughter off to bed and tries to locate Elfen, who returns to his tapestry to elude him. The magician locks his door, and his fellow sorcerers come down the chimney to dance and to escort the magician to their sabbath.

Elfen leaves his tapestry again to enter Lulla's bedroom, but he has lost his talisman and must borrow another alder branch from one of the King of the Alders' daughters in the tapestry. He enters Lulla's room, and they dance. She waves the enchanted branch, and the magician's winged prisoners are freed. When she waves the branch a second time, salamanders and crickets are liberated. The King of the Alders appears and orders all the freed genii to return to his lake through the window. Elfen abducts Lulla just as the magician returns, and he recognizes her kidnapper. He calls for his winged dragon and follows his daughter in a fiery flight (a. 1).

The second act moves to the lake of alders, where the winged creatures have sought refuge. Illuminated projections present a city on a rocky crag, the arrival of Lulla and Elfen, and the moon shining through the branches of the alders bordering the lake. Here, the King of the Alders is sitting with his three daughters clothed in long robes. The liberated butterflies dance with the flowers, and undines emerge from the lake. Lulla recognizes the natural reproduction of the tapestry in her home, and she insists upon returning to her father. She lingers because she is charmed by Schubert's music, and she engages in a dance that imitates the movements of the three princesses moving across the surface of the lake. Elfen waves his talisman, and she is able to dance over the water with the daughters of the King of the Alders. She accompanies them to their grotto.

The magician appears in the sky on his dragon. He is surrounded by his salamanders, and Lulla is delighted to see him, although Elfen is angry. The magician lifts his wand and makes his way toward his daughter until the king stops him to scold him for capturing harmless butterflies. The king declares that he is holding the magician's daughter prisoner as the penalty for her father's cruelty. Overwhelmed by this decision, Lulla dies. The grotto crumbles, and the liberated magician despairs over his daughter's death. He breaks his wand; he throws its pieces and himself into the lake. The Angelus sounds, and the sun rises. Lulla reappears as a dragonfly. She and Elfen fly away across the shimmering lake (a. 2).

The ballet was not a success, and it had to be dropped from the repertory after its fifth billing at the Opéra on 25 December 1907, when it was given on a program with Le Borne's La Catalane.* The five female roles in the composition were filled by Carlotta Zambelli* (Lulla), Antonine Meunier (Elfen, travesty), and Mlles Trouhanova, L. Mante, and L. Piron (king's three daughters) with MM. Vanara (the magician) and Girodier (king) cast in the male parts. Mme Charlotte-Marie Agussol* was the vocalist selected for the singing part, and Mme Catulle Mendès read a commentary in verse on the subject of the ballet before performances.

BIBLIOGRAPHY: Stoullig XXXIII (1907), 27-29; SW 292.

Le Lac des fées was an opera in five acts with a score by Daniel Auber,* a libretto by Eugène Scribe* and Mélesville, and choreography by Jean Coralli.* It had its world premiere at the Opéra on 1 April 1839 and was given on 30 programs between its initial performance and its last presentation on 14 September 1840. It was produced in a version of four acts on 25 October 1839.

The opera opens with Albert and his university companions lost in the Hartz mountains near the lake of the fairies. The latter creatures bathe in this lake and slay all invaders of their privacy. The students decide to return quickly to Cologne, but Albert stays behind (I, 1-3). The fairies arrive upon the scene, and Albert steals Zéila's veil, which protects her from becoming and earthbound mortal. Albert's worried comrades return to find him, and the fairies flee in panic, but Zéila must remain hidden (I, 4). Albert leaves, and the fairies disappear into the sky without Zéila (I, 5-7).

Marguerite welcomes some travelers to her inn and is concerned over her fiance Albert (II, 1-2). He arrives finally, but he is so in love with Zéila that he tries to borrow 25 écus from Issachar to pay his debt to Marguerite so that he can then break his engagement to her (II, 3-4). Unsuccessful, he seeks a way to return to Zéila, who wanders into the inn as a mortal obliged to work (II, 5-7). Marguerite is suspicious of the veil that Albert treats so carefully, but she rejects Rodolphe's proposal of marriage with the explanation that she is about to become Albert's wife. The count notices Zéila, recognizes Albert, and can sarcely believe that this young student is Marguerite's fiance (II, 8-11). Albert senses something familiar about Zéila when she serves his supper, but she insists that she is only a poor servant. He proposes marriage to her (II, 12), however, and jealous Marguerite dismisses Zéila. Albert wishes to leave with her, but he must remain at the inn because of his debt to Marguerite. Issachar lends him the money to discharge his obligation, and Rodolphe buys the bond on Albert's life for double the sum that Albert must pay to redeem himself. Albert and Zéila exit with Marguerite despairing, Rodolphe going off on a hunt, and Issachar counting his money (II, 13).

Albert and Zéila have enough money now to pay off the former's debt, and Albert's friends urge him to leave his attic to celebrate the Epiphany with Zéila (III, 1-2). The feast is observed with singing, dancing, and lavish displays of merchandise. Pikler and his crew circulate through the crowd picking pockets; Marguerite appears in sumptuous dress on the arm of Rodolphe. The Epiphany cakes are distributed; Zéila is chosen queen with Albert as her king to review the parade of artisans and the arrival of the three kings with their gifts. Pikler steals Albert's purse during the excitement (III, 3). Rodolphe demands his money from Albert at the appointed time, and the latter faints in despair after finding himself penniless. Marguerite sees the veil on his person and seizes it because she recognizes it as the fatal object that turned Albert from her. The students rise up in the streets to protect Albert, and violence ensues (III, 4-5). Albert lunges at Rodolphe with his sword, but he strikes Zéila (III, 6).

Albert is now insane and cannot understand that Marguerite is freeing him from his cell in Rodolphe's château because she is angry with Rodolphe for having rejected her in favor of Zéila. His mental condition induces Rodolphe to make him his official fool, but Albert's comments about his captor and the guests at table are insulting and sarcastic enough to arouse Rodolphe's anger. He tries to kill Albert (IV, 1-4), when Zéila enters. She distracts the diners, and her presence restores her lover's sanity (IV, 5). Faced with this new situation, Rodolphe offers Zéila the choice of yielding to him or of seeing Albert executed. She refuses to witness her lover's death and is led away. Marguerite discloses that she has the magic veil, but she cannot trust Albert with it to free Zéila (IV, 6-7). Rodolphe prepares for his marriage to Zéila. Albert urges Marguerite to return the veil to its rightful owner, who escapes with it into the heavens as soon as she receives it (IV, 8).

Zéila continues to think of Albert in her celestial home and complains of boredom because he is not with her. She asks her queen for leave to return to earth and to Albert, and her wish is granted in time to dissuade Albert from suicide (V, 1-4).

The overture of Le Lac des fées was one of Auber's most applauded efforts. Two other memorable moments in the opera are the duet by Zéila and Albert, "Asile modeste et tranquille" (III, 1), and the students' chorus, "Vive la jeunesse!" (III, 2).

The roles of Zéila and Marguerite were sung by Mlle Maria Nau* and Mme Rosine Stoltz,* respectively. The three principal male parts were filled by Gilbert Duprez* (Albert), Nicolas Levasseur* (Rodolphe), and Pierre Wartel* (Issachar). Alexis Dupont and Ferdinand Prévôt were cast as students.

BIBLIOGRAPHY: Chouquet 401; DDO I, 634; B. Jouvin, D. F. E. Auber (Paris: Heugel, 1864), 75-76; Lajarte II, 159; Charles Malherbe, Auber (Paris: Renouard, n.d.), 46-47; Moniteur universel 94 (4 April 1839), 468.

Lacroix, Jules (b. 1809, Paris; d. 1887, Paris), librettist, received an excellent education and embarked upon a literary career without hesitation or interference. He published a long series of novels that brought him fame and fortune during his lifetime, and his poetry was both colorful and technically correct. Like his borther Bibliophile Jacob, he had an interest in literature and devoted his talents to translations of Macbeth, the satires of Juvenal, and the odes of Horace.

His activities for the theatre included Le Testament de César (1849), Valéria (1851), and Oedipe roi (1858) at the Comédie-Française; La Jeunesse de Louis XI (1859) at the Porte Saint-Martin Theatre; and Le Roi Lear (1868) at the Odéon. His only contribution to the Opéra was the unsuccessful La Fronde* of 1853, for which he wrote the libretto with August Maquet.*

BIBLIOGRAPHY: Chouquet 413; GE XXI, 725; Lajarte II, 213; LXIX X, 40; Thieme II, 14.

Lady Henriette, ou la servante de Greenwich was billed as a pantomimic ballet in three acts and nine tableaux. Its score was the fruit of a collaboration by Friedrich Flotow,* Frédéric Burgmuller,* and Edouard Marie Deldevez,* and its libretto was the work of Jules-Henri Vernoy de Saint-Georges* and Joseph Mazilier.* The choreography was created by Mazilier; Pierre Cicéri* designed the sets. The work had its world premiere at the Royal Academy of Music on 21 February 1844, when it was given with the first act of Moïse.*

The action of the ballet begins in 1706 at Windsor castle, where Lady Henriette is completing her toilette. A lady-in-waiting to the queen, she is bored with her boorish fiance, Sir Tristan Crankfort, and she decides suddenly to join a group of villagers on their way to a festival to seek employment (I, 1-3).

The second tableau moves to Greenwich, where bystanders at the fair are watching boxing matches, cock fights, and the dancing. A young and wealthy Welsh farmer named Lyonnel arrives on the scene with his friend Plumkett, their fiancees Mina and Alison, and Mina's rich mother. Lyonnel is quiet and distinguished; Plumkett is loud and strong. The village girls are beginning to find employment, and they must register with the alderman (I, tabl. 2, 1-2). Sir Tristan enters with Lady Henriette and Nancy disguised as villagers. Lyonnel tries to hire Lady Henriette, while Plumkett offers employment to Nancy. The women laugh at their proposals until they see that Sir Tristan is outraged. Spitefully, they accept the positions (I, tabl. 2, 3-5). Mina and Alison are furious to see the comely maidens hired by their fiances, but their indignation only prompts the two men to invite their two servants to dance. It grows late, however, and the countess and Nancy decide that it is time to rejoin Sir Tristan, but the Alderman obliges them to leave with their masters according to contract (I, tabl. 2, 6-7).

The two men and their recently acquired servants are back on Lyonnel's farm, and it is time for him to sign his marriage contract, although he seems more interested in the disguised countess than in Mina. The bride's family leaves, and, when Lyonnel finds himself alone with Lady Henriette, he admits his love for her. She is frightened by his insistence and calls for help. Angered, he forces her to perform a dozen tasks at once. Plumkett behaves in parallel fashion toward Nancy. The men retire, but the countess and her companion remain awake to discuss means of escape. Sir Tristan appears at the window. He has a carriage, and the women flee with him. Dawn breaks, and Lyonnel discovers that the servants have left. He announces that his marriage to Mina is canceled and tears up the contract. He rushes off in pursuit of Lady Henriette (I, tabl. 3, 1-5).

The second act opens in a tavern in Windsor Forest. Plumkett and Lyonnel have joined the queen's guard, and they are among the soldiers waiting to escort Her Majesty on a hunt. Lyonnel is depressed over losing his servant, but Plumkett is delighted to see Nancy arrive with the maids of honor. He runs up to her, but she flees (II, tabl. 1, 1-3). Queen Anne enters with Lady Henriette, her first maid-of-honor. The queen starts the hunt immediately, but the tired countess remains behind to rest. She is bored with Sir Tristan's declaration of love and falls asleep. The rejected suitor withdraws, but Lyonnel enters the room and recognizes her. He awakens her; she upbraids him for his presumptuousness and assures him that she does not know him. She leaves hurriedly, when Plumkett enters still chasing Nancy (II, tabl. 1, 4-6). Shots ring out, and a startled mount bolts with its helpless rider. The hunters leap into their saddles to rescue the helpless rider, but it is Lyonnel who returns with her in his arms. He has saved the queen. She recovers and she knights him. She offers him a jewel, but he asks only that he be allowed to see the ladies in her retinue because he is certain that the woman with her cape and hood wrapped closely about her is his missing servant. The queen grants his request, but he does not see his servant among the maids-of-honor because she has disappeared (II, tabl. 1, 7-9).

The action returns to Windsor Castle, where a ballet is about to begin under the direction of Sir Tristan dressed as Jupiter (II, tabl. 2). Lyonnel posts the guard, and the curtain rises at the castle to present Queen Anne dressed as Junon and ordering the ballet to begin. Lyonnel relieves the guard on the stage only to recognize Venus as his servant. He is unable to restrain himself; he rushes across the stage to embrace her. She faints. The spectators voice their indignation, and he is arrested (II, tabl. 3, 1-2).

Lady Henriette has retired to her boudoir, and she confides to Nancy that the soldier who interrupted the ballet was Lyonnel. Suddenly, there is a loud noise in the outside gallery. Lyonnel has escaped. He runs into the countess' boudoir and begs for sanctuary, but she orders him to leave. He pleads with her and reminds her that she has been the cause of all his trouble. Obdurate, she opens her door and calls for the palace guard. The poor man cannot support this betrayal, and he loses his sanity. Only the timely arrival of the guards prevents him from jumping through the window (III, tabl. 1, 1-3).

The setting moves to the park of the madhouse of Bedlam, where Plumkett and the queen are visiting Lyonnel. Sir Tristan has also come to the asylum only to be confronted by a strange singing teacher and an unpredictable dancing master. A third inmate insists upon telling his horoscope, and he is so annoyed that he draws his sword. The guards place him in confinement because he seems so violent (III, tabl. 2, 1-2). The recreation bell rings, and all the inmates rush into the park to join in a ballet wherein each dancer portrays his own monomania. The chief physician presents his most interesting case to the queen, a woman who believes herself to be the queen of England. Queen Anne and the countess try to help Lyonnel by expressing their gratitude to him, but he can think only of the latter's cruelty. Frightened, he runs away and faints from the strain of this emotional encounter (III, tabl. 2, 3-4).

The queen, her valets, Plumkett, and the doctor return Lyonnel to his home in the hope that he will recover his sanity. Everybody withdraws from his house except Plumkett, who sets a meal before his friend when the clock strikes 8:00 p.m. Lyonnel summons Lady Henriette, who enters dressed as his servant and carrying a basket of fruit. Plumkett pounds upon the table and Nancy appears. The last happy meal taken by the patient is thereby reproduced. The light returns to Lyonnel's eyes when he looks at his servant as he remembers her. He thanks heaven for his good fortune, and Lady Henriette vows never to leave him. The queen, her servants, and the compassionate villagers reveal their presence, and Her Majesty approves the doulbe marriage of Plumkett-Nancy and Lyonnel-Henriette before returning to Windsor Castle (III, tabl. 2, 1-2).

The ballet was comparatively well received in its day, although it has not survived. It was mounted on 32 dates in 1844-45, and it was produced in part on four programs during 1846. It was given its 37th and last billing on 18 June 1847. The cast included Lucien Petipa* (Lyonnel), Hippolyte Barrez* (Plumkett), Elie (sir Tristan Crankfort), Quériau (the alderman), and L. Petit (the constable and the director of the madhouse). The female roles were filled by the elder Marquet (Queen Anne), Adéle Dumilâtre* (Lady Henriette), Maria (Nancy), Sophie Dumilâtre* (Mina), Emarot (Alison), and Roland (Sarah). The three pas de deux in the text were executed by Petipa and A. Dumilâtre, Robert and Maria, Henri Desplaces and A. Dumilâtre. M. Mabille and Mlles Maria and S. Dumilâtre were selected for the pas de trois. Gustave Chouquet recalls that the basic idea of the plot of Saint-Georges' ballet is derived from

Le Ballet des chambrières à louer (1617), and he complains that it is too much in debt to the vaudeville entitled La Comtesse d'Egmont.
BIBLIOGRAPHY: Chouquet 405; Edouard-M.-E. Deldevez, Mes Mémoires (Paris: Le Puy, 1890), 31-33; Lajarte II, 174-75; RBP 226-29.

Laffitte, Léon (b. 28 January 1875, Saint-Geniès; d. September 1938, Paris), vocalist, made his debut in David of Les Maîtres Chanteurs de Nuremberg* on 10 October 1898 almost immediately after completing his studies at the Conservatoire. Although he was attached to the Théâtre de la Monnaie in Brussels during the first part of his career (1905-14), he remained closely associated with the Garnier theatre at other times, and eventually he became one of the outstanding tenors at the Paris opera house.

The year after his debut, he appeared at the Opéra in the title-role of Faust,* as Ruodi in Guillaume Tell,* as Don Ottavio in Don Juan,* as Hylas in Briséis!,* and as Laërte in Hamlet.* He did La Trémouille in Patrie!* in 1900 and Nicias in Thaïs* in 1901. His last five roles in Paris before World War I were Don Alvar of L'Africaine,* Shahabarim of Salammbô,* and Tybalt of Roméo et Juliette,* performed in 1902; Cassio of Othello,* which he sang in 1903; Raoul of Les Huguenots,* done in 1904.

After the outbreak of hostilities, Laffitte was billed in 1915 as Karloo in Patrie!* the duke in Rigoletto,* Rhadamès in Aïda,* Don Rodrigue in Le Cid,* and in the male lead of Samson et Dalila.* He was cast next in the parts of Maître Loys in Le Miracle,* Marcomir in Les Barbares,* and Pylade in Niccolò Piccinni's Iphigénie en Tauride during 1916 (see eighteenth-century volume for Piccinni and Iphigénie en Tauride). He represented Fernand in La Favorite,* Guillaume in Messidor,* Andros in Prométhée, Don Gomès in Henry VIII,* and Lentulus in Roma* in 1917, but, during the last year of the war, he sang only Castor in Castor et Pollux (see eighteenth-century volume for Castor et Pollux).

The restoration of peace saw him interpret Faust in La Damnation de Faust* in 1919 and Canio in Paillasse in 1920. He did his first Wagnerian roles for the Opéra when he filled the parts of Loge in L'Or du Rhin* in 1921 and the protagonists of Lohengrin* and Parsifal* in 1924. He did not appear as prince Assur in Le Jardin du Paradis until 1924 (see twentieth-century volume for Le Jardin du Paradis).

While Laffitte was occupied with the portrayal of these 33 major and minor characters in the 1898-1904 and 1915-1924 intervals at the Garnier Palace,* he found time to create another 18 roles in as many works produced at the Opéra for the first time on the following dates:

Role	Opera	Premiere
Kaddio	Lancelot	7 February 1900
Hylas	Astarte	15 February 1901
Mime	Siegfried	31 December 1901
Toretti	Orsola	21 May 1902
Beppe	Paillasse	14 December 1902
Mouck	La Statue	6 March 1903
André	L'Etranger	1 December 1903
Pédrille	L'Enlèvement au sérail	1 December 1903
Lensky	Eugène Oneguine	9 December 1915
Soloist	Marche héroïque	19 December 1915
Wilhelm	Chant de la cloche	13 January 1916
Landry	Ouragan	17 February 1916
Paolo	Les Amants de Rimini	2 March 1916
David	Le Roman d'Estelle	9 March 1916
Jean Ducos	Les Girondins	26 March 1916
Le Poète	Graziella	6 April 1916
Fernando	Goyescas	17 December 1919
Néron	Néron	27 January 1921

Although some of the 1916 creations were simply an act or a tableau from a longer work, it is evident that the tenor was able to remain occupied during the war despite adverse conditions in the capital. It is perhaps even more obvious that M. Laffitte favored the French repertory despite his willingness to undertake the portrayal of Wagnerian characters. It was doubtlessly his attempt to be a versatile as well as a brilliant and powerful tenor that fostered his popularity.

BIBLIOGRAPHY: KRJ 238; SW 26, 29, 33, 43, 46, 52, 57-58, 63, 69, 75, 79, 82-83, 90, 102-4, 110, 112, 118, 123-24, 133, 135, 140, 148, 150, 162, 164, 165-66, 168, 170, 189, 193, 197, 202, 204, 208, 318, 372, 374-75.

Lafont, (b. 1811, Paris; d. 1861 ?, Paris), née Pauline Leroux, ballerina, was admitted as a young girl to the ballet school attached to the Royal Academy of Music, and she made her debut at the Opéra in a divertissement of La Caravane du Caire on 20 December 1827, but her budding career was interrupted by attacks of rheumatism and injuries (see eighteenth-century volume for divertissement and La Caravane du Caire). She refused to yield to these misfortunes, however, and she returned to the stage to dance the part of a sylphid in the premiere of La Sylphide* on 12 March 1832 before creating Henriette in Nathalie ou la laitière suisse* on 7 November 1832 and Zeir in La Révolte au serail* on 4 December 1833. Her next assignment in Paris was the title-role in the 1835 revival of La Somnambule.* This was followed by three parts: Paquita in the world premiere of Le Diable boiteux* on 1 June 1836, the young girl in La Fille du Danube* on 21 September 1836, and Urielle in Le Diable amoureux* of 1840.

Once more plagued by bad luck, she found herself returned to a position of secondary importance by the success of Carlotta Grisi* in Giselle* on 28 June 1841. Yet she did not grow discouraged and performed in the ballet of La Reine de chypre* of 22 December 1841 and La Péri* of 17 July 1843. She was given the part of Calypso in Eucharis* of 1844, but this ballet enjoyed no success and offered her no fresh opportunity to attain stardom. She did not appear in the ballets of Le Diable à quatre* in 1845 or of L'Ame en peine* in 1846 because she was in retirement by then despite her relatively young age. The unpublished Journal de l'Opéra notes that a special Saturday program was held for her benefit on 25 January 1845. It raised slightly more than 6,000 francs. Mme Lafont was praised by critics in England as well as in France for her unusual ability to mime and to execute difficult steps with energy and precision.

BIBLIOGRAPHY: CB, 71, 79, 87, 91-92, 98-99, 114, 169, 176-77; CODB 323; Ivor Guest, The Romantic Ballet in England (Middletown, Conn.: Wesleyan University Press, 1972), 162; Lajarte II, 143, 145, 147, 150, 154, 164, 169, 176; LXIX X, 60; Mark Edward Perugini, A Pageant of the Dance and Ballet (London: Jarralds, 1946), 180.

Lafont, or Lafond, Marcelin (b. 1800, Bordeaux; d. 23 August 1838, Paris), tenor, was a customs officer in his native city, when his success as a vocalist at local recitals prompted him to embark upon an operatic career. He traveled to Paris to enter the Conservatoire in 1821, and he made his debut at the Opéra on 9 May 1823 as Polynice in Oedipe à Colone (see eighteenth-century volume for Oedipe à Colone). He was received with enthusiasm by his audiences, but he decided that he was not yet well enough trained to perform in the capital, and he left the Royal Academy of Music for an engagement of two years as the leading tenor at the Grand Theatre in Bordeaux during 1826-27.

He returned to the opera house in the rue Le Peletier* on 24 October 1828, when his interpretation of Masaniello in La Muette de Portici* established his reputation beyond a doubt and earned him the position of stand-in for Adolphe Nourrit* at the summit of the latter's career. Lafont's talents were too obvious not to employ in other respects as well, and he was called upon to create three roles at the premieres of three ambitious productions: Raimbaut in Robert le Diable* on 21 November 1831, Ottavio in Don Juan* on 10 March 1834, and Léopold in La Juive* on 23 February 1835.

Lafont's highly promising career came to an abrupt and premature end, when he was preparing to leave Paris with Nicolas Levasseur* to give a series of performances at Bordeaux. He fell ill suddenly and died without warning.

BIBLIOGRAPHY: Chouquet 396, 398; Fétis, Suppl. II, 60-61; Lajarte II, 129-32, 140-41, 147-50; "Mort de Lafont," FM 1 (19 August 1838), 3; SW 73, 129, 184.

La Grange, Anna Caroline de (b. 24 July 1825, Paris; d. April 1905, Paris), vocalist, began her musical career as a pianist, but she decided later to study voice with Bordogni, Mandacini, and Lamperti. She made her debut in Italy, where she appeared in L. Ricci's La Chiara de Rosenberg in 1842 at Varese. She returned to her native land in 1848, but she was not greeted with enthusiasm in Paris, and she went on to enjoy greater success on the stages of Austria, Germany, Russia, and Spain. She also appeared in New York during 1855. She retired from the operatic stage in 1869 to spend the remainder of her active years in teaching.
BIBLIOGRAPHY: Alexandre Bisson and Théodore de Lajarte, Petite Encyclopédie musicale (Paris: A. Hennuyer, 1884) II, 220; Thompson 970.

Lajarte, Théodore (b. 10 July 1826, Bordeaux; d. 20 June 1890, Paris), archivist, studied at the Conservatoire in Paris and subsequently composed a quantity of operettas that have not survived. He contributed Monsieur de Floridor to the repertory of the Opéra-Comique on 11 October 1880, and his ballet entitled Les Jumeaux de Bergame* was billed at the Opéra on 26 January 1886.

Yet it is M. Lajarte's work as a diligent archivist and musicologist that has kept his name alive. His Bibliothèque musicale du théâtre de l'Opéra (1876-79) is still an invaluable bibliographical tool at the least, and it has been reissued in a modern reprint form. His collections of French operatic texts are not as well known, but they are equally valuable. Lajarte was a librarian at the Opéra between 1873 and 1890.
BIBLIOGRAPHY: AEM VIII, 88-89; BBD 959; EDS VI, 1161-2; ELM III, 22; Grove V, 18.

Lalo, Edouard (b. 27 January 1823, Lille; d. 22 April 1892, Paris), composer, studied violin and cello at the Conservatory in Lille before entering the Conservatoire in Paris, where he was a member of François Habeneck's* class in violin.

After finishing his studies, Lalo became more and more interested in composition, and his initial pieces included songs and an opera entitled Fiesque (1866), which took third place in a contest sponsored by the Théâtre-Lyrique. The divertissement from this opera was played in concert during 1872, and it was received with great enthusiasm (see eighteenth-century volume for divertissement). When his Symphonie espagnole (1873) met with an even greater degree of success at the Concert Populaire of 1875, Lalo's reputation as a composer became secure beyond a doubt.

A rhapsody, a concerto, and the overture to Lalo's nascent opera to be entitled Le Roi d'Ys were performed next in Paris, and his ballet Namouna* was given its premiere at the Opéra on 6 March 1882 (see twentieth-century volume for Le Roi d'Ys). This ballet was not applauded without reservation until it was given in concert, but Le Roi d'Ys was soon ready for the stage, and it met with unanimous approval at the Opéra-Comique on 7 May 1888. Also, it went on to enjoy 490 billings at the Comique with revivals in 1902, 1909, 1917. It was finally withdrawn from the repertory after its performance on 6 january 1941, but it was billed almost immediately at the Opéra, where it has been given on 125 occasions between 6 January 1941 and 25 August 1954.

BIBLIOGRAPHY: AEM VIII, 106-8; BBD 960-61; "Bibliographie sommaire de quelques musiciens français depuis 1900," RM 210 (January 1952), 210; EDS VI, 1168-9; CBCM 650-52; EGC 202-4; ELM III, 24-25; Grove V, 25-27; Henry Malherbe, Edouard Lalo (Paris: Heugel, 1921); NEO 361-62; PBSW 62, 186; Georges Servières, Edouard Lalo (Paris: Henri Laurens, 1925).

Lambert, Lucien (b. 1858, Paris; d. 21 January 1945, Oporto), composer, began his musical career by touring as a concert pianist, but he returned to his native Paris eventually to collaborate with Jules Massenet* and François Théodore Dubois* on the "lyric scene" entitled Prométhée, which won the Rossini prize at the Conservatoire in 1885.

Lambert became interested in composing for the theatre at this time, and his opera Brocéliande was produced in Rouen in 1893, while his Le Spahi was booked into the Opéra-Comique on 18 October 1897. His pantomime-ballet La Roussalka* enjoyed the first of its 19 presentations at the Opéra on 8 December 1911, but his other works for the theatre never found their way to the stage except for La Marseillaise, which had three billings at the Opéra-Comique beginning on 14 July 1900, and La Flamenca, mounted at the Théâtre de la Gaîté on 31 October 1903. His

Penticosa and La Sorcière were among his unproduced works.
BIBLIOGRAPHY: AEM VIII, 124-25; BBD 962; ELM III, 26; Grove V, 33.

Lamoureux, Charles (b. 28 September 1834, Bordeaux; d. 21 December 1899, Paris), French conductor and violinist, left his native city to study violin at the Paris Conservatoire, where he carried off first prizes for his skill with this instrument in 1852 and 1854. Later he was able to support himself in the capital by playing violin at the Theatre du Gymnase and at the Opéra before and after the completion of his studies at the Conservatoire.

As a young man, Lamoureux joined forces with Pasdeloup, Colonne, and other musicians to form orchestras dedicated to giving public concerts featuring new or neglected compositions of merit, but, in 1873, he resigned from the Société des Concerts du Conservatoire, because this organization would not ratify his plan to present concerts consisting solely of oratorios. He had money at his disposal by this time, however, and he decided to execute his project independently. He produced Handel's Messiah in 1873 and Bach's St. Matthew Passion in 1874, and he was so successful that he prolonged his program to include Charles Gounod's* Gallia and Jules Massenet's* Eve.

Lamoureux displayed a more active interest in the theatre during 1876, when he joined the Opéra-Comique, but he became involved in a quarrel here before long, and he gave up his position as conductor of the Comique only six months later. The following year, 1877, he was appointed to serve as musical director at the Opéra, and he remained in this capacity until 21 December 1879. At his debut at the Garnier Palace* on 17 December 1877, he directed a performance of Giacomo Mayerbeer's* L'Africaine.* Also at the Garnier theatre, he provided the musical direction for Hamlet* in 1878, and La Muette de Partici* and La Juive* in 1879. He was likewise at the desk for the creation of two new works during his brief tenure at the Opéra: Gounod's Polyeucte* on 7 October 1878; and Victorin de Joncières's* La Reine Berthe* on 27 December 1878. M. Lamoureux returned to the Garnier theatre in 1891 to direct a revival of Guillaume Tell* and to preside at the podium for the first performance of Lohengrin* on this same stage on 16 September 1891.

After the conductor left the Paris opera house in 1879 as a result of an argument with its director, Auguste Vaucorbeil,* he continued to gravitate toward the theatre. He organized the famous Concerts Lamoureux for presentation at the Théâtre du Château d'Eau in 1881, and he obtained permission, perhaps from Richard Wagner* himself, to present Lohengrin* at this same theatre during 1887. This latter "pro-German" undertaking caused a public protest, however, and Lamoureux had to close down his production after its second performance. Subsequently, he resumed giving concerts at the Théâtre de l'Odéon, and, as already indicated, he was back at the Opéra in 1891 to present Lohengrin and to serve as musical director there once again. At the end of his life, the conductor presented Tristan et Isolde* at the Nouveau Théâtre, but he never managed to realize his dream of building a second Bayreuth in France.

BIBLIOGRAPHY: GIR 198-203; Adolphe Jullien, "Chalres Lamoureux," RMI 7 (1900), 153; SW 25, 134, 175, 179, 521.

Lancelot was a lyric drama in four acts and six tableaux with a score by Victorin Joncières* and a libretto by the team of Louis Gallet and Edouard Blau.* Joseph Hansen* established its choreography, and Charles Bianchini designed its costumes. Its sets were created by Carpezat (a. 1, 2), Amable (a. 3, a. 4, tabl. 2), and Chaperon fils (a. 4, tabl. 1). It had its world premiere at the Garnier Palace* on 7 February 1900 in a Pedro Gailhard* production.

The opera is set at Kerléon in King Arthus' palace, where the minstrel Kadio is singing of Arthus' decision to allow Lancelot to decide whether Count Alain or Markhoël is to fill the only empty chair at the Round Table (I, tabl. 1, sc. 1). Arthus enters with Guinèvre, and the two candidates for the seat at the Round Table present themselves. Count Alain discloses that he has agreed to the marriage of his daughter Elaine and Lancelot; Markhoël asserts privately to Lancelot that he will reveal Lancelot's secret love if he does not nominate him to fill the vacancy. Lancelot hesitates but decides in favor of Alain.

The court ratifies his selection (I, tabl. 1, sc. 2-3).

The scene shifts to the queen's apartments, where Guinèvre is upset by the news that Elaine de Dinan is to marry Lancelot. Her worries are compounded, when her lover tells her that their trysts are known to a member of the court. Her lover adds that they must abandon their affair, and the queen accuses him of inventing an excuse to reject her for Elaine. He protests that he does not even know the child, and the queen is appeased. She agrees to meet Lancelot at the usual hour in the forest of Brocéliande, and Lancelot leaves (I, tabl. 2, sc. 1-2). Arthus enters with Markhoël, while Guinèvre is waving farewell to Lancelot. The king is aware of what is happening, and he orders Guinèvre to a convent until he decides her fate (I, tabl. 2, sc. 3-4).

The setting moves to Alain's castle, where Alain and his daughter Elaine have been caring for wounded Lancelot since they found him half-dead in the forest of Brocéliande. Elaine is unaware of his identity, but she has fallen in love with him and is not very eager to accept her father's choice of a husband for her. Lancelot walks for the first time, and he thanks Elaine for restoring him to health (II, 1-2). Also, he assures Alain that he has not revealed his identity to Elaine. Alain tells him that Arthus has decreed the death penalty for him, and he hides him when a group of knights asks for shelter in his castle (II, 3). They are on their way to join Arthus in his campaign against the Saxons, and they disclose that all the king's subjects except disgraced Lancelot are on their way to Kerléon (II, 4). Lancelot is furious over the discredit into which he has fallen; he is upset further by Kadio's report that Guinèvre is in dishonor and dying of shame. Lancelot swears to liberate his queen, and he says farewell to Elaine and Alain, who plan to journey to Arthus' court (II, 5-6).

Lancelot is resting by the Lake of the Fairies. He is tired and too discouraged to continue on his quest to free Guinèvre. He falls asleep, and his dreams of his youth and past prowess are represented in a ballet (III, 1-2).

The scene moves to the convent in which Guinèvre is a prisoner and to which Elaine has come to escape marrying a husband chosen by her father. The queen asks her whether she has news of a knight named Lancelot, and Elaine informs her that he is described by Arthus' subjects as an abject traitor who has betrayed his king, but who will pay for his crimes with his life. Guinèvre flies into a rage and dismisses puzzled Elaine (IV, tabl. 1, sc. 1). A flourish of trumpets announces the arrival of Arthus, who pardons and liberates his surprised queen, although he assures her that he has not forgotten her infidelity. He declares that he never wishes to see her again, and he leaves. She swears to expiate her sins by renouncing the world (IV, tabl. 1, sc. 2-4). Lancelot appears before her to urge her to flee with him, but she rejects his suggestion (IV, tabl. 1, sc. 5). Elaine hears Lancelot and Guinèvre talking to each other, and she recognizes him as the man whom she has nursed back to life. Finally, she realizes that this man is Lancelot, and she disappears in silence. Lancelot leaves the convent (IV, tabl. 1, sc. 6-7), and Elaine returns to tell Guinèvre that the man to whom she was speaking is the man whom she, Elaine, loves (IV, tabl. 1, sc. 8).

Kadio and Lancelot are resting again by the Lake of the Fairies, and the former explains to his master that they are journeying to a place of peace where their hearts and souls will find respite from the trials of life. Alain enters wearing a look of despair and madness. He kneels by the lake and seems to be waiting. Lancelot remains hidden behind the foliage until a barge appears. It is carrying dead Elaine, and Lancelot wonders what is left for him in life. Guinèvre appears and answers, "God" (IV, tabl. 2, sc. 1-2).

Lancelot had a very brief history at the Opéra because it was in the repertory for only three months. It had to be dropped after its eighth presentation at the Garnier Palace* on 24 April 1900. Yet its cast was as competent and as endowed as the authors of the opera could have wished. The female roles were filled by Marie Delna* (Guinèvre) and Rosa Bosman (Elaine). The important male parts were sung by Albert Vaguet* (Lancelot), Maurice Renaud* (Arthus), René Fournets (Alain de Dinan), Jean Bartet* (Markhoël), and Léon Laffitte* (Kadio). The ballet was executed by the corps de ballet of the Opéra led by Mlles Robin and Sandrini.

BIBLIOGRAPHY: AEM 7, 155; EDS VI, 790; "Première Représentation de Lancelot *à l'Opéra,"* Le

Ménestrel 66 (11 February 1900), 42-44; Stoullig XXVI (1900), 1-6; SW 133.

Lapeyrette, Ketty (b. 23 July 1884, Oloron; d. 2 October 1960, Paris), vocalist, studied under the direction of Masson, Hettich, and Bouvet at the Conservatoire in Paris, where she made her debut in the female lead of Samson et Dalila* on 15 January 1908. She became the star contralto of the company at the Garnier Palace,* and she remained at this theatre for 32 years without any serious interruptions except for guest appearances at Amsterdam in 1936 and at Covent Garden in London in 1937. She left the stage in 1939 to join the faculty of the Conservatoire.

After she sang Madeleine of Rigoletto* and Amnéris of Aïda* during the year of her first appearance on the stage of the Opéra, she performed as Uta in Sigurd,* as Fricka and Schwertleite in La Walkyrie,* and as Anne de Boleyn in Henry VIII* in 1909. She did only Queen Gertrude in Hamlet* during 1911, but she was billed as Fidès in Le Prophète* and Posthumia in Roma* during 1912. The war did not interrupt her activities at the theatre. She was cast as Marthe of Faust* and represented La Marseillaise during the production of L'Offrande à la Liberté in 1915; she appeared in the title-role of Théodora* in 1916; she did Véronique of Messidor* and Gaïa of Prométhée in 1917; and Léonore of La Favorite* in 1918.

The return of peace saw her billed as Emilia in Othello* and Pallas in Hélène during 1919, and she sang Erda of Siegfried* and Fricka of L'Or du Rhin* in 1920 (see twentieth-century volume for Hélène). After she performed as the Hôtesse in Boris Godounov* in 1922, she added no new roles to her repertory until 1927, when she appeared as Madame Robin in Le Fifre enchanté,* featured in a gala in honor of King Fouad of Egypt. The last two parts that she executed in works already presented at the Opéra were Marceline of Le Barbier de Séville* in 1933 and Perséphone of Ariane* in 1937.

Mlle Lapeyrette's long association with the Opéra made possible her appearance in 27 premieres at the Garnier between 1908 and 1940. The titles of these works, the dates of their first presentations at the Garnier theatre, and the roles that the contralto sang were:

Roles	**Opera**	**Premiere**
Flosshilde	Le Crépuscule des dieux	23 October 1908
Waltraute	Le Crépuscule des dieux	23 October 1908
Flosshilde	L'Or du Rhin	14 November 1909
Jeanne	La Forêt	13 February 1910
A nymph	Icare	19 December 1911
La Tzigane	Le Cobzar	30 March 1912
Fille-fleur	Parsifal	4 January 1914
La Niania	Eugène Oneguine	9 December 1915
Myrialde	Myrialde	2 April 1916
Vocalist	Une Fête chez La Pouplinière	25 May 1916
Hérodias	Salomé (by Mariotte)	2 July 1919
Pépa	Goyescas	17 December 1919
La Mère	Sept Chansons	10 July 1920
Mrs Quickly	Falstaff	3 April 1922
Padmavati	Padmâvati	1 June 1923
La Sorcière	Le Jardin du Paradis	29 October 1923
La Vieille Femme	L'Arlequin	22 December 1924
La Fée Carabosse	Brocéliande	19 November 1925
Annina	Le Chevalier à la rose	8 February 1927
Feridje	Naïla	6 April 1927
La Mort	La Tentation de St. Antoine	8 May 1930
La Galléga	L'Illustre Frégona	16 February 1931

Souffrance	Guercoeur	21 April 1931
Mona	La Vision de Mona	15 October 1931
Clytemnestre	Elektra	25 February 1932
La Grande Druidesse	Vercingétorix	22 June 1933
La Nourrice	Ariane et Barbe-bleue	23 January 1935
La Nourrice	Médée	8 May 1940

BIBLIOGRAPHY: EFC 180-81; ICM 978; KRJ 240-41; SW 28, 39-40, 48, 51, 53, 60, 63, 66, 77, 83-84, 87, 90, 94, 99, 103, 105, 109-10, 112, 118-19, 124, 146, 148, 153, 161-62, 165, 178, 183, 189, 194, 200, 202-3, 207, 210, 221, 224-25, 278, 375; WOC 260.

Lassalle, Jean (b. 14 December 1847, Lyons; d. 7 September 1909, Paris), bass, studied at the Conservatoire in Paris before making his debut at Liége in 1868. He appeared next in the north and south of France, Holland, and Belgium again before making his Paris debut as Guillaume Tell at the Le Peletier* theatre on 9 June 1872. After the opera house in the rue Le Peletier was destroyed by fire, he performed at the new theatre built for the company of the National Academy of Music. His first two parts here were Guillaume Tell and Hamlet in 1875. The following year, he sang Charles VII in Auguste Mermet's* Jeanne d'Arc* and the title-role of Don Juan.* He was billed next as Pietro in La Muette de Portici* and as Jacques de Lusignan in La Reine de Chypre* during 1877, but then he added no new parts to his repertory until 1881, when he sang Amonasro in Aïda.* This same year he repeated two roles that he had already performed in the rue Le Peletier: Nevers in Les Huguenots* and Nélusko in L'Africaine.*

M. Lassalle was cast in the premieres of five compositions at the Opéra in addition to the roles just indicated:

Role	Opera	Premiere
Scindia	Le Roi de Lahore	27 April 1877

Sévère	Polyeucte	7 October 1878
Henry VIII	Henry VIII	5 March 1883
Gunther	Sigurd	12 June 1885
Le Grand Prêtre	Samson et Dalila	23 November 1892

The bass appeared in London between 1879 and 1893, and he was with the Metropolitan Opera Company during 1891-98. He retired in 1903 to accept a professorship at the Conservatoire. Although he did not appear in as many baritone roles as Dinh Gilly* or Herbert Janssen, he was especially popular because of the range of his voice and the technical precision that he displayed on the stage (see twentieth-century volume for Janssen).

BIBLIOGRAPHY: Henri de Curzon, Croquis d'artistes (Paris: Fischbacher, 1898), 85-94; DEO 253-54; EDS VI, 1257-58; EZF 230-32; GE XXI, 989; ICM 980; KRJ 241-42; Lajarte II, 153, 242, 246-47; Lermina 873; Martin 207; H. Moréno, "Débuts de Mlle de Reszké et de M. Lassalle dans Hamlet," Le Ménestrel 41 (27 June 1875), 236; PBSW 186; Hugo Riemann, Musik Lexikon ed. Alfred Einstein (Berlin: Max Hesses Verlag, 1929) I, 999; RC 453-54; SW 25-26, 30, 74, 107, 109, 112, 116, 125, 152, 180, 186, 197, 203; XYZ 225-28.

Lasthénie was an opera in a single act with music by Louis Hérold* and words by Claude-Etienne Chaillou des Barres.* It was the first score that the composer wrote for the Opéra, but its subject was more suited to a comedy of intrigue than to an opera, and audiences were not especially enthusiastic about it despite the interest offered by several passages in the score. The preface in the libretto of Lasthénie indicates that the subject of Chaillou's work was derived from the seventh chapter of the last volume of Lantier's Voyages d'Anténor en Grèce. The opera had its world premiere at the Roayl Academy of Music on 8 September 1823.

The setting of Lasthénie is a sacred grove outside the gates of Athens, where a temple to l'Amour and l'Hymen dominates the scene. Hyparète visits the temple daily with offerings and prayers that her errant husband Alcibide will stop ignoring her for Lasthénie. The latter enters to reveal that she has a plan to return fickle Alcibiade to his wife's arms (sc. 1-3). The first step in her scheme is to persuade Cléomède to help her by deceiving Alcibiade. He agrees to serve as her accomplice (sc. 4). Cléomède leaves, and Hyparète appears on her way to the temple with her daily offering. She does not know Lasthénie by sight, and the latter is able to volunteer to help Hyparéte without being recognized. The spurned wife takes Lasthénie into her confidence. Lasthénie asserts that Alcibiade is coming to the temple; she suggests to Hyparète that she remain hidden for a time (sc. 5-7). Lasthénie tells Alcibiade that he must help her to reunite Cléomède and his wife, Erinna. Alcibiade agrees because he considers Cléomède his rival for Lasthénie's affections. He offers to escort Cléomède to the altar of l'Amour and l'Hymen to assist him in the repetition of his marriage vows (sc. 8-9).

When Cléomède appears, Alcibiade surprises him by delivering a lecture on marital fidelity. Alcibiade continues in this vein because he believes that he is winning Lasthénie's favor. Cléomède follows Lasthénie's instructions and pretends to regret his wayward behavior; he tells Alcibiade to assure Lasthénie that he has resolved to return to Erinna (sc. 10-11). The doors of the temple swing open, and Hyparète descends its steps. She is covered with a veil and surrounded by priestesses as well as by Athenian women and youths. Cléomède makes a pretense of realizing that there is no escape for him now because Erinna has heard his promises of future fidelity. He feigns confusion and asks Alcibiade to prompt him with the declaration of love and conjugal duty contained in the ceremony. Delighted Alcibiade reads all the vows; "Erinna" removes her veil and reveals herself to be Hyparète. Alcibide realizes that he has been tricked into repeating and therefore renewing his marriage vows. Hyparète thanks Lasthénie even after learning her identity (sc. 12).

The opera was dropped after its 26th performance on 9 August 1826. The two female roles were filled by Gérald Grassari* (Lasthénie) and Mme Sainville (Hyparète) opposite the elder Nourrit (Alcibiade) and Adolphe Nourrit* (Cléomède). The applauded passages in the score were the duet by

Mmes Grassari and Sainville (sc. 6) and the trio, "Se peut-il qu'ainsi l'on outrage" (sc. 11).

BIBLIOGRAPHY: *Adolphe Adam, Souvenirs d'un musicien (Paris: Calmann Lévy, 1881), 32-33; H. Blaze de Bury, Musiciens du passé, du présent et de l'avenir (Paris: Calman Lévy, 1880), 201-3; Chouquet 390-91; DDO II, 640; Benoît J. B. Jouvin, Hérold, sa vie et ses oeuvres (Paris: Heugel et Cie., 1868), 133-34; Lajarte II, 105-6; Moniteur universel 253 (10 September 1823), 1078; Arthur Pougin, Hérold (Paris: Renouard, 1906), 68-69; P. Scudo, Critique et littérature musicales (Paris: Victor Lecou, 1852) II, 274-81.*

Laute-Brun, Antoinette (b. 1 July 1876, Nîmes), vocalist, studied at the Conservatoire in Paris and made her debut at the Opéra on 24 August 1903 as a page in Tannhäuser.* She remained at the Garnier palace* until her retirement from the theatre in 1925. She proved to be an extremely versatile soprano at the very start of her career, and she was accordingly assigned to a wide range of roles during the course of her association with the Opéra.

After her debut in 1903, she sang a minor role in Les Huguenots,* Helwigue in La Walkyrie,* Siebel in Faust,* and Inès in La Favorite* in 1904; and, in 1905, she performed Stefano in Roméo et Juliette* and Jemmy in Guillaume Tell.* She also did four parts in Armide this same year: Sidonie, Lucinde, a Plaisir, and the naiad (see seventeenth-century volume for Armide). She was then billed in three additional parts in 1906: Urbain in Les Huguenots,* Siegrune in La Walkyrie,* and Eunoé in Ariane.* She did only Marguerite in Faust and Crobyle in Thaïs* during 1907, because she married the composer Georges Brun this year besides going on a tour of Belgium with Jean Noté.*

When Mme Laute-Brun returned to Paris, she sang the high priestess in Hippolyte et Aricie in 1908 as well as the priestess of Aïda,* the shepherd of Tannhäuser, Hilda of Sigurd,* and the voice of the bird in Siegfried* during 1909 (see eighteenth-century volume for Hippolyte et Aricie). The soprano then did not add any new parts to her already large Garnier repertory until 1916, when she was cast as Diane in Niccolò Piccinni's Iphigénie en Tauride and Rafaela in Emile Paladilhe's* Patrie!* (see eighteenth-century volume for Piccinni and Iphigénie en Tauride). After the war, she appeared as Taanach of Salammbô* and as the Infante of Le Cid* during 1919, and her last two roles at the Opéra were Télaïre in Castor et Pollux in 1921 and a child in La Flûte enchantée in 1925 (see eighteenth-century volume for Castor et Pollux and La Flûte enchantée).

Mme Laute-Brun's long tenure at the Opéra, interrupted only by her trip to Belgium and several guest appearances in the provinces, made it inevitable that her striking soprano voice and versatility would lead to her participation in premieres at the Garnier theatre. The following list presents in chronological order the world premieres in which she shared at the Opéra and the characters she represented on these occasions:

Role	**Opera**	**Premiere**
Chromis	Ariane	28 October 1906
Antonia	La Catalane	24 May 1907
Le Hêtre	La Forêt	13 February 1910
Nymph	Icare	19 December 1911
Première Fée	Le Sortilège	29 January 1913
Benedetta	Scemo	6 May 1914
Vocalist	Carême prenant	16 April 1916
L'Ange de la concorde	La Fête triomphale	14 July 1919
Léïla	Antar	14 March 1921

This second list indicates the roles she sang in works given their world premieres previously at another opera house but in which Mme Laute-Brun appeared for their initial productions at the Garnier on the date indicated:

Role	**Opera**	**Premiere**
Ouvrière	L'Etranger	1 December 1903
Jeune Fille	L'Etranger	1 December 1903

Oenoé	Prométhée	15 December 1907
Volgunde	Le Crépuscule des dieux	23 October 1908
Nausithée	La Fille du soleil	3 April 1910
Concetta	Les Joyaux de la Madone	12 September 1913
Ecuyer	Parsifal	4 January 1914
Fille-Fleur	Parsifal	4 January 1914
Une Voix	Le Soleil de nuit	29 December 1915
Une Voix	La Tragédie de Salomé	1 April 1919

A tally of these characters represented by Mme Laute-Brun reveals that her Garnier repertory consisted of no fewer than 46 roles.

BIBLIOGRAPHY: EFC 175-76, KRJ 243-44; SW 28, 37, 39, 41, 57, 62, 66, 82, 88, 90, 99, 115-16, 118, 123, 128, 169, 171, 190, 193, 199, 202, 204, 208, 225, 250, 325-26, 332, 365-66, 375.

Le Lazzerone was an opera in two acts with a score by Jacques Halévy* and a libretto by Jules-Henri Vernoy de a Saint-Georges.* It had its world premiere at the Royal Academy of Music in Paris on 29 march 1844. Although the work was in only three tableaux, Philastre, Cambon, Séchan, Diéterle, and Despléchins worked on its sets. The story was based upon the fable of La Fontaine dealing with the man who ran after fortune and the man who waited for it in his bed. The title of the work indicated an idler in Italian, and the word itself was most often applied to unemployed bystanders on the waterfront of Naples.

The opera begins in the port of Naples, where sleeping Beppo is awakened by a chorus of pilgrims. Beppo complains about the perpetual noise made by Neapolitan singers, but he breaks into song himself to priase the pleasures of sleep. The improviser Mirobolante enters followed by a boisterous crowd demanding a performance, and he begins to relate in verse the story of Venus' birth. One of the crowd denounces him as a fraud, and his audience is about to throw him into the bay when Beppo calls the police (I, 1-3). Beppo tells Mirobolante that a poet has a dangerous and unrewarding trade, and he adds that he has found success in sleeping because good fortune comes to him who waits. Mirobolante objects that sleeping never made anyone rich, but Beppo reminds him that he can dream of good food and his sweetheart, when he is asleep. Mirobolante remains unconvinced, but he is grateful, and he asks Beppo to share in the wealth that he is about to inherit from ailing Josué Corvo (I, 4). Josué gives Beppo a heavy sack to take to the bank, but Beppo refuses to carry it because of its weight. Mirobolante offers to deliver it, but Josué fears that he will run away with it. He prefers a messenger who is tired and ready to sleep (I, 5). Beppo's sweetheart Baptista enters; she agrees to marry him if he will find a way to support a wife. He assures her that he has had an encouraging dream of living in a palace and owning a sumptuous carriage. Baptista is charmed (I, 6-7). Mirobolante returns with the news that Josué is about to die. The improviser is certain that he will inherit the dying man's wealth, which he gained by murdering his ward years earlier. Fortunately, Mirobolante adds, no one knows the identity of the victim, and, consequently, no one knows the rightful heir to Josué's estate. Now, however, the gold cross around Beppo's neck reveals him to be the true heir to Josué's money. Thus, the improviser concludes, no one can prevent him and Beppo from dividing the sick man's assets.

Mirobolante does not have to wait long before he has the opportunity to promise Josué that he will save him from the gallows. Josué objects to this inference that he is guilty of a crime until Mirobolante mentions the name of Margarita written on Beppo's gold cross. He recounts the details of the murder. He shows him his nephew, Beppo. Josué laughs and replies that his ward was a girl (I, 8-9). Baptista returns to disclose that the cross hanging from Beppo's neck belonged to her mother. She reveals that she has papers at home that he can examine for the facts surrounding her birth (I, 10-11).

The second act begins at Baptista's home, where Mirobolante assures his hostess that her birth certificate will bring her great wealth. She is not impressed by the prospect of being rich because she is happy with Beppo and her flowers, but she agrees to give Mirobolante half her estate as a lawyer's fee. Beppo is anxious about these arrangements because he fears that he will lose Baptista when she becomes wealthy. Baptista agrees wholeheartedly that money may endanger their happiness, and she burns her birth certificate so that they may live together in peace (II, 1-2). When astonished Mirobolante learns that they have destroyed Baptista's birth certificate because they do not wish money to interfere with their love, Mirobolante reminds Beppo of all the comforts that his wife will forfeit. The picture that he draws of the impoverished life that she will lead is too painful for him to bear. He decides to volunteer for military service (II, 3-4).

Crafty Mirobolante plans now to marry Baptista to gain possession of her future wealth. When the girl enters with her friends, he announces that Beppo has deserted her for Rosina. He proposes marriage to the disillusioned girl and gives her the golden cross as proof of Beppo's inconstancy. She consents to marry him (II, 5-6). Mirobolante tells Josué that his ward is alive. Josué is skeptical, but Mirobolante recites from memory the text of Baptista's birth certificate while pretending to read it. Josué confesses his crime, but he learns that he has been tricked when he snatches a blank paper from Mirobolante's hand. The latter has made the certificate a matter of record, however, and Josué is obliged to admit defeat for the second time. Yet he is bold enough to propose marriage to Baptista, and the two suitors argue for her hand. She invites each of them privately to meet her at the church of Santa Chiara (II, 7).

The setting shifts to the street where Josué's residence and Santa Chiara are located. Beppo has fallen asleep on a bench while returning to the barracks, and Baptista comes upon him when his is declaring his love to her in his dreams (II, tabl. 2, 1-2). Josué Curvo and Mirobolante approach Baptista with confidence. They recognize each other and argue over their rights to Baptista's hand. The Angelus rings, a signal that Baptista is 21 years old and free to choose her own husband. She asserts that Beppo has won her heart. The chorus arouses Beppo to tell him that he has won Josué's palace and Baptista's love. He is convinced that he is dreaming until Baptista speaks to him. He is prompted to remind Miro bolante that fortune comes to those who wait for it (II, tabl. 2, 3-4).

Le Lazzerone did not prove to be a popular offering at the Opéra, and it was withdrawn after its 16th performance on 31 March 1845. Its score was not deficient, but certain critics felt that the music was better suited for presentation at the Opéra-Comique. Some of the brighter moments in the work were provided by Beppo's two arias, "Rien n'est si doux que la paresse" (I, 2) and "Quand on n'a rien" (I, 6), and Baptista's chansonette, "Achetez-moi roses nouvelles" (II, 2). Mme Rosine Stoltz* created the part of Beppo, while the other roles were filled for the first time by Mme Julie Dorus-Gras* (Baptista), Paul Barroilhet* (Mirobolante), and Nicolas Levasseur* (Josué Corvo). The lack of a tenor displaced by Mme Stoltz cast as Beppo might also have served to diminish the impact made by the composition.

BIBLIOGRAPHY: Adolphe Catelin, F. Halévy: notice biographique (Paris: Michel Lévy, 1863), 10-11; Chouquet 405; DDO I, 641-42; F. Halévy, Souvenirs d'un ami pour joindre à ceux d'un frère (Paris: Napoléon Chaix, 1863), 25; Léon Halévy, F. Halévy, sa vie et ses oeuvres (Paris: Heugel et cie., 1863), 37-39, 55; Lajarte II, 175.

Le Borne, Fernand (b. 10 March 1862, Charleroi; d. 15 January 1929, Paris), composer, remained in Paris after he completed his studies under the direction of César Franck,* Camille Saint-Saëns,* and Jules Massenet.* His chamber music won a prize in 1901, and some of his orchestral works were completed at a relatively early age, but the time and energy that he devoted to the composition of these pieces did not interfere with his ambitions for contributing to the stage.

The composer's first four operatic works were produced initially in four different countries: Daphnis et Chloé (1885), Brussels; Hedda (1898), Milan; Muddara (1899), Berlin; and Les Girondins (1905), Lyon. When Les Girondins had finished its run in Lyon, it was brought to the Théâtre Lyrique de la Gaîté in Paris on 12 January 1912, but only its fourth act was produced at the Opéra on 26 March 1916 because of problems generated by the war. The sole composition by Le Borne that was given in its entirety at the Garnier Palace* was La Catalane* of 24 May 1907, which enjoyed nine presentations in this theatre before it was dropped from the repertory on Christmas day of 1907.

Le Borne's authorship for the stage also includes Cléopâtre (Rouen, 1914) and Néréa (Marseilles, 1926).

BIBLIOGRAPHY: AEM VIII, 415-16; BBD 984; ELM III, 45; Grove V, 99.

Lecocq, Charles (b. 3 June 1832, Paris; d. 24 October 1918, Paris), composer, enrolled at the Conservatoire in Paris in 1849. Here, he distinguished himself as a student by winning prizes for fugue, harmony, and accompaniment.

Lecocq left the Conservatoire in 1852, but he seemed unable to gain a foothold in the theatre until he won an operetta competition sponsored by Jacques Offenbach,* who produced his winning work at the Bouffes-Parisiens on 8 April 1857. When Lecocq tried to gain acceptance for his other works, however, he found that theatre managers were not interested in his scripts.

Finally, in 1859, he managed to have his Huis clos staged, but it was a failure. He refused to be discouraged, however, and he kept trying to have a composition accepted until success at last came his way with Fleur de thé (1868). The composer then had a series of nearly 30 works produced. La Fille de Mme Angot* was among them, and the success of this operetta was incredible. It had its world premiere on 4 December 1872 in Brussels, where it broke all attendance figures. It was brought to Paris for a run at the Folies Dramatiques on 21 February 1873, but it was not booked into the Opéra-Comique until 28 December 1918. An operetta, only its second act was given at the Opéra on a gala program honoring French aviation on 28 April 1912.

M. Lecocq presented a second series of 16 light and sparkling operettas between 1887 and 1911, but none of these works found its way to the stage of the Opéra. Mam'zelle Angot, Massine's ballet based upon La Fille de Mme Angot, was billed into the Garnier Palace* on only two occasions in 1954, when it was presented by the Sadler's Wells Ballet Company.

BIBLIOGRAPHY: ACPM 564; AEM VIII, 447-48; BBD 986; ELM III, 52; Grove V, 103-4; PBSW 63, 187.

Lee, Mary Ann (b. 1823, Philadelphia; d. 1899), ballerina, studied ballet with Paul Hazard in her native city before she bacame acquainted with James Sylvain in New York during 1839. Sylvain was a partner of Franziska Elssler* during the latter's American tour, and he taught the ambitious Miss Lee the ballerina's famous steps, that is, the Cracovienne, the Cachucha, the Bolero. The American dancer had already appeared on the stage in Philadelphia, Baltimore, and New York, and she felt that she could push back her horizons by visiting Paris to study with Jules Perrot* in 1844.

Miss Lee set to work learning the French style of dancing and the manner in which the corps de ballet at the Opéra presented Giselle,* La Fille du Danube,* and La Jolie Fille de Gand.* She was bursting with ideas when she disembarked in New York in 1845 only months after her departure for Europe. She toured the United States with her new and genuine repertory of French ballets. George Washington Smith was her partner for Giselle at the Howard Atheneum in Boston on 1 January 1846. Things were going well, but the strain of learning so much so quickly, of traveling and living out of a trunk, and of dancing despite all problems had undermined her health. At first she was forced to relax her pace, but she was obliged almost immediately to renounce her schedule in favor of sporadic appearances. Her program ground to a halt in 1854. Yet she had established one thing beyond all doubt between 1846 and 1854. She and Augusta Maywood,* also a student of Paul Hazard, were the leading American dancers of the era.

BIBLIOGRAPHY: ACPM 565, CODB 319; DDD 133; EDB 207; Madeleine Bettina Stern, We the Women (New York: Schulte, 1963), 5-26; Wlater Terry, Star Performance (New York: Doubleday, 1954), 92-95.

Lefebvre, Charles Edouard (b. 19 June 1843, Paris; d. 8 September 1917, Aix-les-Bains), composer, studied at the Conservatoire in Paris, where he won the Prix de Rome in 1870. After the completion of his residence in Italy, he toured the Orient, and he returned to France to win the Prix Chartier in 1884. He joined the faculty at the Conservatoire in 1895.

The musician's interest in the theatre induced him to write two operas, Le Trésor produced at Angers in 1883, and Zaïre, given initially at Lille in 1887, but it was not until

25 May 1894 that his Djelma* was billed into the National Academy of Music for its world premiere.

Djelma was the only opera that M. Lefebvre had produced at the Opéra, but his music was used once again in the score of the ballet entitled Danses de jadis et de naguère,* to which 27 other composers also contributed in 1900.

BIBLIOGRAPHY: AEM VIII, 464-65; BBD 989; ELM III, 54.

Lefebvre-Duruflé, Noël-Jacques, Lefebvre DIT (b. 19 February 1792, Pont-Audemer; d. 3 November 1877, Pont-Authou), librettist, studied law in Paris and became involved in politics after he had lost his position in the office of the Minister of State in 1815 because of the Bourbons' return to power. He helped to found Le Nain Jaune, and opposition journal during the Restoration, but he lost interest in the political situation as soon as he married M. Duruflé's daughter because his father-in-law placed him in a remunerative post in his manufacturing organization. He ran for office unsuccessfully during the reign of Louis-Philippe, and he was elected to the national legislative body in 1849. Ultimately, he entered the senate and was made an officer in the Legion of Honor during the Second Empire. The change of governments in France in 1870 sent M. Lefebvre-Duruflé back to private life, and he returned to an active career in business until the failure of the corporation of which he had become president. He was arrested in February 1873 because of his involvement in this affair, but he was released later on his own recognizance doubtlessly on account of his age. Then, on 2 December 1873, he was found guilty of breaking the law governing corporations and was fined 10,000 francs. The following year, he was excluded from the Legion of Honor.

Lefebvre-Duruflé's writing inlcuded a history of Russia published in 1812 and a description of the northwestern coast of France that appeared in 1831. He was also the author of translations into French of several English novels. His sole contribution to the repertory of Opéra was his collaboration with Victor-Joseph Etienne Jouy on the libretto of Zirphile et Fleur de Myrte* in 1818 (see eighteenth-century volume for Jouy).

BIBLIOGRAPHY: Chouquet 388; GE XXI, 1128-29; Lajarte II, 92-93; LXIX X, 316; Wks II, 3425, 6095.

Legallois, Amélie-Marie-Antoinette (b. 1804, Paris; d. ?), ballerina, made her first stage appearance at age four or five in Jean Aumer's Les Amours d'Antoine et de Cléopâtre (1808), where she was cast as one of the hero's children by Octavie (see eighteenth-century volume for Aumer and Les Amours d'Antoine et de Cléopâtre). Unaffected by this experience, she took her first lessons in ballet at the dancing school supported by the Opéra. She completed her program here in time to make her mature debut as the heroine in the pantomime-ballet of Clair* in 1822 at age 18. Her success was impressive and immediate, and she was selected to create roles in the following compositions given their premieres on the dates indicated:

Work	**Premiere**
La Somnambule	19 September 1827
La Muette de Portici	29 February 1828
La Belle au bois dormant	27 April 1829
Manon Lescaut	3 May 1830
Robert le Diable	21 November 1831
La Révolte au sérail	4 December 1833
L'Ile des pirates	12 August 1835
Le Diable boiteux	1 June 1836
La Fille du Danube	21 September 1836

These creations and the appearances Mlle Legallois made in the revivals of works like Moïse* (1832) bespeak her efforts to please her public, but it is a sad fact that the dancer failed to convince audiences that she was capable of filling Mlle Emilie Bigottini's shoes (see eighteenth-century volume for Bigottini). It is for this reason alone that she had to remain

content with lesser billings despite the influence of General Lauriston, her lover.
BIBLIOGRAPHY: CB 53, 65, 92, 99, 114; DDD 133; GE XXI, 1137-38; Ivor Guest, Romantic Ballet in Paris (Middletown, Conn.: Wesleyan University Press, 1966), 56-72; Lajarte II, 128-30, 133, 140-41, 147, 151, 154; Parmenia Migel, The Ballerinas from the Court of Louis XIV to Pavlova (New York: Macmillan, 1972), 109.

La Légende de Joseph was a ballet in a single act with a score by Richard Strauss* and a libretto by Harry Graf Kessler and Hugo von Hofmannsthal. Mikhail Fokine* created the choreography, and the sets were designed by José-Marie Sert, while Léon Bakst* was responsible for the costumes. It was created at the Opéra on 14 May 1914 by Serge Diaghilev's* Ballets russes,* and it was the first ballet in which Léonide Massine danced for this comany.

The curtain rises on the ballet to disclose a great hall with a long table on a raised platform, where Putiphar, his wife, and his guests are participating in a sumptuous banquet reflecting the host's enormous wealth and almost limitless power. Yet he is bored, and even the treasures of the Orient and a program of boxing fail to arouse his interest. Finally, the shepherd boy Joseph enters to perform an inspired pas seul, and Putiphar's wife takes such an extraordinary interest in him that Putiphar purchases him from the sheik. Putiphar's wife presents the shepherd with a collar studded with gems, and suspicious Putiphar terminates the feast. Putiphar, his wife, and his guests leave, while Joseph stands at respectful attention, and the sheik leaves the palace with his slaves and remaining merchandise.

The sun has set, and Joseph is alone in the hall. He prays and goes to sleep on a couch. A woman with a lamp approaches his bed and gazes upon him in silent rapture. Then, as if prompted by feelings of guilt, she extinguishes her lamp. Joseph awakens and believes that he is gazing at an angel. He moves toward her, and she kisses him. Frightened, he runs cowering into a corner to pray. She grasps at his cloak, but he rejects her in contempt. Anger overtakes her, and she tries to choke him, but he forces her to her knees.

Guards are attracted by the noise of the struggle, and Putiphar's wife orders them to arrest Joseph. Putiphar himself enters with his men, and they throw the shepherd into chains. Putiphar's wife kisses her husband and points at Joseph. Putiphar flies into a rage and gives the order for his prisoner to be executed. The executioners heat their sharpened irons, but Joseph remains unmoved and absorbed in prayer. An angel appears in a dazzling light and leads the youth away. The guards, executioners, and other bystanders are frozen with fear. Putiphar's wife is overcome, and her face reveals her terror. She grasps the rope of pearls about her neck and pulls it tighter and tighter until she chokes to death (a. 1).

At more than one interval, the ballet seems to be more a drama with incidental dancing than a ballet with a historical background, and this shift in emphasis might have been instrumental in preventing the work from becoming more popular. Also, the biblical story appears to have been shifted to Venice in the sixteenth century because Bakst modeled his costumes after the raiment seen in the paintings of Paolo Veronese. Joseph and the merchants, however, were clad in clothes of the East. The work enjoyed only six presentations at the Opéra, but it had enough intrinsic appeal for later choreographers to create other versions, for example, Heinrich Kroller, George Balanchine, Antony Tudor, Heinz Rosen. At the Opéra, the members of the Ballets russes who appeared in it included Maria Kousnetzoff* (Putiphar's wife), Vera Fokina* (the Sulamite), A. Gregorieff (the merchant sheik), and M. Frohman (the angel).

Boris Kochno notes that Grigoriev lists the date of the initial performance of La Légende as 17 May 1914, while Massine suggests that it had its world premiere on 14 May 1914. Records in the Opéra note that the Ballets russes returned to the Garnier stage in 1914 to mount ten programs there in May and June. Diaghilev's dancers produced six compositions that had not yet been offered to the public; Les Papillons* and La Légende de Joseph were billed on 14 May 1914 for the first time.

BIBLIOGRAPHY: BB 146-48; Paul Bekker, Kritische Zeitbilder (Berlin: Schuster V. Loeffler, 1921), 98-106; BK 95; BOP 153; CB 598-602; Mary Clarke and David Vaughan, The Encyclopedia of Dance and Ballet (New York: G. P. Putnam's Sons, 1977),

208; CODB 320; Michel Georges-Michel, Ballets russes, histoire anecdotique (Paris: Éditions du nouveau monde, 1923), 28-30, 58-62; HAZ 206-7; Michael Kennedy, Richard Strauss (London: J. M. Dent Sons, 1976), 195-96; Boris Kochno, Diaghilev and the Ballets russes, trans. Adrienne Foulke (New York & Evanston: Harper & Row, 1970), 94-97; Ernst Krause, Richard Strauss, the Man and His Work (London: Collet's, 1964), 435-41; Serge Lifar, Serge Diaghilev: His Life, His Work, His Legend (New York: Da Capo Press, 1976), 208-9; Glora Manor, "The Bible as Dance," D Mag 52, no. 12 (December 1978), 73-76; Norman del Mar, Richard Strauss, a Critical Commentary on His Life and Works (New York: Macmillan Co., 1962-72) II, 124-50; Ernst Roth, Richard StraussL Buhnenwerke (London: Boosey & Hawkes, 1954), 33-34; Richard Specht, Richard Strauss und sein Werk (Leipzig, Wien, Zurich: E. P. Tal & Co., 1921) II, 321-39; SS 178-79; Richard Strauss, Buhnenwerke, Stage Works, Oeuvres lyriques (London: Boosey & Hawkes, 1954), 32-35; idem Recollections and Reflections, ed. Willi Schuk, trans. L. J. Lawrence (London: Boosey & Hawkes, 1953), 164-67; SW 294; TDB 295-97.

Lejeune, Gabrielle, vocalist, enrolled at the Liege Conservatory to prepare for her career as a singer, and she made her debut as an operatic soprano at the Théâtre de La Monnaie in Brussels in 1892. She moved to Paris before long, when she received a contract from the Opéra-Comique, and she sang at Convent Garden regularly between 1895 and 1909. She performed at the Manhattan Opera House in 1906 and 1907, and, on 25 February 1911, she made her first appearance at the Garnier Palace* in the role of Magdelaine in Les Maîtres Chanteurs de Nuremberg.* Her subsequent roles at the Opéra included Crobyle in Thaïs* and Guerhilde in La Walkyrie* during 1911 and Galla in Roma* in 1912. The only part that she created at the Garnier Palace was Nikona in Siberia,* which had its world premiere there on 9 June 1911.
BIBLIOGRAPHY: EFC 187; SW 417.

Lenepveu, Charles Ferdinand (b. 4 October 1840, Rouen; d. 16 August 1910, Paris), composer, went to Paris to study law in accordance with his father's wishes, but the few music lessons he took from Marie-Emmanuel-Augustin Savard* in the capital led him to enroll in the Conservatoire. Here, he studied under Ambroise Thomas* and won the Prix de Rome in 1865. In Rome, he composed an opera entitled Le Florentin, which proved unsuccessful when it was staged at the Opéra-Comique in 1874.

Lenepveu made a minimal contribution to the repertory at the Opéra. He was one of 28 musicians contributing to the collaborative effort that the Ballet de l'Opéra presented at the Trocadéro on 22 September 1900, Danses de jadis et de naguère,* which was billed at the Opéra on 11 November 1900 and seven dates thereafter.

BIBLIOGRAPHY: AEM VIII, 614-15; BBD 998; ELM III, 59.

Leoncavallo, Ruggiero (b. 8 March 1858, Naples; d. 9 August 1919, Montecatini), composer, studied under Beniamino Casi and Lauro Rossi at the Conservatory in Naples. He left this institution in 1876 to attend the rehearsals of his first opera, Chatterton, in Bologna, where the producer disappeared with whatever assets were intended for the staging of his work. The young musician now found himself financially distressed, and he was obliged to go on a tour of Europe to earn some money by playing the piano in cafés.

Leoncavallo had not yet given up hope of seeing one of his operas produced, and he entered into an agreement with the Ricordi publishing house. The publishers made him wait for three years, however, and he lost patience. He went to see the famous publisher Sonsogno, to whom he offered a new manuscript entitled Pagliacci. It was produced with great success on 21 May 1892, and Leoncavallo's career was launched.

None of Leoncavallo's works written after 1892 found its way to the stage of the Opéra, but Pagliacci in its Italian and French versions has been billed at the Garnier Palace* under the title of Paillasse* on 131 occasions between 14 December 1902 and 20 November 1936.

BIBLIOGRAPHY: AEM VIII, 634-42; BBD 1000-1001; CBCM 866-68; EDS VI, 1398-1402; EGC 211-12; ELM III, 60; PBSW 71, 75-76, 95, 101, 187.

Le Peletier, a theatre located in the Paris street of the same name, cut through the property of the banker Delaborde in 1786. The theatre was erected during 1821 and 1822 to provide a facility for the

Opéra, which found itself obliged to leave the salle Louvois after the duke de Berry's death. The architect Deleret placed it on the site where the duke de Choiseul's mansion and the Gramont property had been situated.

The opera house was built hurriedly because it was thought that the company would use it for only a short time. It was constructed in rectangular form and was designed to accommodate nearly 1,800 spectators. The first program presented there consisted of Les Bayadères and Le Retour de Zéphire on 16 August 1821 (see eighteenth-century volume for Les Bayadères and Le Retour de Zéphire). Also, in a stroke of genius, its management staged Aladin ou la lampe merveilleuse* on 6 February 1822 to celebrate the installation of illuminating gas in the theatre.

Strangely enough, this supposedly temporary facility housed the Opéra until the night of 28-29 October 1873, when a fire of unknown origin demolished the entire structure in a conflagration lasting for 24 hours. The theatre had served the public for more than 52 years during which time Dr. Véron had opened the dance foyer to subscribers, Nestor Roqueplan had produced nearly 35 new operas and ballets, and Emile Perrin had staged for the first time such capital compositions as Robert le Diable* (1831), La Juive* (1835) Les Huguenots* (1836), La Favorite* (1840) Le Prophète* (1849) Le Trouvère* (1857), Tannhäuser* (1861), and L'Africaine* (1865). Almost in spite of itself, as it were, the opera house left its stamp on posterity, and it inspired a feeling of nostalgia in subsequent generations of melomaniacs. Napoleon III supported the theatre with an annual contribution of 100,000 francs; seats in the orchestra cost 10 francs. The entire 1821-73 repertory included more than 150 new compositions by such composers as Daniel Auber,* Hector Berlioz,* Félicien David,* Domenico Gaetano Donizetti,* Charles Gounod,* Jacques Halévy,* Giacomo Meyerbeer,* Giuseppe Verdi,* and Carl Maria von Weber.* The ballet boasted stars of the calibre of Francesca Cerrito,* Charles Saint-Léon,* Carlotta Grisi,* Mlle Carolina Rosati,* Mme Amalia Ferraris,* and Mlle Eugènie Fiocre.* The list of 1821-73 singing stars at the Opéra was equally as impressive: Marc Bonnehée,* Jean-Baptiste Faure,* Louis Gueymard,* Louis Obin,* and Mmes Marietta Alboni,* Caroline

Carvalho,* Marie Sass,* Fortunata Tedesco,* and Michelle Viardot.*
BIBLIOGRAPHY: *Jacques Hillairet, Dictionnaire historique des rues de Paris (Paris: Les Editions de minuit, 1963) II, 37-38; André Lejeune and Stéphane Wolff, Les Quinze Salles de l'Opéra de Paris (Paris: Librairie théâtrale, 1955), 29-30; Charles Nuitter, Le Nouvel Opéra (Paris: Hachette, 1875), 14-15.*

Leroux, Xavier (b. 11 October 1863, Velletri; d. 2 February 1919, Paris), composer, was a pupil of Jules Massenet* at the Conservatoire in Paris, where he distinguished himself by winning prizes in pianoforte and harmony. He captured the Prix de Rome in 1885 with his cantata entitled Endymion.

Leroux was named professor of harmony at the Conservatoire in 1896, and he remained on the faculty of this institution until his death. Also, he edited the review Musica and composed a number of non theatrical pieces. Yet his primary interest remained the stage, and he had his first opera, Evangeline, produced in Brussels as early as 1895. It was at the Opéra-Comique that Leroux's talents first became evident to Parisian audiences; he had no fewer than five titles booked into this theatre between 1903 and 1924. The number of performances enjoyed by each of these works at the Opéra-Comique is indicated in parentheses after its title:

Title (performances)	**Premiere**
La Rein Fiammette (59)	23 December 1903
Le Chemineau (106)	6 November 1907
Le Carillonneur (11)	20 March 1913
Les Cadeaux de Noël (23)	25 December 1915
La Plus Forte (9)	11 January 1924

The composer's contribution to the repertory of the Opéra was by no means as impressive. The act of Théodora* (1907) already given in Monte Carlo was repeated at the Garnier Palace* on 20 October 1910, but the fragmentary presentation of this work and the 23 representations of Astarte*

beginning on 15 February 1901 were the only occasions when Leroux's work was billed at the Opéra. This is not an imposing record if one remembers that Leroux had his works billed on 208 programs at the smaller opera house.
BIBLIOGRAPHY: AEM VIII, 658-60; BBD 1002; EDS VI, 1415-16; ELM III, 62; NEO 372-73; PBSW 187.

Leuven, Adolphe, Count Ribbing, DIT de (b. 1800, ?; d. 14 April 1884, Paris), librettist, was the son of Count Ribbing, who had been banished from Sweden in 1792 and had then come to live in France. Young de Leuven met Alexandre Dumas in 1825 at Villers-Cotterets, and he collaborated with him on his first work for the theatre, a vaudeville in a single act entitled La Chasse et l'amour.

After this inauspicious start, de Leuven went on to do 200 or so titles for the theatres of Paris during his lifetime if his vaudevilles and light comedies are tallied with his more ambitious works. His noteworthy compositions for the Opéra-Comique at the start of his career included Le Panier fleuri (1839), L'Automate de Vaucanson (1840), and Les Deux Voleurs (1841) and Mlle de Mérange (1841), both with L. Lhérie. His most successful contributions to the repertory of this theatre were the librettos of Le Songe d'une nuit d'eté (1850) with Rosier and of Maître Pathelin (1856) with Ferdinand Langlé. His activity as an author at the Opéra-Comique resulted in his being named codirector of this theatre with Ritt in 1862-70 and with Du Locle in 1870-74. His earliest hits at the Théâtre-Lyrique were La Promise (1854) and Fanchonnette (1855). His contributions to the repertory of the Opéra were limited to a pair of compositions, and only one of them inspired much enthusiasm. Le Diable à quatre* of 1845 had more than a hundred billings, but Vert-Vert* of 1851 had to be dropped after fewer than a score of presentations.
BIBLIOGRAPHY: Chouquet 406, 412; Lajarte II, 179, 210; LXIX X, 437; Thieme II, 151-52; Wks, III, 267.

Levasseur, Nicolas-Prosper (b. 9 March 1791, Bresles; d. 7 December 1871, Paris), vocalist, entered the Conservatoire at Paris on 29 December 1807 and became a member of Garat's singing class on 5 February 1811. His bass voice made an immediate impression, and, after distinguishing himself as a student, he made his debut at the Imperial Academy of Music on 14 October 1813, when he sang the part of the pacha in La Caravane du Caire.* Curiously enough, this one work proved to be the sole composition in tragic repertory suitable for his elegant and poised voice. The other works were pitched too high. Thus, despite his resounding success at his debut, he could not equal his first triumph in subsequent performances.

The frustrated bass broke with management because he was annoyed to find his promising career stalled suddenly, and he left France to sing in London during 1816. When he returned to the French capital, he found himself classified as a replacement, that is, subordinate to the leader of the bass section and superior to the latter's stand-in. He was not overjoyed with this arrangement, but he remained at the Opéra until 1822, when he obtained permission to visit Milan. In the latter city, Giacomo Meyerbeer* asked him to do a role in Marguerite d'Anjou, and he accepted to find himself enjoying his second triumph. After the termination of his leave, he returned to the Opéra, but management transferred him to the Théâtre-Italien to do bass parts here with Pellegrini and Zuchelli. The singer was now obliged to bide his time for another five years while enjoying only moderate success.

Gioacchino Rossini* was director of the Italian theatre in Paris at this time, and he was attempting to arrange affairs so that operas in the Italian tradition might replace the usual lyric tragedies that were standard fare at the Opéra. His purpose was simple, and his strategy was clear. If he could manage to bring about this coup, he could have his own works given at the Royal Academy of Music instead of having to remain content with seeing them billed at the Théâtre-Italien. He had already maneuvered Mme Laure Cinthie-Damoreau* into the Opéra, and he arranged for her and Adolphe Nourrit* to support the production of his Le Siège de Corinthe.* He knew that he needed a bass to complete his team, and Levasseur was moved over to the Opéra to provide the third star in Rossini's crown. Ultimately, therefore, Levasseur found success through his performances of Rossini's work, and he was acknowledged to be the top bass in the operatic hierarchy of France for the same reason.

Once Levasseur was at the Opéra, he sang in the premieres of 22 operas by the leading composers of the day. The following catalogue of the parts he sang after doing the title-role of Rossini's Moïse* indicated the extent of his activity and the measure of his success at the Opéra:

Role	**Opera**	**Premiere**
Moïse	Moïse	26 March 1827
Le Gouverneur	La Comte Ory	20 August 1828
Walter	Guillaume Tell	3 August 1829
Olipur	Le Dieu et la Bayadère	13 October 1830
Le Docteur Fontanarose	Le Philtre	20 June 1831
Bertram	Robert le Diable	21 November 1831
Maître Andiol	Le Serment	1 October 1832
Leporello	Don Juan	10 march 1834
Le Cardinal	La Juive	23 February 1835
Marcel	Les Huguenots	20 February 1836
Spadoni	Stradella	3 March 1837
Cosme de Médicis	Guido et Ginevra	5 March 1838
Rodolphe	Le Lac des fées	1 April 1839
Matteo le père	La Vendetta	11 September 1839
Bazu	Le Drapier	6 January 1840
Balthazar	La Favorite	2 December 1840
Raymond	Charles VI	15 March 1843
Juan de Sylva	Don Sébastien, roi du Portugal	13 November 1843

Josue Corvo	Le Lazzerone	29 March 1844
Brabantio	Othello	2 September 1844
Ismaël	Richard en Palestine	7 October 1844
Ruthwen	Marie Stuart	6 December 1844

The titles of the works in which Levasseur created the forgoing characters and the dates of the premieres of these compositions reflect impersonally but precisely the story of the bass' rise to fame and fortune. Rossini gave him his first opportunity to create a part that fit his voice, the title-role of Moïse. The onrushing sweep of romanticism did the rest, with Levasseur riding the crest of the movement at the Opéra. When it came time for him to retire, he could look back and boast that he had been one of the important figures in the execution of the romantic repertory with Adolphe Nourrit, Prosper Dérivis,* Henri Dabadie,* and Mmes Cinthie-Damoreau and Marie Taglioni.*

Levasseur was appointed to the faculty of the Conservatoire as professor of declamation in 1841, and he withdrew from the stage of the Opéra in 1845.

BIBLIOGRAPHY: AEM VIII, 677; Chouquet 392-96, 398-406; EZF 239-40; Fétis V, 290; GE XXII, 131; Jacques Gheusi, "Les Créateurs de Moïse à l'Opéra de Paris in 1827," Opéra de Paris 11 (1 October 1983), 18; ICM 999; Lajarte I, 339 and II, 125-26, 131-41, 144, 147-50, 152-53, 155-57, 159-62, 164-65, 172-78; Victor Magnier, "Nicolas-Prosper Levasseur," FM 9 (17 May 1846), 155-56; PBSW 55; Alphonse Royer, Histoire de l'Opéra (Paris: Bachelin-Deflorenne, 1875), 87-88.

Limnander de Nieuwenhove, Armand-Marie Ghislain (b. 22 May 1814, Gand; d. 14 August 1892, Moignanville château in Seine-et-Oise), composer, was sent to the Jesuit school in Fribourg to complete his primary studies and became interested in music during his stay in Switzerland. When he returned to Belgium, he married and settled down in Malines, where he founded a musical society that featured a choral group for which he wrote a number of compositions. The works that Limnander did for his group, now called the Réunion Lyrique, focused attention on his talents for the first time.

Yet the composer was honest enough with himself to admit that he was in need of additional instruction in composition, and he went to Paris to continue his studies and his career. He made two trips to the capital, one in 1846 and the other in 1847, and he decided to make Paris his permanent home on the later journey. His Les Monténégrins was performed with great success at the Opéra-Comique in 1849, and this composition, along with Le Château de la Barbe-Bleue (1851), brought him recognition as a skilled librettist, although the political situation interrupted the successful run of the later work after 25 billings. Encouraged by the reception accorded to his first two theatrical pieces at the Opéra-Comique, he gave Le Maître Chanteur* to the Opéra, where it was mounted initially on 17 October 1853. It was not until 1859 that Limnander had Yvonne produced at the Opéra-Comique, and he had no titles posted at the Opéra after 1853. His other works included religious and patriotic compositions usually requested by the Belgian government or done to honor the duke de Brabant.

BIBLIOGRAPHY: Chouquet 413; Fétis V, 302-3; Lajarte II, 214-15; LXIX X, 524; Wks 11508.

Llpkovska Lydia (b. 1887, Poltava, Russia; d. ?) was a lyric coloratura soprano who trained for an operatic career at the St. Petersburg Conservatory. She appeared in this city for the first time as Gilda at the Maryinsky Theatre during 1910, but she sang in other cities of Europe as early as 1909. She appeared frequently in Paris, where she was cast in the title-roles of Lakmé and Manon* as well as in such parts as Violetta in La Traviata, Mimi in La Vie de Bohème, Rosine in Le Barbier de Séville* (see twentieth-century volume for La Traviata and La Vie de Bohème). She was booked into the Opéra for the first time on 26 June 1909, when she sang Juliette, and she returned to the Garnier Palace* in 1913 as Gilda in Rigoletto* and Ophélie in Hamlet.*

BIBLIOGRAPHY: EFC 183; SW 418.

Liszt, Franz (b. 22 October 1811, Raiding, Hungary; d. 31 July 1886, Bayreuth), composer, arrived in Paris for the first time in December 1823, and, although he crossed the Channel in 1824 to play for George IV, he managed to arrange for his opera entitled Don Sanche to be given at the Royal Academy of Music on 17 October 1825. Unfortunately, this attempt at success in the theatre proved futile, and Liszt's work in a single act had to be withdrawn from the stage after a few performances. It has never been published.

Liszt remained in Paris until 1835, but he was never tempted to submit another opera to the jury at the Opéra, although he conducted opera performances at Weimar between 1848 and 1859. More recently, however, his work has been heard at the Garnier Palace.* Darius Milhaud used his music when he was scoring Alexandre Benois'* ballet entitled La Bien-Aimée, which was performed at the Opéra on 22 November 1928 by the ballet company managed by Mme Ida Rubinstein (see twentieth-century volume for Milhaud, La Bien-Aimée, and Rubinstein).

The first Méphisto-Valse by Liszt was played at the Garnier Palace on 19 March 1953, when it served as an interlude on a program of Faust-music entitled Faust 53, which included selections from the Faust-works of Hector Berlioz,* Boïto, Bondeville, Charles Gounod,* Robert Schumann,* and Richard Wagner* (see twentieth-century volume for Boïto and Bondeville). Lastly, Liszt's transcription of Rigoletto* provided material for the score of a pas de deux that was produced under the sponsorship of the ballet company from the Opéra in Geneva on 15 March 1957. It is curious that this ballet was never danced at the Garnier Palace, because its choreography was created by Serge Lifar (see twentieth-century volume for Lifar).

BIBLIOGRAPHY: AEM VIII, 964-88; BBD 1023-27; DGM 309-53; EDS VI, 1541-44; EGC 214-19, ELM III, 81-91; James Gibbons Huneker, Liszt (New York: Scribner's, 1931); GIR 296-303; MCDE I, 543-60; MM 374-94; NEO 379; PBSW 95; Humphrey Searle, The Music of Liszt (London: Williams and Norgate, 1954); Thompson 1020-25.

Litvinne, Félia (b. 1861, Russia; d. 12 October 1936, Paris), vocalist, whose true name was Kanny Schutz, and who also sang under the name of Litvinova, studied in Paris under Mme Barth-Banderoli, Sbriglia, and Victor Maurel.* A soprano, she made her debut in the French capital at the Théâtre des Italiens in 1885 in Jules Massenet's* Hérodiade. She appeared the following winter at the New York Academy of Music and toured Russia later with engagements in St. Petersburg and Moscow. She was billed at the Metropolitan Opera House in 1896 and 1897, at Covent Garden in 1899 through 1901, and at La Scala in 1908.

Mme Litvinne made her debut with the company of the Paris Opéra as Valentine in Les Huguenots* on 29 March 1889, but her constant traveling did not allow her to remain at the Garnier Palace* for long periods of time. She sang Sélika in L'Africaine* and Rachel in La Juive* there in 1889, for example, but she did not return to the Opéra until 1907, when she did the title-role in Christoph Willibald Gluck's Armide, Brunehilde in La Walkyrie,* and Isolde in Tristan et Isolde* (see eighteenth-century volume for Gluck and Armide). She sang Aïda in 1908 at the Garnier, however, and she was cast in no fewer than five parts in 1909: Brunehilde in Siegfried,* Cathérine in Henry VIII,* Dalila in Camille Saint-Saëns'* work, Brunehilde in Le Crépuscule des dieux,* and Vénus in Tannhäuser.*

The soprano was in Monte Carlo in 1911 to perform in the title-role of Saint-Saëns' Déjanire* on 14 March for the world premiere of this work, and she created this same part at the Opéra on 22 November 1911. The other role she gave for the first time at the Garnier theatre was the female lead in Judith de Béthulie, staged initially in Paris on 26 March 1916 (see twentieth-century volume for Judith de Béthulie). The last performance that Mme Litvinne gave at the Opéra was as Brunehilde in Sigurd* in 1916. When she retired, she was considered one of the most accomplished Wagnerian sopranos of her day.

BIBLIOGRAPHY: APD 462, EFC 160-63; KRJ 255-56; Félia Litvinne, Ma vie et mon art (New York: Arno Press Reprint, 1977); H. Moréno, "Débuts de Mlle Litvinne à l'Opéra," Le Ménestrel 55 (31 March 1889), 98-99; PBSW 188; SW, 41, 67, 71, 129, 207, 215, 226; WOC 262.

Livry, Emma (b. October 1842, Paris; d. 26 July 1863, Paris), ballerina, was the natural daughter of Célestine Emarot, a danseuse at the Opéra, and baron Charles de Chassiron, a member of the Jockey Club. She attended a girls' school in Paris and enrolled in Mme Dominique's dancing classes as a young child. After her father had broken off with her mother, she was fortunate enough to find a strong protector at the Opéra in the person of her mother's second lover, the powerful Viscount Ferdinand de Montguyon. It was through the latter's influence that it was decided that Emma should make her debut in a major role, and the viscount and Alphonse Royer,* director of the Opéra, signed an agreement stipulating that Emma Livry was to appear before the public for the first time in La Sylphide* during the absence of its star, Mme Amalia Ferraris.*

Emma Emarot began to prepare for her debut in the summer of 1858, and Montguyon eliminated any obstacles that threatened to delay her initial appearance before the public. Finally, her debut was scheduled for 20 October 1858, and management decided simultaneously that she should be billed as Emma Livry. Montguyon took matters in hand once again at the start of October and saw to it that his mistress' daughter received proper publicity. Le Figaro referred to her as a second Taglioni and a youthful sensation who was French, not Italian or Russian. These notices were apparently effective, because Emma danced to a full house. Her performance inspired the press to use such phrases as "sculptured marble" or "the wings of a frail bird" to describe the 15 year-old ballerina's debut, which was distinguished by its "lightness" and "elasticity" and "ethereal grace." Marie Taglioni* returned to Paris to receive Emma Livry as her guest in her apartment on 16 November and to see her in La Sylphide on 17 November.

One of Mlle Livry's rewards for her work was a new contract calling for a salary of 10,000 francs and an engagement for the next 12 months, despite the malicious rumors being spread about the means by which she had obtained preference at the Opéra. She went into rehearsal almost immediately for the divertissement in Herculanum,* which had recently been completed by Félicien David* (see eighteenth-century volume for divertissement). She was cast as Erigone in the bacchanal in the third act, and her performance on 4 March 1859 was praised once again for its lightness and ethereal quality. Critics compared her to Taglioni for the second time, and management was esstatic over the charm that she exerted upon spectators. Her engagement was extended to three years, and her annual salary was raised to

18,000, 24,000 and 30,000 francs for each successive year. Circumstances continued to work in her favor, when Carolina Rosati* left the company, and only Ferraris remained to enjoy greater prestige in the corps de ballet of the Opéra.

All that Emma Livry could desire now was to obtain a ballet that was "her" ballet just as _La Sylphide_ and _Giselle_* had come to be associated with Taglioni and Carlotta Grisi.* This lack was soon remedied by _Le Papillon_,* for which Jacques Offenbach* had set Jules-Henri Vernoy de Saint-Georges'* words with choreography by Marie Taglioni. It was given its premiere on 26 November 1860 before the emperor. The work did not come up to the high expectations of the public, unfortunatley, but Emma Livry's progress in her art was manifest. She was called "a star of the first magnitude"; she was praised once more for her airy performance and credited with ample grace and artful precision. Above all, she evoked comparison with her steadfast friend, Taglioni, and it was asserted that she had now attained to maturity. Montguyon is said to have embraced her joyously after her performance and to have said, "You were only a caterpillar, but I have made you a butterfly." The baron de Chassiron had just returned to Paris, and he had also purchased a ticket for the premiere of _Le Papillon_ without knowing that the star of the evening was his own daughter. When he learned later that Emma Livry was in fact his daughter, he offered her a portion of his fortune, but the ballerina refused his belated offer.

Mlle Livry suffered an injury during the performance of _Le Papillon_ on 18 October 1861, and she was obliged to rest for an interval of time that was extended by her refusal to appear in a revival of _La Muette de Portici_* and by her demand for a raise in salary to 42,000 francs. In the meantime, Charles Gounod's* _La Reine de Saba_* went into rehearsal without a premiere danseuse because management refused to meet Emma's demands. Ultimately, the star settled for 30,000 francs, and _La Reine de Saba_ opened on 28 February 1862. It failed, but Emma was not held responsible for its shortcomings, and she was assigned the title-role in _Zara_. This new work went into rehearsal on 28 october 1862, but Mlle Livry was also busy with additional undertakings that autumn. She appeared in _Herculanum_ for the last time on 12

November 1862, and she started rehearsing the part of the mute heroine of La Muette de Portici on the evening of 15 November. She was awaiting the moment of her entrance in the second act when her unfireproofed costume moved into the sphere of a gaslight. She was a mass of flame in an instant and ran across the stage in panic. No one had the presence of mind to come to her aid until a theatre fireman named Muller threw a blanket around her. She was still alive and was taken home on a stretcher to endure months of pain. She lay on her face for four months, and straw was placed on the street before her apartment in the rue Laffitte so that she would not suffer from the passage of traffic. Montguyon was at her side constantly, and she received the most competent and compassionate care that Paris could provide. She seemed to improve in the summer, and she was taken to the country. Suddenly, she fell victim to erysipelas, and her pain became unbearable again. She died on 26 July 1863 and was buried from Notre-Dame de Lorette three days later. Marie Taglioni, Mme Dominique, Théophile Gautier,* and nearly everybody else connected with the Opéra attended the service. Interment was in the Montmartre cemetery, and Lucien Petipa* delivered the funeral oration.

BIBLIOGRAPHY: ACD 292; CB 289, 294-95; CODB 329; DDD 138; EDB 217-18; M. Escudier, "Emma Livry," FM 27 (2 aout 1863), 239-40; EZF 242; Ivor Guest, The Ballet of the Second Empire (Middletown, Conn.: Wesleyan University Press, 1974), 2-4, 123-41, 143-60, 177-79; Quatrelles L'Epine, Une Danseuse française au XIXe siècle: Emma Livry (Paris: 1909); André Levinson, Ballet romantique (Paris: Editions du Trianon, 1929), 49-52; Parmenia Migel, The Ballerinas from the Court of Louis XIV to Pavlova (New York: Macmillan, 1972), 232-38; Lillian Moore, Artists of the Dance (New York: Thomas Y. Crowell Co., 1938), 89, 155-59.

Lohengrin is an opera in three acts and five tableaux with words and music by Richard Wagner.* It was given its world premiere at the Hof-Theatre in Weimar on 28 August 1850, and it was taken subsequently to the Théâtre Royal de la Monnaie in Brussels in 1870, to the Academy of Music in New York in 1871, to Convent Garden in London in 1875, to the Metropolitan Opera in New York again in 1883, to the Eden-Théâtre in Paris in 1887, and to the Théâtre des Arts in Rouen in 1891. Then, on 16 September 1891, it was billed for the first time at the Garnier Palace* in a French version by Charles Nuitter.* Lapissida was in charge of this Paris production that featured sets by Amable, Carpezat, Gardy, Lavastre. Charles Bianchini created the costumes. Charles Lamoureux* conducted the orchestra described in detail in the first Paris edition of the libretto. After enjoying more than 300 presentations before World War I, the work has been billed with sustained frequency at the Opéra with revivals in 1922, 1947, 1954, and 1959. It has been staged on approximately 700 occasions at the Opéra.

The French version of the opera begins on the banks of the Escaut River near Anver, where King Henri I is mobilizing his forces to drive the hostile Hungarians from his lands. The time is the middle of the tenth century. Frédéric has been charged by the prince of Brabant to protect his young son Gottfried and daughter Elsa, but the older child Elsa returned one night from the forest without her brother Gottfried, and it is believed that she did away with him. The regent Frédéric has canceled his planned marriage to Elsa, therefore, and has married Ortrude, daughter of King Rabad. Frédéric lays claim to the lands of the prince of Brabant, and Henri summons Elsa to appear before him as a result of this suit (I, 1). Elsa refutes Frédéric's claim, but she is too distraught to defend herself. She can only pray that her honor will be upheld by the knight in shining armor whom she has seen in a dream and who has promised to help her. Frédéric accuses her of pretending to be delirious; he demands to fight her champion to the death according to the code. Elsa chooses her visionary knight to defend her honor, and Lohengrin approaches in a skiff drawn by a swan (I, 2). He prepares to defend Elsa, and she vows to marry him without knowing his name or background if he is victorious. The field of honor is marked off; the herald announces the rules of combat. Lohengrin strikes down Frédéric but spares his life, and Elsa's innocence is proven (I, 3).

The scene shifts in the second act to the castle of Anver near the church, where Frédéric is lamenting his dishonorable state and reproaching his magician wife for his sorry predicament because he believed her lie that she saw Elsa drown her brother. Deceived, he turned his back on Elsa only to marry the author of his shame and misfortune. The sorceress answers his reproaches by assuring him that he can overcome Lohengrin by learning his identity, a feat that can be performed by using Elsa as an unwitting accomplice. Frédéric agrees to follow Ortrude's plan (II, 1), and the latter asks Elsa why she has created so much misery and misfortune. She prays silently to Wotan for help in her scheme, and gullible Elsa forgives her for any injury she might have done to her. In her innocence, Elsa also asks Ortrude to join her and Lohengrin in the church at dawn for their wedding. Ortrude sews the first seeds of doubt in Elsa's mind by telling her to be careful lest Lohengrin disappear as quickly as he came (II, 2). A herald announces that the king has banished Frédéric and has given the territory of Brabant to Lohengrin. When it is revealed that the war must be undertaken immediately, the nobles demur. Frédéric tries to win them to his side, but they reject him (II, 3). Ortrude stops Elsa on her way into the church; she angers her by challenging her to reveal her future husband's name and origin. She suggests malevolently that he is of dubious birth and character (II, 4). The king demands to know the reason for the disorder in front of the church, and Elsa asks Lohengrin to confess his identity despite her promise not to question him. He berates Ortrude for corrupting Elsa, and Frédéric intervenes with the accusation that he was defeated by trickery. Lohengrin continues to conceal his identity. Elsa is filled with anguish, and King Henri urges him to speak, but he is adamant. Frédéric suggests to Elsa that they could make Lohengrin confess, if they were to make him jealous. She rejects his plan, but Frédéric is unshaken despite this rebuff even after the bridal pair enters the church (II, 5).

The last act is set in the nuptial chamber, where a chorus of attendants honor the bride and groom. After the singers' departure (III, 1), the couple swear eternal love and describe their happiness. Elsa begs her husband to reveal his name, and she grows uneasy over his reluctance to answer her directly. She insists, but he will not yield to her request. She weeps on account of his apparent obstinacy and the implied threat that he may abandon her. She protests that even now the swan may be approaching to transport him to another land (III, 2). Frédéric and his men rush in with drawn swords, but Lohengrin slays him immediately, and the other assailants surrender. Lohengrin orders Elsa to dress in white to appear before the king because he is about to reveal his name to Henri (III, 3).

The setting returns to the meadow of the first act, where the king is surrounded by his Saxon nobles and the counts of Brabant. They are about to march off to war (III, 4) and attribute Elsa's sadness to their departure (III, 5). Lohengrin enters with Frédéric's body and accuses Elsa of betraying her oath by persuading him to reveal his origins. He acknowledges that he is Lohengrin, son of Parcival and knight of the Holy Grail of Monsalvat. He is to leave Never because the Grail summons him now that his identity and nature are known. The swan appears, and he gives Elsa his sword, horn, and ring to give to her brother, if he should return to her (III, 7). Ortrude reports to Elsa that the swan is Gottfried, who reappears as himself as soon as Lohengrin frees the swan of its chain. Lohengrin is led away to the Grail by the dove as the curtain falls (III, 8).

Lohengrin is described frequently as the last romantic opera because it exploits the pageantry of the Middle Ages while presenting a benevolent king ruling justly over his subjects and trying to solve problems created by a sorcerer and her corrupt accomplice. The work is similarly compared with Tannhäuser* from time to time because it employs Germanic legend and folklore while developing musical motifs to achieve unity between the music and the libretto. Essentially, however, Lohengrin is different from Tannhäuser. Its music is more antiphonal than woven into a single instrumental unity. Also, the earlier work evolves from the conflict between sensual ecstasy symbolized by Venus and monastic discipline represented by Elizabeth and the pilgrims; the drama offered by Lohengrin is lodged in the divinely endowed protagonist seeking human support and love that a distrustful and faithless humanity cannot offer. The protagonist must renounce all hope in Elsa despite her innocence because she is incapable of loving him on his terms of trust. Lohengrin, therefore, presents a greater tragedy through its insistance upon the irremediable weakness of humanity unable to respond to devine love and its own redemption.

The roles of Elsa and Ortrude were sung by Rose Caron* and Caroline Fierens, respectively, for the premiere of Lohengrin at the Opéra, while the title-role was filled by Ernst Van Dyck* making his debut at the Garnier theatre on this occasion. The other principal roles were done by Maurice Renaud* (Frédéric de Telramund) and Jean-François Delmas* (Henri I) with Douailler as the herald. Rose Caron became famous for her many subsequent representations of Elsa, and later singers to do this same role at the Opéra have included Louise Grandjean (1896), Jeanne Hatto* (1908), Maria Kousnetzoff* (1908), Yvonne Gall (1910),* Germaine Lubin (1922), Lotte Lehmann (1929), Germaine Hoerner (1931), and Régine Crespin making her debut on 10 August 1951 (see twentieth-century volume for Lubin, Lehmann, Hoerner, and Crespin). Lohengrin has been sung subsequently at the Opéra by more than a score of tenors among whom were Albert Alvarez* (1892), Jean de Reszké* (1893), Paul Franz* in his debut at the theatre on 1 February 1909, Lauritz Melchior (1932), Charles Fronval (1947), and Calude Hector (1955) (see twentieth-century volume Melchior). Frédéric was done later by Jean Noté* (1893), Marius Chambon (1905), Charles Camban (1933), and Charles-Paul (1948).

BIBLIOGRAPHY: Paul Bekker, Richard Wagner: His Life in His Work, trans. M. M. Bozman (Westport, Conn.: Greenwood Press, 1971), 170-216; Alice Leighton Cleather, Parsifal, Lohengrin and the Legend of the Holy Grail (London: Methuen & Co., 1904); Siegfried Goslich, Bieträge zur Geschicte des deutschen romantischen Oper swischen Spohrs "Faust" und Wagners "Lohengrin" (Leipzig: Kistner u. Siegel, 1937); Gerhart Johann R. Hauptmann, "Lohengrin" (Berlin: Ullstein & Co., 1913); Albert Heintz, Richard Wagner's "Lohengrin" (Berlin: Verlag der "Allgemeinen Musikzeitung," 1894; André Himonet, "Lohengrin": étude historique et critique, analyse musicale (Paris: Mellottée, 1925); August Jahn, Leitfaden zur Richard Wagners "Lohengrin" (Leipzig: F. Reinboth, 1894); Adolphe Jullien, Musiciens d'aujourd'hui (Paris: Librairie de l'art, 1892), 86-101, 445-54; KCOB 202-16; Theodore Maximilian R. von Keler, "Lohengrin" (Girard, Kansas: Haldeman-Julius Co., 1923); Maurice Kufferath,

"Lohengrin" (Paris: Fischbacher, 1895); MCDE II, 1101-2, 1116-18; OQE 450-56; PBSW 15, 59-61, 147-48, 226-27; Arthur Pougin, "Première Représentation de Lohengrin à l'Opéra," Le Ménestrel 57 (20 September 1891), 298-300; Arthur Prüfer, Einführung in Richard Wagners "Lohengrin" (Bayreuth: C. Giessel, 1937); Joachim Raff, Die Wagnerfrage (Braunschweig: F. Vieweg, 1854); Arthur Seidl, Wagneriana (Berlin u. Leipzig: Schuster v. Loeffler, 1901-2); SSBO 216-19, 335; Stoullig XVII (1891), 19-33; SW 134-36; Edward M. Terry, A Richard Wagner Dictionary (Westport, Conn.: Greenwood Press, 1971), 62-67; Thompson 1039, 2174; Wolzogen U.H.P. Neuhaus, Richard Wagner's "Tannhäuser" u. "Lohengrin" (Berlin: T. Barth, 1873.

Louise is described as a "musical romance" in five acts, although the 1900 edition of the libretto presented it in four acts and five tableaux with the second act divided into two tableaux. Its libretto was written by Saint-Pol-Roux and Gustave Charpentier,* but Charpentier alone composed its score. Mme Mariquita provied the choreography for the Crowning of the Muse of Montmartre in the third act. It had its world premier at the salle Favart, where the company of the Opéra-Comique mounted it for the first time on 2 February 1900 with sets by Lucien Jusseaume and costumes by Charles Bianchi. G. Rochegrasse designed the outfit worn by the Pleasure of Paris figure, and Henri Carré was in charge of the chorus, while L. Landry directed the actor's singing.

The composition opens with Louise and Julien discussing their mutual love across the alley separating their attic apartments, when Louise's mother returns home to pull her daughter from the window (I, sc. 1-2). The angry parent denounces Julien as a worthless idler despite Louise's protests, but she becomes calm when her husband comes through the door. The father produces a letter from Julien, and he suggests that they make an effort to know Louise's suitor better. The mother objects immediately that Julien is a drunkard and a profligate. Louise's father reminds his daughter that her parents are thinking of her future welfare, when they disapprove of Julien. Tearful Louise agrees to forget her lover (I, 3-4).

The scene shifts to a row of market stalls at the foot of Montmartre. It is 5:00 a.m. on an April day, and a milkmaid, a newspaper girl, and a coal picker are setting up their wares. A ragpicker is complaining of the hardships suffered by the poor, and a man in evening clothes representing the Pleasure of Paris enters reciting poetry. A junkman tells the girls how he lost his three daughters to the poet (II, tabl. 1, sc. 1). Julien appears with some artist friends to whom he confides that he plans to kidnap Louise if her parents oppose her marriage to him. His friends leave; Louise and her mother enter on their way to Louise's place of employment as a seamstress. The mother leaves (II, tabl. 1, sc. 2-6), and Julien pursues Louise. She refuses to quit her job and family, although she agrees to become his wife (II, tabl. 1, sc. 7).

The second tableau of the second act transpires in a garment loft, where the woman are singing or talking about the problems they encounter in their work. They notice that Louise is quiet, and they ask whether she is in love. Louise denies all emotional entanglements, and her coworkers sing of the delights of being in love. Suddenly, Julien is heard singing a serenade in the street. He reproaches Louise for not accepting his love, and his song amuses the sewing girls for a time. Upset, Louise leaves the shop to rejoin Julien (II, tabl. 2, sc. 1-3).

Louise and Julien are rejoicing over their love, freedom, and happiness in their own home on Montmartre. They watch the lights of the city and swear eternal love to each other, while the parents in the neighborhood condemn them for their moral laxity. Unannounced, the figure of the Pleasure of Paris appears in the doorway, and one of the Muses enters to hail Louise. A crowd of street urchins heaps roses upon her, and a dancer moves around her. The Pope of Fools sings of her beauty. The shopgirls and artists of Montmartre ask her to be their queen, and the lovers reaffirm their love for each other amidst their apotheosis to a rolling of drums. Louise's mother appears in the garden, and everybody grows quiet. The celebrants leave (III, 1-3), and Louise's mother tells Julien that her husband is ill. Only Louise can save him. Julien receives a guarantee that his wife will return to him, and Louise departs with her mother (III, 4).

The last act returns to the home of Louise's parents, where her mother is working in the kitchen, and her father is complaining of the injustice and disillusionment that oppress him. The mother denounces free love and asserts that Louise must remain with her ailing father (IV, 1). Louise's father kisses her, but she fails to return his affection and asks for permission to go back to Montmartre. Her mother warns that she is courting disaster if she refuses to insist upon marriage. Louise can think only of her freedom, however, and she ignores her parents' advice. Her father tries to prevent her departure, but she defies him, and he orders her from the house. She leaves (IV, 2). He calls after her and curses Paris (IV, 3).

Louise was a popular work, and it was never really dropped from the repertory. It enjoyed 956 performances at the Opéra-Comique during the first half of the twentieth century. It celebrated its 100th presentation as early as 22 February 1901, and, on 17 January 1921, it was billed for the 500th time at this same theatre. Its principal roles were created by Marthe Rioton (Louise), Blanche Dischamps-Jehin* (the mother), Alphonse Maréchal (Julien), and Lucien Fugère (the father). Maurice Utrillo created new sets for the observance of its 50th anniversary at the Opéra-Comique in 1950.

BIBLIOGRAPHY: AEM II, 1103-7; EDS III, 545-48; Raoul Follerau, "Gustave Charpentier," Le Ménestrel 94, no. 30 (22 July 1932), 313-15; KCOB 1252-57; MSRL 42-43; NMO 381-401; OQE 57-58; PBSW 71, 100; SSBO 326-27, 332, 361; Thompson 1043, 2175-76; WOC 108.

Louise Miller was billed as an opera in four acts with a score by Giuseppe Verdi* and a libretto that was a translation by Benjamin Alaffre* of the original Italian by Cammarano. The latter had based his composition upon the work by youthful Friedrich Schiller entitled Kabale und Liebe. The Italian opera had had its world premiere at the San Carlo Theatre in Naples on 8 December 1849, and the French version was produced for the first time at the Imperial Academy of Music on 2 February 1853. It failed to arouse any prolonged interest among paris spectators, however, and it had to be dropped from the repertory after its eighth presentation on 21 March 1853, when it returned only 4,144, francs, 88 centimes, to the box office.

The first act of the opera is set near Miller's house, where Louise is waiting for the young stranger in the village with whom she has fallen in love, although her father is not as enthusiastic about him as she is. Laura and the chorus offer bouquets of spring flowers to Louise, and Rodolphe enters to declare his love to her, but Miller is still filled with misgivings (I, 1-3). Miller is about to go into church, when Wurm asks for his daughter's hand, but Miller replies that his daughter is free to marry whom she chooses. Wurm warns him against the dangers of allowing Louise to select her own husband. Count Walter's son is deceiving her. Miller is consumed with grief to hear that a nobleman is misleading his innocent daughter by promising to marry her (I, 4-5). Wurm tells his master, Count Walter, of his son's folly in pursuing the peasant girl Louise, and Walter regrets his crime without disclosing the nature of his misdeed (I, 6-7). He orders his son to tell the wealthy duchess that he loves her and will marry her (I, 6-8), but Rodolphe cannot bring himself to obey his father, and he asks the duchess to forgive him for not asking her to marry him because he loves another woman. The rejected duchess is furious and infers to Rodolphe that he cannot make a fool of her with impunity (I, 9-10).

The second act continues at Miller's house, where Louise is wondering why her lover has not come to see her. Miller informs his daughter that her sweetheart is Count Walter's son, who is marrying the duchess before sundown. Rodolphe enters and swears his undying love to bewildered Louise, who regains her confidence when Rodolphe swears that he will marry only her (II, 1-3). Count Walter berates his son for tarrying in Louise's house, and he warns him that he loves her. The count insults Louise; Miller and Rodolphe draw their swords, and the count calls his soldiers. He orders Louise and her father thrown into prison. Rodolphe asks his father to be less vengeful, but he ignors his son. Old Miller advises the lovers to pray only to God and to ignore the heartless count, but Rodolphe threatens his father that he will reveal how he came to possess a title and wealth. The count turns pale and orders Louise freed. Miller remains a prisoner (II, 4-5).

The chorus relates to Louise that her father has been locked up in the citadel, and she wonders how she can save him (III, 1). She is in the count's castle now, and the latter's secretary Wurm informs her that her father is in prison for treason. He can be saved from the block, he adds, if Louise will write a letter stating that she never loved Rodolphe but wished to become his mistress because of his wealth and position. She refuses, but the thought of her father's cruel death changes her mind. He then adds that she will have to swear to the duches that it was he, Wurm, whom she loved. Louise despairs, and Wurm reveals in an aside that he will save her father, and then perhaps she will fall in love with him one day (III, 2-3). The count assures the skeptical duchess that Rodolphe never loved Louise Miller, and Wurm enters with Louise. The duchess asks her whether she is in love, and she replies that she loves Wurm. The curious duchess presses for details, and Louise begins to tremble, but she persists in her falsehood to the end despite her feelings of revulsion and terror. The deluded duchess is exultant (III, 4-6). Rodolphe has read Louise's letter but refuses to believe it and summons Wurm, whom he challenges to a duel with pistols. Frightened, Wurm fires into the air, and guards rush in to find Rodolpeh raging at his father's secretary. The count suggests that he marry the duchess, but Roldophe thinks only of suicide (III, 7-8).

Louise is in her bedroom, where Laura is trying to comfort her. Although Louise is writing, she notices through the window that the church is lighted, but Laura cannot bring herself to tell her friend that the illumination is for Rodolphe's wedding. Miller enters and thanks his daughter for her generous sacrifice; he asks her why she is writing a letter at so late an hour. She gives it to him to read. It invites Rodolphe to die with her at midnight. Miller is overcome with grief and begs his daughter to resist the idea of suicide. Obedient, she destroys the letter, and the father and daughter decide to flee together to find a new life elsewhere. Louise prays (IV, 1-3), but Rodolphe interrupts her to show her the letter he has and to ask her whether or not she wrote it. She replies that it was she who wrote the letter. Rodolphe drinks from a goblet of wine he has placed upon the table and invites Louise to drink with him. He curses her infidelity, but she assures him that he has fallen into error, and she asks his forgiveness for misleading him. He rejects her explanations and asks only to die in peace because they have swallowed poison. Louise describes her reasons for writing the letter, and they both curse the predicament into which they have fallen. Miller enters; Louise asks his forgiveness and dies. The count breaks into the house with his men only to find Louise dead, Rodolphe dying, and Miller mute with grief (IV, 4-6).

The male roles of this lengthy opera set in seventeenth-century Germany were filled by Louis Gueymard* (Rodolphe), Morelli (Miller), Merly (Count Walter), and Depassio (Wurm). Louise was sung by Angiolina Bosio,* who took leave of the company on 27 March 1853, while the part of the duchess was done by Mlle Masson.

BIBLIOGRAPHY: *Franco Abbiati, Giuseppe Verdi (Milan: Ricordo, 1959) II, 10-43; A. Basevi, Studio sulle opere di Giuseppe Verdi (Florence: Tofani, 1859), 155-70; Ferruccio Bonavia, Verdi (London: Dennis Dobson Ltd., 1947), 45; France-Yvonne Bril, Verdi (Paris: Hachette, 1972), 35; Julian Budden, The Operas of Verdi (London: Cassell, 1973) I, 417-46; Eugenio Checchi, G. Verdi (Florence: G. Barbera, 1901), 109-14; Chouquet 413; Frederick J. Crowest, Verdi: Man and Musician (London: John Milne, 1978), 95-103; DDO II, 660, 667; Carlo Gatti, Verdi, the Man and His Music (New York: G. P. Putnam's Sons, 1955), 115-18;Gianandrea Gavazzeni, "Notes sur l'évolution du style de Verdi dans Luisa Miller," Opéra de Paris 9 (15 May 1983), 7-9; Vincent Godefroy, The Dramatic Genius of Verdi (London: Victor Gollancz Ltd., 1975), 169-86; Paul Hume, Verdi, the Man and His Music (New York: E. P. Dutton and Metropolitan Opera Guild, 1977), 144-48; D. Humphreys, Verdi: Force of Destiny (New York: Henry Holt, 1948), 117-21; Dyneley Hussey, Verdi (London: J. M. Dent & Sons, 1973), 63-66; KCOB 546-48; Lajarte II, 212-13; George Martin, Verdi, His Music, Life and Times (New York: Dodd, Mead and Co., 1963), 255-63; MCDE II, 1070; G. Nicolo, "Louise Miller à l'Académie Impériale de Musique," FM 17 (6 February 1853), 45-46; OQE 374-75; PBSW 65-66; Giuseppe Pugliese, "La Rédaction du livret de Luisa Miller," Opéra de Paris 9 (15 May 1983), 4-5; Pierre Petit, Verdi, trans. Patrick Bowles (London: John Calder, 1962), 58-62; Max de Schauensee, The Collector's Verdi and Puccini (Philadelphia: J. B. Lippincott, 1962), 41-42; SSBO 214-16, 224; Thompson 1047, 2177; Francis Toye, Giuseppe Verdi: His Life and Works (New York: Alfred A. Knopf, 1946), 255-63; Robert A. Tuggle, "Why Luisa Miller?" ON 36 (11 October 1971), 21-24.*

Louvois, the theatre, was the scene of a brief sojourn by the Opéra between the time that the artists left the salle Favart on 11 May 1821 and the date of their moving into the Le Peletier* theatre on 16 August 1821. They gave only two concerts and two operatic programs in this facility built by Brogniart in 1791.
BIBLIOGRAPHY: André Lejeune and Stéphane Wolff, Les Quinze Salles de l'Opéra de Paris (Paris: Librairie théâtrale, 1955), 28-29; Charles Nuitter, Le Nouvel Opéra (Paris: Hachette, 1875), 14.

Loventz, Amélie (b. 23 July 1871, Paris; d. ?), soprano, studied voice and piano at the Brussels Conservatoire under the direction of M. Warnots. She made her theatrical debut as Marguerite de Valois in Les Huguenots* at Marseilles in 1889, and her performance was so impressive that she was invited to make her first appearance at the Paris Opéra in the same part on 9 November 1890. Her disciplined soprano voice and its impressive range won Mlle Loventz a contract to perform at the Garnier Palace,* and she remained with the company for seven years. Her repertory included the following 13 roles that she sang at the Opéra:

Role	Opera, Year
Colombe	Ascanio, 1891
Raphaela	Patrie!, 1891
Mathilde	Guillaume Tell, 1891
Anahita	Le Mage, 1891
Gilda	Rigoletto, 1892

Inès	L'Africaine, 1892
Juliette	Roméo et Juliette, 1892
Eudoxie	La Juive, 1892
Helwigue	Walkyrie, 1893
Isabelle	Robert le Diable, 1893
Crobyle	Thaïs, 1894
Héléna	La Montagne noire, 1895
Marguerite	Faust, 1896

BIBLIOGRAPHY: EFC 164; Martin 225; SW 25-26, 42, 88, 105-6, 115-18, 129-30, 138, 151, 170-71, 181-85, 189-91.

Lucas, Hippolyte-Julien-Joseph (b. 20 December 1807, Rennes; d. 14 November 1878, Paris), journalist, studied and practiced law to please his father but changed his mind before long to pursue a career in journalism in Paris. His first project as a journalist was to translate articles from the Edinburgh Review and to report on the doings of the British Parliament for Le Globe. Simultaneously, he wrote for Le Bon Sens, Le National, L'Artiste, La Revue du progrès, and La Nouvelle Minerve. His familiarity with the English language and the literature of England did not tempt him to exploit the contemporary romantic interest in England because he was more attracted to the writers of Spain and translated plays by Lope de Vega, Pedro Calderon, and Pedro Alarcon for the stages of the Odéon and the Comédie-Française in 1843-44. He turned next to the ancient theatre and did Les Nuées (1844), Alceste (1847), and Médée (1855) within the next decade.

Lucas' scholarly interests became more manifest in the last half of his life, when he published a history of the Comédie-Française in two volumes in 1843 and a collection of what he considered to be "dramatic and literary curiosities" in 1855. The results of his research on the sources of Pierre Corneille's Le Cid appeared in 1861. These investigations were facilitated by the fact that Lucas had become librarian of the Arsenal collection in Paris.

When it is remembered that Lucas was the author of these creative, journalistic, and scholarly publications, it is difficult to know how he managed to do so many texts for the theatre at the same time. He contributed more than 25 titles to Paris theatres between 1831 and 1850 alone, and his compositions were billed at the Opéra, the Odéon, Mme Saqui's theatre, the Variétés, the Vaudeville, the Ambigu-Comique, the Choiseul, the Beaumarchais, and the Comédie-Française. His offerings at the Opéra included L'Etoile de Séville* of 1845, La Bouquetière* of 1847, and the translation he did of the original Italian libretto of Domenico Gaetano Donizetti's* Betly* of 1853. His big hit at the Opéra-Comique was Lalla-Roukh (1862), for which he wrote the words with Michel Carré.*

BIBLIOGRAPHY: Chouquet 407-9, 414; GE XX, 727; Lajarte II, 179, 185, 215; LXIX X, 760; Ludwig Pfandl, Hippolyte Lucas, sein Leben und seine dramatischen Werke (Liepzig-Reudnitz: A. Hoffmann, (1908); Thieme II, 190; Wks III, 268.

Lucie de Lammermoor is an opera with a score by Domenico Gaetano Donizetti* and a libretto by Salvatore Cammarano based upon Sir Walter Scott's The bride of Lammermoor. It had its world premiere in the original Italian version as Lucia di Lammermoor at the San Carlo Opera house in Naples on 26 September 1835, and it was given in Paris for the first time in this same form on 12 December 1837 at the Théâtre-Italien. It was produced at Her Majesty's Theatre in London on 5 april 1838, but only its second act was heard a few weeks later on 19 April 1838 at the Opéra in the rue Le Peletier.* The French version in three acts by Alphonse Royer* and Jean Vaëz* was mounted initially in Brussels on 5 September 1839 at the Théâtre Royal de la Monnaie. The third and fourth acts of the Italian version were sung at the Opéra on 24 April 1841 for a gala program designed as a benefit for the singer Gilbert Duprez,* but it was not until 20 February 1846 that the French version was performed there in its entirety. Mme Maria Nau* created the part of Lucie on this occasion with the male roles being filled by MM. Duprez (Edgard), Paul Barroilhet* (Asthon), Brémond (Raymond), Paulin (Arthur), and Chenet (Gilbert).

The curtain rises on Lucie de Lammermoor to disclose a crossroads in a forest of Scotland, where Gilbert and a band of hunters are pursuing a stag. Asthon complains to Gilbert of Lucie's love for the enemy of his house, Edgard Ravenswood. Asthon is especially angry because he has been planning to marry his sister to Arthur, nephew of the king's minister. Gilbert informs Asthon that the lovers plan to visit the nearby spring to exchange rings, and Asthon swears to slay Edgard (I, 1-2). The hunters return to the spring for refreshment, and Arthur asks Asthon whether Lucie is marrying him willingly. Asthon assures him that his sister has rejected his rival, and Arthur discloses that his uncle has assigned Edgard to a mission to France. Gilbert promises Asthon that he will slay Edgard before he can complete his tour of duty abroad. The hunters resume the hunt (I, 3-5), and Gilbert is left alone to greet Lucie on her way to meet her lover. She gives him a purse to stand watch (I, 6), and she remains alone by the spring to lament her brother's opposition to her love for Edgard. The latter enters to inform Lucie that he has been ordered to France, and he insists that he is going to ask her brother for her hand. They vow undying love and exchange rings (I, 7-8).

The second act moves to Asthon's castle, where Gilbert is reporting on his trip to France. Edgard believes that Lucie has been unfaithful to him because Gilbert has managed to intercept her letters. Also, Gilbert has had a counterfiet ring made to match the ring that Lucie has given to Edgard. Asthon rejoices (II, 1). Lucie reproaches him for being indifferent to her plight. He assures her that Edgard has forgotten her. She contradicts him; he summons Gilbert, who shows Lucie the counterfiet ring. She is deceived and despairs. A fanfare is heard across the moat. Asthon announces Arthur's arrival, and he urges his sister to marry him to restore the glory of their house. She leaves with threats of suicide on her lips (II, 2).

Arthur promises to restore his future brother-in-law to a position of power in the state, and he signs the wedding contract. Lucie returns to sign the same document, and she accuses her brother of lying to her when Edgard returns suddenly. She faints (II, 3-4), and Edgard vows vengeance, while Asthon orders Edgard's execution. The attendant minister prays that God's intervention will resolve the tragic situation in which the lovers find themselves, but Edgard and Asthon draw their swords. The minister manages to suppress the quarrel, and Edgard asks for Lucie's hand. The minister shows him the contract signed by Lucie and Arthur. Lucie admits that her signature is genuine, and astonished Edgard returns her ring. She begs him to listen to her explanation, but he curses her and her brother (II, 5).

The third act remains in Asthon's castle, where a masked man uninvited to the wedding demands to see the host. It is Edgard demanding satisfaciton on the field of honor. Asthon rejects his challenge on the grounds that it is prompted by jealous anger because Lucie has wed Arthur. Edgard insists, and Asthon agrees to meet him at dawn (III, 1-3). The wedding guests announce in a chorus that Lucie has left for Arthur's castle (III, 4), but the minister enters with the shocking news that Lucie has gone mad and has stabbed her husband. Lucie rushes into the room in disarray and calling for Edgard. She believes first that she is near the spring in the forest, and next she harbors the illusion that she and Edgard are about to be married in the chapel (III, 5-6). Asthon enters, and she mistakes him for Edgard. She explains to him how she came to sign the fateful wedding contract. Asthon is overwhelmed by grief over Arthur's death and Lucie's madness (III, 7).

The setting moves to a "Melancholy spot," where the moonlight is shining on Edgard and Asthon's seconds standing among trees and tombstones. Asthon's representatives inform Edgard that their man cannot meet him because his sister is dying. Edgard despairs when he learns that Lucie keeps calling for him in her agony. He is about to run to her bedside, when the tolling bells and the minister announce her death. Edgard stabs himself and defies Asthon to keep him from Lucie in death. Asthon laments the crumbling of his world, but his peers remind him that he is responsible for the bloodshed and madness visited upon his house (III, 8-11).

Donizetti's work was a success in Paris. It went on to enjoy 85 presentations at the Opéra by 23 December 1850, and its 100th billing at this theatre was posted on 28 July 1852. It was brought to the Garnier Palace* for its premiere at this theatre on 9 December 1889, its 270th presentation at the Opéra for which Nellie Melba* sang Lucie. Yet it seemed at this time that the Opéra was losing interest in the composition, because it was retired from the repertory after its 13th performance at the new opera house, and it was not revived there until the late Lily Pons appeared as Lucie on 15 May 1935 (see twentieth-century volume for Pons). Subsequently, Solonge Delmas filled this role for the 300th presentation of Lucie de Lammermoor by the Opéra at all its theatres on 1 June 1951. The original Italian version of Lucie di Lammermoor was returned to the Opéra for another 14 presentations more recently in 1969 and 1970. Strangely enough, Royer and Vaëz had translated Donizetti's work to provide a text that could be used by theatres not enjoying the gilt-and-velvet budgets granted to the national opera house, and, when Lucie was not being staged at the Garnier, Parisians could hear it at the Variétés (1898), Renaissance (1899), Gaîté (1908), and Champs-Elysées (1913).

The artistes who have interpreted the role of Lucie over the years include Mmes de Roissy, Norbet, Fortuni, Hamakers, and Bovy, and Edgard has been sung by MM. Espinasse, Gueymard,* Puget, Sapin, Affré,* and Volpi. In our time, Lily Pons, Solange Delmas, and Joan Sutherland have become associated with Donizetti's ill-starred heroine (see twentieth-century volume for Sutherland).

The score of the opera is rich in dramatic and musical moments in the French version, of course, because Royer and Vaëz did not allow their task to interfere with the score. French audiences applaud three moments in the first act alone: Lucie's "O fontaine, ô source pure" (I, 7); the duet between Edgar and Lucie beginning with "II me hait" (I, 8); Edgard's larghetto, "Juge toi-meme: Sur la tombe de mon père" (I, 8). The second act is distinguished by the duet of Lucie and Asthon, "Quand mon coeur se désespère" (II, 2), and the chorus, "Suivons l'amant qui nous conduit" (III, 3) as well as by the famous sextet scene inspired by the marriage contract and beginning with Edgard's "J'ai pour moi mon droit" (III, 5). The madness scene is classic, of course, but the third act is also remembered for other passages, for example, Edgard's "Tombe de mes aïeux" (III, 8) followed by his aria, "Bientôt l'herbe des champs croîtra" (II, 8), and his last words "O bel ange, dont les ailes" (III, 10).

BIBLIOGRAPHY: Adolphe Adam, <u>Derniers souvenirs d'un musicien</u> (Paris: Michel Lévy fréres, 1859), 295-310; William Ashbrook, <u>Donizetti</u> (London: Cassell, 1965), 166-71, 215, 416-17, 424-25, 485; <u>L'Avant-scéne</u> 55 (September 1983), 1-139; Guglielmo Barblan, <u>L'Opéra di Donizetti nell'eta romantica</u> (Bergamo: Banca mutua popolare di Bergamo, 1948), 115-28; Camille Bellaigue, <u>L'Année musicale: octobre 1889 à octobre 1890</u> (Paris: Delagrave, 1891), 33-40; Chouquet 407; DDO II, 662-63; Giuliano Donati-Petteni, <u>Donizetti</u> (Milan: S. A. Fratelli Treves, 1939), 173-89; Louis C. Elson, <u>Famous Composers and Their Works</u> (Boston: J. B. Millet Co., 1900), 152-53; Escudier, "<u>Lucie</u> à l'Académie royale de musique," <u>FM</u> 9 (22 February 1846), 59-60; Arnaldo Fraccaroli, <u>Donizetti</u> (Verona: Arnoldo Mondadori, 1945), 200-203, 230; Angelo Geddo, <u>Donizetti: l'uomo, le musiche</u> (Bergamo: Edizioni della Rotonda, n.d.), 163-75; J. Goury, "La (Fausse) Reprise de <u>Lucia</u>," <u>Opéra</u> 10, no. 87 (1970), 9; KCOB 453-61; Lajarte II, 180-81; P. de Lapommeraye, "Théâtre des Champs-Elysées: <u>Lucie de Lammermoor</u>," <u>Le Ménestrel</u> 89, no. 2 (14 January 1927), 12-13; "<u>Lucia di Lammermoor</u>," <u>ON</u> 33, no. 14 (1 February 1969), 17; Jerome Mitchell, <u>The Walter Scott Operas</u> (University: University of Alabama Press, 1977), 105-44, 365; H. Moréno, "<u>Lucie de Lammermoor</u> à l'Opéra," <u>Le Ménestrel</u> 55 (15 December 1889), 394-95; OCM 24-25, 153, 286-93; OQE 78-80; PBSW 53, 109, 141-43, 149, 227; Nino Piccinelli and Ruggero Y. Quintavalle, <u>Donizetti: la vita, le opere</u> (Bergamo: II Conventino, n.d.), 82-83, 197-202; Lea Rossi, <u>Donizetti</u> (Brescia: La Scuola, 1956), 130-51; SSBO 177-78, 181, 183, 190; Kenneth Stern, "Madness," <u>ON</u> 41, no. 10 (15 January 1977), 9-14; SW 136-37; M. Tassart, "What Paris Thought of Joan Sutherland," <u>Music & Musicians</u> 8 (June 1960), 18-19; Thompson 1046, 2176-77; Herbert Weinstock, <u>Donizetti and the World of Opera</u> (New York: Pantheon, 1963), 109-13, 348-50.

Lumbye, Hans Christian (b. 2 May 1810, Copenhagen; d. 20 March 1874, Copenhagen), composer, won the reputation of being "the Northern Strauss" with his orchestra specializing in marches and dance music. His work was heard at the Opéra in Paris because he had scored Harald Lander's <u>C'était un soir</u>, which was produced at the Garnier Palace* on 14 June 1937 by the Copenhagen Opera Company (see

twentieth-century volume for Lander). Lumbye's music for Auguste Bournonville's* Napoli was also played on 14 June 1937, when this ballet was programmed as a companion piece for C'était un soir (see twentieth-century volume for Napoli). Later, on 15 September 1976, Napoli was booked into the salle Favart for a ballet program organized by Ashley Lawrence. His Konservatoriet was also included on this Ashley program.
BIBLIOGRAPHY: AEM VIII, 1311-12; BBD 1051; ELM III, 108.

Lureau-Escalaïs, Maria-Annette (b. 24 February 1865, Montreuil-sur-Bois; d. ?), soprano, studied for three years at the Paris Conservatoire, where she won prizes for singing and opera in 1882. A student of Crosti and Louis Henri Obin,* she made her debut at the Opéra on 27 November 1882 as Marguerite in Les Huguenots.* Her stage presence was without flaw, and her ability to dominate almost any situaiton in the theatre became quite evident when she sang Juliette on one occasion without ever having rehearsed the part. Also, her virtuousity became manifest on 19 February 1886, when she filled the roles of Alice and Isabelle in Robert le Diable.*

Mme Lureau-Escalais had only a brief career at the Opéra despite her talents:

Role	**Opera, Year**
Mathilde	Guillaume Tell, 1883
Isabelle	Robert le Diable, 1883
Marguerite	Faust, 1883
Inès	L'Africaine, 1883
Alice	Robert le Diable, 1884
Eudoxie	La Juive, 1885
Gilda	Rigoletto, 1885
Elvire	Don Juan, 1887
Ophélie	Hamlet, 1888
Juliette	Roméo et Juliette, 1889

The soprano left the Opéra to keep an engagement at the Grand Théâtre in Marseilles during 1894 and never returned to the Garnier.
BIBLIOGRAPHY: EFC 157; Martin 232; SW 25-26, 73-75, 84-85, 105-6, 108-9, 129-30, 189-91.